A CONCISE DICTIONARY OF MIDDLE EGYPTIAN

A CONCISE DICTIONARY OF MIDDLE EGYPTIAN

BY

RAYMOND O. FAULKNER

D.LIT., F.S.A.

Lecturer in Ancient Egyptian in University College, London

GRIFFITH INSTITUTE

ASHMOLEAN MUSEUM · OXFORD

1988

ISBN 0 900416 32 7

This book was published with a subsidy from the Trustees of Sir Alan Gardiner's Trust for Friends and for Egyptological Purposes

REPRINTED 1972, 1976, 1981, 1986, 1988

First printed lithographically in 1981 by Biddles of Guildford from sheets originally set and printed in Great Britain at the University Press, Oxford

Reprinted 1988 by Butler & Tanner Ltd, Frome and London

To

DR. MARGARET MURRAY

who first taught me Ancient Egyptian

in gratitude and affection

PREFACE

FOR a number of years it has been borne in upon me by experience in teaching and in conversation with colleagues that an urgent Egyptological requirement of the present day is an Egyptian dictionary which on the one hand shall contain those words which a third-year undergraduate or an epigraphist in the field is most likely to meet in the course of his regular work, *with textual or bibliographical references*, and yet which shall be sufficiently concise to be reasonably portable and not excessively costly. In the nature of things no attempt to combine these incompatibles can be wholly successful, but the need for such a book seemed to me to demand that the effort be made; apart from the invaluable Vocabulary to Sir Alan Gardiner's *Egyptian Grammar* there is no modern dictionary of Ancient Egyptian in English, and no modern general vocabulary in any tongue which provides references apart from the costly *Wörterbuch der ägyptischen Sprache* in several volumes, which is not only the very reverse of portable, but is also beyond the reach of most students and scholars of the present day, who to consult it must perforce have access to a specialized library. This book is therefore addressed primarily to the younger practitioners of Egyptology, though it is hoped that others may sometimes find it useful.

The present work has been designed as a concise dictionary of Middle Egyptian, since it is that phase of the language which has the widest general application. For the purpose of this book the term 'Middle Egyptian' has been taken as including texts from the Heracleopolitan period to the end of the Eighteenth Dynasty, omitting the Late Egyptian locutions which begin to appear from the reign of Amenophis II onward. This exclusion applies also to words or meanings not recorded before the Nineteenth Dynasty, with a few exceptions the reasons for which will be clear. It has proved desirable, however, to include references to Old Egyptian sources rather more frequently, since these at times shed light on the original significance of a word or provide instances of obvious relevance to Middle Egyptian usage; also the older texts often show the basic forms of words that have undergone phonetic change by the Middle Kingdom. On the other hand, old words which do not appear to occur in

Middle Egyptian texts have not been recorded here apart from a very few instances where the reason for inclusion will again be obvious. On the other hand, certain Middle Egyptian words and phrases have been omitted by intent. These comprise most of the technical terms of the mathematical and medical texts which do not belong to everyday parlance; for these, the specialized works on such texts should be consulted. In order to save space I have omitted also those words whose meaning is unknown, as well as the names of unidentified species of animals, plants, and minerals; the broad categories of these items can often be gathered from the determinatives, and their inclusion would have added unprofitable bulk to the book. When such words have been included, it is usually because they have received discussion in print. The names of only the most important deities and localities have been noted; for the others, works on religion and geography should be consulted.

The method adopted to display the words is in essence that of the Vocabulary to Gardiner's *Egyptian Grammar*; first comes what may be considered a typical writing of the word in question, and this is followed by (*a*) the transliteration into modern characters; (*b*) the meaning, marked with a double underline; (*c*) a reference or references to texts displaying that meaning, or to works where the word is discussed; and (*d*) variant writings, also with references. These last do not pretend to be exhaustive, but display only significant differences; thus the occasional omission of a determinative, or the interchange of 𓀜, 𓂝, and 𓂡 have not usually been noted. In those scenes from tombs where we see pictures of animals and the like with their names written above them, I have where possible treated these pictures as determinatives, justifying this course by the close interdependence of script and picture in Ancient Egypt.

The alphabetic arrangement of this dictionary is that usual in works of this nature, with the proviso that I have followed Gardiner in treating 𓊃 and 𓋴 as one letter *s*. Where the existence of original 𓊃 (*z*) can be established from Old Egyptian texts, the earlier reading has been indicated in brackets at the first occurrence of a stem, e.g. *ꜣsẖ* (*ꜣzẖ*). Apart from such instances, the interchange of 𓊃 and 𓋴 as sole variant has usually not been noted. Following the practice of Erman and Grapow, *Wörterbuch der ägyptischen Sprache*, causative verbs in *s* have been entered under that letter and not under the parent stem.

In order to attain maximum compression, the meanings given do not attempt to indicate the finer nuances, but generally are on broad lines; in some more important instances the provision of a larger number of references than usual will enable the student who looks them up to ascertain for himself something of the finer shades of meaning. On the other hand, there are words such as *sp* and *s̱ḥr* where the demands of clarity have necessitated the quotation of original passages, usually in transliteration. The bibliographical references to be found scattered throughout this book, sometimes as a 'blanket' citation covering the whole range of meaning of a word, are mostly confined to the last half-century, the earliest work to be cited extensively being Gardiner's *Admonitions of an Egyptian Sage* (Leipzig, 1909). As a rule, though not invariably, a given citation refers to the most recent discussion of a word. The variant writings, if any, are normally collected at the end of each article, but often they are embodied in the text in order to avoid an unnecessary repetition of references.

The abbreviations employed are explained in the lists which follow. Since the nature of a word is usually obvious at a glance, such abbreviations as n. (noun), adj. (adjective), and the like have been inserted only where circumstances demand them; the adjective-verb has been deemed to be but an extension of its basic adjective and has not been distinguished from it. Among the verbs, only the geminatae and ultimae infirmae classes have been specified as such; all unspecified verbs are to be regarded as immutable.

In a compilation such as the present work, containing more than 5,000 entries, the compiler in the nature of things owes much indeed to the researches of others. To mention names here would be invidious, but a glance at the list of works cited will show clearly enough the extent to which the present author has depended on the labours of other scholars, and to all such, whether personally known or unknown to him, he now makes due acknowledgement. To the Trustees of Sir Alan Gardiner's Settlement for Egyptological Purposes is owed an especial debt of gratitude, inasmuch as it is they who have made possible the publication of this work at a very moderate price.

R. O. FAULKNER

October, 1961

ABBREVIATIONS OF LEXICOGRAPHICAL TERMS

abbr.	abbreviation.
adj.	adjective.
anat.	anatomical.
art.	article.
aux.	auxiliary.
c.	common gender.
caus.	causative.
coll.	collective.
comp.	compound.
dep.	dependent.
det.	determinative.
encl.	enclitic.
f.	feminine.
fig.	figure, figurative.
foll.	following, followed.
gem.	geminatae.
gen.	genitival.
imper.	imperative.
inf.	infirmae.
infin.	infinitive.
interj.	interjection.
interrog.	interrogative.
intrans.	intransitive.
L.E.	Lower Egypt.
L.Eg.	Late Egyptian.
lit.	literally.
m.	masculine.
math.	mathematical.
med.	medical.
M.K.	Middle Kingdom.
n.	noun, note.
n. div.	nomen divi.
neg.	negative.
n. loc.	nomen loci.
non-encl.	non-enclitic.
num.	numeral.
obj.	object.
O.K.	Old Kingdom.
ord.	ordinal.
o's	one's.
P.	Papyrus.
p., pp.	page(s).
part.	particle.
pl.	plural; plate of publication.
poss.	possessive.
prep.	preposition.
pron.	pronoun.
qu.	quoted.
q.v.	quod vide.
restd.	restored.
rt.	recto.
sg.	singular.
sim.	similarly.
s'one	someone.
s'thing	something.
suff.	suffix.
s.v.	sub voce.
trans.	transitive.
U.E.	Upper Egypt.
var., varr.	variant(s).
vb.	verb.
vs.	verso.
wtg.	writing.

ABBREVIATIONS OF TEXTS AND BOOKS CITED

Act. Or.	*Acta Orientalia.*
Adm.	*Admonitions of an Egyptian Sage*, P. Leyden 344, quoted by column and line. Quotations by page of Gardiner's edition (e.g. *Adm.* p. 99) refer to the writing-board BM 5645. For the commentary on these texts see *GAS* below.
AEO	A. H. Gardiner, *Ancient Egyptian Onomastica*, text volumes.
Äg. Stud.	*Ägyptologischen Studien*, ed. O. Firchow (Festschrift in honour of H. Grapow).
Alphabet	K. Sethe, *Der Ursprung des Alphabets*, in *Nachrichten . . . Göttingen*, 1916.
Amarna	N. de G. Davies, *The Rock Tombs of El Amarna.*
Anc. Eg.	*Ancient Egypt* (journal).
Ann. Serv.	*Annales du Service des Antiquités de l'Égypte.*
Barns, *Ashm.*	J. W. B. Barns, *The Ashmolean Ostracon of Sinuhe.*
Barns, *Ram.*	Id., *Five Ramesseum Papyri.*
Bauer	F. Vogelsang, *Kommentar zu den Klagen des Bauern.*
BD	E. A. W. Budge, *The Book of the Dead*, 1898 edition. Vol. I, Text.
Bersh.	P. E. Newberry, *El Bersheh.*
BH	Id., *Beni Hasan.*
BM	British Museum stelae, &c., quoted by the old registration numbers.
Breasted, *Development*	J. H. Breasted, *Development of Religion and Thought in Ancient Egypt.*
Brunner, *Siut*	H. Brunner, *Die Texte aus den Gräbern der Herakleopolitenzeit von Siut.*
Bull.	*Bulletin de l'Institut français d'archéologie orientale du Caire.*
Caminos, *Lit. Frag.*	R. A. Caminos, *Literary Fragments in the Hieratic Script.*
Caminos, *L.-Eg. Misc.*	Id., *Late-Egyptian Miscellanies.*
Cenotaph	H. Frankfort, *The Cenotaph of Seti I.*
Ch. B. I	A. H. Gardiner, *The Chester Beatty Papyri No. I.*
Ch. B. Text	Id., *Hieratic Papyri in the British Museum, Third Series. Chester Beatty Gift.* Vol. I. Text.
COA	T. E. Peet and others, *City of Akhenaten.*
CT	A. de Buck, *The Egyptian Coffin Texts.*
D. el B.	E. Naville, *The Temple of Deir el Bahari.*
D. el B. (*XI*).	Id., *The XIth Dynasty Temple at Deir el Bahari.*
D. el Geb.	N. de G. Davies, *The Rock Tombs of Deir el Gebrawi.*
Dav. *Ptah.*	Id., *The Mastaba of Ptahhetep and Akhethetep at Saqqareh.*
Dav. *Rekh*	Id., *The Tomb of Rekh-mi-Rēᶜ at Thebes.*
Dend.	W. M. F. Petrie, *Dendereh.*
Desh.	Id., *Deshasheh.*
Dream-book	Chester Beatty Papyri No. III.
Eb.	The Ebers Medical Papyrus.
Edel	E. Edel, *Altagyptische Grammatik*, Vol. I.
EHT	A. H. Gardiner, *Egyptian Hieratic Texts of the New Kingdom. The Papyrus Anastasi I and the Papyrus Koller.*
Erläut.	K. Sethe, *Erläuterung zu den aegyptischen Lesestücken.*
Garten.	L. Keimer, *Die Gartenpflanzen im alten Ägypten.*

GAS	A. H. Gardiner, *Admonitions of an Egyptian Sage*, commentary.
Gauthier, *Dict. géogr.*	H. Gauthier, *Dictionnaire des noms géographiques contenus dans les textes hiéroglyphiques*.
GES	B. Gunn, *Studies in Egyptian Syntax*.
Gîza	H. Junker, *Gîza*.
GNS	A. H. Gardiner, *Notes on the Story of Sinuhe*.
Goyon	G. Goyon, *Inscriptions rupestres du Wadi Hammamat*.
Gr.	A. H. Gardiner, *Egyptian Grammar*, 3rd edition.
Griff. *Kah.*	F. Ll. Griffith, *Hieratic Papyri from Kahun and Gurob*, text volume. For the individual papyri see under *P. Kah.*
Hamm.	J. Couyat and P. Montet, *Les Inscriptions hiéroglyphiques et hiératiques du Ouadi Hammâmât*.
Harris	The Harris Papyrus No. I, ed. W. Erichsen.
Hatnub	R. Anthes, *Die Felsinschriften von Hatnub*.
Helck	H. W. Helck, *Der Einfluss der Militärführer in der 18. ägyptischen Dynastie*.
Herdsm.	*The Herdsman's Tale*, A. H. Gardiner, *Die Erzählung des Sinuhe und die Hirtengeschichte*, pls. 16–17.
Hier.	F. Ll. Griffith, *A Collection of Hieroglyphs*.
Hier. Les.	G. Möller, *Hieratische Lesestücke für den akademischen Gebrauch*.
Hier. Pal.	Id., *Hieratische Paläographie*.
Hymnen	A. Erman, *Hymnen an des Diadem der Pharaonen*, in *Abhandlungen der königlichen preussischen Akademie* . . ., 1911.
Ikhekhi	T. G. H. James, *The Mastaba of Khentika called Ikhekhi*.
Inscr. dédic.	H. Gauthier, *La Grande Inscription dédicatoire d'Abydos*.
Iouiya	E. Naville, *The Funeral Papyrus of Iouiya*.
Israel	Stela of Meneptaḥ naming Israel, Spiegelberg, *ZÄS* 34, 1.
JEA	*Journal of Egyptian Archaeology*.
JNES	*Journal of Near Eastern Studies*.
JRAS	*Journal of the Royal Asiatic Society*.
Kamosĕ	Stela of King Kamosĕ referring to the war against the Hyksos.
Ḳen-amūn	N. de G. Davies, *The Tomb of Ḳen-amūn at Thebes*.
Komm. Pyr.	K. Sethe, *Übersetzung und Kommentar zu den altägyptischen Pyramidentexten*.
Koptos	W. M. F. Petrie, *Koptos*.
L. to D.	A. H. Gardiner and K. Sethe, *Egyptian Letters to the Dead*.
Lac. *Sarc.*	P. Lacau, *Sarcophages antérieurs au Nouvel Empire*.
Leb.	A. Erman, *Gespräch eines Lebensmüden mit seiner Seele*, in *Abhandlungen der königlichen preussischen Akademie* . . ., 1896; revised text *JEA* 42, 22 ff.
Les.	K. Sethe, *Aegyptische Lesestücke zum Gebrauch in akademischen Unterricht*.
Leyd.	Stelae, &c., in the Leyden Museum, quoted by Museum number.
Lischt	J. E. Gautier and G. Jéquier, *Mémoire sur les fouilles de Lischt*.
M.u.K.	A. Erman, *Zaubersprüche für Mutter und Kind*, in *Abhandlungen der königlichen preussischen Akademie* . . ., 1901.
Meir	A. M. Blackman, *The Rock Tombs of Meir*.
Mél. Masp.	*Mélanges Maspero*.
Mereruka	Chicago University Oriental Institute, *The Mastaba of Mereruka*.
Merikarēʿ	*The Teaching for King Merikarēʿ*, P. Leningrad 1116A.
Mill.	*The Teaching of Ammenemes I to His Son*, P. Millingen.

Misc. Acad. Berol.	*Miscellanea Academica Berolinensis*, 1950.
Mitt. deutsch. Inst.	*Mitteilungen des deutschen Instituts zu Kairo.*
Naga ed-Dêr	D. Dunham, *Naga ed-Dêr Stelae.*
Nauri	F. Ll. Griffith, *The Abydos Decree of Seti I*, in *JEA* 13, 193 ff.
Nav. *Todtb.*	E. Naville, *Das ägyptische Todtenbuch der XVIII bis XX Dynastie.*
Neferḥotep	M. Pieper, *Die grosse Inschrift des Königs Neferḥotep in Abydos.*
Neferti	*The Prophecies of Neferti*, P. Leningrad 1116B.
Northampton	The Marquis of Northampton and others, *Report on Some Excavations in the Theban Necropolis during the Winter of 1898–9.*
P. Berl. . . .	Berlin Papyrus No. . . .
P. Boul. XVIII	Boulaq Papyrus No. XVIII, quoted by the section numbers of Scharff's transcription, *ZÄS* 51, 1** ff.
P. Ed. Smith	J. H. Breasted, *The Edwin Smith Medical Papyrus*, commentary. For references to the original text see under *Sm.*
P. Kah.	F. Ll. Griffith, *Hieratic Papyri from Kahun and Gurob*, plate volume.
P. Ram.	Ramesseum Papyri, ed. J. W. B. Barns.
P. Wilbour	A. H. Gardiner, *The Wilbour Papyrus*, Vol. II (commentary).
Paheri	J. J. Tylor and F. Ll. Griffith, *The Tomb of Paheri at El-Kab*, bound with E. Naville, *Ahnas el Medineh.*
Peas.	*The Story of the Eloquent Peasant.*
Piankhi	The stela of victory of King Piankhi.
Plural	R. O. Faulkner, *The Plural and Dual in Old Egyptian.*
Posener	G. Posener, *Catalogue des Ostraca hiératiques littéraires de Deir el Médineh.*
Pr.	The Prisse Papyrus.
PSBA	*Proceedings of the Society of Biblical Archaeology.*
Pt. (L. I)	P. Brit. Mus. 10371/435 (duplicate text of *The Maxims of Ptaḥḥotep* in the Prisse Papyrus).
Pt. (L II)	P. Brit. Mus. 10509 (as above).
Pyr.	K. Sethe, *Die ältagyptischen Pyramidentexte.*
Qadech	C. Kuentz, *Bataille de Qadech.*
RB	A. de Buck, *Egyptian Reading-book.*
Rec. Champ.	*Recueil d'études égyptologiques dediées à la mémoire de Jean-François Champollion . . .*
Rec. trav.	*Recueil de travaux relatifs à la philologie et à l'archéologie égyptiennes et assyriennes.*
Rekh.	P. E. Newberry, *The Life of Rekhmara.*
Rev. d'ég.	*Revue d'égyptologie.*
Rhind	T. E. Peet, *The Rhind Mathematical Papyrus.*
Rifeh	W. M. F. Petrie, *Rifeh and Gizeh.*
RIH	E. de Rouge, *Inscriptions hiéroglyphiques copiées en Égypte.*
Sah.	L. Borchardt, *Das Grabdenkmal des Königs Saȝḥu-reʿ.*
Saqq. Mast.	M. A. Murray, *Saqqara Mastabas.*
SDT	K. Sethe, *Dramatische Texte zu den altägyptischen Mysterienspielen.*
Sebekkhu	T. E. Peet, *The Stela of Sebekkhu.*
Sethe, *Amun*	K. Sethe, *Amun und die acht Urgötter von Hermopolis*, in *Abhandlungen der preussichen Akademie . . .*, 1929.
Sethe, *Lauf*	Id., *Altägyptische Vorstellungen von Lauf der Sonne*, in *Sitzungsberichte der preussischen Akademie . . .*, 1928.
Sethe, *Rechts*	Id., *Die ägyptischen Ausdrucken für rechts und links . . .* in *Nachrichten . . . Göttingen*, 1922.

Sethe, *Steine* — K. Sethe, *Die Bau- und Denkmalsteine der alten Ägypten und ihre Namen*, in *Sitzungsberichte der preussischen Akademie* . . ., 1933.

Sethe, *Zahlen* — Id., *Von Zahlen und Zahlworten bei den alten Ägyptern*, in *Schriften der Wissenschaftlichen Gesellschaft Strassburg*, 1916.

Sh. S. — *The Story of the Shipwrecked Sailor*, P. Leningrad 1115.

Sheikh Said — N. de G. Davies, *The Rock Tombs of Sheikh Said.*

Sin. — *The Story of Sinuhe.*

Sinai — A. H. Gardiner and T. E. Peet, *The Inscriptions of Sinai*, 2nd edition, revised by J. Černý, quoted by inscription number.

Siut — F. Ll. Griffith, *The Inscriptions of Siût and Der Rîfeh*, quoted throughout by plate number.

Sm. — The Edwin Smith Medical Papyrus. For the commentary of Breasted's edition see *P. Ed. Smith* above.

Stud. Griff. — *Studies Presented to F. Ll. Griffith.*

T. Carn. — Carnarvon Tablet No. 1, see A. H. Gardiner, *JEA* 3, 95 ff.

Tarkhan I — W. M. F. Petrie and others, *Tarkhan I and Memphis V.*

Teti Cem. — C. M. Firth and B. Gunn, *Teti Pyramid Cemeteries.*

Th. T. S. — Theban Tombs Series.

I. Nina de G. Davies and A. H. Gardiner, *The Tomb of Amenemhēt.*

II. Norman and Nina de G. Davies, *The Tomb of Antefoḳer and his Wife Senet.*

III. Id., *The Tombs of Two Officials of Tuthmosis IV.*

IV. Nina de G. Davies and A. H. Gardiner, *The Tomb of Ḥuy.*

V. Nina and Norman de G. Davies, *The Tombs of Menkheperraʿsonb, Amenmosĕ and Another.*

Ti — G. Steindorff, *Das Grab des Ti.*

Top. Cat. — A. H. Gardiner and A. E. P. Weigall, *A Topographical Catalogue of the Private Tombs of Thebes.*

TR — P. Lacau, *Textes religieux égyptiens*, quoted by spell number and line.

Unters. — K. Sethe, *Untersuchungen zur Geschichte und Altertumskunde Ägyptens.*

Urk. I. — K. Sethe, *Urkunden des alten Reichs.*

IV. — Id., continued by W. Helck, *Urkunden der 18. Dynastie.*

V. — H. Grapow, *Religiöse Urkunden.*

VII. — K. Sethe, *Urkunden des mittleren Reichs.*

Wb. — A. Erman and H. Grapow, *Wörterbuch der ägyptischen Sprache.*

Westc. — *Tales of the Magicians* in the Westcar Papyrus.

WZKM — *Wiener Zeitschrift für die Kunde des Morgenlandes.*

Wortforschung — A. Erman and others, *Zur ägyptische Wortforschung*, in *Abhandlungen der deutschen Akademie*. . . .

Žába — Z. Žába, *Les Maximes de Ptahhotep.*

ZÄS — *Zeitschrift für ägyptische Sprache und Altertumskunde.*

ZDMG — *Zeitschrift der deutschen morgenländischen Gesellschaft.*

Addenda and Corrigenda

Page

1 *3wt* *length*: *add* *of space*, *Pyr.* 324.

11 *ỉʿnw*: to *ỉ. n* 'greet' *add* *CT* I, 226 *f.*; to 'woe to' *add* James, *Hekanakhte*, p. 109.

12 *ỉw* *be boatless*: *add* *be helpless*, *CT* IV, 81 *d*, cf. *JEA* 35, 95, n. 13; *be deprived of*, *BD* 149, 6.

14 *ỉwḥ* *moisten*: *add* *flood* land, James, op. cit. p. 18.

14 *ỉwtn* *ground*: *add* *mud*, Harris, *Minerals*, 199.

29 *ỉs* *tomb*: *add* *archive*, Goedicke, *Königl. Dokumente*, 100.

31 *ỉšrw* *precinct of Mut*: *add* *water-meadow*, *Bull.* 62, 50; Pap. Reisner III, 35.

35 *ỉdw* *pestilence*: *add* *Kemi*, 18, 78.

40 *ʿbt* *attachment*: add *ʿbt.ỉ rmṯt* 'my human connections', *CT* II, 164 *c–d*.

42 *ʿf3*: for 'devour'(?) *read* *tear off*.

Page

42 ꜥm swallow: under ꜥm ỉb, for 'be discreet', etc. read 'become faint'; 'neglect', James, Ḥeḳanakhte, p. 110.

46 ꜥḥꜣ fight: add ꜥḥꜣ ṯw, ꜥḥꜣ ṯn 'take care', op. cit. 111; ꜥḥꜣ ḥr 'be wary of', CT IV, 69 f.

50 ꜥgt a varnish (?): add but see Harris, Minerals, 63.

55 wꜣḏ a green stone: add often malachite, op. cit. 102. 143.

58 wꜥrtw administrator: reading ꜣtw proposed, Rev. ég. 15, 128.

58 wꜥrtyt administratrix: add or var. of ꜣtyt 'nurse' (?), loc. cit.

58 wꜥḥ: for 'carob bean' read earth almond, tuber of Cyperus esculentus L., Edel, Qubbet el Hawa, II Abt., I Bd., 2 Teil, p. 22.

68 wḫdw pain: add cf. JEA 49, 183; Kemi, 18, 77.

69 wsṯ be dilapidated: add trans. vb. ruin, Merikarēꜥ, 122.

80 bỉꜣ: for 'bronze' read iron, Harris, Minerals, 50 ff. See Graefe, Untersuchungen zur Wortfamilie bjꜣ, Köln, 1971.

95 psš-kf ritual instrument: read psš only: kf is the name of its material, cf. Abu Sir Pap. 20; Harris, op. cit. 228; JEA 57, 203.

Page	
98	fḫt wig(?): for 40 read 140 d.
103	mꜣtt mandrake(?): add but see Bull. 56, 60; ZÄS 96, 12; von Deines and Grapow, Drogennamen, 216.
104	mỉn today: add here, hither; mỉnꜣ 'here', 'hither'; 'like this', 'accordingly', James, Ḥeḳanakhte, pp. 111-2; likewise mỉnw, Edel, Altäg. Gramm. §754, 2.
108	mnw kind of stone: add quartz(?), Harris, Minerals, 110.
110	mnšt yellow ochre(?): add or red o.(?), op. cit. 147.
113	mḥ cubit; mḥ flax: read mḥꜥw?, cf. James, Ḥeḳanakhte, 112.
115	mḫnmt carnelian(?): add or jasper(?), Harris, op. cit. 111.
117	msnḥ rotate: add ZÄS 93, 55.
125	nꜣ this, these: add adv. here, hither, James, op. cit. 112; Edel, op. cit. §754, 2.
128	nbwt the isles: at end add Vercoutter, L'Égypte et le monde égéen préhellénique, 15 ff.
134	nn this, these: add adv. here, hither, James, op. cit. 112.

Page	
152	rḫ-nsw *king's acquaintance*: *add* Edel, *Qubbet el Hawa*, II Abt., I Bd., 2 Teil, p. 92.
154	*rtḥ* *confine*: *delete* det. .
155	*rdi* *give*: to *rdi ḥr wꜣt* 'show the way' *add* 'thrust aside', *Adm.* 4,1.
161	*ḥ3w* *vintage*: *read* .
169	*ḥm* *Majesty*: at end *add* but see *ZÄS* 75,112.
169	*ḥmt* (?) *copper*: *add* cf. Harris, *Minerals*, 50ff.
170	*ḥm3gt* *carnelian*: *add* or *garnet* (?), op. cit. 118.
171	*ḥnt* *swampy lake*: *add* *watercourse*, *ZÄS* 88,88.
178	*ḥsmn* *bronze*: *add* cf. Harris, op. cit. 64; also *amethyst*, ibid. 121.
182	*ḥd* *injure*: *add* *degrade* official, *Merikarēʿ*, 47.
183	*ḫ3w* *plants, flowers*: *add* '(a boat)  with lotus-plants on its ends (lit. 'heads')', i.e. bow- and stern-pieces end in l.-p., *CT* VII, 259 *b*.
190	*ḫft* *in front of*: *add* of speech *to* s'one, *GNS* 32.

Page

195 ḫnd calf of leg: add cf. AEO I, 17 (No. 280).

197 ḫsf draw near: delete 'draw near' and substitute opponent.

204 ẖry-s3: delete 'who is behind, Pyr. 1226.'

206 st seat: under (3) add st-nṯryt 'divine state', CT I, 143c; 146e; st-ḥ3 'liability to corvée (?)', Urk. I, 210, 6; st-ḫt 'meal', Pyr. 1182; st-swꜥb 'cleanliness', CT I, 62c; st-sk3 'ploughing', Urk. I, 210, 14.

208 s3 knife: delete this entry: the word is ns3.

209 s3wy gold two-thirds fine: add reading and meaning denied by Harris, Minerals, 38.

214 sꜥb: for 'saw out' timbers of ship read take to pieces, of boat; also add circumcize, JEA 49, 183.

216 sw3 pass: delete 'remove, m from' and transfer the ref. Pyr. 679 to the first line, between 'trans.' and '1351'.

218 swt he, it: add as possessive n. in swt·f 'what is his', Pyr. 2042.

251 sk3 cultivate: add cf. James, Ḥekanakhte, p. 18.

Page	
252	*sgnn*: for 'tallow' *read* *ointment*, Caminos, *L. Eg. Misc.* 82; Helck, *Materialien*, 700.
266	*šf-tbt* (?) *sixth month*: *add* cf. *Ann. Serv.* 43, 173 ff.
271	*šsꜣt*: for 'nightfall' *read* *night* *sky*, ZÄS 86, 111.
272	*šsm*: for 'leather roll' *read* *baton*, and *add* var.  CT III, 114 *b*; cf. Davies, *Rekhmirēꜥ*, p. 31.
276	*ḳꜣdw* (*ḳd*) *plaster*: *add* *gypsum*, Harris, *Minerals*, 91.
276	*ḳꜥḥ* *bend* arm: *add* *turn* one's back, *Neferti* 43; cf. Posener, *Littérature et Politique*, 153.
280	*ḳntt* *a yellow pigment*: *add* *orpiment*, Harris, op. cit. 153.
286	*ḳnḥ* *dark*: *add* *darken*, ZÄS 86, 113.
301	*tḫn* *injury* to eye: *add* *pierce* sky, of pylons, Louvre C3, 6.
306	*ṯn-r* *reminder*: James, *Ḥeḳanakhte*, 114 suggests *explanation*.
311	*dbn* *mortar*: Harris, *Minerals*, 207 suggests *potter's clay*.
320	*ḏꜥbt* *charcoal*: *add* *soot*, op. cit. 160.

Page

320 dꜥmw **fine gold**: *add* Harris, *Minerals*, 44 ff., prefers **electrum**.

321 dwꜥ: for 'lancet (?)' *read* **surgical knife** and *add* refs. *Pyr.* 660. 661 (var. ).

321 ḏbt **brick**: *add* Harris, op. cit. 30. 207.

324 drwy **paint**: *add* op. cit. 157.

327 nbi 'reed', measure of 2 cubits: *add* Hayes, *Ostraca and Namestones*, 36.

Note

A number of the references cited above are due to Mr. C. H. S. Spaull, to whom I tender my grateful thanks.

R. O. Faulkner.

 3 (1) vulture: (2) bird in general, var. , JEA 34, 12.

 3 encl. part., Gr. § 245; JEA 34, 12.

 3 tread (?) a place, Westc. 9, 16;  r-gs 'go off with (?)' s'one, 12, 25.

 3t striking-power of god, etc., var. , JEA 34, 13.

 3t moment, instant, Sin. B 57. 299; Urk. IV, 969, 1; 1016, 8; m 3t-f 'in his m.' = in the act of doing s'thing, Lr. 5, 10; sim. Urk. IV, 122, 15; 246, 8; m km n 3t 'in the twinkling of an eye', RB 64, 12: time in general, Lr. 7, 9; Urk. IV, 9, 1;  3t 'spend a while', Westc. 2, 6; RB 64, 11;  3t nfrt 'spend a happy t.', Lr. 12, 4. Varr.  Urk. IV, 1016, 8; 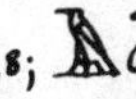 122, 15;  969, 1;  9, 1;  246, 8;  1430, 14.

 33 mound of ruins, BH I, 26, 195; cf. JEA 34, 15.

 33t3 Nubian chieftain (?), JEA 34, 15.

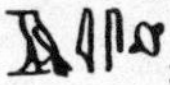 3is viscera, varr. 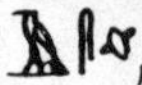, 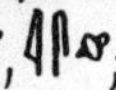; 3is n dnnt 'brain', JEA 33, 48.

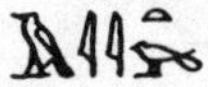 3yt blanch (?), var.  (?), JEA 16, 65; 22, 43; 34, 16.

 3cw container for papyri, etc., Urk. I, 42, 8; var. det.  ZÄS 57, 7*.

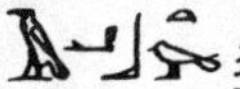 3cbt oppression, Urk. IV, 510, 13; var. dets.  122, 15.

 3w (1) adj. long: of space, Pyr. 729; TR 19, 33; Urk. IV, 424, 1 (det. ); of time, Urk. IV, 587, 8 (); 1084, 11; Peas. B1, 108. 128; Adm. p. 107; h3b 3w 'continual crookedness' JEA 28, 18 (i); fig. 3w ib 'joyful', Urk. IV, 5, 13; 116, 13; 3w hr 'farsighted', Peas. B1, 271; 3w drt 'generous', Les. 80, 21.

(2) n. length: of space, Urk. I, 4, 10; 108, 5 (det. ); Sh. S. 26; Urk. IV, 613, 2 (det. ); of time, Merikarēc 54; r-3w(-f) 'all', 'entire', Gr. § 100, 3.

 3wt length, of time, in m 3wt dt 'in the l. of eternity', 'in perpetuity', Urk. I, 37, 14; IV, 173, 3 (); 832, 14; fig. 3wt ib 'joy', Urk. IV, 15, 2; 223, 10.

 3wt gifts, Sin. B 187; Urk. IV, 108, 1; 408, 13 (det. ); var.  Pyr. 399.

 3wy vb. 3 inf. extend the arm, Westc. 8, 1 (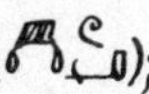); Urk. IV, 498, 3; 612, 13; present an offering, BD 450, 10; announce s'one, n 'to', Pyr. 1141. 1142 ([illegible]);

arouse o'self, JEA 17, 23 ( ); 3wy ḏrt 'lay hands on', JEA 2, 175, n. 5.

3wt-ꜥ gifts, Sin. B 175; Urk. IV, 520, 5; cf. GNS 63.

3w death, in ntt m 3w 'who is deceased', P. Kah. 10, 6.

3wt long knife, CT I, 197.

3wḥ do violence, r 'to', Siut, pl. 13, 34.

3b vb. intrans. tarry, stay, Sin. B 95: trans. avoid, CT I, 284; cease, Eb. 93, 6.

3bw cessation, Sin. B 299; Urk. IV. 98, 10; RB 65, 1-2.

3bw brand slaves or cattle, var. det. , Caminos, L.-Eg. Misc. 230; scorch the skin, Sinai, 90, 7.

3bt brand (n.), Pyr. 675; det. Dream-book, 11, 1. Cf. Caminos, loc. cit.

3bt coll. family, TR 2, 1; varr. BM 159, 11; Les. 79, 13.

3bi vb. 3 inf. desire, wish for, Leb. 141; Urk. IV, 834, 1; 975, 6; var. 28, 1.

3b3b be delighted (?), P. Kah. 34, 18.

3by panther, Urk. IV, 8, 13; varr. 336, 17; 373, 10; 702, 16; cf. ZÄS 44, 19.

3bw elephant, Urk. IV, 893, 15; var. 104, 2.

3bw ivory, Sh. S. 165; det. 949, 4; varr. Urk. IV, 424, 11; 1149, 8.

3bw n. loc. Elephantine, Sin. B 226; varr. Urk. I, 107, 10; IV, 834, 4; 1122, 13; 396, 7; JEA 17, 58 (14); Mill. 2, 10; Adm. 3, 10. Cf. AEO II, 2*.

3bḫ vb. trans. unite, n 'to', P. Kah. 3, 2; mix, m 'into', of compounding drugs, Eb. 104, 20; ḥr 'with', 56, 20; join a god, Urk. IV, 54, 17 ( ); the stars, 1847, 15; link (?) arms, Pyr. 743 ( ): intrans. mingle, m 'with', Urk. IV, 365, 2; 518, 16; ḥnꜥ 'with', 501, 16; be merged, m 'in', Sin. R 8; engage in battle, Les. 83, 11.

3bd month, Sh. S. 114; RB 59, 9; 114, 10; abbr. in dates, Gr. p. 203.

3bd monthly festival, Urk. IV, 27, 4; det. CT I, 16.

ꜣbḏw *n. loc.* Abydos, Leyd. V 4, 2; varr. Les. 70, 17; 68, 5. Cf. AEO II, 36*.

ꜣbḏw a fish, Mu. K. 2, 5; cf. JEA 19, 137 (var.).

ꜣpd (1) duck, JEA 38, 128: (2) bird in general, Sh. S. 51. 185; Peas. B1, 176; abbr. BH I, 34; in offering formula, Gr. p. 172.

ꜣpd rush forward, Urk. IV, 1291, 5.

ꜣfꜥ gluttony, Pr. 1, 4.

glutton, Pr. 1, 8.

ꜣfry boil (vb.), Eb. 42, 7.

ꜣm vb. (1) trans. burn up, Sh. S. 131; Adm. 2, 10; Urk. IV, 613, 17: (2) intrans. burn, of brazier, Pyr. 558.

ꜣmỉ mix, Eb. 4, 5; 14, 4-5.

ꜣmꜥ a perching bird, JEA 18, 151.

ꜣmꜥt ramus of jaw; fork of bone, varr. , , cf. P. Ed. Smith, 512.

ꜣmm (1) vb. 2 gem. seize, grasp, Pyr. 1739; Urk. IV, 6, 1; 1280, 17; TR 59, 3; attack, r s'one, Sin. B 120: (2) n. grasp, P. Ram. III, B 15.

ꜣmmt grasp (n.) Urk. IV, 9, 4; 372, 8; 618, 1.

ꜣmmw gripings (med.), P. Kah. 5, 35.

ꜣms, see under ỉwms 'falsehood'.

ꜣms (1) n. a club or mace, Pyr. 522; 1166; Urk. IV, 1734, 18; RB 60, 8: (2) vb. wield the ꜣms, Pyr. 274.

ꜣr drive away, ḥr 'from', Les. 84, 4; Urk. IV, 972, 7 (); oppress the poor, Merikarēꜥ, 47 ().

ꜣryt staff, BM 586.

ꜣhw misery, trouble, Peas. B1, 254; Leb. 18 (); Adm. p. 105 (); pain, Eb. 37, 15 (); 37, 16 (); injury, Sm. 4, 16 (); illness, Sm. 13, 11; 17, 13 ().

ȝhw sufferer, Merikarēʻ, 39.

ȝhmt sorrow, Tarkhan I, 79, 48.

ȝhd quiver, palpitate, GNS 30; be weak (?), det. , cf. P. Ed. Smith, 512.

ȝḥ kind of bread, Eb. 14, 13; BH I, 35; Urk. IV, 754, 11; var. Pyr. 38.

ȝḥt field, arable land, Sin. B 306; P. Kah. 4, 2.6; Pr. 10, 10; Urk. IV, 2, 4 (det.); 6, 7; 1110, 11; earth, mould, Urk. IV, 57, 9; 837, 7; 1152, 6; RB 122, 15. Var. pl. Th. T. S. I, 27.

ȝḫt Inundation-season, var. , Gr. p. 203; Urk. I, 25, 12.

ȝḫ papyrus thicket, Gr. p. 481, M 15.

ȝḫ-bit n. loc. Chemmis, Urk. IV, 16, 15; 237, 10; varr. , Pyr. 1214. Cf. JEA 30, 52.

ȝḫ spirit, Urk. IV, 194, 14; varr. 150, 4; 446, 6; V, 40, 3; ZÄS 57, 137.

ȝḫ the spirit-state, Urk. IV, 547, 8; var. ZÄS 57, 137.

ȝḫ (1) vb. be, become a spirit, Urk. IV, 518, 7; V, 4, 7; JEA 2, pl. 3, C3. (2) adj. glorious, splendid, Urk. IV, 276, 5; 299, 2; 864, 14; beneficial, useful, profitable, Pr. 5, 7; 10, 10; 17, 5; Siut, pl. 11, 4; Peas. B1, 293; Urk. IV, 47, 6; 485, 2; ȝḫ ib n 'be serviceably minded towards', 890, 9; ȝḫ n ... 'it will be well with ...', 65, 17; 133, 16; V, 4, 14; ȝḫ n‹i› m ib.f 'I found favour in his heart', Sin. B 106. Var. Urk. IV, 47, 6: (3) n. fame (?), Urk. IV, 62, 8.

ȝḫt what is good, profitable, useful, Pr. 5, 7; 17, 5; Urk. IV, 57, 6.8; ȝḫt n 'do good to', Urk. IV, 194, 7 (); 750, 8 ().

ȝḫw power of god, etc., TR 19, 23 (); Urk. IV, 160, 5 (); 221, 3; V, 78, 16 (); BD 482, 3 (); mastery over work, Pr. 5, 9. Cf. JEA 24, 127, n. 5.

ȝḫt arable land, Urk. IV, 482, 9; varr. RB 110, 10; 112, 8.

ȝḫt uraeus-serpent, Pyr. 302; Urk. IV, 613, 15; var. RB 57, 4.

ȝḫt eye of god, RB 58, 8.

ȝḫt flame, BD 369, 9; 378, 6.

ȝḫyt still-room (?), COA III, p. 171; var. Äg. Stud. 1.

ȝḫt horizon: (a) where sun rises and sets, Pyr. 585 (); Urk. V, 28, 3; TR 16, 11 (): (b) tomb of king, Sin. R 6; B 36; Westc. 7, 8; ʿḫmw nw ȝḫt 'images of the h.' = sacred images, Sin. B 287. Cf. Bull. 17, 121.

ȝḫty (1) n. horizon-dweller, ep. of god, Urk. IV, 361, 13; var. Pyr. 346; Urk. IV, 159, 17; pl. V, 27, 14; ZÄS 57, 137; of a remote people, Urk. I, 128, 16; 130, 1 (); RB 74, 12 (); (2) adj. horizon-dwelling, in nṯrw ȝḫtyw 'the h.-d. gods', Urk. IV, 142, 13; 1779, 16.

ȝḫw sunlight, sunshine, Urk. V, 55, 9; varr. Leb. 65; Urk. IV, 19, 11; 518, 3; earlier , q. v.

ȝḫȝḫ grow green, of trees and plants, Amarna, VI, 27, 5.

ȝḫȝḫ stars, Pyr. 1143; BD 153, 10.

ȝḫȝḫ spars (?) of ship, Urk. V, 173, 12.

ȝḫf fever of appetite (?), Pr. 1, 8; cf. JEA 32, 73, n. 6.

ȝḫfḫf be fiery (?) of eye, TR 57, 7.

ȝḫʿ scratch, scrape; carve, engrave, ZÄS 45, 131.

ȝḫʿt scratch, scar (n.), loc. cit.

ȝs (1) intrans. vb. hurry; flow fast, of water, ZÄS 48, 40; ȝs i͗b 'impatient', BD 257, 5-6: (2) trans. vb. hasten, hurry o'self, Pyr. § 337, 1; overtake, Sin. B 22. 169: (3) adv. quickly, Pyr. § 205, 4. Var. Paheri, 3.

ȝs bald-headed vulture, Leb. 87; cf. Orientalia, 7, 67.

, varr. of i͗ss 'bald' and ȝis 'viscera'.

ȝst n. div. Isis, CT I, 18; varr. ibid.; TR 43, 4; Pyr. 960.

ȝsb (ȝzb) fierce, glowing, of radiance, Pyr. 324; var. Urk. V, 43, 11.

ȝsbyw flames, BD 134, 3.

ȝsḫ sickle, Barns, Ram. pl. 24, 21.

ꜣsḫ (ꜣzḫ) reap, Urk. V, 161, 16; Pyr. 657 (det.); Sheikh Said, 16 (det.); BH I, 46; I, 29.

ꜣšr (1) vb. roast, Adm. 5, 8; Eb. 14, 1; t ꜣšr 'toast', Pyr. 78; BH I, 17: (2) n. roast meat, a roast, Sin. B 89; P. Kah. 5, 7. 8; Siut, pl. 7, 302 (det.).

ꜣšrt roast joint, Urk. IV, 825, 16; BH I, 18; var. det. Pyr. 214.

ꜣḳ perish, Leb. 107; Pr. 4, 4; Peas. B1, 259. 295; Adm. 3, 13; 6, 3; come to grief, Leb. 74.

ꜣḳw ruin (n.), Adm. 3, 13; misfortune, Pr. 11, 4 ().

var. of ỉḳḥw 'battle-axe'.

ꜣk be bent, of elbow, Pt. (L I), 27.

ꜣkr n. div. earth-god Aker, Pyr. 796; Urk. V, 205, 17; the earth itself, Pyr. 325; pl. earth-gods, Pyr. 393 (det.); 2202; TR 59, 3 (det.); BD 140, 4 (det.).

see under ꜣyt 'blanch (?)'.

var. of ꜣdw 'aggressor'.

var. of ꜣṯyt 'nurse'.

var. of ꜣṯwt 'bed'.

ꜣṯf be crowned, Urk. IV, 965, 1.

ꜣṯfw atef-crown, RB 119, 11; varr. TR 20, 16; 20, 18; Hymnen, 15, 4.

ꜣṯ nurse (vb.), Pyr. 371; TR 13, 8; CT I, 48 (also var.).

ꜣṯyt nurse (n.), CT I, 48; var. P. Ram. III, B 27.

ꜣṯwt bed, L. to D. I, 4; varr. Ti, 133; Adm. 14, 1.

ꜣṯp load a ship, etc., Urk. I, 109, 5; Sin. B 244; Peas. R 7; Urk. IV, 18, 9 (); Sh. S. 146; a cargo into a ship, Sh. S. 166 (); Leb. 69); be heavy-laden with trouble, Leb. 127; Peas. B1, 70. 276 (); Urk. IV, 1076, 10; Adm. p. 104.

ꜣṯpw (< ꜣṯpw) load (n.), Adm. 1, 2; 5, 12; p. 100; cargo, Peas. B1, 259 (); P. Kah. 30, 38 ().

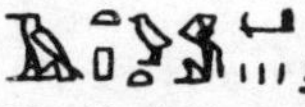 3tpwt load (n.), M.u.K. vs. 3,5; cargo, Urk. IV, 2145,13 ().

 3tp coffer, Adm. 8,5.

 3d quiver, palpitate, perhaps corrupt for 3hd, GNS 30.

 3d (1) intrans. vb. be savage, of crocodile, Urk. IV, 945,16 (det. ); be aggressive, Les. 84, 4.6.7; be angry, r 'with,' Urk. IV, 1091,2; hr 'at', 1091,3; 3d ib r 'be oppressive to,' Pr. 6,1: (2) trans. vb. attack, TR 18,34: (3) n. anger, Les. 80,16. Cf. ZÄS 53,97.

 3dw aggressor, Peas. B1, 181.297; Urk. IV, 969,7; varr. 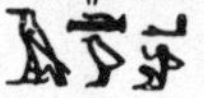 Peas. B2,60;  Urk. IV, 972,5.

 3d decay (vb.), TR 25,2.

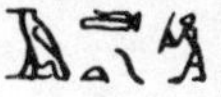 3dt prepare a sleeping place, Adm. 9,1; var.  14,2.

 ỉ reeds, Bersh. II, p. 19; leaves of reeds, Eb. 49,2 (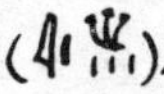).

 ỉ suff. 1 sg. I, me, my, varr. 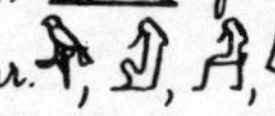, Gr. §34; sportive wtg. , p. 478, M2.

 ỉ (1) interj. O!, var. , Gr. §§ 87. 258: (2) vb. say, JEA 21,177: (3) n. utterance, Pyr. 1708.

 ỉ3t back of man or animal, P. Kah. 7,26; Sin. B141 (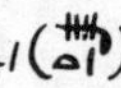); M.u.K. 2,5; 4,8 (); middle of river, BH I, 25, 23-4 (); of lake, Westc. 6,11.

 ỉ3t standard for cult-objects, Pyr. 1287; Urk. IV, 99,13; BD 166,11.

 ỉ3t (1) mound, JEA 34,15; P. Wilbour, 33;  'snakes of the mounds,' Caminos, Lit. Frag. pl. 2, 2,13 = p. 11: (2) ruin, JEA 39, 21 (3ỉ); varr. 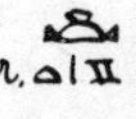 BD 185,16; 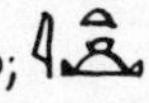 RB 57,12.

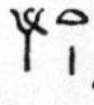 ỉ3t office, function, Les. 68,8; 71,10; Siut, pl. 9, 359; Urk. IV, 209,2; varr. 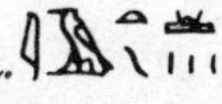 Westc. 9,11; pl.  Urk. IV, 1425,13; ỉ3t nbt 'every o.' = every official, 1113,1.

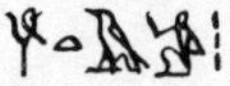 ỉ3tyw office-holders, Urk. IV, 1382,3.

 Ỉ3t n. div. a milk-goddess, var. , Pyr. 131.

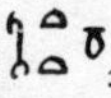 ỉ3tt milk or cream, varr. 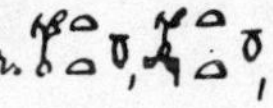, Gr. p. 509, S40; dsrt ỉ3tt, see under dsrt.

 ỉ3ỉ vb. 3 inf., adore, ZÄS 79,86.

 i3w adoration, BD 2,2; varr.  RB 59,15;  110,14;  Urk. IV, 430,17; 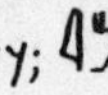 2038,14;  142,8. Cf. ZÄS 79,87.

 i33 mounds of rubble, Rec. trav. 29,164,7; cf. JEA 34,15.

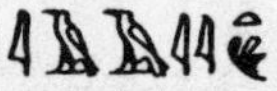 i33yt rod, Peas. B1,22; varr.  R 72;  TR 39,5;  Pyr. 866;  CT I, 49.

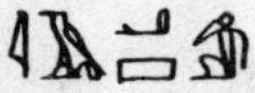 var. of ʿš 'summon'.

 i3wi (1) vb. be aged, BH I,8,8; attain old age, Pr. 17,10-11: (2) n. old age, Sin. B168; Pr. 4,2; varr.  Urk. IV,10,6;  1021,5.

 i3wt old age, Pr. 16,6; Westc. 7,17; Urk. IV, 113,8; var.  48,7.

 i3w old man, Westc. 7,25; Urk. IV,1078,11; var. 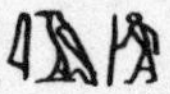 Les. 72,22.

 i3yt old woman, TR 20,35; varr. 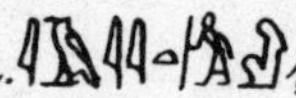 Rekh. 8,23 = GNS 60; 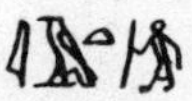 Urk. IV, 1344,7.

 i3wt herds, Urk. IV, 1309,6. Later wtg. of ʿwt 'small cattle'.

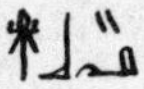 i3by (1) adj. left(-hand), east, eastern: (2) n. the left side of, Sethe, Rechts. Varr. 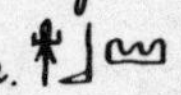 BH I,25,34; 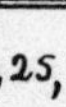 Urk. IV, 262,12; 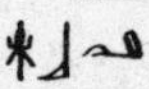 1104,10; 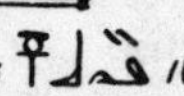 1672,12.

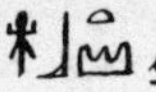 i3bt the East, Pyr. 306 (, ); Bersh. I,15 (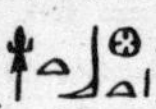); Urk. IV, 19,9; 437,12; V,51,11.

 i3bty (1) adj. east, eastern, Pyr. 344 (); BH I,25,35 (det. ); Urk. IV,661,1; 825,12 (det. ); V,147,4; left-hand, Westc. 8,20 (det. ): (2) n. the East, Sin. B208 (det. 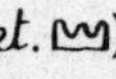); RIH 23 (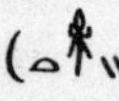); BD 368,7.

[illegible] i3btyw Easterners, Sin. R85; var. [illegible] Urk. IV, 613,3.

[illegible] i3btyw the east of, Sin. B14; varr. [illegible] R39; [illegible] Urk. IV, 834,13.

[illegible] i3b the east wind, var. [illegible], Pyr. 554.

[illegible] i3bt the east wind, Siut, pl. 11,22; var. [illegible] Pyr. 554.

[illegible] i3btt the East, P. Kah. 13,13; BD 197,1 (det. [illegible]); m i3btt 'in the east of', Urk. IV, 420,7 ([illegible]).

[illegible] i3btt snare(?), Eb. 1,17. Cf. ibt 'bird-trap' below.

ỉꜣm *bind the sacrifice*, varr. 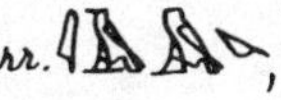 ,  , SDT 113.

ỉꜣm *offer*, n 'to', Neferhotep, 30.38.

, 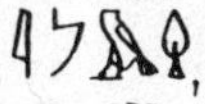 , see below s.v. ỉmꜣ.

ỉꜣrw *rushes*, Pyr. 130; BD 465, 16; sḫt ỉꜣrw 'Field of R.' in the Beyond, Urk. V, 26, 6; BD 223, 15.

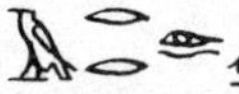

ỉꜣrr *be dim* of eye; *be weak*(?) of heart, var. dets.  , SDT 205.

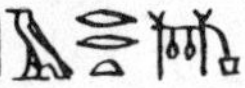

ỉꜣrrt *vine*, Urk. I, 103, 14; var. 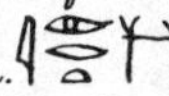 IV, 73, 11. Cf. Garten. 62. 157.

ỉꜣrrt *grapes*, Sh. S. 47; Sin. B 82; cf. ZÄS 58, 45; 59, 71.

ỉꜣḫw *sunshine*, Pyr. 304. 751. 1078; *radiance*, Pyr. 324. 513; as god, det.  , TR 18, 6; var.  18, 5. Earlier form of ꜣḫw 'sunshine'.

ỉꜣs *bald*, varr. ,  , 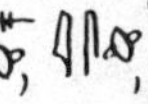 , ZÄS 63, 154; Orientalia, 7, 67.

ỉꜣš *call, summon* s'one, with n, Sh. S. 170; Sin. B 248; Pr. 7, 1; Les. 76, 5. Cf. ꜥš below.

ỉꜣḳ (?) *leap* (vb.) Urk. IV, 259, 17.

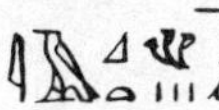

ỉꜣḳt (1) *leeks*, Westc. 9, 20; Eb. 64, 6: (2) *vegetables in general*, Sh. S. 48.

ỉꜣkw *the aged*, BD 240, 6.

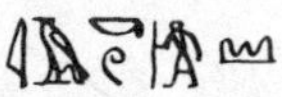

 var. of ỉkw 'stone-quarry'.

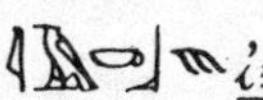

ỉꜣkb *mourning*, Urk. V, 104, 6; var.  104, 9; pl. *wailings*, BD 243, 1.

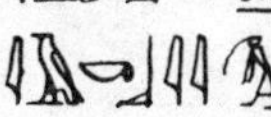

ỉꜣkby *mourners*, BD 177, 11.

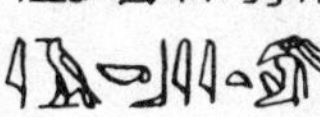

ỉꜣkbyt *mourning woman*, BD 352, 14; var. dets. 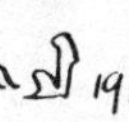 19, 8.

ỉꜣṯ (1) *be injured*, ZÄS 57, 3* 7*; *be distorted*, P. Ed. Smith, 198-9: (2) *be missing*, r 'from', Urk. V, 173, 13; *abate*, of fever, Sm. 17, 13. Var.  ZÄS 57, 3*.

ỉꜣṯw *shambles*, Urk. V, 79, 5; varr.  79, 12;  80, 10.

ỉꜣṯyw *mutilation*, Peas. B1, 177.

 var. of ỉd 'boy'.

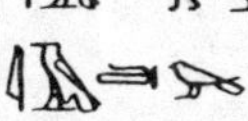

 var. of ỉdw 'pestilence'.

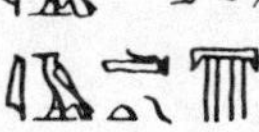

ỉꜣdt (1) *dew*, Eb. 6, 9 (abbr.); 77, 21; fig. use, Urk. IV, 385, 2; *pouring rain* in thunderstorm, 615, 15 (): (2) *pestilence*, Adm. 2, 5; P. Ed. Smith, 512;

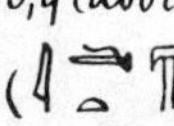

affliction, Caminos, Lit. Frag. pl. 1, 1, 2; influence, op. cit. pl. 4, 8. 9 (det.).

iꜣdt net, Westc. 5, 11; Sm. 20, 10; Caminos, Lit. Frag. pl. 3, 4, 8. Cf. GAS 87.

iꜣdt tract of land, Peas. B1, 143.

ii vb. ult. inf. come, of persons, Sin. B 129; Westc. 8, 11. 12; of things, Sh. S. 31. 155; of old age, Urk. IV, 113, 8; of time, Peas. B1, 183; Siut, pl. 11, 10; of future events, Peas. B1, 271; B2, 122; Urk. IV, 481, 16; return, Sin. R 15; Sh. S. 7; Urk. IV, 767, 3; aux. vb., Gr. § 483, 1.

Idiomatic uses: 'Welcome', Gr. §§ 313. 374; 'him in whom fault had occurred', BH I, 7, 8; 'come in peace', TR 6, 1; Bersh. I, 17; 'return safely', Sh. S. 10; BH I, 8, 13; Urk. IV, 329, 16; ii·w m ḥtp 'Welcome', L. to D. n. on II, 3; 'as the consequence, outcome of', GNS 41.

Varr. m. u. K. 9, 2; Westc. 8, 12; Urk. IV, 113, 8; Peas. B1, 171.

iyt mishap, Peas. B1, 57; trouble, B1, 184; harm, B1, 108. 109; wrong which is done, B1, 98. 103. Varr. Peas. B1, 128; B1, 154; Mill. 2, 9.

ii (?) old neg. part., JEA 34, 27.

iꜥ tomb, Pyr. 616.

iꜥ ascend, n 'to', Pyr. 1016. 1687; arise, of royal dignity, Urk. IV, 255, 9. Cf. ZÄS 46, 98.

iꜥi vb. 3 inf. wash, Sh. S. 13; Westc. 10, 11; Peas. B1, 279; Urk. IV, 547, 1; of 'washing' for gold, BM 569; wash out an inscription, Amarna, V, 26, 24; iꜥ ib 'satisfy' s'one, Urk. IV, 1751, 9; Sin. B 149; 'slake o's ardour', Peas. B1, 206; Urk. IV, 9, 9; 'vent o's feelings', Pr. 6, 2; iꜥ ḥr (1) 'wash the face': (2) 'be vengeful', GNS 34. Var. Urk. IV, 9, 9.

iꜥw washing: (1) 'breakfast' (lit. 'mouth-w.'), P. Kah. 5, 34; varr. Pyr. 60: (2) 'angry speech', Pt. (L. II) 3, 4; varr. Pr. 7, 4.

iꜥw breakfast, Pyr. 1876; var. JEA 31, pl. 4a, 10; cf. ibid. p. 9, n. 1.

iꜥꜥw cover up an inscription, Amarna, V, 26, 24.

iꜥb bowl, Gr. p. 528, W10; later , q. v.

iꜥb heap up corn with a pitchfork, GNS 112.

iꜥb vb. (1) intrans. be united, Pyr. 398; ḥnꜥ 'with', Urk. IV, 951, 11; assemble, of persons, Pyr. 164; BH I, 25, 104; Urk. IV, 566, 11; BD 133, 10: (2) trans. join s'one, Pyr. 584. 631; unite limbs, bones of dec'd., Pyr. 617; BD 407, 1; present, n 'to', Urk. IV, 325, 15; 873, 17; iꜥb ḥꜣt 'inter', GNS 59.

iꜥf wring out clothes, BH I, 29; II, 4.13; squeeze out grape-juice, Bersh. I, 31; moisture, Eb. 57, 11.

iꜥn baboon, Pyr. 1462; Bersh. II, 11; varr. BH II, 6; P. Ram. III, A 33; Urk. IV, 329, 9; Edel, §128; fem. iꜥnt, Bersh. II, 11.

iꜥnw (1) greeting (?), L. to D. IV, 2; 'gr. to...', 'hail to...', loc. cit.; TR 35, 2; (2) woe, GAS 103. Cf. JEA 16, 151.

… var. of ꜥr 'mount up'.

iꜥrt uraeus, Pyr. 265; Urk. V, 18, 14; Hymnen, 7, 2; varr. ZÄS 46, 100; Urk. IV, 385, 12.

iꜥrt abode of god, Urk. IV, 218, 14.

iꜥḥ moon: as satellite, Urk. IV, 18, 10; as god, 13, 16. Varr. Pyr. 1001; Urk. IV, 813, 5; 13, 16; 1583, 15.

… see under ꜥš-ḥꜣt 'pilot'.

iw is, are, cf. Gr. p. 551.

iw hump-back, BH II, 32.

iw vb. ult. inf. come: of persons and living creatures, Sin. B 257; Peas. R 51; B1, 60.88; Westc. 3, 11; of things, Westc. 11, 14; Urk. IV, 498, 17; of time, Sin. B 310; P. Kah. 5, 34; of future events, Urk. IV, 481, 15; of abstracts, e.g. truth, Adm. 3, 12; satiety, Peas. B1, 242; trouble, B1, 57; weakness, Pr. 4, 3; return, Leb. 137; Urk. IV, 88, 15; cf. JEA 16, 68; aux. vb., Gr. §483, 2.

Idiomatic uses: 'Welcome to me!', L. to D. II, 3 (n); 'come in peace', Bersh. I, 15; 'arrive safely', Urk. IV, 56, 16; 975, 4; 'no fault of mine came out,' Urk. IV, 151, 2; 484, 8; 'never was any fault found in me,' BM 614, 6-7; sim. ibid. 14, cf. Clère, Äg. Stud. 38; 'it is finished' at end of text, Gr. § 189; 'a rising man', § 194.

iw island, Sh. S. 109; Sin. B 211; Urk. IV, 86, 9; cf. AEO I, 10*; P. Wilbour, 27.

iwi vb. 3 inf. (1) intrans. be boatless, Pr. 8, 2; BD 261, 4; Peas. B1, 137 (det. X): (2) trans. strand, leave boatless, Pyr. 1176 (); BD 281, 3.

iw lament, BD 183, 7; cry out, CT I, 148.

iw dog, P. Kah. 7, 15.

iw wrongdoing, Leb. 111. 143; Urk. IV, 1107, 6 (); injustice, Pr. 6, 4; Peas. B1, 95. 102; iw n nṯr 'sin against God', Urk. IV, 123, 7; 505, 10; ẖr(y) iw 'victim of wrong', Pr. 9, 5. Cf. ZÄS 81, 8.

iwꜣ ox, Westc. 4, 13; Urk. IV, 351, 17 (); in pl. long-horned cattle in contrast to wndw 'short-horns', Urk. IV, 695, 13; 720, 12.

iwꜣ beef, Urk. VII, 5, 18.

iwꜣyt female representative, substitute, JEA 37, 111.

iwyt wrongdoing, Peas. B1, 264; Urk. IV, 505, 1; RB 112, 13; Les. 72, 21 (); m iw(y)t 'wrongfully' BM 614, 10 (); ꜥḳ n iw(y)t 'fall into wrongdoing', Pr. 11, 13.

iwyt house, Louvre C 15; sanctuary, Urk. IV, 835, 4; quarter of town, GAS 49; in pl. public places, Adm. 6, 10.

iwiw dog, Cairo 20506; var. BD 215, 2.

iwꜥw thigh of man, BD 215, 5; leg of beef, Siut, pl. 6, 276 ().

iwꜥ inherit, CT I, 15; Urk. IV, 199, 15; inherit from s'one, RB 111, 4 (); Cairo 20543, a, 9; succeed s'one, Pyr. 301 (,); act as heir = perform his funerary duties, JEA 16, 154.

iwꜥw heir, Leb. 52; Urk. IV, 14, 15; of endowed stela and statue, 1032, 5. Varr. (pl.), Peas. B2, 101; Urk. IV, 811, 14; 1032, 5.

iwꜥt heiress, Urk. IV, 224, 10.

ỉwꜥt inheritance, heritage, BH I, 25, 18; varr. I, 32; Sin. R 71; B 47; Urk. IV, 807, 2; 17, 4; 563, 14.

ỉwꜥ reward (vb.), Urk. IV, 2, 2; 4, 9.

ỉwꜥyt troops, JEA 39, 44; varr. Urk. IV, 648, 5; 1735, 7.

ỉwꜥw ring, Urk. IV, 997, 5; abbr. 892, 5. See also ꜥwꜥw.

ỉwbt crumb of bread (i.e. not crust), Eb. 15, 11; cf. JEA 22, 105.

ỉwf (ỉf) flesh of man, Pyr. 193 ( ); Urk. IV, 114, 15; Eb. 1, 5 ( ); meat, Pyr. 566; Sin. B 88 ( ); Westc. 4, 15; of fish, Eb. 80, 8. Cf. AEO II, 234*.

ỉwms misstatement, Gr. § 194; varr. Les. 84, 9; RB 115, 2.

ỉwn complexion, Berlsm. 6; colour, Hymnen, 3, 2; RB 113, 12; nature, disposition, Bersh. II, 21, top, 5 (det.); Merikarēꜥ, 31. 40; Urk. IV, 119, 5 (dets.).

ỉwn pillar, Pyr. 524; Sin. B 196; Urk. IV, 819, 7; 1296, 1; a man is 'a p. of his family', BM 159, 11; sim. Les. 69, 23; 74, 4; Bersh. II, 13, 13; ỉwn mwt.f 'p. of his mother', ep. of the young Horus and a priestly title, ZÄS 41, 88; Unters. II, 36, 54; ỉwn knmt a priestly title, PSBA 16, 135; ỉwn n fnd 'the nasal bone', Sm. 5, 10.

ỉwnyt pillared hall, Urk. IV, 365, 3; varr. 384, 5; 1295, 15.

ỉwnt bow, Sebekkhu, 5; var. Pyr. 1644.

ỉwntyw tribesmen (lit. 'bowmen'), P. Kah. 1, 5; varr. Les. 82, 13; Urk. IV, 195, 15; 200, 2; rarely sing. 7, 3; 9, 5; dual, 139, 4.

Ỉwnt n. loc. Denderah, AEO II, 30*.

Ỉwnỉ n. loc. Hermonthis, var. , AEO II, 22*.

Ỉwnyt n. loc. Latopolis (Esna), AEO II, 10*.

Ỉwnw n. loc. Heliopolis, AEO II, 144*; Ỉwnw šmꜥw 'Thebes', JEA 42, 12.

ỉwnn sanctuary, Urk. IV, 16, 1; 384, 2; var. 834, 2.

ỉwr conceive a child, Adm. 2, 4; BD 148, 9; 153, 11; become pregnant, Urk. IV, 226, 3 ( ); Westc. 9, 10; P. Ram. IV, C 2 (det.).

ỉwryt beans, P. Kah. 5, 31; var. Eb. 9, 18; cf. Barns, Ram. p. 26.

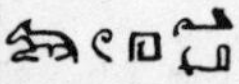 iwh load (vb.), Westc. 11,8; Adm. 4,11.

 iwḥ moisten, Urk. IV, 837,7 (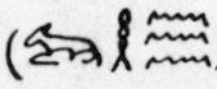); Eb. 70,1; 94,3; BD 403,7; water field-plots, Siut, pl. 19,23; inject a liquid remedy, P. Kah. 5,14; 6,2.8.

 iwḥw inundation, ZÄS 53,106.

 iwsw balance, RB 117,2; 119,10 (det. 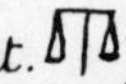); Peas. B1, 96.148; Urk. IV, 1076, 6; var. 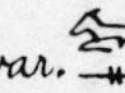 Les. 81,7. Cf. JEA 9,10, n.4.

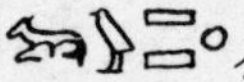 iwšš gruel, AEO II, 231*.

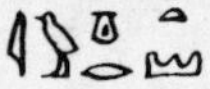 iwgrt see under igrt 'realm of the dead'.

 iwty who...not, which...not, fem. 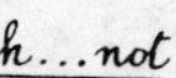, Gr. §§202-3; 307,2; 443; older 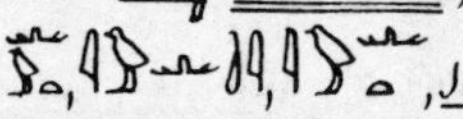, JEA 34,23; ḥr iwtt 'because...not', Gr. §223; iwty n.f 'he who has nothing', §203,1; iwty sw 'he who is nothing', §203,2; sp n iwtt 'to no purpose', GNS 52.

 iwtt what is not, does not exist, RB 116,10; ntt iwtt 'everything', Gr. §203,4; varr. 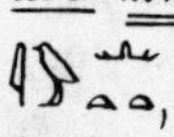, 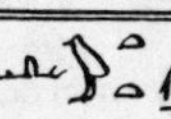 Pyr. 1146.

 iwtyw corruption, Urk. V, 76,9.

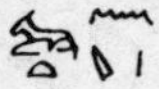 iwtn ground, Urk. IV, 840,1; iwtn n pr 'gr. of a house' on which it is built, JEA 14,299(8); floor, flooring, ibid; Urk. IV, 842,12.

 iwd separate X r 'from' Y, Sh. S. 153; Sin. B 224; Pr. 7,11; with double obj., Sin. R 28-9; Adm. 4,14; cf. GAS 41; r iwd ... r 'between ... and ...', Gr. §180.

 iwdt separation, Peas. B1, 254.

 ib (1) heart: physical, Sin. B 38; Peas. B1,166; Urk. IV, 115,3; seat of thoughts and emotions, Sin. R 9; B 183; Peas. R 42; Urk. IV, 364,13; 969,3; ib.k m-c.k 'with self-possession', Sh. S. 16; cf. AEO II, 250*; Wortforschung, V,6: (2) mind, understanding, intelligence: ib tmw n sḫ3.n.f sf 'the m. is at an end and cannot remember the past', Pr. 5,1; in ib.i sḫnt st.i 'it was my u. which advanced my position', Leyd. V 4,6; nty ib ḥft.s 'that which is intelligible,' RIH 24,7 = GAS 97-8; ib n nsw 'm. of the king' (title), Urk. IV, 927,13; ḥr ib n 'in the opinion of', Peas. B1, 104: (3) will, desire, Sin. B 125; Pr. 7,9; RB 110,10;

Merikarē', 131.134; ỉb 'do the w. of', P. Kah. 34,2-4: (4) mood: pty ỉrf pꜣ ỉb 'what is this m.?', Westc. 9,13; ỉrr·t pꜣ ỉb ḥr m 'why are you in this m.?', 12,21-2: (5) idiomatic uses: n ỉb n 'for the sake of', L. to D. V, 2 (n.); (r)dỉ m ỉb 'determine'; rdỉ ỉb m-sꜣ 'be anxious about'; rdỉ ỉb ẖnt 'give attention to', see below s.v. rdỉ: (6) vb. wish, with foll. infin., Gr. § 292.

ỉb kid, Rekh. 6.

ỉbỉ vb. 3 inf. (1) intrans. be thirsty, Mill. 2,12; Adm. 7,11: (2) trans. thirst after s'thing, Adm. 2,10 (dets.). Varr. BM 101; Hatnub 16,11; P. Kah. 5,47.

ỉb thirsty man, Sin. B 96; var. RB 119,2.

ỉbt thirst, Sin. R 47; varr. Sin. B 21; Pr. 1,5; Urk. IV, 482,12; 511,11; Eb. 39,12.

ỉb think, suppose, Sh. S. 57; varr. Peas. B2,117; Urk. V, 177,9.

var. of ỉbw 'refuge'.

var. of ỉbꜣ 'dance'.

ỉbꜣ draughtsman, var., Gr. p. 534, Y6.

ỉbꜣ dance: (1) vb. BH I, 26, 186; Pyr. 1947; Urk. IV, 19,10; 259,8: (2) n. BH II, 7. 13. 17; Urk. IV, 308,12.

ỉbꜣw Barbary sheep, BH II, 4; varr. TR 22,83; 81.

var. of ỉbr 'ladanum (?)'.

ỉbw refuge, shelter, P. Kah. 2,15; Peas. B1,129; varr. Urk. IV, 1089,3; RB 114,7.

ỉbw tent of purification, Grdseloff, Das äg. Reinigungszelt; Ann. Serv. 51,129.

ỉbwy halliards (?) of ship, Urk. V, 156,11; varr. 192,7; 192,9.

ỉbnw alum (?), Rec. trav. 15,199.

ỉbr ladanum (?), Eb. 27,6; varr. Sh. S. 140; ZÄS 64,48; cf. Bull. 19,25.

ỉbr stallion, Urk. IV, 663, 10; cf. Caminos, L.-Eg. Misc. 219.

Ỉbht n. loc. a Nubian locality, var. , Gauthier, Dict. géogr. I, 64.

ỉbhty Ibhet-stone, var. , Sethe, Steine, 50.

ỉbḥ tooth, P. Kah. 5, 15; 7, 38; BD 97, 16; tusk, Urk. IV, 373, 7 ( ).

ỉbḥ stream, m 'with' liquid, Neferti 52 (det.); Eb. 100, 13; be suffused, ḥr 'with' blood, Eb. 100, 9.

ỉbḥw libationer, Urk. IV, 386, 17; var. Cairo 20712.

ỉbs headdress of king, Urk. IV, 1277, 20; var. 1286, 16.

ỉbṯ bird-trap, Teti Cem. I, 136; var. BD 289, 3.

ỉp (1) vb. count, reckon up, ZÄS 57, 7*; Urk. IV, 659, 5; 975, 11; V, 124, 11; make reckoning, ḥnꜥ 'with', BM 614, 11; assess dues, Urk. IV, 973, 3; pay, Peas. B1, 178; Urk. IV, 1119, 17; allot, n 'to', Pyr. 216. 1831; RB 112, 5; exact, r 'from', Urk. IV, 1120, 1; detail s'one for work, BD 28, 15; claim, m-ꜥ 'from', JEA 17, 59 (39); examine persons, Pyr. 590. 1287; TR 38, 11; Peas. B1, 70; Urk. IV, 119, 11; things, BH I, 7, 9; Pyr. 1033; recognize s'one, Pyr. 580. 582. 895; revise schedules, JEA 4, pl. 8, 4; take heed of, Urk. IV 754, 1; set in order bones of dec'd., Pyr. 1297. 2016; intrans. muster, assemble, of persons, Pyr. 766; ỉp 'collect o's wits', 'recover o's senses', Pyr. 2084; TR 12, 7; of an intelligent young man 'having his wits about him', Urk. IV, 160, 7; 1279, 9.

(2) n. accounting: ỉw ỉp m-ꜥ·ỉ m pr-nsw 'a. was in my hand in the Palace', Les. 79, 10; estimation: tpy-ꜥ m ỉp rḫyt 'foremost in the e. of the plebs', ZÄS 60, 64.

ỉpt census, Urk. I, 16, 14; Siut, pl. 5, 244.

ỉpw payments, Urk. IV, 1119, 16; 1128, 16.

ỉpt grain-measure of 4 ḥḳꜣt, Gr. §266, 1; P. Wilbour, Index.

Ỉpt-swt n. loc. temple of Karnak, Sethe, Amun, §§ 15 ff.

ỉpt name and festival of the 12th month, Urk. IV, 44, 17.

ỉpt (1) harem, varr. , , ZÄS 45, 127; ỉpt rst 'the Southern H.', temple of

Luxor, Sethe, Amun, Index: (2) secret chamber of temple, varr. , , JEA 11, 2.

: for words written with these groups see under wp.

ỉpȝ private office, Les. 81, 18.

ỉpȝt private office, BM 614, 10.

Ỉpw n. loc. Ekhmīm, var. , AEO II, 41*.

ỉpw demonstr. adj. m. pl. these, Gr. §110; Plural, §59; dual , , ibid. §61.

ỉpf demonstr. adj. m. pl. those, var. , Plural, §59.

ỉpn demonstr. adj. m. pl. these, var. , Gr. §110; Plural, §59.

ỉptw demonstr. adj. m. pl. these, Gr. §110; Plural, §60; dual , , ibid. §62.

ỉptwt demonstr. adj. f. pl. these, Plural, §60; dual , , §62.

ỉptf demonstr. adj. f. pl. those, Plural, §60.

ỉptn demonstr. adj. f. pl. these, var. , Gr. §110; Plural, §60; dual , , , , §62.

ỉpdw furniture, Rekh. 18; var. Urk. IV, 1046, 10.

ỉf see under ỉwf 'flesh'.

ỉfd quadruple (vb.), Urk. IV, 2029, 15.

ỉfdt a four, quartette, Gr. §260.

ỉfd rectangular, Bersh. I, 14, 6; Urk. IV, 1122, 8; Rhind, 44, 1.

ỉfd cloth, Peas. R 48.

ỉfdy couch, Westc. 10, 12; var. Adm. 14, 2.

ỉfd flee, Urk. IV, 658, 1; 697, 14; wtḫ m ỉfd 'flee headlong', RB 65, 9; ỉfd ḥr ssmt 'travel by horse', Urk. IV, 2160, 1 ( ).

ỉm there, therein, therewith, therefrom, Gr. §205, 1; ntyw ỉm 'the dead', RB 110, 14.

ỉm form, shape, Pyr. 909; Urk. IV, 246, 2; CT I, 106 (,); side, Pyr. 1114; cf. ZÄS 64, 9.

ỉm moan (vb.), Adm. 5, 5; cf. GAS 35; var. CT I, 215.

ỉmt *groaning, grief,* Adm. 3, 14.

ỉmw *grief,* Sin. R 11; var. ⸗ Caminos, *Lit. Frag.* pl. 10, 3, 1.

'Imt *n. loc.* Tell el-Farꜥûn (Nebêshah), AEO II, 171*.

ỉmt *wine of* 'Imt, var. ⸗, SDT 179.

ỉmt(y) *foster-child of the King of L. E.,* BH I, 25, bq; var. I, 33.

ỉm *gesso* (?), Les. 76, 10.

ỉmyt *pigment,* ZÄS 64, 94.

ym *sea,* var. II, AEO I, 7*.

ỉmy *who, which is in,* varr. Gr. §§ 79. 80; foll. adjj. with superlative meaning, §97; *in which is,* JEA 28, 66; cryptic wtgs. O, Northampton, p. 10*.

ỉmy-ỉb *favourite,* BM 614, 2; Urk. IV, 449, 4; var. 46, 14; 49, 7.

ỉmy-ỉs *councillor,* BH I, 44, 1; var. Urk. I, 123, 12.

ỉmy-ꜥ *regional officer* (?), Caminos, *Lit. Frag.* p. 32.

ỉmy-wrt *starboard of ship* Gîza, IV, pl. 5; Urk. IV, 310, 2 ( ); var. fem. ỉmt-wrt Urk. V, 151, 8; *west side of locality,* Th. T. S. IV, 38, A3; Rec. trav. 20, 215; *the West,* Pyr. 2085; Urk. IV, 414, 3 (det.); *designation of priestly phyle,* Urk. IV, 254, 1.

ỉmy-wt *name of Anubis-fetish,* Caminos, *Lit. Frag.* p. 30, n. 8; *as ep. of Anubis,* passim.

ỉmy-bꜣḥ *who is in the Presence,* Siut, pl. 9, 346; D. el B. 114; *who existed aforetime,* of god, Urk. IV, 111, 9; *ancestor* (usually pl.), 85, 11; 518, 13.

ỉmt-pr *will, testament,* P. Kah. 12, 1. 3; varr. Pr. 10, 5; Urk. IV, 1111, 6.

ỉmyw-mw *aquatic animals,* Amarna, VI, 15, 4; cf. Caminos, *Lit. Frag.* p. 11.

ỉmt-nḏst *stern of ship,* Urk. V, 151, 7; cf. ZÄS 54, 3.

ỉmy-r *overseer,* var. , Gr. §79, cf. ZÄS 81, 8; JEA 41, 121. Usually foll. by specification of office, e.g. ỉmy-r kꜣt 'o. of works', Urk. IV, 52, 1. 8; 448, 10. 13; ỉmy-r pr 'steward', 150, 16; 400, 8; ỉmy-r-pr wr 'high steward', Peas. R 40, cf. AEO I, 45*; ỉmy-r mšꜥ 'general', AEO I, 25*; JEA 39, 33 ff; 'foreman' of gang, 39, 38: fem. , Lac. Sarc. I, 17. 19.

imy-rn·f list of names, P. Kah. 13, 1; var. Urk. IV, 11, 4.

imy-hrw·f who is on duty for the day, of sentry, Sin. R 45.

imy-ḥȝt who, which is in front, Cairo 20088; Eb. 104, 1; which was before, of time, Urk. IV, 766, 6; Eb. 41, 1; ḥȝty·k n imy-ḥȝt 'thy former heart', Urk. IV, 115, 4; imyw-ḥȝt 'those of former times', Adm. p. 97 (det.); Urk. IV, 59, 3; imt·sn ḥȝt 'those which preceded them' = their originals, Urk. IV, 99, 14; sim. JEA 39, pl. 2, 23, cf. p. 20 (3d); pattern, mould of conduct, Peas. B1, 193. 218.

imt-ḥȝt·f 'she who is on his front' = the royal uraeus, Urk. IV, 83, 16.

imy-ḫnt chamberlain, varr. , , AEO I, 23*.

imy-ḫt (usually pl.) following after, of time, Siut, pl. 19, 35; who are in attendance on, Urk. IV, 520, 12; V, 10, 5 (det.); in sing. member of the bodyguard (?), JEA 39, 39 (,); those of later times, posterity, Urk. I, 46, 12 ( ); IV, 57, 15 ( ); Adm. p. 97; in sing. he who shall come after, Pr. 15, 11 ( ).

imy-st-ʿ acolyte, Urk. IV, 100, 14; pl. helpers, Pyr. 398. 558.

imy-sȝ attendant, Peas. B1, 186; B2, 116; P. Kah. 18, 48.

imyw-tȝ snakes, BD 138, 11; imyw-tȝ-mw 's. of land and water', Caminos, Lit. Frag. p. 11.

imi imper. give!, place!, cause!, var. , cf. Gr. p. 553.

imi neg. vb., var. , Gr. §§ 342 ff.

imy in n(·i) imy 'of (mine)', 'belongs to (me)', var. , Gr. §§ 113, 3; 114, 4.

imiwti between, Pyr. 683. 1125; among, 1205 ( ); m-imiwti 'between', Gr. § 177. Older form of imytw below.

imytw between, in the midst of, varr. , ; also m-imytw, r-imytw, var. r-imy, Gr. § 177.

imȝt female ibex, Dav. Ptah. II, 19; BH II, 4; also female of any wild animal, ZÄS 54, 136.

im3 (> *i3m*) a tree, Pyr. 699; varr. ibid.; Sm. 14, 4; Urk. IV, 43, 14. Not 'date-palm', P. Wilbour, 31, n. 6.

im3 (> *i3m*) kind, gentle, *n* 'to', JEA 37, 109; well-disposed, *n* 'to' a temple, Siut, pl. 16, 9; pleasing, *n* 'to', Pyr. 791 ( ); be gracious, *n* 'to', of goddess, Caminos, Lit. Frag. pl. 2, 2, 10 ( ); be delighted, charmed, *r* 'with', Pyr. 1802 ( ); *im3-ib* 'be well-disposed', *n* 'to', Les. 75, 20; Siut, pl. 19, 26 ( ); Urk. IV, 149, 16; *im3 ḥr* 'gracious of countenance', RB 110, 15 ( ).

im3t charm, kindliness, graciousness, Pyr. 562 ( ); Siut, pl. 4, 228; Les. 80, 22 ( ); Urk. IV, 612, 4 ( ); *nb im3t* 'possessor of ch.', Louvre C 172 ( ); *wrt im3t* 'great in gr.', ep. of queen, Urk. IV, 26, 14; 224, 14 ( ); favour toward (lit. 'of') s'one, BH I, 25, 117-8 ( ).

im(3)w brilliance, splendour, BM 552; varr. Urk. IV, 15, 4; RB 113, 10; 113, 12; Urk. IV, 1847, 16.

im(3)w tent, Urk. IV, 659, 6; varr. 656, 13; 1303, 13; Amarna, V, 26, 5; Sin. B 110; hut, Caminos, Lit. Frag. pl. 2, 2, 3.

im3ḫ spinal cord, var. , Gr. p. 465, F 39.

im3ḫ honour, veneration, Pyr. 811; Sin. R 5; Pr. 17, 11 ( ); the blessed state of the dead, Sin. B 191; Peas. B 1, 322; Urk. IV, 113, 7; *im3ḫ r* 'h. is due to', Pyr. 1289; cf. JEA 31, 115.

im3ḫt honour, Les. 81, 16.

im3ḫy vb. 4 inf. be honoured, *ḥr* 'by', BH I, 9 ( ); 24 ( ); 44, 3; *n* 'by', Siut, pl. 4, 227 ( ).

im3ḫw revered one, of the blessed dead, Pyr. 1203; BH I, 7, 12 ( ); Urk. IV, 59, 4 (pl.); of the aged living, Westc. 7, 20 ( ); P. Kah. 2, 8 (pl.).

im3ḫyt revered one, of dead woman, Bersh. II, p. 25; var. BH I, 12.

imw ship, P. Kah. 27, 12; 33, 16; Adm. 7, 12; varr. Urk. IV, 132, 7;

ZÄS 68, 8; Gr. p. 498, P1; ship-load, Caminos, L.-Eg. Misc. 311.

ỉmn create, Pyr. 1095; RB 114, 5.

Ỉmn n. div. Amūn, cf. Sethe, Amun.

Ỉmnt n. div. Amaunet, cf. ibid, Index.

ỉmn (1) adj. secret, hidden, Leyd. V 4, 2; Siut, pl. 5, 239; 16, 25; var. det. Pyr. 399: (2) vb. conceal, hide, Pyr. 434. 516; Adm. 7, 2.

ỉmnt secret (n.), Cairo 20446.

ỉmnw secret (n.), Peas. B1, 182.

ỉmnt secret place, Urk. IV, 384, 6.

ỉmn (1) adj. right (-hand): (2) n. right side; the West, Sethe, Rechts. Varr. Pyr. 888; 730.

ỉmnt the West, Hymnen, 9, 2; Sin. B 214; Leb. 38; Urk. IV, 65, 9; 484, 13; personified as goddess, BM 614, vert. 3 (bis); CT I, 127; varr. BM 614; Bersh. I, 15; Urk. IV, 995, 10; D. el B. 115.

ỉmnty right (-hand), Westc. 8, 19 (det.); BD 457, 1 (); western, Sin. R 18; BH I, 26, 146; Urk. IV, 402, 1; the West, Pyr. 821 (); RIH 23; Urk. IV, 891, 3 (det.); BD 142, 11.

ỉmnty the west wind, Sin. B 14; varr. , Pyr. 554.

ỉmntt the West, Urk. IV, 423, 1; BD 29, 2; 278, 14 (det.); var. 30, 7.

ỉmntỉ Westerner, Pyr. 471; usually pl. Urk. IV, 17, 1; 613, 3; used of the dead in ḫnty ỉmntyw 'Foremost of the W.', ep. of Osiris, passim. Varr. pl. , Pyr. 759; Les. 73, 22.

ỉmnyt daily offerings, JEA 33, 27; var. Urk. IV, 204, 1.

ỉmr be deaf, Pr. 4, 4.

ỉmḥt netherworld, Urk. IV, 116, 11; used of tomb, 484, 14 ().

ỉms (1) in ỉms ỉb 'kindly disposed', 'pleasant', n 'to', Urk. IV, 807, 11-12; var. BH I, 7, 7: (2) var. of ỉwms 'misstatement'.

ʾImsti n. div. Imseti, one of the four sons of Horus, Pyr. 2078; Urk. V, 155, 14; varr. , Pyr. 1097; BD 57, 13.

imdr rampart, P. Kah. 2, 14.

in (1) prep. by, of agent: (2) non-encl. part.: (3) interrog part.: (4) emphatic form of prep. n, cf. Gr. p. 553: (5) so says... JEA 21, 179. Var. Urk. IV, 6, 2.

ini vb. 3ae inf. (1) bring, fetch, Sin. B 42. 178. 181; Sh. S. 114. 129; Westc. 8, 9; Urk. 342, 16; 702, 4; carry off, bring away, Sin. R 15; B 30; Urk. IV, 36, 7; 659, 14; of being 'carried away' by an impulse, Sin. B 39. 185; bring about an event, Peas. B1, 255; Leb. 57.

(2) remove s'thing bad, Urk. IV, 390, 16; Eb. 88, 10; int rd '(the rite of) removing the foot(print)', Th. T. S. I, p. 93; JEA 24, 87; 25, 215; overcome trouble, Caminos, Lit. Frag. p. 11.

(3) reach, attain a place, Urk. IV, 1280, 1.6; in drw 'a. the limit(s)' of a place, BH I, 8, 9; RB 111, 4; of skill, Pr. 5, 9; of strength, Urk. IV, 189, 14; sim. in r drw, Pyr. 416; Mill. 2, 11; in r-ʿ 'a. the limits' of lands, RB 114, 9.

(4) buy, Stud. Griff. 123; in m 'sell', loc. cit.

(5) appoint, r 'to' an office, BH I, 25, 71; Les. 98, 21; Urk. IV, 55, 13.

(6) use, Pyr. 886. 887; Peas. B1, 213; h. 15, 9.

(7) Idiomatic uses: in m 'have recourse to', Rec. trav. 39, 105; in pḥwy, in drw, 'make an end of', 'vanquish', JEA 30, 16; see also Caminos, L. Eg. Misc. 513; it in 'move restlessly', Pyr. 1459; for further uses cf. JEA 24, 124. — Var. Urk. IV, 702, 4.

ʾIn-ḥrt n. div. Onuris, varr. , , Junker, Onurislegende.

inw produce of region, Peas. R 35; Sh. S. 175; tribute of subject lands, Urk. IV, 523, 5.6; 671, 6; gifts from palace, BH I, 26, 153-4; diplomatic g. from foreign powers, Urk. IV, 668, 6; 700, 16; 701, 11; dues to be paid, P. Kah. 26, 35; quarry of hunter, Sin. B 90. Var. BH I, 26, 153-4.

inyt refrain(?) of song, P. Kah. 2, 10.

inw matting, Caminos, Lit. Frag. p. 12.

inw pattern, model, Urk. IV, 120, 5.

int the bulṭi-fish, var. , Gr. p. 476, K1.

ini vb. 3ae inf. delay, TR 2, 25; hold o'self aloof, r 'from', CT I, 231.

in eyebrows, Sh. S. 65; prob. error for inḥ, q.v.

int valley, Th. T. S. I, 9; Urk. IV, 19, 10; 85, 11; 386, 15; var. 654, 9.

in cordage of ship, Les. 68, 7; Urk. V, 173, 14; var. 174, 14.

inyt materials (?) for handicrafts, Adm. 3, 8.

inꜥ chin, Pyr. 1308. Later ꜥnꜥn, q.v.

inꜥt chin, cf. P. Ed. Smith, 515.

inb wall, Sin. R 45; var. Sin. B 17; 'Inb-ḥḏ 'White Wall', name of Memphis and its nome, AEO II, 122* f.; 'Inbw ḥḳꜣ eastern frontier fortress, GAS 112, n. 2.

inbt fence, stockade, Sin. B 116; CT I, 60; var. det. Sin. R 141.

inb wall off a place, Urk. IV, 2155, 11.

inbꜣ be dumb, Eb. 100, 15.

inp decay, TR 25, 6.

inpw royal child, Urk. IV, 1281, 8; varr. (of princess!) 260, 17; 219, 4; 157, 7.

'Inpw n. div. Anubis, Peas. B 2, 115; varr. JEA 2, pl. 2, 4; Les. 73, 4.

inm skin of man, Les. 86, 7. 8; Urk. IV, 339, 17; V, 66, 11; of animal, Sin. B 198 (det.); Urk. IV, 329, 10 (det.); 696, 1; hues of sky, RB 113, 12–13, cf. Breasted, Development, 316, n. 1; of cloth, Caminos, L.-Eg. Misc. 213.

inn indep. pron. 1 pl. we, var. , Gr. § 64.

innk thyme (?); water-mint (?), Barns, Ram. p. 17.

inr stone, Sin. B 300; Urk. IV, 1295, 1; rock, Urk. IV, 894, 2; slab, block of material, TR 20, 62; Urk. IV, 701, 13; 732, 16; m inr wꜥ 'consisting of a single s.', 932, 15; cf. also 366, 17; inr n mꜣt 'granite', Leb. 60–1; inr n 'sea-shell', ZÄS 64, 49;

inr ḥḏ 'limestone', Sethe, Steine, 7; inr (ḥḏ nfr) n 'sandstone', op. cit. 13. Abbr. Sin. B196; var. Urk. IV, 1729, 7.

inry shudder, varr. , , cf. P. Ed. Smith, 512.

inhmn pomegranate (tree and fruit), Urk. IV, 73, 12; varr. Eb. 19, 19; 16, 16. Cf. ZÄS 45, 34; Garten, 47. 151.

inḥ eyebrows, M. u. K. vs. 4, 9; Eb. 103, 15; Sm. 3, 11; var. det. Sm. 4, 2.

inḥ (1) surround, enclose, Urk. IV, 660, 16; 758, 12: (2) rim a vessel with gold, 22, 16; 23, 5 (det. a piece of rim).

inḥꜣst lotus-leaves(?), Adm. 15, 12; Caminos, Lit. Frag. pl. 1, 3, 3; Dream-Book, 2, 5; cf. Ch. B. Text, 11, n. 8.

inst calf of leg, shank; of man, M. u. K. vs. 5, 4; of animal, Siut, pl. 8, 314 (det.); of bird, P. Kah. 5, 4; hence not 'hock' as JEA 29, 17, n. c.

insy bright-red linen, P. Kah. 4, 3; varr. Urk. V, 40, 17; 43, 10; cf. AEO I, 65.

ink unite the Two Lands, P. Kah. 1, 3; collect, gather together, Pyr. 993 ( ); 1473 ( ); Urk. IV, 21, 14 ( ); RB 114, 11 ( ); Paheri, 7, top; embrace, Pyr. 1341. 1629; Th. T. S. I, 10. 27; intrans. come together, of persons, Pyr. 164.

ink indep. pron. 1 sg. I, Gr. §64; belonging to me, §114, 3; varr. , etc., §64.

inty trans. hinder: intrans. linger, ZÄS 49, 102, n. 1.

intnt hold back, restrain, ZÄS 45, 61.

inṯ fetter (vb.), varr. , , CT I, 70.

inṯt fetter (n.), Pyr. 285; var. BD 186, 13.

indw misery, Adm. 6, 8; var. 5, 9.

ind the afflicted man, Les. 79, 5.

ind be afflicted, Hatnub, 16, 10; 20, 12.

ind-ḥr 'hail to ...', Gr. §272.

ir (1) full form of prep. r: (2) non-encl. part. as to, if, cf. Gr. p. 554. For cf. rf.

ỉry adv. thereof, thereto, var. …, Gr. §113, 2.

ỉry adj. relating to, Gr. §79. See the compounds below.

ỉry-ꜥt hall-keeper, Kemi, 1, 81; BM 831.

ỉry-ꜥꜣ door-keeper, Urk. IV, 129, 13; varr. … V, 67, 5; … RB 121, 10-11; cf. AEO I, 90*.

ỉry-pḏt bowman, JEA 39, 41.

ỉry-nfr-ḥꜣt keeper of the diadem, BM 101; var. O.K. … Urk. I, 118, 5.

ỉry-rdwy one in attendance on, Urk. IV, 994, 2; Amarna, III, 28.

ỉry-hp custodian of laws, JEA 27, 76.

ỉry-ḥꜣt pilot, AEO I, 94*.

ỉry-ḥmw helmsman, Urk. IV, 1851, 4; BD 3, 2. Cf. AEO I, 94*.

ỉry-ḫt overseer, administrator, BH I, 30; Urk. IV, 1104, 10.

ỉry-sꜣ keeper of cattle-pens, AEO I, 97*.

ỉry-šdm functionary, Urk. IV, 1088, 14; var. … 1106, 11.

ỉrt-šnbt pectoral, Caminos, Lit. Frag. pl. 9, 2, 9.

ỉri companion, Pyr. 2061; fem. … Paheri, 7, 3.

ỉryw crew of boat, Urk. IV, 895, 11.

ỉrt duty of s'one, Sin. B 246. 290; Urk. IV, 1152, 9; use, purpose of s'thing, Urk. IV, 975, 9. Varr. … Les. 68, 9; … 71, 7; … Urk. IV, 28, 9; … 752, 9; … 975, 9.

… var. of ꜣr 'drive away'.

ỉrt eye, Sin. B 279; ỉrt nb 'every eye', Urk. IV, 495, 7; = 'everyone', 1006, 16. The reading of the masc. dual …, e.g. Sin. B 169; P. Kah. 7, 36; Pr. 4, 3, is not known.

ỉri vb. 3ae inf. (1) create, beget human beings, Sin. R 8; B 72; Pr. 7, 10; ỉr n, fem. ỉrt n, 'engendered by', in filiations, Gr. §§ 361. 379, 3; make, construct concrete things, Sin. B 17. 305; Les. 70, 17; 71, 4. 6; Urk. IV, 207, 11; 437, 4. 13; ḫsbḏ ỉryt 'artificial lapis-lazuli', Urk. IV, 701, 2; make decrees, laws, written documents, Siut, pl. 6, 260; P. Kah. 11, 10; Mill. 1, 1; Eb. 1, 9; Urk. IV, 1045, 4; ỉr m sš 'put into writing',

Urk. IV, 1111, 15; 1112, 4; abstracts, e.g. trouble, Peas. B1, 98.102; a (fair) name, B1, 64; sim. Sin. B299; Urk. V, 104, 6; M. u. K. 2, 3; Pr. 7, 9; actions, e.g. an assault, Sin. B101; a flight, B277; a noise, Westc. 12, 3; sim. Sin. B192; Sh. S. 55; Les. 71, 13; Urk. IV, 5, 7; 194, 15.

(2) do: (a) with obj., e.g. good, Sin. B74-5; evil, Les. 69, 22; justice, Peas. B1, 68; iry.i m 'What can I do?', Adm. 2, 9; sim. Westc. 11, 6; Sin. B183; Adm. 3, 7; ir ib 'do the will of', P. Kah. 34, 2-4; ir ḥꜥw 'do attendance on', Sin. B282-3; ir wpt 'do business', Sin. B117; Pr. 7, 3; JEA 4, pl. 8, 7; ir wpt ḥnꜥ 'punish', L. to D. IV, 4-5 (n.); ir ḥr 'do the bidding of', JEA 4, pl. 8, 9, cf. p. 34, n. 7; ir ḥst 'do the pleasure of', Peas. B1, 3; D. el B. 107; cf. GES 9: (b) without obj. 'do (anything)', L. to D. II, 4; 𓁹𓇋𓇋 'I will do so', answer to order or request, D. el. B. 107; irr ḥm.k m mrr.f 'Your Majesty will do as you wish', Sin. B236; 'the land turns round mi irr nḥp as does a potter's wheel', Adm. 2, 8.

(3) act, take action, Peas. B1, 156; B2, 124; Leb. 114; act as, in the capacity of, an official, etc., Westc. 9, 12; Pr. 5, 3; Sh. S. 183; Peas. B1, 129-30; Urk. IV, 545, 7; exercise an office, Westc. 9, 11; Sin. B235; Les. 72, 12; Urk. I, 106, 9; appoint officials, Peas. B1, 296; Urk. IV, 1112, 9.

(4) achieve a result or purpose, Mill. 1, 3; Westc. 4, 11-12; Sin. B52.203.

(5) in medical contexts: prepare a remedy, P. Kah. 5, 14; Eb. 38, 6; apply a remedy, Eb. 46, 10; treat an ailment, Rec. Champ. 401.

(6) in mathematical contexts: ir ꜥ3y x r y 'work out the excess of x over y', P. Kah. 8, 51-2; ir x sp y 'multiply x by y', 8, 34; ir x [hieroglyphs] 'square x', JEA 15, pl. 36, 14, 4.6.

(7) used pregnantly, succeed, Pr. 8, 5; make prosperous, maintain, L. to D. VI, 8 (n.)

(8) various: lay out a garden, Sin. B305; sim. Urk. IV, 73, 10; cultivate crops, JEA 16, 69; perform a miracle, Westc. 11, 11; a dance, Sin. B194; prepare food and

drink, BH I, 8, 20; Sin. B 84; garner corn, Urk. IV, 743, 1; read aloud a book, BD 497, 12; recite a spell, M.u.K. 6, 7; spend, pass time, Sin. B 29; Sh.S. 41; Peas. B1, 31; Westc. 2, 6; celebrate a festival, Les. 70, 7; Urk. IV, 199, 10; traverse lands, GNS 97; conduct an expedition, JEA 35, 48; inflict a wound, L. to D. V, 1; marshal a force, Bull. 30, 101; ỉr m 'be busy with', Ikhekhi, p. 44; ỉr sp ḥnꜥ 'deal with', Pr. 14, 7; sim. 14, 9; ỉr kꜣt m 'adopt a profession as', Les. 83, 2. For various technical or idiomatic uses not included above, e.g. ỉr ỉrw 'levy a tax', see under the second element.

(9) with various prepositions: ỉr m 'make into', Urk. IV, 617, 3; Eb. 5, 15; 31, 15; 'change, transform into', Westc. 9, 27; Sm. 21, 9; 'act in accordance with', Sh.S. 20: ỉr mỉ 'act like', Mill. 2, 1; 'do, act in accordance with', Westc. 6, 22; Les. 71, 1-2; ỉr mỉ mꜣꜥt n 'do what is right for', JEA 38, 21, n. 4; ỉr mỉ ḫpr 'act properly', 'do as should be done', JEA 12, 126; ZÄS 60, 75; infin. ỉrt mỉ ḫpr 'the correct procedure', JEA 12, 126: ỉr n 'do for', 'act on behalf of', 'help', L. to D. I, 1 (n); JEA 9, 21, n. 1; 'serve' God, Adm. 5, 3; a superior, Urk. IV, 123, 12: ỉr r 'make for' a place, Westc. 12, 14; 'deal with' an accusation, Peas. B1, 257; 'do, act against', 'injure', L. to D. n. on I, 1; JEA 9, 21, n. 1; 'arrange to' do s'thing, Peas. B2, 124; 'act with a view to' a purpose, GES 10; ỉr ḫt r 'do s'thing against' = 'set upon' s'one, P. Kah. 4, 1: ỉr ḥnꜥ 'act in conjunction with', Peas. B2, 124; Leb. 114: ỉr ḥr 'steer to' a direction, D. el B. 73: ỉr ḫft 'act in accordance with', P. Kah. 29, 43; Urk. IV, 1074, 14; 'deal with' a task, Urk. IV, 421, 1.

(10) auxiliary verb, Gr. §§ 338, 1; 485.

ỉr doer (of good), Leb. 116.

ỉrr (evil-)doer, Peas. B1, 193.

ỉrw shape, form, TR 19, 29; Urk. IV, 16, 10 ( ); 220, 1 ( ); nature, 547, 12.

ỉrw cattle-tax, BH I, 8, 17; ỉr ỉrw 'levy the c.-t.' BH I, 30 ( ); Urk. IV, 75, 14 ( ).

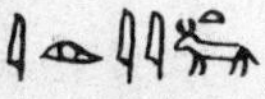 iryt milch-cow, Urk. IV, 743, 12-14.

 iryt tax-corn, Urk. IV, 72, 6.

 var. of i3rrt 'vine'.

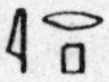 irp wine, Sin. B 82; var. dets.  BD 223, 9;  D. el B. 109.

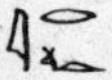 irf full form of encl. part. rf, q.v. so too 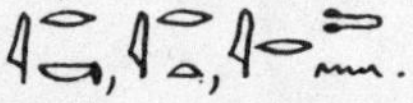.

 irtyw (1) adj. blue: (2) n. colour, P. Ed. Smith, 194 ff.: (3) a blue mineral (?), Eb. 30, 5; Adm. 3, 11 ().

 irtyw blue-dyed linen, Berlin 45 (coffin of Sobkʿo); D. el B. 130.

 irtyw mourning, Adm. 1, 8; 4, 13; cf. GAS 21.

 irṯt milk, Pyr. 32; varr. 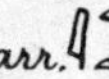 Urk. IV, 188, 11;  Sin. B 27.

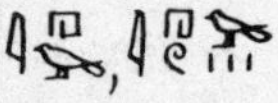 varr. of 3hw 'misery', 'pain'.

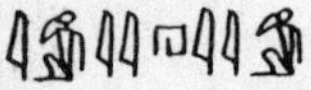 yhy Oho!, P. Kah. 4, 5; older 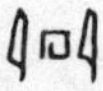 Pyr. 654.

 ihw camp, Urk. IV, 655, 15.

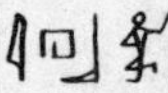 ihb dancing ritual, var. , JEA 32, 19.

 ihbw ritual dancers, JEA 32, 19; var.  BD 74, 3.

 ihm restrain, Leb. 18; var.  Leb. 49; Cf. JEA 25, 220.

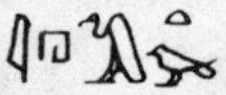 ihmt detention, JEA 25, 220.

 ihm linger, lag, Peas. B1, 56-7; B2, 104. Cf. GNS 58, n. 1.

 ihhy rejoicing, Urk. IV, 917, 5; RB 120, 6 (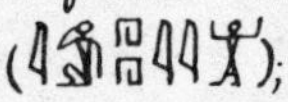); ihhy 'rejoice', Urk. IV, 580, 6;  ihhy n 'acclaim' s'one, BD 354, 12-13; RB 111, 1 (det. ); 114, 4.

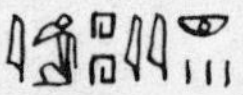 ihhy a festival, P. Kah. 24, 28-9; 25, 33-4.

 iḥ bull, Pyr. 1717; var. det. [illegible] 1544; 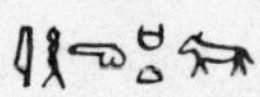 'cow', Urk. IV, 1735, 17.

 iḥt cow, Dream-book, 5, 16; D. el. B. (XI), III, 9, aa.

 iḥ Ah!, interj. expressing relief, GAS 101.

: for words written with this sign see under ʿḥ.

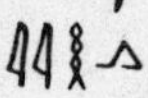 yḥ Hey!, Gr. §258.

 var. of ʿḥ3 'fight'.

ỉhy sistrum-player, ep. of son of Ḥatḥōr, BD 215,12; Urk. IV, 580,4; title of priests of H., Th. T. S. I, 20; JEA 39, 53 (q); Urk. IV, 1856,9.

ỉḥw stable, Urk. IV, 1282,8; ḥry-ỉḥw 's.-master', JEA 39, 43.

ỉḥw a measure of metal, Urk. IV, 1668,18.

ỉḥw weakness, Pr. 4,3.

var. of ꜥḥwty 'cultivator'.

ỉḥms attendant, Cairo 20143, c 1; 20598.

ỉḥtt land-tax, BH I, 8,21.

ỉẖ (1) non-encl. part. then, therefore: (2) interrog. what?, cf. Gr. pp. 554–5.

ỉẖỉ make to flourish, Urk. IV, 1541,5.

ỉẖmt bank of river, Pyr. 279; Peas. B1,6 = R 57; of fortress, Urk. IV, 312,11.

ỉẖm extinguish, annul, ZÄS 54, 19. 27 f.

ỉẖmw ignorant ones, Urk. IV, 201,1.

ỉẖmw-wrd the unwearying stars (i.e. not circumpolar), TR 22, 90–91; varr. BD 40,6; RB 110,12; cf. JEA 21, 5, n. 2; Caminos, Lit. Frag. pp. 44–5; as adj. qualifying sbꜣw 'stars', Urk. IV, 1847,15.

ỉẖm-sk indestructible star (i.e. circumpolar), Pyr. 782; BM 101; usually pl., Pyr. 733; TR 22,90; RB 110,11–12; as adj. qualifying sbꜣw 'stars', Pyr. 1123. 2051; JEA 14, 240,7; cf. JEA 21, 5, n. 2; Caminos, loc. cit.

ỉẖẖw twilight, dusk, Pyr. 751; varr. BD 134,15; 142,13; Sin. B 254. Cf. GNS 97.

ỉs (ỉz) imper. go! Peas. R 47; Westc. 8,9; Urk. V, 174,17; varr. Pyr. 1267; 1861; ỉs ḥꜣḳ 'easy prey', Urk. IV, 6,4; 691,11; ỉs ḥꜣḳ m 'work devastation among', 613,16.

ỉst (ỉzt) boundary-stone, landmark, Pyr. 1142. 1236; var. Bersh. II, 13,11.

ỉs (ỉz) (1) tomb, JEA 10, 226, n. 3: (2) council chamber(?) in 'councillor(?)',

BH I, 44; var. O.K. [hieroglyphs] Urk. I, 98, 8: (3) workshop, BH II, 6; Urk. IV, 453, 6; 503, 12. Varr. [hieroglyphs] Urk. I, 174, 16; [hieroglyphs] Sin. B 195; [hieroglyphs] Urk. IV, 30, 8; [hieroglyphs] 503, 12.

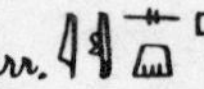

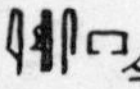

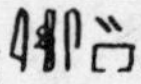

[hieroglyphs] ỉst (ỉzt) palace, Urk. IV, 256, 16; var. [hieroglyphs] Eb. 2, 4; [hieroglyphs] 'Elder of the P.', Pyr. 560; varr. [hieroglyphs] ibid.; [hieroglyphs] Bersh. I, 7.

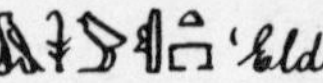

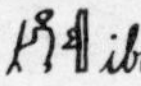

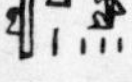

[hieroglyphs] ỉst (ỉzwt) crew of ship, Westc. 8, 4; Sh. S. 7; RB 60, 12 ([hieroglyphs]); company of soldiers, RIH 26, 14; of rebels, Urk. IV, 6, 14 (det. [hieroglyph]); gang of workmen, Sheikh Said, 16 ([hieroglyph]); Neferḥotep, 13.

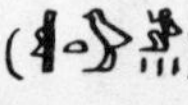

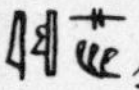

[hieroglyphs] ỉs be light of weight, in fig. sense, Peas. B1, 159; B2, 103; lie light, ḥr 'on', B1, 134 ([hieroglyphs]); ỉs ỉb 'light-minded', B1, 209.

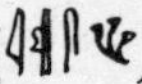

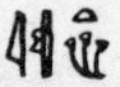

[hieroglyphs] ỉst lightness, fig. of tongue, JEA 35, 42 (l).

[hieroglyphs] ỉs (1) encl. part.: (2) interrog. part, cf. Gr. p. 555.

[hieroglyphs], [hieroglyphs], see ỉꜣs 'bald', ꜣỉs 'viscera'.

[hieroglyphs] ỉs old, ancient, Eb. 26, 12; 47, 16; 49, 1; Urk. IV, 1082, 4; var. 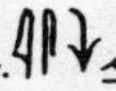 [hieroglyphs] Siut, pl. 15, 7.

[hieroglyphs] ỉsw ancient ones, Les. 72, 10.

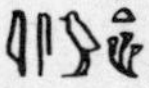

[hieroglyphs] ỉswt ancient times, BH I, 25, 45; 26, 136; var.  [hieroglyphs] Urk. IV, 1120, 5.

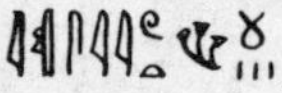

[hieroglyphs] ỉsywt old clothes, rags, Adm. 3, 4; 7, 11.

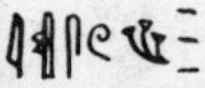

[hieroglyphs] ỉsw reeds, Eb. 79, 11; Caminos, Lit. Frag. pl. 2, 2, 15.

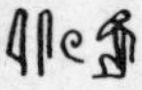

[hieroglyphs] ỉsw non-encl. part., Gr. § 232.

[hieroglyphs] ỉsw reward (n.), Urk. IV, 163, 1; 303, 7 ([hieroglyphs]); 1153, 1 ([hieroglyphs]); m-ỉsw, r-ỉsw 'in return, as payment for', Gr. § 178 ([hieroglyphs], [hieroglyphs]); [hieroglyphs] Urk. IV, 270, 17.

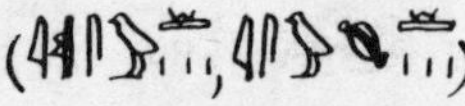

[hieroglyphs] ỉswt(y) representative, Urk. IV, 601, 4, of king as r. of sun-god.

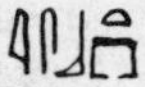

[hieroglyphs] ỉsbt throne, Amarna, III, 13; stool, VI, 30 (det. [hieroglyph]); var. 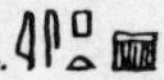 [hieroglyphs] Urk. IV, 1837, 14.

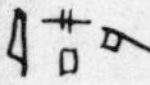

[hieroglyphs] ỉsp (ỉzp) hew, cut, Caminos, L.-Eg. Misc. 406; var. 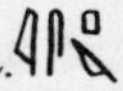 [hieroglyphs] Sm. 8, 18.

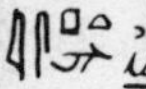

[hieroglyphs] ỉspt quiver for arrows, P. Kah. 19, 16; 20, 47 (det. [hieroglyph]); var.  [hieroglyphs] Urk. IV, 1311, 16.

[hieroglyphs] ỉspr whip, Urk. IV, 1393, 6.

[hieroglyphs] ỉsft (ỉzft) wrong, wrong-doing, falsehood, Pyr. 265 ([hieroglyphs]); BH I, 25, 36; Leb. 123; Cairo 20512, b 5; Urk. IV, 835, 13; V, 23, 3; 57, 6; RB 112, 14.

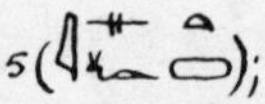

ỉsfty evil-doer, Urk. IV, 945, 14; V, 39, 17.

ỉsr (ỉzr) tamarisk, Pyr. 1962; varr. BH I, 25, 52; Peas. B1, 22. Cf. Garten. 55.155.

ʾIsr Assyria, AEO I, 191*.

ỉsḳ vb. (1) trans. hinder, Les. 79, 16; Tarkhan I, 79, 45: (2) intrans. linger, P. Kah. 38, 12 (dets.); wait, r 'for', Urk. IV, 1548, 2.

ỉsk non-encl. part., var. , Gr. §§ 119, 3; 230.

var. of part. ỉsṯ.

ỉstn strap up, bind, Westc. 12, 5; JNES 14, 23, 13; cf. Ch. B. Text, 3, n. 3.

ỉsṯ non-encl. part., varr. , , cf. Gr. p. 555; Les. 86, 3.

ỉš saliva, Sm. 3, 8-4.

ỉšt possessions, Pt. (L II), 3, 14; JEA 4, pl. 8, 8; (morning) meal, Pyr. 404. Varr. Siut, pl. 8, 313; L. to D. II, 7.

ỉšnn warcry, Sin. B 140.

ʾIšrw n. loc. precinct of Mut at Karnak, Gauthier, Dict. géogr. I, 108.

ỉšst interrog. what?, var. ; ḥr sy ỉšst 'wherefore?', Gr. § 500.

ỉšd a tree, Urk. IV, 591, 16; var. 597, 14; cf. JEA 32, 50; earlier f. Urk. V, 50, 17; 51, 8; fruit of ỉšd-tree, Pyr. 95 (); Eb. 23, 8; 45, 11 (); of various trees (abbr.), Eb. 74, 20; 75, 1.2; 84, 18.

ỉšdd sweat, Urk. V, 151, 16.

ỉḳr (1) adj. (a) of persons, trusty, trustworthy, Sh. S. 1; Pr. 11, 9; skilful, Sh. S. 188; Urk. IV, 969, 14; 974, 7; excellent: s'one is 'e. of plans', Sin. B 48; sim. Siut, pl. 9, 350; Urk. IV, 67, 11; 481, 13; 505, 13; ꜣḫ ỉḳr 'e. spirit', of dead, BD 461, 4; wꜥ ỉḳr 'uniquely e.', Urk. IV, 495, 14; pleasing: of speech, Siut, pl. 5, 242; Urk. IV, 67, 12; ỉḳr ḥr ỉb n 'well-p. to the heart of', Pr. 17, 1; well-to-do, Pr. 7, 7. 10; 10, 8; superior in rank, Pr. 5, 11; cf. Äg. Stud. 52: (b) of things concrete or abstract, excellent, Sin. B 106; Eb. 95, 16; Paheri, 3; swḥt ỉḳrt nt ʾImn 'unblemished egg of Amūn', ep. of king, Urk. IV, 811, 15; bw-ỉḳr 'excellence', Siut, pl. 5, 249; Pr. 11, 9; Peas. B1, 212; adv. r ỉḳr 'exceedingly', Gr. §205,5.

(2) n. wealth, Pr. 7,8; virtue, excellence, Pr. 5,13; Les. 69,16; Siut, pl. 4,220; pl. 'virtues' of s'one, Urk. IV, 60,14; n ỉḳr n 'by v. of', Gr. §181.

 ỉḳr trustworthy man, Urk. IV, 121,3; wiseacre, Sh. S. 184.

 ỉkḥw battle-axe, JNES 14,28; det. [illegible] Urk. IV, 726,17; var. 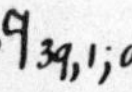 39,1; det. [illegible] 39,3.

 ỉḳdw builder, Urk. IV, 1152,8; ỉḳdw-nswt 'potter', AEO I, 72*. 73.*

 ỉkw stone-quarry, GNS 17.

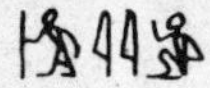 ỉky quarryman, var. 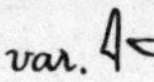, GNS 154; abbr.  JNES 18,32.

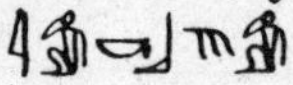 var. of ỉꜣkb 'mourning'.

 ỉkm shield, Sin. B61.134; Urk. IV, 719,1 (det. [illegible]); var.  Lac. Sarc. II, 157.

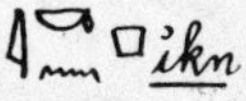 ỉkn cup, Pr. 1,5; jar, Urk. IV, 665,16; 717,16 ().

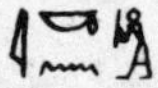 ỉkn draw water, Westc. 12,18. [26].

 ỉknw hoe, P. Kah. 20,45.

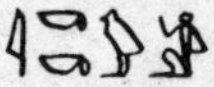 ỉkkw councillors(?), Bersh. II, 13,16.

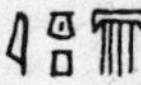 ỉgp (1) n. clouds, Pyr. 500.1774; BD 204,9; gp n mw 'cloudburst', Merikarēʿ, 73; Piankhi, 93: (2) vb. be overcast, of sky, Pyr. 393 (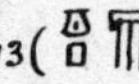); soar cloudwards, Pyr. 891. 1225.1560.

 ỉgr, 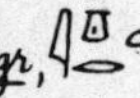 ỉgrt, see below s.v. grw, grt.

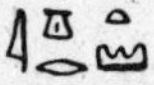 ỉgrt realm of the dead, BD 14,6; var.  262,2.

 ỉt barley, Les. 84,10; Urk. IV, 689,10;  'b. of L. E.', P. Kah. 30,41;  'b. of U. E.', Urk. IV, 195,2; corn in general, JEA 27, 24, n. 3; ỉt m ỉt 'barley', ibid. Varr. Pyr. 657;  120.

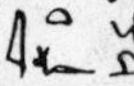 ỉt(ỉ) father, Sin. B 47; Peas. B1,62; Urk. IV, 2,10; dets. acc. to context, e.g.  Westc. 7,21; 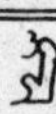 Urk. IV, 697,5; in pl. 'forefathers', Westc. 7,22; varr.  Pyr. 136; 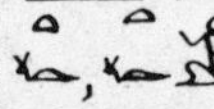 Ann. Serv. 43,315;  (in [illegible] (ỉ)t·f 'his father'), Pyr. 483; 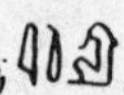 CT I, 49.

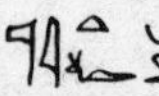 ỉt-nṯr god's father, a title, varr. 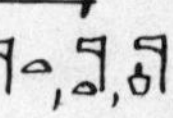, AEO I, 47*; JEA 43,35.

 ỉty sovereign, Sin. R1; varr.  Les. 77,2;  Urk. IV, 16,15; 

Pyr. 511; 1406; Urk. IV, 169, 2; 1410, 5.

ỉtyt queen-regnant, Urk. IV, 462, 15; 'queen of thousands', ep. of crown of U. E., Hymnen, 4, 5.

'Itm(w) n. div. Atum, Sin. B 207; varr. ZÄS 46, 140; BD 4, 1.

ỉtmw suffocation, GNS 106.

ỉtn sun, Sin. R 7; B 233; Urk. IV, 266, 5 (); 887, 16; 896, 5; more specifically disk of sun, 1277, 8; ỉtn n hrw 'd. of day', RB 114, 2.

ỉtnt solar goddess, Th. T. S. I, 30.

ỉtn be in opposition, m 'to', Pr. 2, 2; 13, 11; oppose, with dir. obj., Sin. B 184 (); Neferhotep, 37.

ỉtnw opponent, Pr. 15, 6; var. Urk. IV, 341, 14; ỉtnw pḏwt 'opposer of bows', ep. of Khnum, 194, 9.

ỉtnw secret, mystery, GNS 66; var. Siut, pl. 16, 12 (Tomb I).

ỉtrt (1) row of men, Urk. IV, 1104, 8; 1546, 11; of shrubs, Caminos, Lit. Frag. pl. 2, 2, 15; of shrines at jubilee, 'conclave of U. E.' and 'c. of L. E.', JEA 30, 27; ỉtrty 'the two c.', Urk. V, 108, 3 (det.): (2) chapel, Urk. IV, 825, 12; niche for statue, 1063, 1; box for ushabtis, JEA 23, 188, n. 1.

ỉtrw river, Peas. B1, 60; Sin. B 233 (det.); varr. Westc. 4, 10; BH I, 25, 33; Urk. IV, 186, 13; Caminos, Lit. Frag. pl. 3, 4, 5; RB 113, 5; Adm. 2, 6.

ỉtrw measure of length, 'schoenus', Gr. § 266, 2.

ỉtrw seasons, in k3t ỉtrw 'seasonal work', Urk. IV, 1161, 5; varr. , (without k3t), 124, 5; r ỉtrw·f 'at his (proper) times', 834, 10 (); r ỉtrw·s mty 'at her proper seasons', Les. 86, 18–19.

ỉṯḥ drag, Sin. B 194; Adm. 13, 11; P. Kah. 31, 25 (dets.); draw the bow, Sin. B 63; P. Kah. 1, 5; Urk. IV, 1290, 3; pull off bonds, CT I, 45; pull out eye, Pyr. 60 (det.); tongue, T. Carn. 5; draw off blood, Eb. 96, 13; draw out inflammation, Sm. 14, 3.

ỉtḥ fortress, Siut, pl. 11, 18; Hatnub, 29 13.

var. of ʿtḥ 'strain'.

var. of ỉtt 'fly up'

ỉṯỉ vb. 3 inf. take for use, Westc. 3, 4 ( ); 11, 8; take possession of an inheritance, etc., Sin. B 46; Peas. B1, 93; P. Kah. 3, 1; Urk. IV, 16, 15; 17, 4; 343, 10; take, conduct, n 'to', 1108, 4; take away, carry off, Sh. S. 77; Peas. B1, 14. 59; BH I, 8, 19; Siut, pl. 11, 9; Urk. IV, 1199, 10; rob, Leb. 112; JEA 9, 14, n. 2; remove o'self, Pyr. 1098. 1174. 1484; arrest offenders, Peas. B1, 104. 296; conquer, Sin. B 71; Les. 83, 24; Urk. IV, 5, 14; 556, 9; 1279, 6; spend, pass time, Pr. 19, 7; Urk. IV, 76, 15; excel, GNS 37; move, use o's arm, Pyr. 463. 676. Idiomatic uses: ỉṯ m 'take possession of', JEA 27, 147; ỉṯ … expression for disorderly or erratic movement or conduct, JEA 24, 124 f.; e.g. ỉṯ ỉn 'move unceasingly', Pyr. 1459; nn ỉṯt ỉnt 'without moving to and fro', Sm. 3, 17; the army charged m ḫn n ỉṯt ỉnt 'with a ragged chorus of shouts', Urk. IV, 710, 12; 'my mind ḥr ỉṯt ỉnt 'turned this way and that', 365, 6; ỉw tꜣ pn m ỉṯt ỉnt 'this land wavers', Neferti, 37:—ỉṯw m ʿḫḫw 'one caught in the dusk', Sin. B 254; ỉṯ ḥpt 'travel by boat', Pyr. 873. 1346; ỉṯ ḥr 'avert the face', Pr. 14, 10; ỉṯ gst 'take o's run' = move regularly, Pyr. 1167; ḫpr-ỉṯ.f 'a born conqueror', JEA 32, 55; nn ỉrt sḫn m ỉṯt 'without resting from movement', Urk. IV, 1280, 7.

ỉṯw thief, Peas B1, 164.

ỉṯꜣ steal, Peas B1, 192.

ỉṯꜣ thief, Peas. B1, 235; BD 467, 6.

var. of ỉtn 'sun'.

var. of ỉtnw 'opponent'.

ỉtt fly up, Pyr. 2042; CT IV, 59 m; varr. ibid. 58 i, BD 202, 13.

ỉd boy, BD 398, 6; var. 185, 10.

ỉdyt girl, Westc. 12, 14.

ỉdỉ vb. 3 inf. be deaf, Pyr. 499; TR 1, 55; Eb. 99, 15. Also var. of ỉdr 'stitch'.

ỉdỉ vb. 3 inf. cense, Pyr. 276. 295.

ỉdt censing, incense-burning, Pyr. 365. 1390; Les. 82, 22; sweet savour, fragrance, Urk. IV, 221, 4; 339, 15; BH I, 17; influence, JEA 4, pl. 9, 8.

ỉd assault (?) (vb.), TR 14, 2.

ỉdt wrath (?), Hamm. 114, 7.

ỉd bull, Pyr. 1545.

ỉdt (?) cow, varr., AEO II, 258*; Urk. IV, 1020, 9. 10.

ỉdt (?) womb, vulva, var., Gr. p. 466, F 45; 492, N 41; AEO II, 259*.

ỉdꜣ smooth a new-made pot, BH II, 7; cf. Mitt. deutsch. Inst. 3, 82.

ỉdw pestilence, varr. GAS 25; GNS 32; Urk. IV, 1547, 15.

ỉdb river-bank, riparian land, P. Wilbour, 26; AEO I, 13*; shore of flood, Pyr. 508; of sky, 1167; dual 'the Two Banks' = Egypt, 406; Siut, pl. 13, 7; varr. Pr. 5, 4; P. Kah. 3, 4; Urk. IV, 59, 1; 'the B. of Horus' = Egypt, 501, 1; 'the lands of the Hau-nebut', 21, 4; cf. AEO I, 208*.

ỉdmỉ red linen, BD 308, 3; var. Urk. IV, 1380, 3.

ỉdn serve instead of, replace, Pr. 1, 6; BH I, 8, 8; govern, JEA 39, 18 (dets.); serve as lieutenant-commander, Urk. IV, 897, 15.

ỉdnw deputy, usually foll. by specification of rank or office, e.g. ỉdnw imy-r kꜣt 'd.-overseer of works', Urk. IV, 52, 17; ỉdnw n mšꜥ 'lieutenant-commander of the army', AEO I, 25*; JEA 39, 46; sometimes used alone when the specific function was clear to the writer, e.g. P. Kah. 12, 14; Urk. IV, 897, 17.

ỉdn proxy, in m ỉdn 'as p. for', P. Kah. 13, 29.

ỉdn lay out (?) enclosures, Urk. IV, 57, 13.

ỉdr herd of cattle, Sin. R 143; Adm. 9, 2; Bersh. I, 18; of elephants, RB 58, 16 (det.); of geese, Urk. IV, 745, 2 (det.); var. 85, 5; 'bull of the h.' = of best grade, 196, 1; var. 699, 13; 'cattle-list', JEA 4, pl. 8, 5. Cf. AEO II, 260*.

idr (1) vb. stitch: (2) n. stitching, varr. , , P. Ed. Smith, 229 ff.

idr withhold, m 'from', Urk. IV, 159, 5.

idryt punishment, Urk. IV, 1108, 14; var. RB 119, 12.

idḥw the Delta marshes, Bersh. II, p. 19; var. dets. Urk. IV, 519, 17; Adm. 1, 4; cf. JEA 30, 52.

idḥy marsh-man, Sin. B 255; varr. R 65; B 122.

idrt hall (?) in tomb, Urk. IV, 1174, 17.

ꜥ (1) arm, Sin. B 3; Sh. S. 87; Urk. IV, 114, 14; hand, Sin. B 192. 284. For m-ꜥ, ḥr-ꜥwy, etc., see under the first element.

(2) region, province: ꜥ rsy 'the southern r.' of the Sḫt-iꜣrw, Pyr. 1084; sim. 1087; 'the Southern P.' = Upper Egypt, ZÄS 51, 122; ꜥ mḥty 'the northern r.' of the sky, Pyr. 1000; 'the Northern P.' = Lower Egypt, ZÄS 51, 122; ꜥ ḫꜣst 'the desert r.', Urk. IV, 8, 7.

(3) condition, state, Peas. B 1, 276; Adm. 6, 11; Urk. IV, 18, 11; also dual ꜥwy, Pr. 10, 12; cf. ZÄS 51, 122.

(4) item, piece: ḥbsw ꜥ 5 'five p. of clothing', Urk. IV, 894, 4; ꜥ n ṯbwt n ḥḏ 'a pair of white sandals', Gr. §94; ꜥ n ꜥnḫ 'means of subsistence', Peas. R 125. Cf. Bull. 27, 180, n. 5; 41, 133, n. 3.

(5) track, trace, L. E. var. , JEA 31, 6, n. 2.

ꜥ warrant, certificate, Pyr. 408 (also); Urk. I, 211, 11; 232, 14; record, register, Pyr. 467. 1519; st ꜥ 'place of records', Urk. I, 60, 2; sḏꜣt nt ꜥ 'seal used on r.', 64, 10; sš ꜥ n nsw 'king's r.-scribe', P. Kah. 14, 47.

ꜥ dyke, P. Kah. 2, 12; Urk. IV, 1113, 4; var. Siut, pl. 15, 6.

ꜥ wooden rod, Caminos, Lit. Frag. p. 12.

ꜥ bowl, op. cit. pl. 11, 7.

ꜥ var. of ꜥw 'dragoman'.

ꜥt limb, member of body, Sin. B 3; Eb. 1, 5; Urk. IV, 519, 15; 1278, 14.

ꜥt room, chamber, Sin. B 289; Westc. 10, 7; Urk. IV, 975, 9; later house, AEO II, 206*; 'slaughter-h.', 'brew-h.', 'bake-h.', BH II, 6; 'school', Siut, pl. 14, 67; 'the Holy Chamber' = the celestial hall of judgement, JEA 42, 32 (23); 'orchard', Urk. IV, 1417, 18; 1418, 2.

ꜥꜣ column, pillar, TR 21, 78; varr. P. Kah. 13, 12; Urk. IV, 857, 17; as part of ship, TR 27, 31.

ꜥꜣ(i) great: of size, Sh. S. 164; Westc. 2, 1; Urk. IV, 524, 7 (…); 762, 7 (…); 1048, 3 (…); V, 50, 16; of the 'high' Nile, Les. 68, 17; Herdom. 16; sbḥ ꜥꜣ wrt 'a very g. cry', Sin. B 265-6; of rank or degree, Sin. B 146. 246; Pr. 13, 6; Bersh. II, 13, 2; of quality, Sin. B 65. 215; Peas. B1, 321; Hatnub, 24, 2; Les. 81, 17 (…); of quantity, Bersh. I, 18; Urk. IV, 5, 7; plentiful, much, Sin. B 82. 85; rich in possessions, Siut, pl. 4, 228; of age, senior, P. Berl. 9010, 3; fig. ꜥꜣ ib 'be arrogant', Pr. 5, 8; 7, 7-8.

ꜥꜣ magnate, Les. 82, 2; elder son, P. Berl. 9010, 3 (…); ꜥꜣ n pr 'major-domo', AEO I, 34*.

ꜥꜣ greatness, Sh. S. 140; speak m ꜥꜣ 'boastfully', Urk. I, 224, 18.

ꜥꜣt a great thing, Bersh. I, 14, 2; Peas. B1, 103; m-ꜥꜣt-n, n-ꜥꜣt-n 'inasmuch as', Gr. §181; r-ꜥꜣt 'greatly', §205, 5. Varr. BH I, 25, 45; BM 614, 11.

ꜥꜣw greatly, Gr. §205, 4; varr. Peas. R 75; Les. 76, 13.

ꜥꜣy excess, r 'over' = math. 'difference', P. Kah. 8, 51-2; var. Rhind, 72, 2.

ꜥꜣtt in nrw kꜣw n ꜥꜣtt nbt 'guardian of all the cattle', Les. 69, 17.

ꜥꜣ here, Gr. § 205, 1; there, yonder, JEA 28, 5 (e); 35, 62. Varr. P. Kah. 32, 5; JEA 28, 5.

ꜥꜣ door, BH I, 26, 200; varr. Adm. 14, 3; Urk. IV, 168, 16; BD 136, 14; Urk. IV, 1295, 3; in dual 'double door', 'two-leaved door', BD 89, 10; 377, 1; iry-ꜥꜣ 'door-keeper', see above, p. 25.

ꜥꜣwy-r the two leaves of the door, Urk. V, 28, 13; varr. BD 55, 13; BH I, 26, 202.

ꜥꜣ ass, Peas. B1, 14; Les. 79, 9 ( ); Urk. IV, 325, 5 ( ); 'she-ass', 1735, 18.

ꜥꜣt costly stone, Urk. IV, 665, 13; 701, 13; 705, 14; 913, 2; metal, Les. 61, 12 (det. □).

ꜥꜣt stone vessel, D. el Geb. I, 13; var. Urk. IV, 637, 12; pl. Pyr. 1957.

ꜥꜣt linen cloth, Sm. 16, 19; P. Ram. III, B17.

ꜥꜣꜥ valour (?), JEA 34, 17.

ꜥꜣꜥ evil influence causing disease, JEA 21, 39.

ꜥꜣb: of things, pleasing, desirable, Peas. R 42; of persons, pleasant, Pyr. 471 ( ); Urk. IV, 844, 15 ( ); selfish, Pr. 11, 2.

ꜥꜣbt selfishness, Pt. (L. II), 5, 13.

ꜥꜣbt food, provisions, Siut, pl. 4, 228; Urk. IV, 86, 6 (dets.); offerings, 343, 11 ( ); 1544, 2 ( ); construed as sing. 769, 5.

ꜥꜣpp Apep, serpent-demon, TR 35, 1; BD 2, 16; 29, 6.

ꜥꜣm throwstick, Urk. IV, 335, 6.

ꜥꜣm Asiatic, Sin. B 265; Urk. IV, 615, 6 (det.); RB 60, 8; varr. JEA 4, pl. 9, 7; BH I, 30; Urk. IV, 743, 4.

ꜥꜣmt Asiatic woman, M. u. K. 2, 7; P. Kah. 13, 15; var. Urk. IV, 743, 4.

ꜥꜣgt hoof, Pyr. 1124; var. Eb. 65, 21.

ꜥꜣg thrash, Peas. R 73; B1, 186 (without); Siut, pl. 11, 9 (without).

ꜥꜣd in — n sḫt 'fertile soil (?)', Hamm. 114, 13.

ꜥꜣdt kind of bread (?), P. Kah. 19, 11; var. 20, 13.

ꜥꜣd be pale, pallid, Eb. 42, 9; var. Adm. 2, 2.

ꜥꜥ royal barge, Caminos, Lit. Frag. pl. 11, 2.

ꜥꜥỉ jabber, JEA 22, 37, n. 2.

ꜥꜥw flutter, of heart, Eb. 41, 21; 42, 9.

ꜥꜥwy sleep (vb. and n.), Urk. IV, 1077, 1; 1379, 13 ( ); 1547, 16; Hatnub, 49, 6; (det.); ꜥꜥwy n ḳdd 'a wave of sleep', Urk. IV, 1542, 13.

ꜥꜥb bowl, Urk. IV, 770, 15; 1296, 5. 6. Later wtg. of ỉꜥb.

ꜥꜥb comb the hair, GNS 111.

var. of iꜥf 'wring out'.

ꜥꜥny camp, Urk. IV, 656, 6; 661, 7.

ꜥꜥny coop up, confine (?), JEA 3, 106.

var. of iꜥn 'baboon'.

var. of iꜥrt 'uraeus'.

ꜥw dragoman, varr. , , Gr. p. 506, S 25; imy-r ꜥw 'caravan leader', JEA 39, 34.

ꜥwt crook, BH II, 7.

ꜥwt coll. small cattle, i.e. sheep and goats, Herdsm. 10 ( ); Adm. 5, 5 ( ); Urk. IV, 699, 14; goats only, BH I, 30 ( ); Les. 79, 9 ( ); 79, 21 ( ); ꜥwt ndst 'goats', Urk. IV, 664, 13; 705, 8; ꜥwt ḥḏt 'sheep', 664, 14; 705, 7; ꜥwt ḫꜣst 'wild game', Sin. B 89; Th. T. S. I, 9; ꜥwt špst 'noble cattle' = mankind, Westc. 8, 17; rarely of (large) cattle, Sin. B 119; herds in general, RB 114, 7; 117, 4 ( ); Adm. 12, 3; men, CT I, 155 ( ).

ꜥwꜣi vb. 4 inf. steal goods, Peas. R 43; B1, 292; Urk. IV, 64, 13; rob s'one, Hatnub, 22, 7; Peas. B1, 18. Varr. Urk. IV, 64, 13; rarely ZÄS 59, 27; JEA 16, pl. 29, 3: n. robbery, CT I, 52.

ꜥwꜣt robbery, Peas. B1, 106.

ꜥwꜣy (1) robber, Peas. B1, 302; B1, 143 ( ); Adm. 2, 9 (dets.); M.u.K. vs. 4, 2 (det.): (2) he who is robbed, in nḥm ꜥwꜣy 'rescue the r.', Sin. B 97; P. Kah. 3, 8; Urk. IV, 968, 14; 1011, 14 ( ).

ꜥwꜣyt female robber, M.u.K. vs. 4, 2.

ꜥwꜣ-irr.f brigand, Peas. B1, 235.

ꜥwꜣy reap, Urk. IV, 667, 12.

ꜥwꜣ look after, care for (?), Urk. IV, 21, 11; var. 1911, 7.

ꜥwꜣ go bad, rot, AEO II, 236*.

ꜥwꜣyt a fermented drink (?), AEO II, 236.*

ꜥwꜥw ring, Urk. IV, 892, 15; var. 38, 14.

ꜥwn be covetous, ḥr 'for', Pr. 10, 8; despoil s'one, m 'of', Urk. IV, 133, 4; ḥr 'of', Peas. B1, 231-2.

ꜥwnw plunderer, Peas. B1, 248; var. B1, 101.

ꜥwn-ib be rapacious, Peas. B1, 165. 292; Pr. 10, 5. 6; rapacity, avarice, Peas. B1, 66, 281; Pr. 10, 1; Siut, pl. 5, 231.

ꜥwnt stave, Peas. R 13.

ꜥwg parch grain, Eb. 12, 12; 54, 13.

ꜥb horn, Pyr. 914; Sin. B 54; Urk. IV, 266, 4; var. Pyr. 283; bow, GNS 105; 'overseer of horn and hoof, feather and scale' = all kinds of livestock, BHI, 7, 3; cf. Rec. trav. 38, 61.

ꜥb meal, Caminos, Lit. Frag. pl. 1, 2, 9; 2, 2, 9.

ꜥb, varr. of iꜥb 'unite'; m-ꜥb 'in the company of', Gr. § 178; 'amidst', Urk. IV, 990, 10; 'together with', 334, 7; also var. of ꜥbꜣ 'present'.

var. of ꜥbꜣ 'offering-stone'.

ꜥbt attachment: 'Good is perished, nn ꜥbt-f 'there is no a. to it', Peas. B1, 197.

ꜥbt a funerary ritual object, Meir, III, p. 28, n. 8.

ꜥbt var. of ꜥbwt 'forked staff'.

ꜥbw victims, Urk. IV, 1292, 16.

ꜥbw purification, Urk. IV, 262, 10; Th. T. S. IV, 35 ( ); purity, RB 117, 9 (det.).

ꜥbw impurity, L. to D. 10, n. 3; var. Pyr. 1332.

ꜥbw offerings, Urk. IV, 351, 14; varr. 350, 4; 1449, 5.

ꜥbw-r breakfast, Urk. IV, 59, 7; varr. 560, 10; Siut, pl. 1, 51.

ꜥbꜣ sceptre, Pyr. 197; var. 368.

ꜥbꜣ command a ship, Urk. V, 155, 16.

ꜥbꜣ present, n 'to', TR 21, 65 (…). 66; Urk. IV, 325, 15 (…); without obj., make presentation, n 'to', Siut, pl. 9, 386 (…); present o's hands in ritual gesture, Les. 68, 9 (…); provide, m 'with', Urk. IV, 1294, 8 (…).

ꜥbꜣ offering-stone, Sin. B 196; varr. … Pyr. 1156; … Cairo 20061; … Les. 79, 2; … Urk. IV, 100, 17; … 27, 3.

ꜥbꜣ glitter, Urk. IV, 340, 1; 869, 4.

ꜥbꜥ boast, m 'of', Pr. 7, 6; Paheri, 3; boasting, exaggeration, Les. 84, 12; BH I, 41; Urk. IV, 430, 1; var. dets. … 751, 11; … 973, 9; var. … 1693, 13; … Les. 82, 12.

ꜥbꜥb become excited (?), Urk. IV, 1546, 16.

ꜥbꜥb threshold (?), Urk. IV, 1650, 17.

ꜥbꜥb appear (?), shine (?), Urk. IV, 1684, 6.

ꜥbw lettuce, Caminos, L.-Eg. Misc. 77. 341.

ꜥbwt staff of office, var. …, Pyr. 955. 1471; pitchfork, Gr. p. 517, (O 30).

ꜥbb use the pitchfork, Leyd. V 6, 14.

ꜥbb knock (?) on door, Urk. IV, 661, 13.

ꜥbḫn frog, Eb. 52, 21.

ꜥbš wine-jar, Th. T. S. II, 32; var. det. … Siut, pl. 1, 50.

ꜥpi vb. 3 inf. traverse a waterway, Pyr. 1541; pass, ḥr 'by', ZÄS 51, 121; fly, Urk. IV, 159, 13 (det. …).

ꜥpy the Winged Disk, JEA 30, 46.

ꜥpnnt slug (?), var. …, also det. …, JEA 18, 151; Barns, Ram. 20.

ꜥpr provide, equip, m 'with', Urk. IV, 175, 4; 386, 1; 692, 3; V, 165, 10; man a vessel, Bersh. I, 14, 7; Westc. 5, 2; Urk. IV, 1546, 12; acquire, JEA 35, 96, n. 2; incur injury, Sm. 1, 24. Varr. … Les. 76, 14; … TR 19, 28; … Urk. V, 165, 10.

ꜥprw equipment, Urk. IV, 186, 12; 691, 8.

ꜥprw jewellery, Urk. IV, 634, 12; varr. … 633, 6; … 669, 2.

ꜥprt equipment of offerings, Bersh. II, 1; 9, 3.

ꜥprt kind of jar, Eb. 4, 9; var. P. Kah. 26, 9.

ꜥprw sailors, RB 60, 12; Urk. IV, 304, 17 ( ); 309, 12; workmen, JEA 13, 75; Neferhotep, 13 ( ).

ꜥpr an Asiatic people, Urk. IV, 1309, 1.

ꜥpšꜣy beetle, JEA 20, 187.

ꜥfꜣ devour (?), var. det. , CT I, 30.

ꜥfꜣy encampment, Sin. B 115. 146. 201.

ꜥfꜣy sweet clover (?), JEA 20, 41.

ꜥff fly, TR 51, 25; Urk. IV, 39, 1; 892, 15; var. det. TR 58, 5; abbr. Sm. 19, 6.

ꜥfn cover (vb.), Dream-book, 2, 4; var. det. CT II, 4.

ꜥfnt royal head-cloth, Pyr. 729; var. dets. Urk. V, 162, 7; Westc. 10, 11.

ꜥfty brewer, BH I, 29; varr. Cairo 20161, c 28; Cairo 20095; Leyd. V6. Cf. ZÄS 37, 84; fem. loc. cit. n. 2.

ꜥfd (1) vb. lead, of roads, r 'to', Westc. 7, 26: (2) adj. attractive (?), Leb. 37, cf. JEA 42, 34 (36).

ꜥfdt chest, Urk. I, 139, 12; varr. V, 81, 12; Westc. 9, 5.

ꜥm (1) swallow, Eb. 4, 20; 22, 4; Urk. V, 66, 14 ( ); breathe in, absorb, BD 289, 2; Eb. 54, 9; of the earth 'swallowing up' a ruined shrine, Urk. IV, 386, 5; ꜥm ib 'be discreet', 'dissemble', 'regret', JEA 35, 40, n. 6; 'forget', 'be unconscious', SDT 166: (2) know, Urk. IV, 652, 9. Abbr. Urk. IV, 1383, 19.

var. of ꜥmꜥꜣt 'throw-stick'.

ꜥmꜥ smear (vb.), AEO I, 11*.

ꜥmꜥt mud, muddy ground, mud-flat, AEO I, 10*.

ꜥmꜥꜣt throw-stick, TR 22, 69. 70; var. 22, 71.

ꜥmꜥꜣ throw the throw-stick, Meir, I, 2; var. D. el. Geb. I, 5.

ꜥmꜥm smear (vb.), Westc. 7, 16; cf. AEO I, 11*.

ꜥmꜥm container for bread, etc., P. Kah. 19, 11-13; 20, 11.

ꜥmm brain, JEA 33, 47.

ꜥnt nail of finger or toe, Pyr. 1999 (det.); Neferti, 23; Eb. 78, 10; claw, Pyr. 1212; TR 11, 3; Sm. 8, 15; 'trim the nails,' BH II, 4.

ꜥnt pick (n.), Rec. trav. 39, 165.

ꜥnt ring of gold, Urk. IV, 950, 3; socket for jar, 637, 5.

ꜥn beautiful, Urk. IV, 52, 16 (det.); 1724, 15 (det.); bright, of face, 1280, 8; pleasing, m 'to', of persons, 984, 3; Pr. 16, 10; be kind, n 'to', Pr. 15, 7.

ꜥn the pleasant man, Pr. 12, 3; Urk. IV, 970, 13.

ꜥny writing-board, BD 366, 5.

ꜥnꜥ var. of iꜥn 'baboon'.

ꜥnꜥy complain, Pr. 7, 3; complaint, Pr. 15, 6.

ꜥnꜥn complain, Urk. IV, 1108, 6; complaint, 1114, 3.

ꜥnꜥn chin, M.u.K. 4, 1. Earlier inꜥ, q.v.

ꜥnw n. loc. ꜥAinu, source of limestone, BH I, 26, 175; varr. Urk. IV, 294, 13; 25, 9. Cf. AEO II, 128*.

ꜥnb reed-stalk for matting, Urk. IV, 1124, 7 (det. taken from ꜥnbyt below).

ꜥnbyt measure for the above, Barns, Ram. pl. 24, 20.

ꜥnn vb. 2 gem. turn back, Peas. B1, 299; B2, 96; Westc. 11, 15 (det.); M.u.K. 1, 10; come back, return, Leb. 83; Sin. B 58; Urk. IV, 519, 2; bring back, Peas. B2, 116.

ꜥnḫ sandal-strap, Gr. p. 508, S 34.

ꜥnḫ (1) vb. live, Sh. S. 114; Peas. B1, 275; Westc. 7, 17; nṯr ꜥnḫ 'living god', Leb. 142; bꜣ ꜥnḫy 'living soul', Urk. IV, 113, 11; ꜥꜣw ꜥnḫw 'live donkeys', 891, 5; sḳr-ꜥnḫ 'captive', see s.v. sḳr; ꜥnḫ m 'live on, by' food, etc., Sin. B 165. 187. 236; Urk. IV, 1292, 2; ꜥnḫ ḥr 'live in' a foreign land, Sin. B 162; ꜥnḫ n‹.i› 'As... lives for me', oath, Gr. §218; 'may he l., be prosperous and well', §§ 55. 313; ꜥnḫ dt 'may he l. for ever', § 313; as obj. of , § 378.

(2) n. life, Sin. B256; Les. 69,9; Urk. IV, 15,6; 'given l.', Gr. § 378; 'repeating l.' = living again, ep. of dec'd., § 55; nb ʿnḫ 'lord of l.', (a) ep. of deity, Siut, pl. 5, 239; Urk. IV, 480,15; (b) euphemistic for 'sarcophagus', 113,9 (det.); 481,4 (det.); ʿnḫ 'make provision for' s'one, Peas. B1,82; RB 114,2.

ʿnḫ person, Les. 74,13; ʿnḫ n niwt 'citizen', 70,5; Siut, pl. 15,5; fem. ʿnḫt n niwt, P. Kah. 39, 3.15; ʿnḫw nw mšʿ 'common soldiers', JEA 39, 38.45; ʿnḫ n tt ḥḳ3 'recipient from the royal table', JEA 24,88, n.5.

ʿnḫw the living, Urk. IV, 117,5; varr. 563,15; 283,14; 133,8.

ʿnḫ captive, Urk. IV, 36, 2.6; varr. 35,17; 1368,18.

ʿnḫ-t3wy n. loc. name of Memphis, Gauthier, Dict. géogr. I, 149; AEO II, 123*.

ʿnḫ swear, Urk. IV, 86,1; 139,12 (); 365,14; oath, 80,17.

ʿnḫ garland, Urk. IV, 150,9; 1178,9; varr. 136,14; , 1012, 5.11.

ʿnḫw blocks of alabaster, Hatnub, 22,14.

ʿnḫwy ears, Pr. 4,4; Urk. IV, 149,6; 961,13.

ʿnḫ mirror, Adm. 8,5.

ʿnḫt eye of deity, RB 121,6; var. Urk. IV, 1830,19.

ʿnḫt corn, GAS 49; varr. BD 466,12; RB 57,14.

ʿnḫt goat, Siut, pl. 5, 247; JEA 16, pl. 29,7; abbr. Urk. IV, 75,15.

ʿnḳt n. div. Anukis, Les. 85,10; Urk. IV, 202,15; 823,16.

ʿntyw myrrh, Sh. S. 151; Sin. B288; ʿntyw w3d 'fresh m.', Urk. IV, 346,14; ʿntyw šw () 'dried m.', Urk. IV, 702,5; () Eb. 23,15; ḳmyt nt ʿntyw 'resin of m.' = raw m., Urk. IV, 346,13. Varr. 339,8; 1214,15. Cf. GAS 62; JEA 23,27.

ʿntywy in sš n — 'myrrh-scribe', P. Kah. 20,60.

ʿnd few, GAS 30; scarcity, fewness, Peas. B1,112; Pr. 10,7; be diminished, Pt. (L II), 3,1.

ʿndt the few, of people, Adm. 12,14.

ꜥnd an unguent, Urk. I, 60, 4; var. IV, 502, 5.

ꜥndw jar, GAS 40.

ꜥndw dawn, BD 46, 8; varr. 146, 10; 283, 4; Pyr. 1679.

ꜥr mount up, ascend, r 'to' a place, Sin. R6; Urk. IV, 835, 4 (dets.); n 'to' s'one, BM 614, 17 (); extend, penetrate, of wound, n 'to' bone, etc., Sm. 5, 21; 7, 8. 22; 10, 15. Cf. ZÄS 46, 98; GNS 13.

ꜥrw proximity, var., GNS 12.

ꜥrtyw they who ascend (?), Caminos, Lit. Frag. pl. 14, 1, 2; cf. p. 37.

ꜥr reed pen, Peas. B1, 305; Urk. IV, 127, 8; V, 170, 11; var. IV, 119, 3.

ꜥrt roll of papyrus, Peas. B2, 129; of leather, Urk. IV, 662, 5 (det.).

var. of iꜥrt 'uraeus'.

ꜥrt jaw, Pyr. 30; BD 467, 5; Sm. 8, 14; var. det. 3, 6.

ꜥrt hinder parts of man, TR 24, 8 (det.); hindquarters of animal, Pyr. 1349.

see below s.v. ꜥrrwt.

ꜥrꜥr chin (?), BD 446, 14; cf. Ch. B. Text, 20, n. 7.

ꜥrf n. bag, abbr., Bull. 30, 170; vb. combine, Bersh. II, 21, top, 6; Th. T. S. IV, 6; Urk. IV, 1927, 13 (dets.); 1929, 9 (dets.); enclose, Urk. IV, 346, 6; 617, 7 (det.); contain, JEA 33, 29 (12).

ꜥrrwt gate, Pyr. 392. 952 (det.); Urk. IV, 18, 4 (); leaf of double door, RB 120, 16; 121, 1-2 (); lintel, JEA 4, 147 (); hall of judgement, Peas. B1, 35; P. Kah. 15, 34; Urk. IV, 1073, 3 (); 1107, 5 (); cf. ZÄS 60, 65; dwelling, home, L. to D. VI, 4 (n.) (); JEA 24, 6, n. 10.

ꜥrḳ bent: — sw r-ḫnt 'he was b. up in front', of serpent, Sh. S. 66.

ꜥrḳ don a garment, BD 176, 8; varr. 296, 3; Urk. IV, 112, 13.

ꜥrḳ know, perceive, gain full knowledge of; be wise, skilled, m 'in', varr., GAS 107; JEA 32, 74, n. 1; ꜥrḳ ib 'clever', Urk. IV, 970, 5 ().

ꜥrḳ swear, P. Kah. 9, 9; 13, 27. 35.

ꜥrḳ basket (?), P. Kah. 36, 19.

ꜥrḳy last day of the month, varr. ..., Gr. §264; ... Urk. IV, 367, 4; ꜥrḳ(y) rnpt 'l.d. of the year', Ann. Serv. 51, 445; Rev. d'Ég. 10, 20, n. 1.

ꜥḥ rope, Pyr. 1376; 1742; var. ... BD 393, 7.

ꜥḥ palace, Westc. 5, 3; 9, 18; Urk. IV, 256, 3; temple, JEA 39, 25; varr. ... Sin. B46; ... Sin. B50.

ꜥḥ entrap, snare, Urk. IV, 284, 2; more often ..., e.g. Bersh. I, 7; Urk. IV, 661, 6; with det. ... 767, 10; 1081, 4; enclose town with ditch, 660, 15.

ꜥḥ wipe off, away dirt, etc., Pyr. 1332; var. ... Urk. IV, 1078, 5.

ꜥḥt farm-land, Urk. IV, 172, 2; 667, 10; 742, 17; var. ... 1110, 13.

ꜥḥwty cultivator, Siut, pl. 6, 280; varr. ... pl. 8, 309; ... BH I, 8, 18; ... Urk. IV, 417, 17; ... (pl.), 124, 17. Cf. AEO, I, 97*.

ꜥḥꜣ fight: (1) vb., Les. 84, 18; Sin. B64; Urk. IV, 3, 10; r 'against', Sin. B134; ḥnꜥ 'with', Sin. B111; Urk. IV, 122, 14; P. Ed. Smith, 148; ꜥḥꜣt 'beware lest...', Gr. § 338, 3; ꜥḥꜣ ... 'ply the sounding pole', Peas. B1, 278, cf. JEA 9, 17, n. 10; ꜥḥꜣ ... (var. ...) 'go to war', Pyr. 574; Urk. V, 51, 1; ꜥḥꜣw ḥr 'those with warlike faces', Pyr. 269.
(2) n., Sin. B123. 131; Urk. IV, 85, 9; ... ꜥḥꜣ 'weapons of war', 615, 8; ... n ꜥḥꜣ 'shirt of mail', 664, 3. Varr. ... Sin. R88; ... Pyr. 574; ... Urk. V, 54, 10.

ꜥḥꜣ warrior, Les. 83, 3.

ꜥḥꜣt coll. warriors, Urk. IV, 997, 17.

ꜥḥꜣw arrow, Sin. B62. 128. 138; varr. ... Urk. IV, 1281, 4; ... 1280, 17; pl. also for weapons in general, Pyr. 1144 (dets. ...); pr ꜥḥꜣw 'arsenal', JEA 39, 36.

ꜥḥꜣt battleground, Urk. V, 13, 16; var. ... 13, 13.

ꜥḥꜣt warship, Turin 81.

ꜥḥꜣ fish lates niloticus, JEA 14, 30.

ꜥḥꜣ-mw sounding-pole, Peas. B1, 258; Urk. IV, 1077, 3 (det ...); cf. JEA 9, 17, n. 10.

ꜥḥꜣwty warrior, P. Kah. 9, 2; varr. Bersh. I, 15; Urk. IV, 8, 2. Cf. JEA 39, 40.

ꜥḥꜥ stand, Sin. R 24; B 10; Peas. R 39; Westc. 10, 2; ꜥḥꜥ m-ḥꜣw 's. in the neighbourhood of' = withstand, oppose, Sin. B 55-6; Urk. IV, 187, 9; ꜥḥꜥ m st 'stand in the place of' = succeed s'one, Urk. IV, 59, 16 ( ); var. ꜥḥꜥ ḥr st, 690, 5; ꜥḥꜥ ḥr sf 'suppress (lit. 'stand on') mercy', Les. 83-4; stand by, Pyr. 230; stand erect, of pillars, Pyr. 389; raise o'self, ḥr 'on' o's side, Pyr. 1047; stand up, rise up, Westc. 6, 22; Th. T. S. I, 1; r 'against' s'one, Peas. B1, 186; with ḥr + infin. 'arise and do s'thing,' Westc. 8, 21. 23; arise = succeed (as ruler), Urk. I, 78, 13; ꜥḥꜥ r 'make accusation against', BD 95, 2-3; attend, n 'on' s'one, Urk. IV, 1108, 3; r 'to' business, Peas. B1, 202. 293; ḥr 'to', JEA 17, 59 (30); wait, JEA 16, 63; r 'for', P. Kah. 31, 3; idiomatic uses: ꜥḥꜥ ib 'persistent', Sin. B 57; ꜥḥꜥ m ꜣbd 'enter on monthly duties,' ZÄS 37, 97; ꜥḥꜥ ḥms 'live', 'pass o's life', Pr. 2, 7; Bersh. II, 21, top, 9; ZÄS 60, 69; ꜥḥꜥ ḥr (='face') 'indulgent', JEA 17, 59 (30); dꜣt ntt ꜥḥꜥ 'balance outstanding', P. Kah. 17, 13; rdi ꜥḥꜥ 'produce' s'thing, Westc. 8, 4; aux. vb., Gr. §§ 476-82.

ꜥḥꜥw ceremonial stations of persons, Les. 75, 7; Urk. IV, 159, 1; 1283, 7 ( ); proper positions of things, Westc. 6, 13; Louvre C 14, 10 ( ); RB 119, 10; r ꜥḥꜥw sn 'in good order', Urk. IV, 525, 12 ( ).

ꜥḥꜥw attendance, service, GNS 110.

ꜥḥꜥ attendant, fem. , GNS 110.

ꜥḥꜥw stand-by, helper, Siut, pl. 19, 35.

ꜥḥꜥ heap, Urk. IV, 335, 11; 524, 7 (pl.); 526, 11; Peas. B1, 105; portion, allotment, Les. 76, 14 ( ); Urk. IV, 748, 14 ( ); 768, 7; quantity (math.), JEA 12, 130; in pl. often wealth, riches, Sin. B 147; Pr. 6, 6; 13, 8; Adm. 2, 5.

ꜥḥꜥ stela, Les. 87, 14; Urk. IV, 1032, 4; var. Les. 87, 18.

ꜥḥꜥ measure for beer, Urk. IV, 755, 6.

var. of mꜥḥꜥt 'tomb'.

ꜥḥꜥw ships, Sin. B 244; Westc. 7, 9.11; Urk. IV, 328, 17 ( ); 1116, 12; as coll. pꜣ ꜥḥꜥw 'the fleet', 8, 9; 1546, 12.

ꜥḥꜥt coll. ships, Urk. IV, 1116, 12.

ꜥḥꜥw lifetime, Les. 68, 13; Urk. IV, 895, 14; ꜥḥꜥw ꜣw 'a long life', 1084, 11; ꜥḥꜥw n ꜥnḫ 'lifetime', RB 60, 1-2; period, space of time, Peas. B1, 31; Pr. 14, 8; m ꜥḥꜥw nfr 'in due time', Westc. 7, 22. Varr. BM 614, 3; JEA 4, pl. 8, 10; Urk. IV, 580, 12; (sic) 1485, 6; 1874, 12.

ꜥḫ brazier, Siut, pl. 7, 302; Urk. IV, 634, 14; 639, 13.

ꜥḫỉ vb. 3 inf. raise up the sky, Urk. IV, 942, 14; hang men, 1297, 9.15.

ꜥḫỉ vb. 3 inf. fly, Sin. G 12; Urk. IV, 1306, 4. See also ꜥẖỉ

ꜥḫt swoop (n.) of falcon, Urk. IV, 1302, 11.

ꜥḫm extinguish fire, Pyr. 247; RB 120, 12; quench thirst, Pr. 1, 5 (dets.); Peas. B1, 247 (det. only); Urk. IV, 482, 12; destroy, Urk. V, 178, 13.

var. of ꜥẖmw 'twigs'.

var. of ꜥẖm 'image'.

var of ỉḫmt 'river-bank'.

ꜥḫḫ vb. 2 gem. evaporate; consume, P. Ed. Smith, 497.

var. of ỉḫḫw 'twilight'.

ꜥẖỉ vb. 3 inf. fly, fly away, Urk. V, 63, 11; var. dets. TR 18, 19; Sin. R 21.

ꜥẖm image of god, var. , GNS 110; JEA 39, pl. 2, 22.

ꜥẖm voracious (?) spirit, Gr. p. 475, I 3.

ꜥẖmw twigs, M.u.K. 5, 6; Eb. 21, 2; det. Urk. IV, 1526, 11; var. Eb. 17, 15.

ꜥẖnwty audience-chamber, GNS 67; imy-r ꜥẖnwty 'chamberlain', AEO I, 44*; ꜥẖnwty dwꜣt 'robing-room', GNS 108.162; JEA 5, 155-6. Varr. Sin. B 251; Hatnub, 22, 3; Urk. IV, 1104, 9; (sic) Les. 80, 15.

ꜥš summon, with direct obj., BD 28, 13; with n, Urk. IV, 1072, 16 ( ).

ꜥš-ḥ3t pilot (n.) Urk. IV, 310, 2; act as pilot, Adm. 12, 5.

ꜥš groan, ZÄS 45, 11.

ꜥš so-called cedar, AEO I, 8, n. 1; varr. Urk. IV, 23, 14; 168, 3; 1795, 11.

ꜥš 'cedar'-oil, BH I, 17; cf. AEO I, 8, n. 1.

ꜥš3 lizard, P. Ram. V, 21.

ꜥš3 (1) adj. many, numerous, Sin. B 83. 92. 155; Urk. IV, 1279, 14; ꜥš3t 'm. kinds of metal', Les. 61, 12; much, plentiful, Sin. B 91; Urk. IV, 693, 8; 694, 4; Adm. p. 108; rich, m 'in', Sin. B 147; Urk. IV, 344, 4; ordinary: ḥm-nṯr ꜥš3 'o. prophet', Les. 70, 4; sim. P. Kah. 14, 52; Pyr. 2087; as adv. often, Gr. § 205, 4.

(2) n. quantity, multitude: ꜥš3 wrt m 'a very great q. of', Urk. IV, 641, 11; ꜥš3 n iyt 'm. of afflictions', Pr. 17, 9; 'Hearken, ye nobles and plebs mi ꜥš3·s as many as ye be', Urk. IV, 390, 2; 'the state of yesterday is like today, and resembles it n ꜥš3 in much', Adm. p. 106. — Varr. Pyr. 1146; Urk. IV, 694, 4; Les. 70, 4.

ꜥš3t multitude of persons, Sin. B 59; Urk. IV, 21, 6; company of guests, Pr. 1, 3; the many, the masses, Adm. 12, 14; Pr. 6, 4; 13, 1.

ꜥš3-r chatter, be loquacious, Paheri, 3; P. Ram. II, vs. 2, 4.

ꜥš3-ḫrw noisy, P. Ram. I, B i, 26; Posener, II, pl. 16 (ꜥš3).

ꜥš3 dove (?), Urk. IV, 755, 1; 770, 7; 827, 11.

ꜥš3 obnoxious (?), Caminos, Lit. Frag. p. 42.

ꜥšty (< ꜥš3ty (?)) abundant, Amarna, III, 19, right.

ꜥḳ enter, m 'into', Urk. IV, 613, 12; V, 53, 6; Eb. 1, 16; 99, 13; 'e. into' s'one's wisdom = benefit by it, Urk. IV, 1194, 12; 'e. into' = obey laws, 903, 13; n 'into' a state, JEA 30, 62, n. 5; r 'into', Sin. B 46; Urk. IV, 262, 12; 1105, 14; of 'coming into' property, Les. 72, 18–19; ḥr 'on' a road, RB 65, 7; 'to' s'one, Sh. S. 174; 'by' a door, RB 120, 13; tp-m 'to' s'one, Westc. 10, 6; ꜥḳ pr 'come in and go out', 'come and go', Urk. IV, 433, 11–12; 1105, 5–9; sim. pr ꜥḳ, 498, 7; charge, m 'into' foes, RB 57, 3; come in, of revenue, income, Siut, pl. 7, 300; Urk. IV, 1114, 9; have the entrée: s n ꜥḳ 'trusted man', 'man having the e.', Pr. 7, 3; ꜥḳ m wstn nn smit.f 'one who strode in freely without being announced', Bersh. II, 21, top, 1 ( ); wꜥb ꜥꜣ ꜥḳ n Imn 'a priest having free entry to Amūn', Urk. IV, 50, 9; ꜥḳ ib 'become intimate', 46, 13; 'enter face to face', ḥr 'to' god, JEA 32, 52; set, of sun, Leb. 73; run aground (?), of ship, Peas. B1, 259.

ꜥḳ-ib intimate friend, Leb. 114. 124. 128; var. Les. 69, 24.

ꜥḳ-r one over-familiar in speech (?), P. Ram. I, Bi, 22.

ꜥḳw friends, Mill. 1, 5; Pr. 11, 3. 4 (without).

ꜥḳyt female servant, Th. T. S. II, 12; var Leyd. V 3.

ꜥḳw loaves, Urk. IV, 745, 16; 769, 12; provisions, food, Sin. B 87 ( ); Pr. 17, 7; Peas. R 3; B1, 83; ꜥḳw (n) 'make p. for', Westc. 9, 20 ( ); Peas. B1, 87; income, revenue, P. Kah. 22, 38; 35, 28; Urk. IV, 30, 16.

ꜥḳꜣ (1) adj. precise, accurate, Peas. B1, 131; Pr. 15, 13; Les. 69, 19; 81, 7; Urk. IV, 507, 6 ( ); ꜥḳꜣ ib 'straightforward', 434, 13; 970, 10; so also ꜥḳꜣ ḥꜣty, Siut pl. 19, 46: (2) vb. intrans. go straight forward, progress, Peas. B1, 107. 262: trans. use aright, of tool, BH II, 7 ( ); fig. of 'using' truth, Pr. 10, 4; correct a fault, P. Ram. II, rt. 4, 2: (3) n. straightness, JEA 42, 15; straight-dealing, straight-forwardness, Peas. B1, 173. 253; Pr. 13, 5; exact sense of speech, Peas. B1, 99; r ꜥḳꜣ 'on a level with', Gr. § 178; 'according to', Urk. IV, 1659, 15.

ꜥḳꜣy a straight-dealer, Peas. B1, 172.

ꜥḳꜣyt true balancing, Peas. B1, 158; m ꜥḳꜣt 'exactly', JEA 4, pl. 8, 8 (var.).

ꜥḳꜣ a rope, Urk. IV, 116, 16; BD 204, 6; var. TR 1, 6; use the ꜥḳꜣ-rope, Urk. IV, 116, 16.

ꜥgt a resinous varnish (?) from Syria, Urk. IV, 670, 9.

ꜥgwt a preparation of grain, Siut, pl. 9, 387; P. Kah. 28, 3; var. Bersh. I, 31.

ꜥgn pedestal for vase, Urk. IV, 22, 14.17

ꜥtḫ strain mash, etc., Sin. B 247; P. Ram. III, A 20; earlier, cf. GNS 92; ꜥtḫ.ti 'in pure essence', JEA 1, 25, n. 9.

ꜥtḫw brewers, Adm. 1, 4.

var. of ꜥḏw 'būri-fish'.

ꜥḏ spool, reel, var., Gr. p. 525, V26.

ꜥḏ be safe, BH I, 8, 15; Sh. S. 7; Urk. IV, 1209, 3; ꜥḏ wḏꜣ 'safe and sound', of persons, P. Kah. 32, 12; Urk. IV, 56, 16; 209, 14; 'prosperous and flourishing', of affairs, P. Kah. 27, 9; 29, 4; Urk. IV, 1106, 2: become whole, Sm. 2, 21.

ꜥḏ perceive, var., GAS 81.

ꜥḏt offence (?) in m rdi ꜥḏt 'do not give o.!' Pr. 18, 1 (emended).

ꜥḏ hack up, destroy, Merikarēꜥ, 70 (det.). 119; Adm. 12, 10.

ꜥḏt slaughter, massacre, TR 19, 19; var. Cairo 20238, 13.

ꜥḏ edge, margin of cultivation, Sin. B 9; varr. R 34; Les. 82, 14.

ꜥḏ fat, grease, Th. T. S. I, 1; varr. Urk. IV, 755, 9; 1142, 12; Eb. 31, 15; P. Ram. V, 14.15; 16. Cf. Wortforschung, V, 25.

ꜥḏ fatten (?), Peas. B1, 133.

ꜥḏw the būri-fish, P. Ram. V, 9; varr. Eb. 82, 9; M.u.K. 8, 6.7; cf. Gr. p. 477, K 3.

ꜥḏ-mr administrator, Gr. p. 477, K 3; varr. ibid.; Sin. R 1.

ꜥḏꜣw adj. guilty, Caminos, Lit. Frag. pl. 5, 14: n. guilt, Urk. IV, 971, 17; 1091, 9; m ꜥḏꜣ 'falsely', JEA 3, 88, n. 1; so also n ꜥḏꜣ, 22, 44 (31); m ir gtḥ m ꜥḏꜣ 'do not be weary f.' = 'don't sham tired!', Paheri, 7.

ꜥḏꜣ guilty man, wrongdoer, Urk. IV, 971, 17.

ꜥḏnt armlet (?), P. Ed. Smith, 167.

ꜥḏnt crucible (?), P. Ed. Smith, 168.

w encl. neg. part. not. Gr. §352A; var. Pyr. 815.

w suff. pron. 3 pl. they, them, their, var. Gr. §34.

w district, region, Urk. IV, 345, 4; 615, 12; 1111, 5; 1135, 15; var. Peas. R 37; 'district-superintendent', Peas. B1, 193; var. P. Kah. 4, 25.

wꜣt cord, Sm. 3, 6. 16. 18.

wꜣ brood, n 'on', Peas. B1, 271; conspire, m 'against', TR 12, 1-2; Hymnen, 15, 5; RB 124, 10.

wꜣ (1) far: adj. Sh. S. 148; Sin. B 163; RB 58, 5; r 'from', TR 18, 24; Urk. IV, 1307, 17; adv. of space, Sin. B 2; Peas. B1, 291; RB 62, 1; of time, long ago, for a long time past, GAS 54. Varr. Peas. B2, 52; Urk. IV, 344, 2; RB 58, 5; Adm. 7, 1.

(2) fall, r 'into' a condition, varr. GAS 53, with many idiomatic uses. Add:– snḏ wꜣ ḥr ḫꜥw. sn 'fear fell on their bodies', Siut, pl. 13, 13; wꜣ r iit 'who were in the act of coming', RB 61, 9; wꜣ. f r tr n rtt 'he has taken occasion to conspire (?)', Urk. IV, 139, 3.

wꜣt (1) road, way, Sin. R 19; Peas. B1, 9 ( ); Urk. IV, 170, 6 ( ); 324, 13; šsp tp wꜣt 'begin a journey', 322, 7; wꜣt n 'prepare a way for', Bersh. I, 14, 3; fig. in 'causing everyone to know wꜣt. f his proper task', Urk. IV, 1152, 12; 'walk on a road' = follow a line of conduct, 118, 6; mdd wꜣt 'adhere to s'one's way' = be loyal, devoted to him, 208, 7; Siut, pl. 4, 221. For see below under r.

(2) side, Eb. 96, 20; P. Kah. 5, 41; Peas. R 46; Urk. IV, 4, 6; ḥr wꜣt nb 'on every s.', Adm. 6, 3; sim. JEA 32, pl. 6, 14.

Wꜣwt-Ḥr n. loc. Roads-of-Horus, name of NE. frontier fortress, JEA 6, 115; var. Urk. IV, 547, 4; cf. Caminos, Lit. Frag. p. 20.

wꜣi roast (?) grain, Eb. 12, 12; Urk. IV, 1871, 12; var. ibid.

wꜣꜥw captain (?) of ship, Urk. IV, 996, 1.

wꜣw wave of sea, Sh. S. 40.110.

wꜣwꜣ: — sḫ 'take counsel', Urk. IV, 2142, 15; var. det. 2028, 9.

wꜣwꜣt cord, Urk. IV, 166, 12; var. det 1295, 11.

wꜣwꜣt fiery one (?), Hymnen, 4, 4.

Wꜣwꜣt n. loc. Wawat, Northern Nubia, Sh. S. 9; Urk. IV, 734, 2; var. RB 60, 10. Cf. AEO II, 270*; JEA 44, 119; Kush, 6, 50.

wꜣb root of plant, Eb. 50, 8; 72, 17; of teeth, P. Kah. 7, 37; socket (?) of eye, Eb. 99, 15.

wꜣb cloth (?), description of sail, Urk. V, 156, 16; swaddling-clothes, Siut, pl. 11, 13.

wꜣbt high-lying agricultural land, Siut, pl. 8, 321; var. ibid. 313.

wꜣbt body of the Red Crown, contrasted with the 'curl', Hymnen, 14, 3.

wꜣm bake (?), Eb. 51, 8; 73, 5.

wꜣrt draw-rope of clapnet, BD 393, 5.6; Caminos, Lit. Frag. pl. 3, 4, 7; cf. p. 15.

wꜣḥ vb. (1) trans. set down, lay down, Westc. 7, 14; Sh. S. 78; Urk. IV, 1144, 5; lay, ḥr 'on', 367, 9; n 'before' s'one, Sin. B 90; apply a remedy, m 'in', Sm. 10, 2; ḥr 'to', Eb. 1, 1; stack timber, JEA 16, 63; stow a cargo, ibid. 63; store up goods, ibid. 64; lay aside, discard, ibid. 64.65; leave aside, overlook, ignore, Kamose, 10.13. 15; JEA 3, 89, n. 1; Urk. IV, 1666, 11; set aside s'thing n 'for' s'one, 238, 12; institute offerings, etc., 174, 4; 740, 6; 769, 7; lay down a building, ZÄS 68, 27; enter s'thing ḥr 'in' a register, Urk. IV, 1109, 3.7; add, ḥr 'to', Rhind, 72, 3; pitch a camp, Urk. IV, 655, 15; set death m 'among' people = kill them, 139, 16; wait x days, RB 66, 7; wait for s'one: 'Drink, don't sip; nn iw.i r wꜣḥ.t I won't wait for you', over servitor offering drink to lady, Paheri, 7; permit, with foll. sḏm.f, Gr. §184, 1.

(2) idiomatic uses of (1): wꜣḥ tp 'bow the head', Hymnen, 16, 4; Urk. IV, 166, 5; 324, 3; wꜣḥ tp m x r sp y 'multiply x by y', Rhind, 46, 1; wꜣḥ tp m x r gmt y 'divide y by x', 26, 2; wꜣḥ tp 500 1/10 .f m 50 'take 1/10 of 500 = 50', 46, 2; wꜣḥ ẖt

'make offering', Urk. IV, 430,11; P. Kah. 26,39; w3ḥ ḥr ḥr 'turn the face to' = favour s'one, JEA 41, 23(8); w3ḥ r t3 'put to the ground' = brush aside, 28,19.

(3) intrans. live long, endure: of persons, Sin. B 270; Peas. B1, 146; Urk. IV, 1054,12; w3ḥ tp t3 'e. upon earth', Siut, pl. 13, 37; 14, 87; w3ḥ p3 ḥḳ3 'as the Ruler e.'s', oath, Urk. IV, 38,10; sim. 488,17; w3ḥ mrt 'e.'ing of love', 16,17; w3ḥ rnpwt 'e.'ing of years', Siut, pl. 17, 59; of buildings, Urk. IV, 303,5; of kingship, 593,5; of justice, etc., Peas. B1, 321; Leb. 22; Urk. IV, 366,15; 1202,12; RB 110,15; lie, m 'in', Urk. IV, 687,12; ḥr 'on', Westc. 6,10; Urk. IV, 1550,5; be patient, Peas. B1, 269.

Varr. Sh. S. 78; Sin. B 90; Urk. IV, 139,16.

w3ḥ-ib be kindly, patient, Les. 69,20; Peas. B1, 209–10; RB 114,6; w3ḥ ib r 'be so kind as to...', Leb. 51-2 (restd.); clemency, benevolence, Sin. B 203, cf. GNS 76; in error for w3ḥ 'enduring', RB 76,9.

w3ḥwt oblations, Bersh. II, 13,25; var. D. el. B. 129.

w3ḥw wreath, garland, Caminos, Lit. Frag. pl. 2, 2, 2; Urk. IV, 548,1 (); 1396,7 (); necklace, CT I, 109 (); Th. T. S. I, 15 ().

w3ḥ fillet of gold, BH II, 4; var. II, 7.

w3ḥt processional station, Urk. IV, 379, 6. 13. 17.

w3ḥyt temenos, Urk. IV, 765,8.

w3ḥyt corn, Urk. IV, 116,15; Eb. 41,12; varr. Urk. IV, 499,4; 1390,14.

w3ḥ flood (n.), Pyr. 1524; var. BD 228,14.

w3ḥi vb. 4 inf. be inundated, of land, Pyr. 1102. 1554; be content, of persons, Pyr. 411. 1187; var. RB 74,12.

w3ḫy columned forecourt, Westc. 8,9; varr. Sin. B 251; (sic) Urk. IV, 1086,12. Cf. GNS 96; JEA 25, 104.

w3s sceptre, Urk. IV, 1547,2; varr. Pyr. 967; Pr. 15,2.

w3s n. dominion, JEA 36,12; Äg. Stud. 2; vb. have dominion, Urk. IV, 225,8; 231,9.

W3st n. loc. nome and city of Thebes, var. , Sethe, Amun, §3; AEO II, 24*.

W3sty the Theban, ep. of god Mont, Urk. IV, 657, 8; var. 1311, 2.

w3si vb. 4 inf. be ruined, decayed, Bersh. II, p. 25; Urk. IV, 102, 3 ( ); 169, 11: n. ruin, Urk. IV, 765, 13 (, through confusion with d‘m); 882, 13; 1820, 2.

w3š vb. be honoured, of gods, etc., BD 169, 8; 298, 7; be strong, ZÄS 57, 7*; Urk. IV, 430, 12: n. honour due to god or king, Urk. IV, 221, 12; 244, 7 ( ). Cf. JEA 39, 18 (x).

w3q shouting (?), Westc. 12, 1.

w3g a religious festival, Siut, pl. 7, 291; varr. 7, 299; dets. Les. 73, 6; Urk. IV, 27, 16; 1912, 18.

w3tw conspirators (?), CT I, 46.

w3d papyrus-plant, Pyr. 569; var. Urk. IV, 1278, 16.

w3d papyriform column, Urk. IV, 933, 7.

w3d amulet in shape of last, RB 120, 7; BD 216, 15.

w3d adj. green, Peas. B1, 22 ( ); Adm. 3, 10; Siut, pl. 19, 33; pale, of lips, etc., Barns, Ram. p. 22; fresh, Urk. IV, 335, 11; 755, 9 ( ); 756, 10; raw, of food, P. Kah. 5, 5; Peas. B1, 246; hale, sturdy, Pyr. 457; Eb. 2, 5; Th. T. S. II, 22; fortunate, happy, Les. 76, 13; Urk. IV, 260, 11 ( ); 261, 15; 324, 12; r w3d 'vigorously', Gr. §205, 5; m w3d 'successfully', Les. 86, 21: trans. vb. make green, Urk. IV, 132, 12; make to flourish, 2157, 15.

w3d fortunate man, Urk. IV, 974, 10.

w3d a green stone, Pr. 5, 10; var. Urk. IV, 688, 9.

w3dt green linen, Urk. IV, 1803, 9; var. 1867, 9.

w3dw success, T. Carn. 8, cf. JEA 10, 197; happiness, Adm. 3, 13 ( ).

w3dw green eye-paint, Pyr. 1681; varr. ibid.; BH I, 17; P. Kah. 5, 50.

w3d (pr-w3d ?) an offering-loaf, Urk. IV, 1157, 13.

w3dt rawness in iw3 n w3dt 'raw beef', Urk. VII, 5, 18.

w3ḏt bow of ship, ZÄS 54, 3.

W3ḏyt n. div. cobra-goddess Edjōyet, Urk. IV, 1446, 1. 9; V, 89, 4; var. IV, 246, 15; AEO II, 188*; 'the two Serpent-goddesses' of U. and L. E., Urk. IV, 16, 13; 287, 6.

w3ḏyt hall of columns, Urk. IV, 157, 13; var. 158, 8.

w3ḏ-wr the sea, Sh. S. 33. 59; Sin. B 211; Urk. IV, 142, 10; varr. 118, 12; 322, 6; 616, 13; 1892, 14.

w3ḏḏt vegetation, TR 19, 18; var. BD 493, 3.

wỉ dep. pron. 1 sg. I, me; varr. , , etc., Gr. § 43.

wỉ mummy-case, GNS 69. 160.

wy admirative part. How ...!, var. , Gr. § 49.

wỉ3 sacred bark, Leb. 144; Urk. IV, 304, 17; BD 479, 11; wỉ3 (n) tp-ỉtrw 'riverine s.b.' JEA 38, 21, n. 3. Abbr. Urk. IV, 307, 15.

wỉn thrust aside, push away, set aside, GAS 100; dets. Urk. IV, 546, 13; 1418, 10.

wꜥ one, Gr. §§ 260. 262, 1; indef. article, § 262, 1; wꜥ ... ky, wꜥ ... snnw.f 'one ... other', § 98; wꜥ ... wꜥ 'one ... other', Sin. B 137; Westc. 8, 22; wꜥ nb 'everyone', Gr. § 103; wꜥ m 'one of' several, § 262, 1; m ... wꜥ 'in one' action or state = do or be s'thing 'all together', GNS 99; m bw wꜥ 'all together', RB 111, 2 ( ); unique, one only, Sin. B 70; Urk. IV, 19, 13; JEA 13, 78, n. 2; 17, 57 (5); wꜥ ḥr ḥw.f 'unique', Gr. § 178; nb wꜥ 'sole lord', Pyr. 276 (,).

wꜥỉ vb. 3 inf. be alone, Sh. S. 41; varr. Pr. 14, 7; Les. 72, 5; Urk. IV, 401, 12.

wꜥty sole, single: smr wꜥty 'Sole Companion', BH I, 17 ( ); I, 16 ( ); Urk. IV, 25, 15 ( ); ẖkrt nsw wꜥtt 'Sole King's Concubine', Siut, pl. 13, 38 ( ); tḫn wꜥty 'a single obelisk', Urk. IV, 584, 10; 1550, 3; sb3 wꜥty 'the lone star', Pyr. 251 ( ); M. u. K. 4, 6-7; wꜥtt.f 'his only daughter', Urk. IV, 361, 7.

wꜥt(y) captive, Louvre C 14, 10.

wꜥty goat, Sinai, 91; var. Siut, pl. 7, 292.

wꜥtt royal uraeus, Urk. IV, 160, 3; 390, 14.

wʿꜣ *curse* (vb. and n.), GNS 66. 160.

wʿʿw *privacy*, in st wʿʿw 'private apartment', Urk. IV, 479, 3; sim. BM 614, 5; speak, hear, etc., m wʿʿw 'in private', Bersh. II, 21, top, 15 ( ); Urk. IV, 410, 12; rear a child 'in solitude', RB 111, 16; *private apartments* of palace, Les. 69, 24; 72, 6; 75, 11 (det.).

wʿʿwt *privacy*, Urk. IV, 546, 5.

wʿw *soldier*, ZÄS 52, 116; JEA 39, 45.

wʿb adj. *pure*, Urk. IV, 343, 12; 415, 2; 641, 1; RB 117, 9: intrans. vb. *purify o'self*, Westc. 11, 18; RB 119, 15; *bathe*, Westc. 2, 25; Urk. V, 23, 4: trans. vb. *cleanse, purify*, Urk. V, 23, 15: n. *purification*, Westc. 11, 18; *purity*, Bersh. II, p. 41; D. el. B. 63. Varr. , Pyr. 127; Urk. I, 87, 14; IV, 415, 2; 51, 3.

wʿb *priest*, var. , AEO I, 53*.

wʿbt *priestess*, Cairo 20240, 6.

wʿb *serve as priest*, Neferḥotep, 32; var. Les. 72, 12.

wʿbwt *priestly service*, Urk. I, 15, 7; var. Adm. 11, 5.

wʿbt *place of embalment*; *tomb*; *kitchen, refectory* or the like, GAS 26; *offering-slab*, Urk. IV, 866, 13 ( ).

wʿbt *meat-offering*, Siut, pl. 6, 276; Urk. IV, 31, 13; varr. + suffix Siut, pl. 6, 275; pl. Les. 73, 10; 74, 22; + suffix 98, 13.

wʿbw *sacred robe*, Urk. IV, 112, 13; BD 443, 8; varr. TR 20, 28; BD 448, 15.

wʿf *bend down* horns of bull, Sin. B 54; *subdue* nations, Sin. B 213; Urk. IV 15, 9 (dets.); 196, 4; 740, 1; *be bent, curled up*, of parts of the body, Sm. 4, 15; Eb. 63, 12.

wʿn *juniper* (?), Urk. IV, 343, 4; var. dets. Eb. 31, 7.

wʿr *flee*, Sin. B 149; P. Kah. 34, 20; *fly*, r 'against' s'one, of well-directed javelin, BD 219, 10; *rush forth*, of child at birth, Westc. 10, 9. 17. 24.

wʿr *fugitive*, Sin. B 149.

wꜥrt *flight*, *Sin.* B 205; varr. B 156; B 277; B 262.

wꜥrw *hastiness of speech*, *Peas.* B1, 208.

wꜥrt *leg*, *Urk.* V, 165, 15; *lower leg*, *Eb.* 42, 2; *P. Kah.* 5, 23.24; *foot*, *Les.* 81, 22 ( ).

wꜥrt *desert-plateau*, var. dets. , , *GNS* 30.

wꜥrt *administrative division* of Egypt, *P. Kah.* p. 21; cf. also *ZÄS* 70, 86; *quarter* of guild, Cairo 20039; BM 844; of necropolis, *Les.* 82, 21 ( ), cf. *GNS* 30; *part*, in wꜥrt r wꜥrt 'p. by p.' = in equal p.'s, of mixing drugs, *Eb.* 61, 2.4.6.

wꜥrtw civil *administrator*, *Urk.* IV, 1093, 4; *JEA* 31, 10, n. 8; military title, *JEA* 39, 41.45; wꜥrtw n ḥḳꜣ 'Controller of the Household (?)', *Urk.* IV, 1112, 15, cf. *JEA* 39, 42, n. 1; wꜥrtw n tt ḥḳꜣ 'Controller of the Ruler's Table', *JEA* 24, 88, n. 5; 179.

wꜥrtyt *administratrix*, Louvre C 168; var. Cairo 20025, *r*.

wꜥḥ *carob-bean*, *Siut*, pl. 2, 63; varr. *D. el. B.* 113; *P. Kah.* 20, 6.

wbꜣ *drill* stone, *D. el. Geb.* I, 13; *M. u. K.* 1, 4; *open*, *Sm.* 13, 9; *RB* 114, 1 ( ); *Urk.* IV, 1801, 12; *BD* 30, 13; wbꜣ ib 'o.-hearted', *Urk.* IV, 1320, 4; 1382, 15; wbꜣ ib n 'o. the heart to', 'confide in', *Bersh.* II, 21, top, 4-5 (sic); *Urk.* IV, 538, 14; wbꜣ mꜣꜣ 'o. the sight' = improve vision, *Eb.* 56, 17; 61, 18; wbꜣ ḥr 'clear-sighted', *Siut*, pl. 17, 49; *Urk.* IV, 429, 5; 1436, 10; *open up, explore* a region, *Urk.* IV, 342, 14 (det.); 345, 2; 1064, 13 ( ); *reveal* a matter, *Bersh.* II, 21, top, 4; *Pr.* 14, 10 ( ); *make revelation to* s'one, with obj. of the person, *Urk.* IV, 353, 11.

wbꜣ *open court* of temple, *Urk.* IV, 584, 10.

wbꜣt *opening*, *BD* 406, 15.

wbꜣ *butler*, *AEO* I, 43*.

wbꜣyt *maidservant*, *Westc.* 12, 9.10; var. 11, 19.

wbn *rise, shine*, of sun, *Sin.* B 233; *Urk.* IV, 362, 15 (det.); 420, 7; 806, 15; *glitter*, of precious metal, 173, 10; *appear*, of god or man, Cairo 20040; Caminos, *Lit. Frag.*, pl. 2, 2, 13; *overflow*, *Peas.* B1, 294; *Urk.* IV, 1996, 12; *be excessive*, of justice, *Peas.* B1, 252.

wbn stride briskly (?), BH II, 4; Urk. IV, 1105, 16.

wbnw eastern, Urk. IV, 1984, 11; the East, 1973, 5; r wbnw 'eastward', 1978, 8.

wbnw wound, var. dets. , varr. , cf. P. Ed. Smith, 523.

wbh be bright, Amarna, I, 37, 1; var. det. Urk. IV, 2010, 6.

wbd vb. burn, Eb. 69, 3; BD 354, 11; heat, Eb. 83, 13. 16; be scalded, BD 133, 16.

wbdt burn (n.), Eb. 68, 6; burning, Adm. 7, 1.

wpt horns, Pyr. 705. 1302; top of head, JEA 22, 106; brow, Gr. p. 462, F13, n. 0; iry-wpt 'wig', Urk. IV, 1165, 5; top of mountain, BD 219, 2; 't. of the earth' = farthest south, Urk. IV, 138, 7; 270, 9; 808, 8; wpt nt ht 'upper abdomen', JEA 22, 106; top-knot, Pyr. 401 ( ); head-dress, 546; zenith, Urk. IV, 1542, 13.

wpi vb. 3 inf. open, Pyr. 92 ( ); Sh. S. 67; BD 239, 6; of women, o. the womb in childbirth, Westc. 5, 11; Urk. IV, 303, 9; wp ḥr 'o. the face' = enable one to see, Pyr. 1807; open up a district, Urk. I, 222, 18; road, RB 65, 6; quarry, Bersh. II, p. 24; inaugurate, JEA 32, 50; part, separate, P. Kah. 6, 9; TR 27, 19; BH I, 30; divide goods, Urk. IV, 339, 6; judge contestants at law, petitioners, Siut, pl. 6, 266 ( ); Urk. IV, 1072, 11; 1082, 12; wp x ḥnʿ y 'judge between x and y', L. to D. III, 4 (n.); Urk. IV, 1118, 8; wp mꜣʿt 'reveal truth', JEA 27, 4, n. 4; discern a secret, Urk. IV, 159, 9; distinguish m rn. f 'by name', 259, 14; take o's place, Pyr. 251; wp st 'specify it' = details of it, L. Eg. var. , Gr. p. 538, Z 9.

wpt judgement, Hatnub, 20, 18.

wpi vb. 3 inf. cut off (?), M. u. K. 9, 4.

wpy decision (?), Urk. IV, 1088, 13; cf. JEA 41, 25 (24).

wpw-ḥr except, but, Gr. § 179.

wpwt (1) household: (2) crowd, Caminos, L.-Eg. Misc. 347; var. P. Kah. 10, 2.

wpwt inventory, schedule, Peas. B2, 135; varr. Caminos, Lit. Frag. pl. 22, 13; Adm. 6, 7; P. Kah. 17, 1.

wpwt message, Sin. B 243; Urk. IV, 120, 2; business, mission, Lk. 7, 3; Sh. S. 90; Sin. B 117; BH I, 26, 186; BM 614, 10; Urk. IV, 1108, 2; wpt ḥnꜥ 'punish', L. to D. IV, 4-5 (n.); behest, Sin. B 167. 177; task, Urk. IV, 1074, 12 (det.); news (?): ḥmwt ꜥbꜥbw m wpt 'women became excited at the n.', 1546, 16.

wpwty (< ipwty) messenger, agent, commissioner, JEA 25, 31; 32, 9; AEO I, 26*; in pl. once bystanders (?), Leb. 85. Varr. Sin. B 94; Urk. IV, 1108, 5; 323, 14; hyr. 1440; 920.

Wp-wꜣwt n. div. Wepwawet, Siut, pl. 4, 217; Urk. IV, 432, 4; as ep. of Anubis, Th. T. S. I, 30.

wpt-rꜥ first day of the month and its festival, JEA 24, 5, n. 9; Ann. Serv. 51, 444; Rev. d'ég. 10, 18.

wpt-rnpt New Year's Day and its festival, Urk. IV, 109, 17; varr. 538, 12; 44, 6.

wpš strew, scatter, Urk. IV, 1682, 16; var. CT I, 340.

wfꜣ lungs, AEO II, 245* ff.

wfꜣ vb. talk about, discuss, GNS 31; be t. a. = 'gain repute', Peas. B1, 108; support a plea, JEA 16, 19, 4: n. talk, subject of conversation, GNS 31.

wmt thick, Eb. 20, 14; wmt-ib 'stout-hearted', GNS 35.

wmt gateway, GNS 95; var. dets. Urk. IV, 1795, 13.

wmt thick cloth, Urk. IV, 742, 15; var. det. 1148, 2; cf. Caminos, Lit. Frag. p. 15.

wmt mass of men, RB 57, 3.

wmtt thick wall, in n wmtt 'circumvallation', Urk. IV, 661, 4; 767, 11; 832, 13; 1795, 14; thickness, RB 64, 8; Urk. IV, 1322, 3 (det.).

wn open, Sin. B 115; Peas. B1, 277; Westc. 12, 1; Urk. IV, 96, 8; open up quarry, etc., Urk. IV, 25, 8; 814, 17; RB 112, 13; rip open, Urk. IV, 894, 10; 'free-moving pole (?)', Peas. B1, 258.

wn-ḥr open the sight of, BM 101, cf. JEA 21, 2, n. 5; TR 21, 102; be skilled, m 'in', Urk. IV, 170, 10; 1152, 9; as n. clear vision (?), Barns, Ram. pl. 5, 9, 2; public appearance, Siut, pl. 7, 303; Urk. IV, 751, 1; sdm m wn-ḥr 'judge in public', JEA 41, 19, fig. 1, 5.

wni vb. 3 inf. hasten, hurry, Pyr. 622; L. to D. I, 9 (n.); RB 114, 7; BD 162, 8; wn ꜥwy 'swift of hand', Les. 82, 6; BM 159, 6; pass by, Rec. trav. 26, 11; pass away, Adm. 12, 4; neglect, GAS 102. Var. Urk. IV, 484, 6.

wnt neglect (n.), Urk. IV, 752, 12.

wn fault, blame, Urk. IV, 68, 3; 414, 12; 439, 4; 484, 10.

wn be stripped off, of eyebrows, BD 401, 16; of branches of trees, Adm. 4, 14 (dets.).

wnyt baldness of eyebrows, M. u. K. 3, 8.

wnt sanctuary in temple, Westc. 7, 7; 9, 2.

wnwt hour: division of time, Gr. p. 206; as general term, wnwt bint 'evil h.' = a bad time, P. Kah. 32, 19; n wnwt 'in a moment', Adm. 7, 4; sim. Urk. IV, 691, 10; 943, 4; have pain m wnwt 'spasmodically', Eb. 39, 3; m wnwt.sn 'in their h.' = in the act of being or doing s'thing, Adm. 12, 5; sim. Urk. IV, 49, 6; with r for m, 1078, 3; imy-wnwt 'hour-watcher', 'astronomer', AEO I, 61*. Varr. RB 57, 5; Urk. IV, 49, 6.

wnwt duty, service, Urk. IV, 973, 16; varr. 959, 13; 121, 4.

wnwt coll. priesthood, Siut, pl. 8, 311; Les. 71, 6 (); 98, 5 (); BM 101 (); Urk. IV, 1799, 17 (); staff of workers, 97, 5 ().

wnwty hour-watcher, astronomer, AEO I, 62*; varr. Urk. IV, 1603, 4; 1603, 18; RB 61, 10; , AEO I, 62*.

wnwn sway to and fro, Urk. IV, 286, 15; 288, 2; nod, TR 19, 41; travel about, Pyr. 698 (det.); TR 23, 69. 70 (det.); BD 155, 7 (det.); move about, of child in womb, Pyr. 780 (); trans. traverse a region, Pyr. 770.

wnb flower, Pyr. 544; var. Urk. IV, 1383, 16.

wnpw triumph (?), Urk. IV, 248, 3.

wnf be joyful, BD 115, 4; 125, 10; wnf ib 'be frivolous', Pr. 12, 4, 15, 6 (det.); later 'be content' or the like, Urk. IV, 1845, 10.

wnm eat, Westc. 7, 2. 21; TR 22, 9 ( ); Peas. B1, 12 ( ); Urk. IV, 520, 1 ( ); Paheri, 3 ( ); eat of, feed on, with m, TR 23, 31 ( ); Urk. IV, 547, 14; consume usufruct of property, Siut, pl. 6, 272, cf. JEA 5, 82, n. 1. — Cf. ZÄS 46, 141.

wnmt food, fodder, GNS 44; varr. Les. 79, 11; Sm. 2, 2.

wnmw food, sustenance, Th. T. S. II, 11; var. Amarna, VI, 27, 8.

wnm fattened ox (?), TR 22, 81; var. 22, 82.

wnmyt devouring flame, RB 57, 6; var. Hymnen, 4, 4.

wnmy adj. right-hand, right: n. right side of, Sethe, Rechts. Varr. Urk. V, 34, 10; 35, 6; IV, 1104, 9.

wnn vb. 2 gem. be, exist, cf. Gr. p. 561; JEA 35, 31.

wnt (1) non-encl. part. that, Gr. §§ 187. 233. 329: (2) encl. part, var. of next below, q. v.: (3) in wnt 'there is (are) not', Gr. §§ 108, 2; 109; 188, 2; JEA 35, 33.

wnnt encl. part. indeed, really, var. , Gr. §§ 127, 4; 249.

wn-mꜣꜥ true being, reality, in various senses: (a) as predicate, wn-mꜣꜥ pw 'it is a real (remedy)', Eb. 63, 3: (b) with suffix, n [rdỉ·tw·ỉ] r wn·ỉ-mꜣꜥ '[I have] not [been placed] on my justification', Urk. IV, 1089, 6; sim. 1088, 7: (c) after genitival n, ỉb·k m-ꜥ·k n wn-mꜣꜥ 'thine own real heart being with thee', Urk. IV, 115, 3; ỉmy-r ḥm(w)-nṯr n wn-mꜣꜥ 'a real overseer of prophets', Siut, pl. 10, 3 ( ); sp·f nfr n wn-mꜣꜥ 'his own right cause', Peas. B1, 203. 293; sim. 270; sš ỉḳr n wn-mꜣꜥ 'a really skilful scribe', Urk. IV, 127, 14; sḫty nfr mdw n wn-mꜣꜥ 'a peasant who is eloquent in very truth', Peas. B1, 75-6 ( ): (d) after prep. m: bỉwt·ỉ pw nꜣ m wn-mꜣꜥ 'such were my virtues in very truth', Urk. IV, 973, 10 ( ); mry nb·f m wn-mꜣꜥ 'one truly loved by his lord', BH I, 35: (e) after prep. r: ỉw ꜥḥꜣ·n·ỉ r wn-mꜣꜥ 'I fought in very deed', Urk. IV, 7, 8 ( ).

Wnn-nfrw n. div. Onnophris, name of Osiris, var. , Misc. Acad. Berol. 44; Urk. IV, 1520, 13.

wnḫ be clothed, m 'in', Pyr. 737. 1182 ( ); RB 122, 13 (dets.); don clothing, Pyr. 879; Mill. 1, 7; assume o's body, Pyr. 221. 224; dress a vase with garlands, Adm. 7, 14.

wnḫ roll of cloth, D. el. B. 109; var. det. Pyr. 57.

wnḫyt mummy-cloth (?), Adm. 2, 6.

wnḫw clothing, Amarna, VI, 27, 4-5.

wnš jackal, Peas. R 15; BH II, 4.

wnš sledge, Ann. Serv. 39, 189; var. L. Eg. JEA 31, 38.

wndw short-horned cattle, Urk. IV, 695, 13; 720, 12; varr. Hatnub, 17, 7; Adm. 8, 11; cf. Caminos, L.-Eg. Misc. 210.

wndw goats, Urk. I, 134, 7; cf. Caminos, loc. cit.

wndwt associates, RB 116, 9; var. CT I, 163.

wndwt hold of ship, var. , Pyr. 602; cf. JEA 30, 7, n. j.

wndwt hollow, depression, var. , P. Wilbour, 31.

wr swallow, Pyr. 1130. 1216.

wr(r) adj. and vb. 2 gem. of size, great, Sh. S. 63; Urk. IV, 56, 9; 365, 4 ( ); of quantity, much, many, Siut, pl. 4, 213; Sin. B 82; Sh. S. 150; wr wy 'how often...', Adm. 3, 9; bw-wr 'the greater part of', Sh. S. 152; of age, eldest, Sin. B 79; BH I, 37; of degree, great, important, Peas. B1, 92. 159. 320; Siut, pl. 4, 215; Urk. IV, 943, 5; imy-r-pr wr 'high steward', Peas. B1, 73; st wrt 'the great seat' = the throne, Sin. B 252; wr r 'too much, too great, for...', Leb. 5. 6.

wr (1) n. greatness of size, Urk. IV, 1672, 19; of quantity, sufficiency of food, Pyr. 560; excess of supplies, Sh. S. 54; Les. 79, 12; t ḥnḳt r wr 'bread and beer in quantity', Urk. IV, 1293, 13; n wr n 'inasmuch as', Gr. §181: (2) adv. much, Gr. §205, 4: (3) interrog. how much?, Gr. §502.

wrt (1) n. greatness of rank: 'whose lord gave him wrwt.f his greatnesses', Siut, pl. 9, 350; what is important: dd.i wrt 'I say s'thing i.', Les. 68, 11-12; ptr wrt r ꜥbt ẖꜣt.i 'what can be more i. than my burial?' Sin. B 159; (2) adv. very, Gr. §205, 4.

 wr great one, magnate, Peas. B1,66; Pr. 7,2 (); Les. 81,18; Urk. IV, 62,2 (); 'the great ones' = 'gods' of a place, BM 614, 18; chief of a company, Peas. B1, 190; ruler of a foreign land, Urk. IV, 185,3; 773,2.

 wr-ib insolent, Pr. 8,10.

 wr-mꜣw 'Greatest of Seers', high-priest of Rēꜥ at Heliopolis, AEO I, 36*; II, 267*.

 wr-mḏ-šmꜥw 'Magnate of the Ten of Upper Egypt', administrative title, Urk. IV, 1104, 8.

 wr-ḥkꜣw 'Great of Magic', ep. of gods, Pyr. 204; of king, Urk. IV, 20,2; fem. wrt-ḥkꜣw, of goddesses, 285,13; of crowns, Les. 75,9 (det. 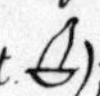); Urk. IV, 1277,16 (dets. 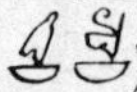); of uraeus, 361,15; 566,2 (det. ).

 wr-ḥkꜣw instrument for 'Opening the Mouth', Ken-amūn, 61; Th. T. S. III, 35.

 wr-ḫrp(w)-ḥm(w) 'Greatest of the Master-Craftsmen', high-priest of Ptaḥ at Memphis, AEO I, 38*; II, 269*.

 wr-swnw master-physician, ZÄS 55, 65.

 wr-diw 'Greatest of the Five', high-priest of Thoth at Hermopolis, ZÄS 59, 104.

 wrt 'Great One', ep. of uraeus, Hymnen, 10,5; of goddesses, Sin. B64; BD 210, 12; 286, 12. 15.

 wrt Crown of Upper Egypt, Urk. IV, 244, 8.

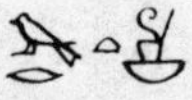 wrt Crown of Lower Egypt, Pyr. 196.

 wrt sacred bark, Les. 71, 18.

 wrt sacred cow, Cairo 20040.

 wri portion of meat, Westc. 4,15; varr.  BH I, 18;  Urk. IV, 1848, 17.

 wryt door-posts, Urk. IV, 520,9.

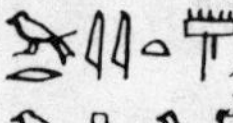 wryt cloth for straining liquids, Adm. 10,1.

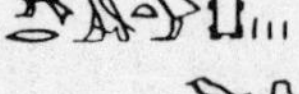 wrmwt roofing, Urk. IV, 389,11; 506,17 (det. ); originally awnings, Pyr. 2100 (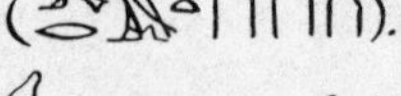).

 wrrt crown, P. Kah. 1,3; Urk. IV, 16,11; 255,7 (det. ); 283,12; as goddess, Sin. B 209 (det. 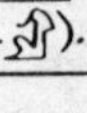).

wrryt chariot, Urk. IV, 615, 8; 657, 5 (det.); varr. 704, 15; 9, 17; 3, 6; 1541, 12; wagon, RB 58, 2.

wrḥ anoint s'one, m 'with' unguent; smear on unguent, GNS 112; Wortforschung, V, 35; var. dets. Urk. IV, 1214, 15.

wrḥ ointment, Urk. IV, 1058, 13; Eb. 86, 18 (det.).

wrḥt ointment, Eb. 78, 15; 82, 13; cf. Wortforschung, V, 36.

wrḥy anointer, Caminos, Lit. Frag. p. 36 with n. 2.

wrs head-rest, P. Kah. 18, 15; Adm. 14, 2.

wrš spend the day, spend o's time, Sin. B q. 158; Peas. B1, 225; Westc. 6, 13; wrš n šw 'stand all day in the sun', of medicaments, Eb. 53, 4; spend much time on a quest, Westc. 7, 6; wake, be awake, Pyr. 875 (det.). 1011. Cf. Rec. trav. 39, 108.

wršy watcher, sentry, GNS 18.

wrd be, grow weary; tire, Pyr. 491. 794; P. Kah. 1, 9 ( ); Urk. IV, 123, 3; 1282, 17; in sense of die, Leb. 153; wrd ỉb 'the heart is w.' = beats slowly, Sin. B 170; Pr. 4, 4; Sm. 3, 3; Eb. 102, 12; 'the weary-hearted' = the inert, ep. of dead Osiris, BD 19, 13; RB 111, 15; ỉḫmw-wrd 'the unwearying stars', see p. 29.

wrdw weariness, Adm. 5, 7.

wḥỉ vb. 3 inf. escape, I. Carn. 13; Urk. IV, 1292, 13; Pr. 14, 12 (det.); miss, of arrow, RB 58, 13; Urk. IV, 1321, 16; fail, RB 60, 6; 111, 12; m 'in', Mu. K. 1, 10; 2, 1; 'by reason of', Pr. 9, 13; be undone, of heart, Kamosĕ, 11 ( ); be lacking, m 'in', Pt. (L. II), 2, 11; Urk. IV, 2144, 4.

wḥt failure, Peas. B1, 292.

wḥꜣḥꜣ arrogance (?), Hamm. 43.

wḥb vb. pierce, Eb. 54, 21: n. hole, Eb. 54, 22.

wḥn throw down fence, etc., CT I, 60 (var. dets. ,); BD 436, 14; GAS 55; an evil spirit, M. u. K. 4, 4; fall off, of scab, Eb. 74, 6; 75, 8.

wḥnn crown of head, Eb. 86, 21; Sm. 2, 21.

var. of wḥ3t below.

wḥ3t cauldron, Pyr. 405; Siut, pl. 7, 292; Urk. V, 60, 8; var. BD 449, 9.

wḥ3t oasis, oasis-region, Urk. IV, 963, 14 (dets.); 969, 13; 1145, 2; cf. AEO II, 236*.

wḥ3tyw oasis-dwellers, Adm. 3, 9.

wḥ3 hew stone, Urk. I, 108, 2; IV, 1448, 5 (); Bersh. II, p. 24 (); pluck flowers, plants, TR 22, 63 (det.); Bersh. I, pl. 27; cut crops, Les. 84, 10; Adm. 5, 13 (dets.); Urk. IV, 689, 10.

wḥyt village, varr. , , , AEO II, 205*; P. Wilbour, 33; pl. det. RB 57, 12.

wḥyt family, kindred, Pr. 7, 7; tribe, Sin. B 94. 113. Varr. Sin. B 200; B 28; B 86.

wḥꜥ (1) loose fetters, etc., Pyr. 349. 593 (); Sm. 11, 5; BD 86, 8; Urk. IV, 166, 12; wḥꜥ ṯst 'l. what is tied' = unravel problems, Les. 69, 21; 73, 2 (); Urk. IV, 47, 12; wḥꜥ Ḥꜥpy 'the l.-ing of the Nile' = the start of the inundation, Dav. Rekh. pl. 122, 33 (A); release s'one or thing, Pyr. 2105 (). 2188 (); Eb. 1, 13; the land was r., i.e created, Urk. IV, 162, 6: (2) return, m 'from', Urk. IV, 116, 1 (); go home after work, Paheri, 3 ().

wḥꜥ-ib capable of action, with r + infin., Urk. IV, 131, 7; skilled, m 'in', 1820, 7.

wḥꜥ investigate, Urk. IV, 1093, 3. 4 (). 5 (). 8.

wḥꜥ fish synodontis schall, Barns, Ram. p. 18; fem. JEA 41, pl. 3, 41.

wḥꜥ fisherman, Peas. B1, 230; fowler, Bersh. I, 17 (pl.); varr. pl. BD 393, 8; Bersh. II, 16; BH I, 32; Urk. IV, 815, 1. Pl. often = 'fishers and fowlers', e.g. Bersh. I, 23; cf. JEA 38, 29.

wḥꜥ distribute rations (?), Urk. IV, 656, 8; cf. JEA 28, 10.

wḥwḥ disappear, of inscription, Amarna, V, 26, 24.

wḥmt hoof, Gr. p. 464, F25.

wḥm ass (lit. 'hoof'), abbr. , loc. cit.

 wḥm (1) repeat an action: wḥm kt ḥst n 'r. another favour to' = favour again, Urk. IV, 31,5; wḥm ꜥnḫ 'live again' after death, BD 104,15; Urk. IV, 964,9 (); wḥm mꜣꜣ 'see s'thing again', 893,5; wḥm ḫꜥ 'be crowned again', D. el. B. 11; wḥm ḥbw 'continue to hold festivals', Siut, pl. 13,22; wḥm mnw 'erect many monuments', Urk. IV, 358,9; nn wḥm ḫꜣstyw Rṯnw r bšt ky sp 'never again will the foreigners of Retjnu rebel', RB 59,10 (with r before infin.; so also RB 60,1; Urk. IV, 895,6); m wḥm 'again', Urk. IV, 1073,17; Eb. 93,15;  wḥm-ꜥ 'repeat', synonym of wḥm, GNS 36; m wḥm-ꜥ 'again', Urk. IV, 114,1.

(2) of speech, usually with det. : repeat, report, Sin. B 216; Westc. 12, 2.7.15; Pr. 7,4; Les. 69,20; BD 104,12; bruit abroad, Sin. B 212; wḥm sꜣ 'sound the retreat', Sin. B 124; wḥm ḏd 'repeat', Eb. 30,16.

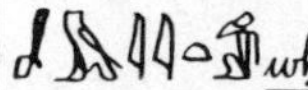 wḥmyt continued howling (?) of wind, Sh. S. 35.104. Cf. JEA 16,68.

 wḥmw herald, reporter, AEO I, 91*; legal registrar, P. Kah. 34,38; wḥmw nsw 'King's h.', AEO I, 22*. Varr. 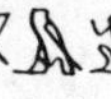 Siut, pl. 7,284;  Urk. IV, 1122,5;  35,1;  4,8.

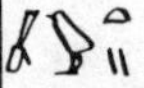 wḥmwty in nn wḥmwty.f 'there will never be his like again', varr. , 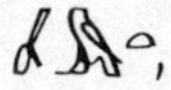, Äg. Stud. 1; JEA 38,59.

 wḥmmyt repetitions of s'thing said, Adm. p. 97.

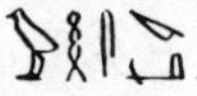 wḥs cut off hair, BD 401,16; kill rebels, 357,4; quell tumult, 481,14.

 wḫ fetish of Ḳ̈ꜣs in U. E., var. 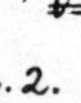, Meir, I, p. 2.

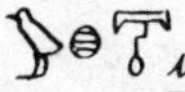 wḫ night, Siut, pl. 11,10; var. 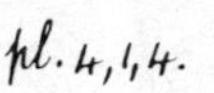 Caminos, Lit. Frag. pl. 4,1,4.

 wḫt darkness, Leb. 71-2.

 wḫꜣ column, Adm. 2,10; Urk. IV, 1379,8; tent-pole, 664,7; 705,13. Varr.  BH I, 26, 196; 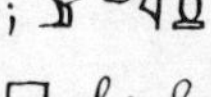 PSBA 22,99, n. *; Urk. IV, 765,13.

 wḫꜣ hall of columns, BH I, 26,194.

 wḫꜣ full blast (?) of storm, Adm. 7,13.

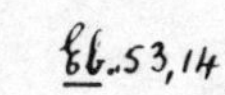 wḫꜣ throw off earth, etc. from o'self, Pyr. 654.1878; BD 152,8; empty out, Ti, 111; Eb. 53,14; shake out linen, BH II, 4.13; beat a mat, Teti Cem. II, pl. 52; purge the body, Eb. 11,3.

 wḫ3 seek, Urk. IV, 1799,2; varr.  Les. 86,10;  JEA 14, pl. 6, 25.

 wḫ3 be foolish, act stupidly, Leb. 18; var.  Merikarē‘, 115.

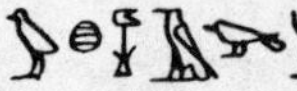 wḫ3 ignorant, incompetent person, fool, Sh. S. 101; Pr. 14,4; Adm. 6,13; varr.  Peas. B1, 218;  Urk. IV, 970,1.

 var. of wḫ 'night'.

 wḫryt dockyard, Urk. V, 151,5; ZÄS 68, 28; carpenter's workshop, D. el Gebr. II, 10 ().

 wḫd be painful; suffer, endure, GAS 104-105; be patient with s'one, Hatnub, 20,17. Var. det.  Urk. IV, 1082,16.

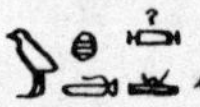 wḫd forbearance, Peas. B1, 272.

 wḫdw pain, Eb. 25,9; 27,7; 31,14; abbr. 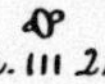 24,14.

 wḫdt pain, Adm. 6,5; Eb. 46,15.

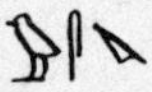 wsỉ vb. 3 inf. saw, BH II, 13; P. Ram. V, 11.

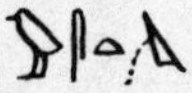 wst sawdust, Eb. 81,18; 92,20; abbr.  83,1.

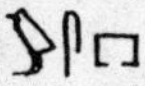 ws (1) crack, chink: (2) small window; 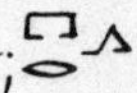 m ws 'height' of pyramid, Ch. B. Text, 71, n. 3.

 wst (wsty?) letter, Caminos, Lit. Frag. pl. 22, 17.

 Wsir n. div. Osiris, BH I, 12; varr. 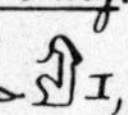 I, 15; 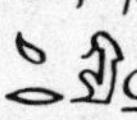 CT I, 2;  Urk. IV, 77,17; 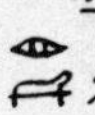 209,1.

 wsf vb. intrans. be slack, sluggish, Peas. B1, 257: trans. neglect, Urk. IV, 353,8 (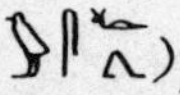); Amarna, V, 26, 22 (); ignore, Leb. 6, cf. JEA 42, 30(b): n. sluggishness, Peas. B1, 281; B2, 107.

 wsfw sluggard, Peas. B1, 284; var.  B2, 109.

 wsrt neck, BD 119, 12 (det. ); 173,3.

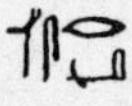 wsr strong, Westc. 10,9; Urk. IV, 94,6 (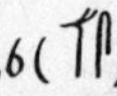); powerful, Urk. IV, 15,4 (det. 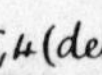); 255,17 (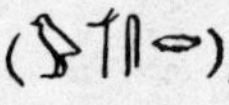); 773,8; BM 614, 14 (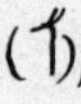); Peas. B1, 116; Les. 68,10 ([illegible]); wealthy, influential, Pr. 6,9; Urk. IV, 766,5; 972,7; wsr ỉb 'stout of heart,' Urk. IV, 111,14; 187,4; 556,15; wsr

rnpwt 'rich in years', Koptos, 12, 3; wsr fꜣw 'rich in splendour', Urk. IV, 1276, 10.

wsr wealthy man, Urk. IV, 1118, 8; varr. Hatnub, 24, 5; Amarna, II, 7.

wsrw strength, power, Urk. IV, 1280, 15; varr. 1541, 7; 89, 7; Peas. B1, 214.

wsrw oar, Urk. IV, 1279, 18; 1280, 4; varr. Westc. 5, 8; (pl.) Urk. IV, 305, 14.

wsḫ cup, Gr. p. 528, W10.

wsḫ (1) adj. broad, wide, Peas. R 45; Siut, pl. 15, 20 (det.); Hymnen, 8, 1; extensive, of movements, Pyr. 886; of monuments, Siut, pl. 15, 4; of riches, Sin. B 146 ( ); wsḫ n.i 'I have space', BD 493, 7; sim. of excavated temple, Urk. IV, 834, 17; wsḫ m 'be proud of', 350, 3; wsḫ ib 'generous', Leyd. V 6, 14; wsḫ st 'spacious of place', JEA 37, 109: (2) n. breadth, Urk. IV, 56, 14; 142, 10 (abbr.); 248, 6; 613, 2.

wsḫ ornamental collar, Urk. IV, 425, 8; 475, 13; abbr. 54, 3; sim. 204, 6.

wsḫ barge, Westc. 8, 5; Urk. IV, 124, 16; var. 125, 5.

wsḫt barge, Sin. B 13.

wsḫt hall, court, Hatnub, 17, 3; Urk. IV, 429, 10; varr. 976, 13; 1092, 7; RB 112, 1. Cf. AEO II, 208*.

wsš (wzš) vb. intrans. urinate, Pyr. 510; P. Ram. III, A 6; Eb. 2, 12a ( ): trans. pass fluid, P. Ram. III, A 8; Eb. 25, 7; P. Kah. 5, 18 ( ).

wsšt urine, Pyr. 127; varr. TR 24, 5; D. el B. 110.

wsš die out, of a race, Hatnub, 20, 2; 23, 3.

wsṯ (wzṯ) vb. be dilapidated, Pyr. 1929 (Neith 758); BH I, 25, 39 ( ): n. dilapidation, Caminos, Lit. Frag. pl. 1, 1, 2.

wsṯn travel freely, Sin. B 115 ( ); Urk. IV, 116, 12; 1063, 14; be unhindered, 1075, 4; m wsṯn 'unhindered', 'with free access', Bersh. II, 21, top, 1; wsṯn ꜥ 'free of hands', Urk. IV, 2092, 7 (dets.); wsṯn nmtt 'f. of movement', 456, 16; wsṯn rd 'f. of foot', 426, 13; wsṯn ḫt 'f. of belly' = gluttonous, Pr. 1, 7; wsṯn sḫrw 'far-reaching of governance', Pr. 8, 14–9, 1; m sḫr m wsṯn 'in arbitrary manner', JEA 38, 29: trans. deal arbitrarily with, ibid.

 wš vb. (1) intrans. fall out, of hair, GAS 62; be destroyed, Leb. 63; abbr.  Eb. 18,1; wš ib 'be helpless(?)', Leb. 85 (det. ); gm wš 'found destroyed', of writings, see s.v. gm; 'H.M. stayed 4 days m wš rdit srf n ssmwt.f because of the necessity(?) of giving rest to his horses', RB 66,7: (2) trans. desolate a place, L. to D. VI, 4, n.

 var. of wsš 'urinate'.

 wš3t widgeon(?), Gr. p. 472, G 42, n. 1.

 wš3 fatten, BH I, 30 (also ); var. 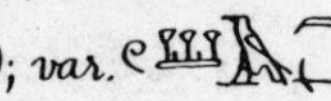 Dream-book, 8,20.

 wš3 utter plaudits (ḥswt), Urk. IV, 502,11; recite praises (ḥknw), 1095,6; 1208,12.

 wš3w darkness, BD 472,7; var. dets. 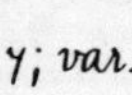 136,1.

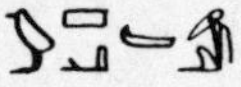 wšꜥ chew, P. Kah. 5,44; Eb. 8,15; Adm. 11,2; eat a morsel, Caminos, Lit. Frag. p. 14; var.  P. Ram. IV, D v,2.

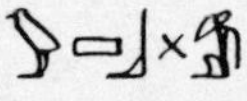 wšb answer (vb. and n.), Sin. B 260.261; Sh. S. 14.16 (det.  only); Leb. 4; Peas. B1, 79.152.216; a. s'one, with n, Sin. B 46; Sh. S. 86; Peas. B1, 50; with ḥr, Urk. IV, 27,9; with direct obj, Les. 84,6; answer for conduct, Urk. IV, 511,17; ir wšb 'make a.', Adm. 12,14-13,1; ir wšb ḥr 'a. for', 'protect' s'one, Urk. IV, 970,16.

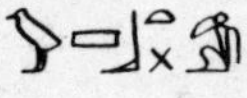 wšbt response(?), Pr. 8,13.

 wšbw comforter(?), Urk. IV, 1078,5; cf. ZÄS 60,70.

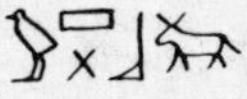 wšb bull, Urk. IV, 1076, 2.

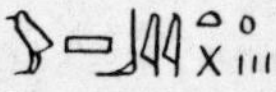 wšbyt beads, M.u.K. 1,1.

 wšm mix, ḥr with, Eb. 33,20.

 wšm prove(?), test(?) s's heart = disposition, Pr. 14,8; cf Žába, 156.

 wšm ear of corn, Hatnub 24,5; var. dets.  Urk. IV, 535,10.

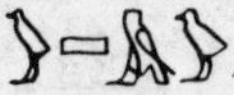 wšmw jar of metal, Urk. IV, 23,4; as beer-measure, 828,7 (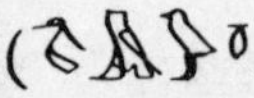).

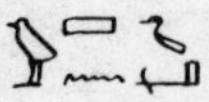 wšn (1) wring the neck of poultry, Sh. S. 145; Siut, pl. 19,27 (det. ): (2) make offering of food and drink, Siut, pl. 5,239.

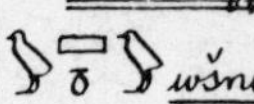 wšnw poultry for table, Dav. Ptah. II, 5; var. 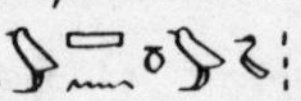 BD 229,2.

 wšr dry up, Sm. 13,9; be barren, of women, Adm. 2,4; be despoiled(?), Urk. IV, 84,1 (det. 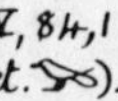).

var. of wšš 'urinate'.

wšd address s'one, Pr. 7,1; Sin. B 254; Westc. 7,14; question s'one, Peas. B1, 216. 220; Sh. S. 15; Les. 75,5 ( ); P. Kah. 13, 23. 28; assent, JEA 27, 86 (11); wšd r mdt 'invite to speak', BH I, 15.

wgi vb. 3 inf. chew, P. Ram. III, B 11; var. Pyr. 1460.

wgyt jaw, Sm. 7,14; varr. 3,18; M. u. K. 2,5.

wgyt talker, 'jawer', fig. use of last, Peas. B1, 253; cf. JEA 9, 17, n. 5.

wgiw ribs (?) of ship, TR 27,20; varr. ZÄS 68, 26; BD 206,14.

wgb (< wbg) rise, of sun, Urk. IV, 1819, 13.

wgp triturate, P. Kah. 6,6.

wgm vb. crush grain, P. Ed. Smith, 497: n. crushed grain, ibid.; AEO I, 14.

wgs cut open, gut fish, etc.; Eb. 66,14; 88,5; Neferti, 31; Caminos, Lit. Frag. pl. 2, 2, 9 ( ); 6, 3, 10.

wgg feebleness, weakness, Sin. B 168; Pr. 4,3; Eb. 100,16; misery, L. to D. V, 1 (n.) ( ).

[ ] wggt woe, Pr. 5,8.

wt (1) vb. bandage, bind, Pyr. 1202; Eb. 35,5 ( ); 39,21; Sm. 7,10 ( ); cf. P. Ed. Smith, 525-6; embalm, Urk. V, 204, 13 ( ): (2) n. mummy-wrapping, Pyr. 1878; M. u. K. 8,7 ( ); Sin. B 192 (pl.); bandage, Eb. 1,12; Sm. 11,5 ( ); 13,21; pl. wrappings, 15,18 ( ).

wt place of embalming in imy wt 'he who is in the p. of e.', ep. of Anubis, BH I, 7; var. imy II, 12; name of Anubis-fetish, Caminos, Lit. Frag. p. 30, n. 8.

wt embalmer, bandager, TR 21,57; BH I, 18; Sm. 5,5 ( ); 7,21 ( ); wt-'Inpw a priest, Les. 70,4; cf. SDT 29.

pl. of wt 'mummy-wrapping' above.

wtḫ flee, RB 58,5; Urk. IV, 139,5; varr. 767,9; RB 65,9.

 wṯḥw fugitive, Urk. IV, 84,12; 508,2.

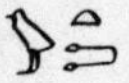 wtt beget, Pyr. 650. 1154; from M.K.  Les. 84,15; Urk. IV, 17,4 (dets. ); 157,4.

 wttw begetter, Les. 68,21.

 wttw offspring, Urk. IV, 84,15.

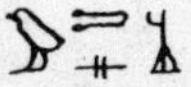 wṯs (wṯz) raise, lift up, Urk. IV, 1662,11; V, 149,11; BD 134,2 (dets. 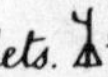); of voice, Urk. IV, 1088,15; of crowns in coronation 82,17 (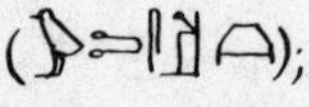); 1278,10; wear crown, Les. 98,17 (dets. 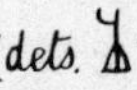); Urk. IV, 85,12; 270,1 (); 361,11; 1543,1 (abbr. 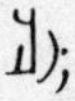); weigh goods, 337,7.15; extol god, Amarna, V, 26, 1.3; display beauty (nfrw) of god or king, Les. 71,4; Urk. IV, 271,11; wṯs-nfrw 'processional bark', 98,1; announce s'one's name, Pyr. 348 (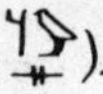).

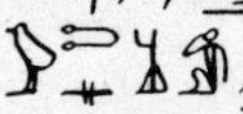 wṯs lay an information, delate, Westc. 12,23; wṯs  'deliver a verdict (?)', Urk. IV, 1088,15.

 wṯsw accused person, Peas. B2,111.

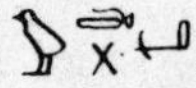 wḏi vb. 3inf. (1) place, put, TR 1,9; Les. 75,17; Eb. 19,6; Urk. IV, 269,4; implant an obstacle, Ann. Serv. 27, 227; plant trees, Urk. IV, 28,4; 353,3; land, m 'with' trees, 57,2; lay a fire, Pyr. 405; appoint as, Pyr. 1690; be bent on a purpose, Peas. B1, 206; wḏ m-sꜣ 'follow after' evil, BM 614,7.

(2) with basic meaning throw: shoot an arrow, GNS 49; utter a cry, Sin. B140 (det. 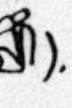). 265; cf. GNS 55; send forth the voice ( or 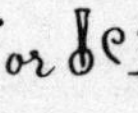), give out a noise (dyt), GNS 55; commit offence, RB 112,11; Urk. IV, 968,15; deal harm, injury, RB 119,12; Adm. 12,13; JEA 6, 301, n. 10; stir up strife, Adm. 7,6; instil terror, Cairo 20089; extend protection, TR 17,39.

(3) in expressions wḏ ꜥ 'extend the hand', r 'to' do s'thing, Urk. IV, 339,6; 'press the hand', r 'against', Eb. 79,4; wḏ ꜥ m kꜣt 'set to work', RB 77,11-12; wḏ rmn 'thrust the shoulder', m 'against', Pyr. 299; wḏ ḥr 'eager', 'bold', GNS 35; wḏ nkn 'do harm', r 'to', Urk. IV, 401,16; 'execute sentence', Westc. 8,15-16; cf. JEA 22,42; wḏ m ḫbd 'show displeasure (?)', Pr. 7,12.

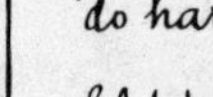 see under wḏb.

wdpw (1) butler: (2) cook, GNS 92; AEO I, 43*. Varr. GNS 92; (sing.), Urk. IV, 153, 5.

wdpwyt serving-maid, Cairo 20016.

wdf delay (vb. and n.), Pyr. 1223; TR 2, 25; Peas. B 2, 122 (); Sh. S. 40 (); Urk. IV, 1070, 6 (); 1110, 14 (); be sluggish, of wound, Sm. 14, 9 (); adv. tardily, Gr. §205, 4.

wdn instal as god or king, Pyr. 1013. 1127. 1686 (det.); record royal titulary, Urk. IV, 160, 11 (det.); 285, 6 (det. X), both with assimilation of n to verb-ending.

wdn be heavy, Urk. IV, 327, 12; 1290, 1; var. dets. BH II, 7; Peas. B1, 128; weigh, ḥr 'on' s'one, of affairs, Adm. p. 108; wdn m (?) 'be weighed down with (?)', Leb. 28 (dets.); become difficult, of conditions, Caminos, Lit. Frag. pl. 2, 2, 11.

wdnt heavy block of stone, Urk. IV, 437, 15.

wdn offer, n 'to', Urk. IV, 871, 6; 1579, 3; varr. 491, 15; Leb. 149; Th. T. S. I, 1.

wdnw offerings, Urk. IV, 1507, 10; varr. 535, 4; 748, 14; Del. B. 95; P. Kah. 38, 11.

wdnt offering, Pyr. 817. 978; var. P. Kah. 4, 3.

wdn offerer, Urk. IV, 451, 15.

wdrt region, Urk. IV, 383, 13; cf. JEA 32, 46, n. 2.

wdḥ pour out, pour off, Pyr. 1148. 2067 (det.); varr. Sm. 2, 25; Eb. 33, 6.

wdḥw offering, Pyr. 1148; var. det. CT I, 126.

wdḥw offering-table, Pyr. 474. 696; varr. Les. 75, 15; Bersh. I, 12; Westc. 9, 26; Urk. IV, 133, 17; 48, 9; Paheri, 1.

wdd gall, gall-bladder, ZÄS 62, 21.

wḏ (1) vb. command, Peas. B1, 48; RB 74, 11; 76, 5; Urk. IV, 184, 7; make a command, n 'for the benefit of', RB 112, 16; wḏ wḏt n 'issue a c. to', Herdsm. 16; wḏ sḫrw n 'govern',

Pr. 6, 4; wḏ.tw + infin. 'it is forbidden to . . .', Westc. 8, 17; enjoin an instruction, ḥr 'upon' s'one, Urk. IV, 196, 7; decree s'one, n 'to' a destiny, 227, 8; allot, decree s'thing n 'to' s'one, BH I, 25, 88; Urk. IV, 166, 1; 198, 3; 808, 14; commit, commend s'one, n 'to', Pyr. 120. 497. 1192; entrust a matter, n 'to', Pr. 9, 1; BM 614, 9. 10; ḥr 'to', RB 58, 8.

(2) n. command, Peas. B1, 268; Les. 72, 13; Urk. IV, 363, 7; 405, 7; written decree, despatch, Sin. B 178. 199; Urk. IV, 208, 10; 1116, 13 (det.); 1343, 11 (det.); precept, Peas. B1, 109; wḏ 'order' to a craftsman, B1, 111.

Varr. BH I, 25, 88; Urk. IV, 183, 3; 45, 16.

wḏt command, decree (n.), P. Kah. 35, 39; Herdsm. 16; varr. BH I, 25, 58; Urk. IV, 1114, 7; 285, 16; 45, 13; 2143, 13.

wḏ-mdw vb. command, control, govern people, with n, Siut, pl. 5, 236; Urk. IV, 257, 10 ( ); 545, 16: n. command, RB 111, 10.

wḏt-mdw command (n.), Siut, pl. 6, 268; Sin. B 49; var. Sin. R 73.

wḏ-tp give orders (?), Pr. 11, 12.

wḏ intrans. vb. act as pilot, TR 22, 39: trans. pilot s'one, Urk. IV, 1847, 10 ( ).

wḏi vb. 3 inf. depart, Urk. IV, 648, 12; stray, of cattle, Adm. 9, 2 ( ).

wḏyt campaign, expedition, Urk. IV, 184, 6; 647, 13; 688, 3 ( ); 689, 5 (det.); journey, 1112, 6.

Sin. B 118 a misreading of ḥww 'cattle'.

wḏ stela, BH I, 26, 137; RB 58, 6; 64, 15; Urk. IV, 1283, 13; varr. BH I, 25, 32; Urk. IV, 133, 13; 697, 5; Leyd. V 88; (sic) Les. 82, 11.

wḏ inscription, Urk. IV, 693, 12; 734, 15; RB 74, 11 (det.).

wḏ jug, Urk. IV, 1150, 7.

wḏ3 (1) adj. hale, uninjured, Sh. S. 79-80; Urk. V, 36, 17; Sm. 4, 13; 18, 4; Les. 69, 2; prosperous, Pr. 1, 1; Urk. IV, 66, 2; 944, 7; V, 63, 6; wḏ3 ib 'be glad', Pyr. 581. 1198; wḏ3 ib-k 'may it please you', formula for announcing news, Sh. S. 1-2; cf. also Urk. IV, 1143, 7; rdi wḏ3 ib 'inform', P. Kah. 22, 5; Urk. IV, 138, 12; ʿnḫ wḏ3 snb 'may he live, be prosperous and hale', Gr. § 313; ꜥḏ wḏꜣ 'safe and sound', of persons, P. Kah. 32, 12; Urk. IV, 209, 14; 'prosperous and flourishing', of affairs, P. Kah. 27, 9; 29, 4; Urk. IV, 1106, 2.

(2) vb. remain over, of balance in calculations, Rhind, 28.—Varr. Les. 69, 2; Urk. IV, 138, 12.

wḏꜣw well-being, prosperity, Urk. IV, 362, 5; varr. 147, 2; 227, 8; an official styles himself wḏꜣw ꜥḥ 'w.-b. of the palace', 969, 8.

wḏꜣ storehouse, Urk. IV, 413, 7; 1144, 13; 1146, 2; var. Caminos, Lit. Frag. pl. 21, 9, 16.

wḏꜣ pectoral (?), Urk. IV, 871, 9; 873, 8; varr. 870, 16; 1859, 12; 1880, 10.

wḏꜣt the uninjured Eye of Horus, var. [hieroglyphs], Gr. § 266, 1; source of notation of measures of capacity, ibid.; used of Eye of Rēꜥ, Urk. V, 37, 13.

wḏꜣyt mythical abode of Amen-Rēꜥ, Urk. IV, 445, 13.

wḏꜣw amulets, M. u. K. vs. 5, 8; 6, 7; Urk. IV, 425, 9 ([hieroglyphs]); 1046, 7 ([hieroglyphs]); protective spell, M. u. K. rt. 9, 7.

wḏꜣ go, set out, proceed, r 'to', Sin. B 282; Westc. 8, 2; 9, 27; 10, 6; 11, 9; Les. 76, 15; Urk. IV, 9, 8; RB 64, 16; of idol carried in procession, Siut, pl. 6, 274; Urk. IV, 308, 6; attain, r 'to' a rank, BH I, 25, 63-4; set, of sun, M. u. K. vs. 4, 3; wḏꜣ r ꜣḫt 'go to the horizon' = die, of king, Sin. B 36; šms wḏꜣ 'funeral cortège', GNS 69. Varr. Les. 76, 15; Urk. IV, 651, 6.

wḏꜥ (1) cut cords, Pyr. 2202; cut off head, Westc. 8, 18 (dets. [hieroglyphs]); Urk. IV, 2092, 18 ([hieroglyphs]); be parted, of lips of wound, Sm. 16, 7 ([hieroglyphs]); 17, 1. 6; cut out sandals, BH II, 4.

(2) judge, Peas. B1, 269; Leb. 23; Urk. IV, 1079, 2; have judgement, ḥnꜥ 'with', L. to D. X, 1, 3; Urk. I, 117, 6; judge between litigants, Urk. I, 133, 4; Peas. B1, 234.

(3) open door, CT I, 33; discern, JEA 4, pl. 37; Urk. IV, 1686, 10 ([hieroglyphs]); assign, devote, n 'to', GNS 69; remove, Pyr. 270. 1470.

wḏꜥ he who is judged, ep. of Seth, Gr. p. 542, Aa 21.

wḏꜥt judgement, Pr. 13, 4; var. dets. [hieroglyphs] Urk. IV, 1381, 13.

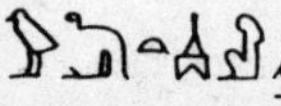 wḏꜥt divorced woman, Peas. R106; var.  B1,63.

 wḏꜥ-mdw (1) vb. judge, Urk. IV, 1074,13; litigate, ḥnꜥ 'with', L. to D. I,10 (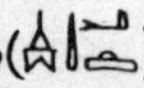); II, 9 ( ); have judgement, ḫft 'against', CT I, 9.13: (2) n. judgement, Urk. IV, 1089,13.

 wḏꜥ-rwt judge (vb. and n.), Peas. B1,217; Pr. 10,10 (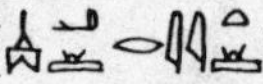); Urk. IV, 1071,17; Paheri, 1,4 (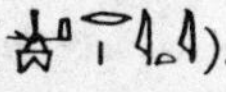).

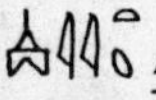 wḏꜥyt mussel(?), JEA 18,153; shell to hold ink (?), Pyr. 2030 (); TR 10,9.

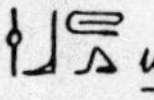 wḏb fold over, Westc. 6,11-12 (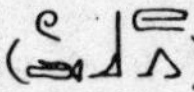); turn, r 'away from', Teti Cem. II, pl. 52; ḥr 'to', Pyr. 115 (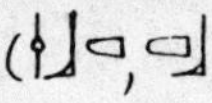); the head, n 'to', 808 (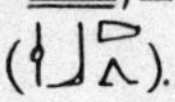). 1723 (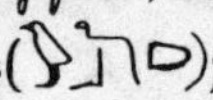); turn back, CT I, 166 (); revert, n 'to', Pyr. 1908; divert offerings, JEA 24, 86; direct action, r 'to a purpose, Pr. 13,3; recur, of illness, Eb. 108,1.

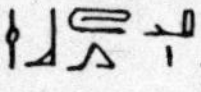 wḏb-ꜥ turn the hand away, desist, compose o'self, JEA 22, 39; turn o'self about, Urk. IV, 1302,8. Var.  Sin. B163.

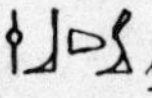 wḏb-rd reversion of offerings from temple to tomb; also the reversion-offering itself, varr. 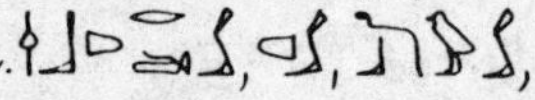, JEA 24,88; 25,215; Gîza, III, 5.

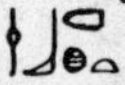 wḏb-ḫt vb. divert offerings: n. reversion-offering, varr. 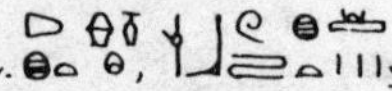 JEA 24,87.

 wḏb in title  ḥry wḏb 'Master of Largess', JEA 24,83.

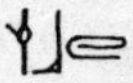 wḏb folded cloth, D. el B. 109.

 wḏb river-bank, Pyr. 291.1008; RB 120,9 (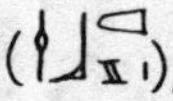); riparian lands, Urk. IV, 118,10 (); Amarna, V, 26, 21; sea-shore, Urk. IV, 687,16 (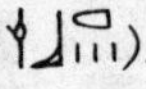).

 var. of wḏf 'delay'.

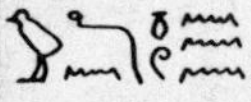 wḏnw flood, inundation, P. Kah. 2, 12; Siut, pl. 11,30; Peas. B1,102; cf. ZÄS 53,134.

 wḏḥ pour out, see wdḥ

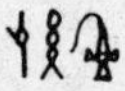 wḏḥ (< wdḥ) cast metal, Urk. IV, 695,1; 731,11.

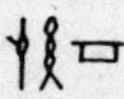 wḏḥ door of cast metal, Urk. IV, 1150, 12.

 wḏḥ vb. wean, Pyr. 729 (). 1119 (). 1344 (). 2003: n. weaned child, Urk. IV, 926,17; of royalty,  157,8; [illegible] 587,7.

[illegible] wḏḥw offering-table, see wdḥw.

var. of bw 'place'.

b3 soul, Urk. IV, 414, 14; 415, 5; varr. Westc. 7, 25; Sin. B 255; Urk. IV, 150, 3. Cf. ZÄS 77, 78.

b3w plur. of last, (1) souls of dead, BD 20, 12; b3w Iwnw 'the S. of On', i.e. of ancient kings, Urk. IV, 361, 9 (, the usual wtg.); of Pe, TR 27, 36; of Nekhen, Siut, pl. 3, 173; of Khemennu, BD 235, 7: (2) power, Sin. B 6* (); Sh. S. 139; P. Kah. 2, 5; Hymnen, 13, 2 (); Urk. IV, 85, 6; deed of power, RB 76, 11.

b3 be, possess, a soul, Pyr. 139. 799; var. Th. T. S. IV, 38, B.

b3 ram, Urk. IV, 224, 17; V, 74, 16; var. 75, 5.

b3 leopard, BH II, 4; var. Peas. R 14.

b3 leopard-skin, Urk. I, 127, 1; cf. JEA 19, 154.

b3 hack up the earth, BD 33, 7; hoe crops, Pyr. 1880 (); destroy, devastate, Pyr. 1837; L. to D. I, 5; Urk. I, 103, 8; IV, 1302, 12.

b3t symbol of Hathōr, Pyr. 1096; var. Urk. IV, 1389, 13; title, Meir IV, 6; BH I, 17.

b3tyt devotee of Hathōr (?), ep. of queen, Urk. IV, 1771, 13.

b3t bush, Sin. B 5. 18; Bersh. II, 16; wisp of corn, Peas. B1, 10. 15.

b33wt virility, GNS 68.

b3y foot-ewer, BM 101; cf. JEA 21, 3, n. 7.

b3iw damp (adj.), Sm. 3, 19; var. 3, 10; cf. P. Ed. Smith, 192.

b3w galley, Westc. 5, 2; P. Kah. 22, 15.

b3b3t inshore eddy (?), Leb. 47; varr. Urk. IV, 76, 9; 51, 7.

b3b3w hole, Urk. IV, 613, 12; 931, 3 (det.); Eb. 97, 18; used of socket of eye, P. Kah. 5, 20; of the seven apertures in the head, Eb. 90, 17.

b3ḥ phallus, Sm. 10, 16; Barns, Ram. p. 27, n. 1; var.

'in the presence of', *Gr.* §178; 'in front of', *Pyr.* 18.34; adv. 'in front', 'formerly', *Gr.*
§205,2; ⌗⌗ 'in the presence of', §178; ⌗ adv. 'before'. 'formerly', *Urk.* IV,
102,4; 344,14; *imy-b3ḥ* 'who is before', see p. 18.

b3ḥ measure of capacity, *Urk.* IV, 1449,5.

B3ḥw n. loc. a region originally W. of Egypt; name later transferred
to the E., varr. ⌗⌗, *AEO* I,118*; ⌗ *Urk.* IV,800,92; ⌗ 187,8.

b3s jar, *Lac. Sarc.* II,13, No.23; var. *Urk.* IV, 206,6.

B3st n. loc. Bubastis, *BD* 254,11; var. *Urk.* IV, 432,9.

B3stt n. div. Bastet, *Urk.* IV,191,1; 432,9; varr. 478,14; *TR* 21,29.

b3s devour, *CT* I,293.

b3ḳ tree moringa arabica, *Ch.B. Text*,49, n.3; var. *Urk.* IV,73,17.

b3ḳ moringa-oil, *Sin.* B83; varr. *Urk.* IV,1143,10; 688,15;
59,10.

b3ḳ oily, *P.Ed.Smith*,376; bright, *Pyr.*1443 ( ); *Urk.* IV, 896,6 (det.
); *BD*463,11 ( ); white, *Pyr.* 252; be dazzled, of sight (ḥr), *Neferti*, 52; clear
of character, innocent, *L. to D. n.* on I,3; *JEA* 28,19 (l̥); fortunate, *Pyr.*955; *Urk.*
IV, 925,10 ( ).

b3k vb. intrans. work, *Urk.* IV,1277,11; n 'for' = 'serve's one, *Sin.* B216; *Pr.* 5,4;
Urk. IV,96,10; 132,5; pay taxes, *Adm.* 3,10: trans. work horses, *Urk.* IV,1281,11; fields,
742,17; carry out a task, *Les.* 76,22; enslave, *Urk.* IV, 83,5; 570,1; in old perfective,
an object is 'worked' (i.e. decorated) with gold, etc. *Westc.* 5,8.9; *Urk.* IV,170,1; 663,12.

b3kw work, task, *Paheri*,3 (also); *Sinai*, 141,6 (det.); workmanship: a vase m b3k n H̱r 'of Syrian w.', *Urk.* IV,665,16; sim.706,6; 733,5;
execution of a design, 1074,8; revenues, taxes, impost, *Adm.*10,4; *BH* I,8,16.17; *Urk.*
IV, 55,8; 734,2; wages, 2030,8.

b3kt work, task, *Les.* 86,21; works of craftsmanship, *Urk.* IV,1391,4; labour
of captives, 185,13; revenues, taxes, *Siut*, pl.19,18; *D. el B.* 131; *Urk.* IV, 412,4 ( ).

bꜣk servant, BH I, 25, 110; Les. 81, 14; Sin. R 3; B 204; bꜣk im 'your humble s.' = I, GNS 64; bꜣk n pr dt 's. of the estate', 'liegeman', P. Kah. 27, 3; 28, 1.

bꜣkt maidservant, L. to D. VI, 2.7; Adm. 4, 12.

var. of bkꜣ 'the morrow'.

see bkyt below.

bꜣkbꜣk a cake, Urk. IV, 506, 9.

bꜣgi vb. 4 inf. be weary, languid, Mill. 1, 12; Eb. 19, 5 ( ); be slack, remiss, Urk. IV, 410, 6; 752, 10 ( ): n. weariness, langour, Pyr. 721. 1500; slackness, remissness, Urk. IV, 61, 17; 115, 15 ( ); 426, 16; 1454, 16 (abbr.).

bꜣgyw the languid ones = the dead, Urk. V, 76, 13; var. 77, 5.

bꜣg sight (?), Westc. 7, 26.

bꜣg thick, of fluids, P. Ram. III, A 31.

bꜣgs thorn-bush (?), Pyr. 1083; var. Eb. 22, 10.

bꜣgsw dagger, Sin. B 128; var. Urk. IV, 13, 15.

see bdt below.

bꜣdt dipper, Sm. 22, 5.

var. of bdꜣ 'jar'.

bit a loaf, Urk. IV, 30, 17; 821, 5; 1553, 12.13; varr. P. Kah. 26a, 15; Urk. IV, 825, 13; bit bšꜣ 'malt (?) l.', 1952, 18.

bit block of stone, Hatnub, 9, 10.

bit vase of oval shape, Urk. IV, 637, 9.

bit bee, P. Kah. 3, 2.

bit honey, Sin. B 83; P. Kah. 6, 7; Urk. IV, 688, 7; var. dets. 1140, 15; 761, 13.

bit crown of Lower Egypt, Hymnen, 2, 2.

bit goddess of Lower Egypt, Caminos, Lit. Frag. pl. 8, 3, 5; 10, 3, 6; 13, 2, 11.

bity King of Lower Egypt, ZÄS 28, 125; 30, 56. 113; varr. Pyr. 724; Les. 69, 14; Urk. IV, 384, 13; pl. bityw 'kings of L. E.' Pyr. 1095. 1488; 'kings' in general,

Urk. IV, 85, 15; 169, 2; 780, 13; 'King of U. and L. E.' Gr. p. 73.

bi good deed, Peas. B1, 109; 'set a good example', Pr. 5, 5; 17, 13.

bit character, qualities, varr. , , , GAS 81; Urk. IV, 66, 15; 1794, 16.

biꜣ bronze (?), TR 22, 96; varr. BD 86, 14; Urk. IV, 638, 12. Cf. JEA 1, 234, n. 2. For see under ḥmt.

biꜣy consisting of bronze (?), Urk. IV, 254, 9; varr. , , , Pyr. 800.

biꜣ a mineral (not metal) in biꜣ šmꜥw 'b. of U. E.'; biꜣ mḥw 'b. of L. E.', D. el B. 110. Varr. BH I, 17; I, 35; sic Th. T. S. II, 32; BD 140, 14.

biꜣt gritstone, Sethe, Steine, 29.

biꜣt beer-vessel, Th. T. S. I, 21.

biꜣt quarry, Urk. IV, 825, 12.

biꜣw mining-region, mine, JEA 4, pl. 9, 2; Sinai, 36, 3; varr. 53, 3; Sh. S. 23-4; Les. 86, 2.

biꜣw produce of mine, BH I, 8, 11. 14; var. Les. 86, 11.

biꜣ heaven, firmament, Urk. V, 55, 5; varr. CT I, 53; Urk. IV, 481, 8; 1819, 2; BM 614, 17; BD 185, 6.

biꜣyt firmament, CT I, 53.

biꜣi vb. 4 inf. wonder, marvel, n 'at', Pyr. 1992; Urk. IV, 347, 13 (sic); 612, 6 (); 1656, 5 (); ḥr 'at', 159, 2 (infin.); 836, 8.

bi(ꜣ)w wonders, marvels, Urk. IV, 339, 1; varr. 342, 16; 1697, 18; D. el B. 125.

bi(ꜣ)yt miracle, Westc. 4, 10; 6, 15; 11, 11; Urk. IV, 405, 1 (); pl. marvels, 329, 1 (); 340, 6 (); 428, 5 ().

bi(ꜣ)ty marvellous person, of king, Urk. IV, 16, 11.

biꜣ in m biꜣ 'no', var. m , GAS 52.

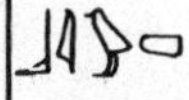 var. of bi3 'heaven'.

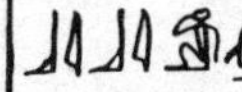 bibi (1) acclamation, BD 435,16: (2) symptom of disease, Eb. 1,6; var. det.  TR 26,4.

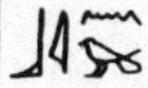 bin adj. bad, evil, Leb. 103.110; Hatnub, 17,10; Pr. 5,2; Peas. B1,123; P. Kah. 32,19; sḫt bint 'a severe beating', Westc. 12,17.25; mw bin 'bad water' = dangerous rapid, Urk. IV, 8,8; bin wy 'How e. is...', P. Kah. 32,12; bin wy n.i 'Woe is me!' Adm. 6,8; bin sdm.k 'e. be your hearing!', P. Kah. 32,16; bw-bin 'evil' (n.), Pr. 5,1; bw nb bin 'all manner of e.', Siut, pl. 11,7: (n.) evil, BH I, 44,3; RB 60,1; Leb. 108; P. Kah. 4,16.

 bint evil (n.), Peas. B1,152; P. Kah. 32,13; Pr. 5,14; 10,3; bint ḥr ib 'what is displeasing', Pr. 7,1.

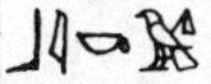 bik falcon, TR 17,39; Sin. R 21; Urk. IV, 113,14; 160,12; bik (n) nbw 'f. of gold', 161,2; Gr. p. 73; fem. 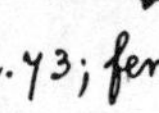 Pyr. 137.

 bik 'falcon'-ship of king, Urk. IV, 9,5; var.  1279,19.

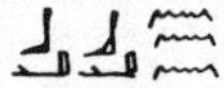 bʿbʿ drink, Pyr. 1286; CT I, 5 (also det. !); Urk. IV, 114,9 (det. ).

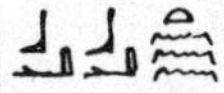 bʿbʿt stream, BD 44,10.

 bʿnt neck, Pyr. 1779; D. el B. 139; var. det.  Urk. IV, 1837,13.

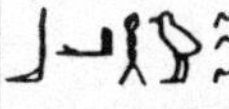 bʿḥw inundation, flood, Pyr. 287; varr.  ibid.;  788;  868;  BM 614,19; 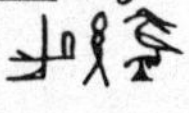 BD 132,5.

 bʿḥ inundated land, Urk. IV, 1795,6.

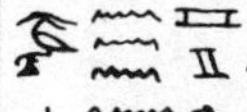 bʿḥ basin for irrigation, COA III, p. 167.

 bʿḥ abundance, Pyr. 1059; varr.  CT I,11; 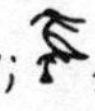 Urk. IV, 1521,9;  BD 227,13; as deity, Pyr. 1065; BD 145,2 (det. ).

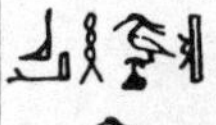 bʿḥi vb. 4 inf. intrans. have abundance, be well-supplied, Urk. IV, 430,13 (); 481,10; 688,1; BD 165,4; be inundated, Urk. IV, 173,11: trans. flood, inundate, Urk. IV, 84,8; 362,14.

 bʿḥ be detested, Leb. 87.

 bw place, Westc. 9,3; Urk. IV, 116,1; 567,3 (); BD 491,12 (); det.  in ref. to desert, Urk. IV, 84,11; late 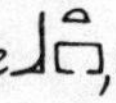, 1283,10; bw nb 'everyone', Gr. §103; m bw wʿ 'all

together', RB 111,2; prefixed to adjj. to form abstract nn., e.g. bw-mꜣꜥ 'truth,' see under the second element.

 bw detest, Urk. IV, 944,12; var. det.  Pyr. 127^w. Older form of bwt below.

 bwt vb. detest, abominate, Siut, pl. 6, 265; Urk. IV, 651,10; 1590,5; 1999,4 (det. ): n. abomination, Pr. 4,1 (); Urk. IV, 390,16; 490,14.16 (); 1799,13 ().

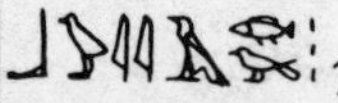 bwytyw those who are abominated, Urk. IV, 83,6.

 bwꜣ magnate, notable, Siut, pl. 13,11 (misread); var.  Urk. IV, 1796,3.

 bwꜣt covert for wildfowl, JEA 16,70; var. , Caminos, Lit. Frag. pl. 3,4,8.

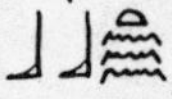, 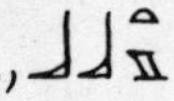 varr. of bꜣbꜣt 'eddy (?)'.

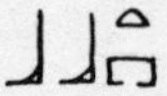 bbt hole, cavity, BD 310,8.

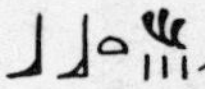 bbt herb inula graveolens, JEA 20,45.

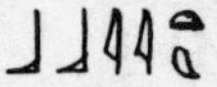 bbyt region of throat, AEO I, 18.

 bbwy collar-bones, AEO I, 18.

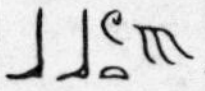 bbwt wig (reaching to shoulders?), P. Kah. 19,51; varr. 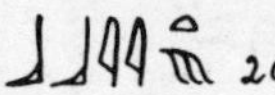 20,49;  Urk. IV, 1164,5.

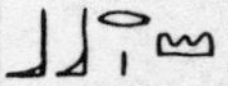 Bbr n. loc. Babel, AEO I, 192*.

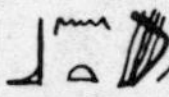 bnt harp, Urk. IV, 174,13; var. det.  23,7.

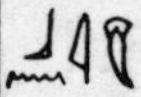 see below s.v. bnr.

 bnw heron, Urk. IV, 113,13; 147,8; V, 16,17; RB 117,9; var. det.  Urk. V, 16,11.

 bnwt (1) a hard sandstone: (2) corn-rubber, Sethe, Steine, 32; GAS 39.

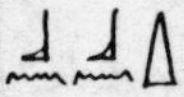 bnbn the sacred stone of Ōn, Berlin Leather, 1,17.

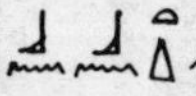 bnbnt pyramidion, Urk. IV, 365,2; 642,11; 738,7.

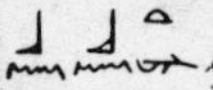 bnbnt stem (?) of ship, ZÄS 68,11.

 bnf gall, var. dets. , , JEA 19,136.

 bnn vb. 2 gem. beget, CT I, 45; BD 68,6; become erect, of male, BD 106,10 (det. );

overflow, Urk. IV, 925, 4 (det.).

bnn bead, M. u. K. vs. 2, 6; pellet, Eb. 59, 9 (det. 0); BD 34, 3. 4.

bnnt pellet, Eb. 35, 9.

bnr dates, Urk. IV, 171, 10; varr. Eb. 22, 17; P. Kah. 6, 8; 15, 67. Cf. AEO II, 225*.

bnrt (> bnit) dates, Les. 73, 15.

bnrt date-palm, Urk. IV, 73, 13.

bniw (< bnrw) date-wine, Eb. 3, 13; var. P. Kah. 5, 57.

bnr (> bni) sweet, pleasant, M. u. K. 2, 4; Eb. 10, 2 (); Les. 81, 4 (); Urk. IV, 297, 11 (); 1087, 8; ḫt bnr 'fruit-tree', Sin. B 241; Urk. IV, 660, 16; s3t⟨·i⟩ bnrt 'my s. daughter', 343, 6; bnr mrwt 'lovable', Les. 70, 7-8; Cairo 20119; fem. bnrt mrwt Cairo 20342; Urk. IV, 580, 16; bnr wy mrt·f 'How s. is the love of him!', RB 112, 9; bnr (i)m3t 'kindly', Les. 80, 22 ().

bnrt sweetness, Sin. R 90; varr. B 65; Urk. IV, 224, 15.

bnrt date-cakes, Les. 76, 14; AEO II, 232*; 'cake-room', Urk. IV, 1141, 16.

bnrytyw confectioners, Adm. 1, 1.

bnrw in r-bnrw 'outside', Urk. IV, 661, 12; so also ḥr-bnrw 655, 5.

bnš doorpost, BD 264, 4; cf. JEA 4, 146; ZÄS 67, 116.

bnty two baboons which greet the rising sun, Urk. V, 81, 6; var. det. IV, 2082, 6.

bnty pair of breasts, JEA 22, 41.

bnt(w)t deep-bosomed, of women, Westc. 5, 10; cf. JEA 22, 41.

bht flabellum, JEA 27, 13.

bh3 flee, Sin. B 63; Urk. IV, 711, 1 (); RB 59, 7.

bh3w fugitive, GNS 34.

bḥ forced labour, Urk. IV, 1374, 9; var. 1962, 15.

bḥn cut off limbs, BD 106, 14; drive off foes, Siut, pl. 5, 246; Urk. IV, 969, 6; BD 2, 15 (det.).

bḥs (bḥz) calf, Urk. V, 156, 8; Herdsm. 9 (det.); varr. Pyr. 27; BH II, 7; 'side of veal', Les. 76, 14.

bḥs hunt, Urk. IV, 893, 15; var. dets. RB 64, 11; 66, 6.

Bḥdt n. loc. (1) town in Delta: (2) Edfu in Upper Egypt, AEO II, 6*.

Bḥdty n. div. He of Behdet = winged sun-disk, Urk. IV, 31, 15; var. JEA 28, 23.

bḫn country mansion, P. Wilbour, 34; AEO II, 204*; Caminos, L.-Eg. Misc. 140.

bḫnt pylon, Urk. IV, 56, 1; varr. dets. (dual), 1654, 11; 365, 4; abbr. 93, 6.

bḫnw the so-called basalt, varr. , , Sethe, Steine, 33; AEO II, 205*.

bḫḫw heat (?), Pyr. 502. 702; BD 125, 3.

see under Bꜣḫw.

bẖbẖ pride (?) as bad quality, Siut, pl. 4, 229.

see above s.v. bḫnw.

bs trans. vb. introduce s'one, m 'into', D. el. B. 33; RB 111, 16 ( ); cf. JEA 39, 19 (gg); instal, Urk. IV, 82, 12 ( ); 157, 9; 1410, 6; initiate, ḥr 'into', 1820, 12; ZÄS 57, 2*; BD 238, 6; inter, Sin. B 197. 259; bring in a state of affairs, RB 112, 8; reveal a secret, Urk. IV, 1783, 12: intrans. enter, M.u.K. 5, 3; Adm. p. 105; m 'on' an office, Adm. 11, 4; n 'to', Pr. 17, 3. Cf. GNS 71.

bs secret (n.), Urk. IV, 484, 11; 1410, 11; Siut, pl. 5, 239.

bsw secret image of god, Les. 70, 17; varr. Urk. IV, 363, 3; 1411, 9.

bsỉ (1) vb. 3 inf. flow forth, of water, RB 77, 13; Urk. IV, 112, 5 (dets.); fig. of food, etc., 501, 7; 1727, 1: (2) n. influx of foreign migrants, 8, 7.

bsw result, consequence, Neferti, 37.

bsw morbid discharges, Eb. 36, 18–19.

var. of bꜣs 'jar'.

bsw flame, Urk. IV, 615, 14 ( ); BD 353, 4; bsw n sḏt 'firebrand (?)', BD 263, 8. 13.

bsꜣ protect, Siut, pl. 19, 21.

bsn (bzn) gypsum (?), SDT 139.

bsk disembowel, Pyr. 1286.

bskw entrails, BD 64, 16; 254, 7 (det.); Pyr. 292 (det.).

bši vb. 3 inf. spit, Eb. 30, 16; spit out, Barns, Ram. p. 9.

bšw spittle, M. u. K. 2, 8.

bš3 malted barley (?), AEO II, 223*; JEA 44, 63; bit bš3 'malted loaf (?)', Urk. IV, 1952, 18.

bšṯ rebel, ḥr 'against', Urk. I, 104, 7; IV, 614, 6 (); 685, 5 (); ḫ3swt bšṯt 'rebellious lands', 139, 1; 269, 15; RB 57, 11; mw bšṯ 'cataract', 'rapid', Urk. VII, 2, 4.

bštw rebellion, Leb. 102; varr. Urk. IV, 138, 13; 1545, 12.

bšttyw rebels, Urk. IV, 1545, 13; 2070, 9.

bḳ be hostile (?), r 'to' s'one, Urk. IV, 62, 2.

see above under b3ḳ.

bḳbḳw recalcitrance (?), Pr. 14, 2; cf. Žába, 155.

bḳsw spine, P. Ed. Smith, 326.

bk3 be pregnant, TR 17, 2; RB 77, 1; dets. , Urk. IV, 268, 7.

bk3t pregnant woman, Hatnub, 20, 17.

bk3 the morrow, Pyr. 345. 1383; morning, Urk. IV, 943, 13 ().

bkyt precinct, JEA 39, 20.

var. of b3gi 'be weary'.

bg3w shipwrecked man, Peas. B1, 138.

, , see under b3gs, b3gsw.

bgsw wrongdoing, Les. 68, 24; Peas. R 165 (); Urk. IV, 470, 8 ().

bt3 wrong, crime, Urk. IV, 61, 8; BD 16, 3. 9 (); JEA 12, 200, n. 7; 21, 44.

bt3 wrongdoer, Urk. IV, 151, 4.

bt3t harm, injury, Urk. IV, 1086, 16.

bt3 see below under bt.

var. of bdt 'emmer', q. v.

btn disobey, defy, Pt. 7, 12; RB 65, 1; ZÄS 60, 72 (); Urk. IV, 1303, 10; btn-ib 'insolent man', Siut, pl. 4, 230; Urk. IV, 969, 5.

btnw defiant man, rebel, RB 65, 2; varr. 56, 12; Urk. IV, 21, 16; 968, 11.

btk sink (?), of the heart, Adm. 3, 4.

btk squalor (?), Adm. 9, 1.

btktk escape (?), var. , ZÄS 58, 25*.

bt vb. intrans. run, CT I, 278; BD 462, 8 (); Sin. B 154 (); P. Kah. 35, 13 (): trans. abandon, forsake, GAS 108; P. Ed. Smith, 200; det. Urk. IV, 117, 14.

btw incurable disease or person, P. Ed. Smith, 200.

bd natron, BD 216, 11.

bdt emmer, earlier , later , AEO II, 221*

bdt bed of gourds, etc., Sinai, II, 135, n. b.

bdš become faint, weak, exhausted, Pyr. 1080 (det.); TR 24, 33; Urk. IV 614, 10; 658, 15; 1302, 12; bdš ḥr 'downcast', 'faint-hearted', Les. 86, 5. 6-7. 15.

bdšt weakness in msw bdšt 'children of w.', ep. of foes of sungod, Urk. V, 51, 9 = 53, 4.

bddw-kꜣ water-melon, var. , Garten, 17. 133.

bdꜣ jar, Ti, 85; BH II, 6; var. P. Kah. 26, 8.

bdꜣ mast-head, TR 24, 15; cf. P. Ed. Smith, 239.

bdꜣ stiff roll of linen, P. Ed. Smith, 239.

p mat, P. Ed. Smith, 481.

p base for statue, Urk. IV, 834, 6.

P n. loc. Pe, AEO II, 188*.

P(y) belonging to Pe: 'spokesman (lit. 'mouth') of every Pe-ite', Siut, pl. 4, 213; Bersh. I, 16; 'gods of Pe', Urk. V, 162, 5; sim. TR 24, 36 (pl.).

pt sky, heaven, Sin. R 7; B 234; Peas. B1, 140; Urk. IV, 15, 13; 886, 14; used of canopy, JEA 22, 37; pt·k tn 'this thine h.' = thy queen, Sin. B 185; iw pt tn ṯ3w 'the weather is windy,' Urk. IV, 156, 4; cf. also Westc. 11, 14. Abbr. Urk. IV, 199, 13.

p3 demonstr. and def. art. m. sg. this, the, varr. , , Gr. §§110–2.

p3y 'he of', Gr. § 111, Obs.

p3y·i poss. adj. m. sg. my, so too p3y·k, p3y·f, etc., Gr. § 113, 1.

p3(w?) aux. vb. 3 inf. with past meaning, varr. , , Gr. § 484.

p3 fly, fly up, BD 164, 2. 10; 179, 9; var. 138, 8.

p3t cake or loaf used in offerings, BH I, 17; Les. 74, 22–3; pl. as general term for offerings, Urk. IV, 28, 5 (); 1800, 12 (dets.).

p3yt lock (?) on door, BD 264, 16.

p3ꜥt irrigable land (?), later (?), AEO I, 12*.

p3ꜥt quail (?), L. to D. III, 2 (n.).

p3wt primaeval time: p3wt t3 'pr. t. of the earth', Urk. IV, 312, 13; 329, 12 (); 545, 3 (); p3wt tpt 'the beginning of time', 146, 9; 165, 14; ep. of holy city in 3bḏw p3wt tpt nt Nb-r-ḏr 'Abydos the pr. place of the Lord of All,' TR 21, 106.

p3wty primaeval god, Urk. V, 78, 14; IV, 517, 17 (); 1217, 10 (); pl. TR 18, 21 (); Siut, pl. 16, 24 (); p3wty t3wy 'pr. g. of the Two Lands', Sethe, Amun, § 14; man of ancient family, Siut, pl. 16, 4 (); Les. 72, 10 (pl.): as adj. primaeval: nṯrw p3wtyw 'the pr. gods', Pyr. 304.

p3w falsehood (?), gossip (?), Les. 79, 18.

p3wt burden, of illness, Eb. 19, 4.

p3ḫ scratch (vb.), Pyr. 440.

P3ḫt n. div. 'She who scratches', a lion-goddess, BH I, 25, 18; TR 11, 3; varr. BH I, 24; Urk. IV, 286, 10.

p3ḫd be turned upside down, Pyr. 685; be turned over, of sole of foot, Sm. 4, 14 (); sim. of dislocation of collar-bone, 11, 18 ().

pꜣs water-pot, TR 10,7; varr. BD 199,6; 458,4.

pꜣḳ a flat thin cake or biscuit, Leb. 75,19; Siut, pl. 8,308; varr. Pyr. 378; Paheri, 3.

pꜣḳt fine linen, Sin. B 153. 293; varr. BM 159,8; Urk. IV, 742,15; Mill. 1,8; Adm. 10,4.

pꜣḳyt shell of turtle, Eb. 67,5; of skull, Sm. 2,9 ( ); 5,1 ( ); flake of stone, Westc. 6,10; potsherd, Eb. 61,18 ( ); 78,17; P. Kah. 7,55 ( ).

pꜣg squat (?), CT I, 18.

pꜣd ball or cone of incense, Pyr. 378; P. Kah. 19,22; var. Westc. 4,14.

pꜣḏ a loaf, Pyr. 310. 314; var. Urk. V, 162,10.

py flea, CT I, 215.

pis tread in (?) seed, JEA 3,100, n. 1.

pꜥt patricians; mankind, AEO I, 98* ff.; varr. Urk. IV, 157,17; 249,3.

pꜥt a cake or loaf, GAS 61.

pꜥw flames (?), BD 353,4.

var. of ꜥpnnt 'slug (?)'.

pw (1) demonstr. this, cf. Gr. p. 565: (2) interrog. who?, what?, Gr. § 498; (3) whichever, Gr. p. xxxv.

pwy demonstr. this, that, Gr. §§ 110. 112.

Pwnt n. loc. Pwēnet, Gauthier, Dict. géogr. II, 45-6.

Pwntyw the people of Pwēnet, Urk. IV, 335,6; 345,14.

pf demonstr. m. sg. that (yonder), varr. , , Gr. §§ 110-2.

pn demonstr. m. sg. this, Gr. §§ 110-2; he of, § 111, Obs.

pnꜥ turn upside down, Pyr. 227. 518; BH II, 4 (abbr.); BD 105,10; turn the eyes, r 'against' s'one, Nav. Totb. 108,5; pnꜥ ḥr 'overthrow' a ruler, Urk. IV, 1312,11.

pnꜥy reversal (?), Siut, pl. 14,79.

pnꜥyt cataract, Urk. IV, 8,9.

pnꜥnꜥ turn over and over, Urk. IV, 1283,1.

pnw mouse, M.u.K. 8,2; Eb. 98,2; BH II, 6.

pns cut off a joint, D.el.B. 107; pull out hair, Eb. 63, 13.

pns clay, Caminos, Lit. Frag. pl. 4,10.

pnst scum (?), Sm. 22,4.

pnḳ bale out a boat, Pyr. 335 (det. …); 950 (det. …); water, Peas. B1, 220; Sm. 22,4; 'b.o. water' fig. for 'unburden o'self' of grievances, Peas. B1, 278 (dets. …); swab up blood, BD 206,12; poke (?) *n* 'at' s'one with stick, 494,5; expend provisions, Peas. B1, 94.

pr house, Sh. S. 134; Peas. B1, 35; Westc. 11,19; household, Siut, pl. 7, 298; L. to D. V, 1; Urk. IV, 3,2; with det. … L. to D. p. 7; *pr.sn* 'home', JEA 36, 111; *nbt pr* 'housewife', BH I, 18; Urk. IV, 921, 4; Th. T. S. I, 9; *ḫt pr* 'property', Siut, pl. 7, 303; Urk. IV, 664, 17; *imy-r pr* 'steward', see p. 18; *imt-pr* 'will', 'testament', see p. 18; palace, Urk. IV, 899, 4; *pr-nsw* 'palace', see below; temple, Peas. B1, 197; Cairo 20543, 19; Urk. IV, 389, 14; *pr n nḥḥ* 'tomb', BH I, 26, 180; *pr-ḏt* 'estate', see below; … *(i)m(y) prwy* 'member of the administration', Urk. I, 81, 16; Bersh. I, 7, 4; Siut, pl. 9, 333-4.

Pr-ꜥꜣ Great House, palace: later Pharaoh, Gr. p. 75; JEA 13, 38; var. … D.el.B. 109.

Pr-ꜥnḫ 'House of Life' = temple scriptorium, varr. …, …, JEA 24, 157.

pr-wr national shrine of U.E. at El-Kāb, JEA 30, 27, n. 3; var. … Les. 72, 4.

pr-bity palace of the King of L.E., Siut, pl. 5, 232; var. … Urk. IV, 545, 14.

pr-mḏꜣt library, JEA 24, 177.

pr-nw national shrine of L.E. at Dep, JEA 30, 27, n. 3; var. … Hymnen, 2, 5.

pr-nbw 'House of Gold' = treasury, Les. 70, 15; Urk. IV, 942, 9; 1115, 3.

pr-nfr funerary workshop, Th. T. S. I, p. 73; var. … Siut, pl. 15, 20.

pr-nsw king's palace, Court, Sin. B 244; Westc. 6, 14; Les. 69, 19; Urk. IV, 81, 3; used of royal bureau, 693, 11; 1113, 3; palace of King of U.E. in contrast to *pr-bity*, Siut, pl. 5, 231; Urk. IV, 545, 13; temple, JEA 39, 25; varr. … Siut, pl. 5, 231; … Urk. IV, 58, 10; … 1106, 13.

pr-nsr national shrine of L.E. at Pe, JEA 30, 27, n. 3; as place of coronation, 39, 25; var. Rekh. 7, 1; without pr, BH I, 7.

pr-ḥry upper part of building, Les. 76, 9.

pr-ḥḏ treasury, AEO II, 215*; var. Urk. IV, 735, 4.

pr-ḫnty harem, var., GAS 47; Urk. IV, 1977, 17.

pr-ẖry ground floor, AEO II, 216*.

pr-šnꜥ labour establishment, AEO II, 209*.

pr-dwꜣt robing-room, var., GNS 109.162; JEA 5, 148.

pr-dšr 'Red House' = treasury of L.E., AEO II, 215*.

pr-ḏt estate, GNS 77, n. 2; varr. ibid.; Meir. III, p. 36.

pryt coll. houses, Adm. 7, 9; Urk. IV, 1379, 12; P. Kah. 39, 31; pryt Pr-ꜥꜣ 'apartments of Pharaoh', Urk. IV, 1842, 3; P. Kah. 38, 10-11; sim. of queen, Urk. IV, 1974, 4.

pri vb. 3 inf. (1) (A) of persons, go, come out, Siut, pl. 6, 278; Urk. IV, 18, 10; 769, 17; 1212, 1; m 'from', Peas. B1, 34; Sin. B 182; Eb. 1, 17; 'into' the day, Urk. V, 4, 3; Les. 75, 19; n 'to', Urk. IV, 150, 9; r 'at', 654, 8; 'into' a ship, 132, 7; r-ḥꜣ 'out', 655, 2; ḥr 'through' a door, V, 27, 15; ꜥḳ pr, var. pr ꜥḳ 'come in and go out', 'come and go', IV, 433, 11-12; 498, 7; 1105, 8-9; pr m ḥtp 'come out cleared' from an accusation, I, 223, 13; pr r ḫntw 'go out of doors', Leb. 82. 131; pr ḥr tꜣ 'go out against a land' in war, Urk. IV, 187, 2; pr ẖnt 'be missing from', I, 14, 9; pr ḥr 'reveal' a secret, ZÄS 47, 96; prt m-ꜥ 'desert from' an army, Urk. IV, 665, 11; pr šp 'turn blind', Peas. B1, 113, cf. JEA 9, 12, n. 5; escape, Leb. 73; m 'from', Urk. V, 80, 11; 96, 9; ḥr 'from', 79, 2; be renowned, of name or person, Pr. 1, 12; Urk. IV, 957, 5; 1082, 6. — (B) of things, come out, Bersh. I, 14, 6; Peas. B1, 319; Urk. IV, 121, 11; Eb. 8, 16; 88, 11; 97, 17; Adm. 12, 4; burst forth, of storm, Sh. S. 32; be issued, of supplies or offerings, Siut, pl. 8, 305; Urk. IV, 48, 9; 768, 14; 1058, 14; 'cut away' a joint of meat, BH I, 35; D. el B. 107; pr m 'come out of the fire' after cooking, Eb. 42, 7; 'go up in flame', Sh. S. 130.

(2) go up, ascend, r 'to', TR 5, 3; Urk. IV, 115, 5; pr r ḥrw 'go up on high', Leb. 59; 'go up

higher', Peas. B1, 4; pr r 'advance against' a position in war, Les. 84, 10; pr h3 'ascend and descend', Pyr. 149; BD 147, 13-14; 'come and go', Sin. B49; Cairo 20539, 4-5; Urk. IV, 116, 4; written RB 113, 3; pr h3 r-gs 'pass to and fro by', RB 77, 16; pr-h3·f 'a popular resort', Adm. 6, 12; 'thronging crowds', Urk. IV, 387, 13. —— be subtracted, Rhind, 28; aux. vb., Gr. § 483, 1. Var. Urk. IV, 150, 9; cryptic wtg. 1805, 7.

prt ritual procession, Les. 68, 7; 71, 12. 13; Leyd. V 6 (det.); Urk. IV, 27, 4; 748, 12; prt '(heliacal) rising of Sothis-Sirius', Urk. IV, 44, 6; 469, 17; 538, 12; 827, 8; prt m ... r 'from ... to', ZÄS 66, 71.

pry hero, champion, Sin. B110; cf. GNS 44.

pry ferocious bull, Sin. B123.

pryt crisis (?), JEA 16, pl. 29, 9.

prw motion, BD 176, 3; procession, RB 117, 8; outcome, result, Pr. 11, 5; BH I, 41, b; Les. 80, 17 ( ); Urk. IV, 118, 8; prw n r 'utterance', Pr. 19, 3; Paheri, 3 (det.); Urk. IV, 351, 6 ( ); 473, 7; 'decision' of judge, 49, 2 ( ).

prw excess, surplus, JEA 9, 19, n. 5; var. det. Urk. IV, 676, 4; prw hr 'more than', GNS 44.

prw land emerged from inundation, Bersh. I, 25.

pr-ᶜ be active, Sin B52; Peas. B1, 116 (ᶜ·k pr); Urk. IV, 1281, 7; 1322, 7; pr ᶜ·k 'get on with your work!', Bersh. II, p. 20; D. el. B. 107.

prt-ᶜ activity, RB 64, 4. 6.

prt-hrw invocation-offerings, later prt-r-hrw, Gr. p. 172.

prt winter, Gr. p. 203.

prt fruit, Urk. IV, 687, 10; seed, Adm. 9, 4 ( ), cf. P. Wilbour, 186. 189; in sense of 'offspring', 'posterity', Les. 73, 10 ( ); Urk. IV, 249, 2; 362, 4 ( ); 1276, 14 ( ).

pri battlefield, Urk. IV, 32, 10; 890, 12; varr. 1290, 7; sic RB 56, 13; 'fighting', Urk. IV, 1698, 11.

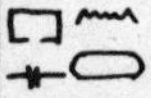 var. of psn 'loaf'.

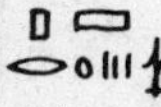 prš minium, red oxide of lead, JEA 21, 39.

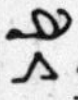 pḥ reach a person or place, Sin. R20; B20; Sh. S. 2.9.11.113; a state, Sin. B258; Urk. IV, 10,6; 151,5; mi pḥ·k wi 'according as you r. me' (i.e. 'my position'), Pr. 19,6; n pḥ·n·tw·f m sḫs 'he could not be equalled at running', Urk. IV, 1279,16; sim. 1378,13; attain wealth, Peas. B1,61-2; pregnantly, without obj., Mill. 1,6; finish doing s'thing, Peas. R59; Urk. IV, 655,8; end by doing s'thing, Pr. 6,9; attack s'one, Peas. B1,316; Les. 84,1; TR 18,33; Urk. IV, 556,1; 1801,1; contest a will, 1070,5 (restd.); spear fish, Peas. B1,207; hit s'one with comment, Peas. B1,219. Varr.  BH I, 8,9;  Les. 75,16;  Urk. IV, 64,9.

 pḥwy hinder parts, hind-quarters, P. Kah. 3,29; 5,9 (); Eb. 31,18; Les. 76,21 (); back of jaw, Sm. 7,14; of house, JEA 14,301; of a locality = its northern part, P. Wilbour, 26; ntyw m pḥwy 'those at the b.' = slaves, JEA 1,35, n. 6; rear, rearguard of army, Hatnub, 17,12; Urk. IV, 654,7; 1302,8; stern of ship, Herdsm. 12; Urk. IV, 98,15, 1279,19; end, in both concrete and abstract senses, Sh. S. 9; Sin. B57. 64.311; Leb. 130; Urk. IV, 85,8; 481,16; 946,11; 974,15 (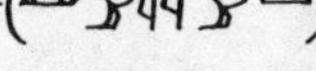); ini pḥwy 'make an e. of', 'vanquish', JEA 30,16; rdi pḥwy 'put an e. to', Pyr. 318; wnwt 6 pḥwy iy 'six hours have elapsed (?)', Caminos, Lit. Frag. p. 16; pḥwy-r 'down to', Gr. § 179.

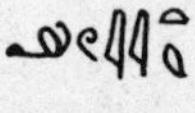 pḥwyt rectum, Eb. 33,9; var. 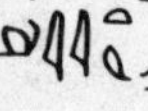 Sm. 22,13. Cf. AEO I, 18.

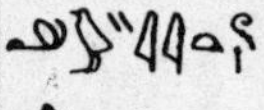 pḥwyt stern-warp of ship, Urk. IV, 1077,2; varr. 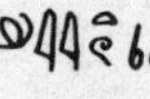 60,8;  TR 27,48.

 pḥt-r ending at, Gr. § 179.

 pḥww the far north, Urk. IV, 270,8; 617,6; pḥww m 'northward to', 902,13; 1129,3; varr. 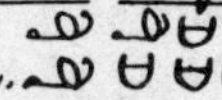 138,8; 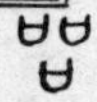 55,5.

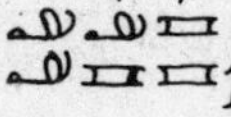 pḥww marshlands, BH I, 34; Urk. IV, 463,7; varr. 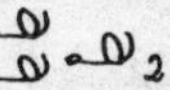 237,9; 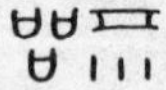 917,16; 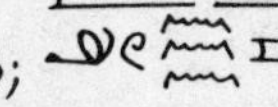 2173,8.

 pḥrt course of runner, RB 114,7.

 pḥrr run, Urk. IV, 942,16.

pḥty physical strength, P. Kah. 3,34; Pr. 4,4; power of king or god, P. Kah. 2,9; Urk. IV, 621,7. Varr. Pr. 4,4; TR 18,3; Urk. IV, 55,3; 161,3; (sic) 255,17; 621,7.

pḥd vb. trans. cut up, cut open, sever: intrans. burst open, of cist, P. Ed. Smith, 329.

pḥdw chair, Urk. IV, 1103,17.

var. of P3ḫt n. div.

pẖ3 kind of grain, Teti Cem. I, p. 96.

pẖ3 a drink, BH I, 17; var. Pyr. 90.

pẖ3 purge, RB 116,2; Hearst, 10,13; reveal a secret, ZÄS 60,74; pẖ3 ẖt 'clean of thought', Hatnub, 24,3 ( ); pẖ3 ib 'clean of heart' Urk. IV, 267,7 ( ); pẖ3 ḥ3ty n 'devoted to', 890,8 ( ).

pẖ3 pavement, Urk. IV, 1081,1.

pẖ3 decking of ship, abbr. , ZÄS 68,12.

var. of p3ẖd 'be turned upside down'.

pḫr (1) turn, turn about (trans. and intrans.), Pyr. 186 ( ). 674 ( ); 2213 ( ); Dav. Ptah. I, 23 ( ); BD 389,12; Urk. IV, 655,9; cf. SDT 74; pḫr ib n 'incline the heart to', Urk. IV, 943,16; pḫr m rꜥ 'noon', 655,14; revolve, of sun, BD 283,11; move about, of limbs, Urk. IV, 114,14; 497,1; surround, enclose, 832,13; 1296,1 ( ); 1656,16; travel around, traverse a region, 352,5; 943,2; RB 111,13; perambulate a hall, Urk. IV, 158,8; circumambulate walls, 1864,11.13; pervade hearts, RB 112,10; unroll a papyrus, JEA 22,106; twist, distort what is said, Pr. 8,7.

(2) with prepositions: pḫr m 'go about in', Pyr. 1122; 'pervade', Urk. IV, 270,7: pḫr n 'serve', Pyr. 304; Urk. V, 87,12; Hymnen, 19,4; 'pass, revert, to', Pyr. 317; Siut, pl. 7, 289 ( ): pḫr ḥ3 'go round about', 'encompass', 'encircle', Pyr. 298. 550. 629; Urk. IV, 203,15; 'convey about' a region, Pyr. 711; 'go round about four times', ritual direction, Urk. IV, 832,9; 'perambulation of the wall', coronation ceremony, 261,6; 262,8; pḫr ꜥwy·i ḥ3·k 'nine arms embrace thee', Th. T. S.

I, 10; pẖr mw ḥ3·sn 'water circulates about them', Eb. 78,7: pẖr m-s3 'follow after' Urk. IV, 971,11 — pẖr m 'persuade with flattery', Siut, pl. 16,13 (); var. pẖr m swn ddt, Les. 80,21 (); 'vice-versa', Eb. 2,3; Urk. V, 36,17.

pẖrt prescription, remedy, Eb. 21,8; 22,1; Sm. 2,2; var. Pr. 10,9.

pẖrt transitory state, description of life, Leb. 20.

pẖrt frontier patrol, varr. , , GNS 91.

pẖrty traveller, Urk. IV, 1112,6.

pẖr-wr n. loc. River Euphrates, RB 58,6-7; varr. 58,4; Urk. IV, 1370,11. Cf. AEO I, 175*.

pẖḥ control (?) horses, Urk. IV, 1281,13.

var. of p3s 'water-pot'.

psỉ cook, Edel, §114; Gr. §281; varr. Eb. 33,7; P. Kah. 5,54; Sin. B88; B27; abbr. Eb. 7,21.

pst mode of cooking, Sin. B92.

psw preparation of food and drink, Urk. IV, 912,6.

psn (pzn) a loaf, var. det. , Pyr. 74; var. Urk. IV, 821,6.

psḥ (pzḥ) vb. and n. bite, Pyr. 233; TR 47,10; Dream-book, 7,18; sting, Eb. 64,6; 97,21; Hearst, 16,8, cf. Ch. B. Text, 56, n.1; ỉb·sn psḥ r ꜥḥ3 'they were biting-eager to fight', Studi Rosellini, II, 86.

psẖ vb. trans. disarray o's hair: intrans. be distraught (det. X), be strewn, m 'with', GNS 14.

pss results of labour, Urk. IV, 2144,4.

psš divide, Pyr. 30 (); Urk. IV, 139,7; BH I, 25,33 (); share, n 'with', Les. 79,12; Siut, pl. 6,272; 8,311; Urk. IV, 1068,7; ḥnꜥ 'with', I. Carn. 3; psš m ḫrw 'break silence (?)', Leb. 76.

psš division, RB 119,8; psš n grḥ 'midnight', Urk. IV, 839,13; cf. Kémi, 1, 30.

psšt sharing out, Peas. B1, 303; Pr. 10,5; 14,13; share, portion, Urk. IV, 82,14; 564,6; 1276,21.

psšw arbitrator, Peas. B1, 248.

psšt carpet, matting of reeds, P. Kah. 30, 44; Amarna, V, 26, 5.

psšty part, division, RB 62, 4.

psš-kf ritual instrument for 'Opening the Mouth,' var. , Meir, III, p. 28, n. 4.

psg vb. spit on, at, Pyr. 142; Urk. V, 35, 12; Sin. B 40 ( ): n. spittle, Pyr. 521 (det.).

psḏ nine, Pyr. 1250.

psḏt group of nine, Pyr. 673; varr. , 794.

psḏt Ennead of gods, Urk. IV, 86, 13; varr. 146, 6; RB 112, 1; Sin. B 207; CT I, 111, contradicting rdg. psḏt-nṯrw of Orientalia, n. s. 28, 34.

psḏt (psḏt-pḏwt?) the Nine Bows = the nations of the world, BH I, 7; var. Urk. IV, 612, 11. Cf. ZÄS 47, 8; Orientalia, loc. cit.

psḏ shine, Pyr. 373; TR 20, 53; Urk. V, 55, 4; JEA 4, pl. 9, 10; varr. Urk. IV, 182; 391, 3.

psḏw back, spine, Pyr. 517; varr. Urk. IV, 1101, 17; 809, 9; 1104, 3; 614, 7; 31, 3; P. Kah. 7, 26.

psḏntyw the new moon and its festival, CT I, 16; varr. BH I, 24; Urk. IV, 27, 4; 469, 16; 657, 2; 1518, 5.

pšn split heads, Pyr. 1963; metal, 305 (dets.); wood, BD 61, 2 (dets.); fracture bones, cf. P. Ed. Smith, 530; separate combatants, Pyr. 1963; slice bread, Caminos, Lit. Frag. pl. 30, 1, 1.

pšš straddle, M. u. K. vs. 5, 7 (det. X); spread o'self, ḥr 'over, Pyr. 580. 825 (det.); spread out awnings, 2100.

, , , see above s. v. p3ḳ, p3ḳt.

Pḳr n. loc. precinct of Osiris at Abydos, Gauthier, Dict. géogr. II, 153; 'district of P.,' Urk. IV, 98, 17; var. Th. T. S. I, 30, B2 (corrected). Cf. ZÄS 41, 107.

pgꜣ open (vb.), Merikarēʿ 36; Neferhotep, 3.7; Urk. IV, 1110, 1 ( ); 1820, 14 ( ); reveal, RB 62, 9; be open, ZÄS 60, 74; of wounds, Sm. 17, 3.8 ( ); pgꜣ-ib 'open-hearted', Cairo 20543, 4 ( ); pgꜣ-ḥr 'honest', BH I, 17; Siut, pl. 6, 263; P. Ram. I, C1, 3 (dets.); cf. Barns, Ram. p. 9.

pgꜣ entrance of building, Peas. B1, 185; of horizon, Les. 74, 11 ( ); mouth of valley, Urk. IV, 654, 9 ( ); arena, Siut, pl. 11, 5; battlefield, RB 57, 8; Urk. IV, 1279, 12; 1290, 13; 1698, 13 ( ).

pgꜣ bowl, Urk. V, 161, 9; var. IV, 761, 13.

pggt toad or frog, JEA 33, 48.

ptpt tread roads, Pyr. 541; trample enemies, P. Kah. 3, 7; Sin. R 43 (det.); Urk. IV, 555, No. 46 (det.); 809, 4; 1277, 3; also written as sphinx (557, No. 62) or bull (No. 64) trampling prostrate foe.

ptr see, behold, Urk. IV, 1311, 4; varr. 97, 16; 1302, 9; 1794, 14; Les. 69, 16; Siut, pl. 4, 220.

ptr interrog. who?, what?, var. , Gr. §§ 256. 497.

miswriting of prì 'battlefield', q.v.

Ptḥ n. div. Ptah, cf. Sandman-Holmberg, Ptah.

ptḥ create, RB 113, 11; cf. JEA 35, 64 (4).

ptḫ cast to the ground, Pyr. 2171 (det.); P. Kah. 7, 21; Les. 98, 12; Peas. B1, 197; put down s'one carried, Pyr. 1348; be stretched out in obeisance, Urk. IV, 897, 9.

pd knee, M.u.K. 5, 1; fig. in wnw nn st ḥr pdw.sn '(monuments) which had not been erected', Urk. IV, 501, 10.

pds box, Westc. 12, 5; varr. 2, 1; Urk. IV, 630, Nos. 8. 9. Cf. Sphinx, 13, 89.

pds stamp flat, flatten, Urk. I, 103, 10 (det.); Eb. 30, 8; Sm. 5, 10; 6, 1.

pdst pellet, Barns, Ram. p. 19.

var. of psdw 'back'.

pdswt sand-dunes (?), Merikarēʿ, 82.

pd stretch cord, Pyr. 684; in foundation ceremony, Urk. IV, 166, 11 ( ); 169, 14 ( ); 765, 14; stretch out arms, JEA 39, pl. 2, 10; man on ground, Adm. 6, 4 (det.); extend o'self in effort (?), Pyr. 1545; draw bow, Urk. IV, 977, 2; diffuse perfume, Pyr. 1754; pd ib 'be glad', 1655; pd nmtwt 'far-striding', GNS 34; pd ḥr (1) 'unwrinkled': (2) 'far-sighted', 'prescient', Caminos, L.-Eg. Misc. 424.

pdt bow, RB 59, 13; Urk. IV, 457, 7; 977, 2; 1279, 15; varr. 712, 2; 1121, 1; 664, 6.

pdty bowman, Adm. 2, 2; var. Urk. IV, 1290, 11.

pdt coll. troop of soldiers, T. Carn. 11. 12; 'troop-captain', AEO I, 112*; JEA 39, 45; 'troop-commander', locc. cit.; var. Urk. IV, 465, 3.

pdty foreigner, Sin. B 121. 276; pl. 259.

pdt coll. foreigners, Adm. 3, 1; varr. Sin. B 63; R 87; P. Kah. 1, 4; see also

pd measure for pigment, P. Kah. 19, 23.

pdt measure for textiles, Urk. IV, 1121, 8; 1125, 8; for incense, 756, 9.

pdi vb. 3 inf. sharpen a knife, Bersh. I, 12, right.

f

f suff. pron. 3 m. sg. he, him, his, it, its, Gr. § 34; dual §§ 75-6.

f3i vb. 3 inf. raise, lift up, Hatnub, 22, 21; Urk. IV, 1144, 4; Hymnen, 8, 1; carry, support, Peas. B1, 91 ( ). 235; Urk. IV, 325, 5; Adm. 1, 2; weigh, TR 37, 3 ( ); Peas. B1, 324; RB 121, 1 ( ); present, Pyr. 1590 ( ); Siut, pl. 2, 107; deliver taxes, tribute, BH I, 8, 17; Urk. IV, 662, 16 ( ); f3 (1) 'sail' (vb.) Sin. B 246-7; P. Kah. 3, 17: (2) 'the wind rose (?)', Sh. S. 34.

f3t financial interest (?), P. Kah. 13, 22. Cf. f3yt 'reward'.

f3yt weight (?), JEA 36, 15 (c).

f3yt reward, JEA 36, 15 (c).

f3yt portable shrine, AEO I, 66; var. JEA 38, pl. 9, ff; cf. JEA 34, 21, n. 6.

fꜣw food-supplies(?), Urk. IV, 269, 5.

fꜣw magnificence, splendour, Siut, pl. 3, 153; Urk. IV, 56, 8; 1276, 10; RB 112, 12: adj. magnificent, Urk. IV, 424, 17.

fꜣk be shorn, Pr. 8, 10 (fig.).

fꜣk shorn man, ZÄS 57, 5.*

fn be weak, faint, GAS 70.

fnfnw recompense(?), Urk. IV, 1151, 4.

fnḫw food-offerings, RB 116, 16.

Fnḫw a Syrian people, Sin. B 221, cf. GNS 85 with n. 1; varr. Urk. IV, 25, 12; 138, 10; BD 263, 7.

fnḫ-ib acute(?), JEA 37, 50 (b).

fnṯ n. snake, Pyr. 432; BD 167, 15 ( ); intestinal worm, P. Ram. III, B 3 ( ): vb. become maggoty, TR 26, 1.

fnḏ nose, Urk. IV, 752, 3; RB 110, 9; varr. Pyr. 291; Sin. B 237.

fndy 'Beaky', ep. of Thoth, var. , PSBA 18, 111.

fḫ vb. trans. loose, release, Pyr. 1285; BH I, 26, 185 (det.); loosen, Sm. 5, 15; of speech, Adm. p. 97; lose, Sin. B 190; Les. 84, 15; cast off, get rid of, Pyr. 207; destroy, obliterate, Pyr. 419. 676; Urk. IV, 1085, 2; leave m-ḫt 'behind' one, Pyr. 250; fail to do s'thing, with foll. infin, Sin. B 170; Urk. IV, 511, 17: intrans. set out, depart, r 'to' a place, Sin. B 29; Les. 86, 16 (abbr.); Urk. IV, 1280, 1. 5: n. ruin of building, Urk. IV, 386, 4.

fḫt wig(?), CT I, 40.

fḫꜥ grasp (n.), Neferti, 61.

fsi vb. 3 inf. cook, Edel, § 114.

fḳꜣ a cake, Eb. 17, 4.

fḳꜣ reward (vb. and n.), Westc. 6, 14; Peas. B1, 301; Les. 83, 7-8; varr. Urk. IV, 507, 16; 894, 3; 1055, 12; 2178, 10.

fk *be empty*, Adm. 6, 4; *be wasted* through oppression, I. Carn. 4 (det.). Cf. fꜣk 'be shorn'.

fkty *shorn priest*, JEA 24, 169, n. 1.

fgn *defecate*, Eb. 12, 4; TR 24, 8; var. BD 398, 9.

ft n. *disgust*, Hamm. 87, 9; vb. *show dislike*, Urk. IV, 1380, 7.

ftft *leap*, Urk. IV, 19, 5; cf. GNS 14.

ftt *obliterate* inscription, Amarna, V, 26, 24 (with for).

ftt *lint*, P. Ed. Smith, 101; var. det. P. Ram. IV, C 3.

fttw *fish* (pl.), BD 395, 10.

fdỉ vb. 3 inf. *pluck* flowers, Urk. IV, 918, 12; *pull up* plants, Bersh. II, p. 23; *uproot* trees, Urk. IV, 352, 11; *pull out* hair, Eb. 63, 18; *remove*, Urk. V, 178, 14 ( ).

fd *sweat* (vb.), Sm. 3, 19.

fdt *sweat* (n.), Sm. 13, 10. 19; Urk. IV, 1282, 18.

fdw *four*, Pyr. 316. 339 ( ); BD 435, 14.

fdt (1) fem. of last, Pyr. 252. 606: (2) coll. *quartette*, CT I, 129.

fdnw *fourth*, Pyr. 316; CT I, 2.

fdḳ vb. *sever, divide, part*, Peas. B1, 129. 173. 257 = B2, 14 (det.); Urk. IV, 1685, 3; *waste* seed, 1666, 12 (dets); *wear out*, of sandals, Hamm. 114, 13: n. *slice, portion*, I. Carn. 3; a warrior ỉr sw m fdḳw 'who made himself into portions' = who was everywhere at once (?), Urk. IV, 1464, 15.

M

m prep., with suffixes , *in*; *with, by means of*; *from, out of*; *as, namely* (m of predication); before suffix conjugation, *when, as, though*, Gr. §162; *together with*, JEA 25, 166; 39, 20. 31. For m-ꜥ, m-m, see below; for m-bꜣḥ, m-ḫt, etc., see under the second element.

m encl. part., var. , Gr. §250.

 m non-encl. part. behold, var. 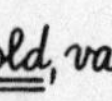, Gr. § 234; usually with suffix, , etc., cf. Gr. p. 570, s.v. mk.

 m interrog. who?, what?, var. ; 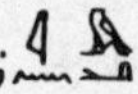 in m 'who?', 'what?', var.  Gr. §§ 227, 3; 496; m m 'wherewith?', mi m 'how?', r m 'to what purpose?', ḥr m 'why?', § 496.

 m neg. imper. do not, var. ; m ir 'do not'; m rdi 'let not', Gr. § 340.

 m imper. take!; m n.k 'take to yourself' often written , Gr. § 336.

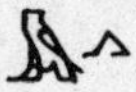 var. of mi 'come!'.

 m3 stern of boat, BD 212, 6.7; 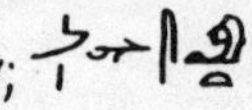 'its bow', Urk. V, 183, 3; 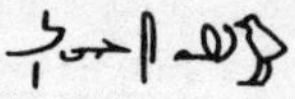 'its stern', 183, 6.

 var. of m3wt 'shaft'.

 var. of im3t 'charm'.

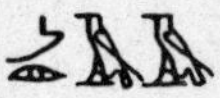 m33 vb. 2 gem. (1) trans. see, Sin. 59. 117. 158; Westc. 5, 15; 8, 11; without obj, Sin. B18 = R44; Pr. 16, 1; Urk. IV, 114, 10; look upon, regard, Sh. S. 28. 29. 179; Adm. 1, 5; Pr. 17, 5; see to the performance of a task, Urk. IV, 57, 3; 437, 13. 15; 521, 10; inspect work, etc., Les. 76, 19; Urk. IV, 79, 17; 1111, 14; 1119, 16; Sm. 7, 15; m3·tw ḥr·f pds ḥr·s 'his face appears (lit. 'is seen') flattened by it', Sm. 6, 1.

(2) intrans. look on at event, RB 77, 3; look, n 'at', Peas. B2, 121; Siut, pl. 16, 6; Urk. IV, 347, 12; r 'toward' = take care of, Les. 79, 5; = take heed of, Urk. IV, 1087, 4 (restd.); m33 ḥr-tp 'oversee', Pyr. 1479.

Varr.  Urk. IV, 1064, 14;  1542, 16; Gr. §§ 299. 439. 448; on geminated form  see § 357 (p. 274).

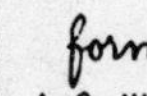 m3w (1) aspect, appearance, Neferhotep, 8; Eb. 107, 16 (): (2) sight, in r-m3w (n) 'in the s. of', Gr. § 178 (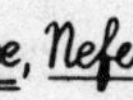, 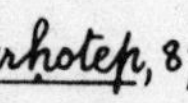); n m3·f 'at the s. of him', Pyr. 266: (3) inspection, in  m3w m 'make i. of', 'look into', Urk. IV, 124, 9; 1006, 16 (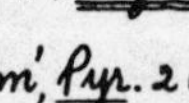).

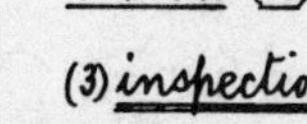 m3w-ḥr mirror, Cairo 28088.

 m3 oryx, Pyr. 806; pl. 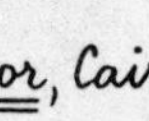 BH I, 30.

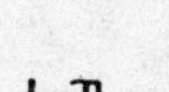

mꜣ-ḥḏ oryx, BH I, 30; Urk. IV, 741, 12.

mꜣi lion, Urk. IV, 893, 12; Westc. 7, 5 (det.); varr. (pl.), Sh. S. 30; RB 64, 12; Urk. IV, 184, 17; 718, 1.

mꜣt lioness, TR 11, 3.

mꜣ-ḥsꜣ (mꜣ-ḥzꜣ) lion, Pyr. 1124; varr. Eb. 66, 9; Urk. IV, 617, 12; 1660, 9; 1666, 15.

mꜣy foetus, Amarna, VI, 27, 6.

mꜣꜥ (1) adj. and vb. true, of speech, BH I, 7 (); 'truth', Pyr. 4, var. BD 264, 5; real: ḥm mꜣꜥ 'a r. coward', Les. 84, 4 (); ḫsbḏ mꜣꜥ 'r. lapis-lazuli', Sh. S. 65-6 (); sim. Sin. R 2; Urk. IV, 98, 14; 167, 9; just, righteous, RB 115, 1; Urk. IV, 1010, 4; true, loyal, n 'to', 414, 11; 899, 7 (); 1010, 12; rightful, of property, Urk. I, 71, 17; rightly belong, n 'to', of kingship, RB 112, 4; pleasing, ḥr ib 'to the heart of', Urk. IV, 289, 12; 396, 5; be in order, of balance, BD 467, 8.

(2) adv. truly, really: mty mꜣꜥ 'one t. precise', Peas. B1, 96-7; Les. 81, 7; imy-ib n ḥnwt.f mꜣꜥ 't. a favourite of his mistress', Urk. IV, 46, 14; ḥsy mꜣꜥ 'one r. favoured', Bersh. I, 21, lower, 8; rightly: st mꜣꜥ 'who acts r.' JEA 39, 53 (l). For wn-mꜣꜥ see p. 62 above.

mꜣꜥ-ḫrw vb. be justified, vindicated, r 'against' s'one, Hymnen, 10, 5; BM 101 (); CT I, 9; Urk. IV, 67, 1; L. to D. IV, 5; ḫrw.f mꜣꜥw 'he is v.', RB 112, 4; sim. Urk. IV, 66, 17; as ep. 'justified' after name of dec'd, 547, 3-5 () et passim; as ep. of Horus, RB 112, 1 (); be triumphant, Th. T. S. IV, 23: n. justification, vindication, Th. T. S. I, 12; Urk. IV, 77, 6; triumph, P. Kah. 1, 1; Les. 70, 18 (); Urk. IV, 59, 1; 1279, 6. Cf. JNES 13, 21.

mꜣꜥt truth, BD 260, 9; Peas. B1, 67. 182 (); Urk. IV, 971, 4 (); m mꜣꜥt 'truly', Sin. B 268; Leb. 25; right-doing, righteousness, Urk. IV, 48, 12 (); 492, 6. 7 (); RB 112, 14 (); justice, Peas. B1, 252, 307; Urk. IV, 40, 13; rightness, orderly management, JEA 43, 14, n. 7; as goddess, Cairo 20539, I b, 2 ( ); Urk. IV, 167, 10; dual in wsḫt nt M3ꜥty 'hall of judgement' in the Beyond, RB 116, 2 ( ); Urk. IV, 116, 9; BD 246, 5 ( ); 'prophet of Maꜥet', Urk. IV, 1030, 8; 1149, 1.

m3ꜥw adv. aright: ꜥnḫ m3ꜥw 'living a.', Les. 68, 12-13; sim. ꜥnḫ n m3ꜥw, Neferhotep, 10.

m3ꜥtyw just men, Leb. 122; the righteous = the blessed dead, Urk. IV, 414, 8 ( ); BD 359, 7.

m3ꜥ vb. present, offer, Neferhotep, 4; Urk. IV, 112, 3; 772, 6; make presentation, n 'to', RB 112, 10; Urk. IV, 368, 13: adj. fit to be offered, Urk. IV, 122, 1. Var. det. D. el B. (XI), I, 24, 7.

m3ꜥw products, Bersh. II, p. 46; Urk. IV, 720, 16 ( ); offering, Westc. 4, 13; Urk. IV, 80, 15; 171, 11; tribute, gifts, 18, 8; 271, 17.

m3ꜥ temple of head, P. Kah. 7, 63-4; M.u.K. 4, 2 ( ); rdi m3ꜥ r (1) 'put the t. to' a place to eavesdrop, Westc. 12, 4: (2) 'pay attention to', Peas. B1, 32; ḥ3ꜥ m3ꜥwy n 'turn o's attention to', Urk. IV, 1082, 14; d3i m3ꜥ r 'pay heed to', Caminos, Lit. Frag. p. 17; tp-m3ꜥ 'beside', 'in the neighbourhood of', 'accompanying', Gr. § 178; tp(y)-m3ꜥ 'opponent', CT I, 55.

m3ꜥ vb. trans. lead, guide, direct; send, despatch; throw out rope from ship, JEA 17, 59; steer ship, TR 27, 43 (det.); extend limbs; paddle water (of swimmers), P. Ed. Smith, 426: intrans. set out on journey, Les. 86, 13. Varr. Les. 86, 2; BD 32, 7.

m3ꜥ bank of river or lake, Peas. R 84; P. Kah. 23, 15. 16; varr. Urk. IV, 57, 2; Caminos, Lit. Frag. pl. 9, 2, 3-4; Urk. IV, 1821, 13.

m3ꜥw breeze, Peas. B1, 55; varr. Urk. IV, 535, 15; BD 489, 2.

m3ꜥw kind of wood, Adm. 3, 11.

m3wt shaft of spear, Pyr. 1212; Caminos, Lit. Frag. pl. 1, 2, 10 ( ), cf. p. 29; staff, Urk. IV, 666, 15; stalk of corn, BD 368, 1. 3; measuring-rod (?), Urk. I, 216, 11 ( ). Cf. JEA 41, 16.

m3wt *rays* of light, *Urk.* IV, 424, 11; var. 806, 14.

m3wy adj. and vb. 4 inf. *new*, *Peas.* B2, 129 ( ); *Westc.* 5, 17; *Urk.* IV 168, 3 ( ); *Ken-amūn*, 45 ( ); *be renewed*, *BD* 41, 3; 165, 12; 188, 7; *Pr.* 4, 3.

m3wt *a new thing*, *RB* 78, 4 ( ); *m m3wt* 'newly', 'anew', *Urk.* IV, 170, 17 ( ); 740, 6; 749, 4; 855, 16; *n m3wt* as adj. 'new', 894, 17; 'anew this day', var. O.K. , *L. to D.* VI, 5, n.

m3wt *new land*, *Amarna*, V, 26, 21; cf. *P. Wilbour*, 27.

M3fdt n. div. *Mafdet*, a cat(?)-goddess, *JEA* 24, 89.

m3m3 *dom-palm*, *Urk.* IV, 73, 14; varr. (pl.), *RB* 60, 14; (pl.), Caminos, *Lit. Frag.* pl. 10, 3, 8; variety of same, *Urk.* IV, 73, 17.

M3nw n. loc. *the Western mountain*, Gauthier, *Dict. géogr.* III, 7.

m3r *dispossess* s'one, *m* 'of', *Hatnub*, 22, 8.

m3r *wretched man, pauper*, *BH* I, 8, 19; varr. *Hatnub*, 20, 7; *Peas.* B1, 233; B2, 112; *Urk.* IV, 1161, 12; 1045, 10.

m3ir *misery*, *Peas.* B1, 280; *Leb.* 128; *Adm.* 13, 6; *Urk.* IV, 1076, 10.

m3rw *viewing-place* in sun-cult, *JEA* 42, 58.

m3ḥ *wreath*, *Urk.* IV, 22, 4; V, 137, 14 (det.); *Th. T. S.* I, p. 111, n. 3.

m3ḥ *pasture*, *Herdsm.* 10.

m3ḥ *sheaf*, *Sheikh Said*, 16; var. (pl.), *BH* I, 29.

m3ḫ *burn*, *GNS* 50. 158; var. *Louvre* C14, 12.

m3st *knee* of man; *hock* of animal, *JEA* 45, 104; var. *Pyr.* 378.

m3s *kneel*, var. , *JEA* 45, 104.

m3ḳt *ladder*, *CT* I, 58; varr. , ibid.; *BD* 203, 1.

m3tt *mandrake*(?), *JEA* 19, 133. 137.

m3tyt *female mourners*, var. dets. , Caminos, *Lit. Frag.* p. 28.

m3ṯ *granite*, Sethe, *Steine*, 17; varr. *Leb.* 61; *Urk.* IV, 843, 4; 622, 14.

 m3ṯ proclaim, CT I, 141; varr. 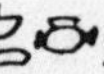 Urk. IV, 261, 3; 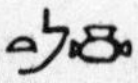 BH I, 25, 69.

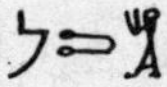 m3ṯ acclaim, Louvre C 15, 7.

 mi imper. come!, var. , Gr. § 336; 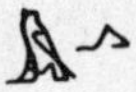 Pyr. 2000.

 mi(w) waters, Urk. IV, 616, 9; Sm. 6, 3.

, 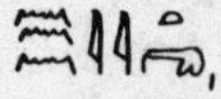, see under mw, mwyt.

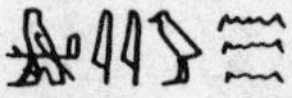 myw seed of man, Urk. IV, 1679, 7.

 mi prep. like, according as, var. 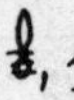, Gr. § 170; m mi 'as if', Sin. R 65; 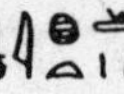 'the like', Sin. B 161.

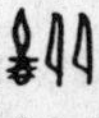 my adv. likewise, accordingly, var. 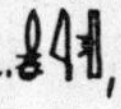, Gr. § 205, 1.

 mi the equal of s'one, Les. 80, 20.

 mit copy of document, Sin. B 178. 204.

 mity equal to, similar to, Gr. § 80; varr. 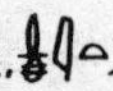 Hatnub, 16, 3; 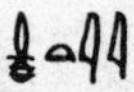 Cairo 20543, 19.

 mitw equal (n.), Peas. B1, 283; Pr. 5, 13; Sin. B 216; JEA 4, pl. 9, 6.

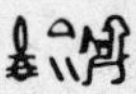 mity likeness, Urk. IV, 1822, 15.

 mitt the like, Sin. B 222. 309; mitt iry 'the l. thereof', Sh. S. 22. 125; Westc. 7, 7-8; m mitt 'likewise', Westc. 8, 22; so too r mitt, Urk. IV, 656, 16; RB 60, 5; m mitt iry, Leb. 66; r mitt iry, Sh. S. 172; Urk. IV, 2, 3.

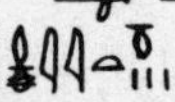 myt a drink, Adm. 13, 13.

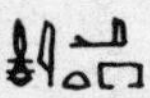 miꜥt loom (?), AEO II, 215*.

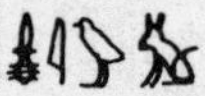 miw cat, RB 119, 7; var. det.  Urk. V, 50, 16; fem. 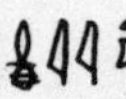 Eb. 65, 11.

 var. of mꜥwḥ 'oar'.

 mibt axe, Ti, 119; var. 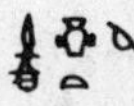 JEA 19, pl. 24. Cf. GNS 52.

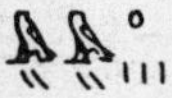 mymy seed-corn of emmer (?), varr. , , P. Wilbour, 113.

 min today, Leb. 103. 104; Gr. §§ 205, 1; 208; m min 'today', § 205, 3; 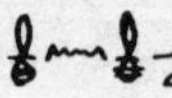, var. O.K. 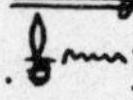, 'anew this day', L. to D. VI, 5, ro.

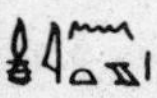 mint kind of land, P. Wilbour, Index, p. 96.

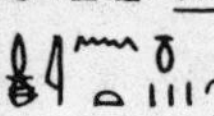 mint daily fare, GNS 41.

minb axe, varr. , , GNS 51. 159.

, varr. of mꜥḥꜥt 'tomb'.

mist liver, P. Kah. 5,5; varr. BH II, 15; Eb. 36,9. Cf. AEO II, 245*.

miswt (mizwt) crown of U. E., Pyr. 724; var. Hymnen, 18, 21.

m-ꜥ prep. in the hand, possession, charge of; together with; from, Gr. §178; m-ꜥ ntt 'seeing that', §223.

mꜥt kind of boat, P. Kah. 22, 13. 14; 33, 12.

mꜥwḥ oar, Pyr. 889; varr. 906; BD 133, 7.

mꜥbꜣ(yw) the Thirty, a judicial body, GAS 50.

mꜥbꜣyt House of the Thirty, varr. , GAS 50.

mꜥbꜣ harpoon, Pyr. 1212; varr. BD 237, 5; Urk. VII, 37, 16.

mꜥf headsman's block, TR 2, 86.

mꜥnḫt pendant, Cairo 28092.

mꜥnḏt day-bark of sun-god, Sethe, Lauf. 21; JEA 20, 162; varr. ibid.; 20, 158, 14; Urk. IV, 366, 7; 1549, 3.

mꜥr fortunate, successful, Leb. 41; Les. 81, 5 (); Siut, pl. 11, 8; 16, 17; RB 59, 7; 60, 5; Urk. IV, 1998, 14 (sic); flourishing, JEA 35, 62: n. success, RB 111, 5; Les. 83, 24.

mꜥḥꜥt tomb, cenotaph, Les. 71, 16; varr. 68, 4; Cairo 20733, c 18; Urk. IV, 27, 16; 1536, 3; cf. JEA 10, 226.

mꜥkꜣ brave, Sh. S. 96. 99.

mw water, Sin. B 27. 233; Sh. S. 14; Westc. 6, 11. 12; 9, 18; rain, Caminos, Lit. Frag. p. 42; semen, RB 111, 15; ḥr mw.f 'loyal to him', Sin. B 75; Urk. IV, 1301, 16; sim. 53, 2; 1099, 2; of god as helper of warring king, 1291, 3; ḏd.i n mw 'I speak in exactness', RB 64, 9. Var. Peas. B1, 220. 279.

mwyt urine, Sm. 10, 14. 17; Eb. 109, 11; var. 49, 7; mwyt 'spittle', 99, 17.

mwy be watery, var. , P. Ed. Smith, 376.

mww class of ritual dancers, var. ..., GNS 70; Th. T. S. II, p. 21.

mwt mother, Peas. B1, 64; Westc. 12, 13; Siut, pl. 13, 33; Sm. 19, 16; varr. Urk. IV, 27, 14; Pr. 10, 2; TR 2, 8; CT I, 17.

mwt n. div. Mut, Urk. IV, 413, 16.

mwt weight, Urk. IV, 1126, 17; RB 114, 2.

mwnf garrison, Urk. IV, 730, 17; palace guard, Mill. 2, 2 ( ); protector of poor, Siut, pl. 11, 3.

mfk3t turquoise, Les. 86, 10; varr. Westc. 5, 16; Urk. IV, 373, 2; 744, 12; 638, 2; cf. Kémi, 1, 99.

m-m prep. among, varr. , , Gr. § 178; adv. therein, § 205, 1.

mm transport cattle, JEA 16, 194.

, varr. of mymy 'seed-corn'.

mmy giraffe, Sh. S. 164; varr. Urk. IV, 948, 4.

mn in m n.k 'take to yourself...', Gr. § 336.

mn vb. (1) intrans. be firm, established, enduring, of king, Urk. IV, 17, 2; 390, 12; sim. of crown, 16, 8; Hymnen, 8, 5; of heirs, Siut, pl. 11, 15; Les. 89, 18; Urk. IV, 1194, 17; of heart = stout-hearted, steadfast, 616, 3; 656, 11; 661, 9; of foot = of stance (fig.), Les. 81, 17; Urk. IV, 18, 13; sim. 545, 15; of other things, concrete or abstract, 131, 16; 430, 8; 518, 14; 1295, 7; Eb. 101, 17; of oath in king's name, Urk. IV, 80, 17; mn w3ḥ 'established and long-living', of king, Bersh. I, 15; 'e. and enduring', of deeds, Urk. IV, 570, 8; mn rwḏ 'e. and prosperous', of queen, Sin. B186; 'firm and enduring', of building, Adm. 2, 11; be fixed, stick fast, m 'in'; be attached, m 'to', P. Ed. Smith, 153; remain, m 'in', Herdsm. 18; dwell, m 'in', Pyr. 247; be vested, m 'in', of property, Urk. I, 12, 15; L. to D. II, 7 (n.).

(2) trans. establish, Urk. IV, 1279, 10; press with fingers, Sm. 13, 13.

mn in r-mn-m 'as far as', Gr. § 180; r-mn 'as well as', 'including', Urk. IV, 1302, 13; 1303, 2; 1305, 8. 10; m mn 'at the fixed rate of', JEA 27, 49, n. 2.

mn so-and-so, someone, Urk. IV, 1108, 7; M.u.K. vs. 3, 4 (also fem.); P. Ram. IV, D ii, 3; of things, mn iry 'a sample thereof', RB 64, 8.

mnt (1) the like, Les. 82, 5 (det. ×); P. Ram. III, B 28; Peas. B1, 231; ir.n.i mnt im.i 'I have proved it myself', Les. 86, 6; n wd.tw irt mnt iry 'it is forbidden to do such a thing', Westc. 8, 17; m t3y mnt 'in this fashion', Ch. B. Text, 65, n. 5; ht mnt 'something', Sm. 1, 4: (2) content of receptacle, P. Louvre 3226, 29, 2 = Gr. p. 199, 2nd ex.

, see under mni 'jar'.

mnt in m mnt 'daily', Amarna, II, 21; VI, 25, 14.

mn be ill, suffer, Eb. 32, 16; Pr. 5, 1; be ill of, suffer from, Eb. 39, 21; Sm. 2, 15; suffer in part of body, Sm. 20, 13; P. Kah. 5, 23; Eb. 103, 6; be troubled about, Pr. 14, 8. Cf. Mél. Masp. I, 342.

mn sick man, Urk. IV, 972, 6.

mnt malady, Turin 159, 5 = Gr. §109; P. Kah. 7, 7 (dets.); Sm. 1, 5; 8, 1; what is harmful, Pr. 17, 6; suffering, Peas. B1, 250; RB 116, 15; 'distress', 'calamity', GAS 103.

mnw pain, P. Ram. I, A4; var. A10.

mnt swallow (n.), Urk. IV, 113, 13; cf. AEO II, 257*.

mnt thigh of man (usually dual), P. Kah. 5, 9; 6, 9; M.u.K. 4, 10; haunch of ox, Siut, pl. 8, 314 (det.).

mni jar, Urk. IV, 635, 3. 16; 828, 10 (); as measure of capacity, Gr. §266, 1 (,).

mni trans. moor ship, Urk. VII, 2, 7 (also dets.); Peas. B2, 102; Westc. 7, 11; fig. Pr. 6, 6; marry, m 'to', Sin. B 78; attach, m 'to' cult-service, Urk. IV, 30, 15; endow, m 'with', Hatnub, 20, 11 (det.); save the drowning, Peas. B1, 137; revive the dead, RB 111, 15: intrans. die, Pr. 2, 8 (det.); Urk. V, 63, 7.

mnit mooring-post, Sh. S. 4; Les. 75, 17 (); Urk. IV, 60, 7 (); Sm. 2, 2 (); whipping-post, Mereruka, pl. 38.

mnỉ death, Urk. IV, 64, 16; 405, 8 (det.); V, 4, 13; Sin. B 310 (dets.).

mnỉwt harbour, Urk. IV, 692, 15; 719, 7.

mnỉt necklace sacred to Ḥatḥōr, varr. , , GNS 100.

mny dual thighs, Eb. 69, 4.

mny corvée, P. Kah. 14, 5; 22, 45.

mnyt root, Eb. 16, 16; 50, 18. 19; of disease, Eb. 25, 9.

mnỉw herdsman, BH I, 8, 18; Herdsm. 10. 13. 14; Peas. B1, 177; cf. AEO I, 66*. Varr. Pyr. 1533; BH I, 35; Urk. IV, 512, 11; RB 114, 6.

mnỉ act as herdsman, Pyr. 936.

mnʿ nurse (vb.), Urk. IV, 230, 15; var. det. Amarna, VI, 27, 10.

mnʿt nurse (n.), Urk. IV, 913, 6; 920, 12; abbr. 1395, 14; dets. CT I, 17; I, 168; used of men, Les. 75, 11; 82, 4.

mnʿy male nurse, Urk. IV, 110, 13; 120, 8; 1432, 14; var. 406, 8.

mnʿt milch-cow, Urk. IV, 72, 4; var. dets. 188, 10.

Mnw n. div. Min, Les. 98, 8; varr. , Pyr. 424.

mnw kind of stone, Urk. IV, 718, 16; 722, 9; var. BH I, 17.

mnw thread, BH II, 13.

mnwt pigeon, prob. varr. , , AEO II, 257*.

mnw pigeons (?), Peas. R 27.

mnw monument, passim; of portable objects, Urk. IV, 22, 3; 1202, 11; var. 1795, 8.

mnwy abundant of monuments, ep. of king, Urk. IV, 369, 15; 554, 1. 3; 1670, 17.

mnw trees; plantation, GAS 88; varr. Urk. IV, 73, 9; 1165, 16; 1004, 7.

see under mnnw 'fortress'.

mnfꜣt coll. trained soldiers; assault troops; infantry; soldiery in general, JEA 39, 38. 44. Varr. Urk. IV, 259, 15; 945, 3; 21, 11; 660, 11; D. el. B. 105.

mnfrt band for arm or ankle, BH II, 7.13; var. dets. Urk. IV, 39,7; 399,10.

mnmn move quickly, of person, Urk. IV, 1105,16; move about, of army, 1112,13; quake, of earth, Sh. S. 60; be shifted, of boundary, Urk. IV, 1111,10.

mnmnt cattle, Sin. R16; B24; Urk. IV, 7,12.

mnnw fortress, Urk. IV, 739,16; varr. 1113,10; 85,3.

Mn-nfr n. loc. Memphis, AEO II, 122*.

mnḥd scribe's palette, Pyr. 954; var. Urk. IV, 509,1.

mnḥ wax, Westc. 3,13; Wortforschung, V, 30; var. CT I, 157.

mnḥ papyrus-plant, TR 22,63; Bersh. II, p. 23; var. M. u. K. 7,3.

mnḥw froth (?) on lips, Urk. IV, 480,2; Hymnen, 3,4.

mnḫ string beads, GAS 31.113.

mnḫ chisel (n. and vb.), Bull. 22,88 ff.

mnḫ potent, of king, etc., Sin. B44; Westc. 9,11; Siut, pl. 4,227 ( ); R B110, 8; Urk. IV, 101,8 (dets.); 114,4; 538,16 (abbr.); trusty, of officials, Sin. B244; efficacious, of commands, counsel, etc., Sin. B49; Les. 69,20; Urk. IV, 60,10; 133,2; 170,12; mnḫ n 'go well with' affairs, I, 224,10; well-disposed, devoted, n 'to', BH I, 26,167; Urk. IV, 113,3; 297,14; sim. mnḫ ib, Siut, pl. 5,242; Urk. IV, 61,16; mnḫ ḥr ib 'pleasing to the heart', Les. 72,8; 73,1; Urk. IV, 142,6, splendid, of buildings, 297,4; of workmanship, 421,12; sbty mnḫ 'a mighty rampart', 184,16; š mnḫw ḥr dḳrw 'a lake embellished with fruit-trees', 433,10; costly, of material, 883,5; lavish, of worship, RB 110,6; excellent, of occasions, Urk. IV, 939,1; of deeds, 1045,2; well-famed, Pr. 15,12; BH I, 26,216; Urk. IV, 945,4; well-established, of endowment, Siut, pl. 6,275; as adv. thoroughly, P. Kah. 6,9; r mnḫ 'thoroughly', Gr. §205,5.

mnḫw excellence, virtues of s'one, Urk. IV, 945,7; 957,4; varr. 465,1; 749,17; Siut, pl. 5,242.

mnḫt willingness of heart, Urk. IV, 40,11; 'do good', 131,7.

mnḫ be joyful (?), m 'over', Urk. IV, 260,7.

mnḫt the third month, Urk. IV, 44, 8.

mnḫt type of fabric, Caminos, Lit. Frag. p. 15; clothing, Urk. IV, 753, 3; var., abbr., Gr. p. 507, S27.

mnst lack (?), BH I, 26, 218.

mns3 (mnz3) jar for liquids, Pyr. 32; BH II, 30.

mnš cartouche, Gr. p. 74.

mnšt yellow (?) ochre, JEA 20, 188; Barns, Ram. p. 33.

mnḳ come to an end, JEA 39, pl. 2, 21.

mnḳt jar (?), Urk. IV, 1848, 15.

mnḳb fan, Pyr. 1151. 1322.

mnḳb (1) cool place, P. Kah. 2, 13: (2) chapel, Les. 76, 23-4.

mnkrt bull's tail worn by king, Cairo 28092.

mntt written for, GNS 41, n. 1.

mnṯ3t pottery vessel, JEA 16, 21.

Mnṯw n. div. Mont, Urk. IV, 87, 16; 247, 1; 1280, 18 (det.); var. Sin. B 206.

Mnṯw Beduin, Pyr. 724; Urk. I, 32, 17; IV, 138, 5; Mnṯw Stt 'B. of Asia', Les. 83, 8; Urk. IV, 5, 4; 808, 8; 'Iwntyw (nw) Mnṯw 'nomad B.', Les. 82, 13; 83, 5; Urk. IV, 200, 2.

mnḏ breast, Pyr. 734. 911; Urk. IV, 237, 16; of male, Pyr. 91; Eb. 38, 11.

mnḏt cheek, varr., JEA 12, 141; ZÄS 62, 20.

mnḏm basket, Peas. B1, 133; var. Urk. IV, 762, 5. Cf. JEA 9, 13, n. 3.

mr adj. sick, ill, diseased, Eb. 1, 11; 2, 11; 35, 10; ḫ3t mrt 'a severe disease', Br. 10, 2; painful, r 'to', L. to D. III, 6 (n.); p. 25; n 'to', IV, 5 (n.); of o's striking-power, Pyr. 253; mr ib n 'have compassion on', 'be sorry for', Pyr. 1109; Sin. B 133; mr ḥr ib n 'be displeasing to', T. Carn. 7; ḫt mr 'calamity', Sh. S. 124: adv. sorely, L. to D. III, 3 (n.) (det.); Eb. 40, 15: n. pain, Peas. B1, 25; Eb. 14, 7; ailment, Sm. 1, 2; 2, 6. 15.

mr sick man, Leb. 131.

mrt pains, Eb. 13, 12. 16. 21.

mr pyramid, Pyr. 1664; Sin. B 300; Urk. IV, 100, 16; varr. 28, 1; 1283, 11.

mr canal, Les. 85, 4; Urk. IV, 89, 7; artificial lake, RB 67, 8; varr. RB 46, 2; (pl.) Caminos, Lit. Frag. pl. 15, 2.

mr libation trough, Urk. IV, 630, 3; var. 1296, 6.

mrw (1) weavers, in 'overseer of w.', BH I, 29; Urk. IV, 924, 17 ( ); 'foreman of w.', 405, 14: (2) servants, underlings, Sin. B 142; Urk. IV, 1444, 8; 'low-class talk', 120, 3: (3) partisans, supporters, Mill. 1, 5; Merikarēʿ 57. 100 ( ); in sing. Les. 68, 24; (sic), Urk. IV, 972, 1.

mrt coll. (1) weavers, Urk. IV, 742, 14: (2) servants, underlings, Sin. B 155; BH I, 25, 10-11; TR 2, 10 ( ); Urk. IV, 41, 5 ( ); 58, 9.

mrw bulls, Caminos, Lit. Frag. pl. 8, 3, 5; 10, 3, 7; 16, 1, 5. Cf. mry 'bull' below.

mri vb. 3 inf. love, Sh. S. 147; Sin. B 66. 107. 123; Urk. IV, 384, 2; 965, 12; want, wish, desire, Sin. B 234. 236; Peas. B1, 127; Westc. 6, 7; with foll. infin., Gr. § 303; with foll. sdm.f, §§ 184; 442, 1; 452, 1. Var. BM 614, 8.

mrwt love (n.), Sin. B 66. 86 ( ). 222; Urk. IV, 16, 17; 19, 3; 20, 3 ( ); will, desire, Peas. B1, 206; Sin. B 233; n mrwt, m mrwt 'in order that', Gr. § 181.

mrwty the well-beloved, Urk. IV, 1614, 13; varr. 15, 15; 857, 5; Siut, pl. 13, 7; fem. Pyr. 534.

mr milk-jar, Pyr. 32, BH II, 15, 11.

mr bind, Westc. 12, 13; Hymnen, 13, 3 (det.); Sm. 3, 18; Paheri, 3.

mrw strip of cloth, P. Kah. 37, 22 (det.); bundle of clothes, Lac. Sarc. II, 16.

Mrt n. div. musician-goddess, var. , GAS 59; JEA 22, 105.

mrt kind of boat, Bersh. II, 6.

mrt street, Les. 82, 14. Cf. mrrt 'street' below.

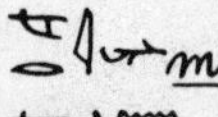 mri sounding-pole, Peas. B1, 278.

 mri run aground, of ship, JEA 9, 17, n. 10.

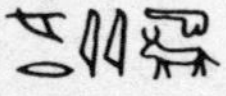 mry fighting bull, BH II, 7; varr. 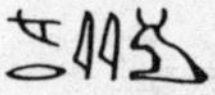 I, 30;  I, p 37.

 mr-wr Mnevis-bull, Amarna, V, 32, 21; varr.  BD 206, 7;  Urk. IV, 1373, 14.

 mryt bank, shore, Peas. R 39; Westc. 7, 11; 8, 2; Leb. 64; Sh. S. 169; RB 63, 7 (det. ); sandbank (?), Peas. B1, 260; quay, JEA 12, 133; 15, 173; height of triangle, locc. cit.; snb mryt 'the coast is clear', Peas. B1, 130.

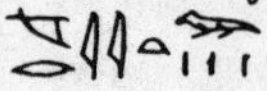 mryt coll. crocodiles, Leb. 75; var. 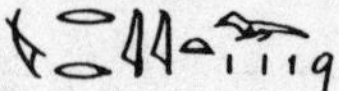 97.

 mryn Syrian warrior, Urk. IV, 665, 9; varr.  895, 4; 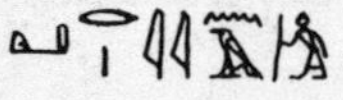 1305, 6; 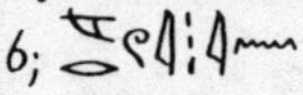 1307, 7.

 mrw kind of wood, Urk. IV, 1149, 9; varr.  373, 4; 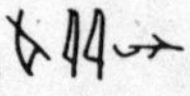 664, 7.

 mrw desert, M. u. K. 2, 8; mrw snb 'the coast is clear', Urk. IV, 656, 15, cf. JEA 28, 11 (qq).

 mrw harbours (?), Siut, pl. 19, 55.

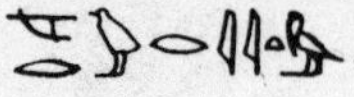 mwryt black stork, JEA 35, 16, no. 7; pl. 2.

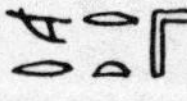 mrt street, GAS 50; avenue of statues, BH I, 44, 2 (dets. ).

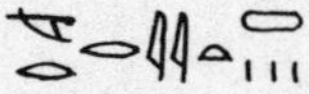 mryt lumps (?) of incense, Sh. S. 164.

 mrḥt oil, grease, Pr. 10, 9; Adm. 8, 4; Sin. B 295; Sm. 2, 8 (); Eb. 2, 13; Urk. IV, 913, 17.

 mrḥ decay (n.), of buildings, Urk. IV, 2027, 6.

 mrkbt chariot, AEO I, 68*; var. 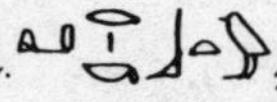 Urk. IV, 1311, 12.

 mhy vb. 3 inf. be forgetful, neglectful, ḥr 'of', Urk. IV, 53, 3; 425, 5; mh ib 'the heart is f.' = has defective action, Eb. 102, 15. Varr.  Urk. IV, 363, 5;  993, 2;  1044, 16;  126, 4.

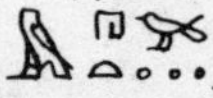 mht forgetfulness, negligence, Hamm. 199; Louvre C 167; mht-ib 'negligence' Pt (L. II), 3, 3; Urk. IV, 118, 5 (); of poor heart-action, Eb. 45, 7; 102, 4.

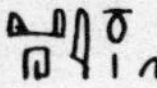 var. of mhr 'milk-jar'.

mhỉt milch-cow, Pyr. 550.

mhwt family, Urk. IV, 1817, 5.

mhwt: dns — 'guarded of speech', JEA 35, 38; 37, 112.

mhn coffer, Caminos, Lit. Frag. pl. 11, 10.

mhr milk-jar, BM 159; Urk. IV, 743, 15; varr. Meir, II, 6; Paheri, 4.

mḥ forearm, var. Pyr. 574; 'small children (?)', RB 66, 4.

mḥ cubit, varr. , , , Gr. § 266, 2.

mḥ-tꜣ land-cubit = 1/100 aroura, abbr. , Gr. § 266, 3; P. Wilbour, 60.

mḥ vb. trans. fill, Pr. 10, 9; Peas. B1, 9; Sh. S. 133; Urk. IV, 413, 7; be full of, Caminos, L.-Eg. Misc. 424; pay in full, ZÄS 43, 34; Stud. Griff. 54 (42); make whole, Urk. V, 32, 3; complete, finish, ZÄS 50, 57; Ann. Serv. 38, 225, n. 2; mḥ nfr 'render good account', Peas. B1, 251; mḥ rdwy 'hurry', Paheri, 3; formative of ordinal numerals, Gr. § 263, 3: intrans. be full, Peas. B1, 276; m 'of', Westc. 2, 1; Urk. IV, 687, 10; ḥr 'of' Sh. S. 116; be complete, Les. 86, 15; Urk. IV, 119, 11; mḥ m 'full measure of', Peas. R 35; mḥ r + infin. 'set about', 'begin doing s'thing', Äg. Stud. 2; mḥ ḫft 'act according to,' Urk. IV, 353, 9.

mḥt the complete Eye of Horus, ZÄS 57, 7*.

mḥ-ỉb one who is trusted, confidant, Siut, pl. 15, 18; Urk. IV, 46, 10; 410, 14; mḥ ỉb m 'trust in', Urk. I, 99, 4. 7; Peas. B1, 236; Adm. 4, 6.

mḥ hold, Urk. IV, 351, 9; seize, lay hold of, with m, Westc. 3, 14; Sm. 8, 15; grasp instructions, Urk. IV, 530, 4; capture, 660, 8. 9; 686, 13; m mḥ 'carry off captive', 4, 6; 6, 5.

mḥ inlay (vb.), Les. 76, 10; Urk. IV, 705, 14; 1859, 12.

mḥỉ vb. 3 inf. be concerned, ḥr 'for', Leb. 78; take thought, ḥr 'for', Sin. B 199; ponder, ḥr 'on', Neferti, 18 ( ): n. care, Leb. 68.

mhy guardian, CT I, 145; varr. ibid.; , , 151.

mḥt bowl, Urk. IV, 634, 17; 828, 4; L. to D. II, 6; var. det. Eb. 93, 16.

mḥt fan (?), Urk. IV, 38, 15.

mḥi̓ vb. 3 inf. (1) drown, bedrowned, Pyr. 615. 766 (); Peas. B1, 137. 238; ib.f mḥ 'his heart is d.' = weak in action, Eb. 102, 15; overflow, of Nile, Siut, pl. 15, 7 (); inundate land, Pyr. 388 (,): (2) swim, BD 105, 5: trans. launch a vessel, Urk. I, 109, 4 ().

mḥt flood-waters, Pyr. 507. 508.

Mḥt n. loc. the Delta marshes, ZÄS 44, 13.

mḥty adj. northern, Sin. B 72; BH I, 25, 33; Urk. IV, 795, 15: n. North, Pyr. 470 (). 814; Peas. R 38; Westc. 4, 9; 11, 7; Urk. IV, 36, 4; mḥt m 'northward to', Urk. I, 101, 11; 105, 13; later mḥt r, Gr. §179.

mḥtt north, Urk. IV, 139, 2.

mḥtyw northerners, Urk. IV, 5, 14; 17, 1; 1278, 17; var. 83, 9.

mḥyt north-wind, Urk. IV, 51, 6; 1164, 13; var. 76, 8; with dets. storm from the north, 'norther', Leb. 72.

mḥyt papyrus-plant, RB 64, 7; 120, 4; Eb. 56, 15; 83, 14 (); clump of papyrus, Caminos, Lit. Frag. pl. 3, 4, 4 ([ ]).

Mḥw n. loc. Lower Egypt, varr. , , , , ZÄS 44, 10. 11: adj. Lower Egyptian, ZÄS 44, 17. 19.

mḥw.s Crown of L. E., ZÄS 44, 20; varr. Urk. IV, 251, 13; 266, 8; Sin. B 271.

mḥy flax, Westc. 12, 13. 17; var. BH I, 29; in O.K. mḥʿi̓, mḥʿw, cf. Edel, §93.

mḥw linen thread, M.u.K. vs. 6, 6.

mḥyt coll. fish, Urk. IV, 1421, 15; varr. 917, 16; 1397, 4.

mḥw hunter, Peas. B1, 205; cf. Caminos, L.-Eg. Misc. 418.

mḥꜣ back of the head, Sm. 1, 7. 8; var. Eb. 91, 19.

mḥwnw slaughterer, Les. 73, 7.

mḥn (1) coil (n. and vb.), of serpents, Pyr. 541 (); BD 144, 14; Th. T. S. I, 30 ():

(2) name of a serpent-spirit, 'the Coiled one', BD 287, 8; 446, 12; used of uraeus, Urk. IV, 951, 2 (det.): (3) a board-game, Ranke, Schlangenspiel.

mḥnyt 'the Coiled one' (fem.), Hymnen, 8, 4; BD 433, 1.

mḥnk partner (?), Peas. B1, 170.

mḫ respect s'one, var. , Siut, pl. 5, 242 (bis).

mḫꜣ make fast, bind, GAS 87.

mḫꜣt balance, Urk. IV, 337, 13; iry-mḫꜣt 'keeper of the b.', BD 96, 4. Varr. Les. 69, 19; Peas. B1, 149; Urk. IV, 119, 10; 454, 1; 49, 3; 533, 14. Cf. JEA 9, 10, n. 4.

mḫꜣ vb. trans. match, equal; adjust, counterpoise; make level: intrans. be like, with n; mḫꜣ ib n 'like in disposition to'; var. dets. , , GNS 49.

mḫꜣw shed, Caminos, Lit. Frag. p. 17.

mḫnmt carnelian (?), varr. , , , JEA 38, 13.

mḫnt face, Pyr. 493; Sm. 3, 10.

var. of mẖr 'low-lying land'.

var. of mẖrw 'business'.

mḫsf peg to secure net, BD 391, 3; 394, 7. 12; 396, 7.

mḫtbt an ornament of gold, Urk. IV, 38, 15; 39, 3.

mḫtmt a closed or sealed receptacle, JEA 41, 13.

mẖꜣ incline o's heart, n 'to', Urk. IV, 260, 4.

mẖꜣ a boat, BM 614, 11.

mẖnt ferry-boat, Peas. B1, 198; B2, 99; RB 119, 3; Les. 79, 16; varr. Pyr. 334; 384.

mẖnty ferryman, Peas. B1, 171-2; varr. Urk. V, 146, 17; CT III, 174; Pyr. 597; 1193.

mẖr low-lying land, Herdsm. 2; var. Urk. I, 77, 11.

mẖr storehouse, barn, Peas. R 4; Adm. 8, 3; Pr. 14, 13; cf. AEO II, 212.*

mḫrw low place, in rdi͗ tp <m> mḫrw 'hang o's head', Westc. 12, 23–4.

mḫrw dealings, business; ordinances; arrangement of building; mḫrw 'govern' a land; 'do s'one's business'; 'provide for' s'one; swḏ mḫrw 'govern', GAS 102; varr. Urk. IV, 656, 7; 1196, 3; 2028, 8; JEA 4, pl. 8, 5.

mẖtw intestines, var. …, AEO II, 252*.

var. of mist 'liver'.

ms (mzꜣ) (1) bring, present, n 'to', of persons and things, Sh. S. 175; Sin. B 269; Westc. 10, 3; Urk. IV, 7, 11; 8, 1; 1086, 13; bring away booty, 1308, 10; extend hand, Les. 73, 7; take aim, RB 58, 13; Urk. IV, 1322, 6 — cf. ZÄS 48, 36; GNS 100. Varr. Hatnub, 17, 3; Urk. IV, 1308, 10; 1781, 6; Ḳen-amūn, 18; Pyr. , 85.

(2) betake o'self, r 'to', Westc. 10, 12; n 'to', JEA 39, pl. 2, 15.

msw: — inr 'stone-carriers'; — wdnw 'offering-bearers', var. , ZÄS 48, 39.

mst a staff, Urk. V, 155, 13.

mst apron of fox-skins, Gr. p. 465, F 31.

msi vb. 3 inf. bear, give birth, Westc. 9, 15. 22; 12, 11 ( ); P. Kah. 6, 22; Urk. IV, 244, 9; calve, of gazelle, RB 77, 3 ( ); lay, of bird, Urk. IV, 700, 14; be born, Sin. B 69 (det.). 276; Urk. IV, 228, 3 ( ); n 'to' parent, Westc. 11, 5; Les. 84, 13. 16; ms n, fem. mst n 'b. to', in filiations, Gr. § 361; create, of god, Urk. IV, 270, 12; 517, 17; bring forth, of field, V, 28, 9; make, fashion, Les 68, 6; 71, 8; 75, 9; Westc. 11, 13; RB 110, 9. 10; JEA 31, 13, n. 2.

ms child, P. Kah. 9, 29; Adm. 2, 14 ( ); usually pl., Sin. B 172. 186. 239; Urk. IV, 690, 2; 'king's children', Siut, pl. 15, 22; var. Sin. B 197.

mst mother, Leb. 77; cf. JEA 42, 36 (64).

mswt coll. children, offspring, Pyr. 141; Urk. I, 11, 16 ( ); young of animals, Urk. IV, 663, 9 ( ).

 mswt birth, BH I, 25, 63; Westc. 10,18 (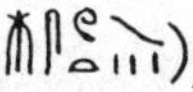); wḥm mswt 'be born again', Urk. IV, 305,6; 812,17; 817,10;  'birth(day) of Osiris', 470,2; 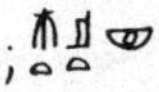 'b. of Isis', 112, 9; 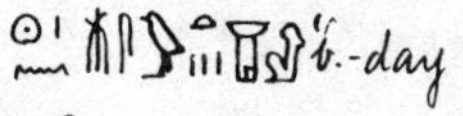 'b.-day of Nephthys', Th. T. S. I, 23.

 mswtt girl-child, Urk. IV, 1344,6.

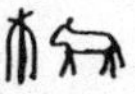 ms calf, Siut, pl. 15,13.

 ms bouquet, Urk. IV, 1383,16.

 ms encl. part. surely, indeed, Gr. § 251.

 msꜣdt nostril, varr. 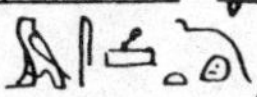, 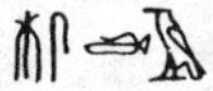, 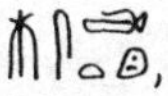, ZÄS 79,88.

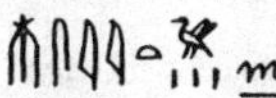 msyt waterfowl, Leb. 93; var. 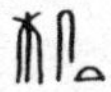 Caminos, Lit. Frag. pl. 6,3,2.

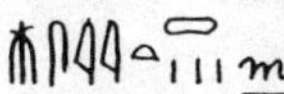 msyt supper, Sin. B 12; Mill. 1,11; Leb. 81; var.  Pyr. 716.

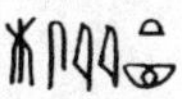 msyt a festival, Urk. VII, 10,9; Siut, pl. 14,82 (); 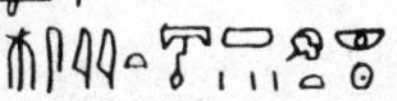 'the First M.', Urk. IV, 483,3; varr. 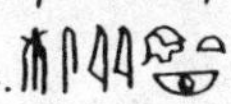 470,2; 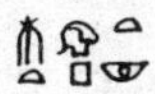 112,9.

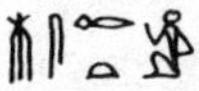 ms-ꜥꜣt prospector (?), Goyon, p. 88.

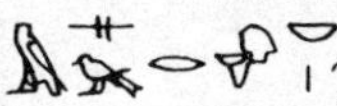 mswr (mzwr) drinking-bowl, Pyr. 930.937; var.  ZÄS 64,2.

 mswḳ kind of bread, JEA 25,166, n. 1.

 msbb turn, ḥr 'to', Siut, pl. 19,29; Urk. IV, 519,5 (det. ); serve s'one, with ḥr, 150,2 (dets. 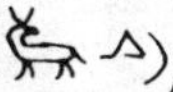); deal (?), ḥnꜥ 'with', JEA 16, pl. 29,10.

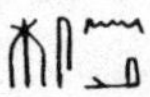 msn spin (?), plait (?), BH I, 29; varr. 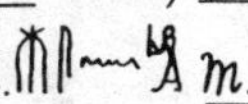 M. u. K. 2,1; 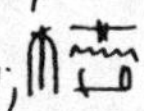 P. Ram. III, B 31.

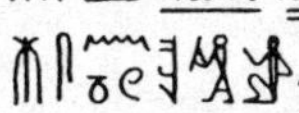 msnw harpooner, Caminos, Lit. Frag. pl. 1,2,2; var.  TR 20, 34; cf. ZÄS 54,50; 57,137.

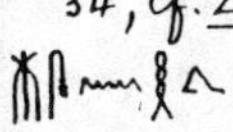 msnḥ rotate; turn backwards; turn away, GAS 27.

 msḥ (mzḥ) crocodile, Edel, § 93; varr.  Westc. 3,12;  Urk. IV, 945,16; fem. msḥt, ZÄS 58,44 (89).

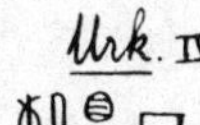 msḫn abode of gods, Urk. IV, 183,13; var. dets.  Pyr. 1180; [illegible] BD 226,4.

[illegible] msḫnt bearing-stool (?), JEA 22,106; birth-place (?), Pyr. 1185 (dets. [illegible], [illegible]); TR 38,12 (dets. [illegible]); breeding-place (?) of cattle, Pyr. 1183; abode of gods, Neferti, 57 ([illegible]); necropolis, Leyd. V 6 ([illegible]).

Msḫnt n. div. Meskhenet, goddess of birth, Urk. IV, 389, 5; var. det. Westc. 9, 23.

msḫtyw adze used in 'Opening the Mouth', Meir, III, p. 28, n. 2.

msḫtyw constellation of the Plough, var. , AEO I, 4*.

mss totter, Urk. IV, 614, 3.

mss tunic, JEA 11, 250, n. 8; det. Urk. IV, 1993, 2; mss n ꜥḥꜣ 'mail-shirt', 664, 3 (det.); 732, 1 (det.).

msšꜣt framework (?) of chariot, Urk. IV, 671, 15.

msḳ leather, Eb. 79, 7; Urk. IV, 671, 14.

msḳt Milky Way (?), Pyr. 279; Urk. V, 79, 15 (det.); 79, 17 (det.); BD 66, 15 (det.); cf. Komm. Pyr. I, 315; II, 20.

mskꜣ skin, Les. 74, 20; leather, L. to D. I, 2; cf. JEA 16, 148.

mski: — n mdt 'slander(?)', Pr. 11, 5.

msktt night-bark of sun-god, Urk. IV, 366, 6; varr. 1549, 4; BD 125, 8; 9, 8. Cf. Sethe, Lauf, 21.

msktw armlet, Urk. IV, 38, 14.16; 39, 3; var. 671, 14.

mstw offspring, Pyr. 935; varr. Urk. IV, 14, 16; 84, 16; cf. JEA 22, 134; fem. mstwt, Pyr. 341.

mstpt portable shrine, D. el. Geb. II, 7; varr. ibid. 10; Sin. B 194.

var. of msꜣdt 'nostril'.

msdt haunch, RB 120, 5; cf. AEO II, 243*.

msdmt black eye-paint, Sh. S. 163; Eb. 33, 3; Sm. 20, 17; var. Th. T. S. IV, 35; JEA 4, pl. 9, 12; Eb. 48, 19; abbr. BH I, 35.

msḏi vb. 4 inf. dislike, hate, Les. 72, 21; BM 614, 8; Pr. 16, 7 ( ); Urk. IV, 461, 5; 758, 9 (det.); VII, 14, 7; m msḏd 'unwillingly', Peas. B1, 99; m msḏd·i 'although I am unwilling', P. Kah. 36, 42; sim. Urk. IV, 969, 3; L. to D. V, 2 (n.).

msḏḏt what is hateful, of conduct, Siut, pl. 18, 13; var. Urk. IV, 504, 13.

msḏw rival, JEA 16, 71; 22, 43; fem. 22, 44.

msḏr ear M.u.K. 4,2; Eb. 92,3; 103,16; var. 92,5.

mšꜥ soldiers, army, Sh. S. 8.170; Sin. R 11; RB 57,1; infantry, Urk. IV, 15+6,10; gang of workmen, JEA 39,38; imy-r mšꜥ 'general', AEO I, 25*; 'foreman', JEA 39,38; imy-r mšꜥ wr 'generalissimo', AEO I, 21*; idnw n mšꜥ 'lieutenant-commander of the army', I, 25*; ꜥnḫ n mšꜥ 'private soldier', JEA 39,38. Var. Urk. IV, 323,15.

mšꜥ n. expedition, varr. , vb. make an expedition, GNS 29-30.

mšꜥ march, Qadech, 221.

mšꜥ kt shoulder-blade, Sm. 12,11; 16,18; 17,2.

mšw sword, Urk. IV, 894,9.

mšrw evening, TR 23,85; Westc. 3,10 (det.); var. M.u.K. vs. 3,3; Urk. IV, 1847,10; 117,2.

mšrwt evening-meal, Leb. 80; var. Pyr. 403.

mšdt ford, Urk. IV, 1310,18; var. Qadech, 351.

mk boat, Amarna, VI, 21,12.

mki guard, protect, P. Kah. 1,2; 2,9; Siut, pl. 4, 226; Eb. 37,4 (det.); look after horse, Urk. IV, 1282,11; mk ḥꜥw.f 'save his own skin', Adm. 9,3; 14,12; mk ḥw, var. ḥw mk, 'guarded and protected, JEA 22,178; 23,160.

mk protector, RB 57,8.

mkt (1) protection, M.u.K. vs. 4,7.8; RB 111,11: (2) correct position, of limbs, etc., BD 447,13; 463,7; Eb. 101,13 (dets.); proper station for standing, BD 473,16 (det.); with det. see under mkꜣt 'support'.

mkty protector, guardian, P. Kah. 1,10; var. dets. Urk. IV, 992,6.

mkꜣt support, pedestal, Urk. I, 184,17; varr. Sm. 2,7; 3,15.

see under mꜥkꜣ.

mkḥꜣ back of the head, Eb. 99,3; M.u.K. vs. 4,9.

mkḥꜣ turn the back to, ignore, Urk. IV, 971,5; eschew evil, RB 112,3; be neglectful, ḥr 'of', Urk. IV, 363,16. Cf. Äg. Stud. 2.

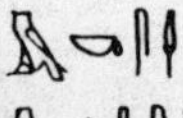 mks a sceptre, Pyr. 134. 1535.

 mks container for documents, ZÄS 53,101.

 mg3 skirmisher (?), JEA 5, 50, n. 6; varr.  Urk. IV, 1593, 4; 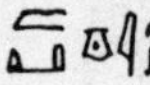 1660, 13.

 mt (mwt) vb. die, Sh. S. 123; Peas. B1, 95; Urk. IV, 690, 4: perish, of ship, Sh. S. 38: n. death, Sin. B 23. 203; Peas. B2, 122; Leb. 12. Varr. 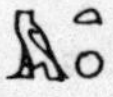 Urk. IV, 496, 4;  965, 13; 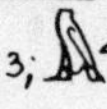 Sh. S. 123;  Cairo 20536;  20030.

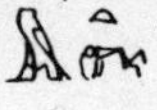 mt dead man, L. to D. IV, 5, cf. p. 12; Eb. 1, 4 (det. ); Adm. 2, 6; mortal man, Peas. B1, 95;  dead woman, L. to D. IV, 5; Eb. 1, 4; sim. 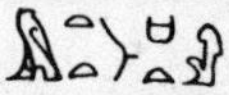 M. u. K. vs. 2, 8.

 mt (1) vessel, duct (anat.): (2) muscle, cf. P. Ed. Smith, 537; Barns, Ram. p. 33.

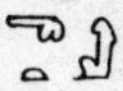 var. of mwt 'mother'.

 mt bolus, Eb. 33, 3. 16.

 mt strip (?) of cloth, in mt ifd 'a rectangular s.', Urk. IV, 1122, 15; varr. 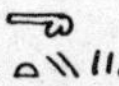 1122, 8;  1124, 12.

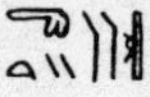 mty straightforward, precise, Pr. 7, 3 (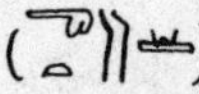); 11, 3; 18, 13 (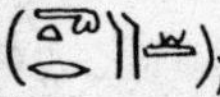); Les. 80, 20; 81, 2; Siut, pl. 19, 46; mty m3ˁ 'one truly p.', 'a s. man', Peas. B1, 96; Les. 69, 18; Urk. IV, 48, 13; 63, 12: exact: st. f mtt 'his e. seat', Urk. IV, 881, 11; sim. RB 114, 13; regular, of seasons, Les. 86, 19 (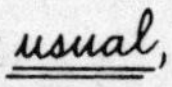); of offerings, Urk. IV, 769, 5; of festivals, 1299, 10; customary, of diet, Sm. 2, 2; usual, of form, Sm. 5, 22. Cf. GNS 85; JEA 38, 16, n. 6: n. exactitude, exactness: s n mty 'a man of e.', BM 562, 8; hrw... r mty 'the exact day of...', Urk. IV, 657, 2; irt ht nbt r mty irw 'doing everything exactly right', 1088, 6.

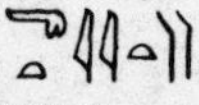 mtyt rectitude, Urk. IV, 994, 7.

 'testimony' see under mt(r)t.

 mtt exact moment, RB 78, 2.

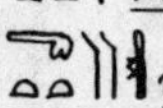 mtt: mtt (nt) ib 'affection (?)', GNS 75, n. 3; Pr. 5, 5.

 mty: — 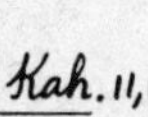 'controller of a (priestly) phyle', P. Kah. 11, 6; var. 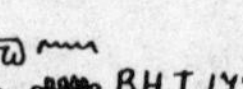 BH I, 17; used of the office, 'p.-controllership', P. Kah. 11, 18.

var. of mtrw 'flood'.

, varr. of mtr 'renown'.

mtwt (1) semen, Eb. 100,7; TR 17,3 (); fig. seed, progeny, Pyr. 145. 466 (); Urk. IV, 1546,2: (2) poison, Pyr. 443; M.u.K. 3,2; ill-will (?), Pr. 7,11.

var. of mṯwn 'arena'.

mtmt discuss, Urk. IV, 434,10; discussion, 364,14.

: for words so written see under mtn.

mtn reward (vb.), GNS 106.

mtnwt reward (n.), Urk. IV, 348,14; 377,8; varr. 369,1; Neferḥotep, 40; CT I, 29.

'precise', 'exact', see under mty.

mtr vb. trans. testify concerning, Sin. R 57 = B 33 (); Urk. IV, 1998,5 (); rarely with dative instead of direct obj., JEA 32, pl. 6, 33; exhibit virtues Urk. IV, 973,8; charge tasks, ḥr 'to', 484,7; instruct, 2156,8; 'witness-stela', JEA 20,54: intrans. be famous, renowned, Sin. B 221; BM 572.

mtr fame, renown, Sin. B 150; varr. Urk. IV, 1823,7; 1532,11; 1532,13.

mt(r)t testimony, JEA 24, 242.

mtrw witness, BD 95,3; RB 118,6; P. Kah. 11,24; Urk. IV, 974,2 (); mtrw m 'a witness in the eyes' = visible testimony, Urk. IV, 503,3.

mtrw flood, AEO I, 7*; var. Amarna, III, 29,13.

mtrt midday, Urk. IV, 839,12; 1542,11.

mt-ḥnt concubine (?), TR 2,11; var. 2,45.

mṯꜣ flout, vex; mṯꜣ ib r 'disagree with' s'one, Äg. Stud. 82 (e).

mṯꜣt land-heritage (?), Urk. IV, 132,8.

mṯꜣm a woman's garment, JEA 4, pl. 8, 3.

mṯwn arena, var. , ZÄS 34,41, n. 7; 43,74; Sphinx, 13,108.

mṯn road, way, Siut, pl. 11,10; Hamm. 114,11; RB 59,2; Urk. IV, 944,17; course, Peas. B1,3. 137; mtn 'obey', Siut, pl. 4,230; mdd mṯn 'be loyal', Les. 68,19; 81,8; tẖ mṯn 'who oversteps the path', Pr. 1,3.

mtn (< mṯn) sheikh (lit. 'path-finder'?), Sin. B 26 (det.). 276.

Mtn n. loc. Mitanni, var. , AEO I, 173*.

var. of mtnwt 'reward'.

mdw staff, CT I,10; TR 23,21; Urk. IV, 440,4; rod, JEA 42,13; mdw ỉꜣw 's. of old age' = supporter of aged parent, Pr. 5,3; P. Kah. 11,18; Bersh. I, 33.

mdw (?) in —— 'goldsmiths', RB 76,7.

mdw (mwdw) (1) vb. ult. inf. intrans. speak, Pr. 4,4; Sin. B2; Westc. 4,18; n 'to', Sin. B257; Sh. S. 15. 73-4; ḥr 'to', Urk. IV, 1542,15; mdw m 'speak against', ZÄS 29,49; 's. about', JEA 24,5, n.2; mdw ḥnꜥ 'dispute with', Leb. 5-6; šm r mdt ḥnꜥ 'go to law with', Urk. IV, 1114,17; rdỉ mdw ḏrp 'interpret writings', 165,15: trans. address s'one, Pyr. 758.

(2) n. speech, word, Sh. S. 18; Sin. B183; Peas. B1,75; Pr. 5,3; plea, JEA 17,59 (32); 'pronounce a spell', 'recitation', abbr. ; 'speech by', Gr. § 306,1. For wḏ-mdw, wḏꜥ-mdw, see under wḏ, wḏꜥ. —— Varr. Pyr. 1120; Urk. IV, 165,15; 1076,3; infin. Sin. B2; Urk. IV, 1114,17.

mdw-nṯr word of God, divine decree, Pyr. 333; Peas. B1,311; in pl. sacred writings, Bersh. II, p. 45; I, pl. 8; Louvre C14,7; Urk. IV, 860,7; written characters, script, Urk. IV, 121,2; 151,5.

mdt speech, words, Peas. B1,72. 98. 153; Pr. 5,6; 7,4; RB 115,1; talk, Urk. IV, 1080,11; mdt nt ḫꜣw mr(w) 'low-class t.', 120,3; 508,7; legal plea, Peas. B1,234; Urk. IV, 1114,12; 1115,11; written word, Les. 82,11; Pr. 15,9; Urk. IV, 966,1; content of letter, Urk. I, 128,5; matter, affair, Les. 70,1 (det.); Peas. B1,41; Westc. 12,7; Urk. IV, 28,11; 46,15; 1113,9; n mdt 'proverb', Peas. B1,19; 'affair', B1,37.

mdwty talker, Merikarēʿ, 23. 27 (M. text); speaker, Urk. IV, 2090, 7 ( ).

mds sharp, of knife, Pyr. 962; acute, of vision (ḥr), BD 328, 15; forceful, of character (bit), Les. 79, 7 ( ); firm-planted, of foot, Urk. IV, 18, 14 (dets.); mds m ib n nb⟨.i⟩ 'one considered acute by ⟨my⟩ lord', Les. 81, 22; mds ib 'spiteful', Urk. IV, 969, 1: trans. cut down quarry, Pyr. 402; BD 329, 1.

md num. 10, Gr. §§259 ff.; wr mdw šmʿw 'magnate of the Tens of U. E.', ZÄS 44, 18; 55, 66.

md deep, Dreambook, 8, 5; BD 458, 9 (det.); Sm. 2, 13 ( ).

mdt depth, Nav. Todtb. 149, 35; var. Urk. IV, 142, 10. Cf. JEA 4, 138.

mdwt bonds, Pyr. 2202.

mdt byre, varr. , , Gr. p. 524, V 19; AEO I, 90*.

mdt stalled cattle, Urk. IV, 72, 4; var. BH II, 30.

mdt oil, Urk. IV, 23, 3; 112, 15; 347, 4. 9; var. 1521, 13. Cf. JEA 23, 31.

mḏꜣt papyrus-roll, Urk. V, 170, 12; Eb. 30, 7 (det.); book: mḏꜣt nt ... 'the b. of ...' as title of text, BD 496, 13; šd mḏꜣt 'read a b. aloud', BD 496, 16; 497, 12; 'god's b.', Pyr. 267; sš mḏꜣt 'b.-scribe', Westc. 6, 21; letter, dispatch, Pyr. 491 ( ); Urk. I, 60, 16 ( ); 128, 5. 10; iry mḏꜣt 'letter-carrier', JEA 13, 75; var. Goyon, p. 55.

mḏꜣt chisel, varr. , ; ṯꜣw mḏꜣt 'sculptor', AEO I, 71*.

Mḏꜣw n. loc. Medja, region of Nubia, AEO I, 73*; II, 269*; ZÄS 83, 38; var. Urk. IV, 142, 5.

Mḏꜣw Medjay, people of Medja; later semi-military desert police, AEO, ZÄS locc. cit. Varr. J. Carn. 11. 12; Urk. IV, 994, 17.

mḏꜣb expel foes, BD 454, 3.

mḏꜣbt bailer of boat, Urk. V, 172, 15; TR 27, 28.

mḏꜣbt drainer for bilge (?), TR 27, 18. Distinct from last.

mḏr shut out storms, P. Kah. 2, 19; wall in treasure, Urk. IV, 1087, 10 ( ).

mḏḥ fillet, JEA 25, 218-9; varr. Louvre C 171; BM 828.

mdḥt *fillet* (?), Urk. IV, 38,15.

mdḥ *invest with insignia*, RB 112,4.

mdḥ *hew timber*, RB 60,14.16; 63,3; *stone*, Sin. L 2; *build ships*, RB 58,1; 60,11. Varr. Urk. IV, 56,13; 98,13; 778,14; 1632,7; BH I, 29.

mdḥ *hewer of stone*, Munich 4,7; *carpenter*, Cairo 20041 ( ); BM 223 ( ); 'head c.', BH I, 29. — N.B. D. el B. 108, Urk. IV, 503,13 = mdḥty nsw 'king's unguent-maker', cf. Wb. II, 190,11, Belegstellen.

mdṯft *chisel used in 'Opening the Mouth'*, JEA 18, 7, n.1.

mdd *press hard on*, JEA 29, 19; Sm. 4,16; *hit*: wd r mdd 'shoot to hit', RB 58,13; Urk. IV,1322,6 ( ); so also stỉ r mdd 1321,16; 1723,15; ỉw wḫз mdd·f 'the fool is hard-hit', Pr.17,4; *strike the mouth in funerary ritual*, Th.T.S. I,17 ( ); rnpt mdd ꜥ 'year of the stroke of a hand', i.e. of distress, Urk. IV, 1823,18; *practise a virtue*, Peas. B1, 212; Siut, pl. 17, 58; Urk. IV, 567,1; *obey orders*, 484,5; 1820,8; *press on*, m 'with' orders, 1822,5; mdd wзt 'be loyal, obedient to', Siut, pl. 4,221 ( ); Urk. IV, 208,7; so also mdd mtn, Les. 68,19; 81,8 ( ); Urk. IV, 86,6.

mddw: r mddw n ỉb n 'according to the will of', BM 614, 8.

〰〰〰

n *prep.* to, for (in dative); of direction *to persons*; *in* sun, dew, a period of time; *because*, Gr. §164; *belongs to*, §114,1; n·(ỉ) ỉmy 'belongs to (me)', etc. §§113, 3; 114,4; n-ntt 'because', §223.

n(y) *gen. adj.* of, belonging to, fem. , m.pl. , cf. Gr. p. 571.

ny *adv.* therefor, for it, Gr. §205,1; *because of it*, Urk. I, 88,1.2 ( ); *used after imperative*, JEA 38, 18, n.6. Cf. PSBA 40,5. As suff. pron. see below.

n *pron.* 1pl. we, us, our, rare var. , Gr. §§ 34. 43.

ny *suff. pron.* 1 dual we two, us two, our, Gr. §34; rarely for suff. 3 dual and pl. they, them, var. , Gr. §§ 34, Obs.3; 486, Obs. 2.

n neg. part. not; n wnt 'there is not'; n is 'indeed not,' 'if not,' 'unless', cf. Gr. p. 572; JEA 35, 33. Written for prep. , Gr. § 164.

nt crown of L.E., Les. 75, 12; Urk. IV, 292, 16; var. Sm. 18, 6.

Nt n. div. Neith, Urk. IV, 1276, 15; varr. D. el. B. 116; Caminos, Lit. Frag. pl. 4, 9.

nt water, Merikarēᶜ, 126; cf. Alphabet, 153.

n3 demonstr. neuter and pl. this, these; pl. art. the, Gr. §§ 110–2; 511, 3.

n3y.i possess. adj. pl. my; so also n3y.k, n3y.f, etc., Gr. § 113, 1.

n3t weaving-room, AEO II, 215*.

var. of ni3w 'ibex'.

n3w breeze, Urk. IV, 1519, 5.

ni vb. ult. inf. trans. drive away, rebuff, Pyr. 1230 d ( ); Peas. B2, 106; avoid, Pyr. 1230 c; throw down an enemy, Pyr. 972 ( ); turn back evil, Pyr. 246; get rid of wrong, Urk. V, 22, 15; parry missile, Peas. B1, 110 (, infin.); darken (?) sun, Pyr. 891 ( ): intrans. shrink (?), m 'from', Adm. 2, 10 ( ).

nit wrong-doing, Urk. V, 22, 5.

ni3w ibex, TR 22, 81; varr. Urk. IV, 741, 12; Sm. 16, 11; abbr. P. Ram. V, 24.

niw ostrich, Pyr. 469; varr. Sm. 4, 20; Urk. IV, 19, 10; Eb. 65, 6.

niw bowl, Eb. 21, 10; var. Siut, pl. 8, 308.

niw primaeval waters, var. , Gr. p. 530, W 24. See also nnw.

niwt lower heaven, BD 37, 13; var. 174, 14. See also nnt.

niwt city, town, Sin. B 66; P. Kah. 12, 4; Urk. IV, 6, 8; abbr. Les. 83, 6; used of Thebes, 'the City', Urk. IV, 979, 12; also niwt rst 'the Southern C.', 1112, 14; niwt nt nḥḥ 'c. of eternity = necropolis, Sin. B 171; L. to D. V, 1; Th. T. S. I, 30, F.

niwty local, of gods, Les. 87, 19; Siut, pl. 14, 85; pl. Les. 69, 8; Urk. IV, 48, 4.

niwtyw citizens, townsmen, BD 437,8; varr. RB 60,4; Bersh. I, 14, 4.

niwiw be glad(?), Urk. IV, 260, 1.

nyny greeting! Pyr. 1362 ( ); Urk. IV, 228,13 ( ); ir nyny 'make gr.', 567,3; 1063,9; ir nyny n 'greet', 347,11; so also ir nyny n ḥr, 1603,9; BD 4,4; 36,5; m nyny 'in greeting', JEA 39, 19; var. m irt nyny, BD 1,8.

nis intrans. vb. make summons, Urk. IV, 509,16; make invocation, 1835,9; nis n 'call to', 'summon', Sin. R 24; Sm. 8,12; Urk. IV, 497,13; so also nis r, Westc. 7,20; 8,12: trans. summon, L. to D. I, 2.13; D. el B. 107; Neferhotep, 12; ḥr rn 'by name', Urk. IV, 2158,14; invoke, Pyr. 786; Peas. B1, 269; dub: nis·tw·f m ḫm-ḫt 'he will be dubbed an ignoramus', Pr. 5,12; recite, Bersh. I, 14,9; BD 486,4; evoke the funeral repast, Sin. B 195; nis ṯnwt 'e. a number' = make a reckoning, Urk. IV, 367,16; 438,14; nis x ḫnt y 'divide x by y', JEA 15, 173, n.1: n. summons, Urk. IV, 430,11; 1827,11. — Var. Urk. IV, 1846,15.

nisw he who is summoned, Westc. 8,11; Urk. IV, 479,3; reckoner, Rhind, 67,2.

nik evil-doer, P. Ram. I, B iv, 4; var. BM 572,4.

nik a serpent-demon, Urk. IV, 445,1; BD 6,7; var. BD 9,7.

nitit impede, TR 2,26; var. 2,25. Cf. ZÄS 45,60.

nitit stammer, Sh. S. 17.

nꜥi vb. 3 inf. travel, Sh. S. 172; Urk. IV, 5,12; VII, 2,7: trans. traverse waterway, Urk. IV, 89,7; convey s'one, Pyr. 1423. 2100.

nꜥt expedition, Urk. IV, 662,1.

nꜥi vb. 3 inf. be lenient, JNES 14, 27.

nꜥyt mooring-post, Urk. IV, 1928,6.

nꜥꜥ smooth, Ch. B. Text, 41, n.5; undecorated, Urk. IV, 717,12; 1309,7 (abbr.): n. smoothness of complexion, Herdsm. 5: vb. mix smoothly, P. Ram. III, A 31.

nꜥw serpent, Urk. V, 175,17; TR 19,21.

nꜥr cat-fish, JEA 14, 28; 17, 67.

nw masc. plur. of gen. adj. n(y), q.v.

Nwt n. div. Nūt the sky-goddess, TR 20, 70; Sin. B 210 (det. !); Urk. IV, 366, 5; sky itself, Urk. VII, 3, 13; IV, 173, 11; RB 57, 10. Var. TR 20, 72.

cryptic writing of m-ḫnw 'within', Th. T. S. I, 1; p. 30, n. 1.

see below s.v. nnw.

nwt adze, var. , Pyr. 311. 315.

nw demonstr. pron. this, these, Gr. §§ 110. 511, 3.

nw time, Eb. 50, 20; P. Kah. 5, 34; CT I, 69 (); ꜥḥꜥw ꜥꜣ n rnpwt 'a lifetime of a long period of years', Urk. IV, 1543, 5; mk ḫpr 'behold, ages have gone by', Meir, III, 23; as adv. for a while, Pr. 15, 7; r nw 'at the proper time', Urk. IV, 1105, 2. 3; 1106, 9. 10; sim. TR 19, 16; BD 140, 5; 280, 8.

nw be weak, GNS 62; Barns, Ashm. p. 17.

nw weakness, Siut, pl. 6, 265; Peas. B1, 107.

nw see, look, varr. , , JEA 31, 113.

nw hunter, Urk. IV, 994, 15; AEO I, 89*; var. dets. Hamm. 126; ZÄS 60, 72; 65, pl. 7, 2.

nwt yarn for weaving, BH II, 13; Westc. 12, 13 (); cord, BD 393, 2 ().

nwi vb. 3 inf. care for, take care of, Leb. 35; Urk. IV, 21, 10; Pr. 7, 11; collect, assemble, GAS 67; JEA 22, 179.

nwꜣ earlier form of nw 'see', q.v.

nwꜣ adze, in — 'a. of Wepwawet' used in 'Opening the Mouth', Pyr. 13; var. Th. T. S. I, 17; cf. Meir, III, p. 28, n. 2.

nwy water, Sh. S. 85. 154; Urk. IV, 173, 10; 1064, 9; flood, Adm. 2, 6. 7; Leb. 65; pool, RB 77, 13. Varr. Sin. B 209; Urk. IV, 1064, 9; RB 77, 13

nwyt waters of canal, etc., Pyr. 1162; Urk. IV, 113, 17; V, 37, 10; pool, Hamm. 1 (); wave, Sh. S. 35. 104; Peas. B1, 59 ().

nwy vb. 3 inf. intrans. return, r 'to a place, Urk. IV, 148, 12; come, n 'to' s'one,

Cairo 1140: trans. bring back s'one, Urk. IV, 21, 13 ( ); 117, 2; 966, 11.

nwn dishevel, be dishevelled, TR 15, 3; BD 170, 11. 12; pull, m 'at' o's hair, Pyr. 1005 ( ).

nwḥ rope, Urk. V, 175, 16; BD 391, 10; Caminos, Lit. Frag. pl. 3, 3. 6; n nwḥ 'rod of cord' = 100 cubits, Gr. § 266, 2; band of metal, Pyr. 138 ( ).

nwḥ bind enemies, Urk. IV, 612, 14.

nwḫ trans. vb. heat, Eb. 49, 21; 66, 6; intrans. be scorched, Cairo 28050.

nws sheet (?) of metal, Urk. IV, 708, 4.

nwd turn aside, Eb. 19, 5; vacillate, Urk. IV, 1076, 8 (dets.); cf. JEA 9, 10, n. 4.

nwdw: nwdw 'swing awry', Peas. B1, 92; 'act perversely', B1, 107; 'make a travesty of', with m, B1, 100; m nwdw 'awry', B1, 262; Urk. IV, 386, 8 ( ); cf. JEA 9, 10, n. 4.

nwdt swaddling clothes of child, Eb. 49, 22-50, 1.

nwdw vb. 4 inf. (fem. infin.) squeeze out oil, Urk. IV, 347, 7; 352, 9.

nwdt ointment, Eb. 64, 9; var. 39, 19-20.

nwdw unguents, Urk. IV, 175, 5; 539, 4; 766, 10; varr. 853, 11; 1058, 14; JEA 4, pl. 8, 4; Bersh. II, 21, top, 8; (sic), BH II, 6.

nwdty ointment-maker, as god, Caminos, Lit. Frag. pl. 13, 2, 5.

nb tie, Sm. 20, 6.

nbt basket, Pyr. 557.

nbwt the isles of the Aegean, Urk. IV, 270, 8; 292, 7 ( ); 346, 6; imyw nbwt·sn 'the islanders', 613, 7; 616, 7; 'the (Aegean) islanders' or 'isles', AEO I, 206*; var. Urk. IV, 83, 7. See further Bull. 46, 125; 48, 107; ZÄS 81, 11.

nb lord, master, owner: 'the L.' = the king, Urk. IV, 17, 2 (det.); 1105, 12 (det.); P. Kah. 13, 28; m nb m sn n ḫnms r-pw 'as l., as brother or as friend', Pr. 9, 8-9 (det.); nb wr 'a great l.', Peas. B1, 92; nb pt 'l. of heaven', BD 2, 2-3; nb ḥmt 'possessor of a fare', Peas. B1, 172; nbw wꜥbwt 'owners of tombs', Adm. 7, 8; nb sꜣt 'master of prudence', Sin. B 48; nb ḥnt 'workman', Peas. B1, 111.

nb-ꜥnḫ 'Lord of Life' = sarcophagus, Urk. IV, 481, 4; 914, 1; var. det. 113, 9.

nb-r-ḏr 'Lord of All', ep. of gods, TR 21,106; BD 13,15; of king, Mill. 1,2 (det.).

nbwy 'The Two Lords' = Horus and Seth, Cairo 20539, b, 3; varr. Urk. IV, 16,9; 138,3.

nbt lady, mistress: nbt.f 'his m.', Cairo 20543,5 (det.); nbt tꜣ 'L. of the land' = queen, Urk. IV, 21,3; nbt pr 'housewife', Th. T. S. I, 9; nbt sbꜣw 'M. of the stars', Sin. B 271; nbt pt 'L. of heaven', B 270 (det.).

nbt-r-ḏr 'Mistress of All' ep. of queen, Sin. B 172; of goddess, Th. T. S. II, 29.

Nbt-ḥwt n. div. Nephthys, Westc. 9,23; var. D. el. B. 46.

Nbty 'The Two Ladies' = Nekhbet and Edjōyet, Les. 98,18; Urk. IV, 251,2; of the two crowns of Egypt, 85,12; 292,17; 566,1; in royal titulary, Gr. p. 73.

nbt lordship, authority of king, Urk. IV, 896,10.

nb any, every, all: nsw nb sḫm-ir.f nb 'any king or any potentate', Les. 98,16; ḫꜣst nbt 'every land', Sin. B 101; 'I wish I had šsp nb mnḫ some potent idol', Peas. Bt. 25; nṯrw nb 'all the gods', Sin. B 210; mnmnt nbt 'all kinds of cattle', R 16; wꜥ nb 'everyone', 'each one', 'each', Gr. § 103; wꜥ im nb 'everyone of them', Sh. S. 99; Sin. B 246; 'everyone', 'everybody'; sim. , Gr. § 103; 'everything', 'anything', ibid.

nbi vb. 3 inf. swim, Siut, pl. 15,22; varr. Urk. V, 55,5; 56,4.

nbw gold, Sin. B 193; BH I, 8,13 (); Urk. IV, 2,2; 'Mansion of g.' = goldsmith's workshop, Les. 75,13; 'Horus of g.', royal title, Gr. p. 73.

nbi vb. 3 inf. melt metal, BH II, 4 (); cast objects in metal, Les. 75,15; Urk. IV, 367,8 (); gild, 339,17 (); 913,12; model, fashion, JEA 6,299.

Nbw the Golden One, ep. of Ḥatḥōr, GNS 104.

nbyt gold collar, JEA 41, pl. 5, 98; var. Gr. p. 505, S 12.

nby goldsmiths, Urk. IV, 1149,17.

Nbt n. loc. Ombos near Ṭukh, AEO II, 28*; Nbty 'He of O.' = Seth, Urk. IV, 531,7; 1547,8.

Nbyt n. loc. Ombi, Kōm Ombo, AEO II, 5*.

nbꜣ carrying-pole, Westc. 7, 12; varr. Paheri, 3; Urk. IV, 2028, 14.16.

nbꜣ wig (?), P. Kah. 19, 50; 20, 48.

nbi n. flame, Hymnen, 9, 4; JEA 32, pl. 6, 3: intrans. vb. burn, Pyr. 2063; Eb. 41, 19.

nbit flaming one, ep. of uraeus, Hymnen, 4, 4.

nbit reed, P. Ram. III, A 31; Eb. 49, 2-3.

nbibi be hot, Sm. 16, 14.

nbnb guard, Urk. IV, 21, 12; var. 1381, 9.

nbs zizyphus, EHT 41*, n. 4; AEO I, 20; det. Bersh. II, 9.

nbd band doors with metal, Urk. IV, 168, 5; 387, 3 (dets.); 766, 1; 1709, 16 (det.).

nbd plait, wrap up, Caminos, Lit. Frag. p. 21.

nbdt tress of hair, BD 445, 14.

nbḏ destructive, Urk. I, 70, 16; 304, 17.

Nbd (< nbḏ) the Evil One, BD 47, 16; 284, 6; 299, 8.

nbdw-ḳd 'those of bad character', enemies of Egypt, AEO I, 134*.

npꜣ be wet, Cairo 28050.

npꜣt a cake or loaf, Siut, pl. 1, 39.

npꜣpꜣ flutter, P. Ed. Smith, 168.

npnpt hem, JEA 22, 40.

npr grain, Pyr. 1065; as god, Mill. 2, 12. Varr. Urk. IV, 469, 11; 925, 6; 1183, 7; RB 112, 7.

nprt brim of well, RB 77, 15; flat slab, basis, JEA 5, 122; var. det. TR 20, 62.

nphw iliac region, JEA 20, 168.

npd slaughter (vb.), Pyr. 746; CT I, 123; var. TR 28, 7.

npdt sharp knife, CT I, 160.

nf demonstr. that, those, varr. , Gr. §110; nfꜣ pw 'thus it was', Adm. 12, 3; mi nf imy-ḥꜣt 'as was described above', P. Kah. 7, 60-1.

nf wrong, wrong-doing, Leb. 129; L. to D. III, 6 (); m nf 'wrongfully', GAS. 44.

nfy wrongfully, varr. , , L. to D. II, 6, n.

nft breath, wind, var. ; cf. P. Ed. Smith, 541.

nfyt fan, Lac. Sarc. II, 16; varr. II, 36; II, 23.

nfw skipper of boat, P. Kah. 22, 13.15; fig. Urk. IV, 1076, 17; later sailor, AEO I, 94*.

nf3 blow, m 'out of' nose, CT I, 338.

nfꜥ remove, GNS 14.

nfnfn unroll (?), Sm. 16, 19.

nfr (1) of appearance, beautiful, fair, M. u. K. 3, 5; Westc. 5, 5; Urk. IV, 219, 2; 329, 2; kindly, of face, ZÄS 53, 115; JEA 39, 53: (2) of quality, good, fine, goodly, Sin. B 28. 81. 203; Peas. R 35; B1, 65. 318-9; Leb. 62; Urk. IV, 767, 14; necessary, JEA 25, 125; nfr ḥr ib 'pleasing', Pr. 7, 1: (3) of character or repute, good, fair, Urk. IV, 119, 8; 481, 2; Sh. S. 159; Pr. 5, 14; kind: nfr.s r itrw.s mty 'she was kinder than at her regular seasons', Les. 86, 18 (): (4) of condition, happy, well, good, Sin. B 31. 76. 205; Pr. 16, 5; hrw nfr 'happy day', 'holiday', Westc. 3, 9-10; Leb. 68; nfr n 'it is well with', Gr. § 141; m ꜥḥꜥw nfr 'in due time', Westc. 7, 22; well-supplied: nfr špss 'one w.-s. with good things', Les. 79, 20; sim. 79, 23; lawful, JEA 16, 171: (5) in fixed expressions: 'good' (n.), Sin. B 74-5; Pr. 5, 1; Peas. B1, 288; Urk. IV, 126, 14 (); 'goodness', Leb. 109; Peas B1, 310-11; Mill. 1, 11; bw nb nfr 'all good things', Westc. 6, 15; 11, 20; Urk. IV, 878, 10; as comment 'all well and g.', P. Kah. 31, 5; m bw nb nfr 'in very g. order', JEA 35, 62; 'good' (n.), Les. 80, 19; 'a happy event', Sin. B 160; Urk. IV, 446, 7; 'a good deed', 181, 17; sp.f nfr n wn mꜣꜥ 'his own right cause', Peas. B1, 203. 293; 'a good beginning', Les. 83, 9; Bersh. II, 8, 7; r tp nfr 'successfully', Les. 70, 2: (6) adv. happily, well, Gr. § 205, 4; mḥ nfr 'render full account', Peas. B1, 251.

nfrt good things, Sh. S. 116; BM 614, 5 (); good, what is good, Peas. B1, 152; BM 614, 8; Les. 69, 20; Urk. IV, 182, 2; 453, 11; 993, 10; kindness, Bull. 30, 99.

nfr beauty, Urk. IV, 278, 14; 361, 9; 611, 6; good, Adm. 15, 14; kindness, Bull. 30, 99; goodness, Siut, pl. 17, 58; Urk. IV, 567, 1; happiness, good fortune, Mill. 1, 3; Pr. 15, 12; Urk. IV, 54, 14; cf. Stud. Griff. 69; do s'thing *m nfr sp 2* 'very well', Les. 86, 21.

nfrw beauty, Les. 71, 20; Urk. IV, 297, 6; 620, 6; Hymnen, 1, 2; goodness, RB 115, 5; Siut, pl. 13, 31.

nfrw young men of army, Urk. IV, 1546, 11; recruits (also *ḥwnw nfrw*), JEA 39, 35 ff. Varr. Urk. IV, 1017, 8; 1018, 6; 924, 12.

nfrwt fair women, Westc. 5, 3; var. JEA 4, pl. 8, 3.

nfrt cattle, Urk. IV, 1023, 12; varr. 1161, 3; 407, 17; 132, 9.

nfr crown of U. E., Urk. IV, 13, 3; 550, 14.

nfr-ḥꜣt diadem, Hymnen, 11, 4; BM 101.

nfr-ḥḏt crown of U. E., Neferhotep, 11; Urk. IV, 296, 3; var. 192, 4.

Nfr-tm n. div. the lotus-god, Siut, pl. 16, 24; var. Cairo 20093, c 1.

nfr zero; *nfr n* 'not'; *nfr pw* 'not', 'there is not', Gr. § 351.

nfryt end, bottom: *r nfryt.s* 'to its e.', Urk. IV, 1813, 20; *ỉꜣt nbt ḥꜣt r ỉꜣt nt nfryt* 'every office from highest to lowest', 1113, 1; sim. 1107, 12; *nfryt r* 'down to', Gr. § 179.

nfryt tiller-rope, Peas. B1, 158. 164.

nfrw ground-level, base, JEA 4, 110, n. 1.

nfrw end: — *grḥ* 'e. of the night', RB 125, 14.

nfrw end, back part of building, JEA 22, 178.

nfrw deficiency, Urk. IV, 1114, 8.

nft slacken bow; detach, loosen (dets.), JEA 22, 40.

nftft leap (vb.), Sin. B 4; cf. GNS 14.

nm who?, var. , Gr. § 496.

nmt slaughter-house, Urk. V, 56, 16; varr. 55, 13; (pl.), 79, 13.

 nm(w) dwarf, varr. , , JEA 24, 186; GNS 70.

 nm go wrong, of plans, Pr. 16, 13; rob, with n, BD 250, 16; steal, with m, Urk. IV, 1031, 11 (det. ).

 nmw vats, Urk. IV, 687, 12.

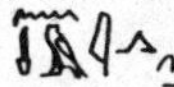 nmi intrans. vb. travel, Urk. IV, 268, 3: trans. traverse, GNS 16. Varr.  Pyr. 1260; 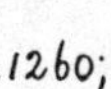 CT I, 53;  Sin. B8;  R32.

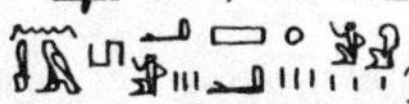 nmiw-šꜥ Sandfarers, Beduin, Sin. R43; varr. 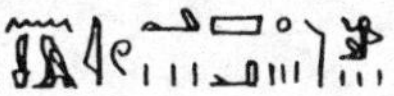 B73; 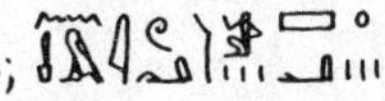 B292.

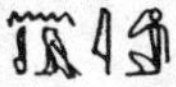 nmi shout, of people, Sin. B141; low, of cattle, B24. Var.  R49.

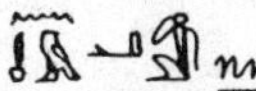 nmꜥ (1) be one-sided, partial, Peas. B2, 104; Les. 79, 19; dets.  Siut, pl. 5, 249;  Urk. IV, 971, 14: (2) question (?) (vb.), Urk. I, 78, 2 (); Leb. 2.3; cf. JEA 42, 30 (1).

 nmꜥ go to sleep, Amarna, I, 36, 2.

 nmwt net, BH I, 34.

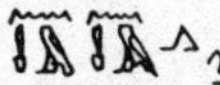 nmnm quake, quiver, Pyr. 393. 721. 1771; go to and fro, 1120; BD 289, 5.

 nmḥ intrans vb. be poor, Amarna, II, 7, 11: trans. deprive, m 'of', RB 116, 12; deduct, m 'from', 117, 2: n. poverty, Amarna, IV, 35; humility, Urk. IV, 2013, 13.

 nmḥ(y) orphan, Peas. B1, 62; RB 116, 12; Les. 79, 14; 82, 4; later private person, freeman of low degree, JEA 19, 21; P. Wilbour, 206. Varr. 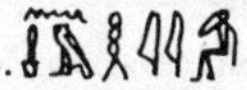 Urk. IV 2143, 15;  PSBA 18, pl. foll. p. 196, l. 15;  (pl.), Les. 82, 4.

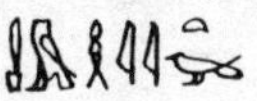 nmḥyt free-woman (?), P. Kah. 9, 4.

 nms royal head-cloth, Urk. IV, 1278, 1; abbr.  1286, 17.

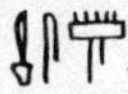 nms clothe with the head-cloth, Th. T. S. I, 17.

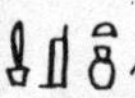 nmst kind of jar, Urk. IV, 22, 8; 23, 2; var.  1870, 1.

 nmt stride over, traverse, Pyr. 325 (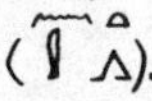). 854. 889 (). 1612; cf. GNS 16.

 nmtt stride, Pyr. 853. 2120; BD 140, 3; pl. Sin. R81; Siut, pl. 4, 219; TR 19, 33; of pose of statue, Louvre C14, 10; journeys, Les. 71, 14; Urk IV, 13, 9; 890, 10; movements, Pyr. 852;

CT I, 52; Sin. B 105; actions, Pr. 17, 2; legal procedure, Pr. 8, 3; BM 572, 9; Urk. IV, 967, 7; nmtwt nt šmt 'order of march', 652, 9; m nmtwt w3ḥt 'with enduring zeal', Urk. VII, 15, 21. Varr. pl. Pr. 10, 4; BM 572, 9; Urk. VII, 15, 21; Les. 71, 14.

nmtyw: ḫfty — 'intruding(?) enemy', var. f. ḫftt, M. u. K. vs. 6, 3.

nn demonstr. pron. this, these, var., Gr. §§ 110-2. 511, 3.

nn neg. part. not, cf. Gr. p. 574; JEA 35, 31.

nny be weary, inert, BD 29, 9; 162, 13 (); drag, of foot, Sm. 4, 14 (); dribble, of fluid, Sm. 10, 22; settle, of flood-water, P. Ed. Smith, 332.

nnw weariness, inertness, of dead, Leb. 45; var. RB 111, 15.

nnyw inert ones = the dead, Adm. 7, 7; varr. Sin. B 195; Leb. 63.

nnw primaeval waters, Gr. p. 530, W 24; as god, Sethe, Amun, § 127. Varr. Pyr. 1078; Urk. V, 170, 13; BD 7, 11. See also nnw.

nnt lower heaven, Pyr. 166; varr. 446; 1691. See also niwt.

nnm vb. err, Peas. B1, 96; Pr. 7, 12; 8, 1; go wrong, of plans, Pr. 16, 13: n. error, Pr. 17, 3. Varr. Pt. (L. II), 3, 15.

nnšm spleen, AEO II, 245*; varr. BH II, 15; Bersh. I, 32.

nnk belongs to me, Gr. § 114, 3; after infin. on my part, § 300, end; cf. JEA 20, 15.

nrt vulture, Pyr. 568; varr. TR 5, 3; Sm. 18, 10.

nri intrans. vb. fear, n s'one, Les. 64, 10; RB 110, 14 (dets.): trans. overawe, Urk. IV, 2081, 19 ().

nrw fear, dread (n.), P. Kah. 1, 5; disturbance (?), Peas. B1, 30. Varr. Les. 64, 6; Peas. B1, 30; Urk. IV, 386, 7; 807, 5; RB 110, 7.

nrw terrible one, Urk. V, 70, 14.

nr charge, m-s3 'after' enemy, Urk. IV, 1302, 11; det. 1311, 7.

nri vb. 3 inf. protect, Urk. IV, 268, 16; infin. 362, 1

nr-ỉḥw(?) ox-herd, Les. 69,17; BD 439, 4-5 (with det.).

nr(ỉ) time; return of the year, Caminos, L.-Eg. Misc. 380; nr(ỉ) 'periodically', Id. Lit. Frag. p. 33.

nh escape death, CT I, 284.

nht shelter, refuge, P. Kah. 2, 16; Urk. IV, 972, 9.

nht magical protection, M. u. K. vs. 5, 8.

nhw protection of king's arm, Les. 68, 22.

nht (1) sycamore, Urk. IV, 73, 11; Sm. 16, 8: (2) tree in general, Urk. IV, 73, 8. 15; 345, 12; 1113, 3.

nhy some, a little, a few, with n, Westc. 12, 26; Peas. B1, 48 (); Adm. 7, 3; Urk. IV, 1302, 9 (); with m, Eb. 47, 18.

nhw loss, Peas B1, 71; Les. 86, 15; Sh. S. 7-8; Urk IV, 7, 5; nhw 'show less of' a bad quality, Peas. B1, 178. Varr. Urk. IV, 614, 2; Les. 79, 20.

nhp pulsate, Eb. 84, 14; det. ⊙ 80, 18.

nhp copulate, BD 224, 2.

nhp rise early in the morning, Urk. IV, 1075, 11; 1390, 10; 2120, 12.

nhpw early morning, Les. 75, 13; GAS 75; var. Eb. 50, 20.

nhp mourn, ZÄS 47, 163.

nhp care, hr 'for', GAS 103; det. Urk. IV, 2157, 14.

nhm shout (vb.), CT I, 144; Les. 78, 18 (det.); Sin. B 201; Urk. IV, 305, 4; 309, 8; thunder, of sky, Pyr. 1150. 1771.

nhm dance for joy (?), Les. 79, 10.

var. of inhmn 'pomegranate'.

nhmhm roar, Pyr. 1150; thunder, BD 105, 16 (det.).

nhnhꜣ quake, Hamm. 114, 7.

nhry noble of Nahrin, AEO I, 173*.

Nhrn n. loc. Nahrin, varr. , , AEO I, 171* ff; Urk. IV, 9, 10.

nhsi (nhzi) vb. 4 inf. wake, Cairo 20520, 32; varr. Pyr. 126; TR 12, 7; Mill. 2, 2.

nhs hippopotamus, Th. T. S. I, 1, 5.

nhdhd throb, P. Ed. Smith, 168.

nḥi vb. 3 inf. pray for, Merikarēʿ, 38; Urk. IV, 972, 14; 2116, 6; GAS 86: n. prayer, GNS 61. Var. Bersh. II, 7.

nḥt prayer, Urk. IV, 367, 8; Adm. 5, 6.

nḥ3 shake (?), Urk. IV, 1818, 5; Eb. 39, 9-10.

nḥ3t palpitations (?) of heart, Eb. 39, 12.

nḥ3 contrary, perverse, GAS 48; alarming, Sm. 2, 3-4 ( ); terrible, Barns, Ram. p. 6; abnormal (?), Sm. 3, 1; nḥ3 n inr 'dry rock (?)', RB 77, 13 ( ).

nḥ3-ib sad man, P. Ram. I, B i, 15.

nḥ3t-ib sadness, Adm. 12, 3; Urk. IV, 1578, 5 ( ); a sad matter, Leb. 56-7.

nḥ3 dangerous waters, Caminos, Lit. Frag. pl. 12, 1.

nḥbt neck, Sin. B 138-9; Sm. 1, 20. 21; Eb. 1, 4.

nḥb harness, yoke; appoint; combine attributes (k3w), JEA 33, 23, n. b; 36, 7, n. 2; Rev. d'ég. 10, 14, n. 3; provide, Merikarēʿ, 86; Urk. IV, 28, 7; requisition, Ch. B. I, p. 35, n. 1.

nḥbw yoke-oxen, Urk. VII, 15, 17. (sic)

Nḥbw-k3w the god N. and his festival, Rev. d'ég. 10, 14, n. 3.

nḥbt bud of lotus, Urk. IV, 954, 1; dets. TR 22, 63; JEA 16, pl. 17, M.

nḥbt lotus-bud sceptre, Cairo 28036; var. Pyr. 134.

nḥp potter's wheel, Adm. 2, 8.

nḥm take away, carry off, Sin. B 104; Peas. B1, 11. 28. 296; assume a dignity or office, CT I, 159. 161; save, rescue, Sh. S. 18; Sin. B 97. 203; Adm. 13, 3; P. Kah. 2, 16; 3, 8; withdraw o'self, Pyr. 1098.

nḥmn non-encl. part. *surely, assuredly,* Gr. §§ 119, 6; 236.

nhn rejoice, Pyr. 1233; CT I, 154; Urk. IV, 259, 9.13.

nhr resemble, Urk. IV, 860, 3; var. Pyr. 1693.

nhr a loaf or cake, D. el. B. 110.

nḥḥ eternity, JEA 39, 110; *s n nḥḥ* 'a man of e.' = an immortal, Peas. B1, 95; *niwt nt nḥḥ* 'city of e.' = necropolis, Sin. B171; *kзt nḥḥ* 'everlasting work', Urk. IV, 1295, 1; as adv. *for ever,* Cairo 20518; so also *r nḥḥ,* Peas. B2, 126; *n nḥḥ,* Urk. IV, 198, 9; *ḥr nḥḥ,* 593, 5; *nḥḥ ḏt* 'for e. and e.', P. Kah. 32, 16; so also *nḥḥ n ḏt,* Cairo 20543, 15; *m nḥḥ n ḏt,* Urk. IV, 283, 13; *nḥḥ ḥnꜥ ḏt,* RB 77, 6; *r nḥḥ ḥnꜥ ḏt,* Urk. IV, 1295, 7; *ḏt r nḥḥ,* 491, 10; *ḏt nḥḥ,* 458, 2; *imt nḥḥ* 'which endures for ever', 299, 2; 1150, 8. Varr. Urk. IV, 198, 9; 499, 15; 389, 17; RB 77, 6; BH I, 26, 176.

nḥsy Nubian, Urk. IV, 84, 1; varr. 743, 4; Les. 84, 20; I. Carn. 3; cf. JEA 7, 121; ZÄS 83, 38; fem. *nḥsyt,* M. u. K. 2, 8; Urk. IV, 743, 4.

nḥḏt tooth, Sm. 3, 10-11; P. Kah. 6, 26 ( ); Sb. 58, 21; *tusk,* Urk. I, 137, 10; Sh. S. 164 (pl.); Urk. IV, 418, 14 ( ).

nḫ vb. succour, protect, Urk. IV, 48, 16; 191, 1; 1078, 6; RB 57, 11: n. *protection,* Urk. IV, 84, 4. Var. Cairo 20539, I, 4.

nḫ miserable, Peas. B1, 117. 204.

nḫwt complaint, lamentation, Peas. B1, 29; Leb. 148; Adm. 2, 4; 3, 14.

nḫ youthful, BH I, 25, 114; *small (?), brief (?),* of sufferings, Caminos, Lit. Frag. pl. 6, 3, 15.

nḫt youth (abstract), Les. 72, 12.

nḫ3 pendulous, Pyr. 2003.

nḫ3w fish-shaped pendant, JEA 11, 212.

nḫ3 knife, BD 448, 12.

nḫ3ḫ3 n. *flail,* Pyr. 1535; varr. BD 482, 10; 13, 11: adj. *pendulous,* Pyr. 729.

nẖꜣẖꜣ ruffle (?) hair, Barns, Ram. p. 22.

nḫb open mine, Sinai, 47. 53; assign property, n 'to', Urk. IV, 2120, 10.

nḫb fresh land, Urk. IV, 1611, 12; cf. P. Wilbour, 28. 178.

nḫb stipulation, Urk. IV, 835, 9.

nḫbt titulary, Urk. IV, 80, 11; 270, 4; varr. 101, 3; 2118, 11.

Nḫb n. loc. El-Kāb, var. , Paheri, 1; cf. AEO II, 8*.

Nḫbt n. div. Nekhbet, Gr. p. 73; AEO II, 8*; var. Urk. IV, 251, 11.

nḫbḫb (1) draw back door-bolt, Pyr. 194; throw open doors, 1361: (2) crepitate, of broken bones, P. Ed. Smith, 254. Var. Sm. 15, 7-8.

Nḫn n. loc. Nekhen, Hieraconpolis, AEO II, 7*; varr. , Pyr. 276; Urk. VII, 65, 1; IV, 1126, 6; BD 235, 1.

Nḫny of Nekhen, Nekhenite, Pyr. 295; varr. ibid.; pl. 1013; Siut, pl. 3, 173.

nḫn shrine, Pyr. 717.

, … varr. of mḫnmt 'carnelian (?)'.

nḫn young, Pyr. 1214; Urk. I, 78, 1; youthful (?), BH I, 26, 189 (det.); X nḫn(i) 'X the younger', Cairo 20058. 20105.

nḫnw child, Bersh. I, 15; varr. RB 111, 16; Adm. 16, 1.

nḫnw youth (abstract), Urk. IV, 131, 5; 993, 16; var. 580, 17.

nḫḫ var. of nẖꜣẖꜣ 'flail'.

nḫḫ vb. be old, CT I, 81m; BD 33, 7: n. old age, CT I, 81o.

nḫt strong, Urk. IV, 85, 8; 102, 12; Peas. B1, 116; stiff, hard, Eb. 51, 21; 52, 2; Sm. 3, 17. 20; victorious, Les. 82, 9 (abbr.); Urk. IV, 654, 7; 809, 1 (abbr.); nḫt ib 'confident', Urk. I, 133, 17; nḫt ꜥ 'strong of arm', Sh. S. 100; 'adult', JEA 16, 199; as n. 'champion', Urk. IV, 1307, 9; 1546, 11; nḫt ḥr 'violent', Peas. B1, 167; Leb. 107; nḫt ḫrw 'reis (?)', Goyon, p. 83, but cf. JNES 18, 30.

nḫt strong man, champion, Sin. B 51. 93. 109.

nḫtt (1) victory, Urk. IV, 189, 8: (2) stiffness, Eb. 82, 7; 84, 1.

nḫtw (1) strength, Pyr. 290; Urk. IV, 161, 17: (2) victory, 593, 11; 659, 13; 1004, 4.9: (3) hostages, 690, 3.

nḫ fluid of body, P. Ed. Smith, 172.

nḫnm one of the seven sacred oils, D. el B. 110.

ns tongue, P. Kah. 1, 7; Peas. B1, 131.166; Urk. IV, 238, 2; ns 'speech', 993, 6.

nst seat, throne, Pyr. 301.906; varr. Sin. B 207; Urk. IV, 1197, 17; 1285, 10; ḫrp nsty 'Controller of the Two Seats', JEA 24, 85.

ns flame, Pyr. 276; D. el B. 114; BD 369, 9. Cf. nsr below.

nsꜣ kind of knife, CT I, 123.

nsywt javelin, var. GNS 52; det. Sin. R 160.

nswt flame, Pr. 12, 2; RB 54, 8.

nsw (< ni-swt) King of Upper Egypt, Pyr. 724; Les. 69, 13 (det.); cf. Gr. p. 50, n. 1; king, Les. 68, 13; Sin. B 270 (det.); Urk. IV, 1546, 13; nsw-bit 'K. of U. and L. E.', Gr. p. 73. Varr. Urk. IV, 194, 10; 95, 17; VII, 59, 9; Pyr. 814.

nsyw kings, Westc. 12, 11; varr. Urk. IV, 15, 8; 344, 14; 1679, 16; specifically of U. E., BD 300, 8.

nsy be king, Mill. 1, 2; Urk. IV 58, 16; 236, 5.

nsyt kingship, Sin. B 186; Westc. 10, 13; varr. RB 76, 12; Urk. IV, 1276, 19; 215, 4; 15, 1.

nsyw priests of Arsaphes (?), JEA 11, 214.

nsb lap up, Urk. V, 76, 9; BD 289, 1; lick, Urk. IV, 236, 14; 239, 8.

nspw wounds, BD 106, 1; 204, 11; 302, 8; var. Lac. Sarc. II, 29.

nsr, see pr-nsr.

nsrt (nzrt) royal serpent, Pyr. 194; Hymnen, 3, 2; varr. Urk. IV, 8, 17; 80, 12.

nsr flame (n.) Pyr. 295; var. ibid.; see also above.

nsrt flame (n.), BD. 58, 14; 99, 1.

nsrf flame (vb.), of uraeus, r 'against' king's enemies, Urk. IV, 390, 15; be inflamed, of wounds, Sm. 9, 20; 14, 2; 17, 11.

nsr anger (?), Pr. 12, 2.

nsr anoint injury, Sm. 2, 22.

nss do damage, n 'to', Urk. VII, 53, 12.

nsty kind of bread, Urk. IV, 1157, 14.

nstyw shrub alkanna tinctoria, ZÄS 64, 51.

nš expel, m 'from', Urk. I, 100, 8 (det.); Peas. B1, 97; ḥr 'from', Merikarēʿ, 47 (dets.); drive apart husband and wife, Pr. 10, 3; put away a woman, Pr. 15, 7.

nšw (1) issue from wound, P. Ed. Smith, 390: (2) pemphigus, Barns, Ram. p. 25.

nšwt mucus, Eb. 99, 6.

nšt hairdresser, Sh. S. S. I, 22.

nšy dress hair, BD 130, 3; 242, 1.

nš3 grains of sand, Eb. 41, 19.

nšw a vessel, BD 494, 5; JEA 23, 186, n. 3.

nšp pant, Peas. B1, 101.

nšmt sacred bark of Osiris, Les. 68, 6; 71, 8; Urk. IV, 1513, 20; abbr. 209, 16.

nšmt green felspar, BD 406, 3; var. dets. 406, 11; cf. Ch. B. Text, 113, n. 10.

nšmwt scales of fish, M. u. K. 1, 2; varr. Caminos, Lit. Frag. pl. 1, 2, 8; det. 2, 2, 2; abbr. in 'overseer of horn, hoof, feather and scale', Les. 69, 14.

nšmt green felspar, BD 406, 11; var. det. 406, 3; cf. Ch. B. Text, 113, n. 10.

nšni rage (vb. 4 inf. and n.), P. Kah. 2, 19; Les. 68, 18; Urk. IV, 1078, 2; 1301, 17; storm, foul weather, Sh. S. 31; Pr. 12, 8; disaster, Sm. 19, 1. 2. Dets. Urk. V, 34, 5; 34, 10; 34, 16; var. Herdsm. 21.

nšnt coll. (?) the doomed (?), Hymnen, 12, 3.

nšnš tear up documents, ZÄS 49, 117.

nkˁwt notched sycamore-figs, var. ..., Act. Or. 6, 288; Anc. Eg. 1928, 65.

nḳwt moisture, P. Ed. Smith, 497.

nḳm be bald, JEA 24, 50.

nḳm suffer, be afflicted, JEA 16, 21.

nḳmt affliction, JEA 16, 19, 6.

nḳr sift, Eb. 60, 11; Sm. 21, 13; BH II, 6.

nḳrw sieve, Sm. 21, 13.

nk copulate, Urk. V, 16, 4; RB 117, 1.

nk3 meditate on, think about, with m, Urk. IV, 46, 16; Adm. p. 101 (...); Caminos, Lit. Frag. pl. 1, 2, 8; with ḥr, Urk. IV, 1381, 8 (...); take counsel, ḥnˁ 'with', 434, 8.

nk3t plot, Urk. IV, 138, 14.

nkn sword, Urk. IV, 1612, 7.

nkn n. harm, injury, BD 402, 1 (dets. ...); 406, 6; Urk. IV, 1033, 5; ir nkn 'do h.', CT IV, 69. 73; wd nkn 'do h.', Urk. IV, 401, 16; 'execute sentence', Westc. 8, 15-16, cf. JEA 22, 42; rdi nkn 'do h.', BD 202, 3-4; dr nkn 'get rid of ill', Les. 75, 14: vb. be injured, BD 192, 8.

nkt n.m. some, a little, Eb. 55, 1; P. Kah. 34, 52; pl. ... n wšwt 's. of the fragments', Sm. 8, 15-16; something, Urk. IV, 1091, 9; 1108, 9; piece, of wood, Sm. 20, 5; profit, advantage, P. Wilbour, 85, n. 5.

ngi vb. 3 inf. break open, break up, GAS 50; varr. ... Adm. 6, 10; ... Eb. 49, 12.

ngt breach in dam, Peas. B1, 277.

ngyt breach (of law), crime, Leyd. V 88.

ngw loss, Urk. IV, 1344, 16.

ng3w long-horned bull or ox, Sin. B120; var. ... Rekh. 6.

ngb turn aside, divert, Pr. 7, 9; 9, 10.

ngmgm conspire, Urk. IV, 1312, 8.

ngsgs overflow, Urk. IV, 951, 13; 1143, 9 ( ); Paheri, 3.

ngg cackle, of goose, BD 179, 10; 493, 12; screech, of falcon, Pyr. 1959.

nty who, which, cf. Gr. p. 546.

ntt conj. that, loc. cit.

var. of nitit 'impede'.

nt-ꜥ n. custom, habit, Westc. 3, 2. 11; rite, ritual, Urk. IV, 450, 13 ( ); JEA 32, pl. 6, 7; Les. 71, 7; routine, Urk. IV, 2158, 3; 2160, 13; duty, 2160, 19; execution of task, Les. 76, 8; rsyt nt-ꜥ 'the regular watch', RB 61, 10; nt-ꜥ.sn n ṯnw rnpt 'their yearly due', Urk. IV, 700, 7. 8: vb. organize, JEA 39, 20 (3 b).

nt-pw it is the fact that..., Gr. §§ 190, 2; 494, 3.

ntb scorch, parch, GNS 154.

ntf (1) indep. pron. 3 m. sg. he, Gr. § 64; belongs to him, § 114, 3: (2) for nty.f 'which he...', § 200, 2.

ntf besprinkle, Peas. B1, 154. 264; Hymnen, 15, 3; Urk. IV, 1483, 12.

nts indep. pron. 3 f. sg. she, var. , Gr. § 64.

ntsn indep. pron. 3 pl. they, var. , Gr. § 64.

ntš besprinkle, Eb. 97, 16; P. Kah. 7, 40.

ntk (1) indep. pron. 2 m. sg. thou, Gr. § 64; belongs to thee, § 114, 3: (2) for nty.k 'which thou...', § 200, 2.

ntṯ indep. pron. 2 f. sg. thou, var. , Gr. § 64.

ntṯn indep. pron. 2 pl. you, var. , Gr. § 64.

nṯr god, Sin. B 43; Sh. S. 113; Pr. 6, 8; used of king, Sin. R 6; Urk. IV, 20, 14; 920, 6; 'the good g.', ep. of king, Misc. Acad. Berol. 50. 52; 'the great g.', ep. of god or (usually) dead king, L. to D. 11. Varr. Eb. 1, 4; Urk. IV, 246, 2; pl. 1847, 3.

nṯrt goddess, Herdsm. 23; Eb. 1, 4 ( ); Urk. IV, 408, 13.

nṯr godhood, divinity, Urk. IV, 141, 4.

nṯrt divine eye, BD 491, 10; JEA 5, 32.

nṯry divine, Urk. IV, 114, 3; 481, 9; 1302, 11; sacred, 398, 10. Varr. 267, 11; 398, 10; D. el. B. 34.

nṯrw sacred pole, ZÄS 68, 13.

nṯry magic cord, M. u. K. vs. 6, 2.

nṯrty adze used in 'Opening the Mouth', Meir, III, p. 28, n. 2.

nṯryt natron (?), Caminos, Lit. Frag. pl. 10, 3, 4-5; var. cf. P. Ed. Smith, 412.

nṯtw bonds, Pyr. 349; CT I, 45; var. ibid.

nḏb sip, Pyr. 123; var. Paheri, 7.

nḏb band door with metal, Urk. IV, 168, 5; 387, 3; 766, 1.

nḏbyt bunt (?) of sail, Peas. B1, 56. 156.

nḏbwt area, extent, Siut, pl. 19, 33; var. Urk. IV, 85, 7.

nḏbḏb sip, Pyr. 123. Cf. nḏb above.

nḏt serf, BM 159; coll. serfs, Urk. IV, 614, 5; 795, 13; det. RB 60, 9.

nḏ grind, Eb. 39, 10; 40, 5; BH II, 6; nḏ 'gr. fine', P. Kah. 6, 4; var. nḏ Eb. 55, 6.

nḏ flour, AEO II, 227*; var. P. Kah. 20, 5.

nḏw miller, Urk. IV, 1811, 10.

nḏtyw maidservants (?), Urk. IV, 2032, 7.

nḏ intrans. vb. take counsel, ask advice, Peas. B1, 144; Les. 81, 9: trans. consult s'one, Urk. IV, 1545, 17; enquire about s'thing, Sm. 8, 1; Urk. IV, 118, 7; call upon king's name, Hamm. 114, 4; utter s'one's name, Cairo 20016.

nḏ vb. save, protect, m-ꜥ 'from', Eb. 1, 8; Les. 71, 12. 17; Urk. V, 147, 5; guard against magic, Pyr. 2029; make good harm, 592: n. (1) protection, RB 62, 11: (2) protector, BD 19, 5; Urk. V, 48, 8. Cf. JEA 37, 32.

nḏ confer office, n 'on', Les. 74, 17; 75, 7; appoint s'one, m 'as', Urk. VII, 32, 9 (sic).

nḏ-r take counsel, consult; question, GNS 83; greet, with n, CT I, 166.

nḏwt-r counsel, Les. 69, 20; BM 572, 10; Urk. IV, 67, 11; consultation, Hatnub, 20, 5; Urk. IV, 649, 4; oracle, 342, 12; greeting, CT I, 166.

nḏ-ḥr (1) greet, Cairo 20539, b 5; Urk. IV, 49, 14; 874, 5; 1113, 2: (2) protect, Hymnen, 17, 1; protector, Urk. V, 48, 17; 117, 7. Cf. JEA 37, 36.

nḏt-ḥr gifts, Urk. IV, 109, 11; 1390, 19; var. 538, 11.

nḏ-ḫrt greet, Sin. B 166; Urk. IV, 1105, 12; pay o's respects, r 'at' the Residence, Les. 74, 12; nḏ.tw ḫrt.ỉ m snb ꜥnḫ 'One enquired after my health and life', Urk. IV, 59, 11; 'Greeting!', Westc. 7, 26.

nḏty protector, Urk. IV, 14, 17; 552, 1; 616, 14; 972, 7; var. VII, 56, 6.

nḏtt protectress, Urk. IV, 280, 8; 300, 1; 362, 2.

nḏ thread, M. u. K. 1, 4; var. BH II, 4.

nḏꜣ parch with thirst, GNS 19. 155.

nḏꜣw chips of stone, P. Kah. 16, 3.

nḏꜣ measure for loaves and dates, Urk. IV, 171, 9. 10; varr. 205, 2; 754, 11. 12.

nḏyt baseness, Peas. B1, 66; Pr. 6, 6; var. Les. 79, 17.

nḏb var. of ndb 'sip'.

nḏm carob-tree (?), Eb. 22, 13; var. Urk. IV, 73, 14.

nḏm sweet, of flavour or odour, Eb. 23, 9; 25, 10; Adm. 8, 4; Urk. IV, 462, 9; pleasant, pleasing, Urk. IV, 122, 16; 464, 14; 920, 10; Siut, pl. 6, 280; a land is nḏm ꜥnḫ 'p. to live in', Paheri, 5; well, hale, Urk. IV, 114, 16; Sm. 1, 3; 5, 8; comfortable, of patient, Sm. 1, 26; 3, 7; of temperature, Eb. 23, 19; nḏm-ỉb 'joyful', m 'over', Les. 70, 8; Westc. 11, 5; TR 19, 38; 'joy', Urk. IV, 117, 11.

nḏmmyt passion, BD 458, 11; var. Pyr. 1248.

nḏnḏ intrans. vb. confer, ḥnꜥ 'with', Sin. B 113; Pr. 5, 8; take advice, m-ꜥ 'from', Urk. IV, 1820, 15: trans. consult s'one, Les. 81, 8: n. advice, counsel, Urk. IV, 1082, 8.

nḏrw vb. 4-inf. grasp, hold fast, Pyr. 380; BH I, 30; II, 7; Urk. IV, 351, 4 ( ); catch, Urk. I, 105, 3; BH II, 13; arrest, Les. 81, 6; Urk. IV, 1104, 16; take possession of, Pyr. 202. 1250; CT II, 120 (also with m + obj.); observe regulations, GAS 77; hold to orders, Urk. IV, 1892, 13; follow journeys, 974, 13; draw tight lips of wound, P. Ed. Smith, 226.

nḏrt imprisonment, Leb. 142; Urk. IV, 1113, 11 ( ); suppression of wrong, Pr. 155.

var. of nḥḏt 'tooth'.

nḏs little, small: of size, Urk. IV, 1299, 5; of degree, psḏt nḏst 'the L. Ennead', BM 552; wnn tp·f pw fd nḏs 'it means that his head sweats a l.', Sm. 3, 19; dim, of eyes, Pr. 4, 3; dull, of ears, Eb. 91, 2; poor, of appetite, 101, 7; ꜥwt nḏst 'goats', Urk. IV, 664, 13 (abbr.); 705, 8; Ḥḳꜣ-ib nḏs 'Hekayeb minimus', VII, 7, 14.

nḏs commoner, citizen, Les. 82, 3; Westc. 7, 12; Leb. 68; JEA 16, pl. 29, 1; in half-contemptuous address, 'good fellow!', Sh. S. 69. 112; nḏs iḳr n r-ḫt 'an excellent man-at-arms', Les. 82, 7; nḏs ḳn 'valiant warrior', Hatnub, 20, 2-3 ( ).

nḏsw low estate, Pr. 13, 6.

nḏsḏs burn (trans.), P. Ed. Smith, 485.

r prep. to; at; concerning; more than; from; as conj. so that; until; according as; indicates purpose or futurity; before suffixes rarely ; cf. Gr. p. 577.

r part, in fractions, Gr. § 265; 1/320 ḥḳꜣt, § 266, 1; 'fractions', ZÄS 57, 7*.

r mouth, Pr. 4, 4; Sin. B 41; Sh. S. 46. 77; Peas. B1, 10. 29; = 'm.-piece' of king, Urk. IV, 549, 9; 901, 1; of Nekhen, 1120, 11; of Pe, 406, 15; opening of cave, etc., M. u. K. 3, 11; Eb. 97, 18; Sm. 14, 10; door, Peas. B1, 284; Sin. B 195; Urk. IV, 661, 13; utterance, speech, Sh. S. 17; Peas. B1, 208; Urk. IV, 118, 13; language, Sin. B 31; intent, Caminos, Lit. Frag. p. 39; (r)di r 'speak', GAS 104; ḏd-r 'caller', Peas. B1, 68; ꜥšꜣ r 'chatter', Paheri, 3; an utterance ḥr r n 'on the lips of' people, = a current saying, GAS 84; m ꜥꜣ r 'boastfully', Urk. I, 224, 18.

r water's edge, Eb. 68,10; var. TR 20,1.

r goose, P. Kah. 27,2; Urk. IV, 745,2; cake in shape of g., 761,11; incense in shape of g., 761,8.

r-ib stomach, JEA 24, 251; AEO, II, 250*; Wortforschung, V, 16.

r-ꜥ(wy) end, limit, Urk. IV, 912,2; 1309,5; 1491,17; as prep. beside, near, Gr. §178; m r-ꜥ 'likewise', Urk. IV, 82,14; mi r-ꜥ 'like', 1292,11; r r-ꜥ 'in the presence of' Les. 79,17-18; r r-ꜥwy.sy n sf 'at her place of yesterday', Ken-amūn, 45.

r-ꜥwy hands, Urk. IV, 161,17; 166,17; 593,12; actions, VII, 60,16; BM 1177,2; var. Caminos, Lit. Frag. pl. 13,2,13.

r-ꜥwy gate, CT I, 69; varr. ibid; I, 77.

r-ꜥ-ḫt combat, Hamm. 43,5-6; 'weapons of war', Urk. IV, 691,8; RB 59,14.

r-ꜥꜣ entry into land: r-ꜥꜣ ḫꜣswt 'E. of the foreign lands'; r-ꜥꜣ rsy mḥty 'E. of South and North'; r-ꜥꜣ ꜣbw 'E. of Elephantine', ZÄS 70,84.

r-wꜣt path, way, PSBA 35, 266.

r-pw conj. or, var. Gr. §91,2.

r-pr temple, chapel, Urk. IV, 1295,7; varr. 832,13; 834,13; cf. JEA 27, 70, n.1.

r-pḏtyw foreigners, Sin. B53; varr. B61; R 85.

r-ḥꜣt river-mouth, Caminos, Lit. Frag. pl. 6,3,17; varr. (pl.), Urk. IV, 1821,13; 889,7. Cf. AEO I 34*.

r-ḥry master, chief, Urk. IV, 545,17; varr. 2089; 405,3. Cf. JEA 39,17.

r-ḫt weapons, Les. 82,7.

see under rssy.

see under rsf.

r-sšy ford (?), Caminos, Lit. Frag. p. 10.

r-stꜣ ramp, JEA 4, 137.

r-stꜣw necropolis, esp. of Gīzah, JEA 4, 137; ZÄS 59,159.

 r-ḏ3w mellay, varr. , GNS 34.157.

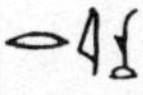 var. of rr 'time'.

 r.i encl. part., see under rf.

 var. of rwt in wḏꜥ-rwt 'judge', q.v.

 rit side, Urk. IV, 1972, 10.

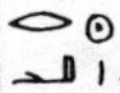 rꜥ sun, Urk. IV, 1013, 11; Leb. 60 (det. );  'every day', Urk. IV, 182, 17; m hrt hrw nt rꜥ nb 'daily', BM 614, 3; Urk. V, 30, 10; sun-god Rēꜥ, Sin. B 206 (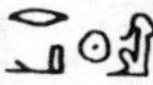). 237 (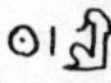); BM 552 (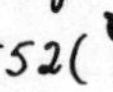); Urk. IV, 15, 17 ().

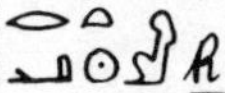 Rꜥt sun-goddess, of queen, Urk. IV, 332, 11.

 rw lion, CT I, 2.

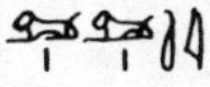 Rwty n. div. double lion-god, CT I, 2; cf. GNS 95, n. 1.

 rwty lion's den, Amarna, VI, 27, 4.

 rwt gate, Pyr. 603. 1713; Sin. R 9 (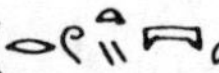 dual). B 285; Urk. IV, 56, 3 (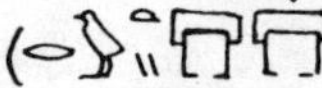). 1105, 16 ()

 rwty outside (n.), BD 497, 9; Urk. IV, 1386, 16 (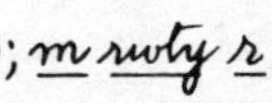); m rwty r 'absent from', 1800, 6; r rwty 'outside' (adv. or prep.), 484, 11; 919, 4; kkwy r rwty 'outer darkness', Hymnen, 6, 4 (det. ).

 rwty outsider, stranger, Hamm. 199, 5; var. 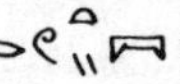 Neferti, 47.

, var. , in wḏꜥ-rwt 'judge', q.v.

 rw3 consider doing s'thing, with ḥr + infin, P. Kah. 30, 14; Urk. IV, 1093, 3 ().

 rwi vb. 3 inf. intrans. dance, Urk. IV, 259, 16; palpitate, of heart, Eb. 101, 12 (): trans. clap hands, Pyr. 2014 ().

 rwt dance (n.), Pyr. 863. 884 (); palpitation of heart, Eb. 101, 11 (det. ).

 rwi vb. 3 inf. intrans. go away, depart, Urk. IV, 1147, 2; pass away, Herdsm. 20; RB 112, 14; advance, r 'against' a land, Sin. B 101 (); serve, n s'one, Les. 75, 18; BD 494, 7 (): trans. expel, drive off, remove s'one or

s'thing evil, Pt. (L II), 3, 14; TR 19, 21; Amarna, VI, 15, 4. 5; leave a place, Sin. B 152 ( ). 247; escape harm, Sin. B 62; Leb. 10.

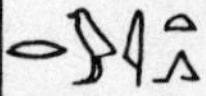

rwi͗t interruption, JEA 4, pl. 8, 8.

rwwt departure, Peas. B1, 255.

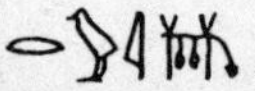

rwi͗ vineyard (?), Peas. B1, 112.

rwyt court of law, Pr. 8, 2. 4; Urk. IV, 967, 7; hall, 1064, 15. Varr.  954, 8; 955, 10; 967, 7.

rwdw stairway, Pyr. 279 (also ); Urk. IV, 424, 1 (); tomb-shaft, Sin. B 304-5 (); cf. GNS 116. See also rdw.

rwḏ cord, Pyr. 443. 684 (abbr.); bow-string, P. Kah. 1, 5 (); in pl. sinews, Urk. V, 157, 3 ( ).

rwḏ hard, JEA 4, pl. 9, 10; P. Kah. 5, 46 (); Urk. IV, 879, 7 (); firm, strong, 114, 15; Westc. 10, 10; Th. T. S. IV, 21; Leyd. V 88; enduring, permanent, Urk. IV, 100, 5 (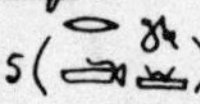); 131, 17; 297, 4 ( ); 300, 6; effective, 118, 13; persistent, Rec. trav. 16, 59 = GAS 68; prosperous, prosper, Sin. B 76 ( ). 186 (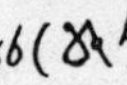); Urk. IV, 974, 5; 1090, 8 ( ); RB 113, 14; successful, succeed, Les. 84, 17-18 (); Urk. IV, 1089, 14; prevail, r 'over', Pyr. 197 (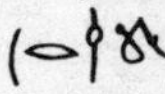); Sin. B 108; rwḏ i͗b 'stout-hearted', Sh. S. 132; Urk. IV, 1281, 11; 'assiduous', Paheri, 3.

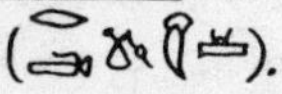

rwḏ strength, firmness, TR p. 9; var.  Urk. IV, 428, 1.

rwḏt success, Urk. IV, 2027, 14; varr. 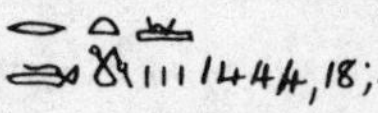 1444, 18; 2049, 20.

rwḏt hard stone, sandstone, Sethe, Steine, 13; var.  Bersh. I, 14, 2.

rwḏ control, administer, Urk. IV, 507, 1.

rwḏw agent, JEA 38, 28; varr. Th. T. S. IV, 7;  Urk. IV, 1442, 20.

rpw rot, Pyr. 1257; TR 26, 2; var.  L. to D. I, 3 (n.).

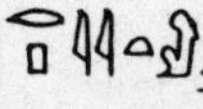

rpyt (1) female statue: (2) female counterpart (?) of deity, JEA 31, 109; presiding goddess of city, Pyr. 207 ( ); CT I, 183 (det.); var. Urk. IV, 31, 10.

rpˁ(t) (1) hereditary noble: (2) heir, var. ; fem. , , , AEO I, 14*; JEA 39, 10.

rf encl. part, var. , sometimes variable for person, , , etc., Gr. § 252.

rm fish, Sh. S. 50; Peas. B1, 61. 207; var. Caminos, Lit. Frag. p. 3.

rmi vb. 3 inf. weep, Peas. B1, 25; Leb. 76; Adm. 5, 5 (det.); Urk. IV, 1118, 9 (abbr.): trans. beweep, Pyr. 163; TR 29, 9.

rmw weeping, Siut, pl. 19, 24.

rmwt tears, TR 25, 9; var. Urk. IV, 1078, 5.

rmw weeper, BD 467, 14; var. Les. 80, 19.

rmn shoulder, Urk. IV, 114, 14; 1278, 1; M. u. K. 4, 3; arm, Urk. IV, 927, 12; 1031, 7; V, 87, 11; in dual also arms of balance, Peas. B1, 166; Urk. V, 55, 15; uprights of ladder, BD 202, 16; side: rmn imnty 'the western s.', Urk. I, 50, 13; rmn n 's. of beef', Westc. 7, 2; rmnwy dw 'mountain-s.', Urk. IV, 388, 11. Varr. BM 614, 7; BM 572, 12; TR 13, 13; Urk. I, 50, 13.

rmn side, half of sheet of water, Westc. 6, 9.

rmn side, gang of rowers, Westc. 5, 18; 6, 4.

rmn in rmn iry dmd 'total of each (?)' (silver and gold), Urk. IV, 1305, 9.

rmn half of 'rod' and 'aroura', Gr. § 266, 2. 3.

rmni vb. 4 inf. shoulder, carry, support, Urk. IV, 413, 6; 1031, 5; BD 450, 14; Pyr. 1241; match, equal, Pr. 5, 12; cf. Äg. Stud. 83 (k); rmn n 'stand beside', 'be friendly with', op. cit. 82 (f): n. bearer, supporter, Pyr. 2122; Urk. IV, 388, 8. Varr. Pyr. 952; TR 23, 73.

rmn processional shrine, Urk. IV, 1952, 5.

rmnwty companion, Pyr. 531; pl. Pr. 5, 13; cf. Äg. Stud. 83 (l).

rmnyt department; domain, P. Wilbour, 110.

Rmnn n. loc. Lebanon, Urk. IV, 700, 8; 739, 17; cf. AEO I, 172-3*.

rmrm chastise, Urk. IV, 1076, 5.

rmṯ man, Amarna, V, 15; pl. men, mankind, Urk. IV, 159, 5 (dets.); Siut, pl. 6, 266; Egyptians, GAS 21; AEO I, 100*. Varr. Pyr. 400; Urk. IV,

1885, 4; 481, 2; 138, 15; I, 60; abnormal wtgs. BH I, 8, 19; Urk. IV, 95, 8; 1024, 7.

rmṯt coll. men, mankind, Siut, pl. 4, 225; 5, 243; Cairo 20335 (dets.); often written (identifiable when qualified by fem. adj.), P. Kah. 12, 12; Pr. 7, 4; Les. 84, 7; Bersh. I, 14, 4 (det.); varr. Urk. IV, 965, 10; Cairo 20530.

rn name, Sin. B 41; Peas. R 1; dets. Urk. IV, 437, 2; (of king), 1295, 7; deeds are recorded *m hrw m rn·f* 'day by day', 661, 16; *imy-rn·f* 'list of names,' see p. 19.

rn young one, of animals, Pyr. 806; BH I, 18. 35.

rny calf, Les. 76, 21; Urk. IV, 1294, 5 (det.).

rnpt year, Gr. p. 203; 5 *ḥryw rnpt* 'the five epagomenal days,' loc. cit.; *rnpwt* 'make years' of life; 'spend, pass years', JEA 20, 159; *rdi rnpwt n* 'give years (of life) to,' loc. cit.; '(the festivals of) the Great Y. and the Little Y.', BH I, 25, 90-1; '(the festival of) the First of the Y.', Les. 73, 6; 'New Year's Day', see above, p. 60.

rnpi adj. and vb. 4 inf. young, P. Kah. 2, 8; Sh. S. 168; Sin. B 167; fresh, of water, Urk. IV, 447, 10; 1373, 15. Varr. CT I, 88; Urk. IV, 85, 5; 616, 3; 1469, 14; 863, 7; (sic), D. el B. 115.

rnpw youthful vigour, Urk. IV, 433, 1.

rnp young man, Sm. 21, 9.

rnp colt, Urk. IV, 663, 11.

rnpwt herbs, vegetables, Urk. IV, 112, 1; varr. 990, 11; 915, 7; 1451, 10; Siut, pl. 2, 123.

rnn rejoice, *m* 'over'; extol, GNS 37.

rnnwt joy, exultation, GNS 38.

rnn caress, Urk. IV, 229, 5.

rnn bring up, nurse, Urk. IV, 200, 11-13; 201, 16; 285, 17; dets. 361, 15; JEA 32, 55 (v).

rnnt (wet-)nurse, Urk. IV, 508, 3; 1060, 13.

Rnnt n. div. the nurse-goddess, Urk. IV, 389, 5.

Rnnwtt n. div. the harvest-goddess, Th. T. S. I, 30, F; JEA 20, 154; varr. Urk. IV, 925, 5; 1541, 18; name of ninth month, 44, 14.

rr time, Pyr. 553. 883; varr. 649; Caminos, Lit. Frag. pp. 33-4.

rri boar; fem. 'sow', JEA 14, 213. 225.

rrt coll. swine, T. Carn. 6.

rrit piggishness (?), Les. 81, 5-6.

rhn lean, ḥr 'on', Les. 77, 14; rely on, trust in, with ḥr, Leb. 121 (det.); Merikarēʿ, 128; Urk. IV, 473, 7 (dets.); 1821, 16.

rhn wade, Pyr. 1162; BD 258, 3 (dets.); 258, 13 (dets.).

rḥw comrades, mates, Neferti, 5. 6; Urk. IV, 327, 11; 1154, 5; ZÄS 60, 71.

rḥwy the Two Companions = Rēʿ and Thoth, Pyr. 128; the Two Combatants = Horus and Seth, Urk. IV, 1072, 11; V, 32, 4; of human contestants, IV, 1439, 8 ( ).

rḥty the Two Female Companions = Isis and Nephthys, TR 25, 8.

rḫ (1) vb. know, Sin. B 114. 205; Sh. S. 121. 148; Peas. B1, 287; with foll. sḏm·f, Gr. §§184. 442, 1; with foll. infin. 'know how to ...', 'be able to ...', Westc. 7, 4; 10, 5; be aware of, Sin. B 32; Urk. IV, 119, 15; learn, Peas. B1, 210; Sh. S. 46; in imperative, Inquire!, ZÄS 57, 105; rḫ m 'know of', Adm. 9, 7; Urk. IV, 368, 7; rḫ x r y 'k. x from y', Sin. B 255-6; Urk. IV, 970, 1; rdi rḫ 'inform', Sin. R 18; B 181; with reflex. obj., rḫ·n‹i› wi is 'I had my wits about me', Urk. IV, 158, 11; rdi·i rḫ·k tw 'I will bring you to your senses!', Sh. S. 72; rḫ ḏt(·f) 'acquire wisdom', Urk. VII, 43, 11; ḥmwt rḫt 'skilled workmanship', IV, 1833, 3; 'wisdom', BM 614, 7. 11; 'wise, learned man', Leb. 145-6; Siut, pl. 14, 66; rḫ-ḫt n rmṯ nbt 'wisest of all men', Peas. B1, 134-5; 'unknowingly', JEA 32, pl. 6, 33.

(2) n. knowledge, Pr. 17, 5; Urk. IV, 57, 17; 58, 2; 969, 16; opinion, Hatnub, 22, 6; Pr. 5, 14; Urk. IV, 1091, 9.

rḫ wise man, Pr. 15, 12; 17, 3; Urk. IV, 386, 1; 970, 1.

rḫt (1) knowledge, Westc. 6,23; var. Urk. IV, 835,12: (2) amount, number, P. Kah. 21, 30. 31; Urk. IV, 664,17; 892,14.

rḫ intrans. copulate, m-ʿ 'with'; P. Kah. 3,32: trans. know woman, Urk. IV, 1409,11 (det.).

rḫ-nsw king's acquaintance (title), Sin. R2; varr. Hatnub 22,1; BH I,7; Les. 75,6; fem. rḫt-nsw, Meir IV,4; BH II,24. Cf. JEA 3,244.

rḫyt subjects of king; common folk; mankind, AEO I,98* ff.; II,272*; varr. CT V,129; P. Kah. 3,6; Urk. IV, 17,8; 133,8; 1118,11.

rḫḫy celebrated, Urk. IV, 119,3.

rḫs slaughter (vb.), Peas. B1,176; var. Les. 73,14.

rḫt wash clothes, BH I,29; Urk. V,162,7.

rḫty washerman, Peas. B1,169; BH I,29; Sm. 22,1.

rḫtt in tꜣwy rḫtt 'the ends of the earth', Urk. IV, 85,17.

rs encl. part., Gr. §252,4.

rs (rīs) wake, Peas. B1,285; Urk. IV, 117,9 ( ); 219,13 ( ); V,170,6; be watchful, vigilant, Leb. 72; Urk. IV, 185,1; 1304,14 (det.); with tp 'head' in tp.i rs 'I was v.', 57,8 ( ); 430,3; sim. 861,7; 1547,16; rs-tp 'be watchful, vigilant', 127,7; 554,15; 656,12; 'foreman', 1153,4; var. 1152,9.

rsw watch, guard of sentries, Urk. IV, 656,9; 661,7; vigilance, I, 105,18 ( ); rsw ḥr 'watch over' s'one, TR 21,81; 'look out for' s'thing, RB 66,4; rs(w)-tp 'vigilance', Urk. I, 129,13; 134,12.

rswt (1) awakening, Hymnen, 2,2; 4,1 ( ); 'set the regular watch', RB 61,10: (2) dream, Sin. B225 ( ); Pr. 11,8; Peas. B1, 217.

rst sacrificial victims (?), Louvre C 14,10; var. Urk. IV, 1291,9.

rsw the South land, Urk. IV, 82,14.

rsw south-wind, TR 22,17.

rsy adj. southern, TR 1,10; Urk. IV, 124,9; 795,7; south of, 4,3; P. Kah. 18,28: n. South, 12,5; Urk. IV, 5,16; 1146,9; n rsy·sn 'to the s. of them', RB 61,10. Varr. Urk. IV, 124,9; 362,11. On 'the South' cf. JEA 43,6.

rs(y)w Southerners, Urk. IV, 1298,5; varr. 5,14; 1248,17.

rsf catch of fowl or fish, Leb. 90; Urk. IV, 446,10 ( ); affluence, Ch. B. I, 40, n. 5.

rssy quite, entirely, at all, var. Gr. § 205,1; Urk. IV, 1380,7.

rš joyful, Sin. B 70; Sh. S. 124; Siut, pl. 13,29.

ršwt joy, Urk. IV, 102,9; 894,14; RB 112,9; varr. Urk. IV, 1845,17; 1575,17.

ršrš rejoice, Urk. IV, 141,2; RB 112,1.

ršršt joy, Urk. IV, 190,15.

rḳ incline, Äg. Stud. 3; turn aside, r 'from', TR 22,36; defy, Neferḥotep, 36.

rḳy fierce (?), JEA 34,45.

rḳw tilting of balance, Gr. p. 269 (BD Ch. 30B,); enmity, Urk. IV, 1278,13; Adm. p. 107.

rḳw opponent, Urk. IV, 269,11 (det.); 341,13; varr. 556,16; RB 58,7; pl. Urk. IV, 938,14; 1670,13.

rḳ-ib disaffected man, Urk. IV, 910,12.

rḳt-ib ill-will, Sin. B 116.

rk encl. part., var. , Gr. § 252,2.

rk time of king, ancients, etc., Westc. 6,16; Urk. IV, 344,13; 939,13; m p3 rk 'in these times', Adm. 2,8; var. Urk. VII, 16,7.

rkrk creep, Barns, Ashm. 30.

rkrk snake, loc. cit.

rkrk a creeping plant, loc. cit.

rkḥ light fire, Pyr. 124.

rkḥ (festival of) Burning, Les. 73,6; rkḥ ꜥ3 rkḥ nḏs 'the Great B. and the Little B.', Urk. IV, 470,1; 483,2; sim. BH I, 24; cf. JEA 41, 123.

rkḥt heat, BD 353,3.

rkḥw flames, BD 351,13.

rtt conspiracy (?), Urk. IV, 139,3. Error for rḳt (?).

rtḥ in 'r.-bread', Th. T. S. I, 18.

rtḥty baker, JEA 41, pl. 5, 102; varr. Eb. 50,17; Goyon, 61,9.

rtḥ confine, restrain, P. Kah. 1,8; Hymnen, 9,2 (det. only).

rtḥ blockhouse, JEA 39, 36.

rṯ encl. part., var. Gr. § 252; pl. var. loc. cit.

Rṯnw n. loc. part of Syria, AEO I, 142*; varr. Urk. IV, 1007,8; in Sin. B always without r, e.g. B 31.

rd foot, Sin. B 16. 170 (); Westc. 7,16; RB 121, 14. 15; int rd 'removing the foot-print', see p. 22 s.v. ini (2); rdwy 'one in attendance on', see p. 25; 'reversion' of offerings, see p. 76; 'rank', 'station', see under st; 'instructions', 'regulations', see under tp; 'Hurry! Stir your stumps!', Paheri, 3; 'Watch your step, mates!', Urk. IV, 327, 11.

rdw stairway, Pyr. 1325; Les. 68, 10-11 (); 82,20 (); Urk. IV, 45,17 (); steps of throne, Pyr. 1296 (); Caminos, Lit. Frag. 9,25 (); tomb-shaft, Les. 80,6 (); Siut, pl. 8, 308 (); cf. GNS 116; 'stairway', AEO II, 211*. See also rwdw.

rd shoot of tree, P. Ram. III, A 19.

rd grow, P. Kah. 2,7; Hymnen, 20,1; Urk. IV, 112,2 (); rd m k[t] 'overgrown with weeds', 2027,8; For 'flourish', 'prosper', see under rwd.

rdi anom. vb. give, Sin. B 27. 96; Siut, pl. 6, 270. 280; 'g. o'self' = reveal o'self, of god, RB 113,13; rdi ḥr 'g. in addition to', JEA 27, 89 (44); put, place, Sh. S. 39. 46; Sin. B 143. 193;

appoint, m 'as,' Sin. B86; Bersh. I, 33; r 'as,' BH I, 25, 46-7; 'to' do s'thing, Peas. B1, 234; send letter, JEA 31, 7, n. 9; cause, permit, grant, with foll. vbs., cf. Gr. p. 579. Also in foll. expressions:-

rdỉ m ỉb 'place in o's heart,' 'determine,' Gr. §§ 184. 303; 'prompt' s'one, Les. 86, 13; Urk. IV, 1282, 5.

rdỉ ḥr ꜥ 'put in the charge of,' JEA 39, 7, fig. 2, 4 = p. 8 (e).

rdỉ ḥr wꜣt 'show the way,' Sin. B251.

rdỉ m ḥr 'command,' Urk. IV, 97, 8; 209, 3; 'appoint,' m 'to,' 897, 14; 'call the attention of,' 364, 11; 'call o's attention to,' 1280, 11.

rdỉ ḥr gs 'lay on o's side,' P. Kah. 7, 39; 'incline to one side' = be partial, biassed, Peas. B1, 98. 149; Urk. IV, 411, 1; 'fell' enemy, 7, 6; 1303, 11.

rdỉ m tꜣ 'bury,' GAS 30.

rdỉ r tꜣ 'cast on the ground,' Sh. S. 53; 'land' from ship, Urk. IV, 9, 6; 'give birth,' Eb. 94, 10; 'leave alone,' BH II, 7; 'neglect,' Leb. 109, cf. Äg. Stud. 84; 'set aside,' n 'for,' Siut, pl. 7, 293.

rdỉ ḥr tꜣ 'cast ashore' rope, Sh. S. 4-5; 'cast forth,' 'expel,' Les. 98, 11; P. Kah. 12, 13.

rdỉ ỉb m-sꜣ 'be anxious about,' Gr. § 178.

rdỉ ỉb ḫnt 'give attention to,' P. Kah. 29, 37; Urk. IV, 1093, 2.

rdỉ ꜥ(wy) n 'give a hand to,' 'help,' Westc. 8, 2; BM 614, 18; Pt. (L II), 4, 5.

Δ☥ dỉ ꜥnḫ 'given life,' part of royal ascription, Gr. § 378.

rdỉ pḥwy 'put an end to,' Pyr. 318.

rdỉ [hieroglyphs] r 'put the temple to' a place to eavesdrop, Westc. 12, 4; 'pay attention to,' Peas. B1, 32.

rdỉ [hieroglyph] 'speak,' GAS 104; nn wnt (s) rdỉt·n [hieroglyphs] ḥr·s 'without neglecting my orders in the matter,' Urk. IV, 353, 10; dd-r 'caller,' Peas. B1, 68.

(r)dỉ ḥꜣt n 'go to' a place, Herdsman, 24.

rdỉ ḥꜣw ḥr 'do more than,' 'exceed,' Les. 86, 14. 20.

(r)di ḥr n 'give commands to', Adm. p. 106.

(r)di s3 (n) 'turn the back (to)', GNS 34-5; rdi s3 r 'put a stop to', 'annul', GAS 103.

(r)di 'draw' a weapon, Sin. B128.

rdi sdt m 'set fire to', Les. 84, 10-11.

rdi tp nfr 'make a good beginning', Les. 83, 9.

Varr. , , , , cf. Gr. p. 579.

rdmt a plant, GAS 33.

var. of r-d3w 'mellay', p. 147.

rdw efflux of body, Eb. 60, 18; Sm. 19, 17. 18; det. BD 134, 2.

h courtyard (?), Pyr. 321; TR 23, 77; M.u.K. 1, 7; cf. Gr. p. 493, 04.

var. of hi 'husband'.

, varr. of h3yt 'portal'.

h3 interj. Ha!, Ho!, var. det. , Gr. § 87.

h3i vb. 3 inf. intrans. come down, go down, descend, RB 76, 10; 77, 4; Peas. R 2; B1, 307; Leb. 107; Urk. V, 42, 12; fall, Sh. S. 130; M.u.K. 5, 2; Eb. 1, 14; Urk. V, 39, 15; befall, of age, Sin. B168; Pr. 4, 2; drip, drop, P. Ed. Smith, 284; accede, r 'to' office, Les. 81, 21; grasp the meaning of, with m or r, Caminos, L. Eg. Misc. 264; 'ascend and descend', Pyr. 209; 'come and go', Sin. B49; 'a popular resort', Adm. 6, 12; 'thronging crowds', GAS 51; 'flag', 'fail', 'cease', ZÄS 60, 67; 'common property', GAS 49: trans. charge down upon enemy, Sin. B53; 60-1; tackle dangerous animal, Urk. IV, 616, 4. Var. 324, 9.

h3t ceiling, Urk. IV, 429, 7; var. pl. Mill. 3, 4. Cf. AEO II, 211*.

h3yt portal, AEO I, 60*; varr. Cairo 20017; 20230; 20056; Urk. IV, 1073, 5.

ḥ3w corvée, P. Kah. 29, 19; var. Urk. I, 210, 5.

ḥ3w time: m-ḥ3w 'at the t. of', Gr. §178; sim. n-ḥ3w, Sin. B 150; imy-ḥ3w.f 'who is in his t.', of reigning king, Cairo 20061; of priests on duty, Siut, pl. 7, 303; 8, 311 ( ); life-time, BM 614, 14 (det.); Urk. IV, 501, 11; neighbourhood, environment: m-ḥ3w 'in the n. of', Gr. §178; n-ḥ3w 'of the e. of', Les. 98, 21; r-ḥ3w 'near', Urk. IV, 584, 10 ( ); 1542, 4 ( ); m-ḥ3w-ḥr 'in front of', Hamm. 114, 8; belongings, Peas. B1, 105; circumstances, B1, 135; affairs, B1, 262; P. Kah. 27, 8; Urk. IV, 1106, 2.

ḥ3w kindred, Pr. 10, 6.7; Urk. IV, 1398, 6; varr. 1825, 3; Leyd. V 1; Les. 79, 13.

ḥ3w species of wild-fowl, Caminos, Lit. Frag. p. 9.

ḥ3b send s'one, Sin. R 13; Peas. B1, 40; Pr. 7, 3; Urk. IV, 1112, 5 ( ); s'thing, 370, 9; ḥ3b n 's. to s'one; ḥ3b r 's. to a place; 's. for', Stud. Griff. 57.

var. of hb 'tread'.

ḥ3bt dance (?), Urk. IV, 83, 15.

ḥ3byt treading under foot (?), M. u. K. 3, 3.

var. of hbk 'beat up'.

see under ḥims.

ḥ3rt herds of game, Urk. IV, 697, 15.

ḥ3kr a religious festival, JEA 4, 126, n. 1; 20, 161; varr. 38, pl. 1, 13; Urk. IV, 27, 5; Cairo 20040.

ḥ3ts kind of jar, var. , BH I, 17.

ḥi husband, Urk. IV, 972, 8; 1078, 6; varr. VII, 16, 12; BH I, 18.

hy interj. Hail!, Gr. §258: n. shout, RB 111, 1 (det.); 'jubilate', Urk. IV, 141, 1.

var. of ḫ3yt 'portal'.

ḥims: m —— 'humbly', Urk. IV, 18, 3; 704, 3; var. 621, 3.

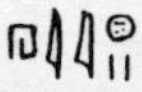 ḥyḥy make acclamation, JEA 4, pl. 9, 8.

,  see under ḥ3w.

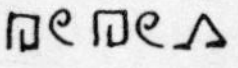 ḥwḥw scurry, Sin. B 229.

 ḥwt be burnt, Siut, pl. 13, 14.

 ḥb plough (n.), Ti, 111; abbr. 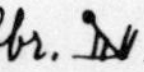 Sheikh Said, 16.

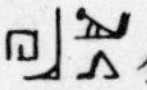 ḥbi vb. 3 inf. tread out grain, Peas. B1, 12; tread a place, Urk. IV, 345, 3; 1290, 7 (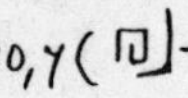); travel, r 'to', Mill. 2, 10 (); enter, m 'into' s'one, of knives, Urk. V, 79, 11; of poison, BD 372, 15-16; ḥb ib 'far-ranging of desire (?)', Urk. IV, 1281, 20.

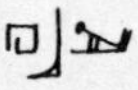 ḥb humiliate (?), Pr. 14, 11; cf. GES 67, 6.

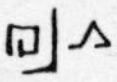 ḥb see ḥ3b 'send' and ḥb 'tread'.

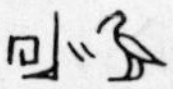 ḥby ibis, Eb. 94, 7; var. 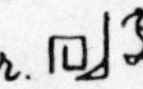 JEA 39, pl. 2, 8.

 ḥbny ebony, Urk. IV, 436, 6; varr.  329, 5; 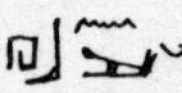 Louvre, C 14, 15.

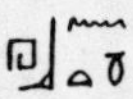 ḥbnt a jar, Urk. IV, 174, 3 (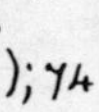); 748, 17; measure of capacity, Gr. § 266, 1.

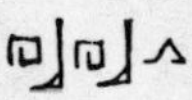 ḥbḥb traverse country, Sinai, 54; Urk. IV, 451, 5; 677, 3 (dets. ); 1547, 17.

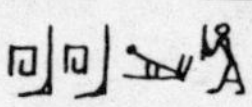 ḥbḥb drive out pain, Eb. 103, 1.

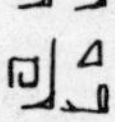 ḥbk beat up, triturate, JEA 29, 6, n. d; var. 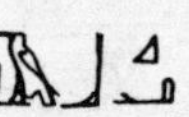 Eb. 21, 11.

 hp law, ordinance, Peas. B1, 65. 274; Urk. IV, 749, 14; 1111, 2; iry hpw 'custodian of l.'s'; imy-r hpw 'overseer of l.'s', JEA 27, 76; hp 'keep, carry out the l.', Th. T. S. p. 71, n. 12.

 ḥm be burning, M. u. K. vs. 2, 3.

 ḥmt fare for conveyance, Peas. B1, 172.

 ḥmw emolument, Barns, Ram. p. 13.

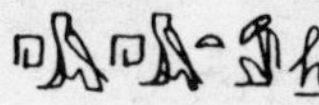 ḥmḥmt war-shout, Urk. IV, 18, 6; 612, 11; 1008, 5 (dets. 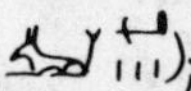); quacking of wild-fowl, Caminos, Lit. Frag. pl. 3, 4, 8. Var.  Urk. IV, 272, 2.

 ḥn box, chest, BH I, 35; Sm. 4, 2; Urk. IV, 388, 1 (det. ); V, 170, 10 (dets. 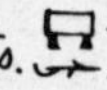).

 ḥn halt, Urk. IV, 1302, 12; cease, ZÄS 21, 127.

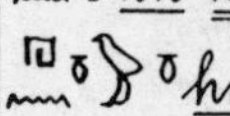 ḥnw jar, Westc. 11, 21; Sm. 22, 5; measure of about ½ litre, Gr. § 266, 1; P. Wilbour, 64.

hnw praise of god or king, Urk. IV, 21, 3; 306, 4; 309, 12; 935, 11; 'jubilation', 141, 1. Var. Cairo 20480.

hnw associates, P. Ram. I, B1, 26; Pt. (L II), 3, 6; Merikarēʿ, 24; family, Th. T. S. I, 25, 6; Urk. IV, 1794, 12 ( ).

hnw waves, Caminos, Lit. Frag. pl. 4, 7.

hnn deer, Urk. IV, 718, 13; det. Eb. 48, 16.

hnn attend to, consider, BM 572, 10 (det.); Urk. IV, 1090, 10; Pt. (L II), 4, 12 (dets.); trust, m 'in', RB 56, 14; assent, n 'to', Louvre C 67, 4 (dets.); approve (?) document, P. Kah. 13, 14; cajole (?), Urk. IV, 1107, 13; hnn ib r 'be well-disposed to', PSBA 18, pl. foll. p. 196.

hr milk (vb.), JEA 4, 33.

hrw adj. pleasing, Urk. IV, 95, 8; 435, 2: vb. 3 inf. be pleased, satisfied, content, hr 'at', 'with', Siut, pl. 6, 276; RB 115, 1; P. Kah. 13, 24; Urk. IV, 993, 8; hr 'with', 1075, 8; hr r sḏm 'be p. to listen', ZÄS 60, 73; hr sḏm·k mdw 'be p. when you hear a speech', Pr. 9, 3-4; be quiet, at peace, Siut, pl. 13, 31; 15, 23; Bersh. II, 13, 11 (det.); hrw 'Take care!', Peas. B1, 1 = R 52; hr ib 'contented', Leb. 126; Urk. IV, 131, 8; hr nmtt 'easy of gait', Les. 82, 18; Urk. IV, 18, 12.

hrt peace, Pr. 6, 10; pleasantness, 11, 12; r hrt 'satisfactorily', Urk. I, 106, 4 (det.); VII, 58, 3.

hrw day, daytime, Sin. B 10. 238; Westc. 12, 9; RB 66, 6 (abbr.); 113, 14; hrw nfr 'happy d.', 'holiday', Peas. B 2, 110-1; Westc. 3, 9-10; Urk. IV, 1163, 14; m ẖrt hrw 'daily', Sin. B 88; Urk. IV, 12, 11; 1176, 1 ( ); so too m ẖrt hrw nt rʿ nb 58, 10 ( ); 992, 4; n hrw r ḫw 'all day until nightfall (?)', JEA 4, 34, n. 1; sentry imy hrw·f 'for the day', Sin. R 45.

hrwyt journal, Urk. IV, 693, 11; 2156, 6.

hrp sink, be immersed: lit. only L. Eg., Wb. II, 500, 27 ff; of heart as symptom, Eb. 101, 15; of 'depressed' fractures, Sm. 2, 13. 16; of displaced vertebrae, 11, 7: suppress o's desires, Pr. 18,12; Urk. IV, 1198,12; VII, 64,7 (det. 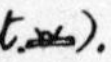).

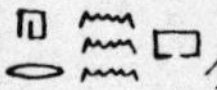 hrmw (?) poultry-pen, Urk. IV, 745,3.

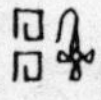 hh blast of fire, Urk. IV, 286,16; 808,17; V, 55,8; of heat of sun, RB 114,10; as symptom of disease, Eb. 100,16. Var. 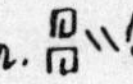 J. Carn. 11.

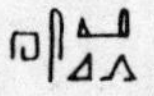 hmḳ (?) wade (?), Urk. IV, 1302,7.

 hḳs steal, Peas. B1, 105.251.

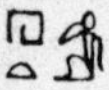 ht call out (?), RB 120,11.

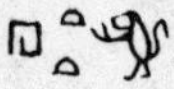 htt adoration, RB 114,11.

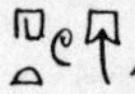 htw (< hṯw) ape, Eb. 16,3; fem. 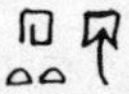 16,4; 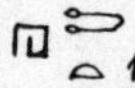 Pyr. 505.

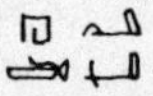 hd attack, Sin. B119 (det. 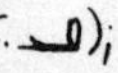); RB 57,8; 59,7; punish, Urk. IV, 971,17; dismiss appellant, 1090, 13.14; obstruct s'one, JEA 38,30; prevail over, with m, Sin. B258: n. assault, Sin. B101; RB 65,4.

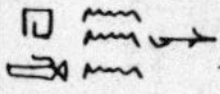 hdmw footstool, Urk. IV, 666,17.

 hdn a plant, Th. T. S. I, p. 94.

 hdhd charge of army, Urk. IV, 710,11.

 var. of 3ḥ 'bread'.

 ḥ3t food, Les. 79,11.

 var. of ḥ3ty 'heart'.

 ḥ3i vb. 3 inf. mourn, Pyr. 1791.2112 (det. ); CT IV, 373 (det. ); Th. T. S. I, 11; wail, Pyr. 744 (); screech, of falcon or kite, CT I, 73.74 (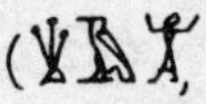, , ); dance at funeral, JEA 41,10.

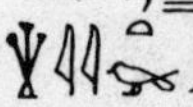 ḥ3yt mourning, RB 111,13.

 ḥ3w mourners, CT IV, 373.

 ḥ3 non-encl. part. would that ...! var. 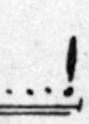, cf. Gr. p. 580.

 ḥ3t tomb, Leb. 53; Adm. 2,7; var.  L. to D. III, 5.

Ḥ3 n. div. the desert-god, BD 463,15; varr. Pyr. 1013; D. el. B. 110; cf. JEA 19, 48, n. 8.

ḥ3 n. occiput, Sm. 1,7; back of ear, 8,21; prep. behind, around, Gr. § 172; r-ḥ3 'behind', RB 61,13.

ḥ3 outside (n.): pr r ḥ3 'go out', RB 59,9; Urk. IV, 117,1 (); 655,2; sim. 1794,15.

ḥ3(y) who is behind = in attendance on, Les 69,24; Urk. V, 27,17; 39,16.

ḥ3y protector, CT I, 158; var. L. to D. X, 2, 8.

ḥ3i outer parts (?) of house, CT I, 163.

ḥ3w-nbw (Aegean) islanders or isles, see above s.v. nbwt 'isles', p. 128.

ḥ3 go ashore, Herdsm. 8.11; run aground, of ship, Peas. B1, 158.

ḥ3y vb. 3 inf. be naked, Hatnub, 20,13.

ḥ3wt nakedness, Peas. B1, 243-4; var. Sin. B152.

ḥ3wy naked man, RB 119,3; var. Urk. IV, 1445,2.

ḥ3(w)t(y) naked man, ZÄS 45, 132.

ḥ3yt bandage (n.), Sm. 4,21; 5,4.

ḥ3yt flood-water, JEA 19,20.

ḥ3yw carrion-birds, Urk. IV, 84,10.

ḥ3w wealth, increase, Les. 68,20 (); excess, surplus, Sh. S. 13; Pr. 7,9; Urk. VII, 62,5; d3t ḥ3w ḫrt-ˁ 'balance of outstanding arrears', P. Kah. 17, 6. 14. 15; ḥ3w n 'most of (?)', Adm. 5,1; m-ḥ3w 'in excess of', Gr. § 178; ḥ3w-ḥr 'more than' in (r)di ḥ3w ḥr 'do more than', 'exceed', Les. 86, 17. 20; Urk. IV, 102,7; ḥ3w-ḥr nfr 'surpassing in beauty', JEA 39, pl. 2, 23; 'abundance of good fortune', Stud. Griff. 69; ḥ3w-ḥr ḫt 'a. of offerings', Urk. IV, 482,17; ḥ3w-ḥr b3kw 'do more than the impost', Paheri, 3; sim. Les. 72,20; m-ḥ3w-ḥr 'in addition to', 'except', Gr. § 178; n-ḥ3w 'excessive', Urk. IV, 2147,6.

ḥ3w vintage, Les. 79,23; cf. Erlaut. 125.

ḥ3w-mr the lower orders, Urk. IV, 1081,10; BD 498,3; mdt nt ḥ3wmr 'low-class talk', Urk. IV, 120, 3; 508, 7.

ḥ3w-ḫt a special offering, Eb. 76, 3; varr. Urk. I, 26, 6; IV, 748, 10.

ḥ3t forehead, JEA 39, 19 (nn); forepart of animal, Pyr. 865; 'meat of the f.', BH I, 17; prow of ship, Urk. IV, 9, 5; 98, 15; vanguard of army, 650, 5; beginning of region, 946, 11; of book, Sin. B 311; Sh. S. 186; foremost, chief, BM 614, 2; Bersh. II, p. 25; Hatnub, 22, 1; Urk. IV, 256, 13; the best of, Bersh. I, 18; m-ḥ3t 'in front of', 'before', Gr. §178; imy-ḥ3t 'who is in front', see p. 19 above; r-ḥ3t 'in front of', 'before', Gr. §178; looking r-ḥ3t 'to the front', Peas. B1, 126; ḥr-ḥ3t 'in front of', 'before', Gr. §178; 'superior to', Sin. B 48; as adv. 'formerly', Gr. §205, 2; ḥ3t 'get in front of', Urk. IV, 895, 3; di ḥ3t n 'go to', Herdsm. 24; ḥ3t-r 'starting with', Gr. §179.

see under r-ḥ3t 'river mouth'.

ḥ3t-ꜥ beginning: ḥ3t-ꜥ m 'b. of' book, Mill. 1, 1; Eb. 1, 1; Pr. 5, 6; ḥ3t-ꜥ ḫr ḫt tpt 'at the b. under the first generation', RB 64, 4; 'I have raised up what was dismembered ḥ3t-ꜥ dr wn ꜥ3mw m-ḳ(3)b T3-mḥw Ḥwt-wꜥrt for the first time since the Asiatics were in Avaris of L.E.', JEA 32, pl. 6, 36-7; p. 47, n. 13.

ḥ3ty-ꜥ local prince, nomarch; mayor, AEO I, 31*; fem. Urk. VII, 28, 15; 39, 16.

ḥ3ty-ꜥ the finest of, GNS 69.

ḥ3t-ḥ3 herdsman, BH I, 30.

ḥ3t-sp regnal year, Gr. p. 203; discussions on rdg. JNES 8, 35. 165.

ḥ3ty heart, AEO II, 250*; varr. Sm. 1, 9; Urk. IV, 1846, 16; pl. ḥ3tyw 'thoughts', 993, 7.

ḥ3tt bow-warp of ship, Sh. S. 4; Urk. IV, 1077, 2; 1867, 12; var. 1909, 9.

ḥ3tt unguent, JEA 6, 58; var. Urk. IV, 339, 14.

ḥ3ꜥyt strife, Sin. B 7; Adm. 7, 6; 13, 2-3 (det.); var. Urk. IV, 8, 6.

ḥ3ꜥꜥ touch, of ship, ḥr 'on' land, Peas. B1, 58 = ḥ3g R 101.

ḥ3ʿb a bad quality, Urk. VII, 65, 19.

ḥ3wty the foremost, Urk. IV, 895, 2; 1882, 3; varr. 1962, 15; 2000, 1.

ḥ3p adj. secret, mysterious, Les. 70, 1 (); Urk. IV, 46, 15; 99, 6: vb. hide, 834, 15; ḥ3p ḥr 'keep silence about' 63, 15; 429, 3; 449, 7; so also ḥ3p ḥt ḥr, GAS 104.

ḥ3p secret place (?), Urk. IV, 1783, 12.

ḥ3m catch fish, etc., BD 229, 9.12; 251, 8; P. Kah. 33, 17; fish waters, BD 233, 11; Leb. 95. Dets. Caminos, Lit. Frag. pl. 2, 1, 4.

ḥ3mw fishermen, Leb. 94.

ḥ3mw kind of wine, BH I, 17; Siut, pl. 1, 52; 2, 109; varr. , , Pyr. 93.

ḥ3rw (1) decoy-duck: (2) bait in general, Caminos, Lit. Frag. pp. 10.18.

ḥ3ḥ3 (1) go astray: (2) stumble, varr. , , P. Ed. Smith, 211.

ḥ3k plunder goods, Sin. B 103.112; Urk. IV, 658, 9; capture towns, 4, 10; 685, 8; 730, 10; carry off captives, Les. 84, 9 (); RB 60, 4; 'easy prey', Urk. IV, 6, 4; 691, 11.

ḥ3k plunder (n.), Urk. IV, 686, 2; 690, 17; 1305, 5.

ḥ3kt plunder (n.), Urk. IV, 4, 11; 690, 15; 730, 12.

ḥ3kw captives, Urk. IV, 704, 9.

ḥ3kw plunderer, Adm. 2, 9; 8, 10.

ḥ3g be glad, Siut, pl. 18, 10; 19, 26.

ḥ3g touch, of ship, ḥr 'on' land, Peas. R 101 = ḥ3ʿʿ B1, 58.

ḥ3g3g rejoice, ḥr 'over', Hymnen, 14, 5.

ḥ3ti cloak, var. , Pyr. 737.

ḥ3tyw fine linen, Sm. 2, 6; varr. P. Kah. 5, 37; M. u. K. 8, 3.

ḥ3ti cloudiness of sky, BD 280, 10; 283, 2.

ḥ3ti bleariness (?) of eyes, P. Kah. 7, 56; var. M. u. K. 3, 9; det. Eb. 62, 19.

ḥ3d *fish-trap*, Urk. V, 79, 6; var. 79, 14: vb. *trap-fish*, BD 233, 14.

ḥ3d *lust* (vb.), *r* 'for', Urk. IV, 219, 16; 1714, 11.

ḥc *flesh*, Pyr. 2114; pl. ḥcw *body*, Sin. B 24 ( ); Sh. S. 64; Urk. IV, 220, 4 ( ); *—self*, with suffixes, Gr. §36; ḥcw nb 'all people', Les. 68, 20; ḥc(w) nṯr 'f. of the god' = king's person, Sin. R 7; Urk. IV, 959, 2 ( ). q.

ḥc *palace*, Urk. IV, 1867, 5.

ḥct *wick*, Gr. p. 525, S 28.

ḥci adj. *joyful*, P. Kah. 2, 1: vb. 3 inf. *rejoice*, Bersh. I, 14, 4; Urk. IV, 259, 7; 271, 4 ( ); 299, 5 ( ); *m* 'at', 'over', Sin. B 66; Urk. IV, 600, 15 ( ); Caminos, Lit. Frag. pl. 2, 2, 13 ( ); *n* 'at', Peas. B1, 272.

ḥcwt *joy*, Louvre C 3, 7; Urk. VII, 4, 2; var. 4, 1.

ḥc3w *children*, Urk. V, 156, 7; varr. IV, 386, 6; Les. 82, 4.

ḥccw *rejoice*, *m* 'over', Urk. IV, 269, 8; 972, 11; var. Les. 64, 14.

ḥccwt *joy*, Urk. IV, 305, 7; 309, 6.

ḥcww *ships*, Bersh. I, 14, 7; varr. Sh. S. 146; Les. 79, 23.

see under ḥbc.

Ḥcpy *Nile*, Les. 68, 17; Adm. 2, 3; as god, Peas. B1, 142; Ḥcpy c3 'high N.', Herdom. 16; Urk. IV, 1841, 10; sim. Ḥcpy wr, Pyr. 292; BH I, 8, 21. Varr. Pyr. 292; Urk. IV 146, 4; 118, 11; (pl.) BH I, 8, 21; ZÄS 45, 141; 47, 163.

ḥcd3 vb. *plunder*, Leb. 112; Peas. B1, 93; Siut, pl. 13, 33: n. *robbery*, Peas. B1, 193.

ḥcd3wt *robbery*, CT I, 212.

Ḥw n. div. *Authoritative Utterance*, PSBA 38, 43; 39, 138; var. Urk. V, 31, 1.

ḫw *royal ordinance*, Urk. I, 108, 10; 109, 11.

ḫww *proclaim*, Pyr. 253; varr. 153; BD 27, 4.

ḫw *food*, Urk. IV, 227, 10; varr. 146, 10; 1526, 5; 1526, 3; 1526, 4; Les. 63, 9.

ḥwỉ vb. 3 inf. beat, strike, smite, Peas. B1, 28; Westc. 12, 10; Sin. R 14; B 72 ( ); P. Kah. 1, 5; Urk. IV, 1107, 7; 1295, 5; defeat in argument, Pr. 6, 3; drive off cattle, RB 114, 7; Les. 84, 10 ( ); drive in mooring-post, Sh. S. 4; flap wings, Pyr. 463 ( ); clap, m 'with' hands, BD 471, 12; gather crops, Pyr. 657; D. el Geb. II, 6; CT I, 286; thresh corn, Bersh. I, 31; throw, r 'against' wall, Adm. 5, 6; tread road, etc., JEA 22, 38; roam the earth, loc. cit.; ḥw sdb 'implant an obstacle', Ann. Serv. 27, 227; ZÄS 63, 75; 64, 136; ḥwt ꜥ 'extending the arm' in dedicating offering, Urk. IV, 870, 16 ( ); JEA 7, 25.— Cf. ZÄS 44, 126.

ḥ(w)t stroke of falcon, Urk. IV, 1666, 7.

ḥwỉ surge up, overflow, of Nile, Adm. 2, 3; Urk. IV, 1651, 15 ( ); Amarna, VI, 25, 10 ( ); BD 440, 4 ( ); rain (vb.), Dream-book, 9, 8.

ḥwyt rain (n.), Westc. 11, 14; Urk. IV, 84, 9.

ḥw-ny-r-ḥr combat, Urk. IV, 1290, 11; 1292, 7; Mill. 2, 2 ( ); Adm. 12, 4.

ḥww class (?) of bulls, Deshasheh, 18; Sin. B 118 ( ); BH II, 7; cattle in general, Meir, I, 10 ( ).

ḥwy non-encl. part. Would that . . . !, var. , Gr. §§ 119, 8; 238.

ḥwt (1) temple, BD 28, 11; 47, 11; 67, 13; cf. JEA 26, 127; funerary chapel, Urk. IV, 28, 1; 447, 5: (2) administrative district, Peas. B1, 86; Urk. IV, 1120, 1: (3) estate, Gîza, III, 190.

ḥwt-ꜥ3t (1) palace, Urk. I, 102, 4: (2) administrative centre of district, Gîza, III, 96: (3) temple, Urk. IV, 607, 4; 745, 14; cf. Ch. B. Text, 110, n. 9; tomb-chapel, BH I, 35.

ḥwt-ꜥnḫ Mansion of Life = royal living quarters, JEA 24, 83.

ḥwt-wryt the Great Mansions = law-courts, GAS 51.

ḥwt-pꜥt Mansion of the Patricians, a shrine, Caminos, Lit. Frag. p. 30.

ḥwt-nt Mansion of the Red Crown, a temple, BH I, 7, 11; pl. I, 17; cf. Ann. Serv. 50, 321.

Ḥwt-nbw (1) Mansion of Gold, temple in Abydos, Les. 68, 6; 75, 13 ( ): (2) alabaster quarries in Hare nome, Hatnub, 9, 7 (det.): (3) sculptor's workshop, Th. T. S. I, 58, n. 1.

ḥwt-nṯr temple, Peas. B1, 195; Westc. 9, 17; varr. Urk. IV, 1156, 14; Pyr. 1277.

Ḥwt-ḥr n. div. Hathōr, Sin. B 207. 237; var. Urk. IV, 345, 7; name of the fourth month, 44, 9.

ḥwt-kꜣ chapel in tomb, AEO II, 211*; in temple, Urk. I, 305, 2 ( ); 'Memphis', AEO II, 124*; var. Les. 64, 16.

var. of ḥtt 'mine'.

ḥwꜣ adj. foul, offensive, Eb. 91, 3: vb. rot, putrefy, TR 26, 1; Eb. 25, 5; smell offensive, Sm. 21, 18; spoil enjoyment (?), Paheri, 7.

ḥwꜣꜣt putrefaction, TR 25, 9; CT I, 304; var. ibid.

ḥwꜥ short, Rec. trav. 39, 101; ḥwꜥ ib 'apprehensive', CT I, 187; Peas. B1, 241. Var. Peas. B1, 108.

ḥ(w)ꜥw short men, Urk. IV, 1073, 13.

ḥwn child, young man, Urk. IV, 241, 12; varr. 1279, 8; BM 552; cf. JEA 39, 16 (h); ḥwnw nfrw 'recruits', 39, 39 ff.

ḥwnt maiden, Urk. IV, 218, 17; 246, 6; var. TR 17, 27.

ḥwn vb. be rejuvenated, refreshed, BM 101; Urk. IV, 365, 17; 752, 3; 939, 14; 1725, 16: n. youthful vigour, 497, 10 ( ).

ḥwn rib-roast, P. Ed. Smith, 395.

ḥwrw poor, humble man, Peas. B1, 20. 232; Pr. 6, 1; despicable person, Les. 84, 8; ḥwrw n rḫty 'a wretch of a washerman', Peas. B1, 169; ḥwrw nw ꜣpdw 'the meanest of the birds', 175-6 (det.). Dets. Urk. IV, 122, 15; 386, 8.

ḥwrw: bw-ḥwrw 'evil' (n.), Peas. B1, 106. 168; ts-ḥwrw 'reproach', Sin. B 41. 227; ḥwrw ib 'poor of understanding', Pr. 6, 3.

ḥwrw speak ill (?), decry (?), Pr. 7, 6.

ḥwtf rob, plunder, var. dets. , GNS 44-5.

ḥb festival, TR 76, 7; varr. Les. 70, 7; Urk. IV, 309, 14; 33, 5; 76, 11;

209, 6; VII, 3, 17.

ḥb-sd jubilee, BM 101; Urk. IV, 565, 16; varr. 292, 9; 199, 10; 1792, 13.

ḥb celebrate a triumph, var. , GNS 55. 159; dets. Urk. IV, 1692, 17; RB 61, 15.

ḥby be festal, make festival, Urk. VII, 54, 7; varr. Hatnub, 23, 2; Bersh. II, 13, 9.

ḥb mourn, Sin. B 142; cf. GNS 55.

ḥbt ritual book, BD 20, 7; var. TR 19, 55; ḥry-ḥbt 'lector', AEO I, 55*.

ḥbyt festival offerings, Urk. IV, 16, 2; 64, 3 (); 1831, 10 (); Les. 68, 8 (); Adm. 3, 9 (); wsḫt ḥbyt 'f.-hall', Urk. IV, 346, 15; 429, 10; 819, 2.

ḥb catch of fish and fowl, BH I, 7, 9; Urk. VII, 54, 9; varr. Del B. 128; Bersh. II, 11; Urk. IV, 917, 17.

ḥbꜣbꜣ waddle, Westc. 8, 21.

ḥbꜥ play 'draughts', with r or direct obj., Urk. V, 4, 12; 95, 15 (); BD 51, 1; 446, 12.

ḥbw target, RB 64, 8; Urk. IV, 1304, 3 (det.); var. 1541, 10.

ḥbbt water, Eb. 73, 19; BD 43, 9; 212, 7; var. dets. Urk. IV, 1829, 16.

ḥbs (1) vb. clothe, Pyr. 741; Pr. 10, 9; be clothed, Pyr. 1988; Pr. 12, 11; M. u. K. vs. 5, 8 (det.); don garment, Adm. 4, 8; furnish house, CT I, 168; hide, cover up, GNS 88; 'covered' = confidential (?), of documents, Urk. IV, 1109, 12; 1110, 5; ḥbs rmn 'c. of arm' = with arms hidden in clothing (?), Les. 72, 6; ḥbs ḥr 'c. the face' = be inaccessible to pleas, Les. 79, 13-14; 80, 22; ḥbs tp 'c. the head', Urk. IV, 944, 16 (dets.); ḥbs ḫt 'keep silence', JEA 37, 50 (n.).

(2) n. garment, Pyr. 966; pl. clothes, clothing, Sin. B 288; Peas. B1, 2; Westc. 5, 12; RB 119, 2 (abbr.); cloth for straining liquids, Eb. 19, 22; P. Ram. III, A 20; covering, Peas. B1, 155.

ḥbswt cloth, Urk. IV, 1121, 8; var. 1125, 6. 8.

ḥbs bear flabellum, Urk. IV, 2014, 8; cf. JEA 27, 13.

ḥbsw bundle (?), P. Kah. 18, 17.

var. of Ḥꜥpy 'Nile'.

ḥpt oar, varr. , , CT I, 94; D. el B. 114; BM 6655; pl. Les. 74, 9; ỉṯ ḥpt 'take the o.' = travel by boat, Pyr. 873. 1346; CT I, 94; dsr ḥpwt 'ply o.'s', 'row', ZÄS 62, 4, n. 3; JEA 20, 162.

Ḥpy n. div. one of the four sons of Horus, Urk. V, 39, 5; varr. 155, 4; 157, 13.

Ḥpw Apis-bull, Urk. IV, 238, 7; varr. , Pyr. 286.

ḥpwty runner, Urk. IV, 617, 15; 1684, 16.

ḥpgt a leaping dance, BH II, 4. 13.

ḥpt travel, RB 113, 14; BD 42, 3.

ḥptt course of sun and moon, BD 49, 3.

ḥpt embrace (vb. and n.), Sh. S. 6 (dets.); Sin. B 143; Urk. IV, 229, 4; V, 48, 6; armful, Sin. B 135; tỉ sy ḥpt·s(y!) ḥr šnbt·k 'while she casts herself (lit. 'embraces') on your breast,' Urk. IV, 1163, 3.

ḥptw cross-timbers of door-leaves, BD 265, 6, cf. Ch. B. Text, 71, n. 7; ribs (?) of boat, BD 205, 14 ( ).

ḥpd open mouth, BD 104, 14; var. RB 119, 7.

ḥf range hills, of lion, Urk. IV, 1302, 2; 1310, 13.

ḥfꜣw snake, Sh. S. 61; var. BD 100, 10.

ḥf(ꜣ)t intestinal worm, Eb. 17, 2; 20, 9.

ḥfꜣt crawling posture, Les. 82, 3; CT I, 180 (det.).

ḥfn num. 100,000, Gr. § 259; great quantity, Urk. IV, 122, 1.

ḥfd climb, Pyr. 751.

ḥfd sit, BD 212, 8.

ḥmt woman, Sin. B 132; Westc. 5, 12; Urk. IV, 15, 3; 'woman', Herdsm. 3;

Westc. 5, 9; *mtt ḥmt* 'dead w.,' M. u. K. vs. 2, 8; **wife**, Sh. S. 134; Peas. R 2; Westc. 4, 8; *ḥmt* 'take a wife,' Urk. IV, 2, 15; *ḥmt-nsw* 'queen,' Sin. R 4; varr. B 264; Urk. IV, 21, 7; *ḥmt-nṯr* 'god's wife,' title of queen, Urk. IV, 34, 15; 192, 11.

see above s.v. *ỉdt* (?).

ḥm encl. part. **assuredly, indeed**, varr. Gr. § 253; *mk ḥm* 'but now behold ...,' L. to D. I, 4 (n.); *ti sw ḥm ỉy·f* 'even now he was returning,' Sin. R 15.

ḥm **coward**, Les. 84, 4.

ḥm **retire, retreat**, Les. 84, 6; Urk. IV, 17, 5; *ḥm* 'Turn back!,' BD 97, 10.

ḥm-ḫt **retreat**, Les. 84, 4. 7.

ḥm **steer**, *ḥr* 'over' water, BD 10, 10.

ḥmw **steering-oar**, Sin. R 38; Peas. B 1, 91; *ḥmw* 'guide the helm,' Peas. B 1, 156. 163; Pr. 12, 5; *ḥmw* 'helmsman,' see p. 25. Varr. TR 27, 30; Sin. B 13; abbr. Les. 75, 22.

ḥmy **helmsman**, Peas. B 1, 126. 221.

ḥmt **stand** (?) **for target**, Urk. IV, 1280, 14; 1281, 1.

ḥm **servant**, Urk. IV, 2, 3; 688, 4; varr. 11, 3; Westc. 7, 15.

ḥmt **female servant**, Urk. IV, 2, 3; 688, 4; var. 11, 3.

ḥm-nṯr **prophet**, AEO I, 30*. 47*.

ḥm-kꜣ **soul-priest**, Sin. B 305; Siut, pl. 6, 248; Urk. IV 28, 9; varr. Gr. p. 453, D 31; Urk. IV, 1520, 1.

ḥm-kꜣ **soul-service**, P. Wilbour, 112.

ḥm **Majesty**: of king, varr. Gr. p. 74; of gods, Westc. 9, 22; Urk. IV, 15, 17; *ḥmw·ṯn* 'your Worships,' of gods or honoured men, Gr. p. 75; in sing. L. to D. I, 7 (n); *ḥm n stp-sꜣ* 'the M. of the Palace,' GNS 83.

ḥmt **Majesty**, of queen, Gr. p. 75; of goddess, Urk. IV, 1074, 7.

ḥmt (?) **copper**, Gr. p. 490, N 34; fig. for firmness of character, Urk. IV, 1087, 10; var. JEA 4, pl. 9, 10. For 'bronze (?)' see under 'Reading unknown'.

ḥmty (?) coppersmith, AEO I, 67*.

ḥmt skill, Pr. 5, 9 (det.); craft of sculptor, etc., Louvre C 14, 8; Eb. 33, 4; Urk. IV, [54,4]

ḥmw be skilled, skilful, Peas. B1, 260; Adm. 4, 8; ḥmw ib 'ingenious,' Urk. IV, 555, 3.

ḥmww craftsman, Pr. 5, 9; Louvre C 14, 8; Urk. IV, 422, 6; expert, Pr. 11, 10; 15, 11; 18, 11; in L. Eg. carpenter, AEO I, 66.* Varr. Sin. B 290; RB 114, 6.

ḥmwt coll. craftsmen, Louvre C 14, 6; Peas. B1, 289; Les. 86, 9; var. Urk. IV, 1006, 7; wr-ḫrp-ḥm(wt) 'master-craftsman,' I, 20, 7; 38, 15; as title of high-priest of Ptah at Memphis, AEO I, 38*; II, 269*.

ḥmwwtyw craftsmen, Urk. IV, 421, 1.

ḥmwy work: ḥmwy pw n ib.i 'it was a w. of my own heart,' Urk. IV, 57, 16.

ḥmt-r (1) magic spell, M. u. K. vs. 6, 1; Sm. 18, 8: (2) etcetera, and so forth, CT I, 16 ( ); Eb. 1, 4; Sm. 19, 5; cf. JEA 38, 26, n. 2.

ḥm3 ball, D. el B. 100; var. Sm. 15, 18.

ḥm3t salt, Peas. R 11; B1, 48; var. Eb. 32, 2.

ḥm3gt carnelian, M. u. K. vs. 2, 6; var. Urk. IV, 1099, 13; cf. GAS 31.

ḥmww fuller (?), var. , Gr. p. 520, U 36.

ḥmwst female counterpart of the ka, SDT 62.

ḥmm surgeon's knife (?), Eb. 106, 16.

ḥmsi vb. 4 inf. sit, sit down, Les. 72, 19; Westc. 12, 8. 20 ( ); Urk. IV, 1103, 17 (det.); JNES 14, 23, 2 (abbr.); dwell, m 'in,' Westc. 7, 1; ḥnꜥ 'with,' 9, 19; ḥms ḥr 'besiege' town, Urk. IV, 3, 7; 184, 17; ꜥḥꜥ ḥms 'stand and sit,' Pr. 5, 2; 'pass o's life,' Pr. 2, 7 ( ); ZÄS 60, 69; ḥms m 'dwell in,' Urk. IV, 116, 11: trans. occupy a place, Pyr. 1182; Urk. IV, 1849, 2 ( ); seat s'one, ḫnt 'at the head of,' Pyr. 895.

ḥmst session, Urk. IV, 349, 10; 1103, 14.

ḥmst seat in sense of 'rank,' 'position,' Les. 74, 18.

(sic) ḥmsw sloth, Sin. B 59; cf. GNS 35.

ḥmsy guest, Pt. (L II), 2, 13; var. pl. Pr. 6, 11.

var. of ḥm3gt 'carnelian'.

ḥn encumber, obstruct, Peas. B1, 7; Urk. IV, 1818, 7.

ḥn provide, equip, Urk. IV, 165, 11; Adm. 8, 3; command, Urk. IV, 353, 8; govern, 2161, 17; control o'self, Pr. 12, 2 (dets.); mouth, 18, 12 (dets.); hands, P. Ram. I, Di, 1; charge s'one with task, Urk. IV, 1074, 16; commend s'one, n 'to', P. Kah. 31, 19; occupy o's hands with business, Urk. IV, 489, 3 (det. only).

ḥnt occupation, craft, Urk. IV, 1148, 13; 1149, 17; business, 453, 8; 1417, 10; services, JEA 39, pl. 2, 25; nb ḥnt 'craftsman', Peas. B1, 111; mk sw r ḥnt·f 'Behold, it shall serve its due purpose', Les. 97, 12. Varr. Urk. IV, 449, 15; 453, 8.

ḥnw military commanders, Urk. IV, 1659, 14.

ḥnwty servant, Urk. IV, 1996, 8. 9.

ḥn go speedily, Pr. 1, 3; cf. JEA 32, 73.

ḥnt swampy lake, var. , JEA 29, 38.

ḥnt cup, BH I, 17; var. I, 35.

ḥnt space of time, Urk. I, 125, 4; lifetime, CT I, 167.

ḥnty dual of last, lit. the two sides or ends: (1) of space, ḥ. itrw 'both sides of the river', Urk. IV, 362, 13 (); ḥ. pt 'the uttermost parts of the sky', BD 166, 14 ().

(2) of time, dt nn ḥ.·s 'eternity without end', Sin. B 212 (); ḥ. rnpwt 'an eternity of years', Urk. IV, 390, 13; 1154, 8 (); rḫ·k ḥ. 'thou knowest eternity', 244, 15 (); m3 n niwt·f n ḥ. 'who looked after his city continually', Hatnub, 24, 1 (); 'the sun-folk who shall come into being n ḥ. in the everlasting future', Urk. IV, 364, 12; sḫ3 w n 3t ḥ. 'who thinks about time and eternity', 2094, 1 (); r nḥḥ ḥ. r dt 'for ever and ever', BD 159, 14; sim. 208, 10-11; 'I foresaw it ḥ. r nn ages ago for now', Urk. IV,

344,3; 'My Majesty shut them up ḥ. r ꜣbdw 7 for a period of seven months', RB 59, 8-9; m kꜣt mꜣwt ḥ. ḏt 'in new everlasting work', Urk. IV, 182, 15.

ḥni rush (n.), TR 22, 63; var. Urk. IV, 1451, 11.

ḥnyt spear, Urk. IV, 719, 1; var. 724, 1.

ḥnꜥ (1) prep. together with, and; as conj. and; rare var. : (2) adv. therewith, together with them, var. , cf. Gr. p. 581.

ḥnw (1) jar, P. Kah. 26, 5; Urk. IV, 665, 14; 952, 6; 1685, 9 ( ); bowl, 666, 4; 759, 17 ( ): (2) chattel, possession, Westc. 6, 7; pl. goods, chattels, Peas. R 43; B1, 28 (det.); P. Kah. 18, 1; Westc. 12, 6.

ḥnwt mistress: ḥnwt.f 'his m.', Urk. IV, 46, 12; ḥnwt tꜣ 'm. of the land', GNS 62; ḥnwt nt ḥmwt nsw 'm. of the king's women', Urk. IV, 603, 9; in respectful address, ḥnwt.i 'madam', Westc. 12, 21. 24; in pl. 'mesdames', 'ladies', 10, 4; 11, 6 (det.). Varr. Les. 80, 13; Urk. IV, 302, 16.

ḥnwt horn, Pyr. 270; var. Urk. IV, 2081, 5.

ḥnw bark of Sokar, Gr. p. 468, G 10; var. Urk. IV, 1909, 8.

ḥnw ribs, P. Ed. Smith, 394.

ḥnb convey land, n 'to', Urk. IV, 746, 2.

ḥnbwt confines of district, Urk. IV, 83, 4.

ḥnmmt (1) the sun-folk of Heliopolis: (2) mankind, varr. , AEO I, 98* ff.

ḥnmnm creep, M. u. K. 1, 9. 10.

ḥnn hoe, Pyr. 1394; var. P. Kah. 20, 44.

ḥnn phallus, P. Kah. 3, 37; Urk. V, 156, 6; CT I, 169 (dets.).

ḥnḥn hinder, detain, M. u. K. 4, 10; Urk. IV, 113, 16; varr. Adm. 8, 6; Urk. IV, 116, 5.

ḥnḥn dawdler (?), cripple (?), Caminos, Lit. Frag. p. 46.

ḥnḥnt swelling, Eb. 103, 19; cf. ZÄS 63, 73. 119.

ḥns narrow, Peas. R 45; Urk. IV, 649, 16; Sm. 7, 13; constricted, Eb. 36, 6 (dets.); 37, 6; ḥns-ib 'meanness', Les. 81, 10 ( ); Leyd. V 6; ḥns-ʿ 'mean', 'ungenerous', Cairo 20025, 10 ( ).

ḥnsk tie up (?), Urk. IV, 83, 13.

ḥnskt (ḥnzkt) braided lock of hair, Pyr. 724 (det.); TR 27, 35; Westc. 5, 16.

ḥnsktyw wearers of the side-lock, Pyr. 360; var. : D. el. B. 115.

ḥnskyt she who has braided hair, BD 237, 9; Westc. 5, 10; cf. JEA 22, 41.

ḥnkt beer, abbr. , Gr. § 59.

ḥnk present s'one, m 'with', Pyr. 761; Siut, pl. 1, 1; offer s'thing, n 'to', Urk. IV, 885, 14 ( ); 1780, 1 ( ); without direct obj. make offering, n 'to', m 'of', 100, 16; 342, 2; 753, 6 ( ); 964, 11 ( ); be burdened, ḥr 'with', Pyr. 1628. On wtg. cf. P. Wilbour, 112.

ḥnk offerings, Siut, pl. 2, 64.

ḥnkt offerings, SDT 148; varr. Urk. IV, 1165, 12; 146, 15.

ḥnkw diplomatic gifts, Urk. IV, 1309, 15.

ḥnkyt bed, Sin. B 294; Mill. 1, 12 ( ); BH II, 16 ( ); bier, Leb. 54; 'bed of life' where the sun sets, Urk. IV, 955, 8.

ḥnkw scale-pan of balance, RB 120, 16–121, 1; det. (?) Peas. B1, 323.

ḥnty vb. 4 inf. be covetous, greedy, Pr. 15, 1; varr. 1, 7; 10, 6; Urk. IV, 1498, 18.

ḥnt greed, Peas. B1, 291; var. BH I, 7.

ḥntꜣ porcupine (?), P. Ed. Smith, 372; var. Eb. 92, 7.

ḥntꜣsw lizard, Eb. 66, 18; 98, 10.

ḥnty commander (foreign), Urk. IV, 1302, 13; 1311, 9 ( ); equerry of foreign prince, Urk. IV, 691, 3 ( ).

Ḥr n. div. Horus, Sin. B 207. 237; of king, Gr. p. 72; f. , of queen, Urk. IV, 361, 4.

Ḥr-nbw *Falcon of Gold*, royal title, Gr. p. 73; f. Urk. IV, 341, 5.

ḥr n. (1) *face*, Sin. B 278; Sh. S. 19. 61; of animal, RB 77, 1; ḥr nb 'everyone', Gr. § 103; (r)di ḥr n 'give commands to', Adm. p. 106; (r)di m ḥr (n) 'lay a charge upon', 'command' s'one, Westc. 9, 19; Urk. IV, 97, 8; 209, 3; 'appoint' s'one, m 'to' office, 897, 14; 'call the attention of', 364, 11; 'My Maj. has commanded rdit m ḥr that an order be given', 352, 2; tp-rd rdy m ḥr n 'instructions enjoined upon', 1086, 11; sim. Les. 76, 18; ḥr 'do the bidding of', JEA 4, 34, n. 7.

(2) *sight*: m ḥr (n) 'in the s. of', Leb. 130; Siut, pl. 13, 31; sim. Urk. IV, 806, 13; 'see m ḥr.k with your own eyes', Peas. B1, 247-8; 'hidden m ḥr.sn from their s.', RB 113, 13; ḥr ḥr 'under the control, supervision of' Urk. I, 84, 16; later ḥr st-ḥr, IV, 16, 9; 209, 2.

Rare var. with suffix Peas. B1, 248. For r-ḥr 'up above' see under ḥrw 'upper part'; for ḫft-ḥr see under ḫft.

ḥr prep., with suffixes, *upon, in, at, from, on account of, concerning, through, and, having on it*, Gr. §§ 91, 1; 165; as conj. *because*, § 165; before infin. §§ 165, 10; 304, 1; 319-20; 482; elliptically for ḥr dd, § 321; ḥr ntt 'because', § 223; ḥr m 'why?', § 496.

ḥry *who, which is upon*, BM 552; Urk. V, 151, 16; *who is higher*, IV, 1104, 15; *upper*, 362, 12; 1550, 18 (); Sin. B 31; *having authority over*, e.g. ḥry sštꜣ 'master of secrets', Les. 69, 18 (); ḥry ḫntyt 'captain of sailors', Urk. IV, 8, 10; ḥry-pr 'majordomo', Westc. 3, 6; Urk. IV, 1416, 11; *headman*, 405, 5 ().

ḥr-ib *in the middle, midst of*, Pyr. 805; 1514; TR 1, 13.

ḥr(y)-ib *which is in the middle, midst of*, Pyr. 1216; Urk. IV, 328, 3; 616, 13; ḥryw-ib.sn 'their middle-sized ones', Pyr. 404; Ḥkꜣ-ib ḥry-ib 'Ḥ. the middle', Urk. VII, 7, 14; *who dwells in*, of god or king, Sin. B 209; Urk. VII, 61, 18; *middle* (n.): m ḥry-ib hrw 'in the m. of the day', IV, 19, 11; cf. also Gr. § 178; *inmost parts* of s'one, Pyr. 582; RB 119, 15.

ḥrt-ib central hall of temple, Urk. IV, 856, 8.

ḥr-ꜥ in default (?), Peas. B1, 174.

ḥr-ꜥ arrears, BH I, 8, 21; remainder, Urk. IV, 1112, 14 ( ).

ḥrt-ꜥ arrears, P. Kah. 17, 3. 4.

ḥr-ꜥwy immediately, var. , Gr. §205, 3.

ḥryw-rnpt epagomenal days, Urk. I, 25, 11; cf. Gr. p. 203.

ḥry-ḫt.f an offering-loaf, Urk. IV, 1952, 19.

ḥry-sꜣ kind of cattle, Pyr. 1544; var. Urk. IV, 1134, 8; P. Kah. 16, 14.

ḥrt-š garden, Urk. IV, 171, 16; 749, 4; 753, 7.

Ḥry-š.f n. div. Arsaphes, Peas. B1, 195; var. P. Kah. 34, 3.

ḥryw-šꜥy Beduin, Urk. IV, 83, 5; dets. ; 372, 11; Les. 82, 13.

ḥry-tꜣ survivor, Leb. 42. 64; Urk. IV, 484, 16.

ḥr-tp on behalf of, Gr. §178.

ḥry-tp who is upon, Urk. IV, 291, 10; VII, 55, 8 ( ); having authority over, VII, 55, 2; ḥry-ḥbt ḥry-tp 'chief lector', Westc. 4, 3; chief, headman, BM 614, 6; Urk. VII, 55, 6; BD 59, 12; master of servant, RB 116, 13 ( ); fem. ḥrt-tp 'chieftainess', Urk. IV, 225, 6; 231, 13; BD 350, 1.

ḥrw upper part, top, P. Kah. 6, 19; Sm. 5, 14 ( ); JEA 15, pl. 36 (14, 3) ( ); n-ḥrw 'upward', Sm. 4, 3; 10, 21; r-ḥrw 'up above', 'upward', Leb. 59; Peas. B1, 4; Sm. 2, 10; ḥr ḥrw 'upraised', of arms, Urk. IV, 618, 6.

ḥryt: m-ḥryt 'above', Sin. R40; 'in advance of', I. Carn. 11 ( ).

ḥrt sky, heaven, Urk. IV, 268, 2; 365, 2; 1198, 1; var. RB 113, 12.

ḥrt tomb, Urk. IV, 10, 9 (det.); 57, 3; 132, 14 (dets.); 918, 16; necropolis, Sin. B303; Urk. IV, 113, 10; 147, 1; 'tomb-garden', Sin. B305-6.

ḥr a rope aboard ship, Urk. V, 192, 15; 193, 2.

ḥr adj. distant, Pyr. 598: vb. be far, r 'from', Pyr. 586; Urk. I, 223, 9; IV, 564, 17; ḥr.ti r, ḥr.tiwny r 'beware of', Gr. §313.

ḥrw-r apart from, besides, as well as, var. , Gr. § 179; without -r, Urk. IV, 8, 1; 1307, 17.

ḥr adj. terrible, Adm. 2, 9; Urk. IV, 184, 17: vb. terrify, n s'one, BD 400, 9.

ḥr terror, dread, Sin. B 280; Pr. 6, 10.

ḥryt terror, dread, Urk. IV, 102, 12; 161, 15; 887, 13; respect, Pr. 7, 5 (dets.); cf. Žába, 125. Varr. Siut, pl. 19, 45; Hatnub, 23, 4; Urk. IV, 64, 5; 1278, 17; 1845, 16; RB 56, 15; ḥry(t)-ib 'terror', Adm. 2, 13.

ḥr prepare, make ready, Urk. IV, 187, 3; 325, 12; be ready, r 'for', RB 56, 14; m-ḥrt 'in readiness for (?)', Caminos, Lit. Frag. pl. 21, 4, 1.

, varr. of Ḥ‘py 'Nile'.

ḥrf kind of bread, Urk. IV, 1157, 15.

ḥrrt flower, Urk. IV, 775, 16; 915, 7; 1668, 19.

ḥrst carnelian (?), JEA 38, 13.

ḥrtt lump of lapis lazuli, Urk. IV, 668, 13; var. 638, 12.

ḥrty vb. 4 inf. travel by land, Westc. 7, 12; var. Les. 84, 20.

ḥḥ (1) n. div., Gr. p. 449, C 11: (2) num. million, a great number, § 259. 262, 2; ḥḥ n 'many', § 99.

ḥḥy vb. 3 inf. seek, search for, Westc. 4, 25; 7, 7; Urk. IV, 7, 12; 26, 17; 85, 9; m ḥḥy n ib 'with ingenious mind', GAS 97; be missing, m 'from', JEA 43, 14, 7. Var. Sin. B 4.

ḥḥ vb used of mast breaking the force (?) of a wave in wreck, Sh. S. 36-7.

var. of nḥḥ 'eternity'.

ḥsi vb. 3 inf. spin yarn, BH II, 13.

ḥst (ḥzt) water-jar, Gr. p. 529, W 14; Caminos, L.-Eg. Misc. 422-3; var. Adm. 11, 1.

ḥsi (ḥzi) vb. 3 inf. favour s'one, Sin. B 206; Peas. B 1, 196; Urk. IV, 134, 13; praise s'one, Peas. B 1, 69; Urk. IV, 58, 2; VII, 30, 13; speech, Pyr. 1299; conduct, Les. 82, 21;

ḥs·ṯỉ 'so please you', Westc. 9, 2; ḥsst 'do what is praiseworthy', Urk. IV, 181, 3; 1139, 12; 'perform rites', ḥr-tp 'on behalf of', 80, 16; 923, 8-9; iry.ỉ ḥst.k 'I will do your pleasure', Peas. B1, 3. Varr. Urk. IV, 77, 1; 40, 12.

ḥst n. favour, Sin. R3; B310 ( ); Urk. IV, 31, 5 ( ); pl. 2, 1; praise VII, 30, 11 (det.); m ḥswt 'as reward for', IV, 200, 3.

ḥsy favoured, praised one, Peas. B1, 68-9; varr. B1, 196; Les. 72, 14; RB 113, 3; f. Urk. IV, 913, 5; cryptic (cf. ḥsỉ 'spin'), BH II, 14.

ḥsty praise (n.), Urk. VII, 30, 9.

ḥsyt concubines, Urk. IV, 1305, 8.

ḥswtỉ favourite (adj.), Pyr. 1212; var. Urk. VII, 37, 16.

ḥsỉ (ḥzỉ) vb. 3 inf. turn back, r 'to' a place; m 'to face aggressively'; m ḥs·f '(coming) to meet him', AEO I, 159*; ḥs ḥr·f 'courageous', Urk. IV, 1292, 7; ḥs ḥr m 'face' an enemy, 85, 10; ḥs sw m irt bw-mꜣꜥ 'he was one who turned to and fro doing good', 971, 8; turn away the evil-doer, 945, 14. Varr. 971, 8; RB 58, 9.

ḥs excrement, Eb. 37, 6; TR 23, 3.

ḥsỉ vb. 3 inf. sing, Urk. I, 45, 14; BH II, 4; varr. Westc. 12, 1; Urk. IV, 1064, 15; imy-r ḥst Pr-ꜥꜣ 'Master of the King's Music', I, 45, 13.

ḥsw minstrel, Leyd. V 2; varr. Th. T. S. I, 15; II, 27; fem. , locc. cit.

ḥs be cold, Peas. B1, 245; Leb. 46; var. Les. 82, 5.

ḥsꜣ (ḥzꜣ) (1) milk, CT I, 168: (2) mucus, P. Kah. 7, 30. 31; Eb. 40, 2 ( ): (3) dough, Ikhekhi, 42 ( ); Bersh. I, 25 ( ); P. Kah. 5, 48 (det.).

Ḥsꜣt n. div. a cow-goddess, Urk. IV, 238, 14; var. ZÄS 60, 75; 'the white thing of Ḥ.' = milk, Les. 73, 15.

ḥsw spell for protection against water, Herdsm. 13.

× ḥsb num. ¼, Gr. §265; ¼ aroura, §266, 3.

ḥsb break, smash, Pyr. 1043. 1144; Sm. 14, 18 (det. …); Urk. V, 170, 11; n. fracture, Sm. 5, 10 (…). 11.

ḥsb count, reckon, Urk. IV, 36, 8 (…); 118, 9; 336, 7; 927, 15; reckon with offenders, V, 55, 12. For tp-ḥsb see under tp.

ḥsbw reckoning, BM 614, 9; account, P. Boul. XVIII, 31 = Gr. p. 201 (…).

ḥsbw doom, Urk. IV, 5, 17.

ḥsb kind of bread, Les. 73, 13.

ḥsb workman, BH I, 8, 14; P. Kah. 31, 4. 25; Urk. IV, 1669, 1.

ḥsp (ḥzp) garden, Gr. p. 488, N 24; AEO II, 216*; var. … Peas. B1, 264.

ḥsmn (ḥzmn) natron, Peas. B1, 47; Adm. 11, 2; Urk. IV, 1076, 12; var. … Pyr. 864.

ḥsmn bronze, Adm. 3, 2; varr. … Urk. IV, 423, 3; … 664, 4.

ḥsmn menstruation, Sm. 20, 13; var. … Eb. 97, 2.

ḥsmn food of some kind, Leyd. V 6, 15.

ḥsḳ cut off head, etc., Peas. B1, 289; Westc. 7, 4; BD 9, 7; 121, 17; cut out heart, etc., BD 31, 2; Urk. IV, 1603, 15; behead man or animal, Pyr. 635. 746; RB 56, 11.

ḥsḳt chopper, BD 394, 15.

… see under ḥnḳt 'beer'.

Ḥḳt n. div. the frog-goddess, BH II, 4. 13; Les. 73, 14; varr. … TR 5, 2; … Westc. 10, 8; … Urk. IV, 389, 5.

ḥḳꜣt sceptre, varr. …, …, Gr. p. 508, S 38.

ḥḳꜣ ruler, Sin. B 99; var. … BM 614, 6; of god or Pharaoh, dets. … Sin. B 17; … Les. 64, 13; … Urk. IV, 16, 3; … 'district governor', Peas. B1, 86; Urk. IV, 1120, 1.

ḥḳꜣ rule over, govern, Sin. B 70; Urk. IV, 16, 7. 14 (…); V, 116, 2.

ḥḳꜣt rulership, Urk. IV, 279, 2; 1276, 16; Merikarēꜥ, 85.

… var. of Ḥḳt 'frog-goddess'.

ḥḳꜣt corn-measure of 4.54 litres, varr. …, …, …, …, …, Gr. § 266, 1.

ḥḳr vb. be hungry, Les. 79, 15; BM 101 (det. …); n. hunger, Sin. B 151; Peas. B1, 243.

ḥkr hungry man, BH I, 8, 20; dets. BD 261, 2.

ḥkꜣw magic, magic spells, Adm. 6, 6; varr. Westc. 6, 8; BD 31, 13.

ḥkꜣy magician, PSBA 39, 31. 139.

Ḥkꜣw n. div. god of magic, late var. , PSBA 37, 253; 39, 134; JEA 24, 128.

ḥkn be joyful, Urk. IV, 14, 15; 566, 3; acclaim s'one, 248, 14 ( ).

ḥknw praise (n.) to god, Sin. B 141; to king, Urk. IV, 101, 4; 753, 17 ( ); thanksgiving, Sh. S. 5; JEA 39, 18.

ḥknw a sacred oil, BH I, 17; var. Sh. S. 140.

ḥt become entangled, of hair, Westc. 5, 15-16.

ḥtt mine, quarry, Sinai, 47. 53; Urk. IV, 25, 8; varr. JEA 4, pl. 9, 5; Bersh. II, p. 24; Urk. IV, 1448, 18; pl. 1448, 5.

ḥtꜣ sail (n.), Peas. B1, 56; Urk. IV, 1546, 8 (det.); in pl. awning, JEA 16, 71.

ḥtꜣ shabby, threadbare, wrinkled, Caminos, L.-Eg. Misc. 290.

ḥtꜣw wrinkles (?), Eb. 87, 16, cf. op. cit. 291.

ḥty smoke, Eb. 54, 9; Sm. 21, 3; Caminos, Lit. Frag. pl. 14, 2, 2.

ḥtyt throat, BD 104, 12; 111, 6; Urk. IV, 482, 12; var. Sm. 11, 23.

ḥtꜥ bed, Urk. IV, 667, 2.

ḥtw bowls, Urk. IV, 871, 8.

ḥtp altar, var. , Gr. p. 501, R4; Urk. IV, 667, 1.

ḥtp offerings, BD 14, 13; var. 3, 8; 'god's o.', Westc. 9, 27; var. Urk. IV, 1553, 18; "forecourt" o.', BH I, 17.

ḥtpt offerings, Urk. IV, 227, 10; 748, 7; BD 35, 2.

ḥtp boon in funerary formula ḥtp-di-nsw 'a b. which the king grants', Gr. p. 170; JEA 25, 34; ideographic wtg. Urk. IV, 46, 6.

ḥtp vb. (1) intrans. be pleased, ḥr 'with', Urk. IV, 580, 3; 618, 17; 835, 16; be happy, Pr. 7, 6; be gracious, n 'to', Sin. B 148. 165. 273; pardon, n s'one, Les. 98, 17. 19; be at peace, Urk. IV, 271, 15; be peaceful, of years, 261, 9; become calm, of sky after storm, Peas. B1,244; rest, m 'in', Urk. IV, 379,6; RB 110,6; r 'in', Urk. IV, 1074,15; go to rest, set, of sun, RB 113,15.16; BD 8,14; ḥtp m ꜥnḫ 'set', of sun; 'go to rest' = die, of persons, JEA 39,53 (f); ḥtp ib ḥr 'be well-disposed toward', Urk. IV, 1293,9.

(2) trans. satisfy, make content, Pyr. 388; Paheri, 5; pacify, Leb. 23; occupy throne, Urk. IV, 83,2; heritage, 1382,6; rest in tomb, Bersh. I,14,12; hall, Urk. IV, 520,6; assume titulary, 896,9. — Varr. Sin. B148; B161; Urk. IV, 580,3.

ḥtpw peace, Urk. IV, 370,17; 1098,14; contentment, Pyr. 508; RB 110,10; good pleasure, JEA 39,17 (l); ḥtp 'make peace', Urk. IV, 704,6; rdi ḥtpw n 'make submission to', JEA 39,19 (hh). Varr. Sin. B205; Sh.S. 11; Urk. IV, 332,9; RB 112,14.

ḥtpt graciousness, Pyr. 34; peace, Pr. 11,4; Urk. IV, 382,12; mercy, Sin. B165.

ḥtpt bundle of herbs, Urk. IV, 771,14; 827,6; det. VII, 54,2.

ḥtpt bowl for bread-offerings, Urk. IV, 827,13.

ḥtptyw the peaceful ones = the blessed dead, D. el B. 114.

ḥtpyw non-combatants, Urk. IV, 698,8; 704,12; varr. 714,5; 665,11.

ḥtmt chair, Gr. p. 500, Q1.

ḥtm provide, m 'with', BD 372,12; 380,13; var. Urk. IV, 248,13.

ḥtm vb. intrans. perish, be destroyed, Peas. B1,223; Urk. IV, 2,6; 518,15; 1491,16; BD 190,14: trans. destroy enemies, Pyr. 293; Urk. V, 51,2; quench thirst, CT I, 90; Eb. 39,12.

ḥtr yoke of oxen, P. Kah. 16,14; var. Urk. IV, 132,9.

ḥtr span of horses, Paheri, 3; pl. horses when inspanned, Urk. IV, 697,16; 710,4; 1306,4; RB 60,4; hence chariotry, Urk. IV, 1546,9; 'they stood ḥr ḥtrw.sn in their chariots', RB 59,5; sim. Urk. IV, 1280,15; rḫ sw ḥtr 'he is one who knows (the management of) a span', 1279,13; t-nt-ḥtr 'chariotry', AEO I, 113*.

ḥtr tax, levy (vb. and n.), Urk. IV, 186, 7; 753, 9; 1114, 9; P. Kah. 21, 20; provide a temple m 'with' workmen, Urk. IV, 1669, 1. Varr. 70, 6; 700, 6; 196, 8.

ḥtr (1) bind together: (2) (med.) be contracted, P. Ed. Smith, 187.

ḥtrw lashings, Pyr. 2080.

ḥts bring to an end, complete period of time, Pyr. 1785; CT I, 173; BD 225, 15; celebrate festival, Urk. VII, 58, 10 ( ).

ḥṯt hyaena, Desh. 9; var. Urk. VII, 36.

var. of ḥṯt 'mine'.

ḥṯ3 kind of bread, BH I, 18.

ḥṯṯ carry under the arm, Caminos, Lit. Frag. p. 15, n. 1.

ḥṯṯt armpit, var. det. , loc. cit.

ḥdb sit, ḥr 'on'; seat o'self; halt, ḥr 'at', GNS 91.

ḥdb overthrow; be prostrate; also det. , loc. cit.; var. CT I, 180.

ḥḏ mace, Gr. p. 510, T 3; var. Urk. IV, 1279, 5.

ḥḏ white, Sin. B 196; Eb. 10, 10; Urk. IV, 701, 13 ( ); bright: ḥḏ t3 'the land becomes b.' = dawn, Sin. B 20. 248; Sh. S. 185. Urk. IV, 896, 4; sim. Adm. 10, 1; ḥḏ ḥr 'b. of face' = cheerful, Pr. 14, 12; JEA 4, pl. 8, 8 ( ); Les. 79, 11 ( ); 80, 20 ( ).

ḥḏ set forth at dawn, var. , GNS 16.

ḥḏ silver, Urk. IV, 174, 3; 423, 10; 701, 12; 733, 5; later also as term for money, Stud. Griff. 124. Var. Les. 71, 5.

ḥḏ white clothes, Sin. B 153.

ḥḏt white linen, Urk. IV, 207, 11; 742, 15; varr. 1148, 2; Adm. 10, 4.

ḥḏt the White Crown, Les. 75, 9; varr. Urk. IV, 256, 6; Les. 98, 17; RB 112, 15.

ḥḏty white sandals, RB 122, 13.

ḥḏ chapel in ḥḏ 'bird-ch.', Caminos, Lit. Frag. pl. 14, 2, 3.

ḥḏt white of the eye, Hymnen, 12, 2.

ḥḏw onions, P. Kah. 6,7; varr. Urk. IV, 548,1; Th. T. S. II, 32.

ḥḏi vb. 3 inf. (1) trans. injure, Peas. B1, 169; M. u. K. 2, 2. 3; Pr. 6,3; destroy, Adm. 10,6; Peas. B1, 274; Urk. IV, 1058, 2; VII, 53, 11; disobey, IV, 974, 3; 1776, 12; annul a contract, Siut, pl. 8, 310; upset concerted action, Westc. 6, 4; waste time, Pr. 7, 9; eclipse: ḥḏ.n nfrw.f bḫnt 'its beauty e.'d the pylon,' Urk. IV, 1823, 1; ḥḏ ib 'be upset (?), annoyed (?),' Pr. 14, 6.

(2) intrans. be destroyed, perished, Peas. B1, 197. 201; Adm. 10, 2; be lacking, Adm. 3, 8. 11; 5, 1; fail, Urk. IV, 351, 6; 994, 3.

(3) n. damage, destruction, BD 458, 6; the land ḫpr m ḥḏ 'has become waste,' Adm. p. 101. — Varr. Urk. VIII, 53, 11; Westc. 6, 4; Adm. 3, 8.

ḥḏdwt brightness, Urk. IV, 15, 14; RB 114, 1; var. BM 552.

ḫ n. placenta (?), Gr. p. 539, Aa 1; child, var. JEA 3, 237: vb. be a child, Eb. 1, 17.

ḫt fire, Sh. S. 55; Westc. 4, 10; Peas. B1, 246.

ḫtt fiery (fem.), Hymnen, 4, 3.

ḫt thing(s): m ḫt wꜥt 'into, as one th.' = altogether, Eb. 4, 8; Urk. IV, 372, 17; 942, 9; ḫt m st 'the th. is in place' = all well and good, JEA 28, 18 (e); ḫt nbt nfrt 'all good th.'s,' Urk. IV, 30, 3; 703, 12; rdi ḫt 'give gifts,' JEA 4, pl. 8, 8; offerings, Urk. IV, 469, 16; 766, 10; ḫt ḫ3wy 'the night-o.', see ḫ3wy; possessions, property, Sin. B 143; Peas. B1, 232; P. Kah. 12, 4; Urk. IV, 1303, 17; 'overseer,' 'administrator,' see p. 25; matter, affair, Urk. I, 53, 1; 104, 12; IV, 118, 11; something, anything, Gr. §§ 92, 2; 103; ḫt nb(t) 'everything,' 'anything,' § 103; 'in every respect,' Pr. 5, 2; mi-ḫt synonym of mitt 'the like,' GNS 60; as obj. of : ir ḫt 'do things,' Les. 70, 2; ir ḫt ḫft 'act in accordance with,' Urk. IV, 1089, 3; 1092, 10; 'workers,' TR 2, 17. 30; 'Lord of Action,' ep. of king, Urk. IV, 13, 14; var.

144,15. Old var.  Pyr. 2030; later 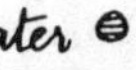 Urk. IV, 1799,6.

 ḫ3 (1) num. 1000, Gr. §§ 259. 262,2; 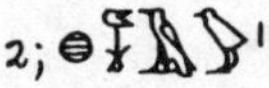 'thousands,' TR 22,66; [illegible] BD 356,10: (2) herd in 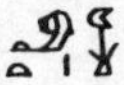 'herdsman,'  'overseer of herds,' BH I, 30.

 ḫ3w plants, Urk. IV, 329,2 (det. [illegible]); 529,4 (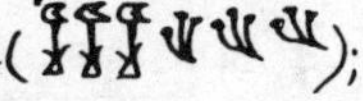); 692,13; flowers, 1996,14 (); RB 62,10 ([illegible]); 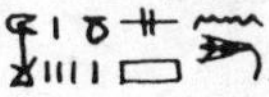 'lotus-f.,' Eb. 43,6; sim. 44,9.

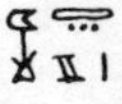 ḫ3-t3 land measure of 10 arouras, abbr. [illegible], Gr. § 266,3; later kind of Crown land, P. Wilbour, Index, 97.

 ḫ3 be young, little, Eb. 1,18.

 ḫ3 office, bureau, Urk. IV, 150,13; varr. [illegible] 152,12;  1119,7;  1117,17; [illegible] 1103,15; 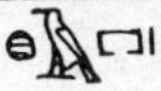 Les. 81,3; [illegible] JEA 41, 21, c. Cf. PSBA 22,99.

 ḫ3t marsh, Sin. B 226. See also ẖ3t.

 ḫ3t corpse, Sin. B 99. 259. See also ẖ3t.

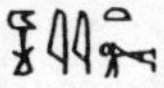 ḫ3yt slaughter, massacre, RB 57,6; var.  795,17. See also ẖ3yt.

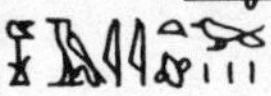 ḫ3yt disease, Eb. 36,14; varr.  Westc. 7,19; 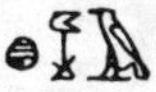 Pr. 10,2. See also ẖ3t.

 ḫ3i vb. 3 inf. measure, Peas. R 3.4; Urk. IV, 339,8; 367,15; cf. JEA 12,136; examine patient, P. Ed. Smith, 104. Varr.  Cairo 20500; 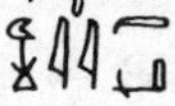 Urk. IV, 669,13;  64,1; abbr. [illegible] Eb. 37,10.

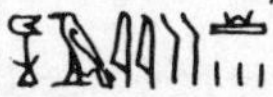 ḫ3yw measurements, JEA 4, 145, n. 2.

 ḫ3y plumb-line, Peas. B1, 91. 92 (); Urk. IV, 1076,8; fig. rule of conduct, Pr. 8,5.

 ḫ3y altar, Les. 77,1. Perhaps miswriting of the next below.

 ḫ3wt altar, Siut, pl. 5, 240; Bersh. I, 14,11 (det. [illegible]); Westc. 9,26; varr. 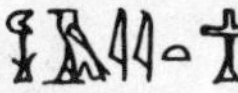 Urk. IV, 27,2; 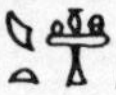 163,7;  RB 113,4; 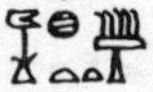 D. el B. 140.

 ḫ3wt altar-chamber, CT I, 164.

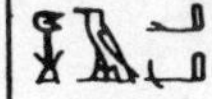 ḫ3ʿ throw, Westc. 3,12; Leb. 13.58; BD 183,2 (det. [illegible]); strike down with disease, BD 356,10 (); cast off bonds, Pyr. 2202 (); abandon property,

etc., Urk. IV, 658, 3; RB 57, 11; despatch messages, Pyr. 400 ( ); thrust, P. Kah. 3, 35; harpoon hippopotamus, TR 20, 31 ( ); Peas. B1, 206; Louvre C 14, 11 (det.); play (?) fish, JEA 9, 16, n. 10; drip sweat, Urk. IV, 1282, 18 (det.); ḫ3ʿ r-bnr m 'eject from', 1312, 9-10; ḫ3ʿ m3wy n 'turn o's attention to', 1082, 14; ḫ3ʿ ḥ3 'leave behind', 1624, 19.

ḫ3ʿ urination, Eb. 2, 17.

ḫ3ʿw discharges (med.), P. Kah. 5, 10. 24.

ḫ3w bowl, Urk. IV, 753, 10; varr. 112, 16; TR 20, 76.

ḫ3wt hide of animal, Peas. R 15; masc. in O. K., Urk. I, 77, 13.

ḫ3wy night, Sin. R 20; B 191; ḫt-ḫ3wy 'the n.-offerings', a festival, BD 71, 7; Urk. IV, 27, 5; 177, 5, 470, 2. Varr. Sin. B 20; BH I, 24; Urk. IV, 470, 2.

ḫ3wy benighted traveller, Adm. 5, 11.

ḫ3b hippopotamus, Louvre C 14, 11.

ḫ3b be bent, of arm, Pr. 13, 12. Cf. ḫ3b 'crooked'.

ḫ3b3s the starry sky, JEA 21, 5, n. 3; var. 21, 8.

ḫ3bt crookedness, Peas. B1, 107. See also ḫ3bb.

var. of ḫfʿ 'grasp'.

ḫ3m bend arm in attitude of respect, Sh. S. 87. 161 ( ); Pr. 5, 11; BM 614, 7 ( ); Urk. IV, 927, 12 ( ); cf. JEA 37, 51 (u); back, Urk. IV, 1073, 4 ( ); bow down, BH I, 9; Urk. IV, 158, 16. See also ḫ3m.

ḫ3nnt: m3m3 n ḫ3nnt variety of date-palm, Urk. IV, 73, 17.

ḫ3rt widow, Peas. B1, 63; var. Siut, pl. 15, 10. See also ḫ3rt.

ḫ3ry be wifeless, Adm. 8, 1.

ḫ3r bolt (?), of horses, RB 61, 13.

Ḫ3rw (Ḫr) n. loc. Khor in Palestine-Syria, AEO I, 180*; var. Urk. IV, 665, 16.

Ḫ3rw Khorian, Urk. IV, 743, 8; var. 649, 10.

h̯3h̯ be speedy, swift, M.u.K. 3,2; Urk. IV, 1541,13 ( ); hasten, hurry, Peas. B2,104; TR 22,25; h̯3h̯ ib 'impatient', Peas. B1,212 ( ); h̯3h̯ r 'quick of speech', B1,208; h̯3h̯ ḥr 'impatience', Les. 80,17 ( ).

h̯3h̯ spear fish, Peas. B1,229. Probably error for h̯3ʿ.

h̯3h̯3 winnow, Sm. 21,11-12; cf. AEO II, 220*.

h̯3s scramble (?), Urk. IV, 658,13.

h̯3s creek (?), Leb. 94; runnel (?), Urk. IV, 919,4 ( ).

h̯3s curl on front of Red Crown (?), Caminos, Lit. Frag. p. 30.

h̯3st hill-country, Sin. B213; Urk. IV, 244,11; 343,16; foreign land, Sin. B28.130.197.202; Urk. IV, 339,1; desert, Sin. B209.292; RB 76,6; 'd. region', Urk. IV, 8,7; 'd. game', Sin. B89; Th. T. S. I, 9. Varr. Urk. IV, 373,11; 334,7; 339,10.

h̯3styw foreigners, desert-dwellers, Adm. 15,2; RB 59,10; 61,5; varr. Urk. IV, 83,6; 711,5.

h̯3syt bryony (?), var. , JEA 20,45; Caminos, Lit. Frag. pl. 4,2; cf. p. 16.

h̯3ty office (?), Urk. IV, 129,13.

h̯3tb have pity, m 'on', Urk. V, 178,17.

h̯3d dough, BH II, 7.

h̯y what, Gr. p. 427; h̯y ḳd·k 'How are you?', JEA 34,38; h̯y ... h̯y ... 'as ... so ...', 3,243.

h̯yt shelter, Les. 82,4.

h̯ʿ hill, Pyr. 542.1022; cf. Gr. p. 489, N28.

h̯ʿi vb. 3 inf. rise, of sun, BD 1,6; 2,4.10; Urk. IV, 362,16; appear in glory, of god or king (esp. of king's accession), JEA 31,24; 39,23; of crown, Hymnen, 14,1; sim. Urk. IV, 287,7; be shining, of king, 16,10; 806,13. Rare var. CT I, 46.

h̯ʿw appearance in glory, JEA locc. cit.; varr. BD 8,4; Les. 68,8.

ḫꜥw crown, JEA 39, pl. 2, 17; varr. (pl.), Westc. 11, 13; Urk. IV, 565, 17.

ḫꜥw (1) weapons: (2) funeral furniture, tomb-equipment: (3) tackle of ship: (4) utensils, implements in general, GNS 115, with n. 3. Varr. Sin. B 136; Urk. IV, 656, 2; 1311, 6; 1302, 10.

var. of ḫꜥm 'approach'.

ḫꜥmw throat, var. , P. Ed. Smith, 313.

ḫꜥr rage (vb.), Urk. IV, 8, 13; 1290, 7.

ḫw: wꜥ ḥr ḫw.f 'unique'; nn wn ḥr ḫw.f 'there is none beside him'; none survived ḥr ḫw.i 'except me', Gr. § 178.

ḫwi vb. 3 inf. protect, Les. 68, 21 (); Urk. IV, 238, 10; 1307, 2 (); 1685, 7 (?) (); exclude o'self from quarrels, RB 122, 5; exempt from dues, etc, Urk. I, 214, 16; 281, 5; 283, 4 (); ḫw mk similarly, JEA 38, 56; set aside property, etc., for a purpose, Urk. I, 15, 1; IV, 1544, 2; avoid, Sm. 20, 9; prevent, with foll. sḏm.f, Pyr. 828 (). 1257. 1654; CT I, 304; 'The Bright Protected One (?)' = the reigning king, JEA 34, 33; ḫw rd 'guarded of gait', Urk. IV, 967, 14.

ḫw protection, M. u. K. 6, 4.

ḫwt protection, Urk. IV, 618, 8.

ḫw fan, var. , in title ṯꜣy ḫw 'f.-bearer', Th. T. S. IV, 38.

ḫwt sanctuary, Bersh. II, 6.

ḫww baseness, wrongdoing, Urk. IV, 1077, 9; RB 116, 2; var. Pr. 1, 4; 15, 5.

ḫwsi vb. 4 inf. (fem. infin.) pound, beat up, Urk. IV, 1141, 12; 1142, 2 (); beat flat ground, 835, 5; build up bricks, 1152, 5 (); fig. of Nile, 924, 10 (det.); build, construct, Sin. B 196 (); B 300; Leb. 61 (); Urk. IV 169, 8 (abbr.); 1823, 4; stir arms, 1154, 5; heart, Neferti, 20.

ḫwd rich, wealthy, Peas. B 1, 125; D. el. B. 110; varr. Peas. B 2, 100; Hatnub, 17, 12; Siut, pl. 5, 247.

ḫwd rich man, Peas. B 1, 89; var. Adm. 8, 2.

ḫwdt wealth of timber, RB 60,13; 61,1.

ḫwdw class of fisherman, Peas. B1,227; var. Bersh. II, p. 20.

ḫbi vb. 3 inf. dance, Westc. 12,1; Urk. IV, 386,6; var. 1162,6.

ḫbt dance (n.), Paheri, 5.

ḫbb dance (n.), Sin. B194.

ḫbw dancers, P. Kah. 24,2; fem. Urk. IV, 2030,6.

ḫbi vb. 3 inf. deduct, subtract, JEA 12,124; reduce, lessen, Pr. 7,9; BD 16,3 (det.); 251,1 (det.); waste time, JEA 13,75 (det.); damage tomb, Urk. IV, 1491,11; exact dues, JEA 27,75 (a); be hushed, of voice, BD 481,3: n. exaction, JEA 27,75 (a). See also ḫbꜣ 'destroy'.

ḫbt deduction, Urk. IV, 1184,11; exaction, 1114,13; lessening of moon, ZÄS 57,3*; sim. of mouth, 57,2*.

ḫbt place of execution, CT I, 70; BD 184,1; 255,5.

ḫbꜣ destroy, lay waste, ravage, Peas. B1,143.230; Adm. 2,11; 3,1; Urk. IV, 697,8; subvert law, Peas. B1,274; ḫbꜣ-ḥr 'downcast', B1,286 (dets.). Varr. L. to D. VI,7; RB 57,12; Urk. IV, 931,2.

ḫbyt carnage, Urk. IV, 9,1.

ḫbbt jar, Adm. 8,4.

ḫbn distort speech, Pr. 17,7; be distorted, of character, Siut, pl. 16,5 (det.); of voice = be found guilty, Pyr. 1041 (); sp ḫbn 'a wrongful act,' Urk. IV, 1383,2 (dets.).

ḫbnt crime, Pt. (L II), 5,10; BD 260,13; accusation, Pyr. 462 (); CT I, 73.

ḫbnty criminal, Urk. IV, 1109,3; dets. 969,4; BD 279,16.

ḫbst (ḫbzt) tail, AEO II, 238*; pl. RB 64,13.

ḫbswt beard, AEO II, 238*.

ḫbstyw bearded ones, Urk. IV, 345,15.

ḫbs hack up earth, Urk. V, 128,1; BD 20,11; var. Pyr. 817.

ḫbsw *ploughlands*, BM 1628, 11; Urk. IV, 1054, 12; varr. 1052, 5; 1093, 2; 1054, 14; 1050, 16.

ḫbd vb. intrans. *be hateful*, Pyr. 296; 'what is h.', Pr. 10, 4; 17, 6: trans. *be displeased with*, Urk. IV, 1491, 12; 1800, 4 ( ): n. *displeasure, disfavour*, Pr. 7, 12; Urk. IV, 1491, 4 (dets.).

ḫpi vb. 3 inf. intrans. *travel*, BM 614, 8; BD 163, 12; ḫp n k3.f 'go to his ka' = die, Urk. I, 227, 7; mrt.f ḫp.s m ḥˁw.s 'love of him coursed through her body', IV, 220, 4: trans. *encounter* s'one, Sin. B 10; Herdsm. 23.

ḫpi *die*, Sm. 19, 7.

ḫpyt *death*, Urk. IV, 1951, 15; varr. , , Cairo 20003.

ḫpw *journeys*, var. , CT I, 107.

ḫpp *strange*, pl. , GAS 97.

ḫpp *stranger*, GAS 97.

ḫppwt *strange things*, GAS 97.

ḫpr vb. (1) intrans. *come into being*, Sh. S. 32; ZÄS 57, 6*; BD 9, 1; n ḫpr.n prw n tp-ḥsb 'no excess is possible to (lit. 'can c. i. b. for') the norm', Peas. B1, 324–5; of illness, n ḫpr.n gsw r.s 'gsw cannot attack her', Eb. 95, 3; ib.sn ḫpr 'their hearts came i. b.' = their will was good, Bersh. I, 14, 5; *become*, with m, Sh. S. 73; Peas. B1, 97; TR 15, 1; *change*, m 'into', Urk. V, 4, 10; Sh. S. 154; BD 163, 15; *grow up*, Sin. B 188. 222; Westc. 12, 22; Les. 70, 21; with det. JEA 21, 3, n. 4; *occur, happen, come to pass*, Sin. R 18; B 35. 37. 160; Sh. S. 22. 125. 130; *take place*, of festival, Urk. IV, 195, 13; *be effective*, Pr. 6, 10 (bis); *go by, be past*: mk nwyw ḫpr 'behold, ages have gone by', Meir, III, 23; sp ḫpr 'a matter which is past', Peas. B1, 273; Pr. 13, 4; sḫrw ḫpr 'bygone affairs', ZÄS 60, 73; [ḫr] m-ḫt p3 hrw 7 ḫpr '[Now] after the seven days had passed', Westc. 3, 17; *come*, of time, Sin. B 11; *continue*, of action: ḫpr r ˁ nb 'the stone-cutting (?) went on every day', Urk. I, 38, 17; *exist, be*, Sin. B 48; Urk. IV, 6, 14; 7, 6; Westc. 9, 18; wšbw mdt m ḫprt im.s 'who answers a word in accordance with what is in it' = what is meant by it, Les. 84,2; as passive of , e.g. Sin. B51; Peas. B1,280; cf. GNS 33.

(2) trans. bring about, Urk. I, 109,11; IV, 340,6; VII, 34,10 (det.).

(3) idiomatic uses: ḫpr n 'accrue to', Urk. IV, 2,1; RB 62,6; mi ḫpr 'act properly'; 'do as should be done', 'correct procedure', JEA 12, 126; ZÄS 60,65; ḫpr m 'amounts to', P. BM 10102, rt. 9 = JEA 14, pl. 35; imi ḫpr 'get it done!', JEA 12, 126; ḫpr.f-iṯ.f 'a born conqueror', JEA 32,55; ḫpr 'fully cooked', 'done', of meat, Meir, III, p.31, n.2. — Varr. Urk. IV, 245,17; 1106,16; TR 52,2.

ḫpr-ḏs.f (1) who came into being of himself, ep. of sun-god, Urk. V, 8,10: (2) fermentation (?), Eb. 34,8; 77,5.

ḫpry children, JEA 21,3, n.4; var. Siut, pl.13,29.

ḫprw form, shape, P. Kah. 1,1 ( ); Sm. 19,6 ( ); Urk. IV, 16,10 ( ); 159,17 ( ); 684,5 ( ); 1061,6; 1276,15 ( ); ḫprw 'assume a s.' 1014,16; BD 23,3 ( ); RB 113,2; ir ḫprw m 'transform (o'self) into', Westc. 9,27; TR 17,1 ( ); Urk. IV, 147,8; BD 181,3; 'have o's upbringing' in a place, Urk. IV, 2,9; modes of being, etc.: sm3.n.f ḫprw.i nbw 'he united all my m. of b.', 161,11; ḫprw ḥr ḫpr 'changes take place', Adm. p.101; ḥ3ty.i n ḫprw.i 'my heart of my different ages', Gr. p. 268.

ḫprr dung-beetle, Pyr. 697; Eb. 88,13; scarab, BD 96,14. Var. Pyr. 366.

Ḫprr n. div. Khopri, young sun-god, Pyr. 888; RB 114,3; varr. Pyr. 1757; TR 19,4; BD 66,5.

ḫprš the Blue Crown, abbr. , Gr. p. 504, S7.

ḫpš foreleg, BD 132,14; 333,7 ( ); D. el. B. 107 ( ); thigh, Urk. V, 131,9. Cf. AEO II, 243*.

ḫpš constellation of Great Bear, Urk. V, 42,3; var. BD 58,10. Cf. AEO I, 4*.

ḫpš strong arm, Sin. B52.105; Urk. IV, 186,16 ( ); 557,3; strength, power, Hatnub, 23,3; CT I, 6 (dets.); Urk. IV, 94,6; 662,11; m ḫpš 'acquire by o's own arm', JEA 16,196.

ḫpš be effective (?), ZÄS 60, 43.

ḫpš scimetar, Gr. p. 513, T 16; battle-axe, Urk. IV, 1562, 8 (det.).

ḫpdw buttocks, P. Kah. 3, 35; Urk. V, 36, 16.

ḫf plunder (vb.), JEA 39, p. 4, fig. 2, 9.

ḫf3t food, Urk. V, 162, 2. 8. 9.

ḫf33t banks of waterway, Westc. 5, 6.

ḫfc fist, Pyr. 431.

ḫfc grasp (vb. and n.), Urk. IV, 17, 4; 617, 4; 887, 10; make captures in war, 3, 17 (); 891, 2; 892, 2 (abbr.): n. booty, 890, 17.

ḫfc a cake, Urk. IV, 1120, 16; 1123, 1.

ḫfḫf flood (vb.), Sm. 18, 4.

ḫft prep. in front of, in accordance with, as well as, corresponding to; as conj. when, according as; with infin. at the time of, when, var. , Gr. §169; r-ḫft 'in front of', §178; ḫft-ntt 'in view of the fact that', §223.

ḫftw adv. accordingly, var. , Gr. §205, 1.

ḫft-ḥr in front of, in the presence of, so too r-ḫft-ḥr, Gr. §178.

ḫfty enemy, Sb. 109, 17; M. u. K. vs. 1, 3; var. Peas. B2, 113; dets: BH I, 8, 10; Leb. 115; Urk. IV, 1166, 12.

ḫm wild (?), of animals, Urk. IV, 1304, 6.

ḫm warm, Les. 82, 4.

ḫm be dry, Sin. B22; Sb. 39, 14; 65, 5.

ḫmw dust, CT I, 90; Urk. IV, 502, 4; 837, 9.

ḫm vb. know not, be ignorant of, Sin. B126; Pr. 6, 9; Urk. IV, 102, 6; 1074, 3; V, 95, 5; with reflexive obj. 'not know o'self' = swoon, Sin. B253; Sh. S. 76; ḫm 'swoon', Ch. B. Text, 59, n. 2; be unconscious of o's limbs, P. Ed. Smith, 325; det. Peas. B2, 47; passive participles Urk. IV, 390, 9; Leb. 124; Adm. 4, 4: n. ignorance, Sin. B205; Pr. 17, 5; Urk. V, 95, 4. For iḫmw-wrd, iḫm(w)-sk, see p. 29.

ḫm ignorant man, Urk. IV, 102, 6; 368, 1; 970, 3; pl. Pr. 5, 7; 'ignoramus', Peas. B1, 219; Pr. 5, 12.

Ḫm n. loc. Letopolis (Ausīm), var. , Gr. pp. 496 (O34); 503 (R22).

ḫm shrine, Urk. IV, 167, 1; vars. 96, 4; 102, 1; 386, 5; 881, 10; RB 114, 13.

ḫm sacred image, Urk. IV, 546, 10.

ḫm demolish buildings, JEA 22, 178; harm s'one, BD 184, 16 (det.); 300, 5; debar, m 'from', 292, 13; exclude, CT I, 212 (det.).

ḫmt cow, Goyon, 53; Cairo 20024, 7.

ḫm33 shrink, Eb. 39, 8; cf. ZÄS 45, 38.

ḫmꜥ seize, grasp, var. det. , JEA 37, 30; penetrate water, of staff, Pyr. 1212; collect, of people: intrans. 24; trans. 615; drive off evil, BD 187, 3 (det.); 269, 12 (det.).

ḫmꜥt butt, grip of oar, Westc. 5, 8.

Ḫmnw n. loc. Hermopolis (El-Ashmūnēn), AEO II, 79*.

ḫmnyw Ogdoad, Urk. IV, 389, 3.

ḫmt num. three, Gr. § 260; vb. do for third time, § 292; treble revenues, Urk. IV, 2029, 15 (); 'she has made her two faces into three', TR 81, 34-5 (collated).

ḫmt-nw ord. num. third, var. , Gr. § 263.

ḫmt-rw (?) num. $\frac{3}{4}$, Gr. § 265.

ḫmt intend, plan, Sin. R 163; B 64. 223; take thought for, Urk. IV, 384, 13; expect, anticipate, GNS 86. Varr. Sin. B 64; B 111; Les. 80, 17; 83, 25; Urk. IV, 367, 10; 384, 13; 487, 13.

ḫmt: m-ḫmt 'in the absence of', 'without', var. , Gr. § 178.

ḫn direct o's hand, r 'against', ZÄS 57, 4*; drive (?) cattle, Bersh. II, 13, 26.

ḫn scowling (?) of face, Hatnub, 23, 4.

ḫn rebel (n.), Urk. IV, 968, 12.

ḫnt: ḫnt 'act of rebellion (?)', Les. 82, 2.

ḫn clap of hands in ḫn 'giving the c.' = beating time, Bersh. I, 12, top.

ḫni vb. 3inf. play music, varr. , CT I, 23; Westc. 11, 17.

ḫnw musicians, Les. 87, 21.

ḫnwt female musician, Meir. IV, 7; var. IV, 4; pl. Les. 87, 21-2; Westc. 11, 24; Urk. IV, 1059, 12 ff.

ḫni vb. 3inf. alight from flight, Pyr. 1971; BD 148, 11 (dets.); Urk. IV, 1526, 11 (); stop, halt, Sin. B 21; Urk. IV, 158, 12; 1547, 5; rest, ḥr 'on', Peas. R 50; Urk. IV, 18, 15; of 'resting' herd, 85, 5 ().

ḫn speech, utterance, Peas. B1, 280; Adm. p. 96; Urk. IV, 1083, 13; matter, affair, 751, 8; 1143, 8; ḫn n itt int 'a ragged chorus' (of shouts), 710, 12 (dets.); ḫn n ꜥbꜥ 'exaggeration', Les. 84, 11-12; ḫn n wšb 'part-song', Paheri, 3; ḫn bin 'a bad business', Les. 98, 9; ḫn n mdt 'saying', 'proverb', Peas. B1, 19; 'complaint', B1, 37; ḫn nfr 'benefactions', JEA 16, 154; Les. 80, 19 (); ḫn (n) nhm 'song of joy', D. el B. 125; Urk. IV, 1095, 7; 2042, l. 11; as non-encl. part., Westc. 12, 24.

ḫnt festival outlay (?), GNS 106-7.

see under ḫnr.

ḫnw resting-place, abode, Urk. IV, 237, 6; 736, 16 (dets.); 1282, 20; 1283, 2.

ḫnw child, BH I, 26, 187.

ḫnws gnat, Eb. 98, 1.

ḫnp snatch, Urk. IV, 84, 11; catch ball, D. el B. 100 (det.); steal, Peas. B1, 99. 123; Urk. IV, 138, 16; pour water, 386, 17; present offering, P. Kah. 25, 8; BD 92, 6.

ḫnp receive seed (), of woman, RB 111, 15.

(sic) ḫnfꜣ arrogance (?), Bersh. II, 21, lower, 12.

ḫnfw a cake, BH II, 15.

ḫnm breathe air, Sin. B 234; smell odours, Peas. B1, 154; Urk. IV, 150, 7; 874, 8; make sweet-smelling, Eb. 27, 13; 48, 1 (dets.); belabour with blows, Adm. 5, 12; be glad, gladden, GNS 97; ḫnmw 'cheerfully', loc. cit; Gr. §205,4.

ḫnmw smell (n.), P. Kah. 7,8; Urk. IV, 339,15; 347,5; varr. 237,11; 1805,7.

ḫnmt red jasper (?), Caminos, L.-Eg. Misc. 424-5.

ḫnms vb. be friendly with, Pr. 14,10; Urk. IV, 116,3 (dets.); BD 239,12: n. friendship, Pr. 9,8; Peas. B1, 272.

ḫnms friend, Sh. S. 184; P. Kah. 4,23; Peas. B1, 85; dets. Pr. 9,9; fem. Cairo 20025.

ḫnms kind of beer, BH II, 15; var. D. el B. 110.

ḫnmtt nurse (n.), TR 21,58; varr. 21,57; 21,59.

ḫnr restrain, BM 159,6; varr. Urk. IV, 1517,12; 938,6; 1373,18.

ḫnrt prison, Westc. 8,15; Urk. IV, 758,16 (); 1109,3; fortress, Hatnub, 23,4; Les. 82,13 (); council-chamber, Urk. IV, 897,6; Bersh. II, 21, lower, 9 (); cf. GAS 47.

ḫnr criminal, prisoner, Peas. B1, 122; varr. B1, 123; Westc. 8,15; Leb. 35.

ḫnr harem, Bersh. II, 21, top, 9; Siut, pl. 13, 29; varr. , , GAS 47.

ḫnrwt women of the harem, Koptos, 12,1; var. Urk. IV, 978,3. (sic)

ḫnr reins, Urk. IV, 711,15; varr. 669,16; 1282,17.

ḫnrtt conspiracy (?), Urk. IV, 139,3.

ḫns (ḫnz) vb. trans. traverse region, Urk. IV, 237,9; 248,1; 386,15; 617,15: intrans. travel, BD 227,15; 466,3; spread, of illness, Eb. 101,21. Var. Pyr. 748.

ḫns move in two directions, JEA 41,13, with n. 5.

ḫnsyt scurf (?), JEA 12, 241.

var. of ḫ3syt 'bryony (?)'.

Ḫnsw n. div. moon-god Khons, Leb. 24; Urk. IV, 432,7 (det.); BD 181,13; name of tenth month, Urk. IV, 44,15.

ḫnš stink (vb.), Eb. 86, 8.10.

ḫnt rack for jars, Pyr. 1482; var. Urk. IV, 873, 4; later sideboard, JEA 41, 15.

ḫnt face, Sm. 3, 18-19; brow, Urk. IV, 559, 9 (no det.).

ḫnt prep. in front of, among, from, out of, var. Gr. §174; m-ḫnt 'in the face of', 'within', 'out of', §178; as adv. 'first' in time, Les. 75, 13; pr m-ḫnt 'come forth', Les. 82, 21-2; imy ḫnt 'chamberlain', see p. 19; m-ḫnt-r 'in front of', GNS 116.

ḫnty: of place, who, which is in front of, Siut, pl. 15, 20 ( ); southern, pl. 10, 12 (ꜣtf ḫntt); south of, Les. 71, 16; of rank or position, who is at the head of, foremost, Bersh. 13, 14 ( ). 22; BM 614, 1; Urk. IV, 228, 10 ( ); esp. in ḫnty imntyw 'F. of the Westerners', ep. of Osiris, passim; pre-eminent in, Koptos, 9; Urk. IV, 234, 2; 362, 10; of degree, principal, of offices, 483, 14 (dets.); 966, 12 (det.); 1094, 14; of time, which is at the beginning of a year, V, 159, 4; of shape, protruding: ḫntyt ⟨r⟩ ḥꜣt.f 'pr. in front', Eb. 37, 18.

ḫnt(y) foreland, Caminos, Lit. Frag. pl. 16, 1, 4; south, southern part, Urk. IV, 807, 17; 902, 6; var. IV 85, 13; ḫntt r 'southward to', Gr. §179.

ḫntw: r-ḫntw 'out', Gr. §205, 3.

ḫntw adv. before, earlier, var. , Gr. §205, 1.

ḫnty outer chamber, AEO II, 208*; m-ḫnt(y) 'indoors', Peas. B1, 127. Varr. Urk. IV, 470, 10; 1845, 12; Adm. 6, 5.

Ḫnty n. div. a crocodile-god, Leb. 79; Peas. B1, 119.

ḫnti-ib be glad of heart, Pyr. 592. 2198; outstanding of mind, Urk. IV, 255, 6.

Ḫnt-mnw n. loc. Ekhmîm, AEO II, 40*.

Ḫnt-ḥn-nfr n. loc. Nubia, Gauthier, Dict. géogr. IV, 182.

Ḫnty-ḫty n. div. P. Kah. 36, 2; name of eleventh month, Urk. IV, 44, 16.

ḫnt-š garden with trees, Urk. IV, 353, 4; name for Lebanon, 169, 17 (det.); 1795, 11. Cf. ZÄS 45, 129. For ḫntš 'orchard (?)' see below.

ḫntyw-š tenants (?), Urk. IV, 407, 15; 412, 7. Cf. ZÄS 45, 129.

Ḫnt-tꜣ n. loc. the Southland, RB 60, 14; 61, 7; 62, 10.

ḫntyw-tꜣ Southerners, Urk. IV, 1279, 3.

ḫnti vb. 4 inf. (fem. infin) sail upstream, travel southward; m ḫntyt 'upstream', 'southwards', AEO I, 160*; out-south o's predecessors, Les. 83, 22. Varr. BH I, 29; Sin. B 94.

ḫntyt southward voyage, Urk. IV, 122, 4; infin. of above, 5, 5.

ḫntš orchard (?), Urk. IV, 207, 6; 746, 2; var. 1379, 16.

ḫntš have enjoyment, m 'of', Urk. IV, 114, 17; 446, 12; be glad, RB 112, 8-9; make glad, Urk. IV, 990, 11; ḫntš ib m 'delight in, over', 1064, 7; JEA 39, pl. 2, 8. Cf. ZÄS 45, 129.

ḫntš walk about freely, Urk. VII, 3, 4.

ḫnd bend wood; twist together flower-stems, AEO I, 66.

ḫnd lower part, calf of leg, Urk. V, 156, 10; BD 205, 8 (dets.); RB 120, 5.

ḫnd tread ways, etc., Urk. IV, 324, 12; 331, 12; 613, 4 (dets.); 1441, 15 (det.); ḥr 'on', TR 23, 7; Peas. B1, 2; P. Kah. 2, 20; tread down foes, Urk. IV, 615, 2; offend (?), Pr. 12, 1. 3.

ḫndw throne, Pyr. 573; varr. Urk. IV, 2081, 17; 257, 9.

ḫnḏ shin of beef (?), var. , AEO I, 17f.

ḫr (1) prep. with; near; under a king; speak to, Gr. §167; by, of agent, §39, end; n(t) ḫr-nsw (favours, etc.) 'from the king', §158, 1: (2) aux. vb. so says, §436; JEA 21, 187.

ḫr non-encl. part. and, further, varr. , , cf. Gr. p. 585.

ḫrt state, condition, Westc. 7, 7; BH I, 29; Urk. IV, 966, 16; 1105, 4; nḏ-ḫrt 'greet', see p. 144; affairs, concerns, Pr. 14, 8; Les. 69, 16; Urk. IV, 63, 15; 127, 7; 1105, 10; requirements, 12, 8; products of a place, I, 123, 17; BH I, 14. 16; irt ḫrt n 'look after' s'one, JEA 31, 33.

ḫrt-ib wish, desire, Sin. B 125; Sh. S. 20; Peas. B1, 38; Urk. IV, 114, 9; favour, BM 614, 5; Urk. IV, 944, 2; 954, 2.

ḫr fall, Sin. B 3. 135. 139; Peas. B1, 291; RB 59, 8; in military sense, Les. 83, 10 (abbr.).

ḫrw enemy, Urk. IV, 9, 11; RB 59, 10-11 (dets.); varr. Urk. IV, 6, 11; 665, 11.

ḫr tomb, necropolis, JEA 22, 186, n. 10; P. Wilbour, 34.

ḫrw low-lying land, BH I, 26, 140; varr. Urk. IV, 31, 4; 1611, 11; Hamm. 114, 4.

ḫryt butchery, CT I, 189; Les. 64, 16; BD 453, 11.

ḫrw voice, Sin. R 25; Peas. B1, 26; Adm. 6, 5; noise, Sin. B 24; Westc. 12, 1; Adm. 6, 1. Var. Sh. S. 57.

ḫrw: ḫrw·sn 'so say they' varr. , , CT I, 92; cf. Gr. §§ 427. 437.

ḫrw·fy says, varr. , , Gr. § 437.

ḫrwy enemy, Peas. B1, 282; Sin. B 54; varr. R 79; P. Kah. 2, 16; RB 111, 4; Urk. IV, 1800, 5.

ḫrwyw war, BD 457, 11; var. JEA 19, 24.

ḫrwyt war, BD 200, 7; var. Cairo 46048.

ḫrp baton of office, Urk. IV, 1104, 6.

ḫrp (1) govern, control, administer, BH I, 25, 11; Les. 77, 2 (det.); Urk. IV, 31, 7; 966, 5; act as controller, Cairo 20543, 19; Urk. IV, 58, 4; 131, 6; direct s'one, of o's heart, Sin. B 229; Urk. IV, 365, 1; 750, 6; drive cattle, Paheri, 3; TR 23, 46; Urk. IV, 1304, 14; lead, get ahead with work, Teti Cem. I, p. 115; undertake works, Les. 71, 7 (abbr.); Neferhotep, 20; ḫrp ỉb 'having authority (?)', Pr. 5, 11.

(2) bring, Urk. IV, 372, 17; 954, 7; provide, Cairo 20001, 6 (abbr.); Les. 79, 9; Urk. IV, 749, 6; make offering of, dedicate, 55, 9; 75, 2; 98, 6; 173, 6.

ḫrp controller, administrator, Urk. IV, 47, 14; Louvre C 172; Bersh. I, 14, 3 (); esp. in titles, e.g. 'c. of works', Urk. IV, 40, 9; 'c. of the palace', JEA 24, 83; 'c. of the two thrones', 24, 85; 'c. of the kilt', AEO I, 40*; 'c. of c.'s', Urk. IV, 966, 10; var. 61, 14; ḫrpw nw dmỉ pn 'the authorities of this town', 126, 1.

ḫrpt dues, taxes, Urk. IV, 412, 3; 1007, 8.

ḫrp district (?), estate (?), Urk. IV, 1105, 10; JEA 38, 18, n. 2; var. Les. 71, 16.

ḫrpw mallet, Urk. V, 204, 3; var. det. Sh. S. 3.

ḫrš bundle, Westc. 9, 21; dets. Urk. IV, 171, 4; 825, 17; also fem. ḫršt, Lac. Sarc. I, 59. Cf. JEA 22, 42.

ḫḫ neck, Adm. 3, 3; Urk. IV, 1304, 18; throat, Sin. B 22; BD 436, 6.

ḫs var. of ḫ3s 'creek(?)'

ḫsy bribe, Urk. IV, 1079, 6; var. 118, 17.

var. of ḫ3syt 'bryony(?)'.

ḫsbḏ lapis-lazuli, Pyr. 513; BH II, 7; JEA 4, pl. 9, 10; var. Urk. IV, 174, 14.

ḫsbḏ blue, Pyr. 253; Siut, pl. 19, 33 ( ); BD 7, 10; blue-black, of hair, BD 14, 7.

ḫsf spin yarn, BH II, 4.

ḫsf vb. (1) trans. drive away, ward off, oppose, Sin. B 17 ( ); Peas. B1, 17; Pr. 5, 12; RB 117, 8; Urk. IV, 969, 17; repel by bad conduct, Pr. 6, 8; repress crime, Peas. B1, 193; Leb. 143; rebels, Urk. IV, 139, 1; redress wrong, Peas. B1, 102. 106; reprove words, Sin. B 183; drive cattle, Pyr. 401; Dav. Ptah. II, 8; divert water, RB 117, 6; avoid anger, Les. 80, 16; prevent, Pyr. 1435; Leb. 146; ḫsf ḫt n 'take action against', Urk. I, 101, 9.

(2) intrans. with foll. prep.: ḫsf n 'punish', Peas. B1, 47. 218; Westc. 12, 10; Les. 98, 14; JEA 4, pl. 9, 7 (det.); 'let him alone ḫsf.f n.f ḏs.f that he may confute himself', Pr. 6, 2; ḫsf r 'contend against', Peas. B1, 296; ḫsf ḥr 'defend', Leb. 24; Pr. 7, 9.

(3) n. punishment, Sin. B 260; disapproval, Pr. 6, 3.

ḫsf-ʿ oppose, Sin. B 98; Urk. IV, 138, 10; opposition, Adm. 7, 6-7.

ḫsft punishment, Peas. B1, 147; var. B2, 94.

ḫsf draw near, Pyr. 203.

ḫsfw: m ḫsfw 'at the approach of', 'in meeting', Gr. § 178; m ḫsf.f 'near him', Pyr. 1425; r ḫsfw 'meet', Sin. B 250.

ḫsfw vb. 4 inf. sail upstream, Pyr. 725; infin. Urk. I, 122, 10;

210, 11; V, 162, 10; VII, 1, 12.

, , see above s. v. ḫm.

ḫsr dispel, drive away darkness, evil, etc., BD 177, 14-15; 280, 10; CT I, 59; P. Kah. 3, 5; Urk. V, 22, 5; clear a road, BD 210, 10; remove dirt, Urk. IV, 835, 2; Varr. BD 54, 5; Urk. IV, 269, 7; Peas. B1, 288.

ḫt wood, Sh. S. 44; Urk. IV, 720, 3; 765, 13; pl. timbers, Pyr. 2080; Urk. I, 121, 14; Bersh. I, 15; mrḥt n ḫt 'w.-oil', Sin. B 295; woodland, AEO I, 12*; tree, Sin. B 83. 297; Sh. S. 156; Urk. IV, 28, 4; n ꜥnḫ 't. of life', embodiment of food, Pyr. 1216; var. n ꜥnḫ Urk. IV, 130, 17; 'staff-of-life plants', RB 112, 7; ꜥt n ḫt 'orchard', Urk. IV, 2152, 8; stick, P. Kah. 1, 4; Urk. IV, 1075, 4; 1080, 14; r-ḫt 'under the authority of', Gr. §178; var. Urk. IV, 1276, 18; pole, Peas. B1, 258; rod, linear measure of 100 cubits, more fully 'r. of cord', Gr. §266, 2; mast, Peas. B1, 57; Urk. V, 156, 5; 'mast', BD 205, 15; a tree, Urk. IV, 73, 16.

ḫtwt coll. furniture, Urk. I, 305, 3; var. Siut, pl. 19, 32; Urk. IV, 1379, 12.

ḫti vb. 3 inf. retire, retreat, Peas. B1, 181; Mill. 2, 3 (det.); 'retreat', Les. 84, 4.

ḫt prep. through, throughout, pervading, Gr. §175; m-ḫt 'accompanying', 'after', 'when', 'afterwards', cf. Gr. p. 586; 'in consequence of the fact that', 'as a result of', JEA 33, 7; see also imy-ḫt above, p. 19; m-ḫt as n. 'future', JEA 32, pl. 6, 8.

ḫtyw-tꜣ who pervade the land, Neferti, 32; BD 394, 3.

ḫtw menials, L. to D. I, 7 (n.).

ḫtt-pr house-servant, varr. , , , L. to D. n. on I, 7.

ḫti vb. 3 inf. carve, engrave, GNS 114. 162; var. Urk. IV, 1938, 4.

Ḫt(ꜣ) n. loc. Hatti, land of the Hittites, AEO I, 127*.

ḫtꜣ creep up to, Les. 82, 13.

ḫtyw threshing-floor, Westc. 12, 14; det. Urk. IV, 687, 14.

ḫtyw platform, dais, abbr. , Gr. p. 497, O 40; terraced hillside, in ḫtyw mfkꜣt 'terraces of turquoise' = Sinai, Urk. I, 113, 5; ḫtyw nw ꜥš 't. of cedar' = the Lebanon, IV, 778, 14; ḫtyw ꜥntyw 't. of myrrh' = Punt, 325, 13; 344, 8; ꜥš mꜣꜥ n tp ḫtyw 'real cedar of the hillsides', 98, 14; 765, 17.

ḫt-ꜥꜣ an edible bird, Westc. 8, 24; poultry in general, Urk. IV, 1293, 13.

ḫtm (1) n. seal, Urk. I, 128, 3 (); Th. T. S. IV, 6 (); hr ḫtm (n) 'with, under, the s. of', Westc. 11, 24 (); Urk. IV, 1109, 14; 1111, 11 (). Cf. WZKM 54, 181.

(2) vb. seal, Urk. IV, 68, 11; 421, 16 (dets.); 1110, 4; 1111, 7; RB 62, 5-6; put a seal ḥr 'on', Westc. 12, 6; Bersh. II, 21, top, 16; contract, m-ꜥ 'with' s'one, Siut, pl. 6, 269. 281; close doors, etc., Sin. R 9; Adm. 14, 3; Westc. 10, 7; 11, 6 (); Urk. IV, 658, 5; 1105, 2; BD 192, 1; include a land in o's dominions, Urk. IV, 808, 2; mix ingredients, Eb. 46, 21.

ḫtm chest, Westc. 12, 5 (); storehouse, Urk. IV, 1105, 2; fort, 661, 1 (); 661, 13 (); imy-r ḫtm 'Superintendent of Fortresses', JEA 39, 46.

ḫtm contract (n.), Neferhotep, 35; P. Kah. 13, 11. 21.

ḫtmt contract (n.), Siut, pl. 7, 296; 8, 305. 312; varr. Urk. IV, 261, 5; Les. 68, 4; 96, 8.

ḫtm valuables (?), Urk. IV, 1114, 1.

ḫtmw (?) cattle, Rhind, 67.

ḫtmy seal-maker, JEA 41, 15.

ḫtmyt sealed chamber (?), BD 143, 14.

ḫtḫt prep. through, Gr. § 178.

ḫtḫt turn back, Pyr. 1071; RB 76, 11; m ḫtḫt 'backwards', Urk. V, 41, 1; nullify, reverse a contract, Siut, pl. 6, 270. 280; come and go, of pain, JEA 20, 185 (10).

var. of ḫtt 'pluck' plants.

var. of ḫwd 'rich'.

ḫdi vb. 3 inf. travel downstream, northwards; m ḫd 'downstream', 'northwards', AEO I, 160*; flow, of water, Urk. IV, 687, 13; n. North, 1973, 14.

ḫdt land-register, Urk. VII, 31, 16.

ḫddw waterfowl, Caminos, Lit. Frag. pp. 35-6.

ḫdy (< ḫwdy (?)) riches, Les. 79, 20.23.

ẖt belly, Sh. S. 68; Pr. 10, 9; womb, Westc. 9, 7; 10, 9; Urk. V, 42, 12; body, Sin. B 39.255; sole of foot, Sm. 4, 15; imyw-ẖt 'thoughts,' Urk. IV, 971, 2; sḫr-ẖt 'thought,' Peas. B1, 209. Var. RB 115, 3; pl., Urk. IV, 201, 1.

ẖt body of gods or men, Siut, pl. 1, 1; Peas. B1, 190; generation, GAS 82; people, Les. 69, 15.

ẖ3t oxyrhynchus (mormyrus kannume), P. Ram. III, A 16; cf. Barns, Ram. p. 18.

ẖ3t corpse, Les. 69, 1; dets. Urk. IV, 617, 3; 64, 16; var. 481, 5.

ẖ3yt heap of corpses, Sh. S. 132; var. Urk. IV, 5, 7.

ẖ3t disease, Eb. 8, 13.

ẖ3t marsh, Sin. R 66, cf. GNS 87.

ẖ33 clothes-peg (?), JEA 42, 39 (111).

ẖ33 resolute (?), Äg. Stud. 113.

ẖ3y thwart s'one, var. det. , CT I, 154.

ẖ3bt curl on , Hymnen, 6, 1; 14, 2 (pl.!); var. Urk. IV, 200, 15.

ẖ3b clavicle, var. dets. , P. Ed. Smith, 348.

ẖ3b sickle, Urk. V, 161, 17.

ẖ3b adj. crooked: n. crookedness: adv. crookedly, JEA 9, 11, n. 8; 28, 18.19; det. Sm. 5, 21.

ẖ3bt crookedness, RB 118, 5.

ẖ3bb crookedness, JEA 9, 11, n. 8.

ẖ3m bend down the arms in respect, JEA 37, 51.

ẖ3mt kind of beer, Les. 73, 13; BM 159, 2; det. Cairo 20410.

ḫ3m-ẖt kind of offerings, Les. 73,16; var. ḫ3mt-ẖt Cairo 20088, c 4.

ḫ3r sack, usually abbr., Gr. § 266,1; varr. Westc. 12,4; Siut pl. 7, 292; leather bag, Caminos, L.-Eg. Misc. 408.

ḫ3rt widow, BH I, 8,20; varr. Hatnub 14,10; Les. 79,15.

ḫ3ḫ3ti storm, Hamm. 114,9.

ḫ3kw-ib disaffected persons, BM 159,5; Urk. IV, 6,12; 256,2; 613,1.

ḫccw measure(?), allowance(?) of milk, CT I, 168.

ḫcm approach, with direct obj, m or n, varr., GNS 33.157.

ḫck shave, BH II, 4.13.

ḫckw barber, AEO I, 69*; var. Urk. IV, 1369,5.

ḫpw figures inlaid in metal, Urk. IV, 388,12; 422,11; abbr. 425,2.

ḫp3w navel-string, navel, varr., JEA 3,203; ZÄS 66,71.

ḫpc chew, Eb. 72,16; 85,17; 86,1.

ḫpn fat (adj.), Hatnub, 17,6; 20,19; 24,3.

ḫmc var. of ḫcm 'approach'.

ḫms bend the back in respect, Hatnub, 49,7; Pr. 5,11; 13,9.

ḫn be blistered, Les. 86,8.

ḫn tent, Urk. I, 130,12; Pr. 1,1; Hatnub, 16,2; ḫn d3mw 'camp(?)', Hatnub, 20,3.

ḫnt hide, skin, Urk. I, 212,5; Peas. R 14; Eb. 40,2; used of Anubis-emblem, Caminos, Lit. Frag. p. 30.

ḫnt burial chamber(?) of tomb, Urk. IV, 1425,6.

ḫn approach, m s'one, Sin. B 137; Siut, pl. 17,45; Urk. IV, 984,2.

ḫni vb. 3 inf. row, Westc. 5,4 (dets.); Urk. IV, 897,1 (det.); convey by water, 6,17; 56,15; 372,14.

ḫnt water-procession, P. Kah. 25,11; Urk. IV, 1299,7; varr. 742,2; det. 1299,3.

ḫnyt coll. sailors, Urk. IV, 1, 16; 6, 9; 306, 9; dets. 1006, 9.

ḫnw sailor, Goyon, 61, 7; var. 56.

ḫnw interior (n.), Sh. S. 175; Urk. IV, 167, 4 (); home, abode, Sh. S. 3. 119; Pr. 9, 8; CT I, 169 (); šm r ḫnw 'go h.', Sh. S. 122; royal Residence, often det. ⊗, Sin. B 232; Westc. 4, 9; 8, 6; Les. 83, 9; m-ḫnw (n) 'within', Gr. §178; 'at, in the house of', P. Berl. 9010, 2.6; cryptic wtg. Gr. §178; p. 531, top; as adv. 'inside', Les. 76, 10; r-ḫnw (n) 'within', Herdsm. 18; Urk. IV, 46, 17; 'into', V, 79, 6; Les. 71, 18.

ḫnw-ꜥwy embrace (n.), Urk. IV, 255, 12; m-ḫnw ꜥ(wy) 'within', 239, 10.

ḫnw brook, Urk. IV, 655, 13.

ḫnwtyw skin-clad people, Urk. IV, 83, 15.

ḫnm vb. (1) trans. join, unite with a god or the dead, Urk. IV, 54, 16; 366, 8; 445, 10; enclose, enfold, Pyr. 1485; Sin. B 208; Urk. IV, 1163, 5; protect, Sin. B 271; take o's place, Urk. IV, 113, 9; enter place, 116, 9; 1524, 13; 1528, 15; unite crowns, 251, 13; 288, 14; 550, 15; wear crown, 13, 3; 192, 14; receive favours, etc., 1014, 1; 1166, 4; enrich, endue, m 'with', GNS 81; of child, lie on s'one's breast, Urk. IV, 913, 6.

(2) intrans. be united, associated, m 'with', Sin. R 7; B 189; RB 115, 6; P. Kah. 3, 1; be provided, endowed, m 'with', Urk. IV, 268, 4; 566, 2. — Var. 251, 13.

ḫnm herd, RB 64, 12; det. Urk. IV, 2050, 5.

ḫnmw citizens, Adm. 4, 8; Siut, pl. 4, 229 (); 9, 352 (); 16 (Tomb I), 17 (); dependants, P. Kah. 12, 5.

ḫnm(t) (dry-)nurse, Urk. IV, 1060, 13.

ḫnm basin (?) for irrigation, COA III, p. 166; P. Wilbour, 30.

ḫnmt well, cistern, Sin. B 102; Les. 84, 10; varr. Urk. IV, 7, 15; 888, 17; 1064, 9.

Ḫnmw n. div. Khnum, Adm. 2, 4; Westc. 10, 14; varr. BH I, 7; Les. 68, 20; dets. Urk. IV, 194, 9; 99, 5; RB 114, 5.

ḫnn vb. 2 gem. disturb, interfere with persons, commands, etc., Urk. V, 87, 8;

Siut, pl. 6, 268; BH I, 25, 98; Adm. p. 102 (dets.); confound truth, Pr. 6, 5; be inflamed, irritated (med.), Eb. 56, 6; 104, 8 (det.); ẖnn-ib 'violent man', Urk. IV, 969, 2.

ẖnnw tumult, uproar, BD 457, 12; Urk. IV, 505, 4; dets. BD 107, 4; 122, 14.

ẖnnw brawlers, Mill. 2, 7.

ẖnty statue, Siut, pl. 4, 224; varr. 6, 273; Urk. IV, 101, 5; 1797, 9; ẖnty ʿnḫ 'living semblance', 279, 7; 1287, 19.

ẖr prep. under; carrying; holding; possessing; at head or foot; in a condition; through, of means, Gr. § 166; subject to s'one's action, Urk. IV, 84, 13; ẖr-ʿ 'in the charge of', see below; ẖr-ḥꜣt see above s.v. ḥꜣt, p. 162.

ẖry which is under, Urk. V, 151, 15; lower, Siut, pl. 8, 308 ('l. stairway',); having, possessing, BD 282, 8; 459, 14; suffering from illness, Eb. 93, 1; bw ẖry·f 'the place where he is', Gr. § 204, 1.

ẖrt possessions, belongings, Urk. IV, 123, 10; 561, 7; BD 259, 2; share, portion, Peas. B1, 93; Pr. 10, 6; Urk. IV, 139, 7 ( ); ẖrt rnpt 'annual allowance', 195, 9; requirements, Sin. B 305; Urk. IV, 1116, 1; due from s'one, Sh. S. 159; duty, Urk. IV, 181, 2; BD 28, 16; skill (?): wr ẖrt m ḥsb tnw 'greatly skilled in the counting of numbers', Urk. IV, 968, 4; sim. 944, 13; m ẖrt hrw 'daily', Sin. B 88; so also m ẖrt hrw nt rʿ nb, BM 159, 12; 614, 3; abbr. for ẖrt hrw, Urk. IV, 992, 4.

ẖrw relatives of family, Les. 98, 21; underlings, Peas. B1, 95; inhabitants of land, Sin. B 103; Les. 84, 10; var. Urk. IV, 140, 13.

ẖrw men, BD 9, 1.

ẖrw base (n.), JEA 15, pl. 36 (14, 3,); lower part, Sm. 8, 18 ( ); under-side, 12, 7; m ḥr m ẖrw 'with downcast face', Leb. 119; n ẖrw 'downwards', Sm. 4, 3; 10, 21; r ẖrw 'below', TR 23, 39 ( ); 'downwards', BH II, 6; M.u.K. 3, 4; ẖrw 'under' trees, Urk. IV, 1193, 11; dd·i swt nꜣ ẖrw 'Further, I say as follows', 1799, 14.

ẖrwy testicles, Urk. V, 32, 16; var. 147, 3.

ẖr-ꜥ under the hand of, in the charge of, Gr. §178; var. Urk. IV, 25, 13.

ẖr(y)-ꜥ n. apprentice, JEA 24, 159: adj. assistant (a. treasurer), P. Kah. 26a, 13.

ẖr(y)-ꜥ halliard (?), TR 27, 40.

ẖrt-ꜥ deceit, RB 64, 10.

ẖrt-ꜥ writing materials, Neferti, 16.

ẖr(t)-nṯr necropolis, Westc. 7, 23; varr. TR 45, 1; Urk. IV, 123, 9; JEA 24, 245; O.K. Urk. I, 9, 5; L. to D. X, 3, 2; 2, 8.

ẖrty-nṯr stone-mason, Siut, pl. 8, 314; pl. Bersh. I, 14, 3; P. Kah. 9, 7; Urk. IV, 1836, 11.

ẖry-ḥbt lector, AEO I, 55*; varr. Neferti, 9; Th. T. S. IV, 35; Urk. IV, 15, 12.

ẖry-ḫt abdomen, Eb. 35, 4; under-side of sky, Pyr. 347. 357.

ẖry-sꜣ who is behind, Pyr. 1226; the hindermost (?), Peas. B1, 326.

ẖr-tp under the head of, beside; ẖry-tp nsw 'chamberlain', var. JEA 27, 144-5; (the spirits) 'who attend Rēꜥ', Pyr. 460.

ẖrd n. child, Leb. 100; Siut, pl. 13, 133; Sin. B78; varr. Westc. 9, 7; pl. Les. 80, 2: vb. be, become a child, Hymnen, 15, 1; Les. 78, 17.

ẖrdt coll. children, Urk. VII, 4, 2.

ẖrdw childhood, Urk. IV, 993, 15.

ẖrd calf of gazelle, TR 22, 77.

ḫs(y) weak, feeble, Eb. 36, 6; Urk. IV, 1280, 2; humble, of rank, Pr. 6, 1; 7, 7; mean, of conduct, Peas. B1, 325; Pt. (L II), 3, 16; Urk. IV, 439, 5; vile, of enemies, 9, 5; 656, 4 ( ); BH I, 8, 10; of speech, Pr. 7, 12; m ḫs 'in evil case', 15, 3; ḫs ḥr ib 'incompetent', Urk. IV, 933, 12; 'crime (?)', Pr. 9, 12.

ḫst cowardice, Les. 84, 4; ritual impurity, Adm. 11, 5.

ḫsy coward, Adm. 7, 7.

ḫsyt wrongdoing, Urk. IV, 507, 2.

ḫsꜣ be unanointed, Hatnub, 12, 13; var. Pr. 8, 10.

ẖsꜣyt kind of spice (?), Eb. 33, 21; varr. Sh. S. 141; Urk. IV, 329, 7; 1375, 16.

ẖsr var. of ḫsr 'dispel'.

ẖks be injured, Urk. V, 32, 3.

ẖkst the injured Eye of Horus, ZÄS 57, 7*.

ẖkr be adorned, P. Kah. 3, 18; Bersh. I, 14, 9; Urk. IV, 256, 4.

ẖkry coiffeur known only in form , q. v.

ẖkrt coiffeuse, JEA 41, 15; concubine, Bersh. II, top, 16; usually in 'king's concubine', Siut, pl. 13, 38; Urk. IV, 1009, 4; as wtg. of ẖkrw nsw 'royal insignia' see next below.

ẖkrw panoply, insignia, Urk. IV, 615, 7 ( ); 978, 4 ( ); 1280, 18; ornaments, 867, 14 ( ); JEA 4, pl. 8, 4 ( ); 39, pl. 2, 18 ( ); 'royal insignia', Les. 75, 9; 'panoply of war', Urk. IV, 657, 6.

ẖkryt insignia, Sin. B 270; cf. GNS 103-4.

ẖtb overthrow, JEA 33, 27 (5).

ẖtt pluck plants, Bersh. II, pp. 19. 23; var. BH I, pl. 29.

ẖdb kill, Sin. B 62; Adm. 5, 12; 13, 3 (dets.).

ẖdr rescue (?), Peas. B1, 138.

ẖdr be in discomfort (?), Pr. 4, 3.

s (z) doorbolt, Pyr. 572; Urk. IV, 498, 11 (det.).

-s suff. pron. 3 f. sg. she, her, it, its, var. , Gr. §34; used for 3 pl., JEA 16, 64 (5).

s ornamental vessel of gold, Urk. IV, 631, 13. 15.

s sheaf of arrows, Urk. IV, 1280, 17.

s (z) man, Sin. B 10; Peas. R 38; Urk. IV, 4, 4. 12; someone, anyone, (no) one, Gr. §102; s nb 'everyone', 'each one', 'each', §103; pregnantly man of rank, Pr. 7, 2; sꜣ s 'a well-born m.', GAS 30; JEA 22, 104; s n ꜥḳ 'trustworthy m.', Pr. 7, 3; pḥ·n·i s n rnpwt 74 'I attained a manhood of 74 years', Urk. IV, 1409, 18. Rare varr. Urk. V, 179, 6; IV, 401, 16; 1148, 12.

st **woman**, Westc. 10, 4; M.u.K. 5, 10; P. Kah. 9, 17; 'woman', Westc. 5, 9; Urk. IV, 4, 11; Leb. 98 ( ); msw wrw st-ḥmt 'female children of princes', Urk. IV, 1305, 7.

st (zt) **pintail duck**, Gr. p. 471, G 39; (sic) st ms 'egg-laying d.', Urk. IV, 1797, 2.

see smyt 'desert'.

var. of sr 'sheep'.

var. of stꜣw 'injury'.

st (1) **seat, throne**, TR 12, 7; Les. 81, 17; Urk. IV, 520, 8; 572, 3; st wrt 'throne', GNS 96; P. Wilbour, 13, n. 1; JEA 34, 21, n. 4; **place**, Sh. S. 153; Sin. B 232. 235; Peas. B1, 98; Urk. IV, 1110, 3; **grounds of house**, Sin. B 155; of tomb, Les. 68, 4; **department, office**, Urk. IV, 257, 10; 1106, 8; COA III, p. 162; **storehouse**, Bersh. II, 7, top, 4; BH I, 7, 9; imy-r st 'overseer of s.', P. Kah. 28, 23; **position, rank of official**, BM 614, 4; Westc. 7, 25.

(2) in expressions st wꜥꜥw 'Privy Council-chamber', Urk. IV, 479, 3; st mꜣꜥt 'Place of Truth' = Theban necropolis, JEA 7, 120; 24, 163; st mꜣꜥ-ḫrw 'Pl. of Justification' = (a) tomb: (b) pl. of divine tribunal, 20, 163; st nt snḏm 'dwelling-pl.', Sh. S. 77-8; st dg 'hiding-pl.', Sin. B 4; r st iry 'in good order', Pr. 7, 11.

(3) prefixed to other words to form abstract nouns (cf. ZÄS 79, 91):–

st-ib 'favourite', BH I, 7, 9; 'f. place', Urk. IV, 183, 12; 'wish', 170, 13; 'affection', BM 614, 1.

st-ꜥ 'stroke' of malignant beings, Eb. 1, 15; 30, 13; for imy-st-ꜥ 'helper', see p. 19.

st-mni '(the state of) dying', Westc. 7, 18.

st-ns 'speech', Urk. IV, 993, 6.

st-r 'utterance', Urk. IV, 967, 6.

st-rd 'rank', 'station', BH I, 17; Urk. VII, 61, 19; var. IV, 992, 16.

st-ḥr 'supervision', in ḥr st-ḥr 'under the s. of', BM 614, 4; Urk. IV, 169; 209, 2.

 st-sm3-t3 'interment,' Westc. 7, 18.

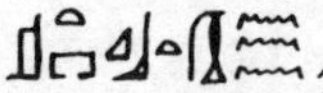 st-ḳbt 'entertainment,' Westc. 4, 25-5, 1.

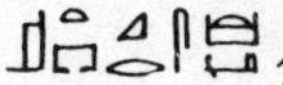 st-ḳrs '(the state of) being coffined,' Westc. 7, 18.

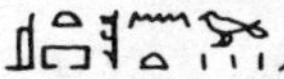 st-ḳsnt 'evil case,' Adm. p. 104.

Var. , Gr. p. 500, Q 2.

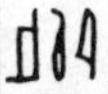 sti? successor, Bersh. I, 33; Urk. IV, 257, 7; fem. 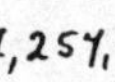 500, 16.

 s3 (z3) son, Sin. B 46; Peas. R 39; Westc. 9, 14; in expressions of filiation, Gr. §85;  'a-son-who-loves,' ritual impersonator of Horus, Les. 68, 5; Urk. IV, 807, 8;  'king's son,' Sin. R 18; Westc. 6, 22; Urk. IV, 13, 1; in sense of 'viceroy,' 40, 14 (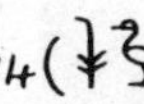); 80, 7; 194, 2; a priest is  'first k. s.,' 105, 15;  'Son of Rēʿ,' Gr. p. 74.

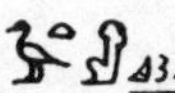 s3t daughter, Sin. B 79; Sh. S. 129; Urk. IV, 669, 1;  'king's d.,' 12, 13.

 s3ty-bity 'the royal twins' = Shu and Tefenet, Urk. V, 168, 16; cf. ZÄS 54, 15.

 s3ty-Gb 'son of Gēb,' Urk. IV, 14, 14.

 s3 land-measure of 1/8 aroura, Gr. § 266, 3.

 s3 maggot, Eb. 78, 8.

 var. of s3tw 'ground,' etc.

 s3 (z3) betake o'self, r 'to,' Eb. 101, 15; var. O.K.  Pyr. 798.

 s3 (z3) cattle-hobble, Gr. p. 523, V 16.

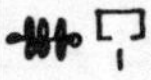 s3 byre, Urk. I, 78, 16; CT I, 98; varr. , 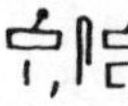, 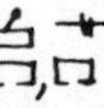 ibid.; 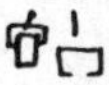 Urk. VII, 23, 6. Cf. AEO I, 97.*

 s3 amulet, Barns, Ram. p. 7.

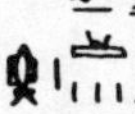 s3 protection, M. u. K. 2, 3; Urk. IV, 491, 9; 1309, 9; varr.  D. el B. 13;  Urk. IV, 239, 17.

 s3 phylē of priests, P. Kah. 11, 16; Bersh. I, 14, 3 (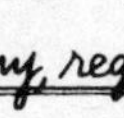); company, regiment of troops, etc., JEA 39, 41. 45; troop of animals, RB 58, 15; 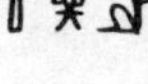 'attendant,' see p. 19; imy-r s3 'foreman,' JEA 39, 41.

 s3w magician, var. , PSBA 39, 33. 44.

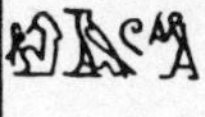 s3w (z3w) vb. 3 inf. guard, Mill. 1, 5; Urk. IV, 361, 17 (); V, 68, 12 ();

Peas. B1, 132 (); ward off, BD 204,12; restrain, Urk. I, 223,10; heed, Sin. B65; sꜣw, sꜣt, sꜣ.ti 'beware lest', Gr. §§ 184. 303. 313. 338,3; varr. O.K.  Pyr. 391;  771.

 sꜣw guardian, warden, Urk. IV, 430,10 (pl. 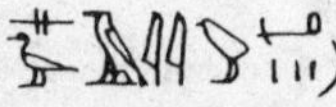); 1109,13; 1723,19.

 sꜣwt watch and ward, Urk. V, 80,11; warding off evil, RB 116,6; sꜣwt 'stand guard against', Urk. V, 51,1 (); 80,9.

 sꜣwty guardian, AEO I, 90*.

 sꜣ back, Pr. 10,9; Peas. B1,182; Urk. IV, 1073,4; m-sꜣ 'at the b. of', 'following after', Gr. § 178; 'having charge of', Sin. B239; 'wearing' sandals, Peas. B1,200; r-sꜣ 'after', Gr. § 178; ḥr-sꜣ 'upon', 'outside', 'after', ibid.; sdm wꜥ ḥr-sꜣ snnw.f 'each shall be heard in turn', Urk. IV, 1104,13; as adv. 'after', 'afterward', Pr. 9,2; Urk. 664,17; sꜣ r.s 'let it be cancelled', P. Kah. 11,20; wḥm sꜣ 'sound the retreat (?)', Sin. B124; kꜣ sꜣ 'presumptuous', GNS 88; di sꜣ 'turn the back', n 'to', GNS 34; rdi sꜣ r 'annul', 'put a stop to', GAS 103; ḥry-sꜣ 'who is behind', see p. 204. Later wtg. , Gr. p. 542, Aa 18. For ḥry-sꜣ 'kind of cattle', see p. 175.

 sꜣ knife, var. , CT I, 123; dets. 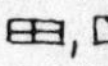,  ibid.

 sꜣt wall, Siut, pl. 5, 235; Adm. 5,6; Urk. IV, 684,10; var.  TR 36,2.

 sꜣi vb. 3 inf. linger, Sin. B151; Peas. B2,127 (); cf. GNS 58; await, JEA 43,112 (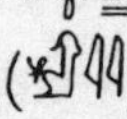, ); creep, TR 51,27 (), cf. GNS 177; 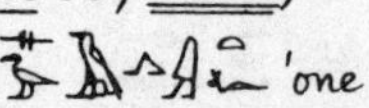 'one whose coming is awaited', later 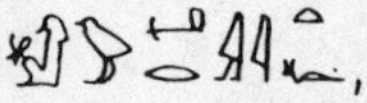, ZÄS 64,72.

 sꜣi vb. 3 inf. (1) be wise, prudent, varr. , , , GNS 33. 157; JEA 39,16: (2) be satisfied, Pyr. 551; Pr. 15,12; Urk. IV, 1999,9 (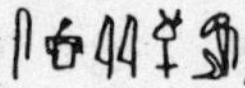); be sated, Peas. B1,124; Adm. 9,1; Urk. IV, 122,17.

 sꜣt prudence, wisdom, Sin. B48; Siut, pl. 3,182; var. 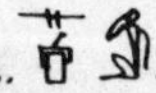 Urk. IV, 1814,5.

 sꜣꜣ wisdom (?), Pr. 12,10; 15,12.

 sꜣꜣ wise man, Merikarēꜥ 33; Neferti, 6.

 sꜣw satiety, Peas. B1, 242.

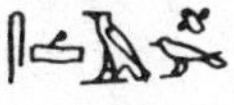 s3 weak: s3-ꜥ 'the w. of arm', 'w. man', Neferti, 54; Merikarēꜥ, 136; Urk. IV, 1078,1; 1079,5; var.  Siut, pl. 19, 19.

 s3i vb. 3 inf. sift flour, etc., Meir, IV, 13; varr. 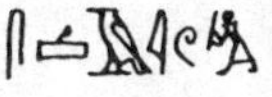 M. u. K. 7, 4;  Eb. 73,5. Cf. Kémi, 1, 140.

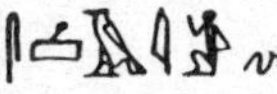 var. of s3ry 'needy man'.

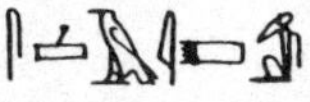 var. of si3 'recognize'.

 s3y prepare (?) bier, Leb. 54.

 s3w beam, baulk, Urk. V, 174, 13; Peas. B1, 91; varr.  B1, 92; pl.  RB 60, 13.

 S3w n. loc. Sais, Gauthier, Dict. géogr. V, 2.

 s3wt loins(?), M. u. K. 4, 9.

 s3wi caus. 3 inf. lengthen building, Urk. IV, 618,13; 1557,10; prolong lifetime, 408,15; 1874,12; friendship, with m, Peas. B1,272; s3w ib (n) 'make glad', Sin. B175; Pr. 10,10; Urk. IV, 411,7.

 s3wy keep an eye on, with ḥr, Urk. IV, 1821,12.

 s3wy gold two-thirds fine, Urk. IV, 168,7.9; 875,8; cf. Sethe, Zahlen, 95.

 S3wty (Z3wty) n. loc. Asyūt (Lycopolis), Siut, pl. 19,45; varr.  pl. 5, 237; O.K.  Pyr. 630. Cf. AEO II, 74*.

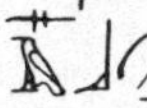 s3b (Z3b) drip, Pyr. 1257; var. 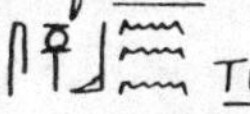 TR 25,6.

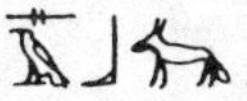 s3b (Z3b) jackal, Pyr. 372; varr. 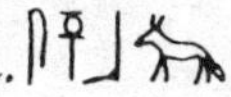 BH II, 4; 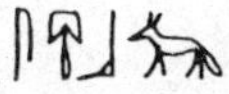 Urk. IV, 617,14; 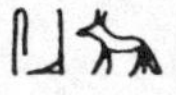 1547,18;  Siut, pl. 3,173.

 s3b dignitary of unknown rank, Urk. IV, 129,5; 130,1; 135,2; prefixed to titles = senior (?), e.g.  's. warden of Nekhen', Urk. I, 101,2; 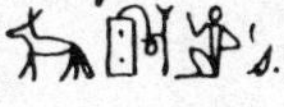 's. scribe', 48,2; 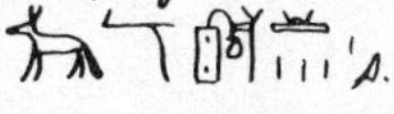 's. superintendent of documents', IV, 1120,10;  'governor' of province, Bersh. I, 7,2; 14,10 (det. 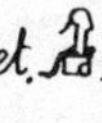); Sin. R1 (); Urk. IV, 952,13 ( 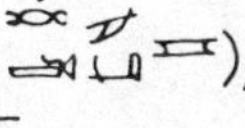);  'Chief Justice (?)', 1169,15; 1172,1; 1174,1; 1913,10.

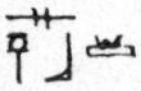 s3b caus. make to tarry, Sin. B95.

s3b cross water, Caminos, Lit. Frag. pl. 14, 2, 1; cf. p. 37.

s3b dappled, of calf, D. el. B. 134; 'many-coloured of plumage', ep. of solar Horus, var. , Gr. p. 464, F28.

s3bt dappled cow, Siut, pl. 15, 11; Urk. IV, 239, 4.

s3bt particoloured snake, Pyr. 1211; var. CT I, 14.

s3p lay out (?) garden, BH I, 26, 206.

s3pt lotus-leaf, TR 28, 3.

s3m caus. burn up, Urk. V, 40, 8; D. el. B. 114; var. Leb. 13.

s3mt lock of hair, Neferti, 42; BD 122, 12.

s3r be wise, Urk. IV, 530, 7.

s3rt wisdom, understanding, var. , GAS 95; JEA 39, 16 (h).

s3(i)r need (n.), Peas. B1, 101; var. dets. B1, 136.

s3rt need, Adm. 14, 2.

s3ry needy man, BM 614, 9; Adm. 12, 3; var. Dend. 6.

s3hhw grumbler (?), Pr. 15, 1.

s3ḥ toe, TR 23, 7; Eb. 78, 6; var. RB 121, 5.

s3ḥ (1) kick, JEA 22, 43: (2) reach, arrive at, with direct obj., Pyr. 723; with r, Sin. B12; s3ḥ t3 (a) 'land' from ship, Sh. S. 34 ( ). 103 ( ); Urk. IV, 56, 17: (b) 'tread the earth', TR 23, 73; 'go to earth' = be buried, Leb. 152.

s3ḥt neighbourhood, var. , in m s3ḥt (n) 'in the n. of', Gr. § 178.

s3ḥ dependant (?), Paheri, 6, see the next below.

s3ḥw neighbours, dependants, GAS 68.

s3ḥ endow m 'with', Sh. S. 178; Urk. IV, 2, 4; 58, 9 ( ).

s3ḥ grant of land, Urk. IV, 1111, 8; BD 14, 13; 434, 11.

S3ḥ constellation Orion, AEO I, 4*; var. Urk. IV, 1546, 13.

s3ḫ caus. spiritualize dec'd, Les. 64, 14; Siut, pl. 8, 313; Urk. IV, 66, 16; glorify god, 368, 16; name, 481, 1 ( ); uraeus, Hymnen, 10, 5; beautify tomb, Les. 68, 4; 82, 20.

s3ḥw *ritual recitations*, Siut, pl. 1, 6 8; var. CT I, 19.

s3ḫ *forcibly drive*, m 'into', Sm. 11, 6.

s3ḥmw *species of bat*, JEA 35, pl. 3.

s3s3 *drive back*, *repel*, var. , GNS 35. 157; JEA 3, 105; *force ship* ḥr 'over' *rapids*, Urk. IV, 8, 9 (dets.); ỉw ỉrty·s ḥr m3 ḥr s3s3 'its eyes looked straight ahead', RB 77, 1; *apply oil*, n 'to', Urk. IV, 112, 15.

s3šrt *a cake or loaf*, var. , AEO II, 229*.

s3ḳ *pull together*, Sin. B 23–4; P. Kah. 1, 11; CT I, 163; cf. ZÄS 60, 66; Barns, Ram. p. 9; s3ḳ ỉb 'self-possessed', Hamm. 113, 8; s3ḳ ỉb r 'set o's heart on', Pr. 11, 9; *be wary*, r 'of', Mill. 1, 3; Pr. 14, 10 (det. only); Les. 80, 19 (abbr.); cf. Žába, 157.

s3tw (z3tw) *ground*, Sh. S. 138; Sin. B 200–1; Urk. IV, 27, 16; *earth* (opp. of 'sky'), Adm. 12, 11; Urk. IV, 1164, 9; *soil*, 834, 15; RB 114, 4–5; *floor*, Urk. IV, 423, 10; 1104, 1. Varr. Urk. IV, 158, 15; 1150, 13; 23, 15; RB 121, 3. See below.

s3tw *floor-boards*, *flooring*, TR 21, 81; Urk. IV, 707, 13; var. O.K. I, 181, 10.

s3-t3 *snake*, Mill. 2, 1.

s3-t3 *reverence* (?), D. el B. 114.

s3t (z3t) intrans. *make libation*, Pyr. 16; BH II, 30 ( ): trans. *pour out water*, Siut, pl. 1, 26 ( ).

s(3)t *libation stone*, Urk. I, 107, 2; Les. 73, 16 (without det.).

s3d *a festival*, Les. 73, 18; var. JEA 38, pl. 1, 13.

sỉ *shuffle*, Sm. 4. 7. 13. 15. For the reduplicated sỉsỉ 'hurry' see below s.v. ss.

sy dep. pron. 3 f. sg. *she*, *her*, *it*, varr. , , Gr. §§ 43. 374, end; pronom. compound *she*, *it*, § 124.

sy *who?*, *what?*, varr. , , Gr. § 499; ḥr sy ỉšst 'why?', § 500, 4.

: for other words written with this sign see under ỉs and sb.

si3t fringed cloth, var. ..., Gr. p. 507, S 32.

si3 vb. recognize, Sin. R 50; Sh. S. 156; Urk. IV, 248, 15; perceive, Sin. B 214; Peas. B1, 298; know, be aware of, Les. 70, 24; Urk. IV, 119, 16; 346, 5; T. Carn. 3; si3 ib 'perceptive', Urk. IV, 971, 1; si3 rd 'wary of tread', 1080, 17: n. perception, knowledge, GAS 85; GNS 83; as god, PSBA 38, 43. 83; 39, 138 (often with det. ...); si3 ht 'wisdom', Urk. I, 39, 15. Varr. ... Sh. S. 156; ... Sin. B 25; ... Urk. IV, 248, 15.

si3 orpiment (?), JEA 19, 135.

si3rr caus. 3gem. dose (?) a patient, Eb. 38, 1. 21.

si3t caus. encroach upon lands, BD 251, 3; cheat, Peas. B1, 105 (abbr. ...).

si3ty mutilator, Urk. V, 57, 2; twister of speech, Peas. B1, 99 (...); cheater, B1, 250 (...). 262-3.

siwy announce s'one, m 'to', CT I, 158; n 'to', Pyr. 340 (...); make a complaint, r 'against' s'one, Pr. 14, 2; hr 'about' s'thing, Urk. I, 78, 12.

siwr caus. make pregnant, Pyr. 1199; var. ... P. Kah. 6, 3.

siwḥ caus. inundate, Urk. IV, 1819, 18.

siwḥ rob (?), Urk. IV, 2148, 5.

sip caus. inspect, examine, Les. 75, 13; Urk. IV, 497, 5; BD 74, 2; 186, 13; revise, BHI, 25, 44; entrust, n 'to', Les. 72, 7; Urk. IV, 54, 11; 142, 5; allot, assign, n 'to', BHI 25, 86; Neferḥotep, 5; Sm. 19, 18; Urk. IV, 1276, 18; destine, n 'to' a fate, 269, 16; 923, 14; organize (?) household, Urk. IV, 1015, 1: n. inspection, Urk. V, 16, 11; 78, 15. Varr. ... Urk. I, 130, 13; ... BD 13, 3.

sipty caus. inspect, Urk. IV, 515, 16 (...): n. investigation, Les. 76, 22; 98, 7-8; ... sipty m 'make i. into', Urk. V, 105, 13; ct sipty rn.f 'the room called "I."' = record room (?), Westc. 9, 5.

sipt(y)-wr inventory, Neferḥotep, 3.

sim3 caus. make well-disposed, n 'to', Urk. IV, 345, 16; varr. ... Pr. 7, 10; ... Pt. (L II), 3, 13; ... Urk. IV, 1381, 14.

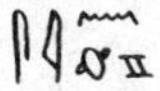 sin n. clay, TR 72,42; Sm. 22,5: vb. be sealed with clay, Urk. IV, 1304,18.

 sint clay seal, in s[d]-sint 's.-breaker,' ritual instrument, Urk. IV, 206,14.

 sinw ropes, Urk. IV, 1867,12.

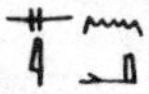 sin (zin) rub, Pyr. 1247; Westc. 7,16 (); P. Kah. 7,41; rub out, obliterate, Urk. I, 7,11 (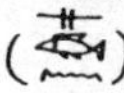); Peas. B1, 309 (); rub together, of ingredients, Eb. 12,2; 34,4.

 sin sever neck, CT I, 72.

 sin caus. wait, n 'for,' var. dets. , GNS 11.153.

 sin vb. run, Pyr. 681. 1532; RB 125,3 (); pass away = die, CT I, 164 (); sin ḥr 'hastiness' of temper, Les. 81,6: n. courier, Pyr. 1532; CT I, 278.

 sint canoe, Urk. IV, 1819,9; cf. Caminos, Lit. Frag. p. 37.

 sind caus. make miserable, Leb. 57-8.

 sihm caus. hold back, GNS 58, n. 1.

 var. of sꜥḥ 'noble'.

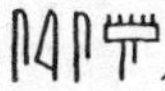 sis 'six-weave' linen, TR 20,91; var. 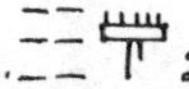 20,92.

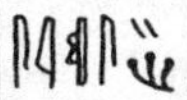 sisy caus. lighten burden, Urk. IV, 1140,1; lessen, Peas B1, 241 (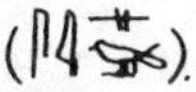).

 sikr caus. enrich s'one, Urk. IV, 38,2; 106,7; 992,15; VII, 2,10; make perfect the dec'd, IV, 1364,17; BD 210,6; make splendid a building, Merikarēꜥ, 127.

 sitn caus. subordinate (?) s'one, n 'to,' Les. 81, 20.

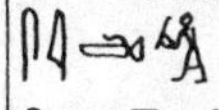 sid caus. make impotent, JEA 4, pl. 9,2 = p. 35, n. 2.

 sꜥꜣy caus. 3inf. make great, of size, Urk. IV, 834,8 (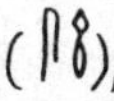); 1048,5; of rank or position, 1172,9 (); RB 114, 15.16; magnify god, Urk. IV, 162,17; truth, JEA 32, pl. 6,9; increase benefits, Westc. 9,26-7; Urk. IV, 163,16; 584,17; RB 64,5; glorify life on earth, PSBA 35, 166.

 sꜥꜣy tremble, Urk. IV, 1509,14.

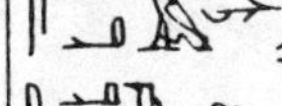 sꜣꜥ gunwale, Caminos, L-Eg. Misc. 161.

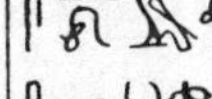 sꜥwꜣ caus. cause to go bad, of drink, Eb. 85,15.

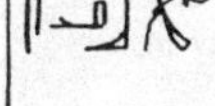 var. of swꜥb 'cleanse'.

sꜥb be equipped, m 'with' weapons, Urk. IV, 657, 6; 1302, 10; 1308, 3 (det.).

sꜥb saw out (?) timbers of ship, Urk. V, 151, 5.

sꜥm caus. wash down medicine, m 'with' drink, Eb. 4, 11. 16; swallow, with m, RB 116, 6; 119, 1; Adm. 6, 1; inlay a material, Urk. IV, 669, 15.

sꜥn caus. beautify, Merikarēꜥ, 122.

sꜥnḫ caus. make live, preserve, Pyr. 1461; Peas. B1, 221; Eb. 1, 10; revive dead, Pyr. 614. 1684; nourish, feed, P. Kah. 3, 5; Siut, pl. 4, 228; 15, 9 (); perpetuate name, BH I, 26, 161; Urk. IV, 12, 10; 128, 12. 16.

sꜥnḫ sculptor, AEO I, 67*.

sꜥnd caus. make little of, Pr. 5, 11; lessen, diminish, Urk. IV, 269, 1; RB 125, 1.

sꜥr caus. cause to ascend, BD 203, 1; make to rise in rank, Urk. IV, 119, 8; cause to approach, of death, CT I, 72; bring to an end o's days of life, I, 158; forward pleas (mdwt), Urk. IV, 46, 17 (); 966, 15 (); affairs (ḫrt), 1833, 19; bring, present, Siut, 18, 5; Urk. IV, 396, 11; 753, 1; 950, 6; sꜥr mꜣꜥt n 'present "truth" to' a god = (1) ritual act, 1540, 15: (2) 'p. "t." to its lord' = act rightly, 338, 5; 1045, 1; sꜥr dwt r ꜥḥ 'act unjustly', 1533, 15; publish (?) report, 1382, 14; obtain (?) royal bounty, 257, 17.

sꜥry ewer on stand, Urk. IV, 635, 10.

sꜥryt uraeus, Urk. IV, 266, 6; 270, 4.

sꜥrk caus. finish off, complete, Hatnub, 3, 3; Urk. IV, 1543, 13 (); put a stop to, Eb. 14, 11; kill (dets.), RB 64, 13-14.

sꜥḥ rank, dignity, Pyr. 1015; BH I, 25, 70 (); 26, 170 (); Urk. IV, 224, 10. 14; BD 284, 4 (); det. , of royalty, Urk. IV, 255, 9. 15; pl. dignities, honours, Pyr. 411; BH I, 26, 128; Urk. IV, 160, 8 ().

sꜥḥ noble, dignitary, Urk. I, 99, 8; varr. IV, 118, 3; 259, 1; VII, 54, 5; used of the blessed dead, RB 110, 15; 119, 6; BD 23, 13 ().

sꜥḥ vb. intrans. be noble, Urk. IV, 1278, 9 (); BD 31, 5 (); of sceptre,

TR 19, 51: trans. ennoble, CT I, 143; Urk. IV, 160, 2; 887, 8.

sꜥḥ mummy, BD 190, 13; var. dets. Urk. IV, 913, 17; Adm. 3, 7.

sꜥḥꜣ caus. make to vie, r 'with', JEA 32, pl. 6, 5.

sꜥḥꜥ caus. raise up prone person, Pyr. 617; Westc. 8, 2; cause to stand, r 'at', Urk. IV, 159, 1; set up, erect buildings, etc., 23, 14; 357, 5; 437, 15; 618, 12; instal king, Pr. 2, 8; accuse s'one; establish crime, r 'against', JEA 21, 144. Varr. Urk. IV, 642, 11; 765, 15.

sꜥsꜥ deface (?), Merikarēꜥ 122 (Moscow and Carlsberg texts).

sꜥšꜣ caus. make numerous, multiply, Sin. B 69; varr. Adm. 14, 13; Urk. IV, 591, 16.

sꜥšꜣ vb. police a district: n. policeman, AEO I, 92-3*.

sꜥšꜣ escort, Adm. 10, 7.

sꜥḳ caus. cause to enter, m 'into', Eb. 1, 6; r 'into', Urk. IV, 658, 13; bring to land, of boats, Peas. B1, 198; bring goods, r 'into' storehouse, Urk. IV, 1144, 13; send in document, Peas. B2, 130 (s restd.); drive animals, r 'to', B1, 24. Var. TR 23, 88.

sꜥḳ-nṯr entry of god in procession, Urk. IV, 741, 1; 768, 8.

sꜥḳy head of family (?), Merikarēꜥ, 59; Siut, pl. 15, 2; cf. JEA 1, 27, n. 8.

sꜥḏ caus. make hale, M.u.K. vs. 6, 1. 2.

swt scirpus-reed (?), emblem of U. E., Gr. p. 73.

sw (1) dep. pron. 3 m. sg. he, him, it, Gr. §43; used in archaistic texts before sḏm.f, p. 424, Add. to §148, 1: (2) pron. comp. 3 sg. he, she, it, §124: (3) non-encl. particle, §240.

swt force of wind, var., JEA 25, 128.

sww dates; sing. day in dates (abbr. ⊙), Gr. p. 203; varr. pl. Urk. IV, 483, 5; 386, 9.

swꜣ (zwꜣ) break, Peas. B1, 58; TR 7, 3; cut throat, Pyr. 270; cut off limbs, etc., Urk. IV, 1108, 14; 2144, 17; cut down trees, 1113, 3; Adm. 3, 5.

 sw3 caus. pass: intrans, Pyr. 468.914; trans. 1351.1560; with m 'on' road, BD 360,11 (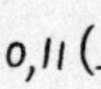); ḥr 'on' road, Peas. B1,8 (); 'over' a case, B1,215; 'over' s'one, Pr. 13,5; 'by' a place, Sin. B1,14 (); 'by' s'one, B1,136; Les. 84,23 (); escape, ḥr 'from', Pyr. 1236; surpass s'one, JEA 16,195 (4); with ḥr + obj. Peas. B1,119; pass away, of dead, Westc. 6,23; of time, 12,9; Sin. B290; remove, m 'from', Pyr. 679; transgress laws, with ḥr, Pr. 6,5; occur: 'new words tmt sw3 which have not o.'d before', Adm. p. 97; sw3t 'what is past', Adm. p. 99; Urk. IV, 750,15.

 sw3w journey, Siut, pl. 11,1.

 sw3w3 caus. ponder, Les. 81,4.

 sw3ḥ caus. make to endure, to last, Pr. 9,8; Urk. IV, 352,10 (); VII, 4,4; make stay in house, Pr. 10,11; lengthen life, Urk. IV, 309,16; 978,5 (): intrans. last long, endure, 366,7.

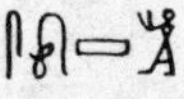 sw3š caus. pay honour to, applaud, JEA 39,18; varr.  Siut, pl. 5,238; 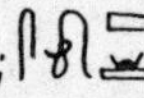 Urk. IV, 309,10;  101,5.

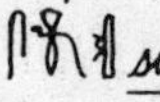 sw3ḏ caus. make green herbage, etc., Peas. B1,142; Les. 68,16; BD 230,6; make to flourish, of person, Bersh. I,15 (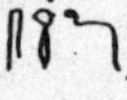); Siut, pl. 9,384 (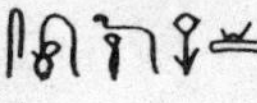); of office, Urk. IV, 209,2; make prosperous, of years, 489,1; richly provide altars, etc., 146,11 (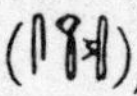); 163,8; Westc. 9,26; refurbish stela, Urk. IV, 27,3. Also for swḏ 'hand over', q.v.

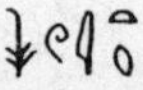 swit pill, Eb. 4,20.

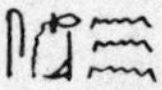 swʿb caus. cleanse, purify, Les. 76,7; Urk. IV, 263,4 (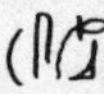); 753,7; V, 23,6; decorate building, m 'with', IV, 737,1; 766,7; consecrate temple servants, 2030,6.

 swb3 caus. open: swb3 ḥr n 'o. the sight of' = instruct, Urk. IV, 422,6; swb3 ỉb 'o. the heart' to wisdom, 1383,6 (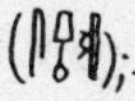); reveal o'self, 1679,7 ().

 swmt caus. make thick, Sm. 22,6; Urk. IV, 758,13; make stout the heart, 890,13 (det. ).

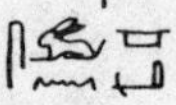 swn caus. open: swn ḥr 'o. the sight' = instruct, Cairo 20712, 3-4.

 swn flattery: pḥr m swn 'persuade by f.', Siut, pl. 16,13; sim. Les. 80,21.

swnt arrow, JEA 41, 15.

swn (zwn) perish, Adm. 5, 2; var. Pyr. 725.

swn affliction, Adm. 5, 14.

swnyt pain, M. u. K. 3, 2.

swnw physician, Eb. 1, 9; 33, 4; 36, 10; wr swnw 'master ph.', Urk. I, 42, 6; V, 61, 10.

swn trade (n. and vb.), RB 62, 10; JEA 31, pl. 2, 12; 7, 11.

swnt price, JEA 13, 189; r swnt 'as the p. of', 'in exchange for', Gr. § 178; swnt 'do trade', Les. 84, 22; JEA 31, pl. 2, 12. Varr. Les. 84, 22; Paheri, 3.

swnw tower, Pyr. 1105; varr. ibid.; ZÄS 47, 125.

swnnw pond, Caminos, Lit. Frag. pl. 12, 1; var. BD 242, 5.

swr (zwr) drink, Pyr. 129; varr. ibid.; Urk. IV, 413, 4; Sin. B 233; Westc. 7, 3; Adm. 13, 13; abbr. Urk. IV, 433, 1; JEA 2, pl. 2, 2.

swr drink-supply, Urk. IV, 1449, 5.

swrt drink-supply (?), Davies, Rekh, pl. 122, 31 (A).

swr caus. promote official, Urk. IV, 1041, 17; increase herds, 238, 13.

swrd caus. weary s'one, Sh. S. 20-1; P. Kah. 36, 7 (dets.).

swhỉ vb. 4 inf. boast of, vaunt, with m, n or direct obj., GAS 28; varr. RB 58, 3; Adm. 7, 14; Urk. IV, 973, 12; 1291, 13.

swh(ꜣ) break up, of ship, Adm. 2, 11.

swhn caus. throw down building, CT I, 162; Urk. IV, 780, 7 (dets.).

swḥ loincloth, Pyr. 533 (also det. ?); BD 449, 1.

swḥ wind, GNS 154.

swḥt egg, Sin. R 93; Urk. IV, 248, 15; 361, 4; Leb. 79 (det.); imyw swḥt 'those who are in the egg', CT I, 167.

swḥt coffin, JEA 21, 143.

swḥt shroud, loc. cit.

swẖ caus. spend the night, Pr. 14, 5.

swḫ3 caus. befool s'one, Peas. B1, 282.

swḫ3y decay (?) (n.), Urk. IV, 848, 9.

swsr caus. make strong, powerful, Urk. IV, 272, 1; BD 210, 12.15; var. Urk. IV, 268, 12.

swsḫ caus. widen, make wide, make spacious, Siut, pl. 11, 12; Les. 71, 22; Urk. IV, 133, 17; 618, 13; extend boundaries, Sin. B71; Siut, pl. 16, 17; Urk. IV, 186, 11; make extensive, of movements, BD 320, 15. Varr. Les. 71, 22; Urk. IV, 83, 3; 1677, 17.

swšr caus. dry (trans.), Eb. 40, 4.

swgm caus. grind, pulverize, var. , P. Ed. Smith, 497.

swt (1) indep. pron. 3 sg. he, it, rarely she, Gr. §64 with Obs.: (2) encl. part. but, §254.

swt (zwt) wheat, var. , AEO II, 223*.

var. of Stḫ 'Seth'.

swtwt walk about, Urk. IV, 116, 2; 520, 12; 1064, 6 (); journey, travel, 3, 6; 91, 14 (); 1541, 12 (); swtwt 'avenue', 'promenade', AEO II, 216*.

swdi caus. 3 inf. plant with trees, Urk. IV, 1795, 15.

swdwd bandage (vb.), ZÄS 57, 7*.

swdf caus. make to linger, Peas. B1, 78.

swḏ caus. hand over, pass on, assign office, etc., Sin. B 234. 239; varr. RB 111, 5; BM 101; Leyd. V 88; Urk. IV, 55, 10; 48, 5. Cf. JEA 33, 7.

swḏ3 caus. make healthy, Westc. 10, 14; Urk. IV, 945, 1 (); keep safe, BD 122, 1; cf. Caminos, L.-Eg. Misc. 446; calm fear, BH I, 77; swḏ3 ib ḥr 'inform about,' Peas. B1, 36-7; swḏ3 tw ib 'inform yourself!' B2 13; swḏ3 ib pw n nb.i 'it is a communication to my lord', P. Kah. 27, 8; 29, 2.

swḏ3 caus. trans. convey, n 'to' s'one, BD 479, 9: intrans. go, 230, 7.

swḏ3 caus. die, Adm. 16, 1; cf. GAS 95.

swḏb caus. wind rope, ḥr 'around', Caminos, Lit. Frag. p. 13.

sb overstep fence, Sin. B116 (corruption of snb?).

var. of s3b 'jackal'.

sbi (zbi) vb. 3 inf. intrans: go, travel, Peas. B1, 202; BH I, 7, 7 (); attain, r 'to', GNS 68.160; watch over, with ḥr, L. to D. IV, 4 (n.): trans. send, Sin. R11; Urk. IV, 323, 17; RB 60, 6; conduct, n 'to' s'one, Westc. 7, 22; r 'to' a place, Sin. B 171.245; spend, pass time, GNS 63.68; attain good repute, Urk. I, 222, 10; IV, 1845, 16.

sbi vb. 3 inf. be faint, Sin. B 255; perish, RB 57, 5; sb n sḏt 'burnt-offering', Sh. S. 56.145; sb n t3 'crumble to dust', Urk. IV, 1800, 7; P. Ch. Beatty IV, vs. 3, 3 ().

sbt burden, Sin. B 291; cargo, Sh. S. 162 ().

sbt wrong, evil (n.), ZÄS 48, 35; var. Urk. IV, 247, 15.

sby uraeus, ZÄS 48, 35.

see under sww 'dates'.

sbw spoils of army, RB 64, 11.

sbw squalor (?), Adm. 2, 8.

sb.tw in quest of, Gr. § 181.

sbt libation-jar, Urk. IV, 1869, 15; 1870, 1.

sb3 star, Sh. S. 129; varr. Sin. B 271; BM 101.

sb3 door, Peas. B1, 34; varr. Urk. IV, 159, 12; 426, 8; 1295, 5; 845, 13; RB 120, 13.

sb3 vb. teach s'one, r 'concerning', Pr. 12, 9; Peas. B1, 287; with double obj. of person and thing taught, Les. 81, 2.8: n. teaching, Pr. 17, 12; 19, 3; sb3 'school', Siut, pl. 14, 67. Varr. Les. 81, 8; Pr. 5, 4; Urk. IV, 993, 17.

sb3 pupil, BM 101.

sb3yt written teaching, Mill. 1, 1; instructions, Urk. IV, 503, 13. Varr. Les. 68, 11; Pr. 4, 1; Urk. IV, 968, 10.

sb3t(y) pupil, Les. 70, 21.

sb3 surveying instrument (?), Siut, pl. 6, 265; abbr. Urk. VII, 6, 6. Cf. Meir III, 36, o. v. p. 28, n. 5.

sb3ḳ caus. cleanse, Pyr. 457; var. TR 57, 9.

sb3ḳḳ caus. give a clear character, n 'to'; commend s'one, n 'to', JEA 28, 19 (l).

sb3gy caus. 4 inf. make weary, Pyr. 260; var. BD 455, 15.

sbi rebel (vb. and n.), ḥr 'against', Les. 69, 1; Brunner, Siut, 50, 65; RB 111, 3; dets. Les 98, 14; Neferhotep, 22.

sbit coll. rebels, Urk. IV, 138, 15.

sbi 'rebel-serpent', a demon, Urk. IV, 1603, 13; 2092, 10. 17.

sbi drink, Urk. IV, 1802, 9.

sbiw flautist (?), Kémi, 1, 139.

sbin alienate relatives, Pt. (L II), 5, 1; property, P. Berl. 9010, 7; Siut, pl. 6, 272 ( ).

var. of sbṯ 'laugh', 'laughter'.

sbn (zbn) glide away, of snakes, Pyr. 225. 237; steer off course, diverge, Peas. B1, 91 ( ). 126. 221 ( ).

sbnw fish, Leb. 89.

sbnt woman who gives suck, Peas. B2, 120.

sbnt cow in suck, Pyr. 716.

sbh3 caus. make to flee, P. Kah. 1, 8.

sbḥ vb. cry out, Sin. B 139; Peas. B1, 30: n. cry, Sin. B 265.

sbẖ jar, Sm. 21, 16; 22, 3.

sbẖ close arms, ḥ3 'about' s'one, Pyr. 585. 636; shut away, r 'from', Urk. IV, 1071, 8 (det.).

sbẖt portal, Westc. 7, 26; Adm. 2, 10; dets. Urk. IV, 174, 9; 422, 2; abbr. 1750, 7.

sbẖt pylon-shaped chest, Urk. IV, 629, 11; 634, 8.

sbšy caus. make to vomit, Eb. 85, 16; 103, 12.

sbk (1) n. calf of leg, Pyr. 1314: (2) adj. splendid, Adm. 10, 6; Urk. IV, 84, 17 ( ); precious, 887, 7; 1685, 9 ( ); Les. 86, 9 ( ); JEA 11, 286, n. 2.

Sbk n. div. Sobk, Hymnen, 1,4; var. Urk. IV, 531, 2.

sbty rampart, Urk. IV, 184, 16; 661, 12; 1297, 9; RB 58, 12; sbty n wmtt 'circumvallation', Urk. IV, 661, 4; 767, 11 (abbr.); 832, 13.

sbty enclosure, RB 66, 5.

sbṯ (zbṯ) vb. laugh, Pyr. 1149 (); Urk. IV, 219, 14; m 'at', Sh. S. 149 (); sbṯ ḥr 'friendly', Siut, pl. 11, 16; Urk. VII, 10, 15: n. laughter, mirth, Pyr. 1989 (det.); Adm. 3, 13; Urk. IV, 2172, 17 ().

sbdš caus. make weak, Hamm. 114, 9.

spt (zpt) threshing-floor, Gr. p. 498, O50.

sp (zp) (1) time: sp 3 sp 4 n hrw 'three and four t. a day', Sin. B298; 4-nw sp 3 m spr n.k 'the fourth t. of appealing to you', Peas. B1, 224; n p3 sp.f tm iw 'his t. has never failed to come', Pr. 14, 11-12; 'twice', graphic sign of repetition, Gr. §207; of reduplication, e.g. = ršrš, q.v.; of similarity, succession or reciprocity, JEA 22, 181. 183; n sp 'together', 'at once', Gr. §205, 3; m sp wc 'with one accord', RB 65, 11; sp n iwtt 'in vain', Sin. B136-7.

(2) matter, affair, case: 'Forbearance sḥtm.f sp ḫpr destroys a m. which is past', Peas. B1, 273; sp bin 'a bad a.', B1, 123; sp pw n ḥsf.tw n D. pn 'Is it a c. for one's punishing this D.?', B1, 46-7; sp.f nfr n wn m3c 'his own due cause', B1, 203; n mh.i ḥr sp n š3t.n.f 'I was neglectful of no m. which he had decreed', Urk. IV, 363, 5; sp ḥnc 'deal with' s'one, Pr. 14, 7.

(3) deed, act: sḫpr sp 'the d. must be effected', Peas. B1, 199; sp nfr 'a good d.', Pr. 15, 11; sp ḫs 'a mean a.', Peas. B1, 325; Urk. IV, 1425, 15; sp.f bin 'his evil conduct', Leb. 110; spw.f nbw mnḫw 'all his excellent deeds', Urk. IV, 1045, 2; sim. Pr. 6, 4; sp.f n rḫ 'his d. of knowledge' = display of skill, Westc. 6, 21; sim. Urk. IV, 57, 17; mcr spw 'successful of d.'s', RB 60, 5.

(4) misdeed, fault: iw sp.f 'him in whom f. had been found', BH I, 7, 8; n iw sp.i 'no f. of mine came out', Urk. IV, 151, 2 (det.); sim. 77, 2; sp.f sw3

ḥr.k 'his m.'s have got beyond you (?)', Merikarēʿ, 26 (Moscow, det.).

(5) occasion, chance: sp tpy 'the First O.' = the creation, BD 9,1; pw sp nfr 'What a happy o.!', Urk. IV, 1078, 13; spw 3 pw r rdit ir.f 'there have been three o.'s to cause him to act', Peas. B1, 155-6 (); tp.i rsw [ḥr] sp n mri 'I am vigilant [for] any ch. of grounding', Urk. IV, 1077, 4; hence mishap: in.n sp 'we overcame a m.', Caminos, Lit. Frag. pl. 2, 2, 11-12; cf. also Bull. 34, 138, n. 3.

(6) venture: n p3 d3yt mni sp.s 'never has wrongdoing brought its v. safe to port', Pr. 6, 6.

(7) success: iw ʿwn-ib šw.f m sp, iw wn sp.f m wḫt 'the rapacious man lacks s., (but) he has s. in failure', Peas. B1, 291-2.

(8) condition: mi sp.s imy-ḥ3t 'in accordance with its former c.', Urk. IV, 140, 17.

sp in sp 'never', foll. by sḏm.f, Gr. § 456.

sp (1) medicine, dose, Eb. 7, 11; 8, 17; 25, 8: (2) portion of food, etc., Pyr. 551. 1674; BD 124, 8; Sm. 12, 14.

spi vb. 3 inf. remain over, Sh. S. 107; Urk. IV, 759, 10; Sm. 21, 12 (dets.); be left out, excluded, Urk. IV, 84, 5; be left over, abandoned, n 'to', Leb. 122; Adm. 4, 5.

spyt remnant, Sin. B 65; var. Urk. IV, 122, 16; m spt ḥr Wnn-nfr 'being what is left over on account of Onnophris', 482, 13.

spw fragments, P. Ed. Smith, 153; 'bundles of wood', Urk. IV, 670, 12.

spt lip, Peas. B1, 166; Pr. 16, 1; Urk. IV, 63, 14 (); 971, 2 (dual); of vagina, Eb. 95, 22; of wound, Sm. 5, 9; of jar, Eb. 63, 18; bank of waterway, Leb. 67; Urk. IV, 655, 13 (); shore, 691, 1 (); gunwale (?), V, 157, 2; edge of horizon, TR 13, 16.

spt ritual (?) object, Urk. IV, 23, 9.

sp3 (zp3) centipede, ZÄS 58, 82.

sp3w birds made to fly = flushed from cover (?), Caminos, Lit. Frag. p. 12.

sp3t district, nome, varr. , Gr. p. 488, N 24; p. 541, Aa 8.

sp3tyw nomesmen, Bersh. I, 14, 9.

spnꜥ caus. overturn, Peas. B1, 112; renew skin, Eb. 84, 3; Sm. 21, 3-4.

spr rib, var. , Gr. p. 466, F42.

spr arrive, r 'at', Sin. B6; Sh. S. 167; Peas. R34; Les. 86, 3 (); reach s'one, with r, Sin. B199; Westc. 7, 13; fig. in 'who committed offence sp·f spr r·f and his deed recoiled upon him', RB 112, 11; come, tp-m 'before' s'one, of royal decrees, Urk. IV, 208, 10; spr r + inf. 'c. to do s'thing', Les. 86, 16; Hatnub, 38 (); spr r ḥꜣty 'come to mind', Urk. IV, 27, 12: trans. reach, V, 96, 10.

spr appeal to, petition s'one, with n, Peas. B1, 88; Leb. 146; Urk. IV, 1110, 11; ḥr a. 'against' judgement, 1089, 13; make petition, BH I, 26, 146 (); Urk. IV, 342, 10.

sprt petition (n.), Peas. B2, 128; Urk. IV, 273, 15; 1524, 6; var. Pr. 9, 6.

sprw petitions, Urk. IV, 971, 12; 1117, 17.

sprw petitioner, Peas. B1, 128; Urk. IV, 1082, 12; varr. 1088, 3; Peas. B1, 284; Pr. 9, 4.

sprty petitioner, Urk. IV, 1110, 7; 1111, 9; var. Siut, pl. 11, 11.

spri caus. 3 inf. make to miss, of missiles, Sin. B135; expel rebel, Urk. IV, 968, 12 (det.).

spḥ lasso (vb.), Urk. IV, 1080, 15; dets. 1076, 1.

spḥw lasso (n.), Urk. V, 55, 13.

spḥ caus. attain, n 'to', Urk. IV, 1091, 13.

spḥt ribs of beef, Meir, III, 21; D. el B. 110.

spḫꜣ caus. purge the body, Eb. 11, 10; fig. of the heart, Pt. (L I) C2 (); Urk. IV, 66, 13 (); make sleek (?) the skin, Pt. (L II), 5, 16.

sphr caus. cause to circulate, ZÄS 60, 69 (det.); brandish weapons, Mill. 2, 1.

sphr caus. register, JEA 27, 20, n. 2; copy, JEA 12, 126; sš sphr 'copyist', BD 28, 3-4. Var. Rhind, title.

sps be tousled (?), TR 57, 9.

spd adj. sharp, Pyr. 270 (); BD 219, 14 (); 229, 14; Urk. IV, 1704, 12; effective, skilled, of persons, BD 152, 9; 298, 7; Urk. IV, 97, 4; of hands, 1723, 11; of fingers, 1152, 8; V, 61, 1; of tongue, Les. 70, 23; Urk. IV, 507, 7; of speech (r), Les. 81, 9; Urk. VII, 65, 15; spd ḥr 'alert', BH I, 8, 10; 'alertness', Urk. IV, 134, 8; 388, 8: vb. display skill, Les. 83, 3; supply food, Siut, pl. 19, 27; restore to order, JEA 19, 24.

spdt effectiveness (?), Pr. 6, 5; cf. Žába, 118 (88).

Spdt star Sirius = goddess Sothis, Gr. p. 205; varr. , , CT I, 188.

spdt triangle, JEA 12, 132.

Spdw n. div. Sopd, Sinai, 115; varr. TR 20, 15; (sic) Urk. IV, 393, 17.

spdd supply, Gr. §274; var. Urk. VII, 2, 6.

sf (zf) cut up, Urk. I, 151, 2; D. el. Geb. I, 9. 12; cut off, Eb. 91, 15.

sft knife, Urk. IV, 666, 6; M.u.K. 3, 4; BD 392, 13.

sf yesterday (n.), Peas. B1, 109; BD 52, 2; m sf 'yesterday' (adv.), Gr. p. 205, 3. Varr. Urk. V, 11, 15; Pr. 5, 1.

sf mix, Eb. 13, 1; m 'with', Urk. IV, 501, 13; ḥr 'with', Eb. 77, 1.

sfw muddle (n.), Urk. IV, 1818, 4.

sf vb. be mild, merciful, Peas. B1, 121. 136; Pr. 13, 4: n. mercy, gentleness, Leb. 107; Les. 84, 1 ( ).

sft clemency, Pr. 13, 12.

sfw the gentle man, Pr. 10, 7.

sf3 hatred (?), Les. 68, 22-3.

sf3t hatred (?), Pr. 9, 3. Cf. Žába, 128.

sf3 be sluggish (?), Pr. 7, 10.

sf3t sluggishness (?), Caminos, Lit. Frag. pl. 3, 4, 7; cf. ibid. p. 15.

sfn be kindly, merciful, Peas. B1, 150. 151; BH I, 7, 8; Urk. IV, 970, 15; 971, 7; dets. Les. 80, 18; ꜥ 84, 1. Cf. Barns, Ram. p. 8.

sfn caus. afflict, Sin. R 188; Siut, pl. 16, 11; Adm. p. 100 (dets.).

sfn3 be drowsy (?), Merikarēꜥ, 79-80.

sfḫ caus. lose, Les. 84, 15; loosen, Sin. B274; release, Eb. 1, 14 (dets.); BD 156, 7; purify, Pyr. 1083 (det.); CT I, 130 (det.); remove evil, etc., Pyr. 850; CT I, 16 (det.); BD 175, 3; lay aside garment, BD 448, 14; part fighting animals, BH I, 30; Bersh. I, 18; offer to god, D. el B. 11: intrans. let go, m 'of', Pr. 12, 7; BD 380, 14.

sfḫy fortress (fem.), COA III, p. 202, n. 3.

sfḫw offerings, Urk. IV, 112, 14; 1803, 8; var. 1488, 8.

sfḫw excretion, TR 23, 91.

sfḫw seven, Urk. V, 46, 15; fem. sfḫt Pyr. 511.

Sfḫt-ꜥbw n. div. 'The Seven-horned', ep. of Seshat, Urk. IV, 339, 12.

sfsf break (?) knives, M. u. K. 3, 4.

sfṯ (zfṯ) slaughter animals, Saqq. Mast. I, 11; Sh. S. 144; Siut, pl. 8, 314; without obj., make sacrifice, Sin. B195; Les. 74, 2.

sft sacrifice (n.), Urk. IV, 163, 8.

sftw butcher, M. u. K. 3, 3; var. Urk. IV, 1022, 10.

sfṯ oil, var., GAS 33.

sm (smt, stm) a priest, AEO I, 39*.

smt hammock, Urk. IV, 2, 16.

sm vb. help, succour, Les. 72, 22; 79, 14; 81, 1; Pr. 15, 12; with n + obj., RB 119, 8: n. deed, event, affair, GAS 46; pastime, Urk. IV, 462, 13; 512, 16.

smw pastures, Bersh. I, 18; Urk. IV, 1373, 3 (constr. as sing.); Sin. B 102; plants, herbage, Urk. IV, 775, 15; RB 111, 6; 112, 8; JEA 16, pl. 17, M4; vegetables, Urk. IV, 171, 4; 749, 6; 1450, 8; herb, Peas. B1, 133.

sm3 (zm3) unite, P. Kah. 3, 2; Sin. B272; Urk. IV, 161, 11; 200, 10. 16; join a company, Pyr. 318; Urk. IV, 1843, 13; heaven r 'to' earth, VII, 65, 8; associate, m 'with', Sin. B121; Les. 72, 14; Urk. IV, 442, 8; ḥnꜥ 'with', Pyr. 647; arrive, m 'in', Sin. B9;

partake, m 'of', Urk. IV, 1165, 3.15; 1516, 10; r 'of', 1011, 3; 1471, 3.11; without prep., 1451, 17; Paheri, 7; make ready a boat, Pyr. 1376; TR 2, 38; dmḏ sm3 'grand total', Urk. IV, 177, 2; varr. dmḏ sm3 m 336, 8; dmḏ sm3 r, BH I, 26, 140-1; sm3 alone, Urk. IV, 1660, 19. Varr. Pyr. 388; Sin. B121; B9; Peas. B1, 309; Urk. VII, 65, 8. For sm3-t3 see below.

sm3t union, Urk. V, 73, 4; var. 73, 5.

sm3y companion, confederate, Sin. B114; TR 2, 9; Adm. 2, 1; var. Hatnub, 20, 20.

sm3yt royal consort, Urk. IV, 216, 11; var. 225, 2.

sm3yt association, confederacy, Peas. B1, 191; varr. Urk. IV, 1081, 3; CT I, 193.

sm3 ramp(?), Hamm. 19.

sm3w (zm3w) lungs(?), Pyr. 410; varr. ibid.; Eb. 16, 18.

sm3w branches of tree, BD 495, 10.

see kkw-sm3w 'twilight' s.v. kkw 'darkness'.

sm3t-ʿ an offering, Urk. IV, 1553, 10; 1952, 14.

sm3t-ʿ3t a textile fabric, Urk. IV, 1125, 6; 1126, 7.

sm3-t3 (1) unite the land, Pyr. 783: (2) land, r 'at', BM 614, 17 (det.); Les. 71, 20; sm3-t3 m 'bring to land', Urk. I, 122, 8 (det.); 199, 3; t3-sm3 'landing-place', Pyr. 1187: (3) be interred, m 'in', Urk. IV, 113, 10; 147, 1 (det.); sm3 t3 im·f 'the earth envelops him', Peas. B1, 309; sim. Urk. IV, 1825, 5: (4) interment, Sin. B193; Urk. IV, 1202, 11; st-sm3-t3 'the state of i.', Westc. 7, 18: (5) 'riverside path', Peas. R 44-5. 49.

sm3 kill, Urk. IV, 812, 3; destroy illness, Eb. 25, 9. Varr. Urk. IV, 814, 16; 795, 8; 809, 3; Peas. B1, 228; Eb. 23, 20.

sm3 wild bull, Urk. VII, 36; RB 64, 13; var. Peas. B1, 207; fem. sm3t, BD 462, 3.

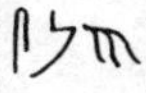 sm3 scalp, Pyr. 697 (also det. ). 2055; Eb. 48,18 (); side, Pyr. 385. 869. 1221.

 var. of s3m 'burn up'.

 var. of sim3 'make well-disposed'.

 sm3 priest who clothed the god, varr. , 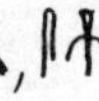, Gr. p. 543, Aa 25.

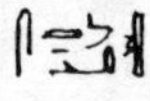 sm3c caus. (1) put in order, correct, CT I, 136 (det. ); Eb. 9,10; 12,17: (2) present, Urk. IV, 158,5; 347,6; 867,9; RB 112,15: (3) survey (?) region, JEA 4, p. 244, n. 2. Var.  Urk. IV, 1846,9.

 sm3c-hrw justify the dead, CT I, 1; the living, Urk. IV, 941,16 ().

 sm3wy caus. 4 inf. renovate, renew, Les. 76,11; Pr. 17,11; varr.  Les. 76,24;  Urk. VII, 56,6; 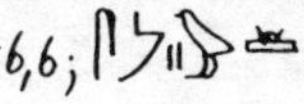 IV, 863,8.

 sm3r caus. impoverish, L. to D. I, 6 (n.); with m + obj. Urk. IV, 1089,10; varr. 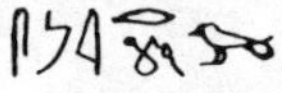 loc. cit.;  1089,14;  1199,9.

 smyt (zmyt) desert, Les. 71,19; necropolis, Urk. I, 15,17; BH I, 7,6; varr. 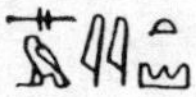 Cairo 20011;  Hier. p. 31; 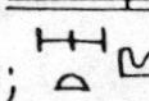, 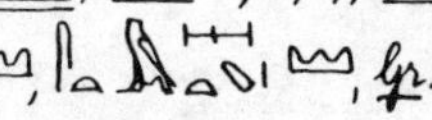, Gr. p. 541, Aa 8; 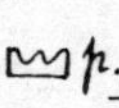 p. 488, N25.

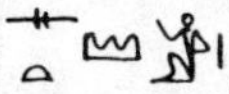 smyty necropolis worker, Siut, pl. 8, 322.

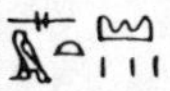 smytyw owners of a desert tomb, L. to D. II, 5 (n.)

 smi vb. 3 inf. report, make report, n 'to', Sh. S. 157; Sin. B51; Westc. 8,7; 11,12; complain, m or r 'against', JEA 20, 163; announce, proclaim, Bersh. II, 21, top, 1; BD 266,6; Merikarē, 94: n. report, Hierat. Les. I, 18, A1; P. Kah. 31,11; acknowledgement of letter, Sin. B 204; smi n mdt 'current news (?)', Adm. p. 107. Var.  Urk. IV, 1112,10.

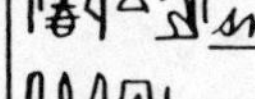 smit charge, accusation, Peas. B1, 257; cf. JEA 9, 17, n. 8.

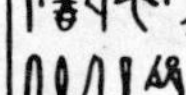 smi whip, Peas. B1, 186.

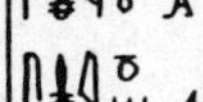 smi chastise, Urk. VII, 54,15.

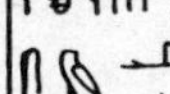 smi curds, Eb. 25,20.

 smc sounding-pole (?), TR 22,39; 27,43.

smꜥr caus. make fortunate, CT I, 182; cleanse, JEA 35, 61 (9) (dets.).

smwn non-encl. part. probably, surely, Gr. § 241.

smn caus. make firm, Pyr. 944. 2080; Urk. IV, 41, 13; smn ib 'fortify the heart', Pr. 1, 6; smn ꜥ ḥr 'm. f. o's hand over' = give authority over, Pyr. 967; smn ḥr n 'control' a land, Urk. IV, 968, 2; establish, make to endure, TR 20, 16; Urk. IV, 15, 7. 16; 17, 3; 28, 5; V, 130, 10; perpetuate name, D. el B. 132; fasten, make fast, Sin. B 122; Urk. V, 156, 9; set in place parts of body, Pyr. 30. 2036; Urk. V, 199, 6; set up stela, inscription, RB 58, 6; Urk. IV, 164, 11; 734, 15; record events, gifts, 661, 16; 662, 5; 1211, 15; confirm office, favours, Les. 98, 23-4; Urk. IV, 46, 1; 1095, 9; affix adornments, Les. 71, 15; make to stay, ḥnꜥ 'with', Westc. 3, 14; set aside, leave to stand, of medicaments, Sm. 21, 15 (dets.); 22, 2; without obj. take station, Urk. IV, 655, 5: n. mainstay of land, Urk. IV, 1087, 6; confirmation of land-holding, 1093, 2.

smnw supports of sky, Urk. IV, 428, 1; rungs of ladder, Pyr. 2080 (dets.).

smn caus. retire, withdraw, Les. 96, 14. 21.

smn goose, Westc. 8, 18. 21.

smnmn caus. shift boundary, Urk. IV, 1111, 13.

smnḫ caus. advance, ennoble s'one, Sin. B 161; Les. 81, 8; make distinguished a name, RB 112, 12; endow, Siut, pl. 6, 271; BH I, 25, 86; Urk. IV, 269, 3; settle endowment, 300, 4; 1045, 6; confirm in writing, Bull. 22, 93; embellish temples, etc., Les. 68, 4; 70, 17; BH I, 25, 8; Urk. IV, 102, 2; restore what is damaged, etc., BH I, 26, 132; Urk. IV, 501, 10; efficiently execute orders, Les. 71, 2; Urk. IV, 162, 15; 1017, 6; publish decree, Urk. I, 296, 2; annals, IV, 383, 13; make effective words, etc., VII, 3, 6; IV, 936, 5; 1160, 4; pull tight cord, D. el B. 107; without obj. set (affairs) in order, Urk. IV, 118, 14; 1214, 1; nfr pw smnḫ ꜥꜣ 'there is no doing any good here', Westc. 11, 23. Varr. Les. 82, 20; Urk. IV, 1169, 4.

smntyw emissaries, Urk. IV, 344, 16.

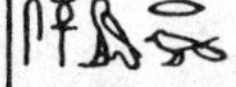 smr caus. cause pain, RB 116, 13.

 smr friend (of king), court title, Sin. R 17; B 280; Urk. IV, 1073, 4; smr wꜥty 'Sole F.', AEO I, 20*; smr tpy 'First F.', Sin. B 307. Varr. pl.  Urk. IV, 256, 11; 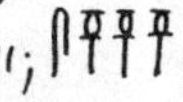 1094, 13.

 smḥy caus. 3 inf. flood land, BD 29, 1; 453, 8;; drown enemy, 349, 1; sink his ship, 247, 10 ().

 smḥy canoe, Caminos, Lit. Frag. pl. 1, 2, 2; var.  Herdsman, 11.

 smḫ caus. forget, ignore, Leb. 68; Les. 69, 9; Urk. IV, 943, 17; L. to D. V, 2 (det. ); var. 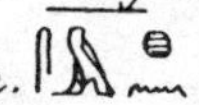 BD 224, 3.

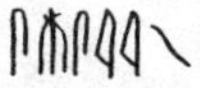 smsy caus. 3 inf. deliver woman, Westc. 9, 23-4; var.  11, 4.

 smsw elder, eldest: adj. Urk. IV, 1709, 3; Westc. 12, 13 (); BH I, 26, 122; smsw r 'older than', Pyr. 306 (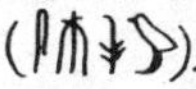). 408 (): n. Pyr. 1526; Westc. 9, 7. 11 (det. ); Urk. IV, 111, 9; smsw ist 'Elder of the Palace', Pyr. 560; Bersh. I, 7; smsw hyt 'E. of the Portal', Urk. IV, 1073, 5 (restd.); abbr. 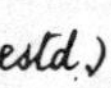 Cairo 20035; cf. AEO I, 60*.

 smt hear, Hatnub, 26, 6; var.  Pyr. 1189.

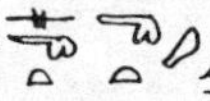 smtmt eavesdrop, BD 254, 11.

 smtr caus. bear witness to truth, RB 119, 9; examine, Urk. IV, 121, 5; 1076, 7 (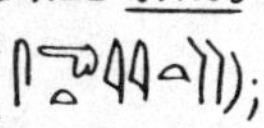); make inquiry, Les. 69, 23 (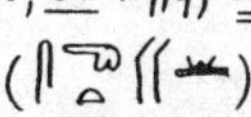).

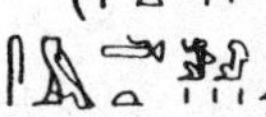 smdt coll. subjects, subordinates, Mill. 1, 3; Urk. IV, 97, 4 (); 121, 3 (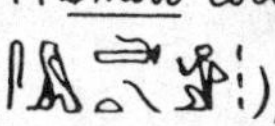); 209, 8. Cf. Caminos, L.-Eg. Misc. 235.

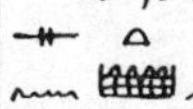 snt (znt) a board-game, JEA 39, 63.

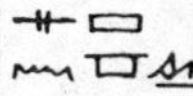 sn (zn) open, Hatnub, 20, 11; 24, 11; varr.  Pyr. 1203; 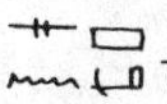 TR 28, 1; 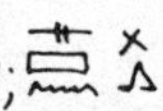 Urk. IV, 116, 8; 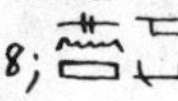 352, 6.

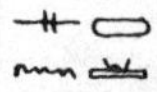 sn reveal, Urk. IV, 1381, 16.

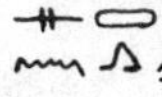 sni vb. 3 inf. pass, pass by, surpass, transgress, GNS 72.160; varr.  Les. 84, 20;  Urk. IV, 247, 10; 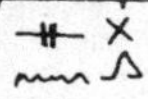 BD 482, 12.

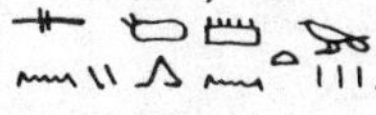 sny-mnt distress, calamity, GAS 103.

sni vb. 3inf. be like, resemble, with r, Adm. p. 99; Peas. B1, 147 ( ); copy, imitate, with r; conform, r 'to' laws, GAS 86.

snt: m snt r 'in the likeness of', 'in accordance with', Gr. §180; dets. Urk. IV, 168, 10.

sni vb. 3inf. cut off heads, Urk. IV, 248, 5; sever necks, BD 191, 8. Cf. ZÄS 50, 97, n. 2.

sn suff. and dep. pron. 3pl. they, them, their, varr. , , ; rarely , , , Gr. §§34. 43; in archaistic texts foll. by sḏm·sn, p. 424, Add. to §148, 1.

sny dual pron. they two, them two, Gr. §§34-43, n. 5b.

sn brother, Westc. 12, 15. 20; Peas. B1, 63; P. Kah. 12, 4; sn·s n mwt·s 'her maternal b.', Westc. 12, 13; sim. Adm. 5, 10; sn·k im, epistolary periphrasis for 1st sg., JEA 28, 18 (c); person sharing in funerary offerings, Gîza, III, 6; var. BH II, 7.

snt sister, L. to D. I, 1; P. Kah. 9, 5; var. Urk. IV, 618, 5.

snwt coll. brethren, TR 2, 27.

snw num. two, Gr. §260; var. Peas. B1, 215.

snnw ord. num. second; ḥr snnw-sy 'again', Gr. §263, 2.

snw companion, fellow, Sh. S. 42; Leb. 106; Urk. IV, 151, 4 ( ); equal, Sin. B 47 ( ); RB 57, 1; counterpart, JEA 4, pl. 9, 6 ( ); dual contestants in court of law, Peas. B1, 234; Urk. VII, 63, 11.

snwt(y) dual female companions, Les. 80, 14.

snt flagstaff, Urk. IV, 1105, 15; pl. 56, 3; 933, 9; RB 63, 1.7.

snwt shrine, often dual, var. dets. , , SDT 234.

snt basis of statue, Bersh. I, 14, 2; var. Urk. IV, 1174, 14.

snt festival of 6th day of (lunar) month, Pyr. 716; varr. TR 5, 7; Urk. IV, 27, 5; 469, 16.

sn smell perfume, Hatnub, 22, 5; breathe air, BD 155, 8; kiss, Sh. S. 133; M. u. K. 2, 2; sn t3 'k. the earth' in obeisance, Sin. B 188; RB 110, 13. Varr. Sh. S. 133; Urk. IV, 229, 3; 243, 6; 278, 14; 662, 9.

sniḥ angler, BH I, 29; var. O.K. Kagemni, 1.

snˁˁ caus. make smooth, polish, BH II, 13; D. el Geb. I, 14 ( ); snˁˁ ib 'soothe', 'calm', Pr. 9, 7; RB 120, 2; nd snˁˁ 'grind fine', P. Kah. 5, 50; Eb. 4, 15 ( ).

snw offerings, Urk. IV, 429, 15; varr. 112, 4; 1414, 16; D. el. B. (XI), I, 24.

snw wine of Pelusium, ZÄS 49, 81; JEA 5, 253.

snw jar, Urk. IV, 1554, 15.

snw poverty, Les. 79, 6.

snwr caus. make to tremble, var. det. , CT I, 104. 120.

snwḥ caus. impassion, JEA 4, pl. 9, 9.

snwḫ caus. boil, Eb. 49, 1; 65, 13.

snwtt bindweed (?), JEA 20, 186.

snwd caus. thrust aside, BD 138, 12.

snb (znb) overstep boundary, etc., Siut, pl. 19, 48; Sin. R 141 (dets.); overthrow landmark, Pyr. 1236 (det.).

snbt (znbt) rampart, Pyr. 1953 (det.). 1955; BD 129, 3 (dets.).

snbw (znbw) battlements, Pyr. 1478.

snbt (znbt) jar, Pyr. 1151; BD 450, 11 (det.); var. Urk. IV, 874, 3.

snb adj. healthy, JEA 16, 19, 4; Urk. IV, 920, 11; M. u. K. vs. 4, 9; pḫrt snbt 'a healing medicine', Hatnub, 20, 12; a year is snbt smw nb 'fruitful in all kinds of herbs', Paheri, 3: intrans. vb. be healthy, well, Peas. B1, 78; P. Kah. 7, 31; Urk. IV, 81, 1; become well, recover, Leb. 130; Eb. 37, 10; 38, 10; snb.t(i) 'Farewell!', Sh. S. 158; snb mryt.k 'that your coast may be clear', Peas. B1, 130; mrw snb 'the terrain is secure', Urk. IV, 656, 15; abbr. in , see under ˁnḫ 'live': trans. vb. heal, ZÄS 53, 11, n. 4; Gr. § 274: n. health, Urk. IV, 611, 11; 874, 12.

snb banish (?) sleep, var. , Neferti, 34.

snbb exchange greetings, Pyr. 1215; Urk. IV, 559, 11.

snf last year, GAS 102.

snf caus. make to breathe, M.u.K. vs. 2, 3; succour, Siut, pl. 19, 25; Hatnub, 14, 10; unload ships, Urk. IV, 323, 1; empty out contents, Peas. B1, 279 (dets.); var. P. Kah. 3, 14.

snfw (znfw) blood, Pyr. 1286 (det.); P. Kah. 7, 29; Eb. 16, 8; var. RB 57, 4.

snfr caus. make beautiful, embellish, Urk. IV, 975, 7; 1294, 14; 1795, 18; restore what is defective, 605, 16 (); carry out business, BM 614, 10; snfr ib 'gladden', Urk. I, 52, 15; 82, 7.

snfḫfḫ caus. loosen, release, D. el B. 116; BD 149, 1. 13.

snm caus. feed s'one; consume food, GAS 63; supply necessities, Urk. IV, 352, 1 (det.); 911, 7 (); 1814, 1 (dets.).

snmw food-supply, Urk. IV, 1184, 13; BD 464, 3 (dets.).

snm greed (?), Peas. B1, 282; var. dets. B2, 41.

snm be sad, GAS 25.

snm pray, n 'to', Urk. IV, 1777, 20; 1833, 14; beg, m 'from', 1830, 4; with direct obj. supplicate s'one, 1827, 6 (dets.): n. prayer, BD 50, 4 (dets.).

snmw squalls of rain, Urk. IV, 84, 9; w3wt snm 'rain-swept roads', 386, 16; cf. JEA 39, 51 (m).

snmyt a rank weed, Peas. B1, 153.

snmḥ caus. pray, make supplication, RB 59, 9; Urk. IV, 1007, 11; 1806, 2; dets. 1803, 3; 2027, 15.

snn likeness, Urk. IV, 412, 11; 1032, 4; image, figure, 426, 10; var. 615, 2.

snnt likeness, Urk. IV, 244, 14.

snn copy of document, P. Kah. 12, 5; var. Rhind, title.

snnw suffer, be distressed, CT I, 81; varr. Adm. 4, 12; BD 115, 6; cf. GAS 40.

snny chariot-soldier, AEO I, 28*; var. Urk. IV, 1344, 1.

snr caus. take care of, Urk. IV, 1282, 11.

snr caus. terrify, with n, Urk. IV, 385, 12 (restd.).

snhy vb. 4 inf. register, record, P. Kah. 14, 5; Urk. IV, 1006, 4.15 ( ); muster troops, Piankhi, 11 ( ); drive (?) birds in fowling, Caminos, Lit. Frag. p. 10.

snh3t shelter, refuge, Hatnub, 24, 8.

snhp caus. rise early, RB 114, 1.

snhp caus. set in motion, Urk. IV, 966, 6.

snhs caus. awaken, Amarna, VI, 15, 5.

snḥ caus. bind, Urk. I, 305, 18; IV, 617, 13 (dets.); entwine, Hymnen, 8, 3.

snḥ3 caus. frustrate (?), GAS 48.

snḥm (znḥm) locust, Pyr. 891; varr. Urk. IV, 1510, 1; RB 119, 16.

snḥm caus. prevent movement, var. , CT I, 52.

snḫn caus. nurse child, CT I, 167; Urk. IV, 231, 8; 579, 8.

snḫn caus. control people, Urk. VII, 54, 6.

snḫḫ caus. rejuvenate oneself, BD 168, 1; renew breath, Urk. IV, 1479, 11.

snḫt caus. make strong, strengthen, Urk. IV, 160, 13; 657, 9; 1154, 11; enrich, L. to D. I, 5 (n.).

snḫtw stiffening, stiffness of limbs, Eb. 82, 14; 83, 8.

snẖt phlegm, M. u. K. 2, 9.

snh3ẖ3 caus. disturb (?), TR 19, 22.

snsy vb. 4 inf. worship, BD 12, 14; Urk. IV, 1818, 12; var. 1063, 17.

snsw worship (n.), Urk. IV, 935, 12; 936, 9; 1874, 5; var. 1878, 16.

snsn vb. intrans. be brotherly, r 'to', Pyr. 645. 801 ( ); fraternize, Urk. IV, 1277, 17; 1286, 13; cf. Caminos, Lit. Frag. p. 36; associate, m-mꜥ 'with', Urk. IV, 1819, 3; ḥnꜥ 'with', 314, F: trans. mingle with, Adm. 2, 5; RB 111, 9; Urk. IV, 2156, 11; be well disposed toward, Les. 68, 14 ( ); agree to action, Westc. 12, 16 ( ): n. brotherly affection, Urk. IV, 1058, 2.

snḏmḏm caus. sharpen, TR 23, 61.

snḳ suck, Pyr. 381. 912; CT I, 17; suckle, Urk. IV, 237, 16; BD 25, 7 (dets.); nurse, JEA 14, pl. 23, 2 (det.).

snkt darkness, Urk. V, 77, 4; obscurity, JEA 4, pl. 8, 7 ( ).

snk-ib haughtiness (?), Urk. VII, 10, 13.

snk tongue, Urk. IV, 238, 2.

snk vb. be greedy, Pt. (L II), 5, 12: n. greed, Merikarēc, 131. See also skn.

snkt longing (?), Caminos, Lit. Frag. p. 14.

snkn caus. injure, damage, JEA 13, 75.

snkkw darkness, var. , CT II, 5.

snktkt gossip (?), Urk. IV, 505, 4.

Sngr n. loc. Babylonia, varr. , , AEO I, 209*.

snty likeness, Urk. IV, 114, 5; 519, 1; var. Westc. 6, 7.

snṯ measure out land, Pyr. 1196; found house, etc., Urk. IV, 300, 2; V, 86, 3 ( ); Amarna, V, 26, 5 ( ); M. u. K. vs. 4, 8 ( ); form limbs, M. u. K. 1, 8; refix eyes of dec'd., Pyr. 644; smn snṯ n 'firmly withstand' (?), Meir, I, 11.

sntt foundation, Leyd. V 88; plan, Urk. IV, 389, 11 ( ).

snty cabin on vessel, Les. 71, 8; var. 71, 15.

sntr caus. cense, Pyr. 127; BD 465, 7 ( ); Th. T. S. IV, 38, B ( ); Sm. 21, 2 ( ); Paheri, 5 ( ); consecrate, Urk. IV, 387, 12.

sntr incense, Urk. IV, 150, 7; 329, 8; varr. 693, 1; 943, 13; M. u. K. 3, 6.

snd a garment, CT I, 109.

snḏ fear: vb. with n + obj., Sin. B 11. 226. 260; Peas. B1, 299; with r + infin. Gr. § 163, 10; snḏ ḥr 'f. on account of', Adm. 12, 11; 'be careful regarding', Urk. IV, 118, 15: n. Sin. B 44. 212; Peas. B1, 298; m snḏ 'through f. of', var. n snḏ (n), Gr. § 181; respect: vb. with n + obj. Pr. 7, 8; Urk. IV, 1091, 4–6; JEA 37, 109: n. Pr. 11, 9. Var. L. to D. I, 3.

snḏt fear (n.), Urk. IV, 18, 17; 64, 4; 965, 15; var. 1845, 16; rnpt snḏt 'a year of terror', 1291, 7.

snḏw timid, frightened man, Sin. B261; Urk. IV, 942, 4; Adm. 11, 13; var. BH I, 7, 7.

snḏm caus. (1) make happy, Urk. IV, 1082, 1; make pleasant, Bersh. II, 13, 10; Adm. 11, 4; Leb. 19 (); BD 135, 10; ease suffering, BD 239, 7; Les. 70, 2; Urk. IV, 47, 2 (); make content, please, Urk. IV, 286, 11; BD 350, 15; give pleasure, n 'to', Pyr. 52. 1836; snḏm ỉb 'make glad', 'please', Urk. IV, 445, 3; 967, 4; BD 439, 11.

(2) sit, be seated, Westc. 7, 12; Urk. IV, 26, 12; 82, 16 (det.); 364, 16; rest, 219, 12 (det.); 1542, 12; st nt snḏm 'dwelling-place', Sh. S. 77-8 (det.).

snḏnḏn caus. incite, JEA 35, 96, n. 7.

sr (zr) sheep, Les. 79, 9; Sin. B198; Urk. IV, 75, 15 (det.); more specifically ram, BD 462, 4; P. Ram. V, 16 (). Cf. Edel, § 128.

sr(ỉ)t ewe, BD 462, 4.

sr nobleman, Siut, pl. 8, 310; JEA 4, pl. 8, 7; Sin. B184 (dets.); magistrate, Peas. B1, 43. 98; Urk. IV, 1103, 16; 1111, 11 (abbr.); 1158, 15.

srwt coll. body of magistrates, Urk. IV, 545, 2; 1112, 9; var. BH I, 30.

sr foretell, Sh. S. 30; Adm. 1, 10 (); Urk. IV, 180, 11; make known, 1892, 14 (); sr ꜥḥꜣ 'challenge to battle', JEA 21, 222.

srwt prophecies, Urk. IV, 500, 12.

sr show (?) s'thing, n 'to', CT I, 191. 229 (var. dets.); s'one, m 'into', Bersh. II, 7.

srw goose, Meir, III, 23; var. BH II, 17.

sr tress; wig; hide of animal, JEA 22, 132.

srt thorn, spine, Eb. 88, 4; 92, 7; Sm. 14, 22.

sryt standard, abbr. , in ṯꜣy sryt 's.-bearer', JEA 27, 13. 17.

sryt cough, var. dets. , , JEA 13, 187.

srwỉ caus. remove, Herdsm. 15; var. Eb. 45, 18.

srwḫ vb. foster, cherish; treat medically: n. treatment, P. Ed. Smith, 99; var.  (sic) Urk. IV, 1282, 11; abbr. Sm. 6, 17.

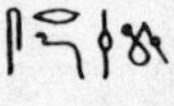

srwḏ caus. strengthen, Pyr. 312; maintain, perpetuate, Pyr. 829 (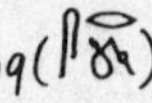); BHI, 25, 5.7 (); Les. 84, 12 (); 84, 14 (); 92, 14; Siut, pl. 16, 10 ( ); Pr. 18, 1; Urk. IV, 879, 9 (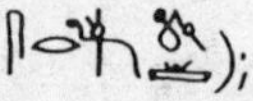); make to flourish, Adm. 14, 1; Sm. 18, 2; restore buildings, GNS 113; make secure, Pyr. 2079. 2080; provide, BD 200, 10; set right wrong, Urk. IV, 247, 15; fulfil contract, Neferḥotep, 35; srwḏ mḫrw 'govern', GAS 102.

srf take one's ease, Peas. B1, 100.

srf rest, relief, Urk. IV, 1541, 16; 1739, 18; 2148, 1 (dets.).

srf warm: adj. Pyr. 870; trans. vb. Eb. 50, 19; 76, 14 (dets. ); n. warmth, CT I, 12; temperature, Eb. 4, 10; 24, 6 (abbr.); inflammation; fever, P. Ed. Smith, 388; mood, Adm. p. 100; srf ib 'deliberate', Urk. IV, 1082, 8 (restd.); 1084, 5; k3 srf 'arrogant', BM 614, 9; ḳb srf 'calm-tempered', ibid, 7; Urk. IV, 970, 15.

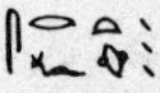

srft fever (?), Eb. 24, 2.

srmi caus. 3 inf. cause to weep, RB 116, 14.

srmt a foodstuff and a beverage, var.  , AEO II, 234*.

srḫ caus. learn about future events, Urk. IV, 1545, 18.

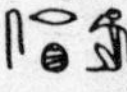

srḫ caus. complain, n 'to', Leb. 125; lay information against, accuse, Peas. B1, 42; JEA 16, 195, 5 (dets. 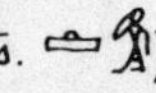); Urk. IV, 484, 9; 511, 8; rdi srḫ 'expose' a crime, P. Berl. 8869, 5 = JEA 28, 17 (restd.).

srḫ guilty person, Urk. IV, 1004, 16.

srḫw accuser, complainer, CT I, 173; Pr. 15, 1 (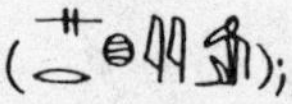); evil spirit, Eb. 1, 5 ( ).

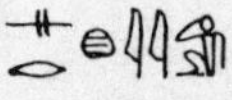

srḫy accusation, reproach, Peas. B2, 8; Pr. 1, 10 (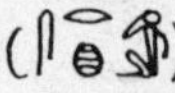); L. to D. V, 2.

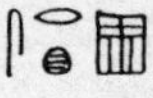

srḫ palace-façade design bearing Horus-name of king, Gr. p. 72; ḥtp srḫ 'assume the royal titles', Urk. IV, 896, 9; rdi ḥr srḫ 'bring to notice', 1381, 17.

srḫ memorial, Les. 75, 21.

srḫ a government department, JEA 13, 75.

srs caus. awaken, L. to D. I, 9 (n., also det.); take command of corps, Urk. IV, 897, 16.

Srḳt n. div. the scorpion-goddess, var., PSBA 39, 33. 140.

srḳ inhale, Pyr. 1158; permit to breathe, of throats, P. Kah. 3, 6 (det.).

srd caus. make to grow, Pr. 12, 9; Eb. 47, 20; 71, 7 (det.); Urk. IV, 146, 14; Amarna, VI, 16, 18; plant trees, Sin. B 297; Urk. IV, 328, 6; 346, 16 (det.); erect monuments, 1485, 13; a temple lake is srd m mnw 'provided with monuments', 1668, 19 (det.).

sh terrorize, Neferti, 19.

shꜣ intrans. vb. be in confusion; n. confusion, GAS 28; trans. vb. confound (?) s'one, JEA 16, 22.

shꜣ hostility, Siut, pl. 15, 23; Pr. 14, 11.

shꜣi caus. 3 inf. bring down, Pyr. 927; Urk. I, 108, 1; Hatnub, 9, 10; make to fall, Urk. IV, 217, 10; Eb. 7, 3 (infin.).

shꜣt discharge (med.), Sm. 20, 16.

shp caus. govern, BD 8, 7.

shri caus. 3 inf. make content, Hymnen, 9, 1; Urk. IV, 545, 17; 969, 10; make peace, 971, 9; VII, 63, 12; Peas. B1, 249. Infin. Pt. (L II), m. 5; Urk. IV, 2156, 2.

shrt ship, ZÄS 79, 89.

sḥ (zḥ) booth, Pyr. 130. 2100; Urk. IV, 1424, 9; hall, Pyr. 560; Urk. I, 33, 17; sḥ-nṯr 'god's b.' of Anubis, Pyr. 1287; Urk. I, 120, 10; Th. T. S. I, 30; as embalmer's workshop, JEA 13, 41; 'shrine', Urk. IV, 296, 6; 421, 10; 427, 15.

sḥ council, JEA 4, pl. 8, 7; Sin. B 184; Pr. 11, 9. 11 (dets.); counsel, Sin. B 133. 182.

sḥy man of good counsel, GNS 34, l. 5.

sḥ3i caus. 3 inf. strip s'one, m of, Herdsm. 24; Adm. 6, 3; reveal secret, Adm. 6, 6; Urk. IV, 484, 11 ( ); 501, 5.

sḥ3p caus. conceal, BD 352, 14.

sḥyt boat (with cabin?), BM 614, 11.

sḥyḥt gallinule (?), Eb. 77, 3; varr. P. Ram. III, B2; JEA 35, pl. 2 = p. 15.

sḥʿy caus. 3 inf. acclaim, Les. 63, 8.

sḥwy collect, assemble, Sin. B 130 ( ); Urk. IV, 6, 12; 649, 8; 1278, 2; RB 65, 8; join up boundaries, Urk. IV, 84, 2 (dets.).

sḥwy collection, Adm. p. 96; summary, P. Kah. 21, 21 ( ); RB 64, 4 ( ); Urk. IV, 690, 15; 780, 4; assemblage of recruits, 1820, 18; sš sḥwy 'scribe of a.', AEO I, 34*.

sḥwʿ caus. shorten, Rec. trav. 39, 103-4.

sḥwr caus. vilify, Urk. IV, 490, 12; var. 122, 13.

sḥb caus. make festive, Urk. IV, 98, 16; 157, 15; adorn, 347, 10; 389, 13; varr. 92, 10; 753, 2; 943, 1.

sḥm caus. put a stop to, RB 111, 11; BD 211, 1; var. Urk. IV, 1683, 13.

sḥm vb. crush, pound: n. trituration, varr. , , P. Ed. Smith 340; Urk. IV, 1871, 13.

sḥn caus. command (vb.), BH II, 24; Urk. IV, 1659, 14; var. 1739, 12.

sḥn decorate (?), Urk. IV, 670, 11.

sḥr caus. fly up, var. dets. , GNS 10. 152.

sḥri caus. 3 inf. remove, exorcise ill, BD 54, 7; 432, 8 ( ); Urk. IV, 240, 5 ( ); Sm. 20, 7; drive away foes, Urk. IV, 209, 17; RB 111, 11; BD 37, 14 ( ); avert face, Pr. 12, 2 (dets.); deliver, m 'from', Sin. B 272 ( ).

sḥsi caus. 3 inf. meet, m s'one, CT I, 108.

sḥḳ3 caus. cause to rule, instal as ruler, Urk. IV, 17, 16; V, 127; 73, 14.

sḥkr caus. make hungry, RB 116, 14.

sḥtp caus. propitiate, please, Sh. S. 142; Pr. 11, 1; Urk. IV, 936, 8 ( ); RB 119, 1; pacify, Urk. I, 126, 3. 11 (det.); 134, 4; 217, 7; satisfy employees, 23, 9; provide for temples, Hat-nub, 17, 9 ( ); Bersh. II, 13, 26; make gracious, n 'to', M. u. K. vs. 6, 3; sḥtp ib (n) 'please', Urk. IV, 911, 8; BD 184, 11; so also sḥtp ḥr n, D. el. B. 114.

sḥtpy censer, Urk. IV, 98, 7.

sḥtm caus. destroy, Peas. B1, 111. 242; varr. Adm. 13, 2; Urk. IV, 969, 1.

sḥtmw destroyer, Peas. B1, 222.

sḥḏ caus. trans. illumine, Les 68, 16 ( ); Urk. IV, 15, 1; 374, 14 ( ); 813, 5; gladden, 614, 5; sḥḏ ib n 'make glad', BD 280-1; so also sḥḏ ḥr, Pyr. 613 ( ); make clear, ḥr 'to', Urk. IV, 241, 7; Sinai, 146; reveal, Th. T. S. I, 5: intrans. shine, Urk. IV, 349, 17; 351, 2; BD 491, 15; make illumination, n 'for', Urk. IV, 357, 7; 518, 3; make explanation, n 'to', Adm. p. 100; become pale, Sm. 4, 4; sḥḏ wr 'great light-maker', ep. of sun-god, Urk. IV, 943, 8 (det. ✶).

sḥḏ inspector (?), e.g. sḥḏ šmsw 'i. of retainers', Les 83, 7; sim. of priests, Urk. I, 9, 4; of prophets, 98, 16; of ships, 92, 9.

sḥḏt chest, P. Kah. 19, 32; 20, 32; BH I, 13; var. M. u. K. vs. 5, 2.

sḥdn caus. vex, Pr. 12, 6.

sḫi vb. 3 inf. be deaf, Peas. B1, 113. 188. See also sḫi below.

sḫi (zḫi) vb. 3 inf. hit, smite, Pyr. 672; Les. 83, 5; beat, Urk. IV, 1076, 3 ( ).

sḫt blow, P. Kah. 1, 4; sḫt bint 'a severe beating', Westc. 12, 17. 25.

sḫ chop off limbs, CT I, 74.

sḫt an offering loaf, Urk. IV, 1952, 16.

sḫt marshland, Westc. 5, 6; field, Sin. B 10; Urk. IV, 124, 16; 182, 3; country beside 'town', BD 185, 10; sḫt 'carry on field sports', Urk. IV, 107, 14; var. I, 88, 3.

Sḫt n. div. the Fen-goddess, Bersh. I, 20; Th. T. S. I, 1; Urk. IV, 917, 17; var. BH I, 34.

sḫty peasant, Peas. B1, 75. 82; fisherman, fowler, GNS 91.

sḫtyw class of cattle, Urk. IV, 953, 17.

sḫꜣ caus. remember, call to mind, Sin. B 222; Peas. B1, 21; Pr. 5, 1; 13, 5; Urk. IV, 27, 10; think about, Sin. B 190; Urk. IV, 27, 14; 364, 17; Eb. 102, 16; mention, n 'to', Sh. S. 128; Peas. B1, 189; Les. 98, 14.

sḫꜣw remembrance, memory, Pr. 16, 12; Siut, pl. 11, 15; 17, 60; mention, Urk. IV, 297, 11; memorial, 1032, 6; Pr. 15, 2. 5. Varr. Sin. B 156; Urk. IV, 430, 8; 481, 2; 297, 11; RB 110, 5.

sḫꜣ caus. spend the night, T. Carn. 13; cf. JEA 3, 106.

sḫꜣḥ caus. hasten (trans.), Westc. 10, 8; var. D. el. B. 107.

sḫꜥy caus. 3 inf. cause to appear, of god or king, Les. 63, 4; 75, 10-11; Urk. IV, 209, 5; 286, 6. 12; 357, 13; display object, 437, 11.

sḫꜥr caus. enrage, Leb. 110.

sḫw breadth, Sh. S. 26-7; Peas. R 46 (dets.).

sḫwy slaughter-house (?), Urk. IV, 506, 16.

sḫwn caus. dispute, Urk. IV, 122, 13; BD 255, 13; det. 255, 4.

sḫws caus. make prosperous, JEA 4, pl. 9, 9; deck out tomb, Urk. VII, 2, 20.

sḫwd caus. enrich, Urk. IV, 80, 15; varr. 163, 14; 413, 8; Siut, pl. 19, 22.

sḫp caus. conduct s'one, n 'to' s'one, Pyr. 2081; r 'to' a place, 373. 2085; bring offerings, BH I, 19; Bersh. I, 12; Urk. IV, 877, 12; display decree, I, 282, 10.

sḫpr caus. bring into being, create, make, Les. 68, 20; Peas. B1, 282. 289; Sh. S. 55; Urk. IV, 15, 14; RB 111, 14; make grow garden, Peas. B1, 264; bring up child, Urk. IV, 812, 8; educate, Pr. 16, 7 (det.); breed horses, Urk. IV, 1282, 16; bring about event, Sin. B 262; effect deed, Peas. B1, 199; foster truth, B1, 167; turn, transform, m 'into', Pr. 10, 8.

sḫm fane, Caminos, Lit. Frag. pl. 13, 1, 4.

sḫm (1) sceptre, Th. T. S. II, 21; BD 287,5; var. Pyr. p. 509, S 42: (2) sistrum, GNS 102.

sḫm mighty one, Power, BM 552; Les. 71,3; BD 364,9; varr. pl. 196,16; 198,3; Hymnen, 6,3.

sḫm adj. powerful, BD 275,14; RB 111,3: vb. have power, Urk. IV, 198,7; BD 308,16; m 'in', Adm. 4,13; BD 89-90; 'over', Hymnen 1,4; BD 62,15; 'by means of', 103,6; 160,1; ḥr 'over', 291,12; give power, n 'to', Urk. IV, 16,13; prevail, m 'over', 710,13; r 'over', 657,16.17; 1291,1; be grim, of face, 1301,17; sḫm ib 'stout-hearted', BD 427,5; sim. RB 56,15; 'violent', Adm. 2,5; 11,13; Urk. IV, 968,16; 'violence', 66,14: n. power, 161,3; grimness, 1409,14. Varr. BD 306,9; Urk. IV, 1289,5; 617,1; RB 111,3.

sḫmt power, Urk. IV, 2161,14.

Sḫmt n. div. Sakhmet, Sin. B 45; varr. P. Kah. 2,20; Urk. IV, 46,11; BD 470,4; Sm. 18,6.

sḫm-ir·f potentate, Urk. IV, 14,13; var. Les. 98,16.

sḫmty the Double Crown, Urk. IV, 565,14; varr. 550,15; 256,4; 200,13; 82,17; 1286,13.

sḫm founder (?), of ship, Peas. B1, 58.

sḫm caus. forget, Urk. IV, 1817,19.

sḫmm caus. make warm, Urk. IV, 1811,3.

sḫmḫ-ib distract the heart of s'one, Urk. I, 45,14; BM 614,2; take recreation, Urk. IV, 109,9; 126,13; 347,1; enjoyment, BM 614,5; Les. 69,15; Urk. IV, 1305,8.

sḫn (zḫn) embrace, Pyr. 575; Urk. IV, 289,15; seek out, Pyr. 1008. 2059; meet, TR 2,5 ( ); occupy a place, Pyr. 310; BD 127,9.

sḫn kidney-fat (?), var. , AEO II, 254*.

sḫn swelling (?), gathering (?), var. , loc. cit.

sḫn bind together (?), JEA 37, 50 (i).

sḫnt (zḫnt) post, Pyr. 1559; 'the (four) p. of the sky', RB 57,10; BD 450,14; var. Urk. IV, 1662,11.

sḫni caus. 3 inf. alight, Pyr. 1216; BD 376,13 ( ); rest, Adm. p. 105; Urk. IV, 1685,8 (det.); 1887,8 (dets.); dwell, 237,10; nn irt sḫn m itt 'without resting from movement', 1280,7.

sḫn resting-place, Les. 88,20.

sḫnw a class of incantations (?), GAS 48.

sḫnš caus. make to stink, BD 96,6.

sḫnti caus. 4 inf. advance, promote, Les. 72,15; Urk. IV, 259,2; 992,14; VII, 66,12; dets. Westc. 7,24; Hatnub, 23,2.

sḫnti caus. 4 inf. take southward, Urk. IV, 1297,13.

sḫr caus. overthrow, Les. 71,13; RB 60,8; Urk. IV, 87,7; throw down, Westc. 8,25; force into place dislocated bone, Sm. 5,17; 9,4; 11,19. Varr. Sin. B 139-40; RB 56,12; 111,3; (infin.) Urk. IV, 140,5.

sḫrw overflowing bowls (?), Adm. 7,11.

see under sḫr 'sweep'.

sḫr (1) plan, counsel, determination: iw mi sḫr nṯr 'it was like the p. of God', Sin. B 43; sḫr·s tp-ʿ 'its former p.', Urk. IV, 312,12; sḫrw imyw-ḥ3t 'the c.'s of the forefathers', Pr. 5,3; sim. Urk. IV, 46,16 (det.); sḫr pn in·n·f ib·k 'this d., it seized your heart', Sin. B 185; sḫr ḫt 'thought', Peas. B1, 209.

(2) governance: di·tw<·i> 3 ḥr sḫr·f 'I am placed under his g.', Sin. B 217; sim. Bersh. II, 21, top, 9-10; Siut, pl. 15, 23-4; Urk. IV, 96,11; sḫr n 'govern', I, 102,9; wḏ n sḫr n 'control the destiny of', Pr. 6,4.

(3) conduct: Do so and so r wnt sḫr·k nn im·f 'until your c. has no wrongdoing in it', Pr. 6,4-5; sḫr·f ḫft wḏ k3·f 'his c. is according to the command of his will', Pr. 7,2; di·i rḫ·tn sḫr n nḥḥ 'I cause you to know the c. (suitable) to eternity', Les. 68,12; m sḫr n wstn 'in arbitrary manner', JEA 38,29.

(4) condition: sḫrw tꜣ 'the c. of the land', Adm. 2,4; di·f wn Kmt m sḫrw·s mi wn Rꜥ im·s 'He causes Egypt to be in the same c. as when Rēꜥ was in it', RB 65,4.

(5) fortune: nn wn rḫ sḫrw·f 'there is none who knows his f.', Pt. (LII) 5,14.

(6) affair: sḫrw ḫpr 'bygone a.'s', ZÄS 60,73.

(7) fashion, nature: ḥꜣp st r sḫrw Dwꜣt 'they are more mysterious than the f. of the Netherworld', Urk. IV, 99,16; ḥr ḳd·sn mi sḫrw mt 'they sleep like the f. of death', RB 114,2; m-ḫt ꜥrḳ·f sḫr rmṯ 'when he had perceived the n. of men', Pr. 2,3-4; r wnn mi sḫr šw 'in order to be like something dry', Sm. 21,18; ky m sḫr 'the other likewise', 21,15.

(8) custom: 'you shall eat your bread at will mi sḫr n wn·k tp tꜣ 'according to your c. when you were on earth', Urk. IV, 520,1; sim. 148,16.

N.B. This word is often written as a plural when the sense in English demands the singular.

sḫrt roll of papyrus, Urk. IV, 2143,9.

sḫry captain of ship, Peas. B1,191; pl. sḫryw 'those who govern', Urk. IV, 146,9; var. : Les. 82,5.

sḫs (zḫz) run, Pyr. 1675; Siut, pl. 11,21; 19,40 (det.); Urk. IV, 1279,16 (); hurry, Urk. IV, 123,3; flee, Adm. 8,13.14; Urk. IV, 508,2; sḫs m-sꜣ 'pursue', 'persecute', GNS 87.

sḫsw runners, Adm. 5,4.

sḫsf caus. create opposition, r 'against', Gr. p. 269 = BD ch. 30B.

sḫsḫ run, Urk. IV, 894,8; m sḫsḫ kꜣ 'at high speed', 1282,18.

sḫt weave, Pyr. 130 (also); BH I, 29; Adm. 7,11-12 (); mould bricks, Urk. IV, 837,8; 1153,10.

sḫt trap, snare (vb.), RB 117,4; Peas. B1,207; Urk. IV, 126,8; close net, Sm. 20,10 (); 'closing the net', BH II, 7; acquire (?) wealth, Pr. 6,7.9.

sḫt stone for patching (?), Urk. IV, 367, 1; 1175, 2.

sḫt ambushing (?): tsm·n·i mšʿ m sḫt 'I trained (?) the army in a.', Les. 82, 7.

sḫty run, Urk. IV, 2000, 12.

sḫd be upside down, TR 44, 1 (det.); Urk. IV, 1078, 16; BD 204, 14; 327, 11; be disordered, of dress, Westc. 10, 2; m sḫd 'head downwards', Urk. IV, 9, 5; 1297, 5; BD 213, 1.

sḫdḫd intrans. be upside down, CT I, 1; TR 44, 2 (det.); hang down, of breasts, Pyr. 2171; m sḫdḫd 'head downwards', TR 23, 11; Sm. 11, 11: trans. hang up, suspend, Pyr. 1516.

sẖi vb. 3 inf. be deaf, Peas. B2, 110; sẖi ḥr 'be neglectful', Urk. IV, 118, 16 ( ); 409, 14; 1079, 5.

sẖ3k strain, squeeze out, GAS 98; det. Eb. 19, 22; abbr. 2, 11a.

sẖʿt hare, BH II, 4. 13; Urk. IV, 1304, 6.

sẖb swallow, Eb. 53, 11. See also sẖp.

sẖbw draught of medicine, P. Ed. Smith, 184.

sẖp swallow, Eb. 24, 6; 27, 10-11.

sẖm be hasty, impetuous, Peas. B1, 211; Siut, pl. 11, 11; Les. 83, 24 (det.).

sẖm comb flax, Paheri, 3.

sẖn demolish, Merikarēʿ, 79. 122.

sẖr sweep, brush over; overlay, m 'with', GNS 117; stroke (vb.) Urk. IV, 232, 10; varr. ibid.; RB 112, 15; (sic) Sh. S. 64.

sẖr milk (vb.), BD 439, 4; Urk. IV, 188, 11; 743, 15 (det.).

sẖrt milking, Goyon, 53.

sẖrw a linen fabric, Urk. IV, 742, 15. Cf. sšrw 'linen' below.

sẖkr caus. decorate, adorn, Les. 68, 9; 71, 11; Hymnen, 2, 5 (dets.); burnish, Sin. B128. Varr. Les. 71, 8; Urk. IV, 1211, 14.

ss vb. burn, Urk. IV, 1437, 10: n. ashes, Sh. S. 72 ( ).

ss hurry, TR 22, 17; varr. 22, 20; op. cit. p. 66, l. 1.

 *ss3i* caus. 3 inf. (1) satisfy, Urk. I, 77, 12; Sh. S. 53; Peas. B1, 94: (2) make wise, Urk. IV, 160, 6.

 *ss3w* provisions, sustenance, Caminos, Lit. Frag. pl. 5, 2; var.  Urk. I, 131, 5.

 *ss3w* satisfaction, RB 112, 8.

 *sswt* a metallic inlay (?), Urk. IV, 692, 11.

 *sswn* caus. destroy, Urk. IV, 613, 15; RB 64, 15; Eb. 1, 5 (dets. ): n. destruction, Pr. 11, 8. Var.  Urk. IV, 8, 6.

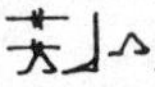 *ssbi* caus. 3 inf. despatch army, Urk. IV, 140, 3.

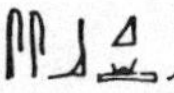 *ssbḳ* caus. honour s'one, Les. 73, 1; RB 76, 5.

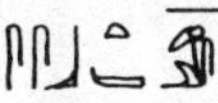 *ssbt* (< *ssbṯ*) make to laugh, Leb. 110.

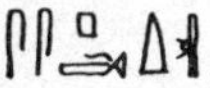 *sspd* caus. make ready, Westc. 3, 7; 7, 9; 11, 20; Urk. IV, 656, 2 (); 835, 17; supply, *m* 'with', 692, 15; 719, 7; prepare food, Adm. 11, 2 (); enliven the downcast, Peas. B1, 286; penetrate (?), *m-m* 'into' secrets, Urk. IV, 1820, 13.

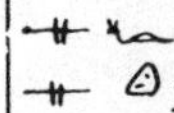 *ssf* caus. soothe, Pr. 1, 10.

 *ssfw* garments (?), Urk. IV, 1867, 9.

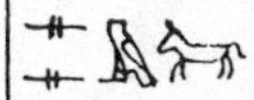 *ssm* horse, Urk. IV, 10, 1. See the next below.

 *ssmt* generically horse, Urk. IV, 663, 8. 9; 688, 5 (det. ); 1282, 8; specifically mare, 894, 5 (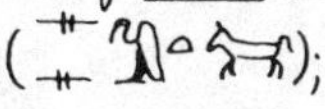); *imy-r ssmt* 'Master of the Horse', JEA 39, 43.

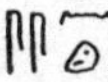 *ssn* caus. breathe, Pr. 5, 2; RB 113, 4; Urk. IV, 76, 8 (det. 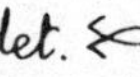); smell, P. Kah. 5, 7. 8; Urk. IV, 918, 11; 1497, 1 ().

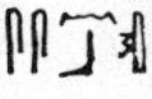 *ssnb* caus. preserve, Th. T. S. II, 11; M. u. K. vs. 5, 9; 6, 2; Urk. IV, 1426, 6; heal, Eb. 33, 13; 71, 11.

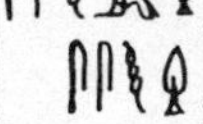 *ssndm* a costly wood, Westc. 7, 13; Adm. 3, 5; varr. Les. 71, 5; 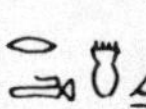 Urk. IV, 720, 3.

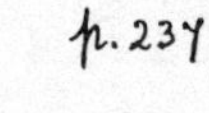 *ssrd* caus. plant garden, Urk. IV, 749, 5. Perhaps a miswriting of *srd*, p. 237 above.

ssḥ destroy enemies, Les. 82,12 (det.); Urk. IV, 55,3; shatter heads, RB 56,11 (det.).

ssḫm caus. strengthen, Les. 84,3.

sst calf (?) of leg, BD 113,2; M.u.K. 5,1; vs. 5,5.

infin. of ssn 'breathe', 'smell', e.g. Urk. IV, 1497,1; 1902,4; 1904,16.

sš (?) (sn ?) open, BD 462,13; varr. 131,8; 19,13. Cf. GNS 73.

sš (?) (sn ?) pass, ḥr 'by', RB 121,3; cf. GNS 72; spread, spread out, strew, GNS 72.161; det. Hatnub, 12,16; det. (of 'spreading' rays), Urk. IV, 391,4; post sentries, 656,9; di sš (?) 'appear', 'manifest o'self', 'draw' weapon, var. , GNS 73.

sš cut linen, JEA 37, 51 (o).

sš threshold, Westc. 7,15; var. BD 428,13.

sš marsh, Westc. 5,5; Bersh. I, 20 (det.); Urk. IV, 463,5.

sšy nest, Urk. IV, 897,12; 898,9 (det.); varr. 157,3; 564,2; , , CT I, 96; 97.

sš (zš) vb. write, Urk. I, 232,14 ( ); RB 112,16; Urk. IV, 252,3 ( ); inscribe, I, 16,4; 67,14; paint, 39,3; Louvre C 15,8; draw, Sin. L2; enrol troops, Urk. IV, 1005,3; 1006,3: n. writing, Sin. B 311; Pr. 2,4; depiction, Urk. I, 7,11; record, 4,15; m sš 'put into w.', IV, 1111,15; 1112,4; smnt m sš 'record in w.', 336,6; imy-r sšw n ḥft-ḥr 'overseer of public w.'s', Goyon, 52; papyrus-roll, Westc. 8,4; letter, JEA 13,75 ( ); P. Kah. 35, 31.38; document, Urk. IV, 1109,10; 1110,5; P. Berl. 9010,5.

sš scribe, Sh. S. 188; Westc. 6,17; Urk. IV, 1109,15; 'painter', 'draughtsman', see ḳdwt; sš·k 'your s.' = 'you' in letters, JEA 31,7, n. 14. Var. (sic) Urk. IV, 1040,10.

, , see under šsꜣ 'be wise'.

, , see under šsꜣt 'nightfall'.

Šsꜣt n. div. Seshat, Urk. IV, 19,14; 1074,7; var. Pyr. 616.

sš3 make progress(?), Peas. B2, 99.

sš3 beseech, n 'from', Urk. IV, 241, 5; 943, 16 ( ); pray, n 'to', 1892, 7 (det.); 2027, 17 ( ).

sš3 prayer, Sh. S. 129.

sšw disk of metal, Urk. IV, 701, 12; varr. 637, 12; 666, 8.

sšw caus. dry s'thing, Eb. 61, 14; 70, 9; 106, 1.

sšw caus. lose by theft, Urk. IV, 2145, 13.

sšw3 caus. impoverish, Adm. 9, 6; deprive, m 'of', 7, 2.

sšp vb. intrans. be white, Pyr. 1566; be bright, Urk. IV, 1847, 16 (det. ⊙): trans. make bright, CT I, 18; lighten darkness, with n, II, 5: n. light, in sšp n 'lighten', loc. cit. See also šsp.

sšm lead, guide, Peas. B1, 254; Urk. IV, 119, 1 ( ); 780, 9 ( ); VII, 6, 7 (det.); RB 59, 2; rule, govern, Peas. B1, 105; Urk. IV, 86, 15; V, 166, 3; show the way, n 'to', I, 127, 9; IV, 247, 6; V, 75, 2; with r + infin. 's. how to' do s'thing, IV, 421, 1; conduct war, work, etc., Les. 82, 8-9; Urk. IV, 389, 1; 449, 15; 536, 16 ( ); instruct people, 102, 6.

sšm guidance, Siut, pl. 17, 57 ( ); RB 56, 10 ( ); Urk. IV, 445, 7 ( ); 974, 4 ( ); procedure, RB 122, 15; Adm. 6, 11; conduct, Pr. 7, 7; 10, 1; Siut pl. 5, 247 ( ); business, Les. 68, 5 ( ); BM 614, 10; Urk. IV, 1113, 14; expenditure, P. Kah. 15, 43; Gr. p. 201 = P. Boul. 18, 31, 5; state of affairs, Sin. R 18; state, condition, Sin. B 173; nature, JEA 42, 15; mi sšm 'after the manner of' Sin. B 225; iry-sšm 'functionary', see p. 25 above.

sšmt leading of procession, D. el B. 63; guidance, Urk. IV, 173, 16 ( ); governance, 250, 8; control, 883, 16 (det.); working out, proof (math.), JEA 12, 126; 'specification' of endowment, Urk. IV, 1796, 17.

sšmw ruler, leader, Peas. B1, 54. 65. 114. 191; varr. Urk. VII, 55, 3; IV, 429, 4; 613, 7; Pr. 8, 14.

sšmt guiding serpent of god, Urk. IV, 267, 9.

sšmw statue, portrait, image, counterpart, JEA 42, 15; varr. 39, pl. 2, 23; Urk. IV, 97, 13; , of goddess, 386, 12.

sšmm caus. warm s'one, Peas. B1, 245; M.u.K. vs. 2, 5 (fem. infin.); heat s'thing, Eb. 54, 13.20.

sšn (zšn) lotus, varr. , , Gr. p. 480, M9; det. Leb. 135.

sšn lotus-shaped cup, Urk. IV, 629, 4.

sšn caus. weave, Caminos, Lit. Frag. p. 13.

sšnw ropes, cordage, Urk. V, 161, 7.

sšrw linen, varr. , ; 'royal linen', 'byssus', Bull. 30, 171.

sšrw linen bags, Bull. 30, 175.

sšrw corn, varr. , , , Bull. 30, 179.

sšrw things; actions; course, manner of action; m sšrw nb 'in every respect'; sšrw m3ˁ 'a successful method'; mi sšrw 'well', 'in good order'; varr. , , , , Bull. 30, 177 ff.

sšr utter, express, Bull. 30, 179. Older šsr, q.v.

sšr (< swšr) caus. dry, dry up, Eb. 65, 15; 82, 21; det. Sm. 16, 10.

var. of šsr 'arrow'.

var. of s3šrt 'cake'.

sšrr caus. 2 gem. lessen, Peas. B1, 251.

sšs3 make wise, Sin. B 216.

sšsp make brightness, BD 176, 10; lighten darkness, 177, 9.

sššr caus. discuss (?), Urk. IV, 1380, 17.

sššt sistrum, GNS 102; JEA 6, 70; varr. Urk. IV, 917, 10; pl. 98, 6.

sšt3 caus. vb. make secret, mysterious, Pyr. 896; Urk. IV, 99, 12; 975, 8; BD 75, 11 ( ); make inaccessible, Pyr. 279; RB 77, 15: adj. secret, BD 29, 14 ( ); 497, 3; 498, 2: n. secret, Urk. IV, 159, 6; 449, 6; Adm. 4, 4; confidential matter, Urk. I, 99, 5; 101, 4; religious mystery, Les. 68, 6; BM 159, 4; Urk. IV, 208, 13; problem, Urk. I, 84, 5; m sšt3 'in secret', 100, 13; 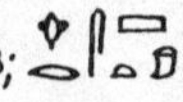 'master of the secrets, Les. 68, 9; var. 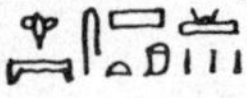 72, 5; cryptic wtgs. , , Gr. p. 459, E 15.16; with descriptive genitive e.g. Urk. I, 82, 10; Meir, IV, 4; Les. 72, 5; cf. Gauthier, Personnel, 27.

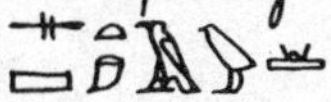 sšt3w secretly, Urk. IV, 97, 14.

 sšd thunderbolt, Urk. IV, 615, 13.

 sšd flash (vb.), RB 57, 2; Urk. IV, 1685, 1; 1723, 14.

 sšd fillet, bandage, P. Ed. Smith, 224.

 sšd put a fillet on s'one, Urk. IV, 1439, 6.

 sšd window, AEO II, 212*.

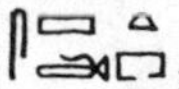 sšdt shrine of falcon, D. el. B. 116; CT I, 258; var. 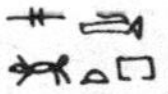 BD 156, 9.

 sšdw drops of moisture, Urk. V, 151, 14.

 sḳ3i caus. 3 inf. make high a building, Urk. IV, 834, 7; 1557, 6 (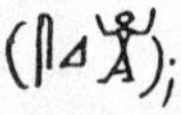); set upright a person, BD 172, 14; 387, 10; exalt a god, Les. 65, 16; king, Urk. IV, 486, 2; extol beauty, 297, 12 (dets. ); victories, 659, 13; prolong lifetime, JEA 39, pl. 2, 17; kingship, ibid. 26.

 sḳ3 basis for shrine, Urk. IV, 633, 1; 640, 12.

 sḳ3ḥ caus. vb. plaster, GAS 76.

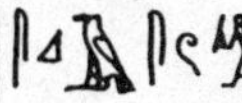 sḳ3s caus. bind, fetter, Wb. IV, 304, 3; check, Caminos, Lit. Frag. pl. 2, 2, 12; string up fowling-tackle, pl. 3, 3, 7.

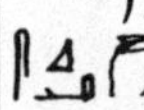 sḳꜥ caus. make to vomit, Eb. 89, 17.

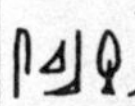 sḳb kind of wood, Westc. 5, 9.

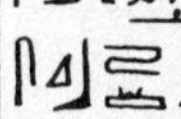 sḳb (< sḳ3b) caus. double supplies, Urk. IV, 1819, 19.

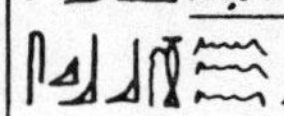 sḳbb caus. make cool, P. Kah. 5, 11; Eb. 31, 7; TR 37, 13; calm disturbed land, Urk. IV, 1312, 16; refresh oneself, 73, 8; 1165, 16; so also sḳbb ib, 918, 8: n. refreshment, 149, 16.

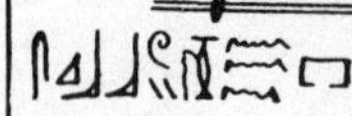 sḳbbwy bathroom, varr. , 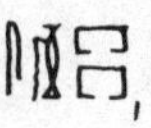, GNS 110.

sḳbḥ caus. trans. refresh: intrans. give ease, n 'to'; live in easy circumstances, JEA 16, 196 (10).

sḳnd caus. enrage, Siut, pl. 19, 21.

sḳr strike head, Pyr. 217; Urk. IV 615, 6; ball, Pyr. 249; D. el B. 100; harp, Ti, 60; drum, Festival Hall, 11; strike down foes, Sin. R 14; Urk. IV, 7, 3; RB 56, 12; clap hands, Pyr. 1974; grasp hand, 802; step out, of feet in dance, 791. 1366; work metal, D. el Geb. I, 14; Hatnub 19, 3; set up stairway, Pyr. 1090. 1108; TR 11, 5; ladder, Pyr. 1431; knead dough, BH II, 7; get rid of s'thing bad, Eb. 45, 10. 14; offer, present, Pyr. 978; D. el. B. 29.

sḳr wound, injury, CT I, 142; L. to D. V, 1; BD 231, 13 (det.); cf. P. Ed. Smith, 204.

sḳr-ʿnḫ captive, Urk. IV, 895, 5; varr. (pl.), Sin. R 15; Urk. IV, 4, 4; 36, 7; 780, 11; 809, 5.

sḳsn caus. make miserable, Urk. IV, 1082, 1.

sḳdy caus. 3 inf. intrans. sail, voyage, of boat, Les. 71, 14; Urk. IV, 814, 13; RB 58, 2; sail, travel, of persons, Peas. B1, 55; B2, 101; Urk. IV, 116, 17; 324, 11; RB 113, 14: trans. row, Pyr. 368 (det.); convey by boat, TR 2, 60; 22, 84; Urk. IV, 2089, 10; sail on waters, 113, 17.

sḳdwt sailing, Urk. IV, 322, 6; varr. D. el. B. 114; Urk. IV, 697, 12.

sḳd sailor, Sh. S. 27; traveller, Hatnub, 17, 14; 25, 17.

sḳd caus. cause to build, Urk. V, 170, 9.

sḳdw builders, Leb. 62. Used of those who commissioned the work, not of the craftsmen (iḳdw).

sḳd slope of pyramid, JEA 15, 176, n. 1.

sḳdwt (?) coll. company of troops, Urk. IV, 1659, 14.

var. of encl. part isk.

sk wipe, Pyr. 372. 626. 966 (det.); wipe out, Sm. 5, 11. 18; 8, 11. 16; wipe away, 6, 10;

sk ḥt 'w.o. the belly' = pour out o's heart, Pr. 9,4 ( ).

ski vb. 3 inf. intrans. perish, Pr. 15,10; Urk. IV, 147,3; 415,8; V, 149,14; ỉḫm-sk 'indestructible star', see p. 29; so also Urk. IV, 366,11: trans. destroy, Sin. B 56; Peas. B 1,118; Urk. IV, 87,11 (det.); Adm. 12,2 ( ): n. accusation, Urk. IV, 40,6; 61,15; 1107,4.

skw troops, companies, Peas. B 1,303; RB 56,14 (det.); Urk. IV, 653,9; ts skw 'marshal the ranks', GAS 20; sim. skw, JEA 21,222; 'controller of gangs', Les. 86,2. Varr. Hatnub, 25,6; Urk. IV, 9,12; 758,9; Sin. B 55.

skw battle, var. , GAS 20.

sk fell (?) trees, Adm. 4,14.

ski vb. 3 inf. pass time, Urk. IV, 62,5; Neferhotep, 25.

skꜣ cultivate, Leb. 69; Urk. IV, 116,13 ( ); 747,9; more precisely plough, 132,9.

skꜣ plough-ox, Adm. 9,4.

skꜣt ploughland, Urk. IV, 499,1.

skꜣ crops, Leyd. V 6,14.

skꜣp caus. cover up, Eb. 43,18.

skp strain medicament, Eb. 96,9.

skm caus. make complete, ZÄS 57,9;* Urk. IV, 1184,11; make up to, with m, Rhind, 22.

skm be, become grey-haired, Eb. 65,8.11.19; 66,2; dets. 65,4; skm ns 'hoary-tongued' = wise, JEA 4, 34, n. 6.

skn be greedy, Peas. B 1,178-9; Pr. 1,9; lust, ḥr 'after', Rev. d'Eg. 7, 80.

skn embroil (?) in quarrels, Pr. 7,4; cf. Žába, 124.

Skr (Zkr) n. div. Sokar, Urk. I, 121,7; BD 14,2; varr. Urk. IV, 432,3; P. Kah. 27,4.

skr adorn (?), Th. T. S. II, 10 = JEA 6, 299.

sksi caus. 3 inf. make to bow down, JEA 32, pl. 6, 12.

sksk destroy, RB 57, 15; Peas. B1, 317 (det.); Urk. IV, 5, 6; 685, 5; var. 729, 13; 812, 2.

sktt (1) var. of msktt 'night-bark' of sun: (2) kind of boat, ZÄS 68, 14.

sktw kind of boat, Urk. IV, 707, 12.

sq command (?) ship, Leb. 26.

 var. of swgm 'pulverize'.

 caus. cause to see, Peas. B1, 213; glimpse s'one, Urk. IV, 117, 7.

sgnn caus. soften, Sm. 2, 8; 8, 5; weaken, Sin. B54; anoint, Eb. 81, 9 (dets).

sgnn tallow, JEA 22, 178.

sgr caus. silence (vb. and n.), Les. 80, 19 (det.); Siut, pl. 4, 229; Sin. R8; Urk. IV, 967, 12. 14 ().

sgrḥ caus. make peaceful, pacify, P. Kah. 3, 4; Urk. IV, 21, 15 (det. only); 1312, 15; satisfy, Siut, pl. 19, 53 (det.); Pr. 18, 5.

sgrg caus. institute offerings, CT I, 126.

sgrgw yards (?) of ship, Peas. B1, 58; cf. JEA 9, 9, n. 6.

st dep. pron. 3 f. it, them, var. , cf. Gr. p. 592.

st pron. comp. they, Gr. § 124.

sti͗ vb. 3 inf. shoot arrow, P. Kah. 1, 4; Siut, pl. 13, 33; person, etc., Sin. B138; Peas. B1, 207; Th. T. S. I, 9; sti͗ r 's. at', RB 64, 7 (dets.); Urk. IV, 1281, 4; 1541, 10; throw, Peas. B1, 111; thrust, r 'into', P. Kah. 7, 23; spear fish, Peas. B1, 228; Urk. IV, 463, 7; kindle light, Siut, pl. 8, 305 ff.; Urk. IV, 148, 13 (det.); set fire, m 'to', I, 103, 16; pour water, IV, 27, 1; 149, 17 (); 1846, 11 (); BM 1164, 8 (); inspect (?) work, Urk. IV, 397, 1; glitter, of sky, 1862, 1.

sty stare (vb.), P. Kah. 4, 2; stare at, Urk. IV, 1409, 8 (); Pr. 6, 11 (det.).

stwt rays, Les. 68, 16; varr. Urk. IV, 615, 1; 421, 4; 426, 2.

stw arrow, dart, Caminos, Lit. Frag. p. 11.

stw target, Urk. IV, 1280, 13; 1281, 4.

stt shooting pains, var. , JEA 20, 184.

stỉ impregnate female, BH II, 4 (); with ḥr + obj. Urk. IV, 238, 8; beget, Pr. 7, 11 ().

styt seed, posterity, Adm. 12, 4.

stt ground, GAS 90.

var. of sṯ3 'drag', etc.

sty-r mid-day meal, see s.v. sty 'odour'.

Sty (Zty) in T3-sty 'Nubia', var. det. , Gr. p. 512 (Aa 32).

Styw Nubians, Urk. IV, 83, 17; RB 60, 9; Iwntyw Styw 'Nubian nomads', Urk. IV, 5, 6; 84, 6 (); sing. (rare), 7, 3; 9, 5; dual, 139, 4 (Iwnty nw Sty).

sty Nubian ochre (?), Ch. B. Text, 18, n. 5; var. Gr. p. 452, D 19.

Sṯyw Asiatics, Sin. R 1; B 17. 25. 245 (); Adm. 14, 11.

Stt n. div. Satis, see under .

st3 caus. vb. heat, P. Kah. 7, 55; kindle taper, Urk. IV, 117, 3 (); 499, 9.

st3t (1) censer: (2) lamp, JEA 17, 61, n. 9.

: for words written with this sign see under sṯ3.

var. of particle ỉst.

stw3 caus. hold up, Les. 74, 15-16.

stwr caus. keep clean, RB 77, 15.

var. of swtwt 'walk about'.

stwt caus. (1) resemble, with n, Urk. IV, 1509, 5 (det. only); with r, 1649, 5; 1668, 9: (2) smooth over, make even, Peas. B 1, 249; JEA 9, 17, n. 2; stwt mdwt 'smoothing of words' = extenuation (?), Urk. IV, 973, 12: (3) praise craftsmanship, 1280, 10.

stbn (< sṯbn) caus. hasten, CT I, 73.

stp cut up animal, D. el B. 107; cut off limbs, ibid.; Pyr. 653. 1286; pick out, choose, Sin. B 79; Urk. IV, 361, 17; 888, 7.

stpw the choicest, pick, Sin. B 80; Sh. S. 94; varr. Sin. B 86; BH I, 8, 12.

stpt coll. choice things of food, Leb. 144; varr. RB 117, 7; Les. 73, 15; Urk. IV, 753, 8; 1418, 6; D. el B. 107.

stpt choice (n.), Peas. B1, 210.

stp vb. be dismembered, ruined: n. ruin, JEA 32, 54 (ṯ).

stp strip of cloth, rag, P. Ed. Smith, 500; varr. P. Ram. III, A 23; M. u. K. 8, 3.

stp-s3 protect, with ḥr, Pyr. 4; with ḥ3, Urk. IV, 222, 4; 225, 13; 260, 14; do escort duty, Pyr. 948; Urk. I, 11, 9; 224, 11; sim. stp-s3, 100, 9.

stp-s3 palace, Sin. R 17; BH I, 25, 100; Urk. IV, 194, 1; varr. Les. 74, 17; RB 61, 1.

stp choke (?), P. Ed. Smith, 314.

stf liquid (?), COA III, 175.

stfw in stfw 'sheet copper', contrasted with ingots, Urk. IV, 708, 2.

stny caus. crown king, Urk. IV, 1686, 16. Perhaps identical with sṯny, p. 256.

stnm caus. lead astray, Peas. B1, 114; confuse, JEA 22, 137: n. confusion, ibid. Var. BD 311, 5-6.

sthi caus. 3 inf. ramble about, Caminos, Lit. Frag. p. 49.

stḥn (< sṯḥn) caus. make dazzling, radiant, BM 552; Urk. IV, 1546, 14 (det.); 1795, 16; varr. 1824, 15; 1668, 19; 2161, 13.

Stẖ n. div. Seth, varr., old, Gr. p. 460, E 20; 449, C 7.

stkn caus. cause to approach, Neferti, 30; BD 20, 13; 190, 6; induct, m 'into', BD 20, 12; r 'into', Urk. IV, 966, 9; cut short time or activities, Caminos, Lit. Frag. pp. 12-13; bring on doom, Urk. IV, 5, 17; execute (?) judgements, 1381, 13.

var. of particle ist.

var. of sti 'impregnate.'

sti vb. 3 inf. strew, scatter, Pyr. 567; Sheikh Said, 16; var. Urk. IV, 615, 14.

stw sower, Bersh. II, 8.

stt jar for beer, Paheri, 7; Urk. IV, 828, 5.

Stt n. loc. (1) Asia: (2) island of Sehēl, var. , Gr. p. 506, S22.

Sttyw Asiatics, Urk. IV, 343, 1; varr. 621, 6; 661, 6.

var. of s3t 'pour out'.

st(y) odour, smell, Bersh. II, 17; Leb. 87. 135 (); Urk. IV, 219, 13; 339, 16 (det.);
 'mid-day meal', Gr. p. 206, n. 5.

st3 measure of capacity, Gr. § 266, 1.

st3 weave, Pyr. 1202; spin yarn, BH I, 29 (); II, 4 ().

st3 vb. (1) of things, drag, CT I, 261; Urk. IV, 753, 16; 1032, 12; ch n st3 'a portable brazier', 639, 13; pull, Pyr. 684. 1070; st3 skdwt 'tow', Leb. 70; pull out, Pyr. 443. 572; reduce swelling, Sm. 5, 12; 6, 20; draw off pus, Eb. 91, 12.

(2) of persons, drag, drag away, Leb. 12; Sin. B 230; Urk. IV, 1107, 14; 1108, 8; admit, usher in, Sin. B 264; Westc. 8, 10; Urk. IV, 140, 16; 1086, 12; bring, Peas. B1, 302.

(3) intrans. flow, Peas. B1, 239; Urk. IV, 118, 12.

Varr. RB 123, 4; 63, 7; 58, 2; Urk. IV, 349, 13; 140, 16; 753, 16; 777, 13; 2006, 5; Peas. B1, 239; Eb. 91, 12; O.K. Pyr. 1070; 245; 685; whence, by misunderstanding, M.K. Sin. B 230; Leb. 70.

st3t (1) aroura of land, varr. , Gr. § 266, 3; P. Wilbour, Index, p. 98; det. RB 117, 1: (2) sheet of metal, Urk. IV, 53, 16; 426, 9.

st3t roller (?) for moving ship, ZÄS 68, 11.

st3w dragging (n.), Urk. IV, 1424, 16.

st3w injury, Mill. 2, 5; Urk. V, 60, 17; varr. 66, 16; 67, 17;

60, 3; 60, 5; 32, 7. Cf. JEA 6, 301, n. 10.

sṯ3m caus. bind up injury, Eb. 67, 22; 70, 2; 108, 2.

Stỉt n. div. Satis, Pyr. 1116; varr. BM 852; Urk. IV, 88, 14; 396, 7.

stp vb. intrans. leap up, Pyr. 947; Urk. V, 147, 4 (dets.): trans. overleap, Pyr. 1321.

stp discharge (vb.), of eyes, P. Kah. 7, 36.

stny caus. 3 inf. distinguish, honour, BM 159, 4; Urk. VII, 2, 11: without obj. make distinctions, Hatnub, 12, 8; 20, 9; nbw n stn 'refined (?) gold', Louvre C 15, 8. Varr. Urk. IV, 970, 2; 1817, 2; JEA 39, pl. 2, 5.

sṯsỉ caus. 3 inf. raise, lift up, RB 114, 3; BD 244, 7 (dets.); 441, 1 (det. only); remove lassitude, RB 111, 15; display beauty, 114, 8.

sṯs staff, Sebekkhu, 5; Hamm. 114, 13 (det.); pl. props for net, Caminos, Lit. Frag. p. 15 (dets.); sṯsw Šw 'the p. of Shu' supporting sky, BD 221, 11-12; Urk. V, 6, 16; 28, 11; fig. clouds, in sṯsw pr m ỉwḫw 'the c. which come forth at dusk', BD 142, 13.

sṯsw raising up, BD 387, 10; var. TR 1, 48.

sṯsw praises, Urk. V, 4, 5; BD 444, 5; var. 18, 4.

stsy be stretched out, prostrate, Eb. 36, 7; Sm. 12, 5. 11 (); 17, 19 (); m stsy 'prostrate', Urk. IV, 659, 3 (); 1303, 11.

sṯt kindle light, TR 20, 68; det. 20, 67.

sd tail, Sh. S. 163; Urk. IV, 894, 11; V, 151, 5. For see ḥb-sd.

sd clothe, Sin. B 292; varr. M. u. K. 6, 7; Caminos, Lit. Frag. pl. 16, 1. 2; CT I, 125.

var. of sd 'break'.

sd3 egret (?), Gr. p. 470, G 33.

sd3 vb. intrans. tremble, TR 19, 2; Urk. IV, 614, 12; 616, 8 (); RB 63, 12 (dets.): trans. make tremble, Urk. IV, 242, 3; shake off (?) symptom, P. Kah. 5, 35.

sd3w trembling, BD 289, 9; var. Sin. B 3.

sdwḥ embalm, var. GAS 33.

 sdb (1) fringe of cloth, JEA 22, 40: (2) a garment, BD 438, 1.

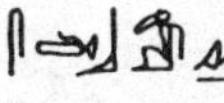 sdb chew, D. el B. (XI), III, 9, Ab; Eb. 34, 9.

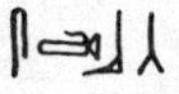 sdb see below s.v. sḏb.

 sdm paint the eyes, Pyr. 54. 55; RB 122, 13 (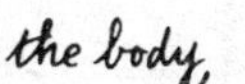); Eb. 59, 10; the body, 52, 1.

 sdm eyepaint, Les. 96, 10; varr.  Eb. 61, 20; 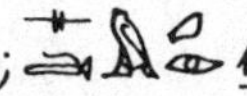 Urk. IV, 1521, 13.

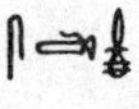 sdmi caus. attach, r 'to', Pyr. 55. 609; of family 'attachment', with n, Les. 79, 13 (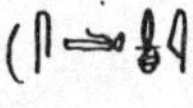).

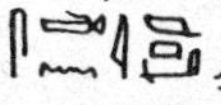 sdni caus. punish, Urk. IV, 269, 10.

 sdḥ caus. bring low the arm of the evil-doer, Urk. IV, 968, 17; Neferhotep, 28.

 sdḥ ease (?) misery, Leb. 18.

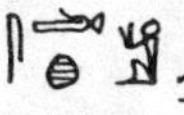 sdẖ caus. conceal, m-c 'from', JEA 16, 149; det.  RB 78, 2.

 sdẖ well (?), Urk. IV, 1578, 11.

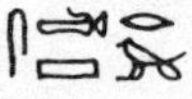 sdšr caus. redden, Hymnen, 12, 3.5; cf. JEA 35, 72.

 sdšrw reddening, Hymnen, 12, 3.

 sdgi caus. 3inf. conceal, r 'from', RB 62, 8; var. 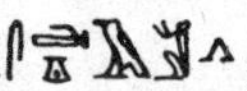 Urk. IV, 385, 13.

 sdgw hidden things, Urk. IV, 501, 5.

 sdg hidden place, Urk. IV, 1071, 9.

 sdtyw weaklings (?), Les. 77, 14.

 sḏ vb. break, Pyr. 249; TR 10, 7 (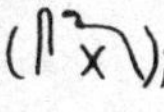); Leb. 79 (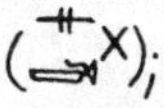); RB 120, 12 (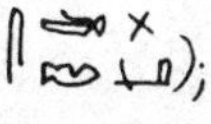); Urk. IV, 1693, 19 (); break into, invade, 85, 11 (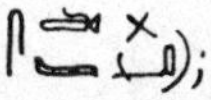); breach wall, 895, 1; break open way, RB 65, 6; break up hailstorm, Pyr. 500; fight, JEA 28, 18 (f); rupture cist, etc., P. Ed. Smith, 157; inflict wound, Sm. 12, 16; 15, 7.8; sḏ r-bnr 'break out', Paheri, 3;  'broken-spirited', 'craven', Les. 84, 8. n. fracture, rupture, P. Ed. Smith, 157.

 sḏt fire, flame, Les. 84, 11; RB 120, 12; Urk. IV, 158, 4; var.  Pyr. 247;   'burnt-offering, Sh. S. 56; 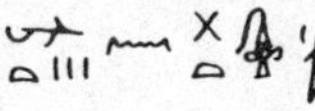 'firewood', Urk. IV, 640, 13.

 sḏ3 adviser (?), Urk. IV, 2090, 6.

sḏ3 travel (vb.) CT I, 86; Bersh. II, 13, 1; BD 280, 16; depart, P. Kah. 4, 4 (det. X); in sense of 'die', BM 614, 12.

sḏ3y take recreation (?), Urk. IV, 1322, 8. See the next below.

sḏ3y-ḥr amuse oneself, take recreation, Urk. IV, 676, 10; RB 64, 11; Th. T. S. I, 9; sḏ3y-ḥr n 'please' s'one, Urk. IV, 456, 2; mdwt nḏmt nt sḏ3y-ḥr 'pleasant and enjoyable words', 122, 16; varr. 451, 6; 955, 16; 1161, 4.

sḏ3yt seal, Siut, pl. 15, 7; var. Les. 75, 15; O.K. Urk. I, 64, 10. Cf. WZKM 54, 177.

sḏ3w (?) rings (?), Urk. IV, 22, 6.

sḏ3w (?) seal-bearer, Les. 90, 13.14; 's.-b. of the King of L. E.', 68, 3; varr. 72, 3; 98, 3; 's.-b. of the god' = (1) representative of king; (2) chief embalmer; (3) a priest at Abydos, Bull. 51, 137 (there read ḫtmw).

sḏ3w (?) precious, GNS 111.

sḏ3wt (?) precious things, treasures, GNS 111.

sḏ3wtyw (?) treasurers, Les. 74, 13; var. Urk. IV, 1116, 3; 'chief treasurer', Les. 87, 20; varr. Urk. IV, 32, 12; 1105, 14.

sḏ3m caus. lie, m-ꜥ 'with' woman, ZÄS 47, 95.

sḏ3mt pick (n.), Urk. IV, 837, 9; 1682, 15.

var. of sḏḥ 'shank'.

sḏ3s: ḥr — 'being in good state', BM 614, 14; Siut, pl. 13, 32; var. 13, 18.

sḏwy caus. slander (vb. and n.), RB 116, 13; Urk. IV, 1533, 15; 1828, 2; Pr. 7, 4 ( ).

sḏb impediment, obstacle, varr. , Ann. Serv. 27, 227; verbal opposition, BD 107, 2; evil, Urk. IV, 269, 16 ( ); guilt (?), 499, 14; 1109, 2.4 ( ); ill-will (?), Pr. 12, 7.9.

sḏb restore to life, Pyr. 167.1824.1872; BD 307, 14 ( ); s'thing to its owner, 299, 12.

sḏb penetrate, of injury, P. Ed. Smith, 260.

sḏfꜣy caus. vb. endow altars, Westc. 9, 26; Neferhotep, 24; provide, m 'for' s'one, Les. 68, 19: n. foundation, endowment, Wilbour, p. 116. Varr. Bersh. II, 13, 10; Urk. IV, 1796, 9; 163, 7; 247, 17; 531, 14; 1688, 13.

sḏfꜣ-tryt oath of allegiance, RB 59, 16; var. Urk. IV, 1304, 2.

sḏm hear voice, etc., Sin. R 25; B 31; Sh. S. 56; hear of s'thing, Sin. B 32; listen, n 'to' s'one, Sh. S. 12; Peas. B2, 104; Urk. IV, 508, 6; obey, with n, Pr. 16, 9; RB 110, 10; understand, JEA 16, 69; judge, Les. 81, 3; Urk. IV, 1092, 6; 1113, 13; satisfy conditions (math.), Rhind, 30 = Gr.[1] § 227, 3. Varr. Les. 81, 3; Urk. IV, 257, 12; 1104, 14; 1845, 18.

sḏmi judge, Pr. 16, 4; Urk. IV, 1111, 16, cf. Gr. p. 274, n. 1; usually pl., e.g. Pr. 5, 3; Peas. B1, 99; BH I, 26, 156; Urk. IV, 1109, 14; hearers in lit. sense, Pr. 5, 14.

sḏm-ꜥš servant, Urk. IV, 925, 16; 1215, 17; fem. 1343, 5.

var. of sdm 'paint' the eyes.

sḏn carry child, varr. , , CT I, 281.

sḏr spend the night, BM 159, 11; Adm. 7, 11; M. u. K. 7, 5; sleep, Peas. B1, 201; Urk. IV, 2, 16; V, 171, 2; lie, Westc. 7, 15. 18; P. Kah. 5, 33; lie down, go to rest, Sin. B 293; Mill. 1, 12; Herdsm. 9; sḏr m sṯꜣy 'lie prostrate', Urk. IV, 659, 3 (det.); be inert, inactive, GES 28; sḏr n iꜣdt 'expose all night to the dew', of medicaments, ZÄS 31, 51 (abbr.); aux. vb. do in the night, Gr. § 483, 1.

sḏrw sleeper, Peas. B1, 216; var. B1, 285.

sḏrt sleeping-draught, RB 125, 14.

sḏrt festival of 'Laying (Osiris) to Rest', JEA 38, pl. 1, 13; Les. 74, 10.

sḏryt sleeping-place (?), Les. 74, 10-11.

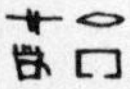 sḏr department (?) of the Residence, Urk. IV, 259, 11.14.

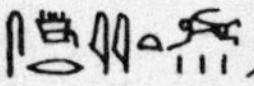 sḏryt slaughter, Urk. IV, 1292, 14; var. dets. 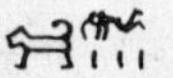 1292, 13.

 sḏḥ shank, shin, varr. , , AEO, I, 17.

 sḏḥ ringed plover, JEA 35, 18 with pl. 2.

 sḏsr caus. consecrate, hallow, sanctify, JEA 32, 51; clear way, Urk. IV, 1043, 6. Var. 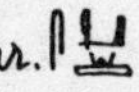 95, 11.

 sḏty child, CT I, 106.112.117; foster-child of king, Les. 70, 21; BH I, 26, 184; Urk. IV, 1072, 1; var. 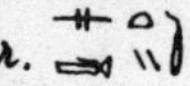 1578, 12.

 sḏd caus. relate, recount, Les. 88, 22; Sh. S. 21.124; Urk. IV, 27, 11; talk, m 'of', Pr. 17, 11; Urk. IV 365, 9; Th. T. S. III, 29; ḥr 'to', Pr. 17, 12.

 sḏdt description, Urk. IV, 437, 7; tale, 1281, 3.

 sḏdw tales, Urk. IV, 344, 10.

 sdd caus. make permanent, Urk. IV, 1523, 6.

 sḏd3 caus. fatten, Meir, III, 4.

 sḏdm caus. make envious (?), Leb. 44.46; cf. JEA 42, 34 (40).

 š lake, pool, Peas. B1, 54; Westc. 5, 2; Urk. IV, 28, 3; garden, ZÄS 45, 129 (); Urk. IV, 447, 5; 1280, 12; ḥrt-š 'garden', see p. 175 above; š-ḥrt 'tomb-garden', GNS 116; basin for liquids, Eb. 60, 13; D. el B. 142.

 št (< šnt?) num. hundred, Gr. §§ 259 f.

 š3 field, meadow, Herdsm. 15; Peas. B1, 142; Westc. 12, 7; country (in contrast to 'town'), P. Kah. 12, 4; ZÄS 72, 42; Ann. Serv. 27, 219; marsh, swamp for fishing and fowling, Caminos, Lit. Frag. pl. 1, 2, 1; 6, 3, 6.17; Urk. IV, 463, 4.

 š3 pig, JEA 14, 212; abbr.  Les. 79, 9; var.  JEA 14, 213.

 var. of š3s 'travel'.

 š3 ordain, order, Sin. B 126.156.229; Pr. 2, 5; Urk. IV, 96, 14; predestine, Adm. 1, 7;

Pr. 14, 2; JEA 32, pl. 6, 11; assign, Urk. IV, 1116, 7 ( ); settle, decide, Sinai, 141.

šȝi bundle (?) of flax, Westc. 12, 17; cf. JEA 22, 43.

šȝyt dues, taxes, Urk. IV, 75, 17; 530, 15; var. 126, 1.

šȝꜥ vb. begin, Les. 86, 14; Sin. B 189-90; Mill. 1, 12; Urk. V, 6, 14. 15; be the first to do s'thing, Eb. 103, 18; spring, originate, m 'from', Caminos, Lit. Frag. p. 7: n. beginning, Urk. IV, 584, 11; šȝꜥ m 'b. from', Gr. § 179; sim. m šȝꜥ m, Urk. IV, 1107, 12; šȝꜥ r 'as far as', Gr. § 179; r šȝꜥ r 'down to', § 180. Varr. Les. 86, 14; Hamm. 114, 11.

šȝꜥ container for corn, AEO II, 212*.

šȝꜥ space, volume, JEA 12, 131.

šȝꜥt void (?) (n.), GES 101, n. 5.

šȝw weight, Bersh. I, 14, 7; worth, value, JEA 42, 14; n šȝw 'apt to', 'fit for'; n šȝw n 'in the capacity of', GNS 47.

šȝw fate, Urk. IV, 5, 17; var. 1344, 3.

šȝw coriander, Caminos, Lit. Frag. pl. 4, 3 = p. 16.

šȝbw meals, food, Urk. IV, 481, 10; varr. , GNS 113; Caminos, Lit. Frag. pl. 2, 2, 9; Urk. IV, 1520, 13; 1797, 12.

see under šwbty 'ushabti'.

šȝm be hot; burn, P. Ed. Smith, 366. 376. Cf. šmm 'hot' below.

šȝmw soiled linen, Peas. B 1, 249.

šȝs vb. intrans. travel, Westc. 7, 9. 11; Neferhotep, 13; go, Westc. 11, 26; 12, 2. 18: trans. tread on enemy, CT I, 212. Varr. , , , L. to D. II, 2, n.

Šȝsw n. loc. desert NE. of Egypt, Urk. IV, 36, 13; 721, 12.

Šȝsw Beduin, AEO I, 193*

šȝš avoid (?), Pt. (L II), 4, 3; P. Kah. 2, 15.

šȝšȝt necklace, Urk. IV, 1123, 16; var. det. 22, 5.

š3š3t bosom, P. Ed. Smith, 349.

š3k bag (?), Urk. IV, 692, 11.

š3ty ship's complement (?), Urk. IV, 1279, 19.

š3d dig, dig out, Urk. IV, 57, 3 (det.); 814, 11; varr. L. to D. n. on II, 2; Urk. IV, 90, 1.

šʿ cut off, RB 77, 4; cut up, Pyr. 653 (det.). 1337; cut down trees, Urk. IV, 326, 17 (dets.); RB 57, 14; hew ship, Urk. I, 108, 4 (det.).

šʿt knife, RB 118, 8; dets. Pyr. 257.

šʿt slaughtering, Urk. IV, 84, 6; V, 30, 16; RB 56, 12; terror, Urk. IV, 18, 5; 248, 7; V, 39, 17; ḥr(y) šʿt 'the violent man', IV, 1410, 13; varr. Cairo 20242; Urk. IV, 84, 6; 139, 5; BD 110, 9; Les. 64, 9. Cf. JEA 37, 29.

šʿt top of the dd-column, JEA 37, 29.

šʿt document, Eb. 49, 1; sš šʿt 'secretary', Urk. IV, 911, 13; 1215, 13.

šʿy sand, BD 29, 2; var. Sin. B 294; nmiw-šʿy 'Sand-farers' = Beduin, Sin. B 73. 292; ḥryw-šʿy 'Sand-dwellers', Les. 82, 13; RB 56, 12; 58, 10.

šʿyt a cake or biscuit, var. , AEO II, 232*.

šʿty weight and value of $\frac{1}{12}$ deben, var. , Gr. § 266, 4.

šʿd cut, Westc. 10, 19; Urk. IV, 667, 15; V, 22, 10 (dets.); cut off, IV, 894, 1.11 (dets.); BD 421, 5; cut down, Urk. IV, 689, 9; 1004, 7; šʿd drt m 'part with', JEA 10, 120, n. 3.

šwt feather, BD 127, 2; varr. RB 111, 14; M. u. K. 1, 2; CT I, 17; 'plumes' as diadem, Urk. IV, 16, 12; 1277, 20; abbr. 200, 16; s3b šwt 'variegated of plumage', var. , Gr. p. 464, F 28; šwt-Dḥwty a herb, JEA 20, 186; 'overseer of feathers and scales', i.e. of fowl and fish, Urk. IV, 514, 10.

šwt side, var. , usually dual, P. Ed. Smith, 400.

šwt coll. neighbours, Pr. 15, 2; Urk. IV, 945, 11.

šw vb. be empty, M.u.K. vs.1,1; Pr.15,1; be lacking, Urk. IV, 519,11; be devoid, m 'of', Pr. 6,8; 16,2; Peas. B1, 253. 291; Westc. 7,19; Les. 68, 24; Urk. IV, 500,2; be missing, m 'from, Urk. V, 19,11: n. lack, Leb. 123.

šwt emptiness, Adm. 7,2; Peas. B1, 82.

šw needy man, Peas. B1,174.

šw blank papyrus-roll, Urk. IV, 1132,14; BD 211,7.

Šw n. div. the air-god Shu, Urk. IV, 1675,5; V, 170, 14.15.

šw ascend, Pyr. 1038 ( ). 1231; CT I, 342.

šw sun, sunlight, Peas. B1, 223; Urk. IV, 117,4; 437,17; Paheri, 3; cf. AEO I, 5.

šw dry, dried, Eb. 20,10; 23,15; 97,18; abbr. Urk. IV, 702,5.

šwyt shadow, shade, varr. , , GAS 59; Urk. IV, 1165,16.

šwyt shade as part of man's personality, Gr. p. 173; spirit of god, Urk. IV, 1542,7 ( ); 'sacred figure', 'image' of god, 56,10; 183,10 ( ); 'Sunshade', kind of small temple, COA III, p. 200; var. ibid.

šw3 poor, Pyr. 475; TR 1,55; var. dets. Pt. (L II), 3,9.

šw3w poor man, Sin. B 309; Mill. 1,6 (dets.); Adm. 2,4.7; var. Urk. IV, 1825,11.

šwiw emptiness (?), default (?), JEA 9, 12, n. 10.

šww an edible vegetable, AEO I, 63*; varr. P. Kah. 7,43; Urk. V, 152,14.

šwb persea-tree, Garten. 31.144; JEA 32, 50; var. Urk. IV, 73,12.

šwbty ushabti-figure, JEA 14, 296; varr. BD 28,9; 28,11.

šwbty a jar, Urk. IV, 733,5.

šwty trader, AEO I, 94*.

šbi vb. 3 inf. mix, Eb. 32,21; mingle with, Urk. IV, 2156,14; Amarna, II, 8; confuse message, words, Urk. IV, 120,2 (det.); 1997,16; di m šb 'give in exchange', JEA 12, 71, n. 8.

šbt value, JEA 12, pl. 17, lower, 4; price, JEA 14, pl. 35, right, vs. 5.

šbw food-offerings, RB 116, 15; varr. Urk. IV, 518, 11; 1045, 7.

šbw necklace, Urk. IV, 38, 14. 16; var. 893, 11.

šbb knead bread in brewing, GNS 92.

šbbt kneaded bread-paste, GNS 92, n. 1.

šbb gullet, P. Ed. Smith, 314.

šbn mix, Eb. 24, 17; *m* 'with', Les. 64, 1; Urk. IV, 22, 12; VII, 4, 2; *ḥr* 'with', Adm. 3, 14; BD 211, 8; Hatnub, 17, 10; consort with (direct obj.), Caminos, Lit. Frag. pl. 13, 2, 3; *wsḫ m šbn* 'collar of mixed (beads)', Lac. Sarc. I, 58; 'mixed cattle' = rabble (?), Les. 80, 16; var. 80, 17.

šbnw various, Urk. IV, 672, 12; varr. 722, 10; 692, 17.

šbšb adjust, divide correctly, GAS 77, JEA 29, 23; set out design, Urk. IV, 1074, 8.

šp vb. intrans. be blind, TR I, 55; Peas. B1, 113. 188: trans. make blind, Peas. B2, 105; Urk. IV, 85, 6 (det.).

špt blindness, Eb. 57, 17. 21.

šp flow out, depart, of morbid fluid or evil spirit, Eb. 90, 16; M. u. K. 1, 4. 10; 2, 7.

špnt a measure of beer, Urk. IV, 821, 7.

špsy noble, august, of gods, etc., Les. 73, 7; Urk. IV, 18, 17; 267, 3; 358, 14; 942, 17; *tꜣ ꜥwt špst* 'the n. herd' = human beings, Westc. 8, 17; splendid, of buildings, etc., BH I, 26, 193; Urk. IV, 56, 3. 13; 167, 15; 386, 5; valuable, of plants, minerals, etc., Sh. S. 48; Urk. IV, 342, 16; 853, 11; *šps n nsw bity* 'one v. to the King of U. and L. E.', ep. of official, Siut, pl. 5, 231; costly, Urk. IV, 174, 13; 425, 8; 427, 6. Varr. Siut, pl. 5, 231; Urk. IV, 220, 17.

šps a noble thing to do, Urk. IV, 221, 2.

špsw costly offerings, BH I, 20.

šps tomb-chapel, Les. 88, 20.

špst ritual jar, Siut, pl. 13, 27.

šps nobleman, wealthy man, Urk. I, 79, 12; IV, 349, 16; Adm. 2, 7; šps nsw 'king's gentleman,' ZÄS 85, 12 ff.

špst noblewoman, Adm. 4, 12; 8, 8; 9, 1; špst nsw 'king's lady.' ZÄS, loc. cit.

špss noble, august, Sin. B 237; RB 110, 3; well-esteemed, Urk. I, 109, 8; 119, 12; rich, Les. 79, 22: trans. vb. enrich, Urk. IV, 268, 13; cf. JEA 39, 20 (ww); Gr. § 274: n. value of s'one, JEA 4, pl. 8, 2.

špss wealthy man, Neferti, 10.

špssw riches, wealth, Adm. 2, 4; 8, 1; precious things, Sin. B 286; Sh. S. 147. 165; Urk. IV, 334, 6; VII, 2, 3; dainties to eat, Sin. B 187; Westc. 7, 21; Urk. IV, 146, 10. Varr. Urk. VII, 59, 2; IV, 670, 14; 1140, 16.

špt a fish (Tetrodon fahaka), Gaillard, Les poissons, 97.

špt vb. be discontented, angry, BM 159, 12; Pr. 14, 9 (dets.); L. to D. III, 3 (n.) (det.); SDT 109 (): n. discontent, anger, BD 35, 4; 485, 4 (det.); špt-ib 'anger,' 34, 10; šptw-ib 'malcontents,' Urk. IV, 370, 7.

šptyt urinary bladder, Eb. 49, 6; 100, 11.

šf respect (?), honour (?), Siut, pl. 11, 8; Hatnub, 22, 11.

šf swell, Eb. 108, 3; Sm. 5, 22.

šft ram-headed figure of Amūn, Urk. IV, 183, 10; 623, 1; abbr. 848, 8.

šfi vb. 3 inf. respect, Les. 84, 8.

šfyt majesty, Urk. IV, 1291, 5; BD 487, 9; respect, JEA 4, pl. 9, 8. Varr. loc. cit.; Adm. p. 102; RB 112, 12; BD 30, 14.

šfc fight (vb.), Urk. IV, 32, 9; 1344, 1.

šfšft ram's head, Urk. IV, 701, 7.

šfšft respect, awe, Urk. IV, 138, 2; 200, 2; 272, 1; dets. Herdom. 7; BD 45, 12; Hymnen, 15, 4.

šfšfyty one greatly respected, Les. 65, 20.

šf-tbt (?) the sixth month, Urk. IV, 44, 11.

šfdyt bier, Th. T. S. II, 21; var. … Adm. 7, 2.

šfdw papyrus-roll, Peas. B1, 305; Les. 43, 11; 98, 16; register, Urk. IV, 1109, 3 (…).

šfdw metal object used in ritual, Urk. IV, 1296, 5; det. … 1296, 6.

šm go, r 'to', Sin. B285; ḥnʿ 'with', B27; Sh. S. 122; opp. of ỉw 'come', Sin. B249; walk, Westc. 7, 4; Peas. B2, 98; set out on journey, Sin. B6. 19; Sh. S. 23; Peas. R 36; pass, of property, n 'to', Urk. I, 36, 15 (…); 137, 4; šm … 'babble', Pr. 7, 12; Urk. IV, 974, 7.

šmt walking, Peas. B1, 201; gait, Louvre C14, 9; movements, CT I, 136 (det. …); Sin. B99; actions, Les. 82, 1; business, BM 614, 13; … šmt 'do b.', ibid. 8. 10; mtnw ḥr ỉrt šmt 'the roads are passable', Adm. 13, 12.

šmw traveller, Sin. R 29.

šmw a class of incantations (?), GAS 48.

šmꜣw foreigners, Caminos, Lit. Frag. pl. 10, 3, 5; Urk. IV, 390, 8; 1545, 13 (dets. …); var. … 740, 1; disease-demons, dets. …, P. Ed. Smith, 385.

šmꜣw distress, Les. 68, 23; disease, P. Ed. Smith, 384 (…).

šmyt walking-stick (?), P. Kah. 19, 45; 20, 43.

Šmꜣw n. loc. Upper Egypt, varr. …, …, ZÄS 44, 8; Gr. p. 483, M 26-8; … wr mdw Šmꜣw 'magnate of the Tens of Upper E.', varr. …, …, …, …, locc. cit.: adj. Upper Egyptian, ZÄS 44, 17.

šmʿ barley of U. E., Peas. B1, 5; B2, 137; Urk. IV, 1132, 11.

Šmʿ·s crown of U. E., ZÄS 44, 20; varr. … Sin. B271; … Urk. IV, 251, 13.

šmʿ make music, Westc. 12, 1; varr. … BH II, 7; … Urk. IV, 1064, 15.

šmʿw musician, Sin. B194; fem. … Cairo 20142, d; … Urk. IV

 šmw summer, Gr. p. 203.

 šmw harvest, Siut, pl. 8, 308; Leb. 69; Urk. IV, 667, 12.13; harvest-tax, P. Wilbour, 24; dets.  Urk. IV, 499, 14.

 šmm vb. 2 gem. be warm, hot, P. Kah. 2, 18; M. u. K. vs. 2, 2; Paheri, 3; Urk. IV, 19, 12; have fever, become feverish, Sm. 9, 1; 10, 2; cf. P. Ed. Smith, 386. Abbr.  Eb. 36, 13.

 šmmt fever, P. Ed. Smith, 386; inflammation, Sm. 14, 14.

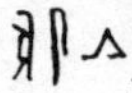 šms follow, accompany, Les. 71, 13; Urk. IV, 3, 5; 13, 9; rdwy.i fḫ.n.sn šms 'my legs have failed to f.' through old age, Sin. B170; serve, Sin. B171; Urk. IV, 17, 13; 86, 5; 173, 12; 1069, 10; bring, Bersh. 14, 1; present, JEA 38, 16, n. 7; šms ib 'f. o's desire', Pr. 7, 9; cf. Žába, 127; swt nt šms-ib 'places of enjoyment', TR 22, 57; sim. Urk. IV, 132, 3; šms hrw nfr 'have a good time', Leb. 68; šms ḳd 'drop off to sleep', Mill. 2, 1. Varr. 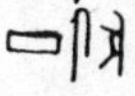 Siut, pl. 19, 26;  Les. 71, 13.

 šmsw follower, retainer, Sh. S. 1; Sin. R2; B180; Peas. R47; B1, 38 (dets. ); šms(w) Ḥr 'F. of Horus' = righteous person, Pr. 17, 10; plur. used of gods, Urk. VII, 56, 19; of primaeval kings, IV, 86, 4. Cf. JEA 39, 36 ff.

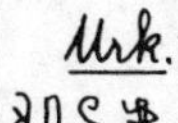 šmsw following, suite, Westc. 7, 22; varr. 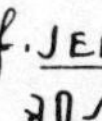 Urk. V, 63, 10;  Les. 68, 10.

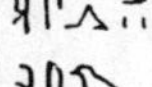 šmswt coll. following, suite, RB 114-5; Urk. IV, 1020, 8; varr. 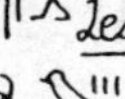 892, 7;  651, 9.

 šmsw worship, JEA 14, pl. 6, 24.

 šms-wḏ3 n. funeral procession, GNS 69: vb. follow the funeral, Urk. IV, 1084, 14.

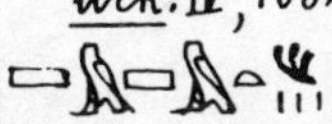 šmšmt hemp(?), Barns, Ram. p. 19.

 šn tree, RB 57, 16.

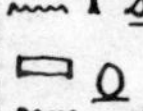 šn ring, SDT 198.

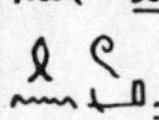 šni vb. 3 inf. encircle, RB 112, 6; Sin. B213 (det. ); Urk. IV, 271, 17; 283, 6 (det.

); enclose, 758, 16; surround, 1303, 10; cover diseased eye, P. Kah. 7, 54 (det.).

šnw circuit, circumference, Urk. IV, 1277, 13; varr. 373, 9; 459, 9; 640, 17; 1692, 5.

šnw enclosure, Urk. IV, 184, 16; 834, 14.

šnw cartouche, Gr. p. 74.

šnw cartouche-amulet, Caminos, Lit. Frag. p. 34.

šnw net, Leb. 9; Adm. 2, 13; Urk. IV, 2, 6; 659, 4 ( ); meshes of net (ỉ3dt), Caminos, Lit. Frag. pl. 13, 2, 7.

šn-wr ocean, Urk. IV, 1278, 19; varr. 86, 9; 617, 7.

šnwt entourage, Peas. B1, 140-1; varr. Les. 71, 23; Sin. B 281; Les. 69, 15.

šnỉ vb. 3 inf. suffer in o'self, Westc. 9, 22; Urk. IV, 1543, 7; suffer from s'thing, 226, 4.

šnw troubles, need, P. Kah. 3, 5; Pr. 5, 4; Urk. IV, 269, 7; 1800, 15.

šnỉ vb. 3 inf. (1) inquire into a matter, Urk. IV, 694, 7; question s'one, 1093, 6; Pr. 14, 7; litigate, Urk. I, 13, 10; šn ḫt r 'institute proceedings against', 13, 3; 100, 13: (2) curse, Sin. B 74 ( ); utter sedition, Leb. 102; exorcise, conjure sickness, M. u. K. 1, 6; Eb. 59, 11.

šnw enquiry, Urk. IV, 1114, 6.

šnt spell, conjuration, M. u. K. 6, 7; Eb. 19, 3; 30, 7.

šn be infested with crocodiles, ZÄS 48, 164; JEA 9, 13, n. 1.

'sheriff', see s. v. šnt.

šnw hair, Sin. B 291; Herdsm. 4; varr. BD 445, 16; Eb. 63, 14; 'coiffeur', D. el B. 109; grass, Bersh. I, 18; Urk. IV, 762, 5 ( ).

šny-t3 fenugreek (?), var. JEA 12, 240.

šnỉ dispel strife, Urk. IV, 269, 14.

šnyt storm, BD 481, 4; varr. Pyr. 336; Urk. IV, 535, 1.

šnꜥ turn back, repulse, repel, RB 123, 3; Urk. IV, 116, 6; 447, 13; Pr. 10, 12; police district, JEA 22, 41; detain, JEA 38, 29; RB 117, 8; dart about, of fish, Peas. B1, 61. Varr. CT I, 182; BM 101; Urk. IV, 1912, 18; Pr. 10, 12.

šnꜥ constable, JEA 22, 41; 'overseer of all police, 39, 41.

šnꜥt detention, Pr. 8, 3.

šnꜥw policing, JEA 22, 41; 38, 29.

šnꜥ breast, D. el B. 116; BD 112, 13; 117, 11.

šnꜥ storm-cloud, Neferti, 25.

šnꜥw (1) storehouse: (2) labour establishment, AEO II, 209*; varr. Siut, pl. 4, 292; Peas. B1, 173-4; Urk. IV, 1142, 15.

šnꜥt storehouse, Urk. IV, 50, 10.

šnꜥ labourer (?), Goyon, 61, 8; Cairo 20473.

šnwt granary, varr. , , Gr. p. 498, O51; AEO II, 214*.

šnbt breast, Urk. IV, 8, 15; 117, 4; varr. 612, 4; 347, 10; Sm. 11, 2; irt-šnbt 'pectoral', see p. 25 above. Cf. P. Ed. Smith, 334.

šnp garment (?) worn by vizier, JEA 31, 115.

šns a cake or loaf, Westc. 4, 15; 6, 20; Urk. IV, 497, 17; var. 1157, 14; det. BD 449, 7.

šnsw slab for offerings, Urk. IV, 498, 1; var. 640, 10.

šnš tear up papers, Urk. V, 170, 12.

šnty heron, Urk. IV, 113, 14; cf. ZÄS 61, 106.

šnṯ revile God, Hatnub, 10, 5; RB 118, 11 ( ); oppose s'one, Pr. 12, 7 ( ); Urk. IV, 1081, 3; punish crime, Leyd. V 88; šnṯ ib 'be angry', Peas. B1, 270; šnṯ ḫt 'vent anger', m 'on', CT I, 192; n 'on', Westc. 12, 9; r 'on', 7, 25.

šnt anger, BH I, 7, 8.

šnṯ sheriff, Naga ed-Dêr, p. 34; varr. Urk. IV, 436, 3; 1105, 10; P. Kah. 30, 11. Cf. JEA 9, 15, n. 2.

šnṯt strife, quarrel, Pyr. 1463; varr. ibid.; Naga ed-Dêr, p. 34; RB 122, 5.

šntw strife, quarrel, CT I, 43; varr. ibid.; Pr. 7, 12; Urk. IV, 61, 10.

šnty quarrelsome man, Pr. 10, 8; P. Ram. I, B1, 9 (); pl. foes of king, Urk. IV, 137, 14; 613, 1; 968, 13.

šndt Nile acacia, Arab. ṣunṭ, RB 60, 14; varr. P. Ram. V, 8; Sm. 16, 8.

šndwt kilt, Pyr. 546; varr. ibid.; Peas. B1, 63; Sin. B 308.

šndty wearer of a kilt, Siut, pl. 7, 296; var. loc. cit., table, l. 5.

šrt nose, nostril, P. Kah. 6, 22; Urk. IV, 944, 1; 1166, 3; dets. M. u. K. 2, 9; BD 446, 6.

šrt kind of grain, Urk. IV, 747, 5. 9.

šr stop up, block, P. Ram. I, B III, 14 = Barns, p. 9; varr. Urk. IV, 385, 17; 2013, 16.

šrr adj. and vb. 2 gem. little, Westc. 12, 14 (det.); Pr. 19, 7; Merikarēᶜ, 107; meagre, Siut, pl. 7, 295; Sin. B 258; younger, junior, P. Berl. 9010, 3; often abbr. , e.g. 'Hekayeb the y.', Urk. VII, 7, 14; short, IV, 691, 10; 1304, 11; Caminos, Lit. Frag. pl. 22, 17.

šrr small, lowly man, BM 1372; Hatnub, 20, 10; var. Adm. 4, 2.

šri lad, Urk. IV, 2, 14; younger son, P. Berl. 9010, 3 (); Urk. IV, 691, 3.

šrit daughter, ZÄS 55, 85.

šrš hurry (?), Meir, III, 8; bolt (?), of horses, Urk. IV, 697, 16.

šs bier (?), Urk. IV, 1814, 12.

šs rope, abbr. , Bull. 30, 164.

šs alabaster; vessels of a., varr. , , , , Bull. 30, 167 ff.

šst alabaster, Urk. I, 107, 17; IV, 1044, 4.

see sšr.

šs3 vb. be wise, Urk. IV, 449, 16; 1080, 16; be conversant, m 'with', Siut, pl. 18, 9; Urk. IV, 97, 7; 363, 4; 1197, 10; ḥr 'with', 74, 12; 151, 15; be skilled, m 'in', 422, 14; know, Adm. p. 106; šs3 ḥr 'skilled', Urk. IV, 118, 4; 121, 2; 1152, 12; di šs3 m 'inform s'one of', Sh. S. 139: n. wisdom, Sin. B 33; Urk. IV, 134, 8; skill, 1283, 2.

šs3t nightfall, varr. JEA 6, 300. 302.

šs3w bubalis antelope, BH II, 4; var. Urk. VII, 36.

šs3w tongue, Pyr. 127; later šsr, see below.

šs3w medical prescription, P. Kah. 5, 20; var. Eb. 36, 4.

šsp (šzp) take, Sh. S. 3; Urk. IV, 151, 14; 615, 8; accept, Peas. B1, 192; Pr. 1, 10; 6, 11; Siut, pl. 4, 225; receive, RB 113, 4; Urk. IV, 76, 11; 324, 4; n 'from', JEA 27, 69, n. 7; assume crown, Les. 98, 17; RB 112, 15; catch fish, Leb. 89; purchase, JEA 21, 143. Also in expressions šsp 3wt-ib 'commencement of happiness', JEA 33, 25; —— 3s 'make haste', Mill. 2, 3; —— i3w 'grow old', JEA 33, 25; —— ꜥḥ3 r 'attack', Urk. IV, 893, 16-17; —— w3t 'take the road', 808, 15; 979, 10; cf. JEA 33, 26; —— tp-w3t nfrt 'make a good journey', Urk. IV, 322, 7; cf. JEA 38, 21, n. 3; —— wnwt nt nfr-ib 'take an hour of recreation', Mill. 1, 11-12; —— wnwt bint 'have a bad time', P. Kah. 32, 18-19; —— bi3t 'perform a miracle', Urk. IV, 157, 16; —— f3 ṯ3w 'set out and sail', Sin. B 246-7; —— nmtwt 'approve actions', Les. 75, 7; —— kḥkḥ 'attain old age', JEA 33, 26; —— ksw 'crouch down', Sin. B 17-18; —— ḏt 'commencement of eternity', JEA 33, 25; —— n ib n 'who are dear to', TR 2, 45. Varr. Pyr. 879; Siut, pl. 4, 225; Urk. IV, 76, 11.

šsp palm of hand, Urk. IV, 84, 1; BD 220, 2; ZÄS 60, 71 (det.); measure of 1/7 cubit, abbr. , , Gr. §266, 2.

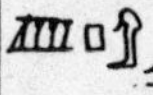

šsp (1) statue, image, varr. ideogr. or det.  ,  , GNS 94.

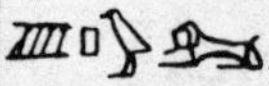

šspw sphinx, Goyon, 61, 14; var.  54; cf. GNS 94. 161.

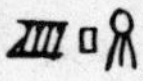

šsp adj. white, BD 494, 11; bright, 176, 7. 9 (det. ☉); 301, 13: n. dawn, P. Kah. 1, 10; Peas. B1, 201; Westc. 7, 18; light, Urk. IV, 518, 2. Older sšp, q. v.

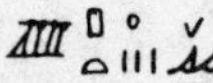

šspt cucumber, cucumis melo, var. det. 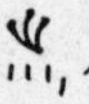 , Garten, 14. 130.

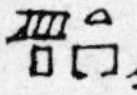

šspt chapel, Urk. I, 107, 5; summer-house, Westc. 3, 7. 8; bedroom, Amarna, VI, 27, 3.

šspt-dḥn chorus, Urk. IV, 978, 12; cf. SDT 176.

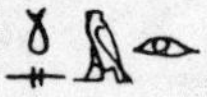

šsm be bloodshot, of eyes, P. Ed. Smith, 282.

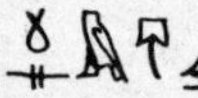

šsm leather roll (?), Urk. IV, 1104, 7; cf. JEA 31, 115.

šsmt sacred girdle, Stud. Griff. 316.

šsmt (šzmt) malachite, varr.  , 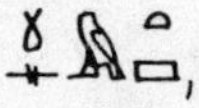 , op. cit. 320.

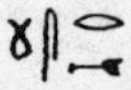

šsr arrow, P. Kah. 1, 4; Sin. B274; Urk. IV, 8, 14; var. 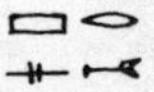 Urk. VII, 55, 10.

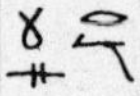

šsr tongue, Bull. 30, 180.

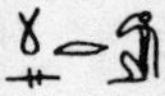

šsr utter, express, Bull. 30, 179; var. 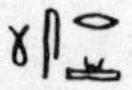 Pr. 15, 10.

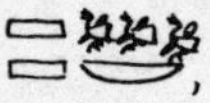

, 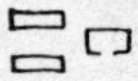 varr. of šsy 'nest'.

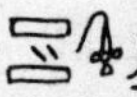

šši vb. 3 inf. refine (?) gold, Urk. IV, 1938, 4.

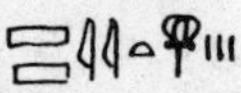

see under sššt 'sistrum'.

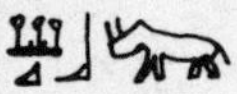

škb rhinoceros RB 64, 16.

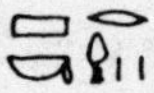

var. of ḫkrw 'panoply'.

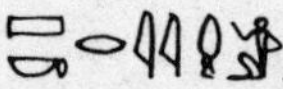

škry (ḫkry) coiffeur (?), JEA 41, 15.

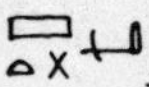

št assessment of taxes, P. Wilbour, 10; ꜥ3 n št 'tax-master', Urk. IV, 1962, 18; cf. loc. cit.

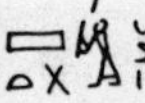

št coll. tax-payers, P. Wilbour, 57.

št3 mysterious, Urk. V, 55, 10; RB 110, 3. 5; secret, Les. 70, 17; 75, 12; Hymnen, 9, 5; Urk. IV, 966, 17; hidden, Siut, pl. 13, 31; Les. 86, 7; difficult, BH II, 14; Bersh. I, 14, 1. 2. Varr. Les. 70, 17;  BD 38, 5;  474, 12.

št3t secrets, Neferhotep, 2; varr. Urk. IV, 134, 8; 74, 12.

št3w secrets, Leb. 30; BD 425, 14 (dets.); 426, 4 (); religious mysteries, Urk. IV, 416, 17 (); 417, 3. 6.

št3 copse, scrub, P. Wilbour, 29, n. 1; 32; brushwood (?), Adm. 3, 11.

var. of štyt 'sanctuary of Sokar'.

štyt chamber, P. Ed. Smith, 248.

štyt leader, stroke of bank of oars-women, Westc. 5, 19; 6, 3.

štyw stroke-oar (?), Westc. 5, 15.

štyw tortoise, Eb. 57, 6; var. 86, 12.

štyw an offering-loaf, Urk. IV, 1953, 4. 5.

štbt crate (?), P. Louvre 3226, 29, 2.

štm vb. be quarrelsome, Merikarēʿ, 147; Pr. 11, 13 (): n. hostility, Sin. B 98 (det.). Cf. Rev. ég. 7, 83.

št equip (?), CT I, 280.

št satchel, var. , CT I, 71.

štyt (sic) sanctuary of Sokar, D. el B. 11; varr. Urk. I, 85, 1; IV, 992, 1; 1850, 8; 1813, 7.

šdi vb. 3 inf. take away, remove, Leb. 58; Adm. 6, 7; 7, 1; 11, 4; Siut, pl. 7, 293; Eb. 23, 19; cut out, RB 58, 6; Urk. IV, 25, 9; D. el. B. 107; Sh. S. 54; dig lake, etc., Urk. IV, 28, 3; 815, 1; 919, 4; M. u. K. 8, 7; rescue, Sin. B 214; Peas. B1, 138; salvage boat, B1, 259; stave off (?) event, B1, 154; pull, ḥr 'on' rope, B1, 164; exact dues, JEA 27, 62, n. 2; ransack a country, m 'of' goods, RB 62, 8; apportion field-plots, Urk. IV, 1111, 12.

šdi vb. 3 inf. read, Les. 80, 4 (); Urk. IV, 122, 11; 1998, 6; read aloud, recite, Pr. 2, 6; Herdsm. 13; Sin. B 200 (det.); Urk. IV, 966, 1 (det.).

šdi vb. 3 inf. suckle, RB 111, 16; Urk. IV, 579, 10; 580, 17; educate, I, 51, 13; IV, 34, 16; Siut, pl. 15, 23; šd nḫn n 'act as guardian to' a minor, P. Kah. 12, 14 (det.);

nourish strife, Mill. 2, 7 (det.); 'fattened goose', Urk. IV, 745, 4; sim. 755, 17; 770, 6.

šd-mdw disturb (?), CT I, 155. 161.

šd-r public proclamation, Urk. IV, 1114, 2.

šd-ḫrw disturbance, Siut, pl. 4, 224; RB 111, 11; 112, 11; Urk. IV, 1816, 7.

šd vulva, Eb. 95, 17. 22 (det. ▭); 96, 3.

šd mortar for pounding drugs, Eb. 21, 12; 77, 3; P. Ram. III, B 7.

šd poultice, Eb. 52, 13.

šdw waterfowl (?), Urk. IV, 1380, 1.

šdt (šdt) dough, Eb. 53, 18. 19; Sm. 21, 16; 22, 2 (det.), cf. P. Ed. Smith, 497; var. O.K. Ikhekhi, 42 (XII).

šd artificial lake, Urk. IV, 1668, 19.

šdyt (1) pool, Bersh. II, p. 23; RB 119, 15. 16; well, AEO I, 8*: (2) plot of land, see below s.v. šdwt 'plot'. Varr. Urk. I, 212, 5; Dream-book, 8, 5.

šdy ditch, Urk. IV, 660, 15; 1307, 12; 1739, 14.

šdyt rubble, Urk. IV, 835, 3.

Šdt n. loc. Crocodilopolis, P. Wilbour, 43.

Šdty n. div. He of Crocodilopolis, ep. of Sobk, Rec. trav. 38, 186; P. Wilbour, 43.

šdw skin as mat, etc., Adm. 9, 1; Urk. IV, 1104, 3. 4 (); water-skin, Rec. trav. 11, 119.

šdw raft, Adm. 4, 10 (also det.); 7, 10.

šdw plot of land, Westc. 4, 9; Peas. B1, 300; Leb. 69; Urk. IV, 116, 13 ().

šdwt plot of land, Peas. B1, 303; var. P. Kah. 21, 7.

šdn be closed, of eyes, BD 89, 12.

šdḥ pomegranate-wine, COA III, p. 164.

šdšd protuberance on standard , ZÄS 47, 88.

ḳ3i adj. and vb. 3inf. tall, high, Sh. S. 156; Peas. B1, 6; Urk. IV, 16, 12 (); 424, 1. 17; 1073, 13; dꜥ ḳ3 'a h. wind', Peas. B1, 245; exalted, BD 176, 1; 473, 14; be raised on high, uplifted, BD 217, 3; 262, 2; ḳ3 ib 'haughty', Pr. 12, 1; ḳ3 nrw 'greatly dreaded', Urk. IV, 1382, 8 (); ḳ3 ḫrw 'high, loud of voice', Peas. B1, 26; Siut, pl. 4, 229; Urk. IV, 1031, 9 (); Les. 86, 21 (infin.); ḳ3 'presumptuous', 'overweening', Sin. B 230; Siut, pl. 4, 229; ḳ3 srf 'high of temper', BM 614, 9.

ḳ3t height, Sm. 14, 11; varr. Urk. IV, 142, 10; 374, 13.

ḳ33 hill, high ground, Pyr. 1652; Urk. V, 6, 17 (det.); Leb. 59 (dets.); varr. TR 1, 28; Urk. IV, 364, 3; Pyr. 1587.

ḳ3yt (1) high ground: (2) arable land, P. Wilbour, 27. 178; det. Amarna, V, 28, 21; abbr. Urk. IV, 207, 7.

ḳ3yt high throne, Urk. IV, 2006, 14.

ḳ3w height, Urk. IV, 1077, 13; BD 182, 16 (); 221, 15; sbḥt r ḳ3 n ḫrw.s 'who cries out at the top of her voice', BD 354, 4-5.

ḳ3t coll. foreign foes, Urk. IV, 896, 11.

var. of ḳ3rt 'door-bolt'.

ḳ33 grains (?), varr. , , GAS 45; Gr. p. 456, D 51.

ḳ3ꜥ vomit (vb.), P. Kah. 5, 36.

ḳ3b intestine, Eb. 42, 12; ḳ3b m3ꜥ n pḥwyt 'rectum', Eb. 38, 16; ḥryw ḳ3b. sn 'who are on their bellies', CT I, 166; interior, middle of land, etc., Mill. 2, 11 (dets.); Urk. IV, 2155, 13 (); V, 68, 12; BD 109, 12; m-ḳ3b 'in the midst of', Gr. § 178.

ḳ3b fold over, double over, Sm. 12, 5. 11; double quantity, Urk. IV, 389, 2 (); 745, 11; 1685, 5; JEA 15, pl. 35 (17, 4, dets.); 'doubled', Rhind, 65.

ḳ3bw coils of snake, Pyr. 1146; var. det. TR 5, 4.

ḳ3bw windings of waterway, Pyr. 2061; varr. Urk. V, 66, 13; 67, 14.

ḳ3bt breast, AEO II, 241*.

ḳ3mdt funeral oration, Mill. 1, 9.

ḳ3r bundle, Caminos, Lit. Frag. pl. 2, 2, 8.

ḳ3rt door-bolt, BD 150, 7; 474, 3; varr. 136, 9; Urk. IV, 116, 8.

ḳ3ḥ mud-plaster, GAS 76.

ḳ3sw bonds, D. el B. 107 (also); BD 105, 12 (dets.); rigging of ship, TR 27, 9.

ḳ3s rope-ladder, Pyr. 2079.

ḳ3s string bow; bind victim; tie rope-ladder, GNS 49; var. Urk. IV, 1603, 14.

ḳ3s vomit, Eb. 40, 15. See also ḳis below.

ḳ3ḳ3-ib vainglorious (?), Hamm. 114, 7.

ḳ3ḳ3w travelling-barge, Peas. B1, 35; Westc. 8, 3.

ḳ3dw (ḳd) plaster, Amarna, V, 26, 24.

ḳi form, shape: m p3 ḳi 'in this fashion', Leb. 50; mdt tn m ḳi·s nb 'this matter in its every aspect', Peas. B1, 41-2; mi ḳi(·f) 'entire', Gr. § 100, 2; m ḳi wc 'all together', T. Carn. 5; mi ḳi 'according to', Urk. IV, 1015, 1; nature: rḫ ḳi iry 'who knew their n.', Urk. IV, 1281, 12.

var. of ḳcḥ 'bend'.

ḳis vomit, P. Kah. 6, 16.

Ḳis n. loc. Cusae (El-Ḳūsīyah), varr. , , , Gr. p. 446, A 38. 39.

ḳc vomit, Eb. 30, 16. Cf. ḳ3c above.

ḳcḥ elbow, Pr. 8, 6; 13, 12; arm, Urk. V, 165, 15; BD 308, 5 (dets.); shoulder, M. u. K. vs. 5, 1; Sm. 2, 8.

ḳcḥt shoulder of beef, Siut, pl. 8, 322.

ḳcḥ corner, P. Kah. 2, 18; Siut, pl. 6, 278; BD 155, 11; bend of stream, Urk. IV, 653, 12; bight of net, JEA 28, 14.

ḳcḥ bend arm (c), Urk. IV, 753, 14; (rmn), V, 87, 11; hand (drt), IV, 401, 12; 470, 13;

769,1; sim. ḳꜥḥ m drt, 121,12 (dets. 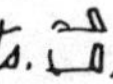); people to o's will, Merikarēꜥ, 27. Varr.  Urk. IV, 28,17;  JEA 16, 195, 11.

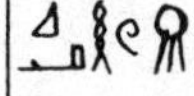 ḳꜥḥw sunshine, Urk. IV, 1811,3.

 ḳꜥḥw: 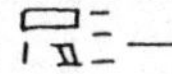 ——— 'fish-ponds', Neferti, 30; cf. JEA 1, 103, n.15.

 ḳw a loaf or cake, Urk. IV, 1130,17.

 ḳwr gold-miner(?), var. , JEA 4, 247, n.3.

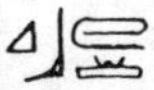 see under ḳ3b.

 ḳb3t crown of head, BH I, 26, 188.

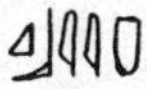 ḳby jar for beer, Siut, pl. 7, 293; Urk. IV, 828,4.

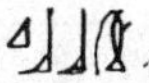 ḳbb adj. and vb. 2 gem. cool, Eb. 36,14; 37,3; P. Kah. 2,17; RB 114,10; Cold, P. Kah. 7,40-1 (dets. 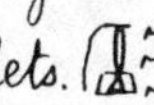); Les. 68,17 (det. 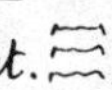); cooling of remedy, Eb. 33,16; calm, quiet, Hatnub, 22,16; Les. 80,16; T. Carn. 5; Merikarēꜥ 68; Pr. 14,5.6; be purified, Pyr. 1204 (dets. ); take one's ease, Neferti, 30; BD 422,6; ḳb ib 'be calm', L. to D. I,8; 'be refreshed', Westc. 5,3.7; ḳb ḥt 'amicable', Hatnub, 10,4; Pr. 10,8; ḳb srf 'calm-tempered', BM 614,7; Urk. IV, 970,15; st-ḳbt 'recreation', Westc. 4,25-5,1. Abbr. 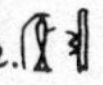 BD 454,4.

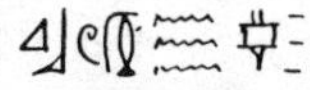 ḳbw cool breeze, Caminos, Lit. Frag. p. 11.

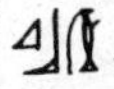 ḳb cold (n.), P. Kah. 7,62.

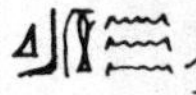 ḳb vb. intrans. pour a libation, n 'to', Amarna, I, 39, n.4 (): trans. pour out water, III, 22; wine, V, 22.

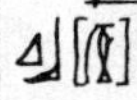 ḳb strew(?): ḥrt ḳb.ti m sb3w 'a sky strewn(?) with stars', Urk. IV, 1686,9.

 ḳbbwt cold water, TR 22,60; varr. 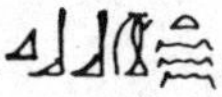 22,62; 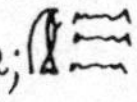 Amarna, VI, 33, MID. 2 (or ḳbḥw?)

 ḳbḥ foot(?), AEO II, 255*.

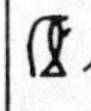 ḳbḥ(?) fountain in n. loc. Ḳbḥ Ḥr 'F. of Horus', Urk. IV, 808,2; sim. 'F. of Seth', 808,1.

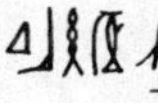 ḳbḥ vb. trans. purify, Pyr. 1995: intrans. present libations, n 'to', BD 486,5 (dets. 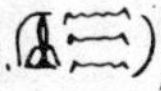); be calm(?), Hymnen, 10,2.

ḳbḥw cold water, Meir, III, 17; BD 454, 4 (dets.); var. Amar. IV, 3, 8; the abbr. , e.g. BH I, 17; Amarna, VI, 33, MID. 2, may stand for either ḳbḥw or for its synonym ḳbbwt above.

ḳbḥw coolness, Adm. 11, 13.

ḳbḥw (?) libation-vase, Urk. IV, 22, 9.

ḳbḥt (?) libation-vase, Urk. IV, 22, 7.

ḳbḥw wild-fowl, Peas. B1, 113; TR 22, 66.

ḳbḥw sky, Pyr. 841; varr. Urk. IV, 1320, 5; BD 174, 12.

ḳbḥ (?) death, Urk. IV, 518, 10.

Ḳbḥ-snw·f n. div. one of the four sons of Horus, TR 27, 4; varr. Urk. V, 39, 5; 155, 15.

ḳf3t fame, JEA 32, pl. 6, 10.

ḳfn bake, BD 208, 13; clot, of blood, P. Ed. Smith, 251.

ḳfn a loaf, Siut, pl. 8, 314. 320.

ḳfnw baker, Louvre C 167; var. (sic) Cairo 20452.

ḳm3 (1) throw, TR 22, 69; Les. 69, 1; Urk. IV, 1587, 19: (2) create, Sin. B 265; Urk. IV, 223, 9 (dets.); 580, 8; beget, 585, 7; P. Kah. 5, 18; produce, Urk. IV, 51, 4; RB 77, 8; carry out teaching, Urk. IV, 272, 9; ḳm3w nw ib(·i) 'my own ideas', 173, 15: (3) hammer out, m 'from' metal, Urk. IV, 53, 16; 422, 10; 426, 9; ḥd twt m ḳm3 'a statue of hammered silver', 666, 11; sim. 1304, 3; RB 64, 8. Varr. Sin. B 265; Les. 69, 1; 72, 9; Urk. IV, 1587, 19; 951, 9; 51, 4; 236, 3.

ḳm3 form, appearance, BD 308, 1; 467, 11; Urk. IV, 1073, 8 (dets.); nature, 246, 9; 255, 5 ( ).

ḳm3w winnower (?), Cairo 20214.

ḳm3 mourn, GNS 86.

ḳm3w class of soldiers, D. el B. 125.

ḳmi *gum ned* (?): ḳmi špt 'g. of lip' = reticent, Urk. IV, 63, 14.

ḳmyt *gum, resin*, Urk. IV, 329,3; 346,13; varr. ... Eb. 41,18; ... 10,10.

ḳmḥ *a loaf*, BH I, 17; D. el B. 110.

ḳmd (1) *devise, invent*: (2) *mourn*, GNS 86.

ḳn *fat* (adj. and n.), Eb. 55, 1 (det.); 73, 21; 77, 10.

ḳnt *yellowness* (?) *in eyes*, Eb. 57, 14; 64,4; cf ḳnit below.

ḳni adj. and vb. 3 inf. (1) *brave*, Sh. S. 132; Sin. B 107; Urk. IV, 2.5; 9, 16; *strong*, RB 114, 6 ( ); M. u. K. 3,3; Siut, pl. 15, 16 (det.); Urk. IV, 414, 17; *sturdy, of child*, Leb. 100; *able, capable*, Les. 79, 6; RB 114, 14; *dutiful, of son and heir*, Leyd. V 88; Urk. VII, 56, 5; *powerful, of speech*, Merikarēᶜ, 32; *stout, of heart*, Siut, pl. 11, 30; Adm. p. 104; *active*, Caminos, L.-Eg. Misc. 445: (2) *conquer*, Merikarēᶜ, 93 : (3) *amount*, r 'to', *of measurement*, Peas. R 46, cf. Caminos, loc. cit : (4) *be profuse*; n. *profusion*, Caminos, loc. cit.

ḳn *brave man*, Mill. 2, 4; Adm. 7, 7; as *military title*, Urk. IV, 34, 2 ( ) 894, 16; 895, 2.

ḳnyt *the Braves, military corps d'élite*, JEA 39, 44.

ḳnt *valour*, Urk. IV, 5, 1. 13; 7, 9; Les. 84, 3.

ḳnn *supremacy*, JEA 32, pl. 6, 2.

ḳn *offence*, RB 112, 11; Peas. B 1, 12 (det. X); Caminos, Lit. Frag. pl. 28, 2 (dets.); Urk. IV, 1109, 8.

ḳn vb. trans. *complete, accomplish*, Pt. (L II), 4, 13; Caminos, Lit. Frag. pl. 13, 1; *cease*, with foll. infin., Israel, 10: intrans. *be provided*, m 'with', Urk. IV, 505, 6: n. *first quality* : dᶜm n ḳn 'fine gold of the f. q.', Urk. IV, 367, 14; sim. 892, 14; mdw r spr n ḳn 'speak to perfection (?)', Pr. 18, 11.

ḳn *mat*, Urk. IV, 1104, 1; det. P. Kah. 30, 45; var. SDT 212.

ḳni *ceremonial garment*, SDT 211.

ḳni *sheaf, bundle*, JEA 37, 114.

ḳnỉ embrace (vb. and n.), Sh. S. 44.133.168; Urk. IV, 921, 1 ( ); 1163, 1; bosom of mother, M. u. K. vs. 4, 1; 5, 7.

ḳnỉw palanquin, Westc. 7, 12.14; var. Urk. IV, 666, 16.

ḳnỉw portable shrine, Les. 71, 4.

ḳnỉt a yellow pigment, BD 374, 1; 379, 11; var. P. Kah. 20, 38.

ḳnỉt yellowness (?), of eyes, Eb. 62, 22.

ḳny be yellow (?), of eyes, P. Kah. 7, 60.

ḳnb bend; bow, incline o'self; subjugate, var. , Stud. Griff. 72.

ḳnbt corner, angle, AEO II, 214*.

ḳnbt court of magistrates, etc., loc. cit; varr. Urk. IV, 1086, 12; 1116, 12.

ḳnbty magistrate, P. Kah. 11, 22; Urk. IV, 1111, 3.

ḳns bury, Urk. IV, 1197, 1.

ḳnḳn beat people; pound up medicaments; beat out, flatten metal; deal wrongly (?), m 'with', GAS 64.

ḳnḳnyt mallet (?), P. Kah. 20, 31.

ḳnd be angry, furious, Les. 80, 18; Urk. IV, 269, 9; 1082, 15.

var. of ḳꜣrt 'door-bolt'.

ḳrt depression, hollow place, P. Ed. Smith, 250; ḳrty 'the two sources' of the Nile, BD 380, 3. Cf. ḳrrt 'cavern'.

ḳrỉ draw near, attend s'one, JEA 39, 16 (g)

ḳrỉ storm, storm-cloud, AEO I, 5*; dets Sh. S. 57; O.K. Pyr. 261; 281.

ḳrf bag (?), Bersh. II, 17.

ḳrf contract, draw together, var. dets , , P. Ed. Smith, 427; det. CT I, 56.

ḳrft bag, Les. 61, 12; Eb. 53, 12; det. 53, 13.

ḳrft contractions (med.), P. Ed. Smith, 427.

ḳrfw facial wrinkles, Eb. 87, 6.

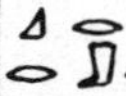 ḳrr vb. 2 gem. fire pottery, BH II, 7; broil (?) food, m 'out of' bones, Pyr. 413 (det. ).

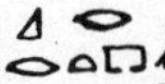 ḳrrt cavern, BD 253, 2; 274, 2; det.  272, 9.

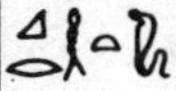 ḳrḥt serpent-spirit as (1) guardian of a place; (2) ep. of princes of ancient family, var. dets. , ; GAS 55; JEA 32, 46, n. 17; pl. serpent-figures in gold, Urk. IV, 1728, 15.

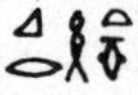 ḳrḥt vessel, Urk. IV, 54, 3; 183, 14; 427, 8; det.  204, 6.

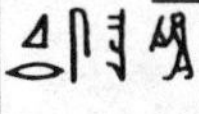 ḳrs vb. bury, Peas. B1, 308; Sh. S. 169 (dets. 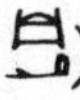); Les. 72, 21; Urk. IV, 1424, 17 (det. ); 1825, 4 (abbr. ): n. burial, L. to D. I, 1; Sin. B 91 (dets. 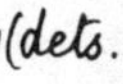); Leb. 43 (det. );  ḳrs '(the state of) being buried', Westc. 7, 18.

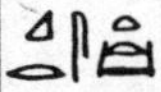 ḳrst burial, Urk. IV, 32, 11; 113, 7; 414, 2; varr. 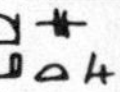 48, 7;  1005, 6.

 ḳrsw coffin, BD 436, 7; varr. 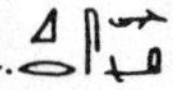 Adm. 7, 8;  Urk. IV, 1424, 16.

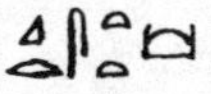 ḳrstt tomb-equipment, Urk. VII, 9, 18; var. 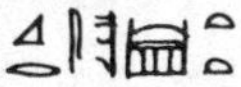 BH II, 7.

 ḳrdn axe, Urk. IV, 669, 15; cf. JEA 15, 249 (32).

 var. of ḳꜥḥ 'bend'.

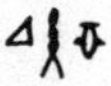 ḳḥ vase or jar, Urk. IV, 1859, 10.

 ḳḥḳḥw metal-workers, RB 76, 7.

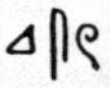 var. of ḳꜣs 'bind'.

 ḳs bone, Westc. 10, 10; BD 100, 14; var. 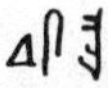 Pr. 5, 1.

 ḳsn painful, Westc. 9, 22; 10, 4; painfully, Eb. 41, 21; irksome, P. Kah. 3, 33 (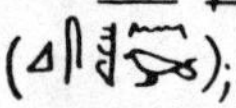); troubled, Cairo 20001; difficult, Pr. 11, 11; Les. 86, 12; dangerous, Urk. V, 198, 13; 199, 12; BD 29, 6; wretched, Pr. 13, 11; 14, 3; m st ḳsnt 'in a difficult place', BM 101; Les. 89, 21; 'in evil case', Adm. p. 104; 'in a bad state' (med.), P. Kah. 6, 27.

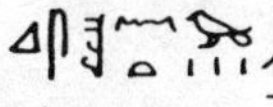 ḳsnt trouble, misfortune, Les. 70, 2; Leb. 15. 20; var.  Mill. 1, 6.

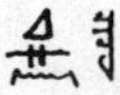 ḳsn pain, GES 192 (22); troubling by foes, RB 61, 6.

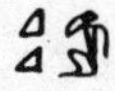 var. of wnm 'eat'.

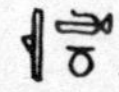 ḳd pot, Eb. 92, 9.

 ḳd use the potter's wheel, AEO I, 73*; var. 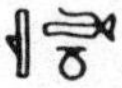 BH I, 25.

ḳd potter (as ep. of Khnum), Urk. IV, 223, 6; 225, 16; 234, 2.

ḳd build, Sin. B 297; Westc. 9, 25; Urk. IV, 767, 11; fashion men, 161, 2; 222, 13; Adm. 2, 4. Varr. Leb. 60; Siut, pl. 5, 236; Urk. IV, 43, 10; 161, 2.

ḳd builder, Urk. I, 20, 17; varr. IV, 129, 2; dets. Adm. 3, 6.

ḳd form: m ḳd·f mty 'in its customary f.', Sm. 5, 22; nature, Pr. 14, 7; Urk. IV, 246, 3; reputation, Pr. 15, 4; Urk. IV, 120, 4; 508, 6; ḳd 'achieve a (good) r.', 'achieve success', JEA 17, 60 (45); 37, 51 (V); ḳd ḥr 'attain a (good) r. with', Urk. I, 222, 10; character, disposition, BM 614, 8; Sin. B 32; Urk. IV, 40, 5; nb ḳd 'man of virtue', GAS 21; dw ḳd r 'ill-disposed toward', JEA 20, 158 (7); extent, GES 101; mi ḳd 'in every respect', Urk. I, 100, 11; mi ḳd·(f) 'entire', Gr. § 100, 2; ḥr ḳd 'entirely', Hatnub, 24, 9; Sm. 21, 11. 17; 'altogether', P. Kah. 3, 33; 'utterly', Pr. 7, 3; m ḳd wꜥ 'all together', Urk. IV, 1823, 8. Varr. Urk. VIII, 6, 19; Urk. IV, 40, 5.

ḳd go round: mw pf ḳdw 'that circling water' = R. Euphrates, Urk. IV, 85, 14; m ḳd·sn nb 'all round them', 1307, 12 ( ); sim. P. Harris I, 4, 2.

ḳd sleep (vb. and n.), RB 114, 2; Mill. 2, 1; Urk. IV, 363, 12; 1887, 9:

ḳdt kitĕ, weight of $\frac{1}{10}$ dbn, Gr. § 266, 4.

Ḳdw men of Kodē, Urk. IV, 649, 10.

ḳdwt drawings, Urk. IV, 1082, 4; sš ḳdwt 'draughtsman', AEO I, 71*; varr. RB 76, 7; Les. 76, 10.

ḳdf gather flowers, sayings, GAS 97.

ḳdtt a conifer (?) from Syria, Urk. IV, 672, 8; Rec. trav. 7, 112.

ḳddw characters (?) of persons, CT I, 192.

ḳdd sleep (n.), Urk. IV, 530, 3; 959, 15; 1542, 13 ( ); pl. ḳddw 'slumbers', P. Kah. 1, 10.

k suff. pron. 2 m. sg. thou, thy, thee, Gr. § 34.

kꜣ non-encl. part. so, then, var. , Gr. §§ 242; 346, 5; 427; 450, 5, d.

kꜣi vb. 3 inf. think about, Sin. B 72; Urk. IV, 365, 4; Pt. (L II), 5, 14; plan, Les. 83, 23; Urk. IV, 269, 16; VII, 48, 14; kꜣ.f 'he will say', Gr. §§ 436. 437.

kꜣt thought, plan, device, var. , PSBA 23, 237; plot, Urk. IV, 138, 14.

kꜣ soul, spirit; essence of a being; personality; fortune, Gr. p. 172; JEA 36, 7, n. 2; will of king, Urk. I, 109, 11; kingship, JEA, loc. cit; in pl. goodwill, Pr. 12, 7. 9. 11; cf. Greven, Der Ka in Theologie und Königskult des Alten Reiches, reviewed JEA 41, 141; phantom: iw pn n kꜣ 'this ph. island', Sh. S. 114. Varr. Sin. B 206; Urk. IV, 242, 6; I, 50, 15; 221, 18.

kꜣ-ḥr-kꜣ fifth month; festival of Khoiakh, ZÄS 43, 139; Th. T. S. I, p. 97, n. 4; var. Paheri, 4.

kꜣw food, PSBA 38, 89; varr. Adm. 5, 1; Urk. IV, 146, 10; Mill. 1, 7.

kꜣ bull, Sin. B 119; Urk. IV, 1020, 11; varr. 238, 8; Bersh. I, 18; Sin. B 118.

kꜣt vagina, P. Kah. 6, 22; Eb. 65, 21; var. Pr. 10, 12.

kꜣt work, construction, Urk. IV, 57, 11; 163, 3; kꜣt sḫt 'the w. of the field', 1161, 4; kꜣt ꜥwy 'handiwork', 173, 17; m kꜣwt mꜣwt 'in new w.', 182, 15; imy-r kꜣ(w)t 'overseer of works', Sin. B 303; Urk. IV, 52, 17; ḫrp kꜣwt 'controller of w.', 97, 2; craft, profession: kꜣt gs 'the c. of the leather-workers', Urk. I, 22, 8; kꜣt m ꜥḥꜣ 'p. as warrior', Les. 83, 2-3; kꜣt nbt nt Mntw 'all the c. of Mont' = of warfare, Urk. IV, 1279, 11. Varr. Leb. 62; RB 113, 16; Urk. IV, 131, 6; 1795, 18; 173, 17.

kꜣt-šwt a lichen (?), JEA 20, 46.

kꜣi boat of Nubian type, Les. 84, 21; 85, 1.

kꜣw sycomore figs, Sh. S. 49; var. Eb. 102, 2. Cf. JEA 16, 69, n. 2.

kꜣwty (1) builder's workman: (2) porter, var. , AEO I, 59*.

k3p burn incense, Pyr. 1017 ( ); TR 20,10; cense gods, Pyr. 1718 ( ); fumigate patient, P. Kah. 5, 3.4 ( ).

k3p hut, Sh. S. 43; hide of fowler, Caminos, Lit. Frag. pp. 10.13; var. pl. 2, 2, 6.

k3pwt covers: ——pt 'c. of the sky' = clouds, ZÄS 57, 32; var. TR 16, 7.

k3pt linen cover of jar, JEA 22, 38.

k3p bandage (n.), loc. cit.

k3p vb. cover; roof over; hide o'self, take cover, loc. cit.; droop, of eyebrows, P. Ed. Smith, 199.

k3p royal nursery: 'child of the n.', Urk. IV, 899, 15; 901, 16; 997, 6 ( ); var. Top. Cat. 38, No. 241. Cf. Helck, 34; JEA 24, 57, n. 1; k3p št3 'secret chamber (?)', Urk. IV, 1815, 5.

k3pw roof, Urk. IV, 23, 15; 841, 17; abbr. 842, 6.

k3pw crocodile, Pr. 9, 3.

k3pw bittern, JEA 35, pl. 2, 15; p. 18.

k3p3p cover (vb.), ZÄS 57, 32.

k3mw vineyard, orchard, AEO II, 215*; var. Kamosĕ, 11.

k3m(w) vintner, Urk. IV, 523, 16; var. 1365, 20. Cf. AEO I, 97*.

k3mw grape-harvest, Sh. T. S. III, 30.

k3nw vineyard, varr. , , Edel, §123.

k3ny vintner, BH I, 29 ( ); Peas. B1, 263.

k3r shrine, Les. 71, 6; TR 21, 4 (dets.); varr. Urk. IV, 445, 3; 168, 15; 130, 16.

k3ry gardener, AEO I, 96*.

k3hs be harsh, overbearing, Peas. B1, 213-4; Pr. 1, 12 (dets.); cf. JEA 37, 109-10.

K3š Cush in Nubia, var. , older , , Kush, 6, 39.

k3k3 bush (?), brush (?), JEA 29, 10, n. b.

ki cry out, ZÄS 58, 17*; Hatnub, 14, 4; 22, 8.

kit shout of acclaim, Pyr. 197; varr. 737; CT I, 185; Urk. IV, 222, 15.

ky other, another, f. , m. pl. ; wꜥ ... ky, ky ... ky 'one ... other'; , var. , 'others', Gr. § 98.

ky monkey, Sh. S. 165.

Kbn n. loc. Byblos, var. , ZÄS 45, 7; AEO I, 150*; Urk. IV, 1344, 5.

kbnt seagoing ship, Urk. I, 134, 15; Hamm. 114, 10; varr. Urk. IV, 323, 2; 707, 12.

kf uncover, unclothe; doff clothes; strip, deprive, despoil GNS 55; strip away, of sail, Peas. B1, 56; clear, of sky, Leb. 139; Siut, pl. 13, 10; gather flowers, Urk. IV, 1383, 16. Varr. , GNS 55; RB 117, 4; , , Urk. IV, 1383, 16; 1509, 15.

kft gash, P. Ed. Smith, 82.

kft (kf(3)t ?) trustworthiness (?), Peas. B2, 86.

kf3 flow forth, M. u. K. 3, 4; 5, 1; var. 1, 2.

kf3 hinder-parts of bird, M. u. K. 4, 1; bottom of jar, Eb. 54, 22; base of abscess, 109, 20.

, varr. of kf 'uncover'.

kf3 be discreet, Merikarēꜥ, 64; kf3 ib 'trustworthy', Pr. 8, 6 (); Adm. 2, 9; kf3 ib ḥr 'trust in', Pr. 13, 8.

kf(3)t: m —— 'indeed', Urk. IV, 1344, 9. 11.

kfꜥ vb. make captures, Urk. IV, 35, 17; 891, 8 (dets.); 893, 8 (det.); make requisition, 2147, 12; 2154, 14 (dets.): n. booty, captures, 711, 4. 10; 895, 8.

kfꜥ shoot at (?) target, Urk. IV, 1281, 1.

kfꜥw warrior, Urk. IV, 898, 17; var. 899, 9.

var. of kf3 'flow forth'.

Kftyw n. loc. Crete (?), var. , AEO I, 203*.

kftiw class of seagoing ships, Urk. IV, 707, 12.

km black, ZÄS 57, 10*; BD 231, 11 (det.); 232, 1; 426, 4; Hymnen, 11, 4; varr. Urk. IV, 168, 7; 1098, 8.

Kmt n. loc. the Black Land, Egypt, Sin. B 26. 32. 34; varr. B 165; RB 59, 3.

Kmt coll. Egyptians, P. Kah. 3, 3. 5.

Km-wr n. loc. Bitter Lakes region, Gauthier, Dict. géogr. V, 202.

kmt a jar, Urk. IV, 640, 16.

km vb. total up to, amount to, Sh. S. 127; Rhind, 22; Merikarēʿ, 101; complete, Sh. S. 118; RB 113, 15; Urk. IV, 58, 13; put an end to, Adm. 14, 2; BD 469, 9; pay, n 'to', P. Kah. 16, 24 ff.; 23, 10. 11 (): n. completion: m km n ꜣt 'in the twinkling of an eye' (lit. 'in the c. of a moment'), RB 64, 12; m km n wnwt 'in the space of an hour', 57, 5; profit, JEA 42, 33 (29); duty, Urk. IV, 973, 17.

kmt completion, M. u. K. vs. 3, 3; final account (?), P. Kah. 31, 1 ().

kmyt conclusion of book, Ch. B. Text, p. 43, n. 7.

kmy(t) fem. coll. herd of cattle, Urk. IV, 1373, 3.

knt dislike (?) of s'one, Pr. 8, 9.

kni vb. be sullen (?), BD 254, 3; Urk. IV, 132, 6 (det.): n. sullenness (?), Bersh. II, 13, 25 (det.).

Knʿnw Canaanites, Urk. IV, 1305, 7.

knm wrap, m 'in', Pyr. 1197; cf. ZÄS 58, 157.

knmt darkness, BD 257, 1.

knmtyw 'they who dwell in darkness', name of a conquered people, Urk. IV, 896, 14; in sing. ep. of a deity, BD 257, 1.

knḥ dark, Urk. IV, 2097, 2.

knḥw darkness, BD 446, 1; 448, 1.

kns pubic region (?), Barns, Ram. p. 25.

krp scrape out inscription, Amarna, V, 26, 24.

khꜣ raise the voice, CT I, 226 (also det.); utter a bellow, TR 1, 39 (det.);

rage furiously, JEA 30,19.

khb harm s'one, M.u.K. vs.6,5; be violent; roar, howl, JEA 30,19.

kḥkḥ become old, JEA 13,187; šsp kḥkḥ 'attain old age', 33,26.

kḥkḥt hacking of cough, JEA 13,187-8.

ks pose (?): ks n sḳr wꜥt(y) 'the p. of striking down a captive', Louvre C14,10.

ksi vb. 3 inf. bend down, Westc. 4,1; Adm. p.104 (dets.); bow down, Pyr. 57; be prostrate, of foe, Pyr. 1632.

ksw bowings, Pyr. 57; m ksw 'bowing', Les. 82,2 (det.); RB 110,13 ( ); Urk. IV, 809,8 ( ); 1098,15; šsp ksw 'crouch down', GNS 18.

ksm defy, browbeat, ZÄS 60,67; Meir, I, 27, n.3; JEA 29,9, n.c; dets. Caminos, Lit. Frag. pl. 3,3,6; profane temple, JEA, loc. cit.

kk be dark, BD 458,9; of child about to be born, Westc. 10,23.

kkw darkness, M.u.K. 1,9; RB 111,8 ( ); BD 174,15; kk(w) 'twilight', Urk. IV, 248,17; CT I, 161 (det.); BD 85,5.

kt (< ktt) pettiness, Urk. IV, 61,12; var. 1815,15.

ktwt cauldrons, Urk. V, 61,4.

ktkt quiet: m ktkt 'quietly', RB 123,14-15.

ktkt quiver (vb.), Amarna, VI, 15,6; Urk. IV, 2013,11.

ktt small, trifling, a trifle: sꜣt ktt 'a s. daughter', Sh. S. 129; ꜣt ktt 'a tr. moment', Pr. 1,4; nh n ktt 'a mere trifle', 1,6; wr ktt 'great and small', 7,4; sim. Urk. IV, 1139,16; hrw ktw 'the day is short', RB 113,14.

ktt girl, Westc. 12,22.

kṯn charioteer, var. , AEO I, 28*.

gꜣw vb. 3 inf. intrans. be narrow, constricted, Eb. 102,10; TR 23,88 (dets.); BD 104,13; 111,5; languish, Peas. B1,100; lack, be lacking, Urk. VII, 3,1; Les. 86,12: trans.

deprive, m 'of', Urk. IV, 613, 13 (det. ); 767, 12 (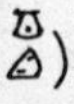).

 g3w lack: n 'through l. of', Gr. §178; dets.  Adm. 11, 11.

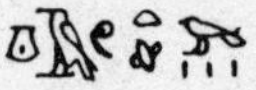 g3wt lack, want (n.), GAS 86; var.  Pr. 13, 7.

 g3wt dues, tribute, Urk. IV, 334, 9; var.  138, 6.

 var. of gb3 'arm'.

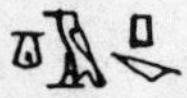 g3p lance (?) an infection, P. Kah. 7, 60.

 var. of gf 'monkey'.

 g3ḥ be weary, BD 138, 14; var.  215, 3.

 g3g3 cackle, Westc. 8, 23.

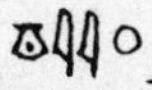 gy an offering-loaf, Urk. IV, 1953, 3.

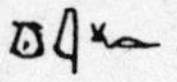 var. of gf 'monkey'.

 gw class of bull, GNS 17.

 see g3wt 'dues' above.

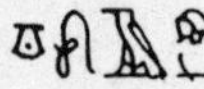 gw3 pull tight, D. el Geb. I, 4; Urk. V, 176, 5; be choked, TR 26, 2; gw3 r 'beseige' city, P. Ed. Smith, 240.

 gw3w3 strangle-hold, Urk. IV, 7, 4; var. 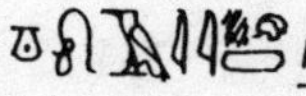 RB 59, 6.

 gw3t chest, P. Kah. 19, 17.

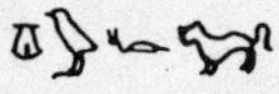 gwf var. of gf 'monkey'.

 gwš become askew, bent, twisted; turn away, abandon, var. dets. , , , , JEA 41, 91 (14); 42, 19.

 gwg shout (?), n 'at', Urk. IV, 1104, 12.

 gb goose, Gr. p. 471, G 38.

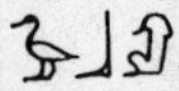 Gb n. div. the earth-god Gēb, var. 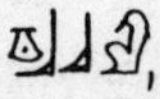, loc. cit.

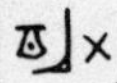 gb deficiency, Hamm. 87, 9; 113, 14 (); deprivation, Urk. IV, 2146, 2 (dets. ).

 gb3 arm, P. Ed. Smith, 357; varr. 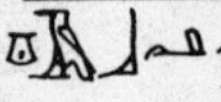 Eb. 37, 11;  Urk. IV, 414, 17.

 gb3 side of room, Westc. 8, 18. 19.

gbb earth, Bull. 30, 180.

gbgb be lame, Eb. 77, 4; M. u. K. 5, 1 (dets.): trans. fell enemy, Pyr. 678 ( ); gbgbw 'headlong', of flight, Urk. IV, 711, 1.

gbgbyt: m ——— 'headlong', of flight, Urk. IV, 658, 1; 'prostrate', RB 59, 8; Urk. IV, 1698, 10 ( ).

Gbtyw n. loc. Koptos, var. , Bull. 30, 181; AEO II, 28*.

gp: —— n mw 'cloudburst', Merikarē', 73; Piankhi, 93. Cf. igp.

gf long-tailed monkey, Urk. IV, 1120, 17; BH II, 6; cf. Caminos, L.-Eg. Misc. 442; varr. Bersh. II, 11; Sh. S. 165; Urk. IV, 949, 1.

gfn rebuff, Pt. (L II), 4, 14; Urk. IV, 1139, 16; var. Urk. VII, 5, 3.

gmt black ibis, Gr. p. 470, G 28; var. pl. Adm. 2, 8.

gmi vb. 3 inf. find, Sin. R 19; Sh. S. 47; Peas. R 38; Westc. 5, 1; use o's hand, RB 61, 12; be able to do s'thing, Sm. 1, 25; 2, 14; control land, JEA 31, 33, n. 1; 'found destroyed', BH I, 26, 162; var. Eb. 18, 1; cf. JEA 39, 20; gm ts 'apt of phrase', Urk. IV, 47, 1; 1817, 9.

gmȝ temple of head, P. Ed. Smith, 276.

gmw mourning, Sin. R 9; cf. GNS 10.153.

gmw weakness (?), Sm. 8, 17; P. Kah. 7, 19.

gmwt weakness, BD 29, 11-12.

gmḥ catch sight of, espy, Sin. B 25; Adm. 7, 12; 8, 5; look, n 'at', Urk. IV, 364, 15; r 'at', Pr. 6, 11; sti m gmḥ ʿšȝ 'pierce (s'one) with much staring', Pr. 6, 11-7, 1; gmḥ wȝ 'far-sighted', 'perspicaceous', Barns, Ram. p. 5.

gmḥt candle, Siut, pl. 8, 305; var. pl. 7, 296.

gmḥt plaited hair, Urk. IV, 200, 16.

gmḥsw hawk, Pyr. 280; varr. Urk. IV, 943, 3; Pyr. 1048.

gmgm smash boxes, Adm. 3, 5 (dets.); ink-wells, TR 10, 9; tear up books, TR 9, 3 ( ); break, of trees, Sh. S. 59.

gn stand for ritual bowl, Urk. IV, 1296, 5.

gnw branches (?) of trees, Adm. 4, 14.

gnwt records, annals, Urk. IV, 86, 3; varr. 166, 3; 500, 13; 358, 15; Gr. p. 514, T19.

gnwty sculptor, AEO I, 66*; var. Gr. loc. cit.

gnbtw a foreign people from Pwenet, Urk. IV, 695, 6.

var. of gfn 'rebuff'.

gnn vb. 2 gem. be weak, Sm. 4, 14; Urk. IV, 502, 8; 1280, 2; be soft, Eb. 105, 2; Sm. 6, 13. Var. Urk. IV, 943, 4.

gnnwt weakness (?), Adm. 5, 13.

gnnwy suet (?), COA III, pl. 93, 234; varr. 235; 236; cf. p. 174.

gnḥ mount poles m 'in' gold, Westc. 7, 13.

gnḥt star, Urk. VIII, 3, 15; CT I, 262.

gnḳ serve, n s'one, Urk. IV, 86, 9.

var. of grg 'falsehood'.

grt encl. part. moreover, now; adv. either, varr. Gr. § 255.

gr vb. be silent, Pr. 4, 4; 11, 9; be quiet, Les. 72, 12; be still, Westc. 5, 17. 18; cease, desist, m 'from', Adm. 6, 1; Les. 84, 2. 3: n. silence, Pr. 5, 14; Urk. IV, 1543, 16.

grw the silent man, Peas. B1, 315; Pr. 1, 1; Hatnub, 49, 7; var. Peas. B1, 298.

grw adv. also; after negatives, further, any more, varr. Gr. § 205, 1.

grḥ vb. complete, finish off work, JEA 4, 137; be satisfied with a bargain, ZÄS 60, 72: n. end, cessation, Adm. 5, 14.

grḥ night, Peas. B1, 202; Urk. IV, 1077, 1; RB 113, 15.

grg vb. snare wildfowl, Caminos, Lit. Frag. pl. 1, 2, 1; 3, 4, 8; hunt, GNS 42: n. hunter, loc. cit.

grgt catch of fish, GNS 42.

grg falsehood, lie, Peas. B1, 132. 183. 241; dets. B1, 67; Urk. IV, 65, 12; varr.

 Urk. IV, 48,14; 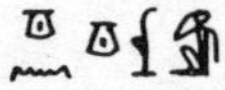 Les. 80,3.

 grgy liar, P. Ram. II, vs. 2,5; Urk. IV, 971,14; 1078,16.

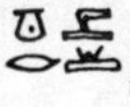 grg vb. trans. found a land, Urk. IV, 95,16; establish a house, household, JEA 16,198; L. to D. n. on VI, 5; people a place, Urk. IV, 172,5; RB 57,13; furnish waste lands with vegetation, Peas. B1,142; settle crown on king's head, Urk. IV, 292,16 (det. ); provide for tomorrow, Peas. B1,183; set in order, JEA 39, pl. 2, 22.24; Merikarē̆ 49; Adm. 5,4: intrans. be ready, Adm. 2,2; grg ib r 'r. to do' s'thing, Bersh. II, 13, 24; ḥ3ty·i grg ḥr š3[t]·n·f 'my heart is set on what he has ordained', Urk. IV, 350,11; grg ḥr 'alert (?)', Siut, pl. 19,50; put o's trust, ḥr 'in', Adm. p. 107; make preparation, Urk. IV, 656,1. Var.  Leyd. V 88.

 var. of g3ḥ 'be weary'.

 gḥs gazelle, D el B. 140; Eb. 98,7 (dets. 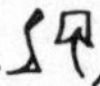); var. 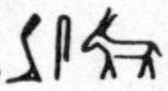 Urk. IV, 741,12; fem. gḥst, RB 76-7.

 gs (1) side, CT I, 292; Sh. S. 85; Urk. IV, 262,12; border of land, Sin. R 17; r-gs 'beside', 'in the presence of', Gr. §178; (i)r-gswy 'beside', Pyr. 477.940.992; ḥr-gs 'beside', 'in the presence of', Gr. §178; ḥr-gswy 'beside', RB 52,10; (r)di ḥr gs (a) 'put (o'self) on (o's) side', BD 402, 8-9; (b) 'lay low' an enemy, Urk. IV, 7,6; 84,7; (c) 'incline to one side', of balance, Peas. B1,149; of norm of speech, B1,98; (d) 'show partiality', of judge, B1,269; Urk IV, 1082,13: (2) half, Gr. §265; ½-aroura, P. Wilbour, 60. Var. 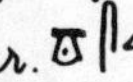 Pyr. 385.

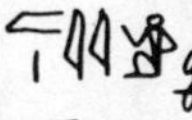 gsy neighbour, Sin. B 151-2.

 gs-pr administrative district (?), Urk. I, 101,12; 102,6; IV, 1114,13 (det. ); Les. 68,3; temple (?), Sh. S. 141.

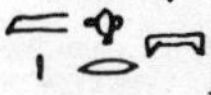 gs-ḥry top, upper part, Urk. IV, 362,12; Eb. 70,4; 94,3.

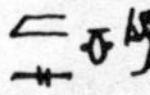 gs anoint s'one, m 'with' oil; smear on unguent, var. 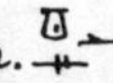, GNS 112.

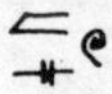 gsw ointment, Eb. 25,11 ff.

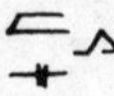 gsi vb. 3 inf. run: wn gs pḥrt 'hasten and r. a course', RB 114,7.

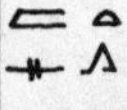 gst (1) speed, Urk. IV, 617, 15: (2) run, course: it gst 'take o's run' = run o's course, Pyr. 1167 (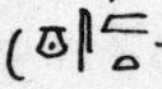); Urk. IV, 580, 2; D. el B. 97.

 gs3 tilt, Peas. B1, 92. 96. 162-3; favour s'one, with n, Pr. 13, 4 (det. ); gs3 n ḥrw 'sink down', Sm. 10, 21; cf. P. Ed. Smith, 331.

 gs3 favourite (n.), Urk. VII, 59, 17; 63, 7.

 Gs3 n. loc. Apollonopolis (Ḳûs), varr. , 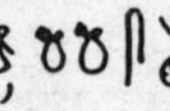, Bull. 30, 181; AEO II, 27*.

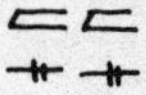 gsgs regulate, RB 113, 15.

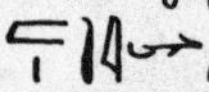 gsty scribe's palette, var. 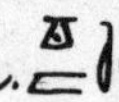, Gr. p. 542, Aa 13;  Urk. IV, 151, 14; 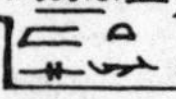 503, 7.

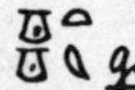 ggt kidney (?), Gr. p. 526, V 33; COA III, p. 173 (13).

 ggwy stare, Urk. IV, 1303, 7; varr.  1509, 9;  1543, 14; infin.  19, 4. Cf. ZÄS 81, 14.

 gtḥ be tired: m ir gtḥ m ˁḏ3 'Don't sham tired!', Paheri, 7 (3rd register).

 var. of suff. pron. 2 f. sg. ṯ.

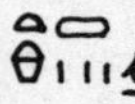 t bread, Peas. R 6; Pr. 6, 8; RB 119, 2; loaf, Westc. 4, 13; Peas. B1, 84; 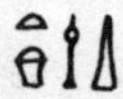 t-ḥd 'white bread', conical loaf used in offerings, Siut, pl. 6, 275; var. det. 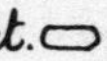 277. Abbr.  in names of other ritual loaves, e.g. 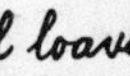 t-(i)m(y)-t3, 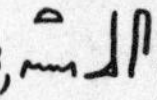 t-nbs, etc., BH I, 17. Varr.  Sin. B 151;  CT I, 65.

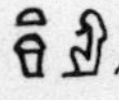 wtg. of Ḏḥwty 'Thoth'.

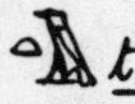 t3 demonstr. and def. art. f. sg. this, the, Gr. §§ 110-2; for 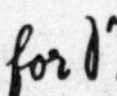 'she of', § 111, Obs.

 t3y.i poss. adj. f. sg. my; sim. t3y.k, t3y.f, etc., Gr. § 113, 1.

 t3 earth (opposed to sky, other world), Sh. S. 29; Urk. IV, 15, 13; 66, 15; 67, 1; land (opposed to water), Peas. B1, 58; Urk. IV, 324, 11; in geographical sense, Sh. S. 11. 148; Sin. R 12; ground, Sh. S. 53; Westc. 7, 5; dual 'the Two Lands' = Egypt, passim; pl. 'flatlands' (opposed to ḫ3swt 'hill-countries'), Urk. IV, 343, 16; Sin. B 213.

T3-iḥw n. loc. Farafra Oasis, Gauthier, Dict. géogr. VI, 4.

t3-wr larboard, Urk. IV, 322, 4; V, 151, 6; varr. , , , Gr. p. 506, S22.

T3-wr n. loc. the Thinite nome, Urk. IV, 111, 13; varr. BM 614, 4; L. to D. V, 2, n.

T3-mri n. loc. Egypt, varr. , , GNS 81.

T3-mḥw n. loc. Lower Egypt, var. , ZÄS 44, 10.

T3-nḥs(y) n. loc. Negro-land, Urk. IV, 334, 9; 948, 15.

T3-nṯr n. loc. God's-land, often of Pwēnet, e.g. Urk. IV, 323, 14; 329, 2; 334, 6; but also of other regions, e.g. RB 58, 1; 61, 2.

t3-rd stairway, AEO II, 211*.

T3-sty n. loc. Nubia, see sty.

T3-šmꜥw n. loc. Upper Egypt, var. , Bull. 31, 126; JEA 21, 29, n. 7.

t3-tmw all men, M. u. K. vs. 5, 1; so also Urk. IV, 17, 5; 367, 17; 895, 13; in Les. 63, 6 and occur in successive ep.'s of Osiris as if distinct the one from the other. Cf. SDT 34.

T3-tmḥ n. loc. southern Libya, AEO I, 114*; var. Sin. R12.

T3-ṯnn n. div. Memphite earth-god, varr. , , etc., SDT 33.

T3-ḏsr the Sacred Land = necropolis, BD 383, 16; 479, 14; 482, 4; var. RB 110, 7.

t3 kiln, Ti, 84; var. P. Ram. III, B 7.

t3 hot, Leb. 47. 88; Eb. 36, 8; hot-tempered, Adm. 5, 3; BD 256, 2; t3 ib 'h. temper', Pr. 12, 3 (det.); so also t3 ht, 11, 5.

t3w heat, Eb. 32, 18; 36, 7; Adm. 11, 13 (dets.); var. M. u. K. 4, 8.

t3yt shroud, CT I, 188; varr. TR 22, 86; 22, 88.

t3yty the shrouded one, ep. of Osiris, BD 322, 2; title of vizier, Th. T. S. II, 17 ( ); O.K. Dav. Ptah. II, 28.

T3yt n. div. goddess of weaving, Sin. B 192; dets. TR 22, 85. Cf. GNS 69.

var. of t3-wr 'larboard'.

 t3mw worm(?), Peas. B1, 131 (fig. use); cf. JEA 9, 13, n. 2.

 t3ḥ mischief-maker, Merikarēʿ, 24; dets. 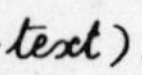 23 (M.-text).

 t3ḥt lees, dregs, GAS 58.

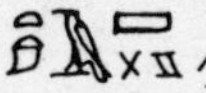 t3š boundary, Sin. B 71. 80; BH I, 25, 41; Les. 84, 5; varr.  Urk. IV, 7, 2; 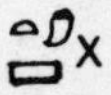 1277, 13; 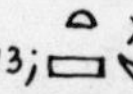 1744, 5.

 t(3)š fix the limits of, BD 27, 16.

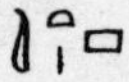 tit pestle(?), Gr. p. 520, U 33.

 tit an amulet, late var. , Gr. p. 508, (V 39).

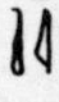 ti non-encl. part., var. , Gr. §§ 119, 4; 212; 243; 324.

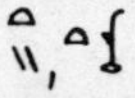 varr. of part. tr.

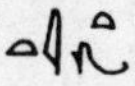 tit image, Urk. IV, 84, 17 (with det. ); 887, 2; form, shape, 157, 11; Th. T. S. IV, 20; figure, Urk. IV, 53, 17; design, 1074, 8; written sign, BH I, 26, 164 (dets.  pl.!); a text is collated ti(t) r ti(t) 's. by s.', Iouiya, pl. 33, 30. Varr. 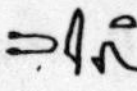 Urk. IV, 157, 11;  53, 17; 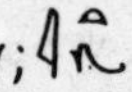 1319, 18; 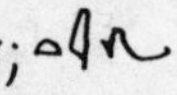 Iouiya, loc. cit.

 ti3 acute pain, Sm. 3, 9. 13; P. Kah. 5, 16; 6, 8.

 ti3 shriek, P. Kah. 6, 25.

 var. of ity 'sovereign'.

 tiw yes, Gr. § 258.

 see under tḥwy.

 tisw quarterstaff, Ken-amun, 18; var.  Urk. IV, 1344, 17.

 tisps a tree and its spice(?), Urk. IV, 329, 7; varr. 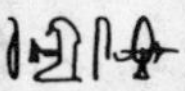 1375, 15; 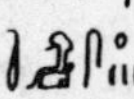 Sh. S. 163.

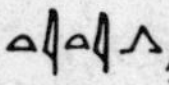 titi trample on foe, Sin. B 61; RB 56, 16; dets.  Urk. IV, 613, 1;  621, 9; [illegible] 1290, 15.

 tw (1) var. of dep. pron. tw: (2) indef. pron. one: (3) demonstr. this, that, cf. Gr. p. 599.

 tw.i pronom. comp. I, also tw.k, etc., Gr. § 124.

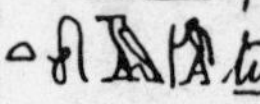 tw3 vb. intrans. lean, ḥr 'on', Pyr. 730. 816: trans. support, sustain, 1156. 1529; L. to D. I, 12 (n.); hold up, Siut, pl. 2, scene 2 (det. 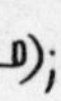); Les. 75, 9; set crown, m 'on' head, Urk. IV, 278, 6 (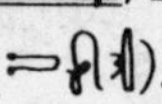).

twꜣ vb. put a claim, n 'on' s'one, Pr. 7,6; claim from s'one, Peas. B1, 299; appeal to s'one, B2,106 (det.): n. claim, Pr. 10,6; Les. 83,25 (dets.). Cf. JEA 9, 19, n. 8.

twꜣ poverty, Urk. IV, 1824, 12.

twꜣ(w) man of low station, inferior, GNS 47; var. Merikarēꜥ, 28.

twꜣwt one of the seven sacred oils, Siut, pl. 1, 32; var. BH I, 17.

twy demonstr. adj. f. sg. this, that, Gr. §§110-2.

twn (< ṯwn) rise, raise, JEA 12, 131.

twr reed, Eb. 55,16; var. Leb. 92.

twr vb. intrans. be clean, Urk. VII, 57,6; Hatnub, 23,2; Les. 71,11: trans. cleanse, GAS 76. varr. Les. 71,11; 65,15; Urk. IV, 752, 11; dets. BD 141, 15.

twr show respect to, with direct obj., Siut, pl. 4, 226; Urk. IV, 1162,15 ( ); with ḥr, Les. 68,23 ( ); Urk. IV, 20,13 ( ). See also tr 'respect'.

twt statue, Sin. B 307; Urk. IV, 378,2; 752,16; image, figure, V, 64, 9. 10; likeness, IV, 534,1. Abbr. 842,13. Various dets. are 46,2; 378,2; 537,15.

twt (1) like, n 'to', Sin. B 52; Peas. B1, 118; Urk. IV, 368,5: (2) suitable, fitting, Berlin Leather, 2,4 = GES 51, n. 4; TR 20,52 ( ); Urk. IV, 943,5; natural, n 'to', Peas. B1, 122: (3) fair, pleasing, CT I, 76 ( ); Urk. IV, 161,10 ( ); be pleased, Pr. 16,1: (4) assembled, united: smꜣ twt m r n ḥm.k 'joined and united in Your Majesty's person', Sin. B 272; a man twt m rmṯt 'who has people around him', P. Ch. B. V, vs. 2,7 = Ch. B. Text, 50, n. 4; mfkt twt n ḥr.k 'turquoise is heaped up before you', Piankhi, 108-9; niwt.f twt sy m iḥy 'his town was wholly in acclamation', Urk. IV, 1160,7; sim. 1200,2; be in accord, ḥnꜥ 'with', Leb. 40: (5) full, entire, complete: gs t(w)t 'the full half of', Urk. I, 105,1; ZÄS 57,7*;

(ỉ) sw t(wt) 'the full equivalent of', Pyr. 81; ỉw·k sbꜣ·t(ỉ), ỉw·k ḥmw·t(ỉ), ỉw·k twt·(tỉ) 'you are instructed, clever and complete', Peas. B1, 260-1; pr twt ꜥpr 'who went forth complete and equipped', Urk. IV, 1540, 11.

twtt likeness, Peas. B1, 261.

later var. of indep. pron. 2 m. sg. twt.

twtn rare pron. 2 pl. you, Gr. §43, Obs. 2.

var. of ṯbt 'sandal'.

tby pay, P. Boul. XVIII, 22, 15 = ZÄS 57, 8**.

tbt payment, reward, JEA 38, 19, n. 4.

tbn bone-marrow (?), Barns, Ram. p. 33.

tbtb hoist, Urk. IV, 658, 4; var. … 658, 7.

tp head, Urk. IV, 16, 8; Sin. B 193. 209; Westc. 8, 18; head (man), chief, Urk. I, 69, 2; Munich, 4, 7 = Gr. §468, 3; tip of toe, Sm. 4, 14; of flagstaff, Urk. IV, 56, 5; end of bone, Sm. 4, 8; example (math.), Rhind, 51. 62; the best of: 'gold of tpw ḫꜣswt the b. o. the lands', Urk. IV, 362, 12; 421, 13; 845, 15; sim. 339, 9; 428, 7; m tp n 'at the head of' an army, 7, 7 (…); r tp (n) 'into the presence of', var. r tp-ꜥ(n), Gr. §178; tp-m 'in front of', 'in the direction of', 'before' (of time), §179; tp-ỉm 'previously', §205, 2; m … tp-n 'from … to', ZÄS 60, 75. For ḥry-tp see p. 175.

tp person, in tp + numeral 'x p.'s', Les. 83, 4. 7; Peas. B2, 136; Urk. IV, 6, 15; tpw sḳrw-ꜥnḫ 'captive slaves', 70, 2.

tp financial principal (?), P. Kah. 13, 22, cf. Griff. Kah. p. 37. See also tpy-r.

tp upon, Gr. §173; … 'daily', RB 116, 11.

tpt uraeus, Urk. IV, 271, 17; 614, 5.

tpy being upon, principal, first, varr. …, …, Gr. §§ 80. 263. 264.

tp-ỉꜣt due time to do s'thing, Urk. IV, 1430, 14.

Tp-ỉḥw n. loc. Aphroditopolis (Atfiḥ), AEO II, 119*.

tp-ỉtrw: wỉꜣ —— 'sacred bark for the river', JEA 38, 21, n. 3.

tp-ꜥ before, of time, Gr. §181; r tp-ꜥ (n) 'into the presence of', §178.

tp-ꜥw(y) adj., usually pl., (a) of place, who are in front of, before, Pyr. 126; (b) of time, who had been before, former, Urk. I, 222, 17; IV, 28, 15 ( ); (c) of rank, who takes precedence of, JEA 32, 15 (sing.): n. predecessors, ancestors L. to D. X, 2, 2 ( ); Urk. I, 46, 10 ( ); IV, 76, 10.

tpt-ꜥ former state, Urk. IV, 1283, 8.

tp-wꜣt journey, JEA 38, 21, n. 3; beginning of reign, Turin 1447 = Gr. § 301.

tp-mꜣꜥ accompanying, escorting, JEA 27, 146.

tp-nfr a good beginning, Les. 83, 9; 86, 16; r tp-nfr 'successfully', 70, 2; 86, 14.

tp-r: t n — 'bread for the mouth', Pr. 6, 8.

tp(y)-r (1) utterance, Urk. IV, 959, 5; 974, 9 ( ): (2) financial principal (?), P. Kah. 13, 24. 37 ( ): (3) base of triangle, Griff. Kah. 37; radius of circle, P. math. Moscow, 18, 2.

tpt-r utterance, Les. 70, 9; 81, 6 ( ); Urk. IV, 165, 13; 322, 10.

tp-rꜥ-mḏ ten-day 'week', Urk. IV, 411, 10.

tp-rnpt: ḥbw.f ꜥꜣw nw — 'his great annual festivals', Urk. IV, 175, 13; ḫnt.f nt — 'his annual voyage', 308, 3. Distinct from tp-tr below.

tp-rsy the South, JEA 43, 6.

tp-rd instructions, regulations, Urk. IV, 58, 1; 97, 6 (det.); 421, 8; 1103, 14; Adm. 11, 4 ( ); duty, Urk. IV, 28, 10; governance, 255, 13.

tpt-rd task (?), Urk. IV, 74, 15; cf. Wb. V, 290, 6.

tp-ḥwt roof, AEO II, 216*.

tp-ḥr(y) master, Sin. B121.

tp-ḥsb reckoning, Urk. IV, 122, 5 ( ); correct method, Rhind, title; norm, standard of speech or conduct, Pr. 5, 7; 8, 5; Peas. B1, 98. 311. 325; rectitude, Peas. B1, 147-8. 274.

tp-ḫnt act of tyranny (?), Les. 82, 2.

tp-n-šsmt-ꜥ specification, Urk. IV, 1796, 17.

tp-šw destitution (?), JEA 32, pl. 6, 26.

to be read as tp-rsy, q.v.

tp(y)-tꜣ survivor, L. to D. IV, 4 (n.); var. Urk. IV, 446, 11; pl. tpyw-tꜣ 'who are on earth', L. to D. X, 2, 6; XI, 3.

tp-tr 'Beginning-of-the-Season' festival, JEA 38, pl. 1, 3; cf. p. 4, n. 12; ḥbw tp-tr 'calendar festivals', JEA 38, 21 with n. 2; ḥbyt nt tp-trw 'calendrical festival offerings', Urk. IV, 195, 4 ( ); 195, 8 ( ).

tp-dwꜣyt dawn, see under dwꜣyt 'morning'.

tpt fine oil, Sin. B 289; Urk. IV, 351, 17.

var. of tpr 'breathe'.

tpỉw ox (?), Urk. IV, 669, 9; var. 699, 12.

tpnn cummin, Eb. 2, 2; var. 5, 11; cf. Garten, 41. 148.

tpr breathe, Les. 68, 18; varr. Urk. IV, 482, 16; Neferḥotep, 36.

var. of tpḥt 'hole'.

tf demonstr. adj. f. sg. that (yonder), varr. , , Gr. §§ 110-2.

var. of ỉt(ỉ) 'father'.

tf saw, var. , JEA 41, 15.

tfỉ vb. 3 inf. leap (?), Leb. 34 (infin.).

Tfnt n. div. Tefênet, Urk. IV, 1675, 5; 1849, 10 (det.); var. BD 15, 5.

tfn orphan, Pyr. 317; Urk. IV, 972, 3. 9.

tmt sledge, BD 38, 14; var. 210, 12.

tm neg. vb., varr. , , , cf. Gr. p. 600.

tm perish, Pyr. 256 ( ); Pr. 5, 1; cease, Pyr. 1948.

tm close the mouth, Pyr. 230; Peas. B1, 286.

see under Ỉtmw 'Atum'.

tm be complete, in old perf. 'complete', 'entire', 'all', Gr. § 317: n. everything, the universe: nb tm 'Lord of All', ZÄS 54, 45; nnk tm 'to me belonged the u.', 54, 47; km3 tm 'creator of all' (det. ııı), RB 114, 2; in iw tr shm.k m tm in.‹i› n.k 'Pray have you power over everything which I have brought to you?', Urk. V, 172, 12–13.

tmw totality of men, everyone, BD 2, 1; Urk. IV, 449, 14; varr. 1817, 7; 967, 16. For 'all men', see p. 293.

tm in obscure title , var. , ZÄS 40, 96.

tm3 mat, varr. , Gr. p. 524, V 19. For the similarly written word for 'cadaster (?)' see under tm3.

tm3yt mat, P. Kah. 19, 15; varr. Urk. IV, 1136, 16; Caminos, Lit. Frag. pl. 10, 3, 2.

see under Tmḥ 'Libyan'.

tms turn the face, r 'to' s'one, Urk. IV, 971, 4.

see under tms.

tmsw panelling, ZÄS 68, 12.

tn (1) demonstr. adj. 2 f. sg. this, var. , Gr. §§ 110–2: (2) var. of dep. pron. tn f. sg.

tn var. of pron 2 pl. tn.

, , see under tn, tnw.

tnỉ vb. grow old, Sin. B 190; Urk. IV, 10, 6; Adm. 16, 1 (dets.): n. old age, Sin. B 258; Westc. 7, 7; Pr. 4, 2; Urk. IV, 64, 9. Var. P. Kah. 11, 19.

tnỉ external signs of old age, Sm. 22, 9.

tnỉ old man, elder, Urk. IV, 58, 1.

tnbḥ turn aside, swerve, shrink, r 'from', GAS 67. 103–4; run at random, of cattle, Adm. 9, 2. In Peas. B1, 97. 161 the det. is an unidentified quadruped.

tnm turn aside, Urk. IV, 363, 13; go astray, Sin. B 96 (det.); err, Peas. B1, 131. 188; deflect, of balance, B1, 148 (det.); be confused, of roads, JEA 22, 136 (7, 8). Var. Urk. IV, 445, 7.

tnmw darkness, gloom, var. dets. , , CT II, 4. 6.

tnmw beer, JEA 13, 189.

var. of tnnt a Memphite sanctuary.

tnt spur-winged plover, JEA 35, pl. 2 and p. 16.

tr time, Sin. R 20; B 12; Urk. IV, 384, 9; season, Les. 86, 3. 4; RB 61, 3; 114, 10; r tr nb 'at all t.'s', Urk. IV, 343, 13; RB 62, 8; so also r trwy (dual), 64, 6; Urk. IV, 1603, 10; m tr nb m nw.f 'at every s. in its time', 1198, 6; r tr r tr.f 'from s. to s.', 1198, 7. Varr. sg. RB 117, 6; JEA 16, pl. 17, M; Les. 86, 4; dual RB 64, 6; Urk. IV, 1603, 10; 430, 17; pl. 834, 10; RB 114, 10; 61, 3. For 'seasonal work' see p. 33; for 'festival', see p. 298.

tr encl. part. forsooth, pray, varr. , , Gr. §256.

tr respect s'one, Urk. IV, 970, 13; greet respectfully, Sin. B 11 ( ); worship god, Merikarēʿ, 112; without obj. show respect, Siut, pl. 19, 28 ( ).

tryt respect (n.), Urk. IV, 1532, 13; var. 1532, 12.

see sdfꜣ-tryt 'oath of allegiance'.

var. of trt 'willow'.

var. of twr 'reed'.

thi vb. 3 inf. intrans. go astray, Merikarēʿ, 11 (restd.); of 'straying' pains, Eb. 40, 6 ( ); transgress, Merikarēʿ, 71. 72; BD 255, 12 ( ); trespass, r 'on' a place, JEA 2, pl. 3, B 1; attack, with r, Urk. IV, 1302, 10 ( ); err, 1021, 10; th ib 'misguided', Peas. B 1, 189; ib th 'the heart is astray', as symptom, Eb. 102, 5.

trans. lead astray, mislead, Sin. B 148. 202; Leb. 11; overstep path, Pr. 1, 3; Merikarēʿ, 52; disobey, Les. 68, 22; Pr. 5, 8; 7, 12; Urk. IV, 974, 4; impugn o's character, 547, 11; falsify (?) account, BM 614, 9 ( ); neglect appointed dates, RB 117, 7; reject petitions, Pr. 9, 6; violate corpse, JEA 2, pl. 2, 6.

thw transgressor, Peas. B 1, 237; var. Urk. IV, 1081, 4.

thm perforate, penetrate, P. Ed. Smith, 125-6; incite (?), JEA 39, 5, n. 4; destroy (?), Urk. IV, 1661, 4 (det.); undertake works, 1962, 14; drive cattle, P. d'Orbiney,

1,9; knock on door, P. Ch. B. I, rt. 17,8.

thm perforation, puncture, abbr., P. Ed. Smith, 125-6.

thr a Syrian warrior, Urk. IV, 686,5.

thwy pea, var., JEA 21,38.

th plummet of balance, Peas. B1,96; Les. 69,19; RB 117,3; det. Urk. IV, 453,17.

thi vb. 3 inf. be drunk, Peas. B1,125; Urk. IV, 688,15; 916,15; dets. Adm. 13,13; drink deep, Urk. IV, 1591,18 (det.).

tht drunkenness, Paheri, 7.

thw drunkard, Pr. 1,9.

thy the second month, Urk. IV, 44,7.

thb immerse; irrigate, GAS 75.

thn n. injury to eye, Eb. 56,6 (det.); 57,8; vb. injure eye, 60,10.

thn obelisk, Urk. IV, 56,11; 366,13; 425,16; abbr. 590,14.

thth disorder hair, Urk. V, 87,4; Herdsm. 25 (det.); crumple papers, TR 7,3 (det.).

tši vb. 3 inf. be absent, r 'from', Urk. IV, 32,10; 892,9; r-gs 'from the presence of', 603,10; be missing, 98,9 (); 912,4; m 'from', 1660,6 (); r 'from', Peas. B1,179 (); desist, Urk. IV, 1452,11; hr 'from' action, Les. 83,13 (); also incorrectly for t3š 'fix the limits of', BD 27,16.

tšw deserter, Urk. IV, 21,14.

var. of t3š 'boundary'.

tš spit out (?), Urk. IV, 1410,11.

tš smash heads; grind corn, GNS 34; split wood, RB 64,7; Urk. IV, 1321,17. Var. Sin. B 55.

tšb smash, Sin. R 80. Possibly corruption of tš above.

tštš crush, Eb. 69,12.

tk3 n. torch, taper, Siut, pl. 8,305; CT I, 262; Urk. IV, 772,2.6; flame, P. Kah. 6,5;

Urk. IV, 495, 6: vb. illumine, Hamm. 114, 5; Urk. IV, 1819, 14. Var. CT loc. cit.

tk3w rite of torch-lighting, Hatnub, 22, 4; Bersh. II, 13, 25.

tkn be near, Urk. IV, 47, 4; m 'to' s'one, 1090, 6; Pr. 14, 1.7; n 'to' a place, Urk. IV, 1110, 15; approach, draw near, without obj., Leb. 71; Peas. B1, 145; with direct obj., Sin. B170; Les. 81, 17; Urk. IV, 616, 10; 1213, 17; with m + obj., Pr. 9, 9; Adm. 2, 6; Urk. IV, 984, 4; attack, r s'one, BD 438, 5; border, m 'on', of situation, Herdsm. 2; st tknt 'environment (?)', Pr. 14, 3-4.

tknw neighbours, Pt. (L I), 97.

tkr opponent, Siut, pl. 4, 230.

tks pierce, Urk. VII, 3, 13; cf. ZÄS 45, 131.

tkk vb. 2 gem. violate frontier, Urk. IV, 556, 2; attack s'one, Adm. p. 102; Urk. IV, 1281, 19.

tkkw attackers, Urk. IV, 614, 10.

, varr. of twt 'full', 'entire'.

ṯ suff. pron. 2 f. sg. thou, thee, thy, later , Gr. §34.

ṯt table, var. , JEA 24, 171. 179.

ṯt board, woodwork, JEA 24, 171.

ṯt coll. staff; gang; partisans, varr. , , JEA 24, 170-1. 179.

ṯ3 fledgling, M. u. K. vs. 2, 2; Amarna, VI, 27, 7 (); fig. for 'child', CT I, 167; Caminos, Lit. Frag. pl. 18, 2 (det.).

ṯ3 pellet, Giza, III, 103; pl. [ooo] Urk. IV, 1584, 5.

ṯ3: ___ ib 'able (?)', Urk. IV, 970, 4.

ṯ3w vb. 3 inf. take up, seize, snatch, GNS 36; don garment, RB 115, 7 (dets.); rob, steal, Pr. 13, 12; RB 118, 2; shave (?), GNS 111; harbour enemies, Les. 98, 10. Varr. Pr. 13, 12; Urk. IV, 1279, 18; 1282, 17.

ṯ3wt theft, Peas. B1, 122; P. Kah. 18, 1; a gathering up of things, Pr. 10, 3.

ṯ3w bearer: ——— 'standard-b.', var. , JEA 24, 13; 39, 45; 'fan-b.', Amarna, I, 30; 'weapon-b.', Urk. IV, 90, 17; 'sculptor', var. , AEO I, 71*.

ṯ3y male, man, Sin. B132; Leb. 99; Herdsm. 14; Eb. 26, 1; Urk. IV, 695, 12; var. JEA 16, 20.

ṯ3y (?) bull-calf, Urk. IV, 171, 13. Or should k3 be read?

ṯ3w book, Urk. IV, 1089, 7; var. Sm. 2, 17.

ṯ3w wind, Sin. B234; Leb. 134; RB 113, 4 (abbr.); air, Les. 68, 18 (det.); RB 111, 6; Urk. IV, 1280, 3; breath, Sin. B236. 275; Peas. B1, 232; Urk. IV, 662, 10; irf pt tn ṯ3w 'the weather is windy', Urk. V, 156, 4. For f3i ṯ3w see under f3i.

var. of Ṯ3-wr 'the Thinite nome'.

Ṯ3w-wr n. loc. an outlying district of Egypt (?), L. to D. V, 2, n.

ṯ3wt sail (?) (n.), Urk. V, 156, 15.

ṯ3b a vessel, Urk. IV, 22, 13; 636, 1; 828, 5.

ṯ3bt loan, var. , L. to D. II, 5, n.

ṯ3m foreskin, BH I, 26, 185; TR 55, 9.

ṯ3m cloak, M. u. K. 6, 7; swaddling-clothes, 6, 1; bandage, Caminos, Lit. Frag. pl. 12, 3.

ṯ3m veil (vb): ——— ḥr 'v. the face' = show indulgence, n 'to' Sh. S. 19; RB 119, 13; Siut, pl. 11, 14 (det.); P. Ram. II, vs. 1, 8; 2, 5.

ṯ3r make fast, GES 5, n. 6; fasten, ḥr 'on' prey, Urk. IV, 84, 12 (dets.); take possession of his lordship (nbt) by king at his accession, Urk. IV, 896, 10 ().

ṯ3rt cabin, ZÄS 68, 21; entrenched camp, T. Carn. 11.

ṯ3ty vizier, varr. , , AEO I, 19*; viziership, GNS 89.

ṯit dais, Urk. IV, 2059, 14; var. 2059, 12.

 var. of ṯf 'saw'.

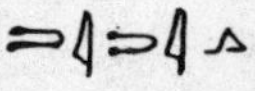 ṯỉṯỉ trot, Urk. IV, 1282, 11; cf. Caminos, L-Eg. Misc. p. 602.

 ṯw dep. pron. 2 m. sg. thou, thee, later 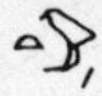, Gr. §43.

 var. of ṯỉt 'dais'.

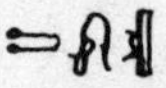 var. of ṯwꜣ 'support'.

 ṯwn gore with horn; stick, m 'into', var. det. 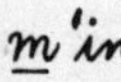, ZÄS 58, 38; 43, 74. See also ṯwn 'rise'.

 ṯwt indep. pron. 2 m. sg. thou, later , Gr. §64, with Obs.

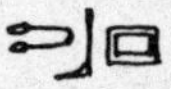 ṯb crate, Meir, III, p. 21, n. 5.

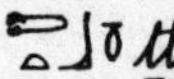 ṯbt vase, Urk. IV, 666, 1.

 ṯbw sole of foot, Pyr. 681; var.  Urk. IV, 1952, 5 (dual).

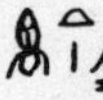 ṯbwt sandal, Gr. p. 507, S 33; sole, Sm. 4, 15. Varr. sg. 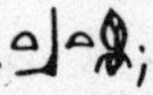; Urk. IV, 18, 14; dual 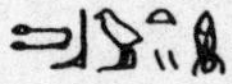 TR 23, 20; 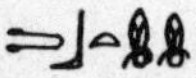 Urk. I, 102, 13; 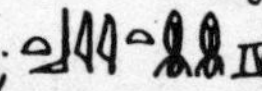 IV, 545, 15;  241, 16.

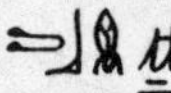 ṯbỉ vb. 3 inf. be shod, TR 23, 19; Urk. IV, 1952, 5 (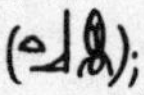); provide with sandals, JEA 38, pl. 9, ff = p. 19, n. 4.

 ṯbw sandal-maker, Gr. p. 507, S 33; AEO I, 68*.

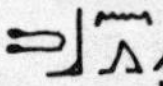 ṯbn be quick, Les. 82, 6.

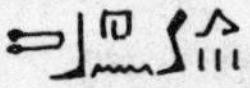 ṯbhn leap, prance, of animals, Amarna, VI, 16, 19; var. 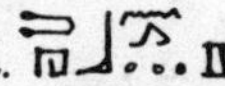 IV, 33 (Apy, 10).

 ṯpḥt cavern, Pyr. 268; Urk. IV, 545, 9 (); 919, 11 (det. 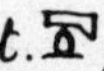); 1516, 6 (det. ); hole of snake, TR 19, 21; Adm. 7, 5; M. u. K. 3, 11.

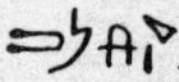 ṯmꜣ cadaster(?), varr. 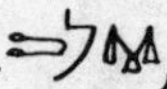, 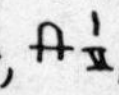, Gr. p. 524, V 19;  Urk. IV, 1113, 14.

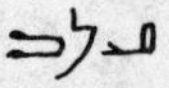 ṯmꜣ-ꜥ(wy) strong-armed, GNS 84; ṯmꜣ ꜥ.k 'your arm is s.', Urk. IV, 248, 4.

 Ṯmḥ Libyan, AEO I, 114*; varr. pl. 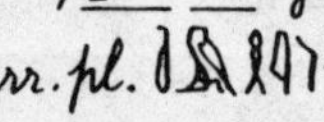 Sin. R 12; 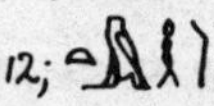 B 38.

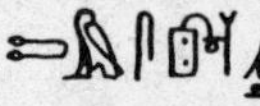 ṯms red, ruddy, Pyr. 911; P. Ed. Smith, 194; also violet, JEA 35, 75. Varr. 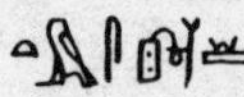 Sm. 3, 20; [illegible] 13, 20; [illegible] 3, 10.

[illegible] ṯms be besmeared, ZÄS 60, 73; abbr. [illegible] Urk. IV, 84, 9.

 ṯmsw injury, harm, Gr. p. 534, Y3.

 ṯn dep. pron. 2 f. sg. thou, thee, later , Gr. §43.

 ṯn suff. and dep. pron. 2 pl. you, your, later , Gr. §§34.43.

 ṯny suff. pron. 2 dual you two, your, early obsolete, Gr. §34.

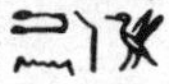 ṯn interrog. where?, whence?; r ṯn 'whither?', varr. 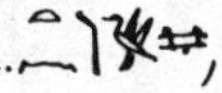, 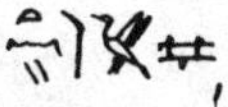, 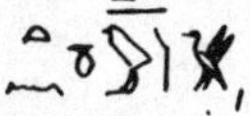, Gr. §503.

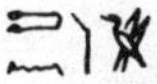 ṯni vb. 3 inf. lift up, TR 18, 27; promote, BH I, 25, 10 (dets. 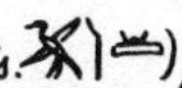); Les. 69, 16; Urk. IV, 1073, 9; distinguish, r 'from', Herdsm. 17; Adm. 4, 1; 11, 3; Urk. IV, 47, 15; be distinguished, of actions, Pr. 17, 2 (dets. ); of speech, Urk. IV, 121, 4; of birth, RB 114, 7; ṯni r 'more than', JEA 33, 28. Varr.  Herdsm. 14;  Urk. IV, 222, 16; 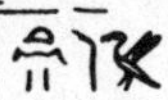 RB 114, 7.

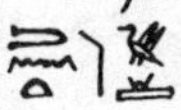 ṯnt difference nt x r y 'between x and y', Urk. IV, 164, 16; m-ṯnt-r 'more than', JEA 33, 28.

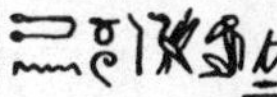 ṯnw distinction: do, say ḫt ṯnw 'things of d.', Pr. 9, 1; 19, 2; ṯnw·f ṯnw·k 'his d. is your d.', BD 476, 13-14 ().

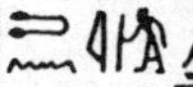 ṯni old man, see s.v. tni.

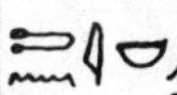 ṯni basin, Urk. IV, 23, 1; 1296, 5; varr. 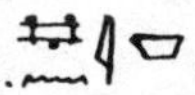 1296, 6.

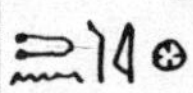 Ṯni n. loc. Thinis, AEO II, 38*; varr.  BM 614, 4;  Urk. IV, 517, 1.

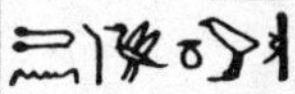 ṯnw number (n.), Urk. V, 178, 10; IV, 795, 10 (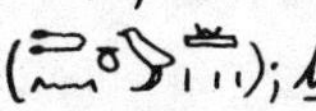); Westc. 7, 5 (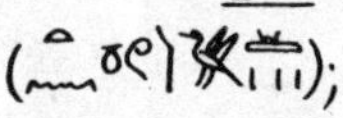); in pl. Urk. I, 133, 14 (); IV, 968, 4 (); nn ṯnw·sn 'they are innumerable', RB 114, 6; counting, numbering, Pyr. 601; each, every foll. by n. of time, Gr. §101; every time that, foll. by sḏm·f, so also r-ṯnw-sp, §181; r-ṯnw, Urk. I, 104, 7.

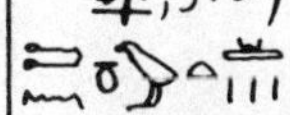 ṯnwt quantity, number, RB 60, 11; Urk. IV, 249, 2; 336, 7; numbering, census, of cattle, Bersh. I, 18; Urk. IV, 238, 13 (det. ); of prisoners, 9, 14 (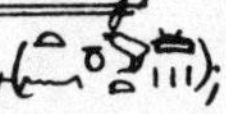); of the dead (a religious festival), BD 81, 14 (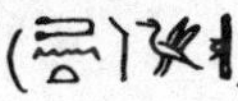); JEA 38, pl. 1, 4 (det. ); Les. 73, 19.

ṯn-r reminder, varr. , , L. to D. I, 2 (n.); JEA 16, 148.

ṯnf enjoyment (?), Paheri, 7.

ṯnft bag, Amarna, VI, 30.

ṯnfyt sail (?) (n.), Urk. IV, 2143, 16.

ṯnm var. of tnm 'turn aside'.

ṯnnt sanctuary at Memphis, Les. 64, 7; varr. Urk. V, 79, 9; Hymnen, 10, 1.

ṯnr eager, Urk. IV, 1559, 6.

ṯnḥr hawk, Peas. B1, 175.

ṯntt sacred cattle, Meir, I, p. 2.

ṯntꜣt dais, Urk. IV, 140, 15; varr. 83, 2; 1385, 6; 1869, 17.

ṯrt willow, Bull. 31, 177; var. Urk. IV, 73, 15.

ṯryt complaint (?), CT I, 173.

ṯrp an edible bird (goose?), Pyr. 746; var. Adm. 11, 1.

ṯrm wink, ZÄS 54, 134; P. Ed. Smith, 199.

var. of ṯbhn 'prance'.

ṯhm harry, Hatnub, 11, 10.

ṯhm hunt, Bersh. II, p. 19.

ṯhw vb. rejoice, Urk. IV, 502, 9; RB 112, 9 (det.): n. joy, RB 110, 13; Urk. IV, 347, 12 (dets.).

ṯḥn meet, RB 61, 9; engage, ḥnꜥ 'with' an enemy, Y. Carn. 4; RB 59, 4; ṯḥn r ꜥḥꜣ ḥnꜥ 'e. in battle with', Urk. IV, 656, 3-4.

ṯḥn lance (?) infected place, Eb. 106, 16.

ṯḥn gleam, Pyr. 699; abbr. RB 113, 12.

ṯḥnt fayence, varr. , , Gr. p. 505, S 15; Urk. IV, 1862, 1.

Ṯḥnw n. loc. Libya, varr. , , , AEO I, 116*.

Ṯḥnw Libyans, Sin. R 16.

ṯḥnw one of the seven sacred oils, AEO I, 117*.

tḥḥ exult, BD 175, 10.

tḥḥwt exultation, Urk. IV, 894, 15; var. 2096, 3.

ṯs sit, Hatnub, 19, 3.

ṯs (ṯz) (1) vertebra, Sm. 10, 18; BD 12, 11 (); 44, 12 (det.): (2) spine, Pyr. 238. 1308 (); BD 29, 6 (det.); tsw bksw 'spine', Pyr. 229. 409.

ṯs neck, L. to D. X, 1, 4.

tst tooth, M. u. K. 3, 10.

ṯst (1) knot, M. u. K. 8, 3; BD 121, 18 (det.); fig. Urk. IV, 1247, 14: (2) vertebra, BD 447, 3; var. det. 36, 9.

ṯs sandbank, Urk. V, 198, 13; Westc. 9, 16. 18; 'the land was m ṯs' in drought', Siut, pl. 15, 9 (); sim. Hatnub, 20, 8-9; 24, 9; rnpwt nt ṯsw 'years of d.', 20, 11.

ṯst ridge, range, Urk. I, 104, 16; IV, 891, 3 ().

ṯs (1) tie knot, cord, M. u. K. vs. 1, 6. 7; Urk. IV, 895, 10; tie on fillet, Urk. I, 98, 12 (); wreath, IV, 1214, 16; weave cloth, BH II, 4. 13; fig. of 'weaving' protection, ḥ3 'about' king, Urk. IV, 567, 4; wḥꜥ ṯsst 'loosen what is tied' = unravel complications, Les. 69, 21; Urk. IV, 47, 12.

(2) join, rejoin, Peas. B1, 257. 289; Westc. 7, 4; knit together bones, Sm. 4, 11; Urk. V, 182, 7; form unborn bodies, TR 17, 9; Urk. IV, 495, 5; BD 387, 9; unite the Two Lands, Urk. IV, 14, 6; build monuments, Merikarēꜥ, 63; model face of sphinx, Goyon, 54 ().

(3) marshal troops (skw), GAS 20; levy troops (d3mw), Hatnub, 24, 6 (); P. Kah. 2, 7 (); Adm. 15, 1; Urk. IV, 924, 12; men for labour, I, 282, 13; order, arrange rites, JEA 32, pl. 6, 7 (det.); knot itself up with confederacies, of Egypt, Adm. 7, 7.

(4) clot, Sm. 5, 19; become constricted (?), Eb. 40, 19.

ṯst coll. troop, battalion, Urk. I, 134, 17; JEA 13, 75; troops, Urk. I, 102, 7; Siut, pl. 15, 17 (); gang of workmen, Urk. I, 136, 17; people of nomarch, Siut, pl. 5, 231.

ṯsw commander, GNS 91; protector of poor, Ḥatnub, 12, 12.

ṯs speech, utterance, P. Kah. 1, 8; Sin. B 184 (det.); Urk. IV, 1090, 16; phrase, sentence, Les. 80, 18 (); Urk. IV, 47, 1; 430, 1; Eb. 1, 3; maxim, Peas. B2, 107; Pr. 5, 6; Urk. IV, 1089, 7; ṯs pḥr 'vice-versa', V, 36, 17; Eb. 2, 3.

ṯs as prefix forming abstract nn.: ṯs- 'fighting', Urk. IV, 1698, 11; ṯs- 'reproach', GNS 31; ṯs- 'crime (?)', Pr. 9, 12.

ṯsỉ (ṯzỉ) vb. 3 inf. raise, lift up, L. to D. I, 9; Sin. B 256; TR 36, 2 (dets.); Urk. V, 149, 11; BD 230, 11; fig. of the heart, Sin. B 23 (dets.); of a new generation, Siut, pl. 13, 29; set up ruined walls, Urk. VII, 56, 7. For ṯs ḏꜣmw 'levy troops' see p. 307.

ṯs support (n.), Les. 82, 3.

ṯst station in life (?), Siut, pl. 13, 10 (det.); 15, 20.

ṯsỉ vb. 3 inf. go up, r 'to' a place, Urk. IV, 893, 3; 'undertake journeys', Les. 73, 13; Urk. IV, 1485, 17 (ṯs).

ṯsỉ vb. 3 inf. be angry, m 'with'; bear a grudge, m 'against', so also ṯs ḥt m, varr. , , , GNS 57. 159.

ṯst complaint, Mill. 1, 7; Peas. B1, 299.

ṯswrt an offering-loaf, Urk. IV, 1553, 11.

ṯsm hound, Sin. B 90. 223 (det.); Sh. S. 165; Urk. IV, 329, 9; f. ṯsmt, P. Kah. 18, 27; Eb. 65, 21.

ṯsm (?) train (?) troops (originally of hounds?), Les. 82, 7.

ṯtf flow down, Urk. IV, 502, 5; overflow, Peas. B1, 294; Pr. 7, 8.

hand, see under ḏrt.

d(w) vb. ult. inf. give; place, put, JEA 45, 102; implant obstacle, Ann. Serv. 27, 227;

strike blow, Pyr. 424; cause, with foll. sdm·f, Urk. IV, 260, 13; d ỉb r 'set o's heart on', Pyr. 807; d r tꜣ 'put on the ground', Bersh. II, 11; 'put in to shore', 'land', Urk. IV, 309, 5; 322, 8 (infin.).

 var. of dwꜣt 'netherworld'.

 dꜣ shake, tremble, Eb. 48, 3; cf. ZÄS 57, 116.

 dꜣwt shaking, trembling, CT I, 17; det. Eb. 48, 3.

 dꜣ copulate, BD 106, 10; cf. ZÄS 57, 116.

 dꜣ become loose, wobble, of decaying limbs, BD 120, 8.

 dꜣỉ subdue lands, Ann. Serv. 17, 228. Cf. dꜣr.

 dꜣỉw loin-cloth, Westc. 10, 2; varr. Pyr. 1214 (is det. 'cloth'); Peas. R 46; L. to D. II, 5; Urk. IV, 1993, 1; cf. ZÄS 49, 106 ff.; JEA 21, 143.

 dꜣbw figs, Sin. B 81; Sh. S. 47; varr. Urk. IV, 438, 11; Sm. 5, 4; nht nt d(ꜣ)b 'fig-tree', Urk. IV, 73, 15.

 dꜣr control temper, Hatnub, 10, 4; Siut, pl. 9, 338 (abbr.); Urk. IV 63, 6; a tribe, Sin. B 93 (); o's wishes, Peas. B 1, 210; dꜣr ỉb 'self-denial', Pr. 1, 4; 'self-control', 5, 12; subdue foes, P. Kah. 1, 3; Sin. B 50 (); suppress evil, Urk. IV, 15, 5; rob s'one, hr 'of' goods, VII, 5, 7; 16, 2; steal goods, Pr. 14, 1.

  dꜣdꜣ copulate, RB 117, 1; cf. ZÄS 57, 116.

, dỉ, see under rdỉ 'give', etc.

 dỉ provisions, Gr. p. 533, X 8.

 dyt papyrus-plant, Sin. B 122. Cf. dt 'papyrus-stem' and dyt 'p.-marsh'.

 dy here, there, ZÄS 50, 99.

 var. of dꜣỉw 'loin-cloth'.

 dỉwt five parts, Urk. IV, 139, 6; cf. Gr. § 260.

 dỉwt gang of 5, BH I, 8, 19, cf. GAS 72; var. Dav. Ptah. II, 7.

 dỉwt (?) shriek, RB 119, 8; Sin. B 266 (); bellow, TR 1, 39 ().

var. of db 'hippopotamus'.

dw infin. of d(w) 'give', 'place'.

dw3 rise early, Eb. 18,14; Adm. p.106.

dw3w dawn, morning, RB 113,13; 114,1; Sh. S. 186 ( ); Urk. V, 6,8 ( ); IV, 1847,9 ( ); tomorrow, the morrow, Peas. B1, 183; Urk. V, 11, 15 ( ); m dw3(w) 'tomorrow', Gr. § 205, 3; dw3(w) sp 2 'very early', Herdsm. 22; nṯr dw3w 'morning star', Pyr. 357; var. BD 222,7; 'morning star', Pyr. 871.

dw3yt morning, BM 552; Urk. IV, 267, 17; Eb. 40,4 ( ); tp-dw3yt 'dawn', 'morning', RB 111,9; 113,2-3; pr-dw3t 'House of the M.' = robing-room, see p. 90; so also ḫnwty-dw3t, see p. 48. Varr. TR 22,51; Urk. IV, 447,16; 657,3.

dw3t netherworld, Pyr. 257; varr. 5; Urk. IV, 1590,11; 1617,12; 11,12; nether chamber in tomb, Th. T. S. I, p. 117, n. 5.

dw3tyw dwellers in the netherworld, BD 319,16; var. 320,3.

dw3 praise, worship (vb.), Les. 68,13; BM 552; varr. Urk. IV, 217,14; 159,15; 142,14; 1847,9; RB 110,11; 110,13. See also dw3-nṯr below.

dw3t praise, worship (n.), Siut, pl. 16, IV, 4; pl. 'praises', Les. 77,19-20; var. Urk. IV, 167,12.

dw3-wr deified royal beard, BM 101; varr. Pyr. 2042; 1428. Cf. JEA 21, 4, n. 2.

dw3-wr adze for 'Opening the Mouth', Th. T. S. I, 17; cf. Meir, III, 28, n. 2.

Dw3-mwt·f n. div. one of the four sons of Horus, Pyr. 552; varr. Urk. V, 39,5; (sic) BD 58, 8-9.

dw3-nṯr praise God, Siut, pl. 5, 238; 11,1 ( ); with n, 'p. G. for' s'one = thank him, Sh. S. 167 ( ). 176; Les. 76,13. For nṯr dw3w 'morning star' see above s.v. dw3w 'dawn'.

dwn trans. stretch out legs, Sh. S. 45; hands, Pr. 7,2 (det. …); stretch bow, Pyr. 673 (…); straighten knees, CT I, 56; body, P. Kah. 5,34 (…): intrans. be stretched out, taut, P. Ed. Smith, 193; be prostrate, Sin. B 253; *m dwn*, of motion, 'straight on'; of time, 'from then on', 'henceforward'; of action, 'habitually', 'continually', JEA 22, 175 f.; 'he stood *m dwn.f* straight up', 176, n. 1.

… var. of *ddw* 'kind of grain'.

db hippopotamus, Peas. B1, 206; var. … Th. T. S. II, 11; f. *dbt* (det. …) Caminos, Lit. Frag. pl. 6,3,5.

db horn of animal, var. …, Gr. p. 463, F 16; wing of army, Urk. IV, 653, 11.12; 657, 10.12.

… var. of *d3bw* 'figs'.

dbỉ vb. 3 inf. stop up, Peas. B1, 233.

… var. of *dbt* 'brick', 'ingot'.

… see *db3*.

dbn vb. trans. go round a place, Sin. B 201; Westc. 12,3; travel round a region, JEA 4, pl. 9,3 (…); Urk. IV, 943,2 (…); Sin. B 181 (…); encircle, *m* 'with', Urk. V, 62,1: intrans. recur, of plants in season, JEA 16, pl. 17, M.

dbnt circuit of ocean, Urk. IV, 1248, 19.

dbnw circumference of sky, Urk. IV, 85, 16; det. ◎ 332, 15.

dbn weight of about 91 grammes, varr. …, …, …, Gr. § 266,4; general term for w. of balance, Peas. B1, 166; Urk. IV, 338, 2.

dbn helmet, Urk. IV, 712,1; cf. Rec. trav. 30, 154.

dbn builder's mortar, P. Ed. Smith, 412.

dbnt lock of hair, M. u. K. 9,6.

dbḥ ask for, beg, Leb. 80; Adm. 7,11; Urk. IV, 370, 17; 1309, 17; requisition, *m* 'from' Treasury, Urk. VII, 3,1; varr. … IV, 662, 10; … 1110, 5; … 1309, 17; … 332, 9.

dbḥw requirements, necessaries, Urk. I, 286, 10; var. … RB 117,1; det. … 118,4.

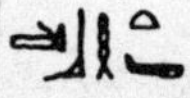 dbḥt necessaries, Urk. VII, 2, 17; var. 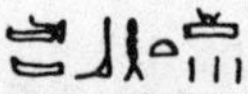 Siut, pl. 19, 53.

 dbḥt-ḥtp funerary meal, Sin. B 195; varr. 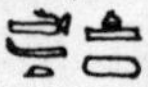 Urk. IV, 26, 9;  842, 11.

 dbḥt-ḥtp altar, Urk. IV, 22, 10.

 dbḥw measure for offerings, Urk. IV, 635, 14; var.  640, 7.

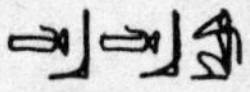 dbdb thump, of heart, Eb. 42, 10.

 Dp n. loc. Dep, Delta city, Gr. p. 73.

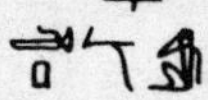 dp taste (vb.) Peas. B1, 215; Sm. 21, 21; experience, Sh. S. 124. 181; Peas. B1, 59.

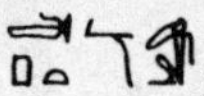 dpt taste (n.), Pr. 5, 1; Sin. B 23; Adm. 5, 2.

 dpt ship, Sh. S. 25; Peas. B1, 57. 126; Urk. IV, 814, 13; fig. 'ship' of state, GAS 29; dpt nṯr 'sacred bark', GAS 33; dpwt nsw 'king's ships', RB 63, 5 ().

 dpt loins, AEO II, 243*.

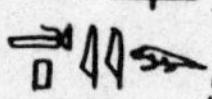 dpy crocodile, Urk. IV, 84, 12; 616, 9; var.  T. Carn. 6.

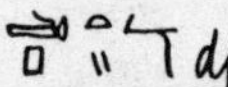 dpty an offering, Urk. IV, 1952, 20.

 var. of dfꜣw 'provisions'.

 dfꜣ-ỉb stolid (?), JEA 32, 73, n. 11; 36, 49; 37, 110.

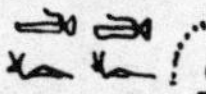 dfdf drip, Pyr. 133; var. 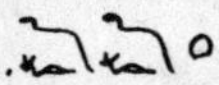 BD 466, 9.

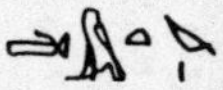 dmt knife, Sm. 19, 7; Urk. IV, 1603, 15; var.  Eb. 40, 6.

 dm be sharp, Urk. IV, 2081, 5 (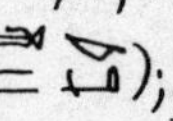); sharpen, Pyr. 962 (det. 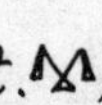); pierce sky, of crown of god, RB 111, 9; of obelisks, with n, Urk. IV, 374, 13 ().

 dm pronounce, proclaim name, Peas. B1, 20; Urk. IV, 131, 9; 440, 15; mention, m 'by' name, GNS 92; be renowned, of office, Les. 72, 16. Varr.  loc. cit.;  75, 4;  Urk. IV, 194, 17;  257, 16;  260, 15; 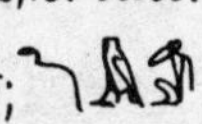 1845, 20.

 dmꜣ stretch, Ch. B. Text, 30, n. 10; be stretched out, Sh. S. 137.

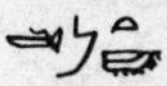 dmꜣt wing, Urk. IV, 617, 8.

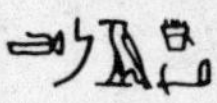 dmꜣ bind together, Urk. IV, 612, 15; 1547, 3; JEA 37, 31; var. 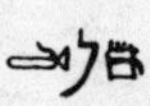 RB 57, 8; abbr.  Urk. IV, 284, 1.

dmꜣ cut off heads, Urk. IV, 896, 12; var. 1277, 5.

dmꜣw groups (?), classes (?), Urk. IV, 1822, 2.

dmỉ vb. trans. touch, Sin. B 200; Sh. S. 79. 137; reach place, Sin. B 16 (det. R 42): intrans. be joined, r 'to', GNS 41 (dets. Eb. 86, 14; Sm. 5, 9); accrue, r 'to', Sin. B 85; cleave, ḥr 'to', Eb. 91, 14; Leb. 150 (dets. sic); suit, n s'one, Peas. B1, 153-4; befall, n s'one, Urk. IV, 1092, 13.

dmỉ town, AEO II, 1*; quarter of t., JEA 33, 26; abode, Peas. B1, 27; Leb. 38. 154; vicinity, Les. 77, 21 (det.); quay, JEA 22, 104; r dmỉ.s 'at its fitting place', 33, 29.

dmỉw fellow-citizens, TR 23, 47.

var. of ỉdmỉ 'red linen'.

dmỉ ornamental fruit-dish, Urk. IV, 763, 10.

dmḏ reassemble dismembered body, Pyr. 318. 617. 980; assemble, bring together people, TR 2, 1. 15; Urk. IV, 257, 13; 612, 12; associate, ḥnꜥ 'with', Pyr. 1023; CT I, 155; Urk. IV, 807, 1; join s'one, Pyr. 645; unite lands, Urk. IV, 83, 10; V, 73, 16; JEA 32, pl. 6, 11; accumulate grain, Urk. IV, 1183, 7; compile spell, BD 87, 13; extend (?) hand, n 'to', Les. 75, 10; old perf. dmḏ, dmḏ.tỉ 'entire', Gr. § 317. Varr. TR 2, 15; 2, 16; JEA 32, pl. 6, 11; Urk. IV, 138, 4; 257, 13.

dmḏ total, BH I, 21; P. Kah. 8, 62; Urk. IV, 1112, 12; abbr. P. Kah. 8, 13. 14; dmḏ r 'total', Urk. IV, 4, 12; dmḏ smꜣ 'grand total', Urk. IV, 177, 1; written * JEA 30, 33, n. 6; varr. dmḏ smꜣ m, Urk. IV, 336, 8; dmḏ smꜣ r, BH I, 26, 140-1 ().

dmḏw crowd, CT IV, 371; var. Berlin Leather, 2, 4; fem. JEA 41, pl. 6, 117; var. pl. 2, 20, cf. p. 12, n. 2.

dmḏt collection of recipes, Eb. 2, 7.

dmḏyt cycle of festivals, JEA 32, pl. 6, 6 = p. 46, n. 5; var. [] Urk. IV, 1410, 1.

dn cut off heads, Urk. IV, 269, 15; 614, 1; kill s'one, TR 33, 5; Urk. V, 55, 14; Hymnen, 19, 1.

dnỉ dam water, P. Kah. 2, 12; construct dam, RB 117, 6; hold back, restrain s'one, Urk. IV, 1279, 2 ( ); RB 63, 1; revet earthen banks, m 'with' stone, Urk. IV, 312, 11 ( ).

dnỉt dam (n.), Peas. B1, 237. 244; RB 117, 6; var. CT II, 7.

dnỉt ditch, canal, JEA 1, 31, n. 2; P. Wilbour, 30.

see under dỉwt 'shriek'.

dnỉt bowl, Urk. IV, 641, 12; 770, 8.

dnỉt basket, P. Kah. 19, 41.

dnỉt a festival, Urk. IV, 445, 8.

dnỉ share out, var. ; sš 'scribe of distribution', AEO I, 33*.

dnỉw share, portion (n.), Urk. IV, 67; det. 2158, 6; cf. JEA 5, 50, n. 7.

dnyt land-register, JEA 5, 50, n. 7.

dnw flaw (?) in stone, Urk. IV, 367, 2.

dnwt families (?), Urk. IV, 1821, 2.

see under dnbw.

var. of dnḥ 'wing'.

dns heavy, P. Kah. 3, 33; Sin. B 169 (det.); Eb. 36, 18; irksome, Adm. 4, 10. 14; burdensome, of years, Adm. p. 101; overburdened, of stomach, Eb. 36, 5; weighty (fig.), Peas. B1, 160. 209; B2, 103; Urk. VII, 64, 7; dns mdwt 'guarded of speech', JEA 35, 38; 37, 112. Var. Urk. IV, 47, 8.

dns heaviness (?), Urk. IV, 848, 14.

dnsw weights of net, BD 390, 13.

dng pygmy, JEA 24, 185.

dnd slaughter animals, BD 62, 3.

dndn traverse a place or way, Pyr. 2099; BM 573, 9; Les. 74, 11.

var. of dndn 'be angry'.

dr (1) subdue enemies, Sin. B 110; RB 57, 4; Urk. IV, 745, 12; expel, drive out people, Adm. 7, 8. 9; Urk. IV, 8, 7; 1199, 8; illness, Eb. 6, 10; remove need, evil, etc., Peas. 69. 107; Urk. IV, 102, 13; 117, 10; 835, 3; repress wrongdoer, V, 22, 5; Siut, pl. 11, 7; wrong-doing, BH I, 25, 36; RB 116, 8; Adm. 12, 5; destroy places, T. Carn. 11; writings, Les. 98, 15; Adm. 6, 9; dr tw 'Damn you!', Th. T. S. II, 11.

(2) lay down flooring, Urk. I, 181, 10; of the earth as floor, IV, 1164, 9; overlay floor with gold, 1150, 13.

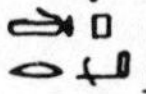 drp vb. trans. offer to god, Urk. IV, 547, 2; offer things, n 'to', Siut, pl. 13, 27 (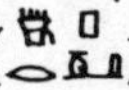); feed s'one, Urk. IV, 415, 7; 1026, 7; present dues, 1115, 1: intrans make offering, Leb. 53; Urk. IV, 100, 17; n 'on behalf of' dec'd., 446, 11; hr 'to' gods, 490, 17.

 drpw offerings, Urk. IV, 499, 11; 519, 11.

 drf writing, script, BH I, 7; Urk. IV, 165, 15; 969, 14; nn drf n ỉwms im 'there is not a line of falsehood in it', 776, 10; title-deeds, Les. 98, 13 (); Urk. IV, 837, 9; 1495, 6 (det. ).

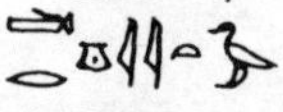 drgyt bat, see under dgyt.

 dhnt forehead, BH II, 7; Eb. 103, 14; of horse, Urk. IV, 1304, 13.

 dhnt mountain-top, Amarna, V, 32, 31 (corrected).

 dhn (1) bow, n 'to', Urk. IV, 1785, 10; dhn tꜣ 'touch the earth with the forehead' in obeisance, GNS 94: (2) appoint, P. Kah. 11, 19; BH I, 25, 107 (det. ); Urk. IV, 3, 9 (dets. ); 663, 2; order burial, V, 12, 9.

 dḥi hang down, Sm. 12, 9 (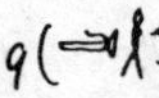); be low, P. Ed. Smith, 355 (); be humiliated, Pr. 12, 1;  dḥ(i) rmn 'humble', Urk. VII, 3, 8; IV, 64, 8. Cf. ZÄS 45, 130; 49, 132.

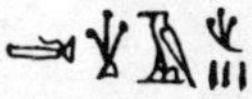 dḥꜣ straw, Paheri, 3.

 dḥr leather, Westc. 12, 5; Urk. IV, 662, 5; 1392, 18; hide, 2148, 12; 2149, 8 (); abbr.  P. Kah. 19, 20; used of tough tissue, Sm. 3, 16.

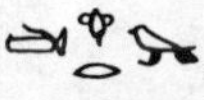 dḥr bitter, Eb. 40, 11; Urk. IV, 1087, 9; bitterness, Sm. 22, 1.

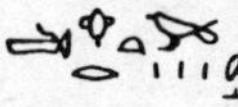 dḥrt bitterness, M. u. K. 2, 4; Urk. IV, 1077, 16; sickness (dets. ), P. Ed. Smith, 475.

dḥty lead, Urk. IV, 686, 16; 706, 9; 744, 14; var. 718, 5.

: šspt nt dḥn 'chorus of singers', SDT 176.

ds jar, Pyr. 10; varr. RB 123, 2; Stamm. 114, 13; as beer-measure, Gr. § 266, 1.

ds knife, Pyr. 270; Pr. 1, 2; Urk. V, 79, 3.

ds flint, RB 120, 10; var. Westc. 9, 5.

dsi vilify, Les. 79, 16.

dšr flamingo, Gr. p. 470, G 27.

dšr adj. red, Urk. V, 43, 10; M.u.K. 1, 1 (det.); dšr ỉb, dšr ḥr 'furious', JEA 35, 72: n. reddening, Eb. 62, 9.

dšrt the Red Crown, Les. 98, 17; Urk. IV, 366, 2; BD 369, 13; varr. Urk. IV, 16, 8; Hymnen, 2, 3.

dšrt the Red Land, the desert, Urk. IV, 270, 17; varr. 1276, 18; 283, 17; BM 614, 6; RB 59, 3.

dšrt red pot, Rekh. 11; BH I, 18.

dšrt wrath, Hymnen, 6, 4.

dšrw wrath, CT I, 21; varr. ibid.; Hymnen, 12, 4.

dšrw blood, BD 293, 4; var. 344, 12.

dk (< dḳr?) flour, Urk. IV, 754, 10; varr. 171, 17; 741, 13; 762, 5; 1554, 7; powder, Sm. 21, 6.

dkr (1) press (?), r 'against': (2) exclude (?), r 'from', var. det. : (3) a process in spinning, GNS 60.

dḳrw fruit, Sin. B 83; Urk. IV, 694, 5; fruit-trees, 433, 10.

dgi vb. 3 inf. hide, Sin. B 4; Pr. 5, 10; var. Adm. 4, 6.

dgi vb. 3 inf. intrans. look, n 'at', GNS 108; r 'at', Pt. (L II), 2, 14 ( ): trans. see, behold, Peas. B 2, 106; RB 114, 9; Urk. IV, 117, 6 ( ); 148, 17 ( ).

dg(3)yt staring (n.), Pt. (L II), 2, 15.

dg3 walk, Urk. IV, 2010, 8.

dgyt *a bird*, JEA 35, pl. 2, 14 and p. 17.

dgyt *bat*, varr. , , Barns, Ram. p. 18; JEA 35, pl. 3.

dgm *castor-oil plant*, Kémi, 2, 100.

dgm *be speechless*, var. det. , P. Ed. Smith, 296.

dgs *walk*, Adm. 2, 12.

ddt *dish*, Urk. IV, 631, 7; 665, 13; 721, 17.

ddỉ *haematite*, JRAS 1927, 497.

, ; varr. of Ḏdw 'Busiris.

Ddwn n. div. *a Nubian god*, Urk. IV, 197, 5; var. 193, 16.

ḏdw *kind of grain*, var. JEA 19, 152; Kémi, 1, 140.

ḏt *cobra*, var. , Gr. p. 476, I 10.

ḏt *body* of person, Pyr. 193; Urk. IV, 1282, 3; fig. of a land, 352, 4; of obelisk, 367, 9; *image, bodily form* of god, 97, 17; 384, 7; statues m nb mty 'each in its own exact form', JEA 39, pl. 2, 23 = p. 20 (3g); as synonym of ḏs 'self' in nḏ·s ḏt·s m-c Stš 'that it may protect itself from Seth', Urk. V, 147, 5; ib·sn fn ḥr ḏt·sn 'their hearts were weak of themselves', IV, 2027, 19; k3·i n ḏt·i 'my own ka', TR 5, 5-6; sim. Urk. IV, 447, 5; smyt nbt iy·ti ḥr ḏt·s 'every desert has come of its own accord', 501, 4; 'for ever', 147, 3; 495, 13; 'for ever', VII, 48, 15; k3t·f n ḏt ḏt 'its everlasting work', 48, 16. For ỉp ḏt, rḫ ḏt, ḫm ḏt, see under the first word.

ḏt *eternity*, Sin. B 212; Urk. IV, 111, 7; cf. JEA 39, 10; ḥrt·f nt ḏt 'his eternal tomb', Urk. IV, 918, 16; as adv. *for ever*, Sin. B 238; m 3wt ḏt 'in perpetuity', 'for ever', Urk. IV, 173, 3; 832, 14; ḏt r nḥḥ 'for ever and ever', Sin. B 180, see further under nḥḥ; for see the next above.

ḏt estate, varr.; so also pr n ḏt, GNS 77, n.2.

ḏt serf, P. Kah. 10, 8. 22; 11, 4; pl. Peas. R 40; P. Kah. 10, 7. 21; 11, 1; Urk. IV, 368, 10. Cf. nḏt 'serf', p. 143.

ḏt papyrus-stem, Urk. IV, 1321, 17. Cf. ḏyt 'p.-plant' and ḏyt 'p.-marsh'.

var. of mḏt 'oil'.

ḏꜣ fire-drill, Sh. S. 54; var. Sm. 13, 6.

hand, Les. 75, 20; handful, Pyr. 124. 1703. Cf. ḏrt below.

ḏꜣt crane, Bersh. I, 20; TR 20, 94.

ḏꜣỉ vb. 3 inf. extend arm, CT I, 74; Urk. IV, 28, 16; with m or r 'against', GAS 82; oppose o'self, m 'to', Pyr. 963; Eb. 1, 15; pierce, transfix, Caminos, Lit. Frag. pl. 2, 2, 7; RB 64, 8; Urk. IV, 1322, 4; reach out, of child's mouth, m 'after' milk, Peas. B2, 119; Urk. IV, 240, 1; sim. 1031, 12; cf. JEA 9, 21, n. 7; take the breast, tp 'to' the mouth, Pyr. 381. 1119. 1427; devour food, Pyr. 736; provide, m 'with' food, JEA 16, 196; ḏꜣ mꜣꜥ r 'pay heed to', Caminos, Lit. Frag. p. 17; ḏꜣ 'be contentious', Urk. IV, 64, 1. 7; 1412, 7; ḏꜣ rd 'impede', Pyr. 311. 315. In Pyr. usual det. is ; in M.K. also, CT I, 74.

ḏꜣỉ vb. 3 inf. ferry s'one across water, Peas. B1, 172; Urk. V, 178, 9; cross sky, Pyr. 128; RB 113, 13; water, 58, 2; 64, 14; obj. not expressed, Sin. B 13; Peas. B1, 199; ḥr mw 'over water', Urk. IV, 4, 7; sim. 1302, 7; rarely of crossing land (tꜣ), Pyr. 1215; fig. ḏꜣ tꜣ 'be busied', 'interfere', r 'with', GNS 115; ḥr 'with', Hamm. 114, 6.

ḏꜣt balance, remainder, Peas. R 4; Urk. IV, 118, 15; Rhind, 28; deficiency, Peas. B2, 94; Urk. IV, 77, 7.

var. of ḏꜣwt in r-ḏꜣwt 'in return for' and of ḏꜣyt 'wrongdoing'.

ḏꜣyt wrongdoing, Pr. 6, 6; varr. CT I, 173; Les. 75, 21; Urk. IV, 1776, 16.

ḏꜣyw opponent, Eb. 1, 15; f. ḏꜣyt ibid.

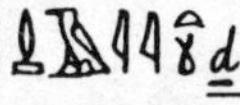 ḏ3yt robe, Adm. 7,11; P. Kah. 39,16.

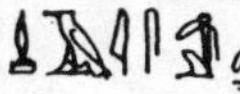 ḏ3is dispute, argue, ḥnꜥ 'with', GNS 42; oppose actions, Sin. B99, cf. Barns, p.11. Var. O.K. 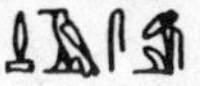 Urk. I, 217,6.

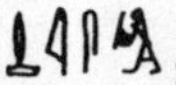 ḏ3is argument, dispute, Siut, pl.16, I,18; var. 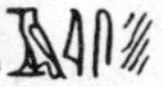 BM 1059.

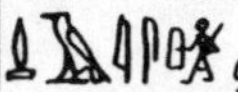 ḏ3is civil war, Siut, pl.11,7.

 ḏ3isw disputant, GNS 43.

 ḏ3ytyw opponents, Urk. IV, 400,16; var. O.K.  Pyr. 1212.

 ḏ3w mat (?), varr. , 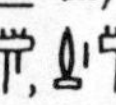, CT I, 264.

 ḏ3w night, Siut, pl.7,298.

 ḏ3wt in r-ḏ3wt 'in return for', varr. , 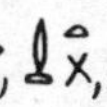, Gr. §180; 'because of', Urk. IV, 1321,8; dets.  RB 58,3.

 ḏ3bḥw type of fisherman, Peas. B1,229.

 ḏ3f vb. heat, Eb. 39,18; burn, Israel, 7.

 ḏ3mw young men, P. Kah. 1,10; Urk. VII, 3,18 (); troops, P. Kah. 2,7; 9,2; Adm. 14,14; ḏ3mw n ꜥḥ3wtyw 't. of warriors', Bersh. I,15 (det.  only); ḏ3mw n ḫrdw 't. of young men', Hatnub, 16,4; ḥn ḏ3mw 'camp', 20,3; 25,5; 27,2. Cf. JEA 39,40. O.K. varr. , 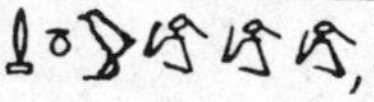, Pyr. 1206.

 ḏ3rt bitter gourd, JEA 20,41.

 ḏ3rw need, JEA 9,18, n.8; 16,22 (det.  only); varr. 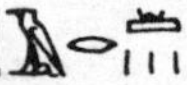 Siut, pl.11,5;  Urk. IV, 1385,20.

 Ḏ3hy n. loc. part of Palestine and Phoenicia, AEO I, 145*

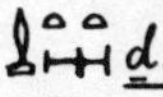 ḏ3tt estate, var. 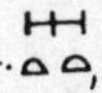, perhaps also 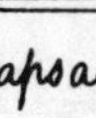, 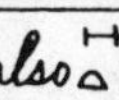, Gr. p.540, Aa 8. For 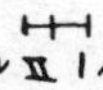 see p.326.

 ḏ3dw audience-hall, Urk. IV, 257,1; 349,10; det.  26,12.

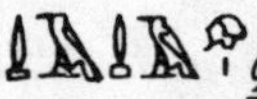 ḏ3ḏ3 head, P. Kah. 5,55; Westc. 8,19; of body of men, Siut, pl.8,311; tip of bow, Les. 82,8. Varr.  Urk. V, 131,9;  Westc. 8,18.

[illegible] ḏ3ḏ3t magistrates, assessors, var. O.K. [illegible], Gr. p.540, Aa 8; Dyn.18 [illegible] Urk. IV, 41,5.

ḏ3ḏ3t lyre, GAS 59.

ḏ3ḏ3w pot, Eb. 46, 17.

ḏyt papyrus-marsh, Gr. p. 481, M. 15. Cf. ḏyt 'p.-plant', p. 309 above.

var. of ḏꜥr 'search out'.

ḏꜥ spear fish, P. Kah. 33, 16.

ḏꜥ storm, storm-wind, Sh. S. 31. 32; Peas. B1, 244; Westc. 11, 14.

ḏꜥ kind of bread, Urk. IV, 1157, 15.

ḏꜥt vein of ore, AEO II, 218*.

ḏꜥb coal-black, Pyr. 1105.

ḏꜥbt charcoal, Adm. 3, 11; Siut, pl. 7, 294; Eb. 73, 11.

ḏꜥm a sceptre, Gr. p. 509, S 40. 41.

ḏꜥmw fine gold, Westc. 5, 9; varr. Urk. IV, 421, 11; Sin. B 252; Urk. IV, 1668, 1. Cf. Caminos, L.-Eg. Misc. 441.

miswriting of w3s 'ruin', see p. 55.

ḏꜥr search out, investigate, Pr. 14, 6; Les. 68, 15; Peas. B2, 93 (dets.); Urk. IV, 1344, 20; 1425, 14 (dets.); seek, 158, 10 (dets.); 861, 5; probe, palpate wound, P. Ed. Smith, 92; plan work, Urk. IV, 395, 2; take thought, n 'for' the future, 57, 15; 384, 12. Varr. 812, 12; 1344, 20; abbr. 926, 13.

ḏꜥryt lock (?) of door, RB 121, 6.

ḏw mountain, Sin. B 15. 122; varr. RB 58, 1; JEA 4, pl. 9, 4.

ḏw adj. bad, evil, Leb. 111; Eb. 24, 8; Urk. IV, 257, 15; sad of heart, Westc. 12, 21: n. evil, Urk. IV, 488, 3: adv. evilly, ZÄS 60, 68; bw-ḏw 'evil' (n.), Peas. B1, 214. Varr. Westc. 12, 21; Urk. IV, 1076, 3.

ḏwt evil (n.), Sin. B 273; Peas. B1, 288; RB 112, 11; 118, 16; sadness of heart, Westc. 9, 12; dirt encumbering ruin, Urk. IV, 835, 2 ().

ḏw the Evil One, Urk. IV, 1819, 7.

ḏwy evil (adj.), var., CT I, 32; bw-ḏwy 'evil' (n.), Siut, pl. 14, 65.

ḏwỉ call upon god, Urk. IV, 470,14; 1777,18; var. 874,6.

ḏwỉ separate (?), Sm. 18,3.

ḏwiw jar, Siut, pl. 8,308; var. Westc. 6,20.

ḏwꜥ lancet (?), Eb. 105,4; 109,15.

ḏbt brick, Westc. 10,2; Urk. IV, 169,10; 879,5; 1295,3; ingot, slab of metal, RB 64,7; Urk. IV, 708,3. Varr. 1321,7; 718,4. Cf. ZÄS 52,130.

ḏbꜣ (1) repay, Urk. IV, 162,16; RB 62,11; make repayment, P. Kah. 3,15; Urk. IV, 561,15; replace, restore, Peas. B1, 48.49 ( ); Westc. 6,6 ( ): (2) clothe, adorn, Les. 68,8; 71,10 (abbr.); Urk. IV, 261,7; provide, CT I, 163; Urk. IV, 547,9; 1445,6; pad, Sm. 3,14; 8,21.

ḏbꜣw payments, Pr. 13,10; Urk. IV, 344,15; reward, 163,2; compensation, Westc. 11,26; bribes, Les. 79,19; Urk. IV, 118,16; 1082,14; r-ḏbꜣ 'instead of', Gr. §180. Varr. Les. 68,5; 96,8; Peas. B1, 318.

ḏbꜣ garment worn by god, D. el B. 11.45 (det.).

ḏbꜣw crowning, Les. 75,10.

ḏbꜣt (1) robing-room, CT I, 164; D. el B. 37.85 ( ): (2) sarcophagus, Adm. 7,8; JEA 10,239, n. 2.

ḏbꜣw altars, Urk. IV, 149,12.

ḏbꜣ stop up, block, Urk. IV, 814,12; var. Pr. 5,2.

Ḏbꜣ n. loc. Edfu, AEO II, 6*.

ḏbꜣ mat of leaves (?), ZÄS 60,76.

ḏbꜣw floats of net, BD 390, 13.

ḏbꜥ (1) finger, P. Kah. 5,46; Sh. S. 14.188; thumb, P. Ed. Smith, 304; ZÄS 73,119; later also toe, JEA 39,117: (2) digit = $\frac{1}{28}$ cubit, Gr. §266,2: (3) num. 10,000, §259. Var. Pyr. 1208.

ḏbꜥ point the finger, m 'at', in reproach, Pr. 1,5; cf. JEA 22,43.

ḏbꜥw reproach (n.), Urk. IV, 61,13; 'do wrong', 1618,17.

ḏbꜥwt *signet, seal*, Urk. IV, 1044, 14; 1184, 16; *ḥr ḏbꜥwt* 'under the s. of', 68, 10; 209, 13; sim. *ḥr ḏbꜥwt*, BM 614, 5. Varr. loc. cit.; Urk. IV, 1044, 14; 1072, 5; 209, 13.

ḏbw *pole* (?) of chariot, Urk. IV, 663, 12; 669, 6. 7.

ḏfꜣw *provisions, sustenance*, Westc. 7, 21-2; varr. Pr. 12, 10; Urk. IV, 51, 5; 146, 10; 117, 5; 1165, 13; 1222, 4; 227, 10; 1819, 19; 1999, 14; BM 1164; deified as *Abundance*, JEA 31, 66.

ḏfꜣ *be provided*, Pr. 8, 8; *abound*, *m* 'in' supplies, I Carn. 12.

ḏfꜣy *a well-provided man*, Hatnub, 23, 9.

ḏfy *penetrate*, P. Ed. Smith, 337.

ḏfyt *penetration*, Sm. 11, 8.

ḏfd *pupil* of eye, Eb. 57, 3; var. BD 212, 13.

var. of *ḏfḏf* 'drip'.

ḏfdft (< *ḏfḏft*) *drop* of liquid, Eb. 59, 22.

ḏms *avocet*, JEA 35, pl. 2 and p. 18.

ḏnb *deflect*, P. Ed. Smith, 250.

ḏnb *crooked*, var. det. , loc. cit.

ḏnb *crookshank, cripple*, BH II, 32.

ḏnb *an offering-loaf*, Urk. IV, 1952, 15.

ḏnbw: —— *rsyw* 'southern territories (?)', var. , Rec. trav. 37, 65; var. [ ] RB 62, 5.

ḏnnt *skull*, Sm. 1, 19. 21; 2, 2 ff.

ḏnḥ *wing*, TR 5, 3; var. Eb. 88, 13; abbr. RB 111, 14.

ḏnḥ: —— *n ḏrww* 'wing-rib (?)', COA III, p. 173, 9 (f).

ḏnḥ *upper part of hind-leg, ham* (?), M. u. K. 5, 1; cf. AEO II, 244.*

ḏnd vb. intrans. *be angry*, Pyr. 631; *ḏnd ib* 'be infuriated', ZÄS 60, 70: trans.

subdue, CT I, 50 (det. ): n. wrath, Siut, pl. 4, 224; BD 21, 9 ().

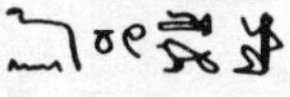 ḏnd angry man, Adm. p. 106.

 ḏnḏn vb. intrans. be angry, Caminos, Lit. Frag. pl. 23, 29 (): trans. subdue, CT I, 50: n. wrath, CT I, 188, BD 355, 16.

 ḏrt hand, Sin. B 54; Westc. 4, 3; trunk of elephant, Urk. IV, 894, 1; handle of jar, 733, 6; 3w ḏrt 'generous', Les. 80, 21. Varr.  Siut, pl. 11, 3;  Urk. IV, 3, 13;  35, 17. Cf. ḏ3t above.

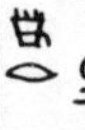 ḏr prep. in (archaic), SDT 24; since, before, until, Gr. §176: adv. at an end, §205, 1; ḏr ntt 'since', §223.

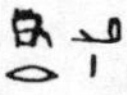 ḏr-ʿ(wy) n. end, limit, Urk. IV, 426, 17 (); 1074, 12; 1308, 9; 1670, 1: adv. long ago, Gr. §205, 3; ḏr-ʿ-r 'right down to', §179.

 ḏr (1) end hunger, etc., Peas. B1, 243. 244. 280; end up as, Westc. 6, 11; aux. vb., Gr. §§ 316. 483, 1: (2) hinder, obstruct, Pyr. 625; 1715.

 ḏr obstacle, JEA 20, 160.

 ḏrt harm (?), M. u. K. 2, 4.

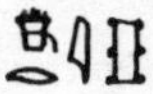 ḏri enclosing wall (?), Urk. IV, 174, 11; 475, 7; var. 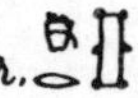 Sin. B 198.

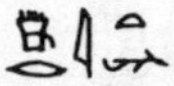 ḏrit wall (?), GAS 28.

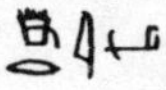 ḏri strong, of staff, Urk. IV, 1344, 17; as adv. strongly in mḥ·tn ḏri sp 2 'press on with the capture' (lit. 'capture ye, s., s.'), 660, 9; grg ḏriw 'make thorough preparation', 2151, 2.

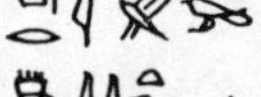 ḏri be hard (?), stolid (?), GAS 106.

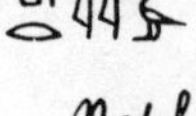 ḏryt kite, Pyr. 463 (); BD 360, 7; ḏrty 'the Two K.' = Isis and Nephthys, Pyr. 230. 308; BD 53, 14; so also ḏrt wrt ḏrt nḏst 'the Great K. and the Lesser K.', represented at funerals by women, Th. T. S. I, p. 41, n. 2; II, pl. 21 (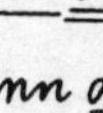); Paheri, 5 (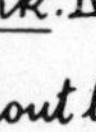).

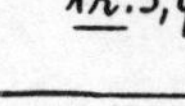 ḏrw boundary, Urk. IV, 118, 9; end, limit, 248, 17; BH I, 8, 9; RB 56, 13 (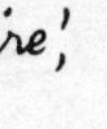); Pr. 5, 9; nn ḏrw(·f) 'without l.', Sin. R 16; B 84 (). 212; r ḏr(·f) 'entire',

'all', Gr. §100, 1; nb-r-d̲r 'Lord of All', ep. of god or king, sim. nbt-r-d̲r of queen, loc. cit.; dd ‹i› nw r d̲r rmṯw nb 'I say this to all and sundry', Urk. I, 88, 6.

d̲rw walls (?), Bersh. II, 21, bottom, 13.

d̲rwt sarcophagus, GAS 28.

d̲rwt hall (?), Adm. 2, 11; cf. GAS 28; varr. ibid; Urk. IV, 1379, 8.

d̲rwy paint (n.), Les. 76, 10; Urk. IV, 670, 10.

d̲rww side, flank (anatom.), AEO II, 254*.

d̲rww wall (?), JEA 10, 227, n. 2.

var. of d̲rf 'writing'.

d̲rtyw ancestors, Urk. IV, 86, 3; 344, 13; 429, 8; var. 584, 17.

d̲rd leaf, late var., Gr. p. 463, F 21.

d̲rd̲ry (sic) strange, Sin. B 202; Neferti, 29 (det.).

d̲rd̲ri stranger, Pt. (L II), 5, 15; var. sic (pl.), Leb. 117.

see below s.v. dḥrw.

Dḥwty n. div. Thoth, varr., late, cf. Boylan, Thoth.

Dḥwtt festival of Thoth, JEA 38, pl. 1, 12; varr. Urk. IV, 469, 17; 27, 6.

dḥrw leather lacings, Urk. V, 151, 17; var. 151, 13. Cf. dḥr 'leather'.

var. of dḥty 'lead'.

ds with suff. pron. (him)self, by (him)self, (his) own, Gr. § 36.

var. of ds 'jar'.

dsw call, n 'to', Pyr. 755; CT I, 272 (also).

dsr (1) adj. holy, sacred, Siut, pl. 5, 237; Adm. 6, 5; RB 110, 3 (); Urk. IV, 345, 4 (); 881, 10; splendid, 607, 6; costly, 913, 2: (2) vb. clear a road, Hamm. 114, 11; Les. 71, 16; separate, r 'from', Pyr. 1778; with double obj., TR 23, 23 (); raise, support, ZÄS 51, 120; 'with upraised arm', ep. of Amen-Rēʿ, Urk. IV,

880,12; ḏsr m 'steer', Les. 74,6-7; ZÄS 62,4, n.3; JEA 20,162. — Cf. JEA 32,51.

ḏsrw seclusion, D. el. B. 115; Urk. IV, 349,12 (); cf. JEA 32,51; privacy, Urk. IV, 967,13 (); m ḏsrw 'in private', Bersh. II, 21, top, 4 (); sanctity, Urk. IV, 18,15; 736,10 ().

ḏsrw holy place, Urk. IV, 150,8; 1686,4; var. 229,1; Ḏsr ḏsrw 'Holy of Holies' = temple of Dēr el-Baḥri, 308,7 (); 409,8 ().

Ḏsrt-imntt 'the Western Holy Place' = Medinet Habu, Urk. IV, 881,1.9.

ḏsrt strong ale, Caminos, L.-Eg. Misc. 425; ḏsrt 'milky ale (?)', Siut, pl. 2, 101; varr. Les. 73,13; BH I, 17.

ḏsrt table of offerings, BH I, 17.

ḏd say, Sin. R 2; B 32.125.261.266; Les. 68,11; speak, Sh. S. 21; Peas. B1, 68; Urk. IV, 1,17; speak of, JEA 6,301, n.3; utter speech, Peas. B1, 72; recite spell, RB 122,12; tell, n 'to', Sin. B 172.173; expect, with foll. infin., Sin. B 7; bid, Sin. B 234; ḏd 'refuse', with foll. infin., Adm. 1,2; ḏd pw 'it means', introducing gloss, P. Ed. Smith, 115; m ḏd 'namely', 'as follows', Gr. § 224; mi ḏd 'according to the saying', Peas. B1, 146; r ḏd 'saying', 'that', Gr. § 224; r ḏd in 'said by', at beginning of letters, JEA 16, 153-4; ḏdw n.f, ḏdt n.s 'called', introducing second personal name, Gr. § 377,1; ky ḏd 'otherwise said', introducing alternative readings or glosses, Urk. V, 8,17; 11,2; 12,8; 'to be pronounced', of spell, etc, var. ; 'said by', Gr. § 306,1.

ḏd the djed-column, Pyr. 1255; Urk. IV, 1860,13; BD 72,2.

ḏd stable, enduring, Pyr. 813; varr. , ibid.; Urk. IV, 165,5; 1095,13.

ḏdt stability, duration, Urk. IV, 230,16; 263,4; usually var. , 86,14; 394,1; 575,11.

Ḏdw n. loc. Busiris, Abu Ṣir Banā, AEO II, 151*. 176*; varr. Pyr. 288; , Gr. § 289,1; JEA 41,81, fig. 1, top.

Ḏdwt n. loc. Mendes, Tell er-Rubaʿ; more often , AEO II, 150*.

ḏdꜣ fat (adj.), Peas. B1, 62; Eb. 33,5; Hatnub, 17,7 (det.); var. Urk. IV, 59,9.

ḏdb (1) sting: (2) incite (det.), late var. , GNS 50.

ḏdf stand on end, of hair, Herdsm. 4; creep, of flesh, Sin. B 228 (det.), cf. Barns, Ashm. 25.

ḏdft snake, Gr. p. 476, I, 14; internal bodily worm, Eb. 20, 7-8.

ḏdḥ shut up, imprison, RB 59, 8; Urk. IV, 767, 6; 780, 5; 1076, 2.

ḏdkw canal(?), channel(?), Urk. IV, 3, 10.

READINGS UNKNOWN OR DOUBTFUL

boy, Urk. IV, 74, 15 (id?, ḫrd ṯ3?).

eyes, Sin. B 169; P. Kah. 7, 54; Pr. 4, 3; var. Gr. p. 450, D 4.

bowl with handle(?), Urk. IV, 666, 3 (ḫntw?).

bull-calf, Urk. IV, 171, 13 (ṯ3y?, k3?).

womb, vulva, see under idt.

3/4, see under ḫmt-rw.

negative particle, see under ii.

ox, bull: when written alone it is often impossible to decide between the readings iw3, iḥ or k3.

rabble(?), see under šbn 'mix'.

train(?) troops, see under ṯsm.

sculptor, see under gnwty.

chief(?), Urk. IV, 48, 15 (ḥry-tp?).

see under ḳ33 and dḳr.

festival of the half-month, var. , Gr. p. 486, N 13.

sandbank(?), JEA 42, 37 (81) (ṯs?); for see under ḏ3tt 'estate'.

copper, see under bi3 and ḥmt.

bronze(?), distinct from last above, Urk. IV, 173, 9.

bundle, P. Kah. 20, 18 (dm3t?). Barns, Ram. p. 25 would read sḫnt.

 wtg. of ḏrw 'limits' (?), Urk. IV, 773, 12.

 leash, Westc. 7,5; 8,26.

 part of papyrus-plant, RB 120,3. Not srt 'thorn'.

 see under sḏ3w, etc.

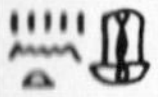 festival of the 5th of the month, Urk. IV, 27, 5.

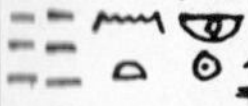 festival of the 6th of the month, see under snt.

 festival of the 15th of the month, Caminos, Lit. Frag. pl. 3,4,5; cf. p. 3; BD 117, l. 4.

Addenda

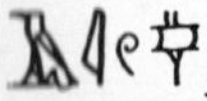 3iw: pt m 3iw 'a windy (?) sky', Caminos, Lit. Frag. p. 18.

 ꜥbḥ fill up, Pyr. 1140. 1902; det. 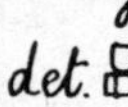 CT I, 298; var. 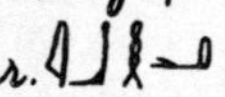 ibid.

 mi3sw (mi3zw) spines, CT I, 289; varr. 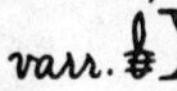 Pyr. 1560;  1999.

 nbi 'reed', measure of 2 cubits, Ch. B. Text, 42, n. 8.

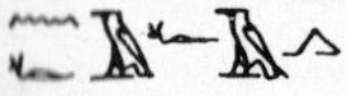 nf3f3 creep (?), CT I, 216.

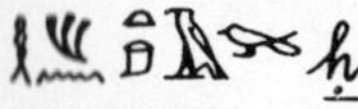 ḥnt3 be in need (?), BD 268, 7.

 ḥmntyw a ship, RB 60, 12; Urk. IV, 1823, 4; var.  1892, 17; O.K.  I, 107, 8.

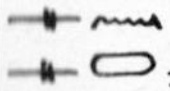 ssn caus. cause to pass, CT I, 401.

To si3t (< si3ṯ) 'encroach upon' add the reference CT I, 403 ().